ELECTRIC WOODWORK

JEREMY BROUN originally trained as a craft teacher at Shoreditch College, gaining a Distinction in Advanced Woodwork in 1966, and also training in metalwork, ceramics and bookbinding. He then taught in secondary schools for six years, his last post being at Millfield, where he taught woodwork and plastics and where he started developing his own ideas in wood.

He set up a small workshop in Bath in 1973, and has been producing both speculative and commissioned work ever since. He has exhibited widely and has won various national awards, including a Churchill Travel Scholarship in 1979. In the following year he was selected for the Crafts Council Index of Makers, and in 1988 he began making (award-winning) films on wood and design. He has written articles on woodworking since 1971, and his first book, *The Incredible Router,* was published by GMC Publications in 1989. His time is taken up by woodworking, writing, making video films and lecturing.

ELECTRIC WOODWORK

POWER TOOL WOODWORKING

JEREMY BROUN

GUILD OF MASTER CRAFTSMAN PUBLICATIONS LTD

First published 1991 by
Guild of Master Craftsman Publications Ltd,
Castle Place, 166 High Street, Lewes,
East Sussex BN7 1XU
Reprinted 1993

ISBN 0 946819 26 2

Designed by Ian Hunt Design
Printed and bound in Great Britain by
Redwood Press Ltd, Melksham, Wiltshire

The following photographs were supplied by courtesy of the manufacturers:

Black & Decker Ltd (Figs 5.1, 17.2, 17.18); Ebac Ltd (Fig 17.8); Fercell (Fig 15.15); Hitachi Power Tools (UK) Ltd (Figs 2.18, 17.20, 17.28); Luna (Ryobi) Tools Ltd (Figs 15.17, 15.18, 17.6, 17.16, 17.21, 17.27); Machine Mart (Fig 5.25); Metabo (Draper Tools) (Fig 16.17); Multico Ltd (Fig 17.19); Rod Naylor (Figs 7.9, 7.10); SMS Woodworking Machinery (Fig 17.29); Trend Cutting Tools Ltd (Fig 7.30); Wolfcraft UK (Fig 15.4(b))

DEDICATION

This book is dedicated to my mother Jean

ACKNOWLEDGEMENTS

I am indebted to the help of various individuals and company representatives who made the writing of this book possible.

First, a special mention to the editor at GMC Publications, Liz Inman, for her support and enthusiasm, and to her assistant, Ian Kearey, who shared the project in the latter stages of production. Thanks also to John Haywood, technical editor, for his advice – and visit – regarding technical matters.

Also, I much appreciated the help of Vince Goodsell of F-Stop Photography for his care, speed and dependability while processing my pictures, and for calming my nerves about F-stops – and also to Anna Bush Crews of F-Stop.

To my friend and fellow designer–maker Andrew Varah, who freely gave his advice on several occasions; to my friend Cherry Coad who featured in some of the photographs, and also to Annabelle Moore. To Geoff Field for his tips about various power tools, and thanks also to my friend Dee Levey for her support and tolerance during this project.

Finally I would like to thank the following companies and individuals for their help, and for supplying tools and in some cases photographs:

AEG – H. Klostermann
Black & Decker – John Bonnet
Black & Decker Service Centre, Bristol – Eddie Scannel, Alan Richardson
Bosch Power Tools – Olowole Kaliko and Richard Peters
General Fixings Ltd – Alan Gait (MD)
Hitachi Power Tools (UK) Ltd – Arthur Taverner (MD), Graham Bickerdyke
Kity (UK) Ltd – John Farrar
Luna (Ryobi) Tools Ltd – Gerry Baker (MD)
Machine Mart – Andrew Wood
Makita Power Tools – Chris Bull
Martin Godfrey (Woodrat jig)
Metabo (Draper Tools) – Paul Jones
M & M Distributions – Paul Merry
Panasonic Power Tools – Stephen Brandrick
Richmond Power Tools – David Mitchell
Record Power Tools – Mark Taberner
Rod Naylor (Dupli-carver router jig)
Skil – D. Carn
Simbles – Derek Dee
Trend Cutting Tools & Machinery Ltd – Jim Phillips (MD)
Wolfcraft – Mike Furness and Stan Robertson
Westminster Trading Co Ltd (Zyliss lathe and vice) – John Mills

All the cutters used by Jeremy Broun in Chapter 7, The Router, and in the projects, were supplied by Trend Machinery & Cutting Tools Ltd, Unit N, Penfold Works, Imperial Way, Watford, Hertfordshire WD2 4YY, telephone 0923 249911.

CONTENTS

NOTES ON MEASUREMENTS

Although the metric system was introduced in 1971 it is still not fully implemented, even in 'the trade'. Buying a sheet of 'eight by four' is a convenient terminology which is preferred by many, although strictly all measurements are specified in metric when purchasing timber. In this book the author has used a combination of both metric and imperial – a conversion table can be found below.

METRIC CONVERSION TABLE

Inches to millimetres

¼" — 6mm	3¼" — 83mm	7¼" — 185mm	19" — 485mm	40" — 1015mm
⅜" — 10mm	3½" — 88mm	7½" — 190mm	20" — 510mm	41" — 1040mm
½" — 13mm	3⅔" — 93mm	7¾" — 195mm	21" — 535mm	42" — 1065mm
⅝" — 16mm	3¾" — 95mm	8" — 200mm	22" — 560mm	43" — 1090mm
¾" — 19mm	4" — 1mm	8¼" — 210mm	23" — 585mm	44" — 1120mm
⅞" — 22mm	4⅛" — 105mm	8½" — 215mm	24" — 610mm	45" — 1145mm
1" — 25mm	4¼"4⅜" — 110mm	8¾" — 220mm	25" — 635mm	46" — 1170mm
1⅛" — 30mm	4½" — 115mm	9" — 230mm	26" — 660mm	47" — 1195mm
1¼" — 32mm	4¾" — 120mm	9¼" — 235mm	27" — 685mm	48" — 1220mm
1⅜" — 35mm	5" — 125mm	9½" — 240mm	28" — 710mm	49" — 1245mm
1½" — 38mm	5⅛" — 130mm	9¾" — 250mm	29" — 735mm	50" — 1270mm
1⅝" — 40mm	5¼" — 133mm	10" — 255mm	30" — 760mm	51" — 1295mm
1¾" — 45mm	5½" — 140mm	10⅛" — 257mm	31" — 785mm	52" — 1320mm
2" — 50mm	5¾" — 145mm	11" — 280mm	32" — 815mm	53" — 1345mm
2⅛"2¼" — 55mm	6" — 150mm	12" — 305mm	33" — 840mm	54" — 1370mm
2⅜" — 60mm	6⅛" — 155mm	13" — 330mm	34" — 865mm	55" — 1395mm
2½" — 63mm	6¼" — 160mm	14" — 355mm	35" — 890mm	56" — 1420mm
2⅝" — 65mm	6½" — 165mm	15" — 380mm	36" — 915mm	57" — 1450mm
2¾" — 70mm	6¾" — 170mm	16" — 405mm	37" — 940mm	58" — 1475mm
3" — 75mm	7" — 178mm	17" — 430mm	38" — 965mm	59" — 1500mm
3⅛" — 80mm	7" — 180mm	18" — 460mm	39" — 990mm	60" — 1525mm

To obtain the metric size for dimensions under 60", not shown in the above table, multiply the imperial size in inches by 25.4 and round to the nearest millimetre, taking 0.5mm upwards
e.g. 9⅛ × 25.4 = 231.8
= 232mm

To obtain the metric size for dimensions over 60" multiply the imperial size in inches by 25.4 and round to the nearest 10mm taking 5mm upwards
e.g. 67 × 25.4 = 1701.8
= 1700mm

KEY TO SYMBOLS

The following symbols are used at the beginning of each project as a quick guide to which power tools can optionally be used in its construction.

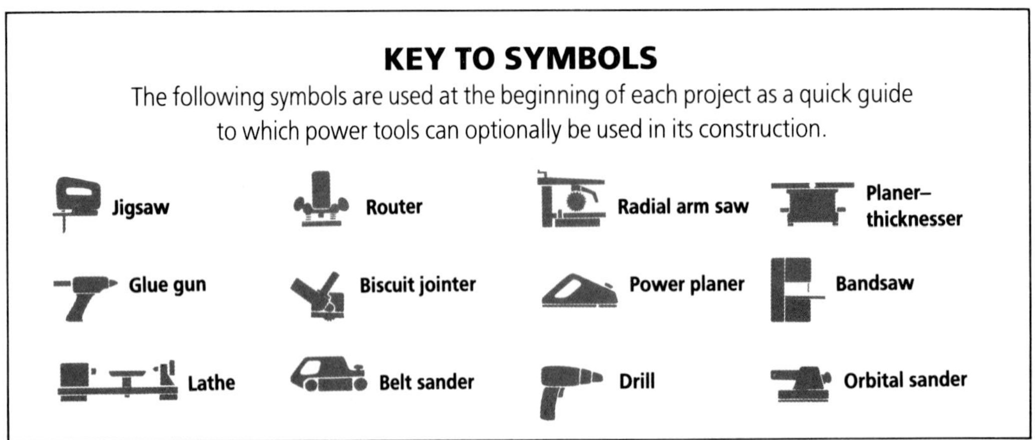

AUTHOR'S NOTE Whereas the various projects designed by the author are offered for the reader to make, it is requested that the reader observe the copyright protection of certain other designs photographed for this book and marked 'Copyright © Jeremy Broun'.

FOREWORD

It is a great pleasure for me to be invited to write a few words about Jeremy Broun's book, almost thirty years on from when we were both at Abbotsholme School. I was then the woodwork master and he was the school's first A level candidate.

It is not easy to write a fresh, comprehensive and convincing book on power-tool woodworking. It is even more difficult to do so for readers ranging in age from the young to the mature, and in ability from the questioning fumble-fingered to the proficient serious woodworker – but Jeremy Broun has done it.

With admirable clarity and guidance Electric Woodwork informs and illuminates on this expanding area of modern craft knowledge. Step by step from the history, the tools, their use and finally through a range of realistic and inspiring projects, he gives insight and expert practical knowledge, born of real, at-the-bench experience, to all who consult these pages.

There is an abundance of detail, often technical, but never confusing. The emphasis on safety is reassuring and clear. The reinforcement of safety in the description of each tool or machine complements the stimulating encouragement the text and illustrations provide. I have been using some of these electric tools for many years and am delighted to find myself both agreeing with and learning from the depth of information revealed.

There is also within these pages an appreciation that woodworking with power tools creates new opportunities for the craftsman. Their correct use brings precision and an expanding range of techniques of which many a dedicated die-hard hand craftsman would be proud. Jeremy Broun understands this and more, and he has the gift of making the complex simple and the written word an almost three-dimensional experience. This is indeed a very good book.

Howard Orme
Eton College, 1991

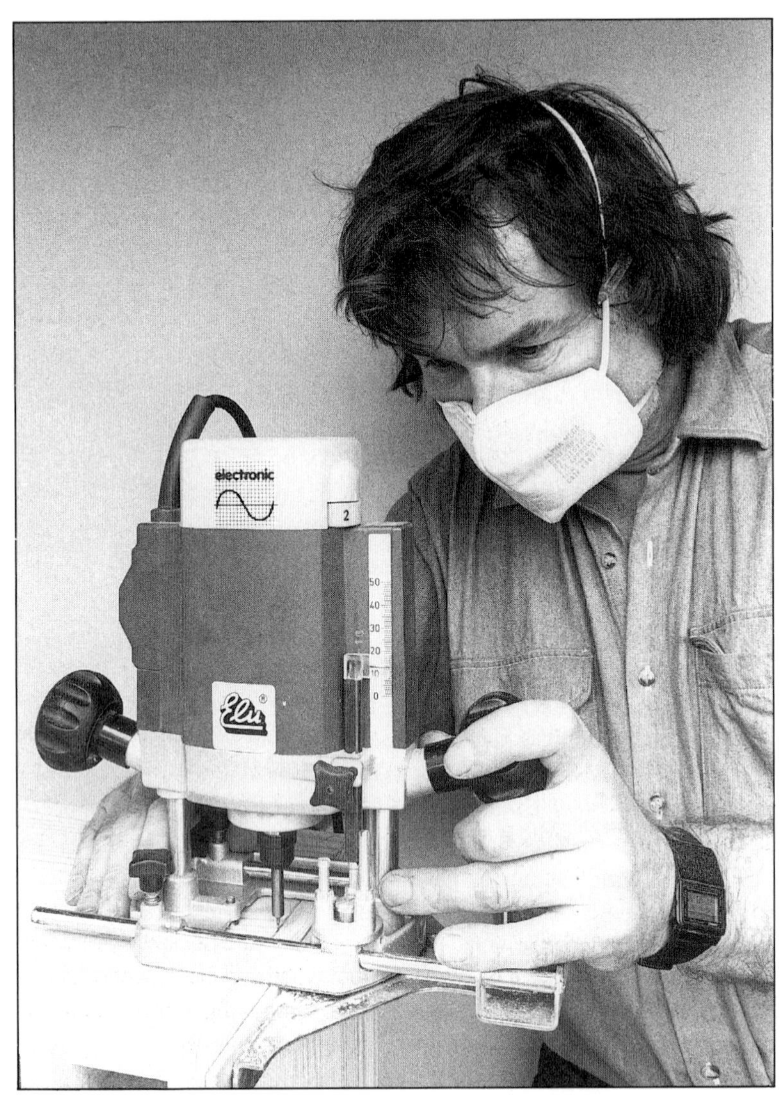

Fig 1.1 The router – the ultimate power tool?

1
INTRODUCTION

When I took up woodworking seriously as a teenager in the early sixties I made holes with a brace and bit, got the wood flat with a wooden jack plane and cut grooves for inlay with a scratch stock. I never dreamt that almost three decades on I would be writing a book called *Electric Woodwork* and that the world of woodworking would undergo such a revolution – the power-tool revolution.

Gone are the days of blistered hands and aching wrists caused by arduous planing or driving in screws manually. Or the frustration of crooked sawing or trying to get wood 'square' with a hand plane, leading to mediocre work. For many such frustration would have put them off woodworking for life (myself almost included). The power-tool revolution has changed all that. It has taken the drudgery out of repetitive handwork, giving faster results for the professional who is working for profit and for the amateur whose leisure time may be equally precious. Above all it has introduced a wonderful freedom for woodworkers everywhere to explore the material and its fashioning techniques in both traditional and innovative ways and to give so many people the opportunity to make things in wood with relative ease.

I have always warmed to the 'small is beautiful' philosophy, and indeed the portable electric power tool is just that – small and beautiful! It is compact and purposeful and can do what much larger and heavier machines did in the past (and sometimes more). It requires a small operating space (you don't need a large workshop). It consumes a negligible amount of electricity (most tools run for a few minutes at the most and consume the equivalent of a few 100 watt light bulbs), and much pleasure in woodworking can be derived from making a little go a long way. This involves the way things are designed – and is a considered approach. So too is my particular choice of tools amidst what could be called a current power-tool bonanza.

I am not offering a catalogue of gimmicky or fashionable gadgets, but approaching the subject comprehensively with creative end-results in mind. A careful selection has been made of a few electric tools, each with a proven track record, with one or two promising tools and accessories included. They work as a *creative team.* And of course the functions of some of these tools overlap, putting the choice of application in the woodworker's hands (or should I say – head).

The tools are portable in so far as they can be carried in the hand or under the arm, and this allows me to include one or two light machines which I consider to be essential in any electric workshop today. One thing is for sure, the chosen tools are seldom idle or wasted. All of the tools featured I have used personally, and they broadly represent what is on the market.

Making things in wood is immensely satisfying, and indeed these days is a therapy for some, as well as a vital activity for others! Apart from a basic level of skill (or dexterity) – which is obviously required – it is largely a matter of having the confidence to have a go and pitch in at your own level ('a man should always reach beyond his grasp').

As it would be limiting to write about power-tool woodworking in simply its driest, most technical sense – this is also a book about design and how it is integrated into the making process. With this in mind, a range of projects aimed at the serious woodworker has been designed around the creative capabilities of the power tools. (I make no distinction here between amateur or professional, male or female.)

The projects vary in difficulty and are open-ended in concept, thus allowing the reader some choice over dimensions, materials and choice of power tools.

2
FROM PITSAW TO LASER BEAM

ELECTRICITY

Electricity has transformed our lives in the 20th century, affecting the way we think, behave and communicate!

We take for granted that at a flick of a switch we have instant light, instant heat and instant television, not to mention the computer and the Black & Decker drill, but in the context of the history of the world this has all happened very recently. In fact, during the writing of this book my grandmother was 101 years old, which means that when she was born the electric lamp had only been invented ten years previously (Swan, Edison 1878), that the radio was yet to come (Marconi 1895) and although the cathode ray tube had been perfected two years before her birth (Braun 1897), television was not to become commonplace until the 1960s. And all this is largely due to the phenomenon of electricity. Electricity is the heartbeat of modern civilization, and indeed modern civilization has discovered that it is also electricity which causes the heart to beat!

Of course the Greeks had observed the phenomenon of electricity as early as 600 BC, when they saw that certain fish flashed in the water. They also noticed the electrostatic power of Baltic fossil resins (amber) which they called 'elektron', but the term 'electricity' was believed to have been first used at the end of the 16th century by William Gilbert, a physician to Elizabeth I. He noted that glass (and other similar materials) when rubbed had the same electrostatic properties as amber.

Then, around the middle of the 18th century, the American Benjamin Franklin further prepared the ground with his famous experiment with the kite and the key in a thunderstorm (Fig 2.1). At the beginning of the 19th century, the English chemist and physicist Michael Faraday discovered the principle of electromagnetic induction, which was to serve as the basis for electricity-producing machines – generators, magnetos and dynamos (Fig 2.2).

Fig 2.2 At the opposite end of two centuries and sitting side by side: Michael Faraday and the electric motor he pioneered; a cordless drill motor by Hitachi Power Tools.

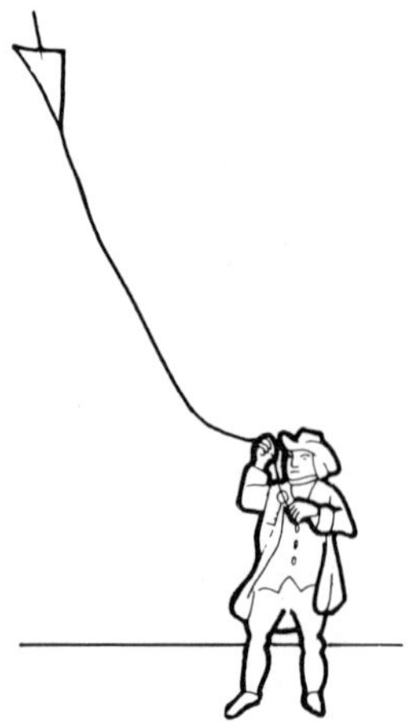

Fig 2.1 Benjamin Franklin flying his kite.

Perhaps the most significant aspect of electricity relating to the world of woodworking is the electric motor (Fig 2.3), which is in essence a dynamo in reverse. But before I get too stuck on electrical tramlines and consider the workings of an electric motor, let us move sideways and take a brief historical glimpse at woodworking.

WOODWORKING IN HISTORY

Up until the Industrial Revolution and the harnessing of steam power, which of course was the key to rapid technical and economic development in Britain in the mid-19th century, woodworking was still predominantly a hand craft. Indeed the pitsaw, although crudely mechanical, was used right up until that time and relied on two men arduously supplying the muscle power to cut logs into planks (Fig 2.4).

Considering the widespread use of timber throughout the ages (there is hardly anything that has not been made of wood, from the great tra-

Fig 2.3 An Electra Beckum 2.2HP single phase electric motor.

ditions of the shipbuilder and the wheelwright, to the cooper, clogmaker and chair bodger – Fig 2.5), surprisingly little had changed in the way timber was fashioned in terms of driving power. Of course there was a steady development of mechanization over the centuries from the adze (a perfect example of a self-guiding jig – Fig 2.6) to the cogged wheel (Fig 2.7), but in the main the handcraft traditions carried on until the Industrial Revolution.

Fig 2.4 A pitsaw.

Now, within a century, we have seen dramatic technological change which has taken us from cutting wood with a pitsaw to the possibilities of cutting wood with a laser beam.

Mass-production techniques based on new materials-forming processes – such as metal casting and plastics moulding (Bakelite) – sowed the seeds of product design in the early 20th century, and this in turn gave birth to the humble electric drill.

Fig 2.6 The adze.

Fig 2.7 A cogged wheel.

Fig 2.5 A chair bodger.

THE HUMBLE BLACK & DECKER

Enter Mr S. Duncan Black and Alonso G. Decker, two young American inventors who in 1916 manufactured the first rotary hand drill – weight at birth: 24lbs! . . . (Fig 2.8). They now weigh considerably less at around 4lbs (under 2kg). What is interesting about this drill is that it had the first pistol grip and trigger switch – interesting because it could only have come from the Wild West!

Rapid industrial expansion and product development led to other major breakthroughs such as the world's first portable ¼in consumer drill in 1946 (Fig 2.9). The fifties saw the beginnings of

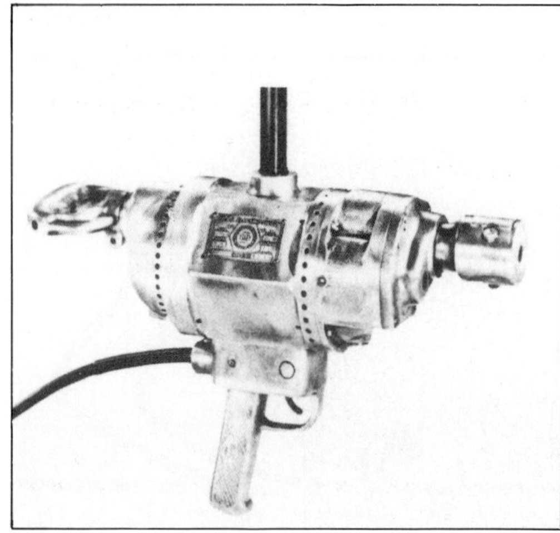

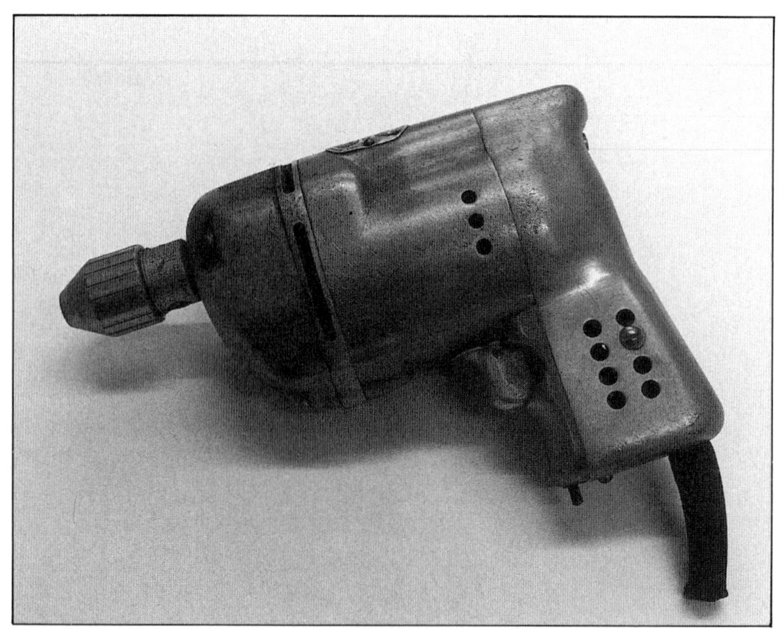

the DIY market as we now know it, with developments to the drill (Fig 2.10) and the introduction of DIY powered tools such as the finishing sander and jigsaw.

Of course the very first Black & Decker drill could hardly be called portable, but subsequent technological developments in aluminium casting – giving substantially lighter casings – plastics injection moulding and the invention of the integrated circuit (the 'chip') led on to the power tool, and indeed machine, which we know today (Figs 2.11 and 2.12). It is interesting to note that the world production of aluminium over the past hundred years has risen a millionfold!

THE TECHNOLOGICAL REVOLUTION

It has been said that if man had never decided to explore outer space there would have been no need to make things small and lightweight! Indeed in 1968 Black & Decker supplied a cordless power head for an Apollo lunar surface drill to remove core samples from the moon (Fig 2.13).

The most rapid advances have undoubtedly been in plastics technology and microelectronics. Rather than being a specific material, 'plastic' is more a term describing a vast family of materials each with entirely different properties, from acrylonitrile-butadienne-styrene (ABS) to polytetrafluoroethylene (PTFE), from Velcro to Teflon, and even plastic wood!

Advances in polycarbonate technology have led to power-tool casings, e.g. glassfibre-reinforced polycarbonate resin, combining superb strength with lightness (Fig 2.14). This is truly a miracle of technology, and a far cry from those cheap plastic washing-up bowls of the 1950s which forever split and thus earned plastic a bad name.

Fig 2.8 The world's first rotary hand drill (courtesy Black & Decker) 1916 (above left).

Fig 2.9 The world's first portable ¼in consumer drill in 1946 (courtesy Black & Decker) (above right).

Fig 2.10 A Black & Decker domestic drill in the 1950s.

CUTTER TECHNOLOGY

Another significant factor in the development of power tools concerns the bit which actually cuts the material – the cutter. Its design and construction are vital to the efficient performance of the tool, whether it be a bit (Fig 2.15) or a blade. The advent of high carbon and alloy steels, and tung-

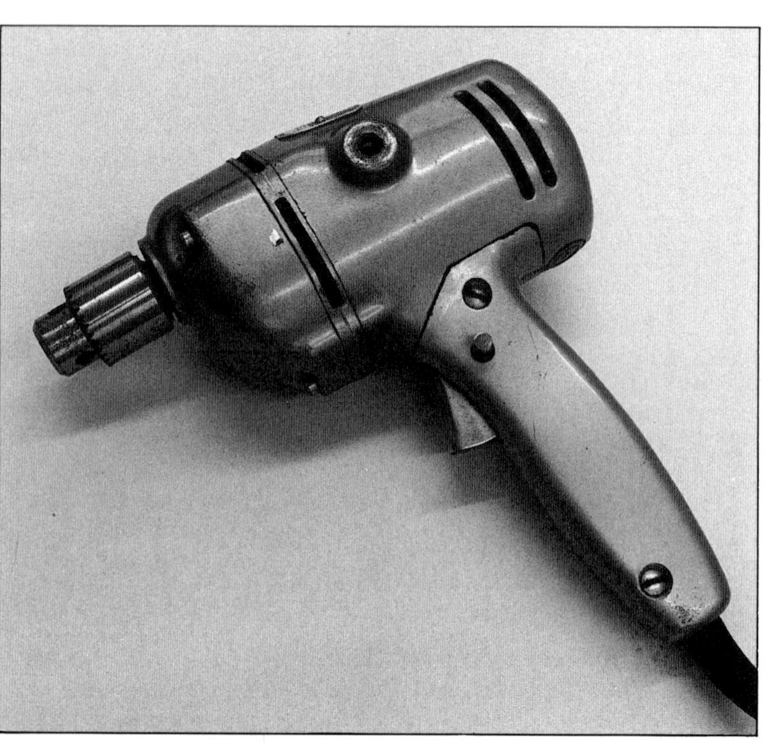

Fig 2.11 The revolution in plastics and aluminium forming (Luna Woody planer-thicknesser with cover taken off).

Fig 2.12 A truly portable electric tool (the Luna Woody planer-thicknesser weighing 17kg).

sten carbide, has resulted in a cutter which is equivalent to the radial tyre on a motor car. Without this kind of tyre the modern high-performance car would simply stay in the garage. Similarly cutters today are made of high speed steel (HSS) and can be tungsten-carbide tipped (TCT), the latter having a far greater life. The modern cutter (Fig 2.16) is designed to perform at the high temperatures caused by the high speed of rotation of the power tool, and cutter design and technology are

Fig 2.13 Cordless power head used on the Apollo Lunar mission in 1971 (courtesy Black & Decker).

Fig 2.14 Superb strength and lightness of the polycarbonate casing of a Hitachi drill.

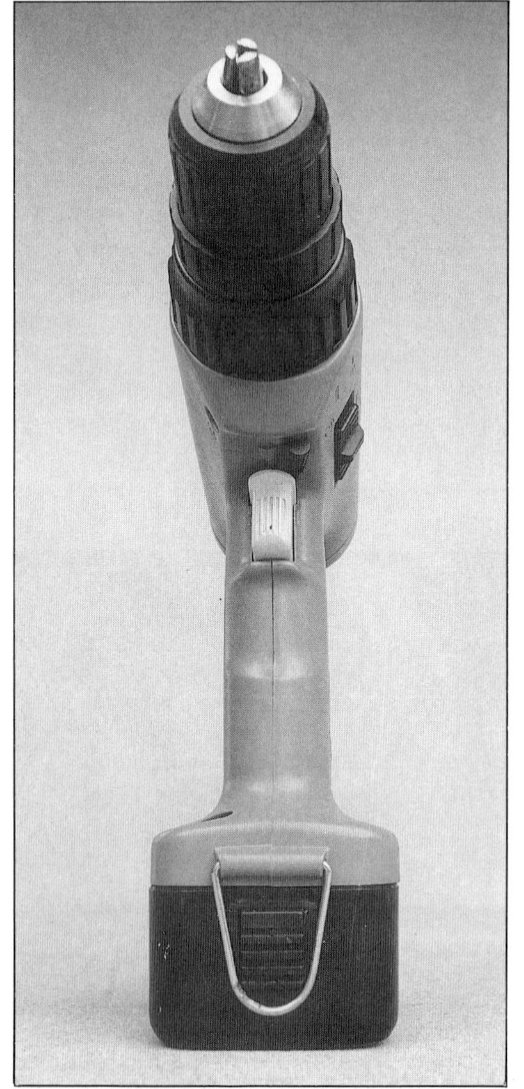

Fig 2.15 A range of tungsten carbide tipped router bits by Trend Cutting Tools Ltd.

Fig 2.16 A TCT circular sawblade.

as important as the power tool which drives it and are also under constant development (Fig 2.17).

'DESIGNER' POWER TOOLS

During the 1980s, to quote Hitachi Power Tools: 'We have seen tremendous advances in virtually every aspect of modern technology . . . from production methods through to computer-aided design.' (Fig 2.18) Perhaps the most significant

Fig 2.17 Bosch grinder set up with an Arbotech wood carver cutter.

Fig 2.18 Cut-away view of a Hitachi grinder.

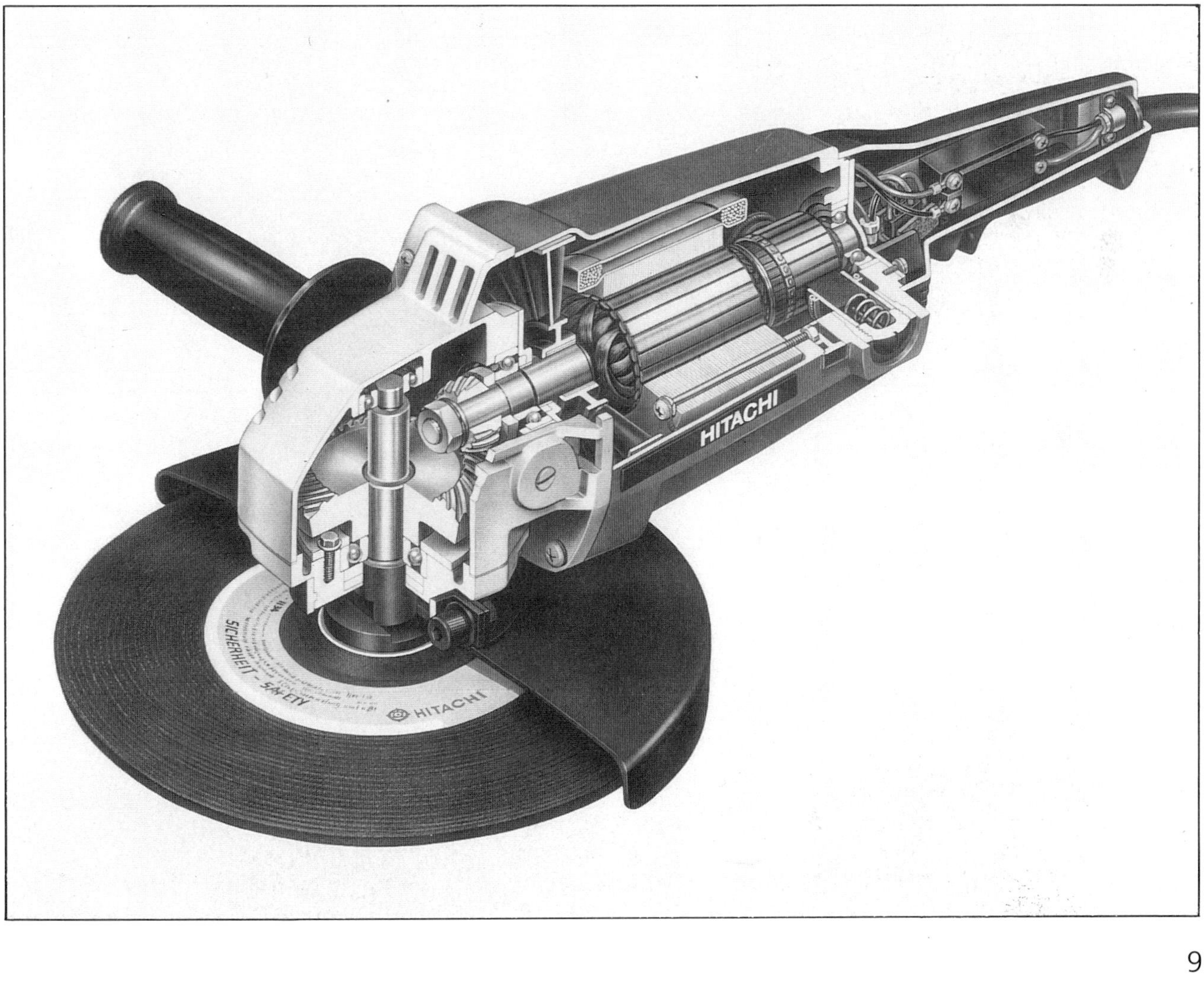

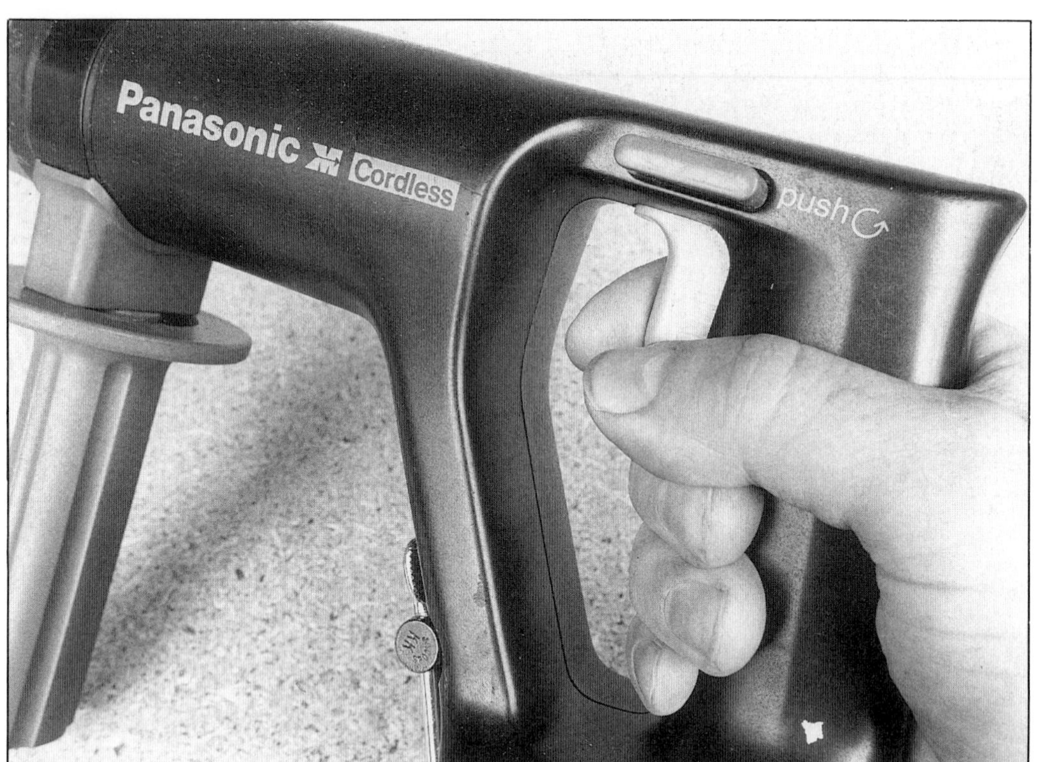

Fig 2.19 Comfort and visual appeal of the Panasonic 'Force 12' cordless drill.

Fig 2.20 The author's Black & Decker power planer – ergonomically designed.

Fig 2.21 The Black & Decker Service Centre in Bristol.

have been CAD and CNC (computer-numerically controlled) technologies, the former allowing a greater range of design factors to be dealt with and the latter allowing greater ease of manufacture. (A machinist can look after four milling machines or lathes at the same time, for example.)

Whereas the early power tools were designed and built 'to do a job', far more things affect design today. Factors such as durability, safety, ease of maintenance, ease of use, comfort, visual appeal (Fig 2.19) – even colour – are important, so it is not just a matter of building a good tool but designing it around the potential user (Fig 2.20). One could ask where it is all leading, now that fashion has entered the world of woodworking!

THE POWER TOOL BONANZA

There are now so many power tools bombarding the market, most of them really quite excellent for what they do, that attracting the eye of the individual has become more important (Fig 2.21), and the consumer woodworker has never had it so good! Choice may be difficult, but the high standards in product design and manufacture today, guided by stringent safety legislation, have resulted in fierce competition offering a real bonanza for woodworkers.

These electric tools range from drills, jigsaws, planers, routers, tackers, glue guns, screwdrivers, lathes, sanders, to the extractors which remove the dust and chippings which the other tools make. And they all share one thing in common – except

Fig 2.22 An electric motor.

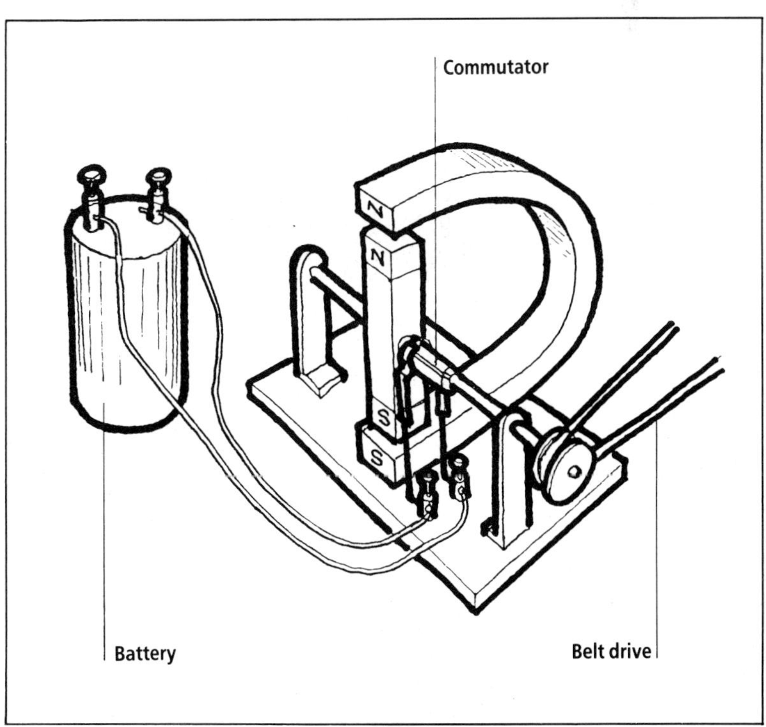

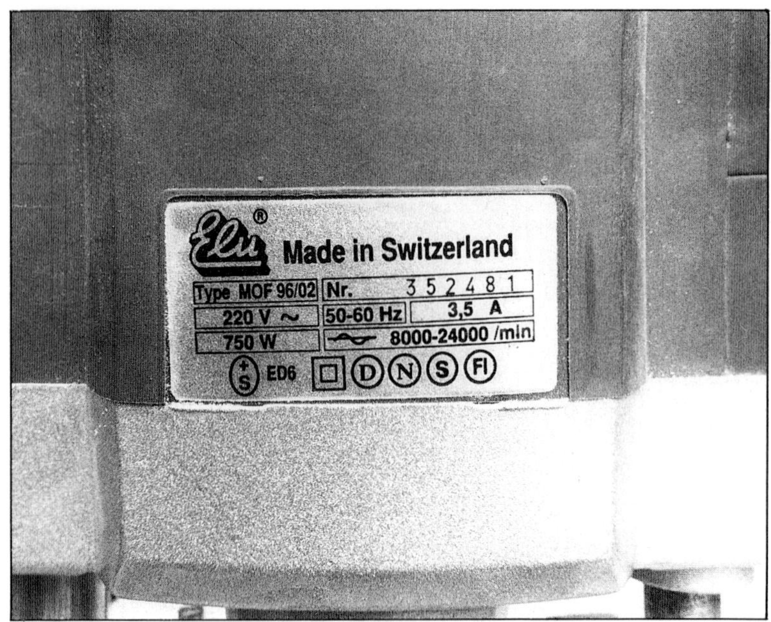

Fig 2.23 Elu MOF96E router with 750 watts input rating.

for the glue gun – (Fig 13.2) they are all driven by the electric motor pioneered by Michael Faraday some 150 years ago and still going strong today.

THE ELECTRIC MOTOR

The basic electric motor uses an electromagnet armature on a rotating shaft which is suspended between the poles of a horseshoe magnet. When the motor is switched on a current runs through the wire, the brush and the commutator into the electromagnet. The similar poles of the armature and the horseshoe magnet repel each other and cause the shaft to turn half a revolution until the poles are opposite – and want to attract each other. The commutator acts as a switch at the half turn, reversing the direction of the current which in turn reverses the magnetic pole so that a continuous motion results (Fig 2.22).

Early power-tool motors were necessarily large, and the significant subsequent developments in technology have been in the design and construction of series-wound motors, mica commutators to moulded commutators, and varnished windings giving greater power for their size. But what of the power of the power tool?

POWER RATING

As all power tools are essentially electric motors, they are power rated in terms of wattage. It is important to understand that the manufacturers specify the *input* wattage – the power drawn into the tool from its source (mains or cordless) and that the actual power of the tool is measured by its *output* wattage – the power which is transmitted through the tool to the bit or blade . . . and manufacturers rarely specify this. Let's take some random examples from the vast array of electric tools and look at their input ratings (Fig 2.23):

AEG circular saw (160mm blade)	1200 watts
Black & Decker electric drill (½in chuck)	550 watts
Bosch portable planer	600 watts
Elu router (¼in collett)	750 watts
Hitachi orbital sander (½ sheet)	350 watts
Kity planer–thicknesser (150mm × 100mm)	740 watts
Luna Woody woodturning lathe	550 watts
Makita mitre saw (255mm blade)	1380 watts
Metabo jigsaw	450 watts
Ryobi radial arm saw (210mm blade)	1250 watts
Skil belt sander	940 watts

This gives a fair indication of the input (continuous) power ratings of some popular tools. Note that machines are generally rated in kilowatts e.g. Kity planer–thicknesser = 0.74kW which is approximately 1 horsepower (1HP). Ryobi produces a 3HP portable router which is as large as you are likely to find in a portable tool.

However, it is the *output* wattage that gives the true power of the tool – the power that is available at the driving end. The power consumed (input) is drawn by the motor from the power source (mains or battery), and due to electrical and mechanical losses within the internal workings of the tool, the transmitted power (output) is less than the power consumed (input). This power differential is referred to as the 'efficiency' of the tool and of course models vary. An example of one particular manufacturer's drill is 500 watts input = 280 watts output. But there is no exact ratio which applies to all power tools of all manufacturers. If you want to know you will probably have to ask!

Power consumption of electric tools

The power that an electric tool consumes when used depends on the service conditions. The harder the service conditions – the greater the pressure applied, the harder the material, the larger the bit diameter, etc. – the greater power consumption will be.

Power consumption at rated load/input

The *rated* input is the power that the tool consumes in continuous operation under load to result in its temperature rising to 85°C above ambient temperatures (in accordance with the International Electro Technical Commission); it is the power in watts which is shown on the rating plate of the tool.

If an electric tool draws more power from the mains than its rated input, it means a higher current is passing through the windings and the motor temperature will increase, resulting in overload and eventual burn-out of the windings (a distinctive smell).

Some tool manufacturers, e.g. Metabo, produce high-quality windings with at least 8 coatings of insulation capable of bearing temperatures of up to 200°C, and feature overload protective devices.

No-load speed

The speed at the spindle of a power tool normally decreases as the load applied increases (a noticeable drop in revs). A typical 500 watt drill rated at a no-load speed of 900rpm may drop to 500rpm at rated load. Some sophisticated power tools – in particular drills – have electronic components which reduce if not eliminate the work-related speed drop.

ELECTRONIC

The use of the term 'electronic' has similarities to the aforementioned 'plastic', and it invariably indicates the presence of some clever little 'chip' which determines some aspect of the performance of the tool, but usually refers to the speed of start-up. It has now become jargon, and it is not alone. Suffice to offer here a few other useful buzzwords for gatecrashers at woodworkers' social events! There is variospeed, full-wave electronic, constamatic speed stabilization, electronic winding-temperature monitoring, electronic torque control, vario-tacho-constamatic electronic speed control and FET electronic speed control. However, perhaps the most relevant here is the popular 'electronic variable' speed facility featured in some drills, routers and other tools, and manufacturers display their own symbol depicting this (Fig 2.24). Essentially it allows the tool to run at a range of stepped-up speeds from an easy start to full revolutions. In the case of a router, for instance, it eliminates the snatch of the tool on start-up and allows different cutter diameters to operate at maximum efficiency and prevent burning (see pages 48–49).

Fig 2.24 The Hitachi 'electronic' symbol.

PAST HISTORIC, FUTURE PERFECT

Whereas the electric motor has been at the heart of the power tool since its conception, the microcomputer has come to generate the pulse. (In an age of 'smart' technology, who knows what newfangled device will be dreamt up next?) Certainly the fastest developing technology at present is in cordless tools (see 'The Cordless Revolution'), and if you consider the key to cordless performance is the size, strength and stamina of the battery, the 'smart-charger' keeps an *intelligent* eye on those lazy battery cells which don't always pull their weight, and through a host of sensing, monitoring and energizing actions ensures it achieves optimum functioning. Perhaps in the future there will be intelligent drills and saws with an electronic brain which can sense the knots in the wood, tell you when to stop drilling, and can prevent the wood splitting! And who knows, there may come a time also when sanders create no dust at all, and the electric drill makes its exit from the workshop to lay to rest in a museum, as wood is fashioned entirely by a laser beam energized by the sun, making no noise at all and programmed by an 'intuitive device'.

But in the space of a century, *despite* these enormous changes, a tool is still a tool in the user's hand. Today, over a hundred years on, we would do well to pause and ponder the cry of the artist, craftsman and philosopher William Morris: 'We must be masters of machines and not their slaves'!

3

THE POWER STRUGGLE

I would imagine there exists in the minds of many woodworkers the feeling that using power tools is 'cheating at woodwork'. In view of the rapid and recent development of electric tools, this somewhat 'Luddite' view is not surprising, but let's consider a little closer what the hand skills versus machine skills argument is actually about.

My own position is that I trained in cabinetmaking hand techniques, but I readily embrace the new technology. I think the important thing is not so much the nature of the tool, but the way it is perceived and used in relation to the finished article.

As I mentioned previously, at the turn of the century William Morris said, 'We must be masters of machines and not their slaves.' Much furniture during the Victorian period was vulgar and heavily proportioned, totally lacking the finesse and spirit of the work of the craftsman who toiled by hand as the machine was exploited for profit, and compromises in materials and quality of manufacture inevitably resulted. Morris was right to protest at the influence of machinery, even though furniture which had previously been the privilege of the wealthy became available to the masses.

Of course if it were not for mechanization we would not enjoy the unprecedented luxury of choice in so many areas of our lives today. Indeed mass-production processes dictate standards of workmanship that the hand craftsman needs to match before a potential customer will even consider purchasing his work. We take for granted the quality of 'craftsmanship' in a nut-and-bolt, or digestive biscuit, each produced in millions on the production line. After all, mechanization is essentially a lever – a device for achieving more work with less effort. A series of cogged wheels, for example, gives more torque – or rotational leverage – than a single wheel.

'RISK' AND 'CERTAINTY'

If we consider some common hand tools, such as chisels, planes, saws and drills, it is difficult to be purist about the idea of 'skill'. A plane, for instance, is a chisel held in a sophisticated jig (Fig 3.1). That jig guides the cutting edge in a controlled way and the skill of hand planing is in exerting the driving power by way of even pressure throughout its journey. Take the plane blade out of the plane

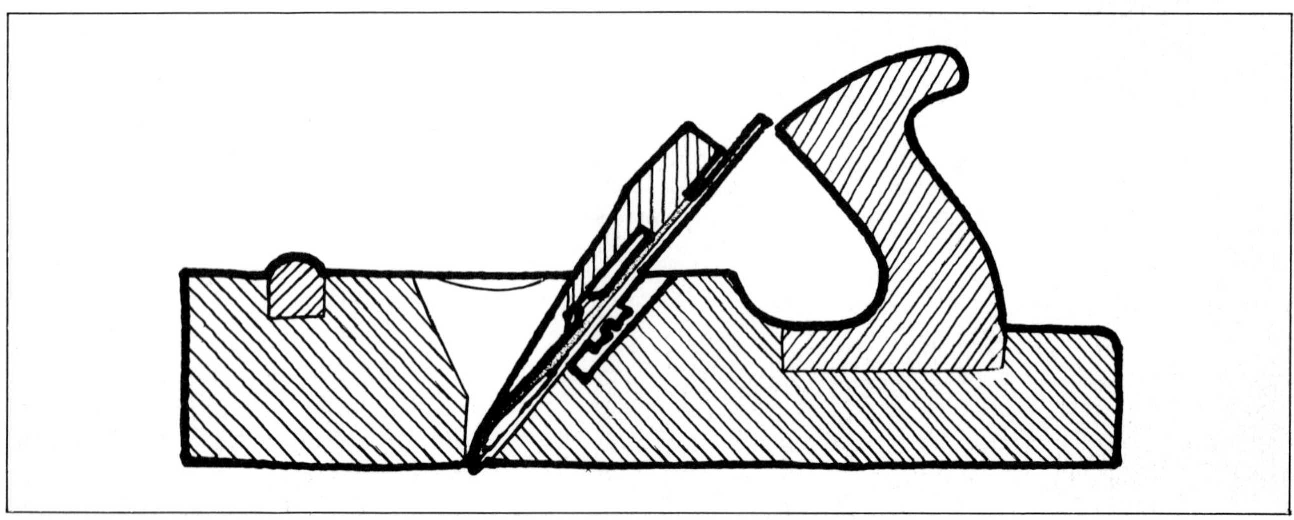

Fig 3.1 Section through a wooden hand plane.

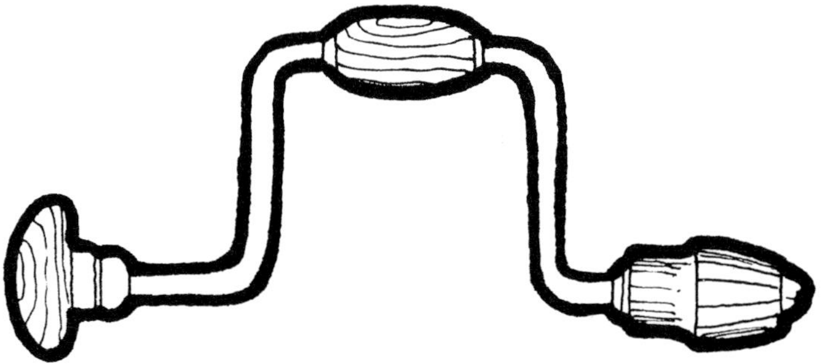

Fig 3.2 Brace and bit.

body and try to achieve a flat consistent cut! What is already a fairly difficult task would be almost impossible.

In his book, *'The Nature and Art of Workmanship,'* David Pye suggests there is the skill of 'risk' and the skill of 'certainty'. The chisel involves the skill of 'risk' and the plane the skill of 'certainty'. A handsaw, by virtue of its large, flat blade area, is a self-guiding jig once the initial cuts have been made. Of course different hand tools present different levels of difficulty. Perhaps one of the most difficult tasks is to saw a piece of wood perfectly 'square', whereas a spokeshave may be relatively easy to master. But the point is that many hand tools demand the skill of 'certainty' not 'risk'.

Where does this leave the power tool? You would be surprised if when visiting the dentist you were met with a Black & Decker drill, but the drill the dentist uses *is* a power tool. And, as David Pye argues, it is the skill of 'risk' which the dentist uses with his drill, because there is no guiding or jigging system other than the steadying of his fingers against your mouth in controlling the path of the drill (not a particularly comforting thought)!

In contrast the woodworker's brace and bit (Fig 3.2) demands the skill of 'certainty' – once it has been correctly aligned, you just keep turning and the path is guided. The source of power, therefore, has nothing to do with the skill needed and in many instances the power tool demands more skill. The Arbotech Woodcarver (Fig 3.3) is a good example of the skill of 'risk' and so too is the Black & Decker Powerfile (see page 189).

While established and respectable woodturners may argue that the gouge is superior to the scraper because it is a 'true' cutting tool, nobody stops to ask if the lathe itself is a 'true' (respectable) tool! It also demands the skill of certainty.

QUICK VERSUS SLOW

But perhaps the point is that all tools are surely equal in so far as they are in essence levers? The creative potential of a router compared to a full

Fig 3.3 Attempting to sculpt a perfect hollow with the Arbotech Woodcarver – the skill of 'risk'.

complement of hand tools (Fig 3.4) is probably no less, no more (although I am slightly biased and would say more!), but the difference is in the speed at which the router performs, as well as its' being many 'levers' in one.

Everything I have ever made with a router I could probably make with hand tools, but it would take a lot, lot longer, and I personally have neither the patience nor the inclination for this, even though (or perhaps because!) in my 'apprenticeship' days I was taught to do everything the hard (slow) way – by hand. But there are others who have been introduced to woodworking in a more relaxed way who prefer the slow and gentle action of hand tools, the resonance of a spokeshave, the perfume of curling shavings as they float off the bench – in contrast to the harsh, aggressive shriek of the power tool throwing dust everywhere!

THE POWER OF THE POWER TOOL

The power tool is the adze (see Fig 2.6) of the late 20th century. The level of skill or difficulty involved is determined largely by the user. Some of my own designs in wood have explored the potential of the power tool quite rigorously because that is the challenge I enjoy.

An example is my 'Zigzag' table (see colour section), where three laminated components meet at the centre to form a zigzag joint. The joint cannot be cut conventionally like a dovetail, one copied from the other. It demands precision marking-out and precision cutting using various hand and power tools. The joint cannot be clamped in the normal opposing direction because it has three components and is therefore equally tricky. The laminates have to be identical as they correspond with both centre zigzag joints and the finger joint at the corners and they would show if they were slightly misaligned. Another example is the Pyramid Drinks Cabinet (see colour section) which also demonstrates the creative potential of power tools.

Ultimately it is the user and the degree of his skill and workmanship which determines how versatile, creative and useful he finds power tools, and of course hand tools will always have their place in the workshop. Indeed, hand marking-out operations are essential in many instances where power tools are used to fashion the wood. The serious woodworker is likely to complement electric tools with hand tools.

The important thing is to discriminate which tool is best for a particular task. Although the choice of power tools today presents an extremely useful and creative set of 'levers', it would be foolish to rely solely on electric tools. They all act as a team to produce the desired object and it is surely this that we are constantly striving towards.

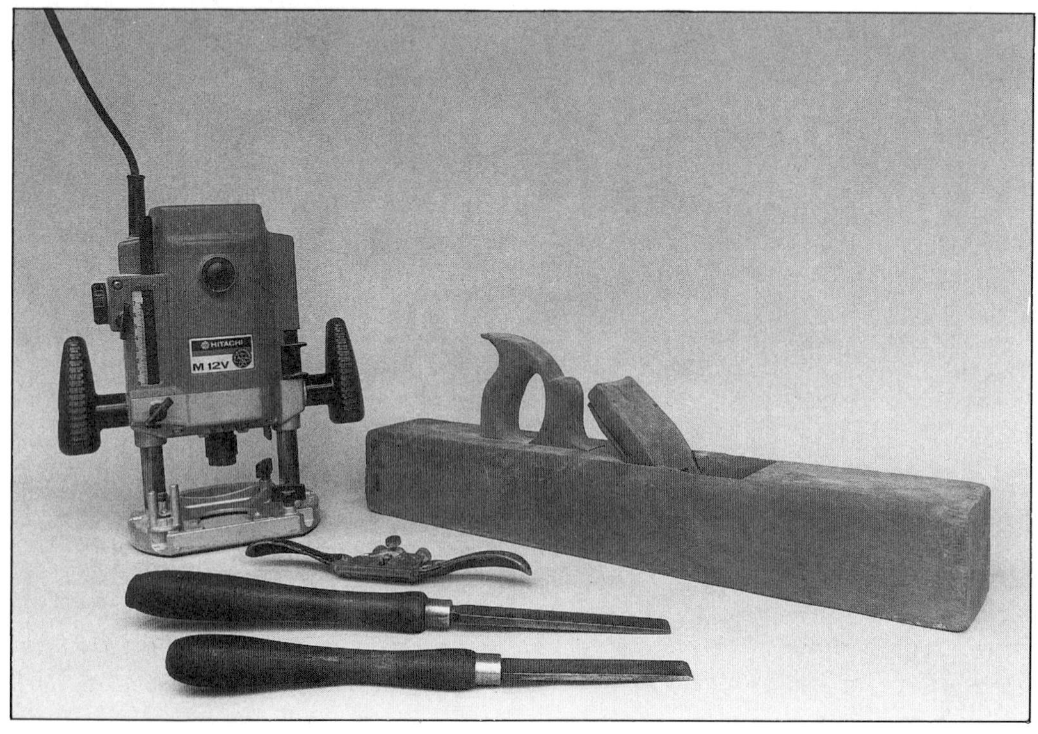

Fig 3.4 A selection of the author's tools.

4 HEALTH AND SAFETY FIRST

Health and safety have come to the forefront in recent years, and rightly so. It is no longer just a question of common sense to use a dustmask or earmuffs or guards on machines, but a matter of serious concern, endorsed by increasing legislation. And that legislation covers both the employed and self-employed (and would probably cover the leisure worker if it could be enforced).

It takes only a second to lose a finger or damage an eye, a few hours to impair your hearing and over several years you could seriously damage your lungs, so the workshop is potentially a very dangerous place.

Inevitably, as more people take up woodworking, whether it be for leisure or business, more accidents will occur. But alongside this is increasing medical and scientific knowledge of the toxicity of certain species of timbers. This is of particular importance for the power-tool user, who may be lulled into feeling that he (or she) is at the more casual end of the woodworking spectrum. But handling electric tools, deceptive by their size, in a small, confined workshop, means it is essential to implement health and safety procedures.

ELECTRIC TOOLS

Electric power tools and light machines are powered by 220–240 volts main electricity, which is enough to kill and certainly enough to cook (I've been cooked once or twice myself!).

▮ It is important that the tool is insulated. A tool rated up to 750 watts (1HP) should carry a 5 amp fuse in its plug. Above this rating it should carry a 13 amp fuse.

▮ When wiring a plug – the first thing to do – it is important that the outer sheathing is clamped in the plug and not the wires (Fig 4.1). This demands careful cutting of the wires to the correct length beforehand, but failure to do so will lead to the wires being gradually pulled out.

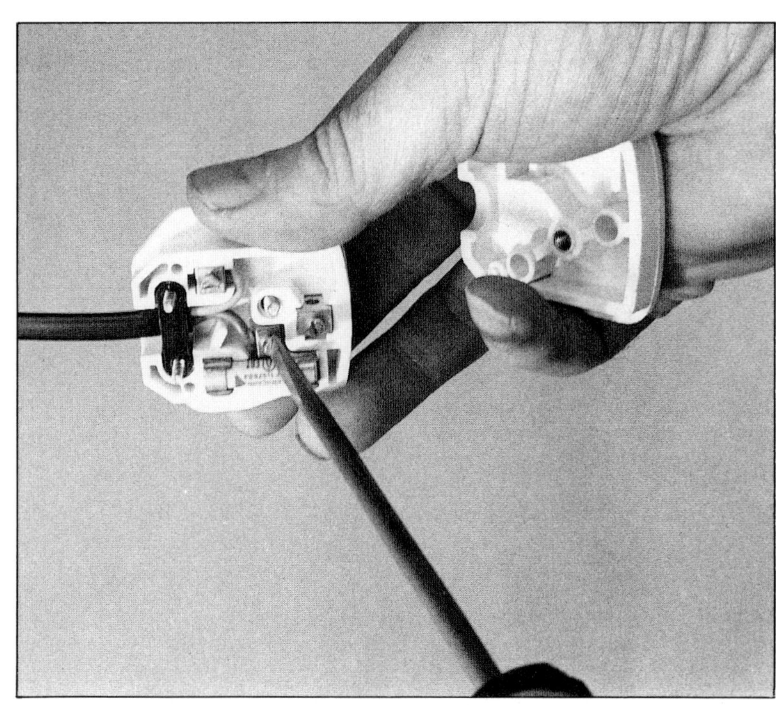

Fig 4.1 Wiring a plug.

▮ Power tools should be plugged into a ring mains circuit (looped) with earth and contact-breaking 'trip' switch at the master unit.

▮ Most power tools nowadays have only two wires – live (brown) and neutral (blue) and no earth. This is because they are 'double-insulated' and all electrical parts are encapsulated in insulating plastic within the enclosed casing. Older metal-cased tools should be earthed, and so too should light machines.

▮ Ideally cables should be heavy duty to take the wear and tear of usage.

▮ Cordless tools, powered by DC current up to 24 volts, are virtually harmless (electrically speaking) and can be used safely outside in damp conditions.

▮ On purchase of any tool the manufacturer's operating manual should be carefully read and specific safety points observed.

Workshop electrics

PVC wiring should be installed and all sockets and connections checked – loose connections and old wiring start fires, see Chapter 15, The Electric Workshop.

Fire

Any woodworking workshop is a potential fire risk – some airborne wood dust can ignite spontaneously! The workshop floor should always be swept at the end of the day and dust extraction is essential, especially if you do a lot of woodworking. A smoke detector (Fig 4.2), fire extinguisher and fire blanket are a sensible and inexpensive investment.

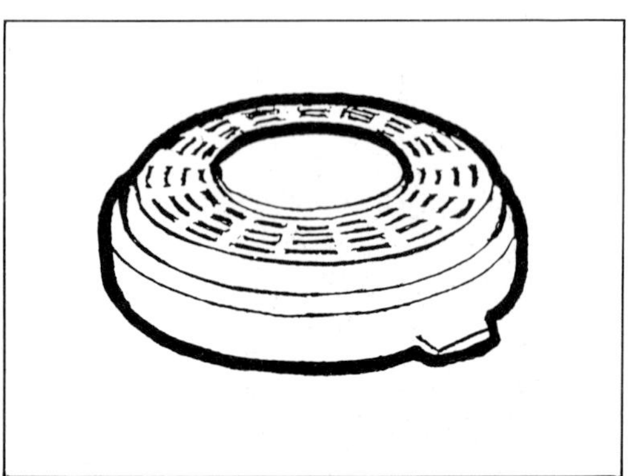

Fig 4.2 A smoke detector.

Dust filtration/extraction

Because so much modern woodworking is done by abrading, the residue is dust, and clearly dust is a menace. Chippings, being larger, are more of a nuisance but less of a health risk. Dust is finer and ideally should be filtered at source. Power tools and light machines have dust/chippings extraction take-off hoods of varying diameters (Fig 4.3). The most efficient dust-extraction system is the large volume filtered unit (wall or floor mounted) which will collect dust and chippings. There are numerous excellent extractors on the market up to about 1000 watts (Fig 4.4).

Because space is limited in my own workshop I have a portable unit which I link up to each machine (Fig 4.5). The smaller vacuum-cleaner-type dust and chippings collection units are suitable for power tools and have smaller diameter hoses, and usually a long-reach of cable. Some models, such as those produced by Elu, have simultaneous switches for the power tool by means of a socket for the tool mounted on the extractor. It pays to buy a good-quality model which runs quietly.

If you use a dust extractor religiously you will find surprisingly little dust in the workshop. Without one the build-up is gradual but extensive, covering (or perhaps the word is – burying!) all of your tools and equipment and eventually leading to dustwebs on the ceiling (I know!). Particles of dust in the air remain there for many hours and are a health hazard if they are inhaled.

Dustmask

Always wear a dustmask as a precaution. Not only are some woods particularly toxic, causing bron-

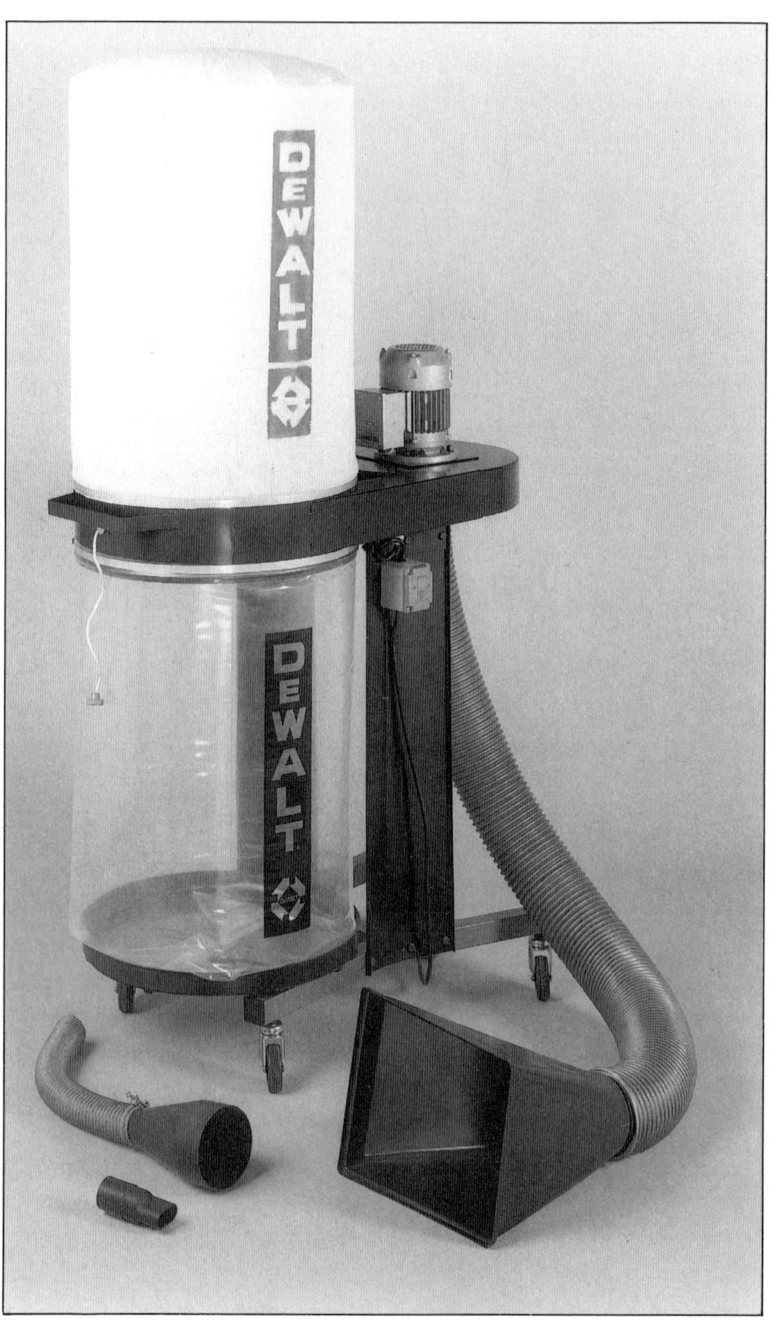

Fig 4.4 DeWalt portable chippings collector.

chial problems, but all dusts are potentially dangerous to health. Dustmasks should conform to British Standard BS6016 (respirators for the woodworking industry). There are various leading suppliers such as Racal and 3M (Fig 4.6). These masks normally have a life of eight hours and should then be replaced.

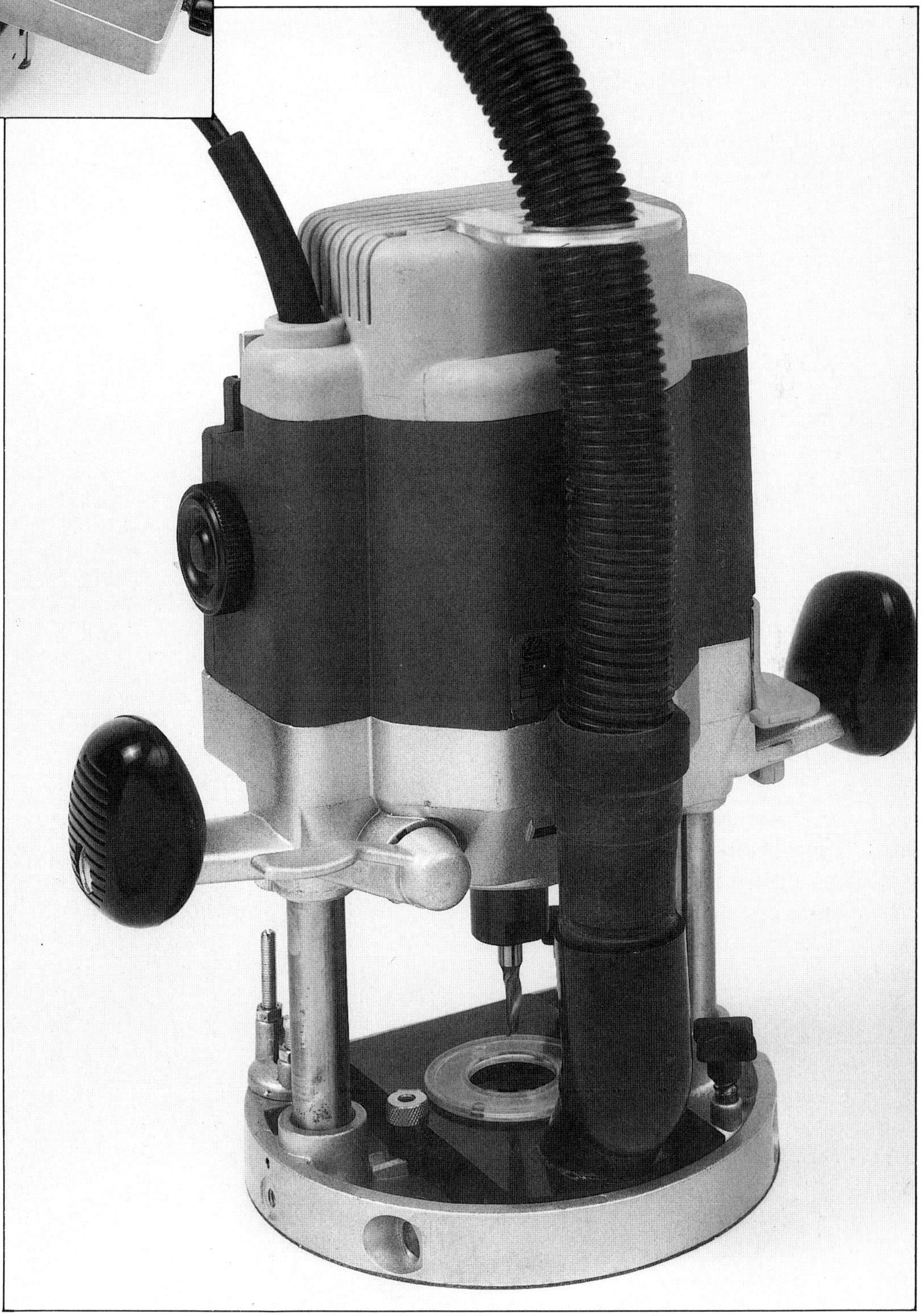

Fig 4.3 Extracting dust at source.

Fig 4.5 Elu EVE 928 portable dust extractor – quiet and powerful.

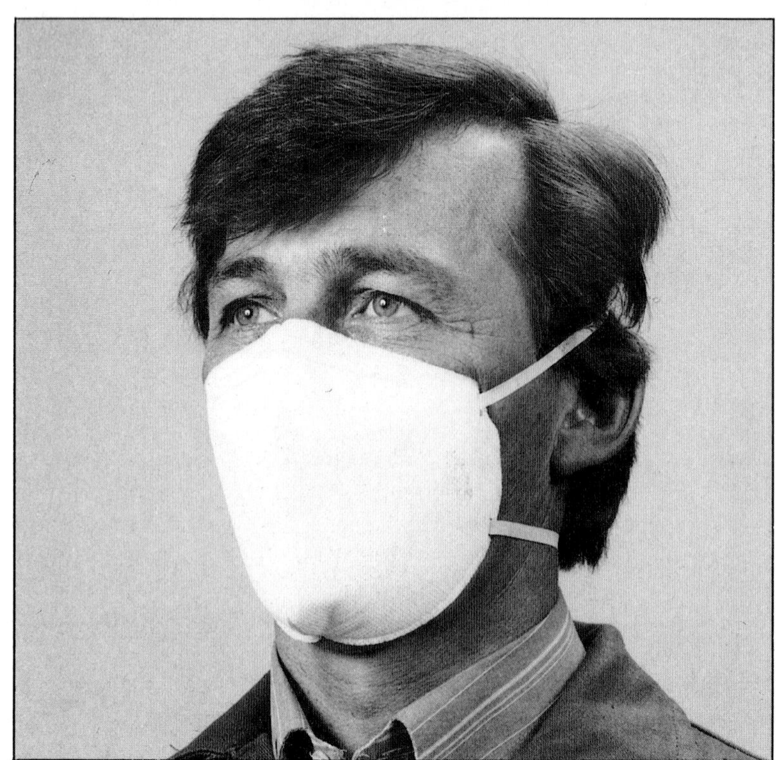

Fig 4.6 Racal 5060 dustmask – an effective deterrent.

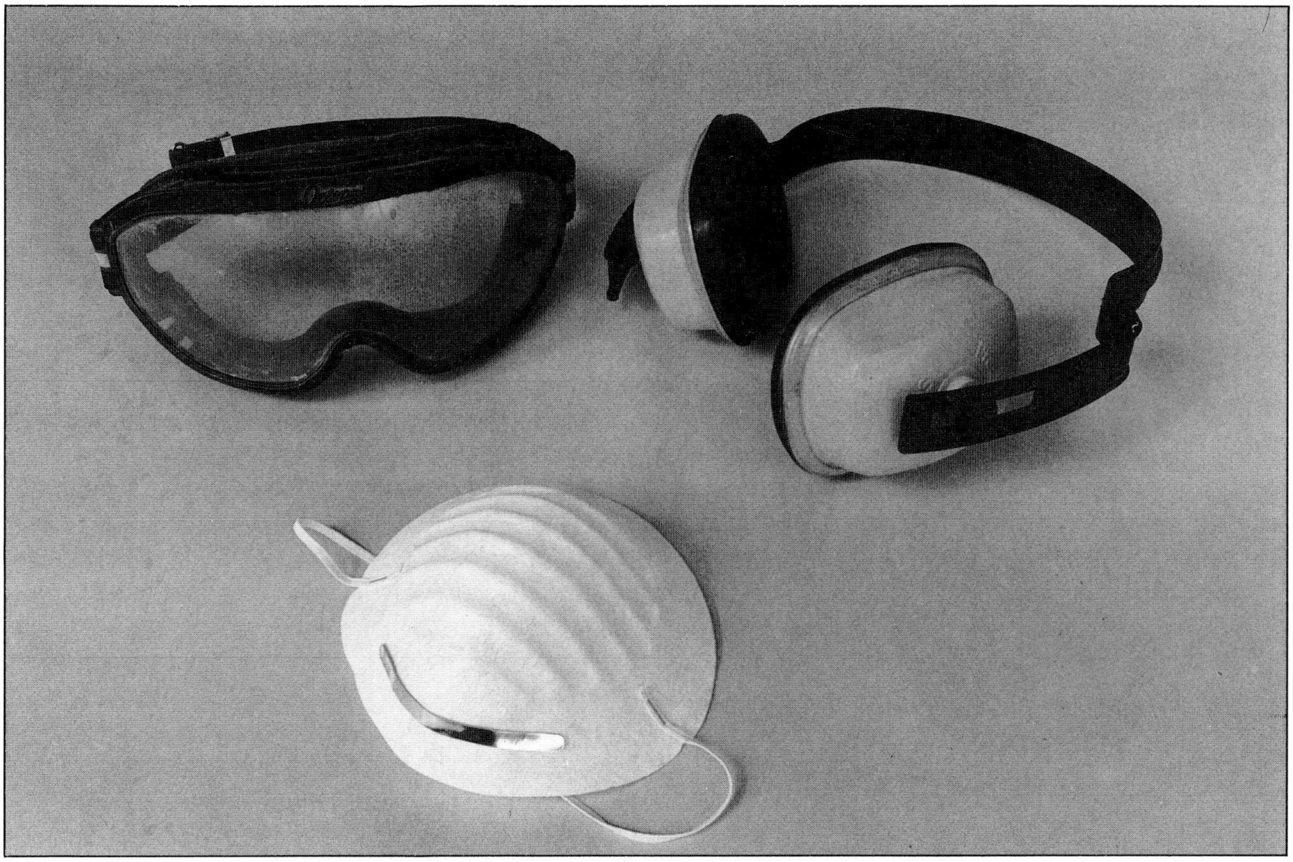

Fig 4.7 Eye, ear and nose protection.

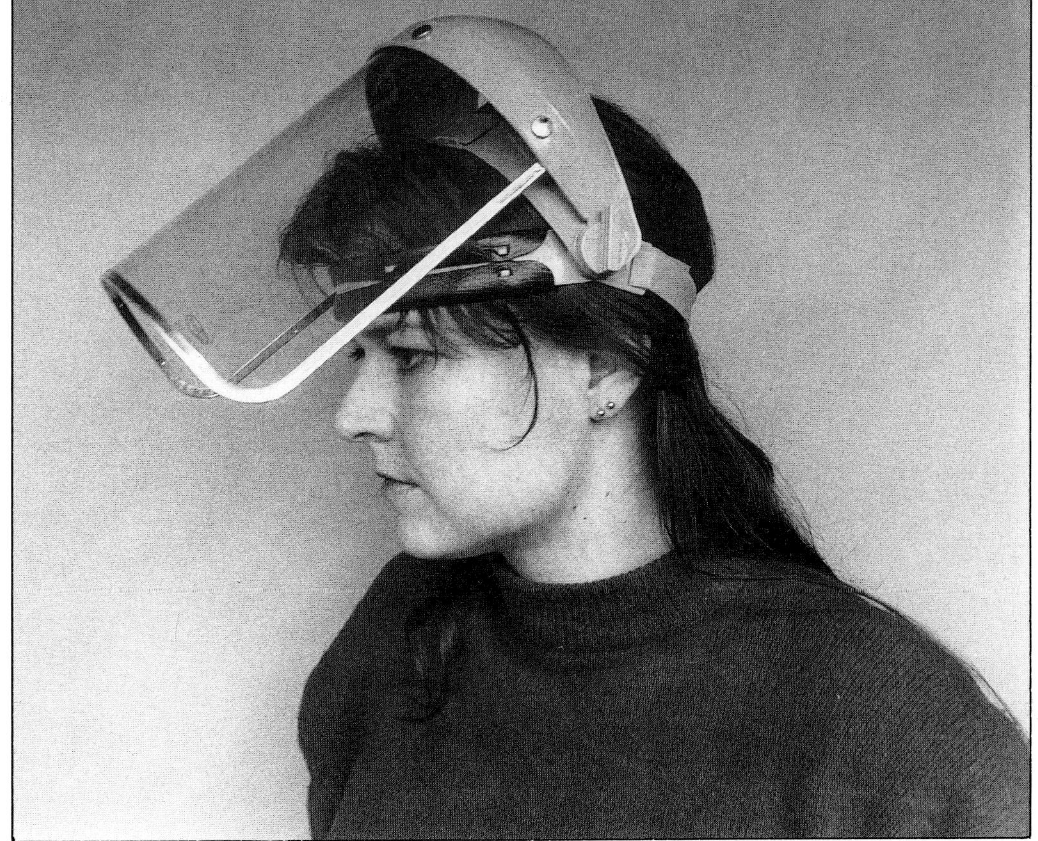

Fig 4.8 Inexpensive full-face, hinging visor.

Earmuffs

Every router and circular saw should be sold with a pair of earmuffs (Fig 4.7). Much electric woodworking is unsociable and earmuffs should be worn at all times. The higher frequencies are clipped which means you can still safely hear the tool you are operating.

Eye protection

Eye protectors range from lightweight spectacles to full face visors (Fig 4.8). Operating some electric tools is more likely than others to cause eye injury, e.g. the lathe, router, circular saws and the grinder fitted with the Arbotech Woodcarver.

Fig 4.9 The Racal Dustmaster 4 Mk 2.

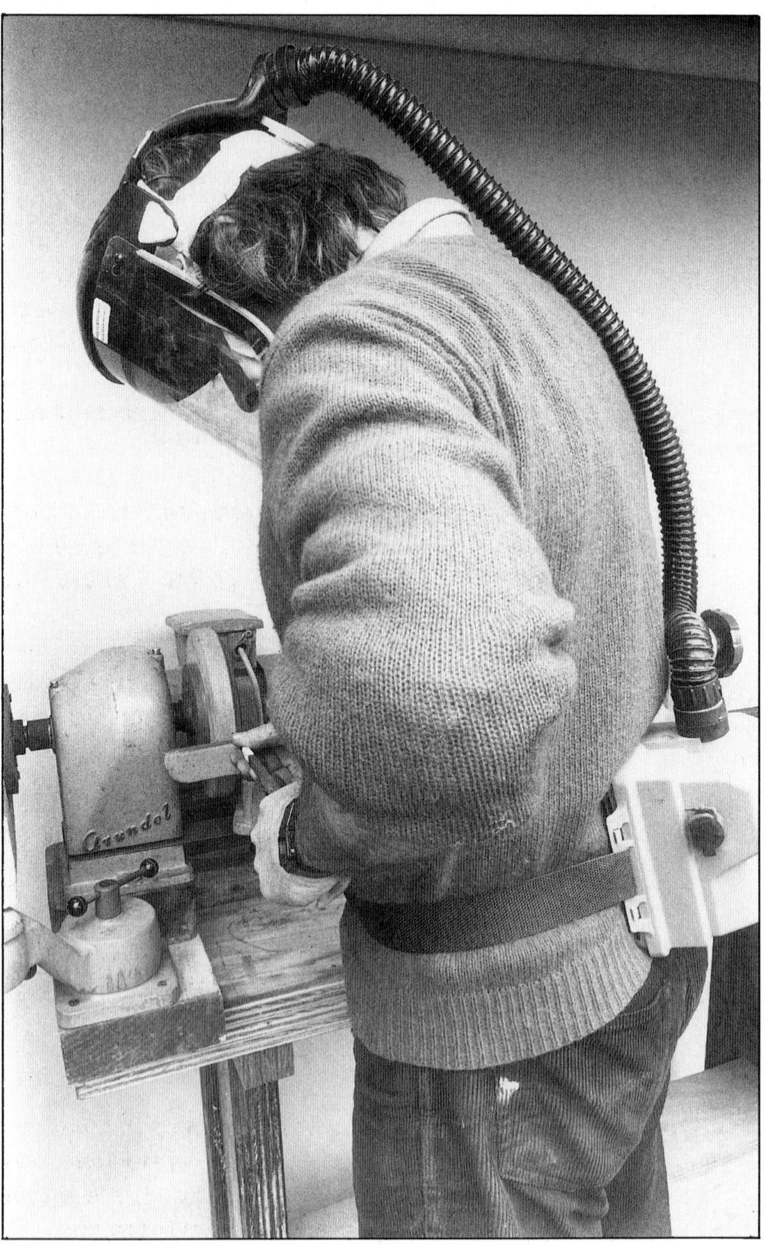

Combined face protection

Racal Ltd make a range of sophisticated integral helmets such as the Dustmaster 4 Mk 2 (Fig 4.9), which is battery powered and runs for approximately 10 hours on one charge. This is claimed to give ultimate protection against nuisance dusts and has a high-impact-resistant visor. I tried one out and found it to be surprisingly comfortable – after my misgivings about being dressed like a spaceman! Perhaps the Mk 3 will have integral earmuffs.

Operating electric tools

Specific points are dealt with in separate chapters, but in the main be aware that **all tools have sharp cutters.** Power should be switched off *before* setting up a tool and *immediately* after using it. Hands or fingers should be kept well away from sharp and moving parts. Manufacturers issue comprehensive operating instructions in each power tool manual.

Guards

Most tools are supplied with guard protection to meet increasing legislation, and common sense and the responsibility and care of the user are essential. I personally find some guards restricting as it helps to be able to see the line you are cutting (Fig 4.10) **but that does not mean I recommend you should remove them.**

First aid kit

A small, compact easily-purchased first aid kit should be hung on the wall at a visible and accessible point. It should include instant bandages, lint, Dettol, scissors and tweezers for those splinters which are a common occupational hazard.

SOME SAFETY HORROR STORIES

1 When I was at college one of my fellow students (a brilliant guitarist) was on teaching practice. While circular sawing some wood for the pupils, he accidentally cut his finger off. The boys were instantly on hands and knees trying to find the finger amidst the wood dust. It was later sewn back on in a hospital which was fortunately nearby.

2 A young trainee woodworker was known amongst his peers to be something of a daredevil. When his instructor turned his back for five min-

Fig 4.10 Clear plastic blade guard on a Ryobi radial arm saw for good visibility when cutting.

utes, the young trainee flicked the switch of a machine planer and 'played with it'. He instantly lost two and a half fingers.

3 Some time ago, while building a kitcar, I managed to drill straight into my finger with a ½in twist drill while drilling through a fibreglass panel. My other hand was supporting the material in the wrong place, out of sight behind the panel.

4 After having half a glass of wine at lunchtime once, in the afternoon I returned to the bandsaw in my workshop. With surprising ease I fed my thumb into the blade. Never, ever, take alcohol when woodworking!

5 Several years ago, as a young woodwork teacher, I was demonstrating bowl turning to a group of pupils. I was using a new tool which had sharp edges (the sides of the blade). My hand was firmly clasped around it when the tool suddenly snatched in the wood, causing the sharp edges to incise deeply into my forefinger. I managed to ask a pupil to quickly fetch the headmaster before I fainted in a heap on the floor! The injury required several stitches at the local hospital.

If ever an accident occurs, and I suppose one of the most common amongst carpenters must be treading on an up-turned nail in a board, it is always best to seek medical advice as to whether a tetanus injection is required.

In addition to the above horror stories, always bear in mind the following:

- Before using new machines, read the manufacturer's instructions. If still baffled then seek advice from the retailer or an experienced woodworker who has experience of the tool concerned. Or simply contact the manufacturer.
- Avoid alcohol or drugs. Do not use machines or hand tools if taking a course of drugs that induce drowsiness, e.g. for hayfever.
- Avoid distractions when machining or using dangerous hand tools. (Lock up all young children!)
- Sensible clothing. Avoid flapping sleeves – literally 'roll up your sleeves'.
- A problem for all who use dangerous machinery is woodworking in isolation. Can we attract someone's attention in the case of an accident or emergency before disaster befalls, or does someone know we are in the workshop?

Your health and safety must always come first, and a short lapse in concentration can easily lead to an accident. Woodworking is potentially a dangerous activity, despite its tremendous enjoyment.

Fig 4.11 A first aid kit is essential.

5

THE DRILL

The electric drill is synonymous with twentieth-century DIY man (and woman). If you didn't go out and buy your Black & Decker when you first set up home then the chances are you were given one as a Christmas present, whether you asked for it or not.

Just as Hoover was to the vacuum cleaner, Black & Decker is to the electric drill. But of course there are many others. Panasonic, perhaps better known for televisions, and Peugeot, who make cars, also make electric drills, and there are countless other excellent drills by Hitachi, Bosch, Makita, Ryobi *et al.* There are more electric drills on the market today than any other power tool, ranging in size, capacity, speed, specific function, chuck type, etc., but essentially they all do the same thing – they drill holes!

Of course the electric drill is the power tool from which all other power tools originated. And that comes as no surprise when you consider that it is little more than an electric motor with a switch, a handle and a chuck on the end of its spindle. The 'bolt-on' accessories to the electric drill are substantial, ranging from sanders, jigsaws, circular saws, flexible drives, to lathe attachments, making it a truly versatile piece of kit (Figs 5.1 and 5.2). But it is also true that although many of these bolt-ons are still available, they have been largely superseded by specific power tools which obviously give superior performance because they are designed exclusively to do a particular job.

TYPES AND SPECIFICATION

From the enormous array of drills on the market, ranging from cheap throwaways to the Mercedes models (usually to be found in the hire shops), it is worth observing a few ground rules (which can apply to other power tools as well).

Fig 5.1 Black & Decker drill.

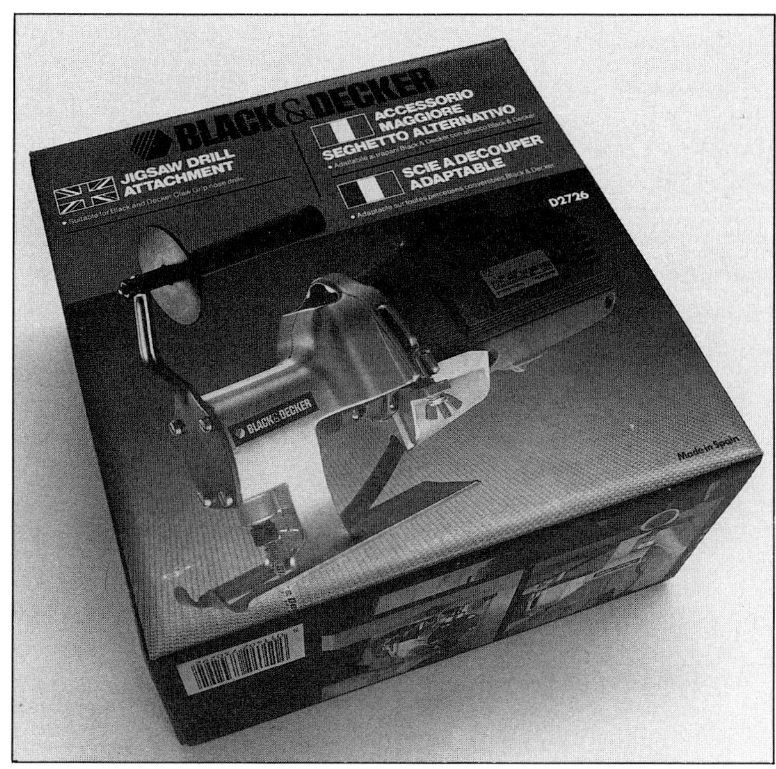

The cheaper drills are likely to have phosphor-bronze bearings instead of needle-roller bearings, thin windings, and are generally lightly fabricated and come under the DIY label.They do not have a particularly long working life. An industrially rated drill will cost more and basically will last longer, but the DIY user may only pick up the drill for a few minutes each month, whereas the professional will be looking for a heavyweight tool which offers sustained reliability. Having said that, manufacturers offer many, many grades and specifications in between. My own collection includes heavy-duty industrial drills and cheaper throwaway models, but strangely one of my earliest and cheapest drills, from the mid-70s, is still going strong today (Fig 5.3)!

Drills are specified by their power (wattage), by their chuck size, and other features such as 'torque control' (Fig 5.4), 'multi-speed', 'reverse action', 'hammer action', 'fast-action chuck', 'variable-speed trigger' (and if you are lucky the tool will drill holes as well!).

Fig 5.2 Attachments for the drill.

Fig 5.3 The author has drilled over 40 000 holes with this drill!

Whereas there are rotary drills, percussion drills, impact drills, reversible drills, driver-drills, thermal-flow drills, etc., the drill of most relevance here is the one which drills wood but can also drill into masonry (for Rawlplug fixings) (Fig 5.5) and is therefore likely to be a **rotary hammer** drill with perhaps two speeds.

If other functions are required it is probably best to have a separate drill specifically designed for tasks such as driving in screws, (see page 36). From a practical point of view it is tiresome to keep changing drillbits – from pilot drills to shank drills to screwdriver bits.

Drills are normally supplied with a removable handle which is clamped around a universal collar of 43mm diameter (Fig 5.6). This collar allows the drill to be mounted in a stand (Fig 5.7) and is common to some routers. The handle also accommodates a simple and effective depth-stop for drilling. (For early Black & Decker drills an adaptor is available for converting to the 43mm collar.)

POWER RATING

Drills range in specified power from under 300 watts to about 1000 watts. 500 watts is a good average and of course that refers to input wattage not output wattage (see page 10) so the actual power is less.

Fig 5.4 Adjustable torque control on the excellent Hitachi D10DF cordless drill-driver. Also featuring the wonderful keyless chuck.

Fig 5.5 A heavy-duty Bosch rotary drill used in masonry.

Fig 5.6 The handle and depth stop on a Black & Decker 600 watt drill.

Fig 5.7 Operating the Wolfcraft drillstand.

Fig 5.8 Tighten all three positions when using a chuck key.

THE CHUCK

The chuck capacity varies from ¼in to ½in and this refers to the spindle diameter of drills and bits. Suffice to say here that in the case of a flatbit the shank diameter is a standard ¼in or 6mm, meaning it can be driven by the smaller chuck capacity drills. However, it is an advantage to have a drill with a ½in chuck.

Most chucks are operated by a geared key (Fig 5.8), and it is important to tighten up the chuck by placing the key in each of the three holes progressively so that the pressure or grip is even on the three chuck jaws. Invariably keys get lost and one of the most sensible recent innovations has been the keyless chuck (see Fig 5.4) which is a real boon. (This type of chuck is also available on some manufacturers' percussion drills.)

DRILLBITS AND ACCESSORIES

Generally made of HSS steel, bits for drilling are available in different types.

Twist drills

By far the most common is the twist drill, which ranges in diameter from about 2mm to 25mm, with 12mm as an average maximum (Fig 5.9). These drills cut cleanly, are self-guiding and are strong – although brittle. In operation the wood debris is cleared through the helical flutings, but the drill should be cleaned with a pin or something similar as resinous woods can cause debris to stick.

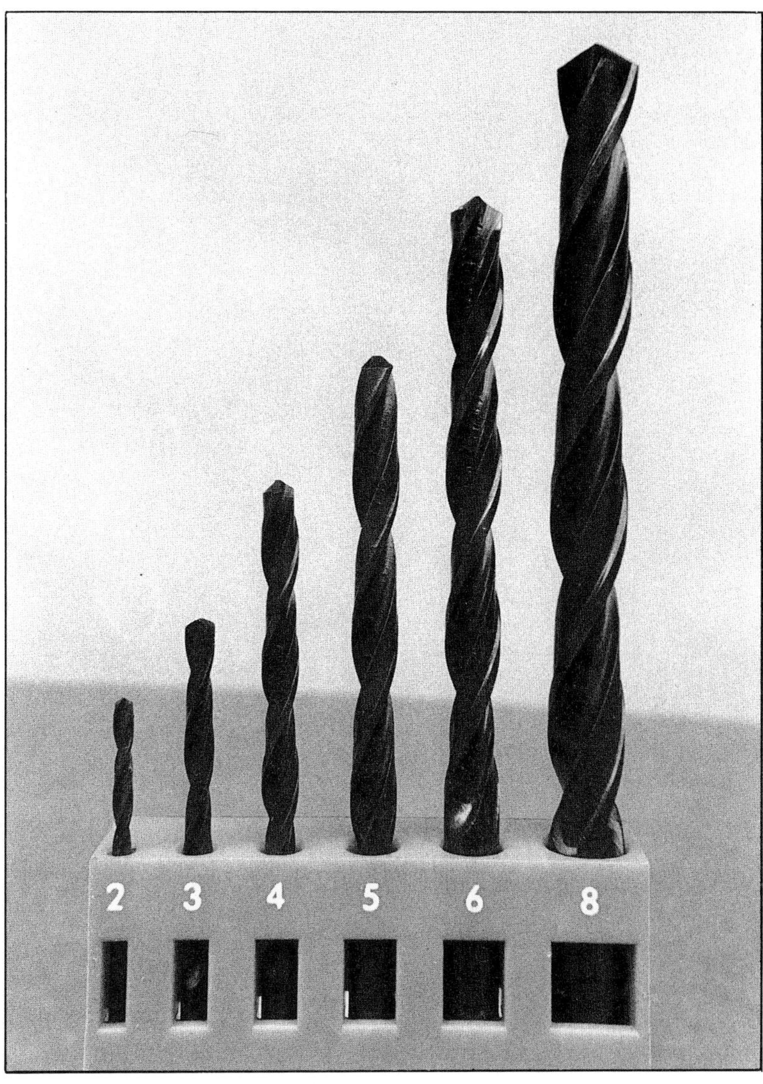

Fig 5.9 Set of twist drills.

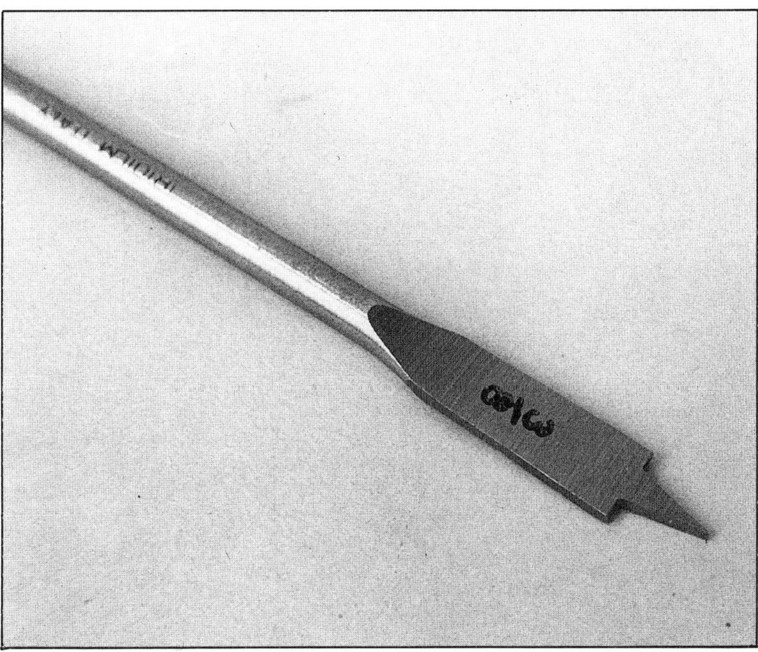

Fig 5.10 Another wonderful invention – the flatbit.

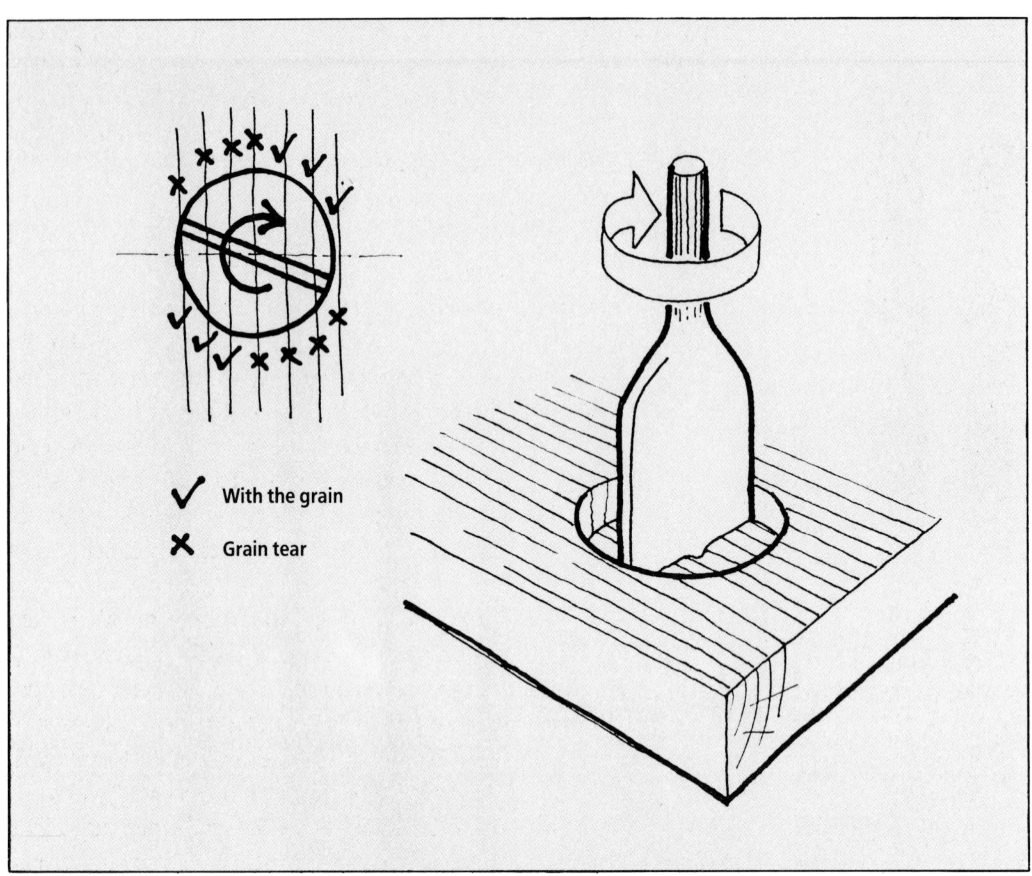

Fig 5.11 The action of a flatbit – keep it razor sharp to avoid grain tear.

Fig 5.12 Grinding a flatbit. The cutting edge matches the profile of the wheel and is tilted slightly upwards to get the right angle.

Fig 5.13 Bradpoint bits make centring easy.

The larger diameter twist drills are not cheap and demand greater torque, so the alternative flat-bit is well worth considering. The expert wood-worker can easily re-grind drills freehand but the cutting angle is crucial. There are drill-grinding jigs on the market (see page 36).

Flatbits

Whereas a twist drill can be used in a hand drill, the flat or spade bit is purpose-designed for the electric drill (Fig 5.10). When they first appeared the experts scorned their efficiency because they effectively scrape the wood and can tear the grain in the cutting circle (Fig 5.11). This is important if the hole is going to show in a finished piece of work and the flatbit is less than razor sharp. Its advantages are that it is relatively inexpensive and ranges in size from about 6mm to 38mm, the larger diameters being most useful. Because of their design the larger bits perform well in an average-powered drill, whereas the torque would have to be enormous if using the equivalent twist drill. They are also easier to centre because they have a sharp centre point. Flatbits can be ground easily (I use a grindstone – Fig 5.12). If kept sharp they

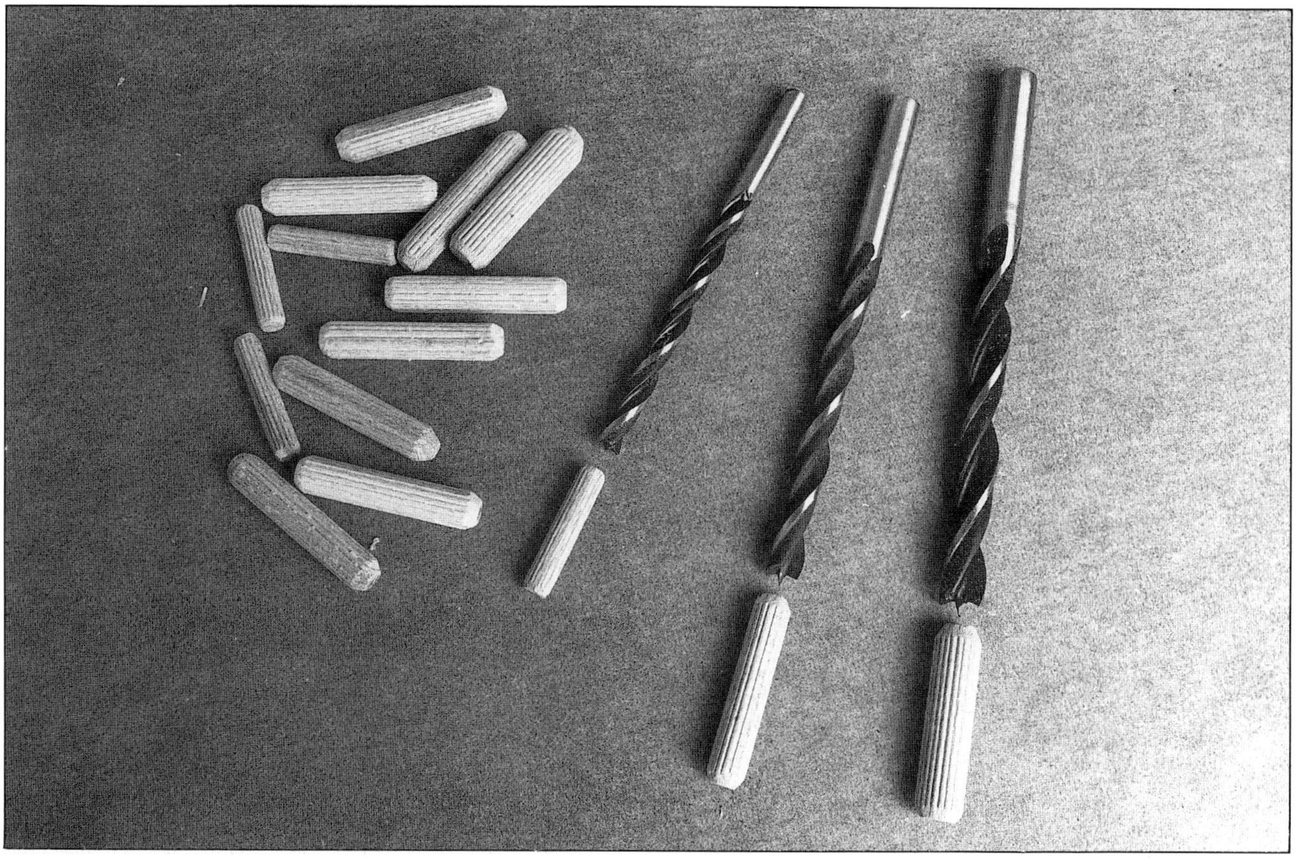

Fig 5.14 Three popular sizes of dowels and drills.

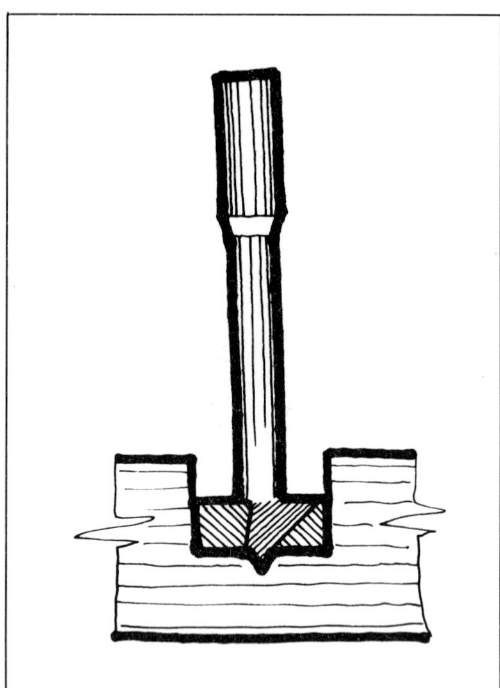

Fig 5.15 Forstner bit – a flat-bottomed hole is cut.

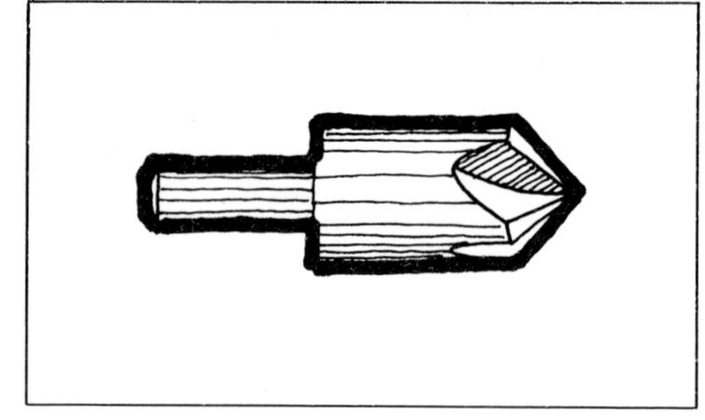

Fig 5.17 Countersunk bit.

should not wander in deep holes. Care should be taken in holding work firm as the shanks can bend, but otherwise they are remarkable hole borers.

Bradpoint bits

Bradpoint or dowel bits are similar to twist drills but have a centre point which makes location precise – they do not wander. They are available in sizes similar to twist drills. Common sizes for using with standard dowel are 6, 8 and 10mm (Fig 5.14).

Forstner bits

Forstner bits overcome the problem of many other drillbits (Fig 5.15) – they leave a relatively clean, flat, bottom to the hole (though the ideal flat-bottomed hole is achieved with a router cutter). Forstner bits are expensive and they drill clean-walled holes to precision. (A derivation of this bit is the hinge-sinking cutter which is purpose-made for cabinet hinges (Fig 5.16).)

Countersink bits

Countersink bits allow screwheads to bed in just under the surface of the timber. They are generally operated at a high speed to prevent vibration and grain tear (Fig 5.17).

Dual-purpose bits

There is a range of dual-purpose bits for drilling and counterboring for sinking screws in, and it is worth considering the requirements and specifications of wood screws (see Fig 5.18), as drilling requirements are crucial if effective fixings are to be obtained.

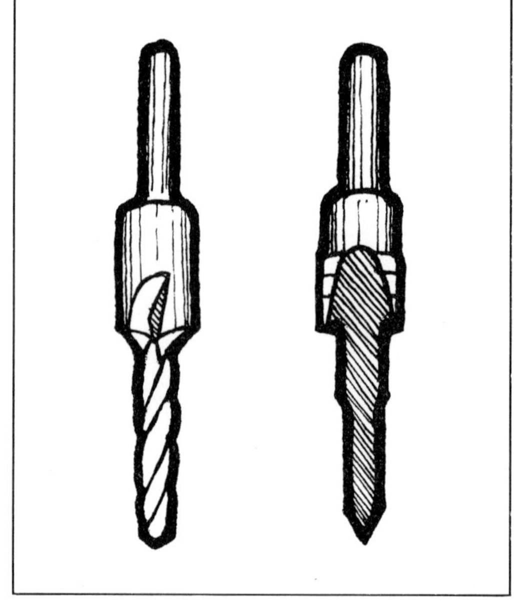

Fig 5.18 Dual-purpose bit.

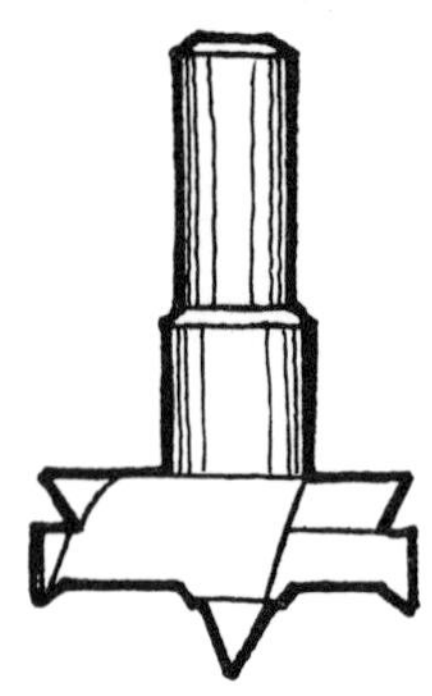

Fig 5.16 Cabinet-hinge sinker.

Hinge-sinking cutters

An HSS flat-bottomed cutter for boring vertical-walled holes, generally of 35mm and 26mm diameter, to accommodate concealed cabinet hinges in MDF or chipboard (Fig 5.16).

Plug cutters

These are two-piece sets enabling a cylindrical core of wood to be extracted from an offcut of the same timber into which its matching hole is going to be bored (Fig 5.20). Plugs are generally used to cap screwheads which are sunk below the surface. The advantage of a wood plug over a short piece of dowel is that the grain direction matches, hence avoiding the different grain direction of the timber movement so commonly caused by exposed dowels. Plugs can look neat.

Hole saws and tank-cutting bits

Although designed for metal, these wide diameter interchangeable HSS cutters screw on to a pilot hole mandrel and are accurate and efficient. Diameters range from 3mm to 50mm (Fig 5.21).

SAFETY AND OPERATION

The drill is a tool which is very susceptible to lazy use, perhaps because it is so often used and therefore familiar. It should **not be held by its cable**, the **chuck key should never be left in the chuck**, and as with other mains-powered tools it **should not be used near water.** The enormous versatility of the drill and its apparent meekness should not lead to it being underestimated. Like any power tool it can do a lot of damage very quickly (see Horror Stories, page 21).

A fairly common problem arises when drilling and fixing wall panelling when battens are used, and cavities filled with fibreglass insulation. The drill can go through the panelling and into the insulation material, immediately wrapping it around the drillbit. But what is more likely to happen is that the drill is instantly snatched out of the user's hand – which could cause a wrist sprain – and the drill flies out of control.

The drill should be held firmly, ideally in both hands (see Fig 5.5) with or without the handle. Holes to be drilled should first be centre punched

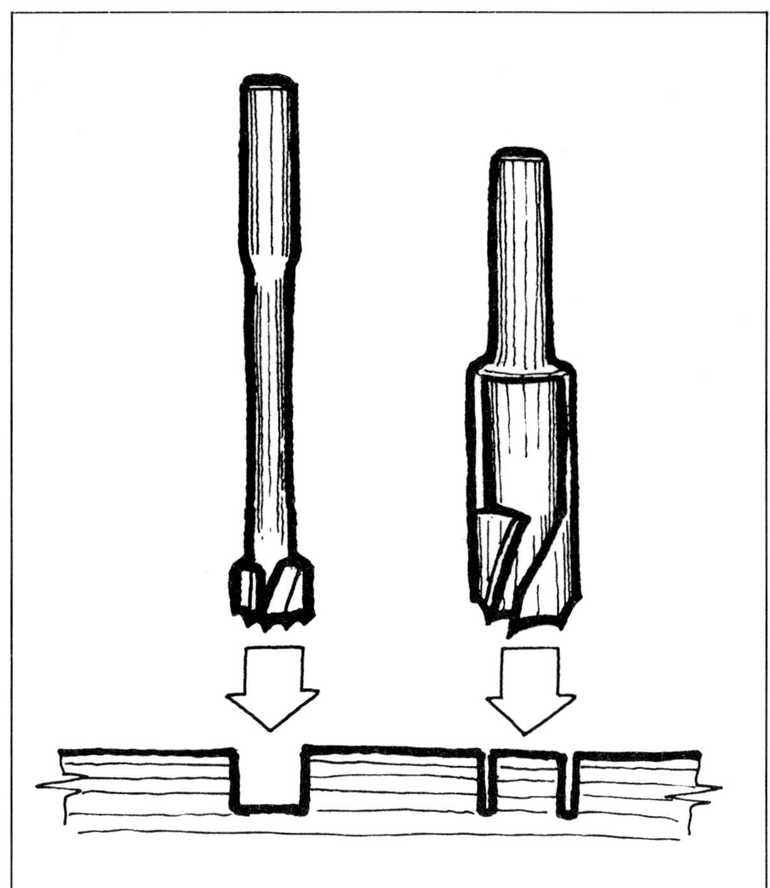

Fig 5.20 Plug cutter.

Fig 5.19 The hinge-sinking cutter.

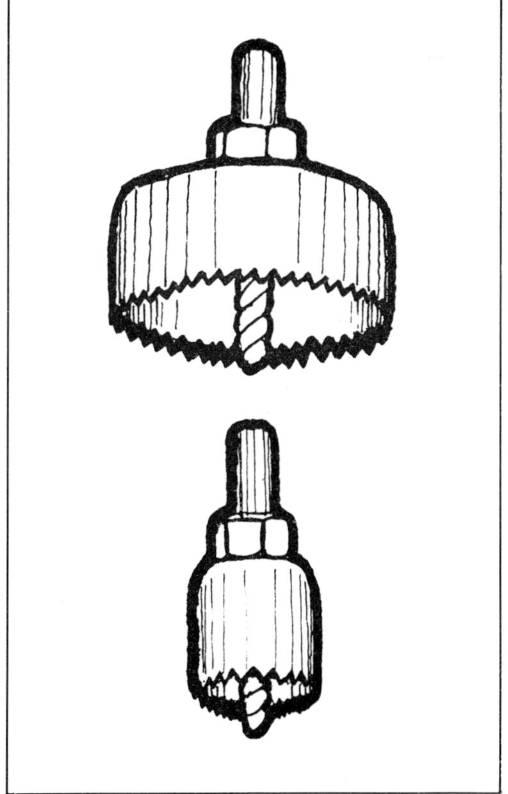

Fig 5.21 Tank cutter.

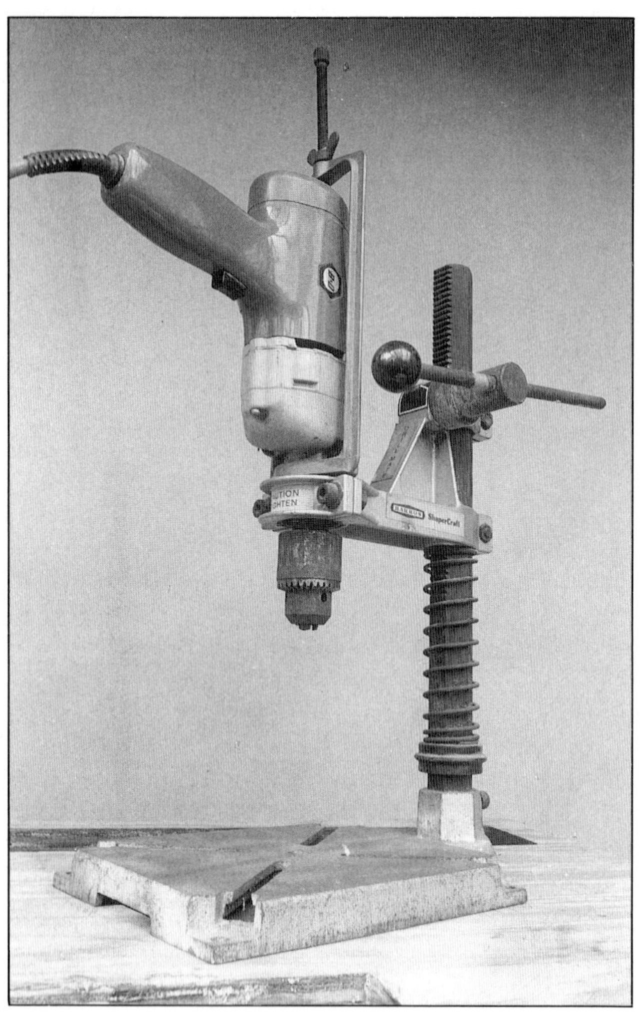

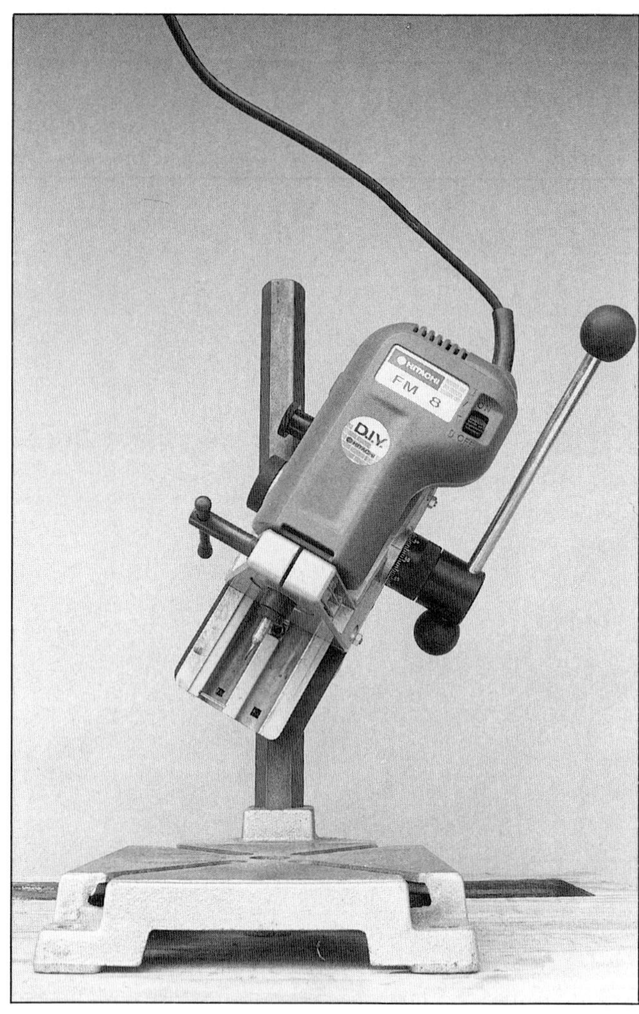

Fig 5.22 The author's battle-scarred drill and drillstand (above left).

Fig 5.23 Hitachi FM8 router mounted at an angle in the Wolfcraft drillstand (above right).

so that the drillbit engages immediately, without wandering. It helps when freehand drilling to first line up a try-square behind to check accurate drill alignment.

Gentle pressure should be applied – you can feel the bit engage with the material. Too much pressure, or jerking, will break the drillbit, which is brittle.

When drilling masonry for fixings it is very easy to jam the drill and sometimes very difficult to get the drillbit out. This is caused by debris clogging in the spiral flutings in the drillbit and the bit should be withdrawn periodically to clear dust and debris.

ATTACHMENTS

Drillstands

Perhaps the most useful of all accessories is the pillar drillstand, which is a relatively inexpensive jig for precision drilling (Fig 5.22) (its purpose-built machine counterpart is much more expensive). Some drillstands have a rack and pinion action and depth-stops. Some allow the drill to be positioned at any angle and the universal 43mm collar allows the optional mounting of a router (Fig 5.23).

Lathes

This is a simple bench-clamped jig marketed by several companies. The 43mm collar takes most drills (Fig 5.24). It is best to use fixed-speed drills for any extended period of time. The lathe attachment is best suited for narrow-spindle and small faceplate work as the 'swing' is limited. It is interesting to note that this type of lathe, driven by a fairly meaty electric drill, delivers more power than some of the small purpose-built lathes (i.e. 1.3 HP).

Drum-sanding kits

A useful kit comprising various diameter rubber drums mounted on a screw-tightened spindle. The abrasive roll is loosely slipped on to the drum, then the spindle nut tightened so that the rubber ex-

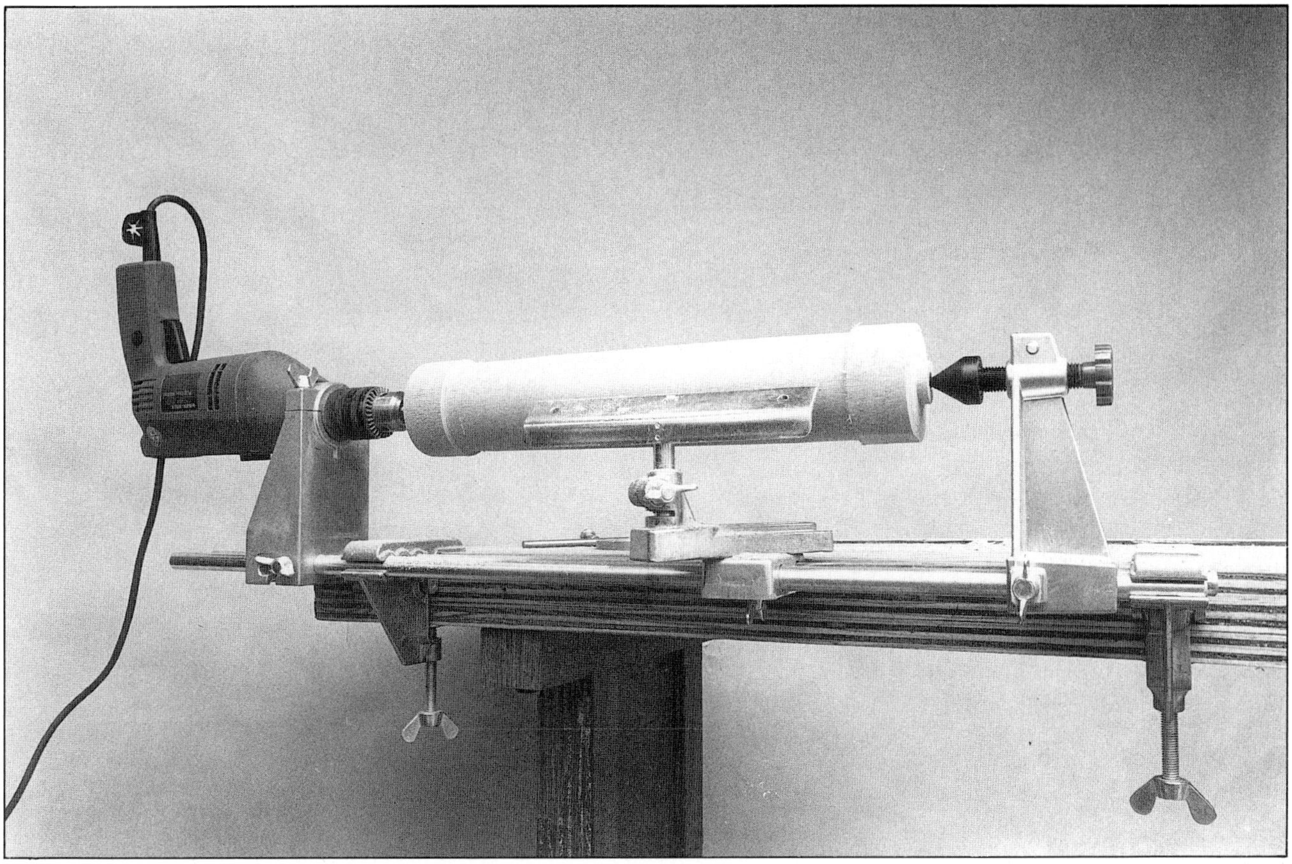

Fig 5.24 A Black & Decker PL20 600-watt drill mounted in a Zyliss lathe attachment – more power than some conventional lathes!

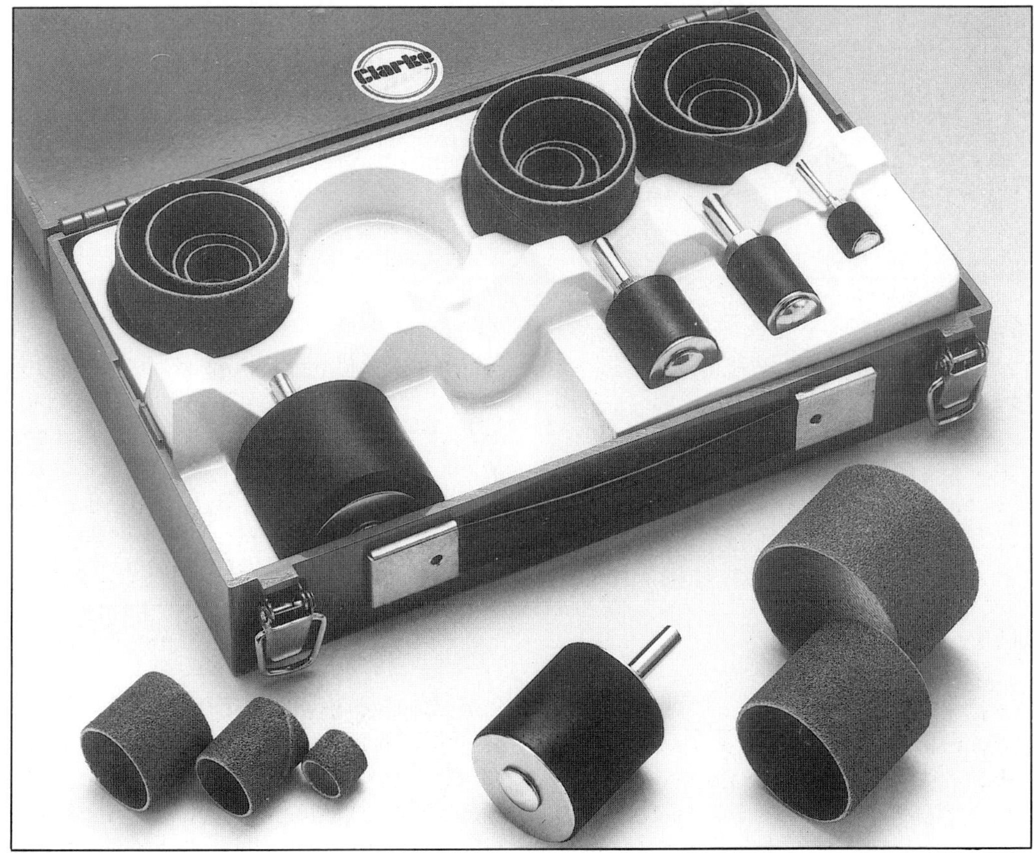

Fig 5.25 A drum-sanding kit.

pands to grip the abrasive roll. These kits can be used for delicate, flat or curved sanding operations. (Supplied by Machine Mart, see page 272.)

Disc-sanders

A disc-sander attachment to a drill or lathe is always very useful as the accurate finishing of end-grain is particularly difficult. Wolfcraft supply an excellent attachment with adjustable table and fence (Fig 5.26) which uses Velcro-backed abrasive sheets which are easily replaced. (Any disc sander less than about 8in diameter is likely to get clogged up too quickly.) A shop-made fabricated table can also be easily made up with the drill and disc mounted in a drill clamp (Fig 5.27).

Tool-sharpening

A useful attachment is a sharpening device for twist drills which is versatile and easy to use. The drill is jigged to be ground at around 120° by a rotary grinding wheel attached to the chuck of the drill (Fig 5.28). A variety of small diameter carborundum grinding wheels can be attached to the chuck of the drill and used for tool sharpening.

Fig 5.27 Drill mounted in a drill clamp.

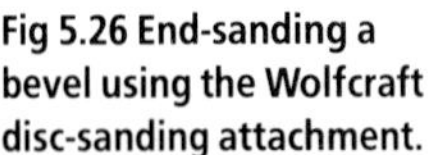

Fig 5.26 End-sanding a bevel using the Wolfcraft disc-sanding attachment.

CORDLESS DRILLS AND DRILL-DRIVERS

Increasingly popular, cordless drills find their way in and out of the workshop – as an extra drill in the workshop, or for tasks away from the mains, in the garden shed or attic, for instance.

Cordless drills are rated from about 2.4 volts to 24 volts with chuck capacities up to ½in. They normally double up as screwdrivers and have torque control settings (a slipping clutch), two speeds, or variable speed, and reverse action. The chucks are either keyed or keyless, although there is a trend towards the latter for convenience. They are very

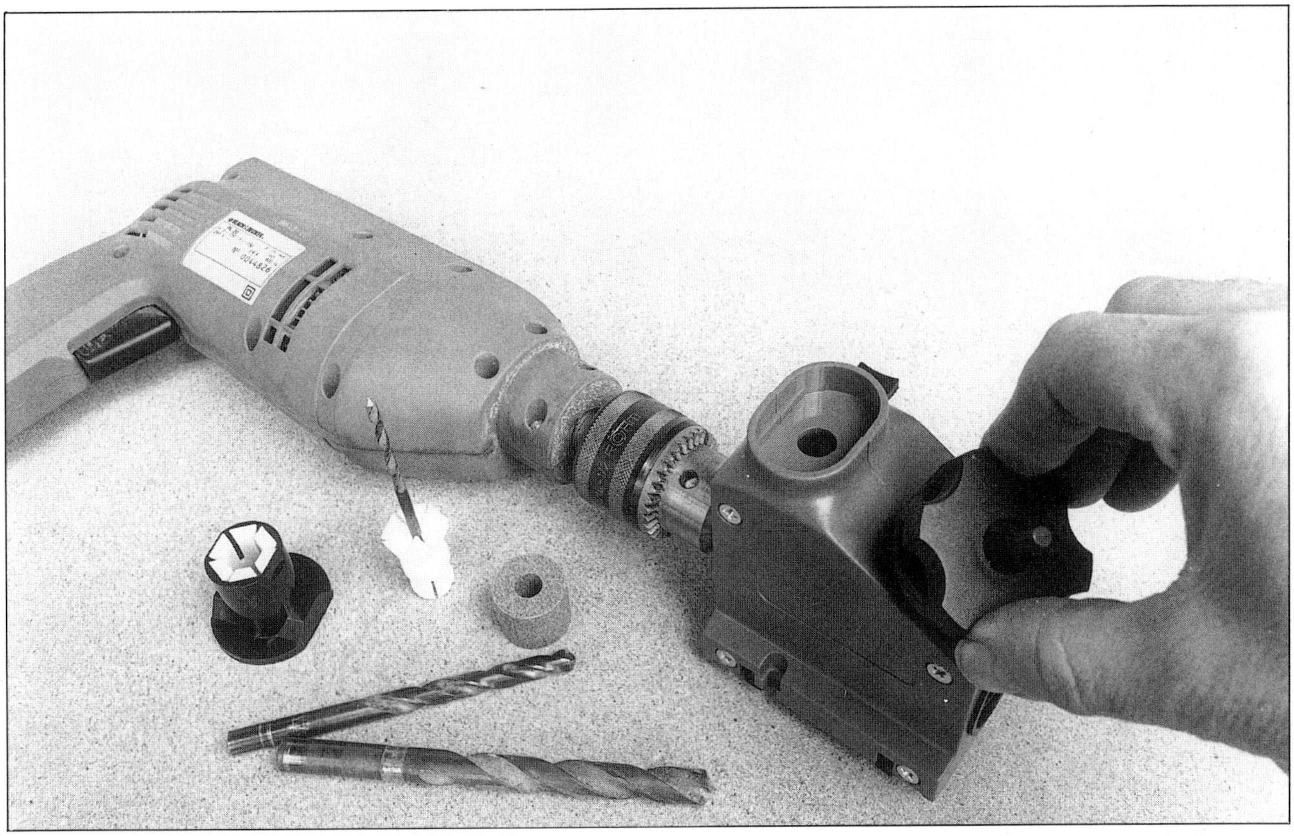

Fig 5.28 The Martek drill-sharpening attachment.

Fig 5.29 Neat little performer – the Panasonic 2.4 volt cordless drill-driver.

Fig 5.30 Accessories for the Panasonic drill-driver (left).

much tools of convenience (see Chapter 16, The Cordless Revolution).

Drill-drivers range from conventionally shaped and sized drills to what I refer to as 'neat little performers' (Fig. 5.29), which are compact yet powerful battery-driven tools (see Chapter 16). They possess either a conventional chuck or a hexagonal collett into which fit a range of screwdriver bits (Fig 5.30).

They are extremely useful, removing much of the time-consuming and wrist-aching work of fixing screws by hand, but it is important to use the right screwdriver bit for the job.

Cordless drill-drivers are powerful enough to cope with up to 300 or so repeat operations, depending on the specification, but obviously the mini versions are more suited to smaller diameter drilling. I find it natural when using a drill-driver to finally tighten up the screw manually, and my Skil screwdriver (Fig 5.31) has a spindle lock. The manufacturer of the Richmond drill-driver (Fig 5.32) does not recommend this practice, however, especially when the tool is cranked.

Some manufacturers produce cordless hammer drills with keyless chucks. All cordless power tools tend to be relatively expensive, and of course part of that cost extends to the battery and charger (see Chapter 16).

APPLICATIONS

The applications of the electric drill are numerous, from simple hole-boring operations in virtually any material, to buffing, polishing, sanding and attaching to the jigs already mentioned. It is a tool seldom used in isolation but as an essential part of an integrated team.

Fig 5.31 The author's Skil electric screwdriver (left).

Fig 5.32 The Panasonic drill-driver in action.

6

THE JIGSAW

The jigsaw is a rather understated power tool (Fig 6.1) and its modest appearance does not immediately suggest its capability, but for its size and with its simple action it is a truly remarkable little tool and I for one would be lost without it. It is a tool designed to cut, with the appropriate blade, any sheet or board material and solid timber (Fig 6.2).

I recall that when jigsaws first became readily available my reaction was similar to when Japanese motorcycles first raced at the Isle of Man TT – the highly revving motors would surely wear out! I reckoned the jigsaw blade, being so small with teeth you could almost count on one hand, would not last the pace and blade replacements would soon overtake the initial cost of the tool. Not so at

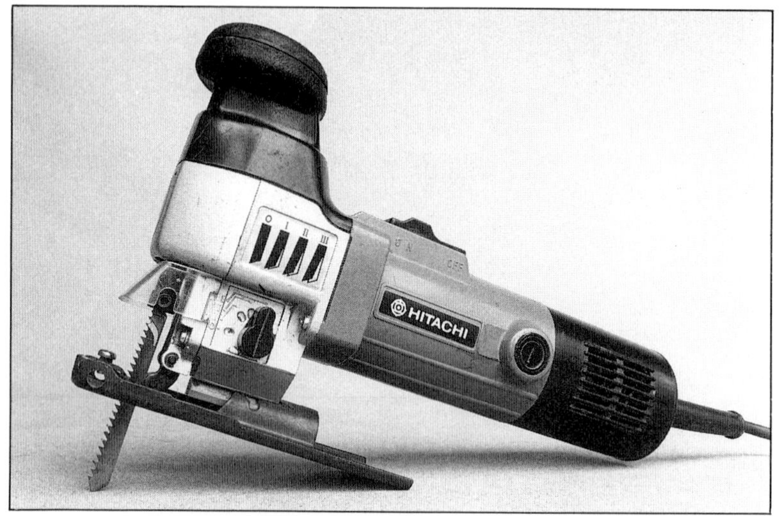

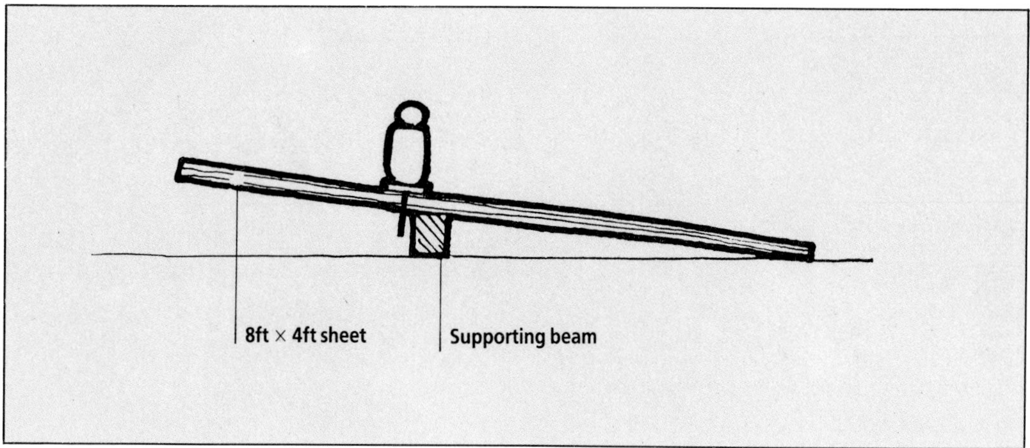

Fig 6.3 Cutting 8ft × 4ft boards with a jigsaw with a supporting batten.

all. The jigsaw has been developed together with blade-cutter technology to present a true 'David' amongst the present-day 'Goliaths' of electric tools.

The simple reciprocating action of the blade allows it to cut through any kind of material up to a reasonable thickness of about 25mm (Fig 6.2). And as with other tools I have pushed this one to the limit – and cut 50mm thick hardwood down the grain on more than one occasion.

The greatest strength of the jigsaw is its versatility – you take the tool to the material rather than vice versa. For example, when reducing 8ft × 4ft manufactured boards to dimension – in restricted workshop space with no one else around to help lift the material – the jigsaw comes into its own. You can simply place the board on the floor with a supporting batten underneath to allow the blade to clear (Fig 6.3).

Fig 6.1 Hitachi CJ65V 400 watt orbital jigsaw (opposite above).

Fig 6.2 Cutting through stout plywood with the Hitachi orbital jigsaw (opposite below).

Fig 6.4 Cutting curves with the jigsaw.

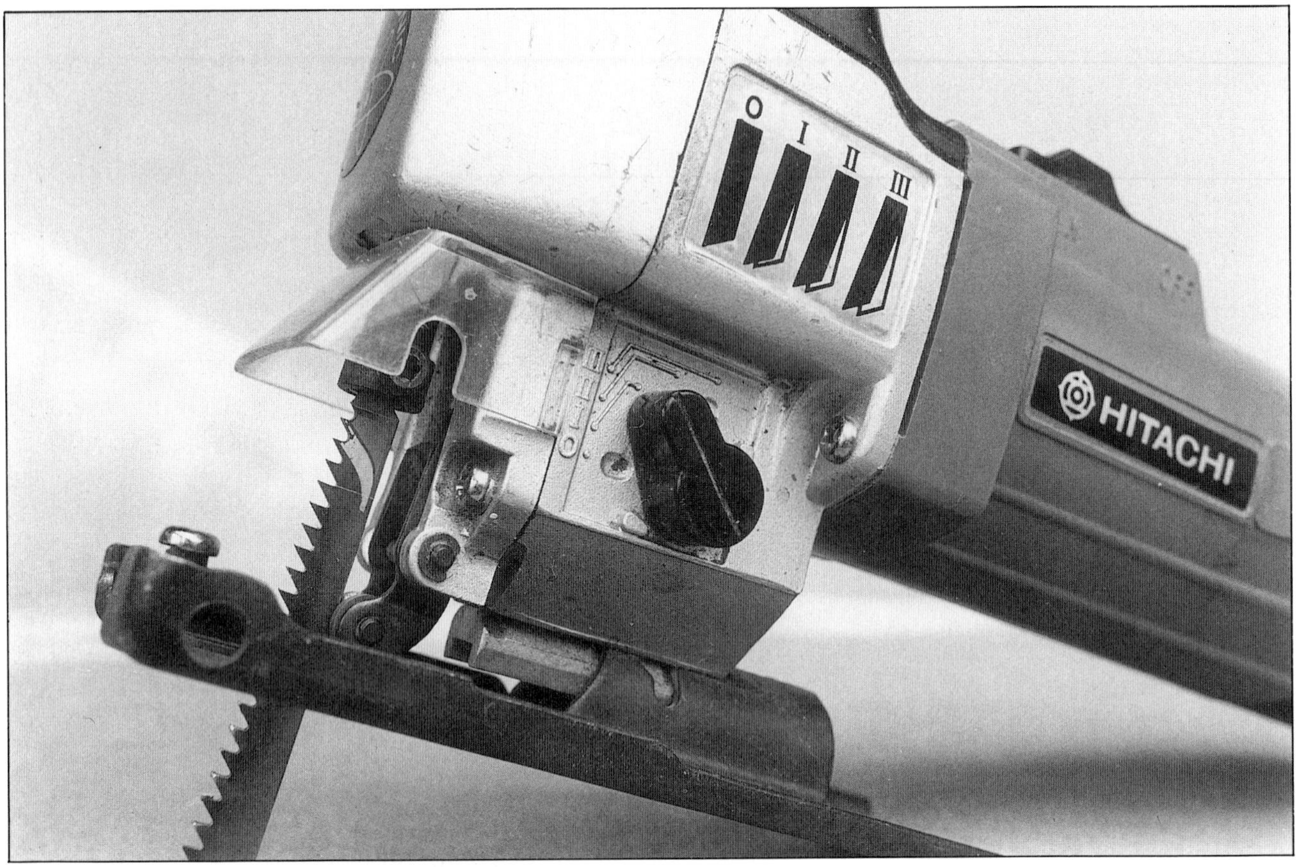

Fig 6.5 Close-up of the Hitachi CJ65V jigsaw.

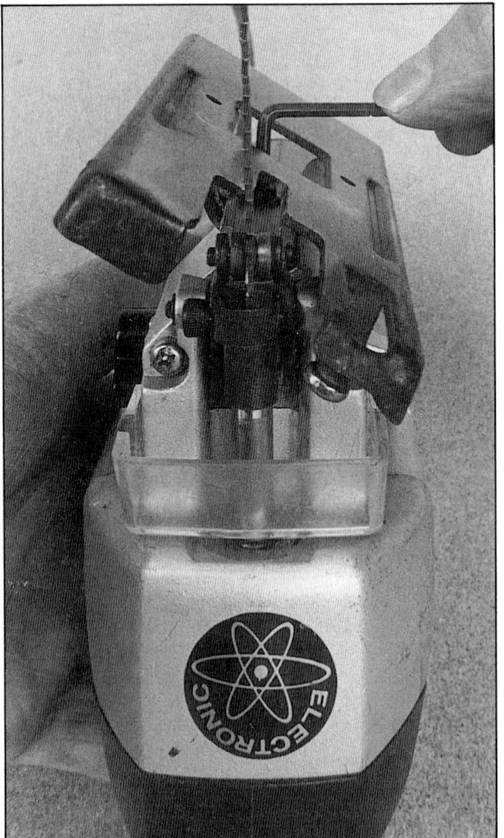

Fig 6.6 Adjustable base-plate locked with an Allen key.

Of course many woodworkers have an aversion to making straight cuts with a tool which is designed for curved cutting (Fig 6.4) (e.g. bandsaw instead of circular saw), but a small but significant consideration is the dust a machine creates, especially when using manufactured board, and the hazardous dust from chipboard and MDF. The slow reciprocating action of a jigsaw, with a fine kerfed blade, minimizes this problem. It is also easier on the ears.

TYPES AND SPECIFICATION

The jigsaw is usually power-rated at between 350 and 650 watts and delivers about 3000 strokes per minute (length of stroke 16–26mm). Models range from DIY to industrial and because of its normally prolonged workload it pays to buy an industrial model with a robust motor (Fig 6.5) and plunger mechanism. This mechanism should have a rear blade-supporting roller. The baseplate is pressed steel, can be adjusted to saw at an angle (Fig 6.6), and links up with a side fence for parallel cutting work. The blade reciprocates in a linear motion and approximately 50 per cent of the teeth are used in the action.

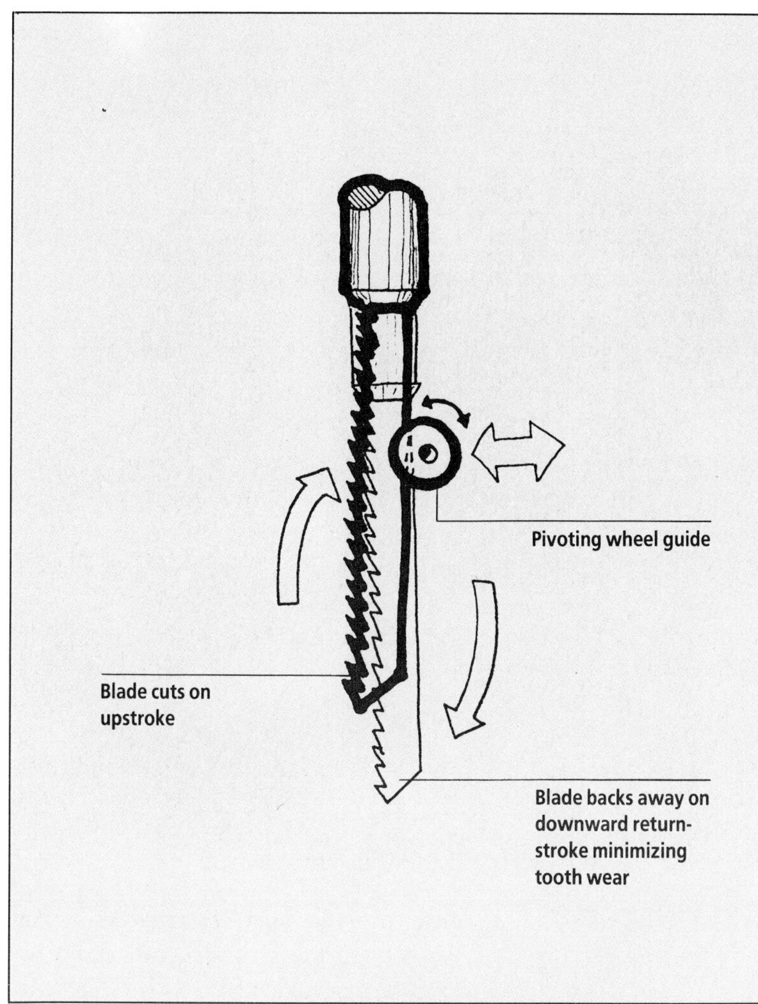

Fig 6.7 The orbital action of a jigsaw.

Orbital jigsaw

The most efficient jigsaws work on an orbital or oscillating blade stroke. Instead of the path of the blade being linear, it is elliptical, whereby it moves forward on the upward stroke to engage in the material, then backwards on the down stroke (Fig 6.7), clearing the dust and enhancing the blade life. The degree of orbital stroke can be adjusted in stages (see Fig 6.5).

Scrolling jigsaw

For cutting particularly tight bends the scrolling jigsaw has a blade-carrier assembly which can be rotated or 'steered' by the knob at the top of the tool.

BLADES

The blade is usually fixed in the plunging mechanism by a grub screw tightened with an Allen key (Fig 6.8). Alternatively, insert and twist the blade then tighten it with a long screwdriver down the top of the plunger tube (Fig 6.9).

Blades vary in length from about 50mm–100mm and are available in a vast array of tooth patterns and profiles or different materials (Fig 6.10). (My observation is that they also vary enormously in price.) Most blades cut on the upward stroke and obviously a coarse-toothed blade will tear the grain (Fig 6.11), especially when cutting

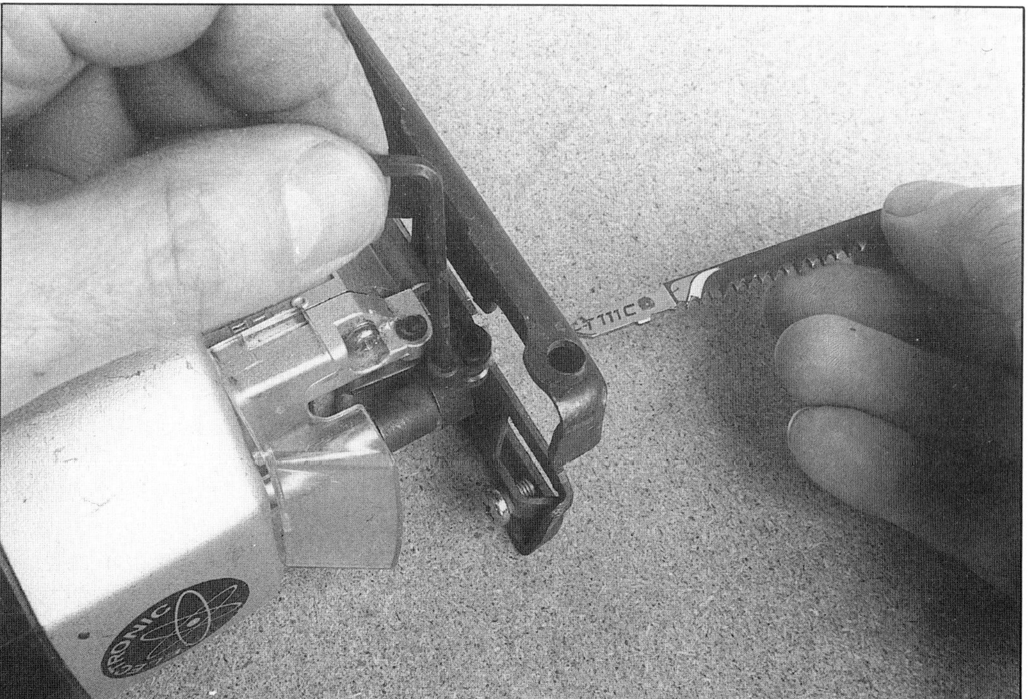

Fig 6.8 Insert the blade and tighten with an Allen key.

across the grain. For general-purpose woodworking a medium-to-coarse blade is suitable.

Blades also vary in thickness. My preference is for a stout blade which is less likely to buckle in use, although I frequently use a metal-cutting blade which has a narrow kerf and minimises grain tear.

Blades are generally made of high-speed steel, are relatively long lasting, and should be thrown away when they begin to dull. It is possible to obtain TCT blades and special steel blades, such as the 'Bi-metal' range by Elu, which are claimed to last up to five times as long (Fig 6.12). Of course in line with general manufacturing policy (confusion!) there are several different blade shank profiles, but fortunately most are interchangeable if the jigsaw has a clamp/grub screw blade-holder.

Fig 6.9 Tightening the blade on a Bosch jigsaw.

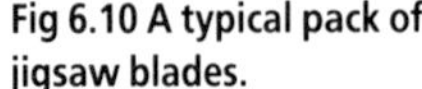

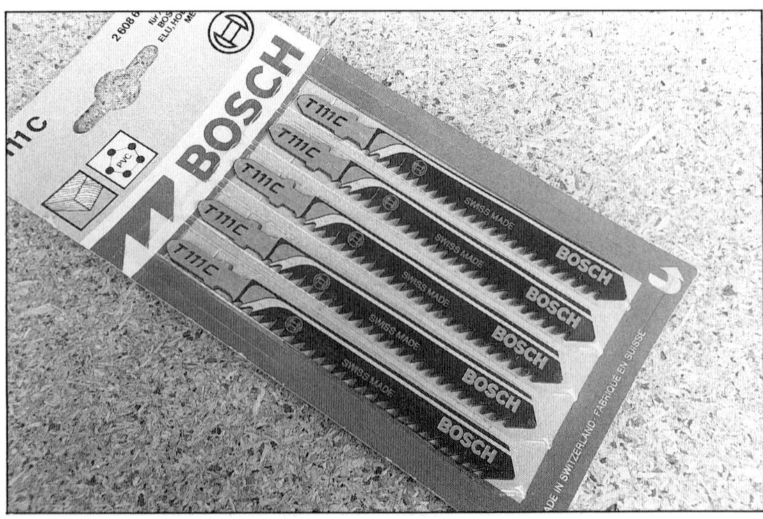

Fig 6.10 A typical pack of jigsaw blades.

SAFETY AND OPERATION

The jigsaw is a relatively safe tool but there are one or two specific points to note. Make sure the cable is well out of the way of the blade, both above the material and below. Make sure the cable does not trap in the sawcut behind – it is best to trail the cable to one side. Keep your fingers well away from the blade and do not overwork the tool as blades are brittle and will snap easily.

The most difficult task is in compensating for the vibrating action of the tool. When operating the jigsaw it has to be pressed firmly downwards into the material otherwise the saw will jump. If jumping does occur, momentarily relax the pressure to eliminate the vibration then press firm. It is quickly mastered as the tool is so small and unthreatening.

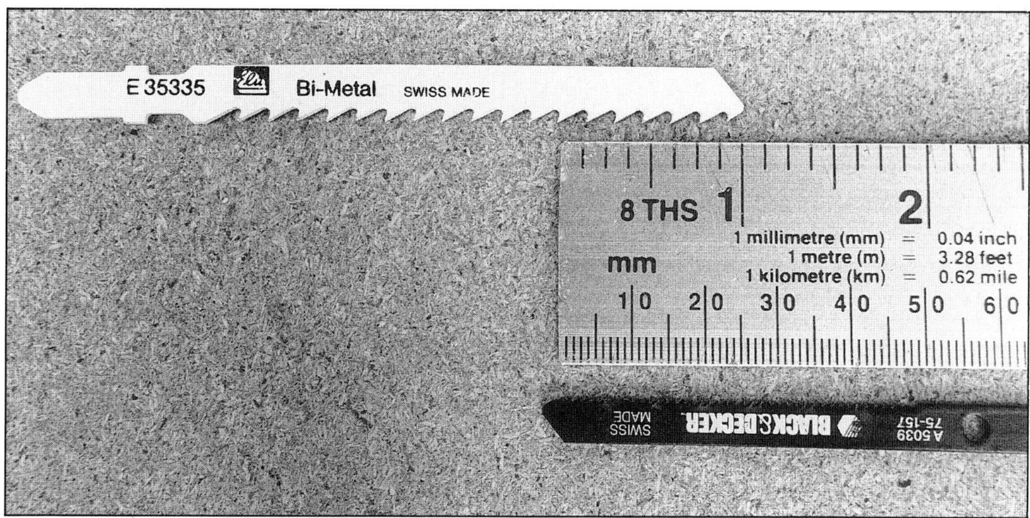

Fig 6.11 A fairly coarse-pitched blade. Although efficient it will tend to tear the grain.

DUST EXTRACTION

On most jigsaws an air-flow directed from the motor fan to the cutting area keeps dust and debris from building up around the blade and obliterating the line. Separate dust extraction is possible via a purpose-made flexible hose.

APPLICATIONS

The jigsaw is a useful tool for various applications where the bandsaw cannot be used. In particular for cutting large work (curved or straight), for internal cuts – such as floorboards and kitchen sink orifices (Fig 6.14) – and for cutting timber board across the grain. I do not particularly recommend starting an internal cut straight off the saw as it often simply buckles the blade. Instead I drill a hole first (Fig 6.13).

Perhaps my most exclusive work with the jigsaw (that which cannot be done *as well* with any other tool) is crosscutting boards both in straight cuts and around curved profiles, and reducing large manufactured boards to smaller pieces.

In 1980 I produced a design for a drinks cabinet. It was made from a single board of 2in thick ash

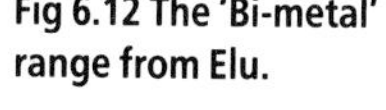
Fig 6.12 The 'Bi-metal' range from Elu.

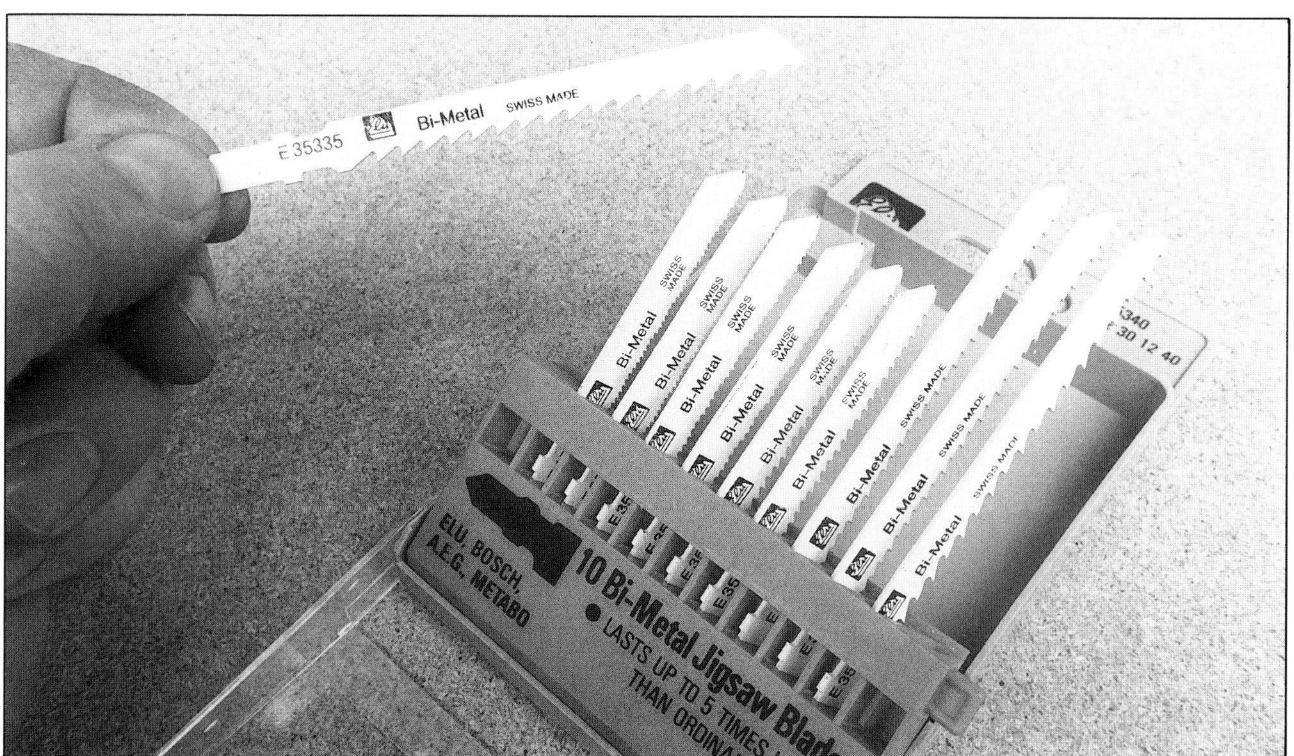

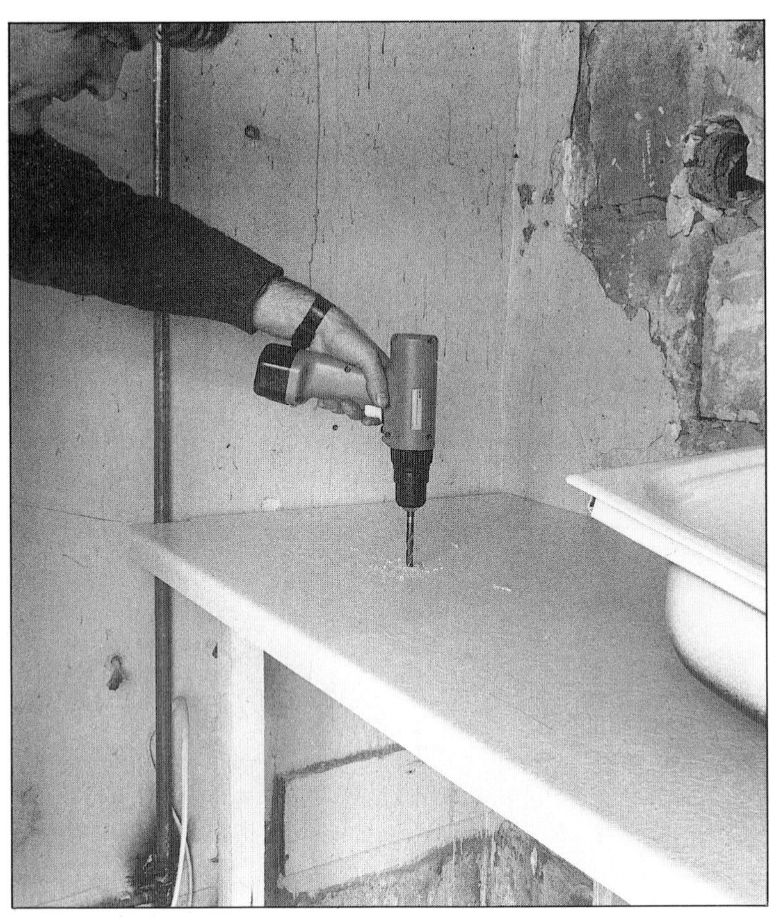

from which I made my own 'veneers'. I used two or three electric tools, and the jigsaw was one of them. The 'veneered' front panel was cut into four doors and a centre flap (see colour section) by first routing a 1.6mm groove (batten method) to outline each door, then cutting through the 25mm thick panel with a jigsaw loaded with a metal cutting blade (Fig 6.15). It was the only tool to do the job, especially as there were internal cuts to be made. It was slow, but accurate, and the saw kerf was just fine enough to allow each door to be trimmed afterwards (with a router) to the original groove wall. That's what you call pushing the technology all the way!

I think it makes the point that you do not need lots of different sophisticated heavy-duty machinery to produce inventive work. On the contrary smaller tools seem to allow far more creative freedom.

Of course the jigsaw can be jigged up as a table saw in the inverted position and the work taken to the saw, as in the Triton and Wolfcraft Pioneer workcentres. Some manufacturers supply small jigsaw tables which simply clamp on to a bench (Fig 6.16).

Cordless jigsaws (see Chapter 16) have a lot of potential, especially if working in remote places

Fig 6.13 Drill a hole for the jigsaw blade to start cutting.

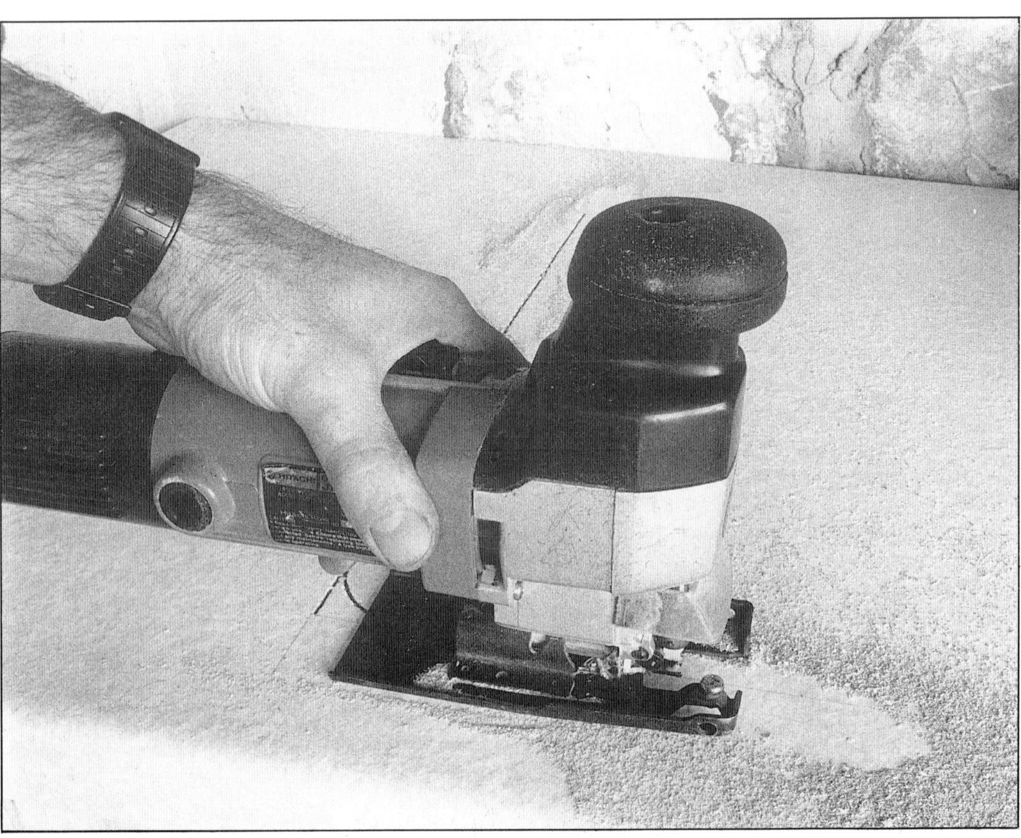

Fig 6.14 Using the jigsaw to cut a kitchen sink orifice.

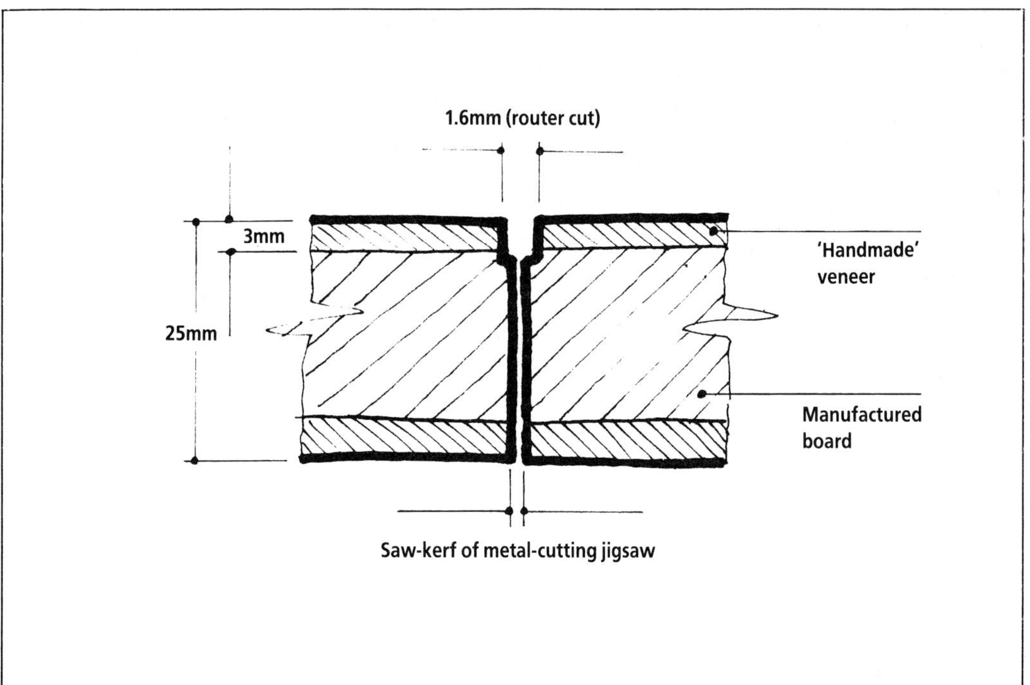

Fig 6.15 Section through the door panel of the Pyramid Drinks Cabinet.

such as the attic, or when roof building. Intended for convenience rather than stamina they operate for approximately 15 minutes on one charge.

CONCLUSION

The jigsaw is a priority tool in my opinion. It is worth purchasing a good-quality orbital model which gives the accuracy and robustness needed for varied and creative work. There is no other saw which can cut such tight circles – indeed it can be used to cut irregular sized holes (see Electric Lamp, page 252) – and its versatility generally is hard to beat, especially when reducing to size large manufactured boards.

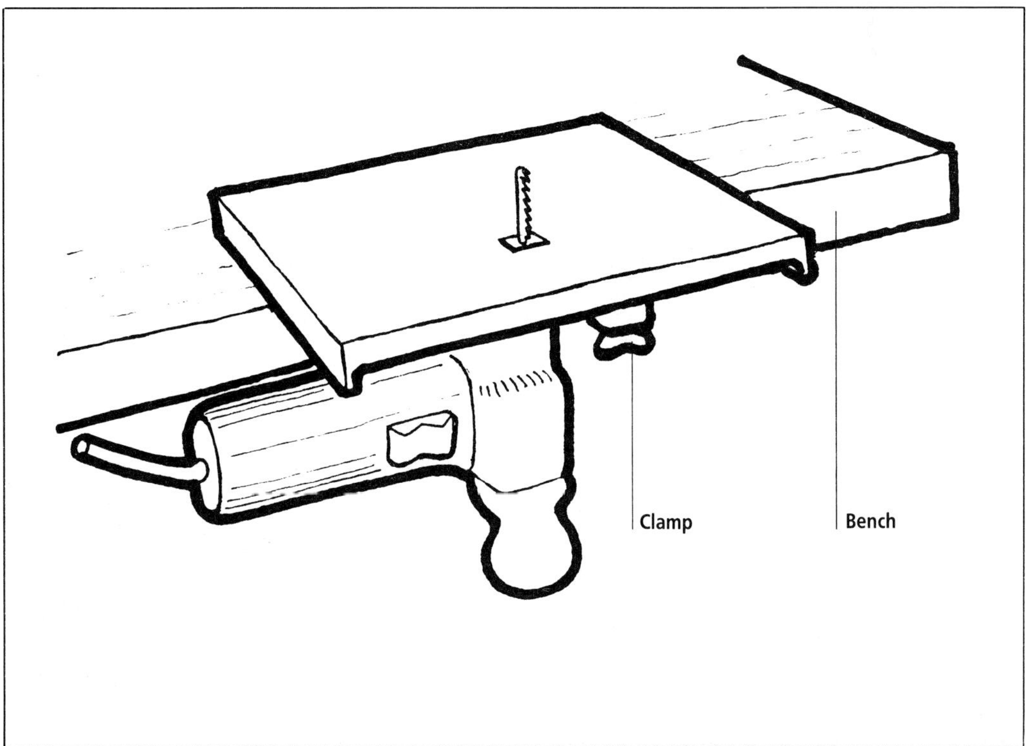

Fig 6.16 A bench-mounted inverted jigsaw table.

7

THE ROUTER

I would almost go as far as to say that the router is the ultimate power tool, as indeed it is many tools in one. The router is basically a high-revving electric motor which drives a shaped cutter at the end of its spindle (Fig 7.1). The body of the router is a motor with handles on it, which is connected to a retractable (plunging) baseplate, which makes contact with the surface of the wood. The cutter is lowered into the wood through an opening in the baseplate and the hole it makes is transplanted into a groove as the tool is drawn across the wood (Fig 7.2). Add to this a variety of jigging methods (e.g. fences and templates) (Fig 7.3), a million different cutters (Fig 7.4) and a choice of power capacities ranging from 400 watts to 2HP (Fig 7.5) and you have a tool of *infinite* creative potential.

Using a variety of jigging devices the router will cut and shape wood to virtually any form. Indeed it is the jigs or guiding methods which are at the heart of its creativity. The router will smooth wood flat, profile and trim edges, cut grooves, rebates, flutings, and make specific joints.

Coupled to purpose-made jigs, such as the Woodrat, it will cut impressive dovetails from the miniature to the massive (Fig 7.6). Mounted over and swinging from the JKB Universal Routing Table it will make large shallow bowls (Figs 7.7 and 7.8), and bolted to the Dupli-carver copy-carving jig (Figs 7.9 and 7.10) it will transform plastic gnomes into tasteful and convincing wood sculptures!

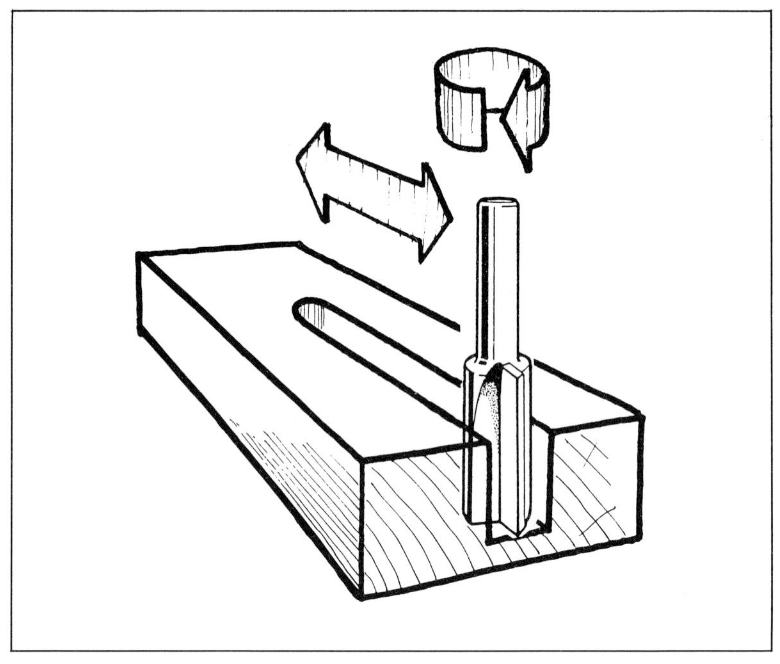

Fig 7.2 A hole is translated into a groove.

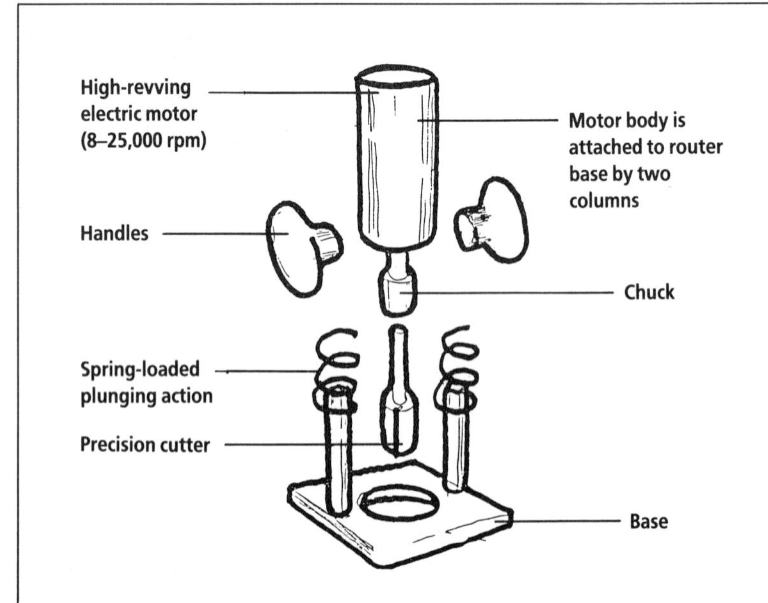

Fig 7.1 The basic concept of the router.

I was first introduced to the router by chance in 1974 by a salesman, and to date the majority of my designs have evolved from the use of this remarkable electric tool. Put another way, it is hard to imagine how else these pieces could have been made when so many of the traditional boundaries have been extended by the router. But for those more at home with tradition the router is still an incredibly useful tool.

The modern plunging router is a high-revving machine. At around 25000rpm its tiny cutter does a lot of work very fast. The term 'electronic' refers to the variable speed of the router, usually in a series of steps from 8–25000rpm. The advantage is not so much the easy start-up which eliminates snatching (you should be wide-awake in any case), but the varying speeds can suit different materials

Fig 7.3 The straight fence acts as a guide.

and different cutter diameters. In general a slower speed prevents the material burning with any size cutter and gives more efficient performance for large-diameter cutters.

POWER

Routers are rated according to their power (wattage) which determines their physical size. We can broadly categorize them into three groups:

400–750 watts (¼in collett or chuck)
750–1300 watts (¼in, ⅜in collett)
1300–2000 watts (½in collett)

(Note that 1 horsepower is approximately 750 watts.)

While it is true that a more powerful router can achieve more, the difference is not as dramatic as one might expect. Lower-powered routers will just

Fig 7.4 The tip of the iceberg when it comes to the choice of cutters.

Fig 7.5 David and Goliath – a Makita trimmer and Hitachi 1800 watt electronic router.

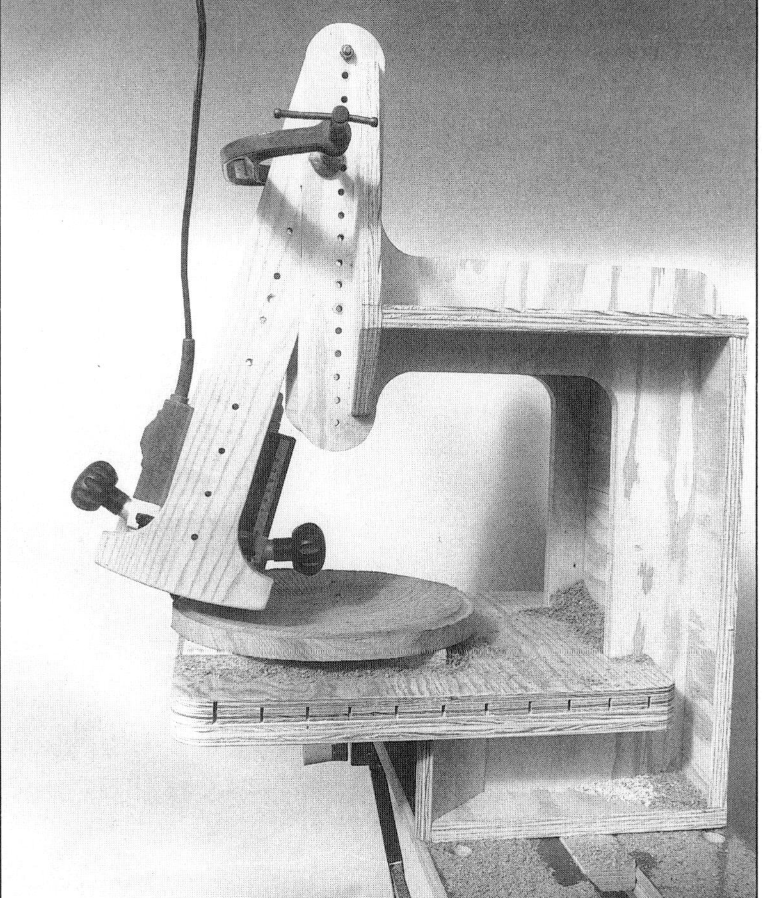

Fig 7.6 A massive dovetail cut on the Woodrat router jig.

Fig 7.7 Making a fluted dish on the JKB pendulum jig.

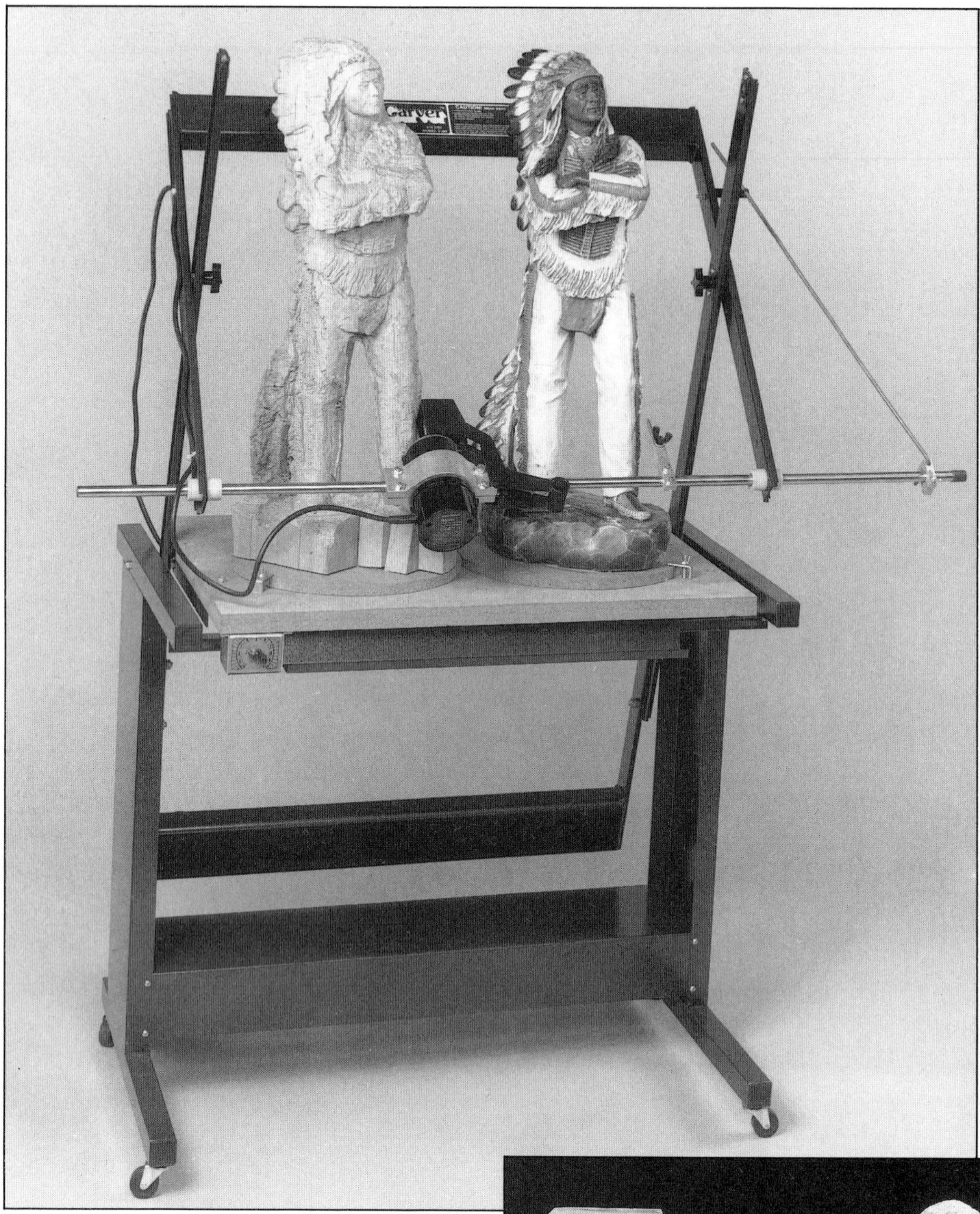

Fig 7.9 The Dupli-carver F200 three-dimensional copy-carving jig.

Fig 7.10 Precision, accuracy and versatility of the Dupli-carver router jig.

take longer to cut a feature (e.g. a groove cut in a series of steps rather than in just one pass).

Apart from power the main difference is in the shank diameter of cutters. They are available in ¼in, ⅜in and ½in diameter shanks and apart from being stronger, the later diameter shanks offer a wider range of cutters. Collett sleeves enable ¼in and ⅜in cutters to be held in ½in collett routers. (Note that ¼in = 6.35mm.)

Of course, like drills and other electric tools it is advantageous to have more than one router, perhaps a small and a large one, and one mounted in a table (Fig 7.11).

Fig 7.8 The 20th-century adze!

Fig 7.11 Using the Elu router table.

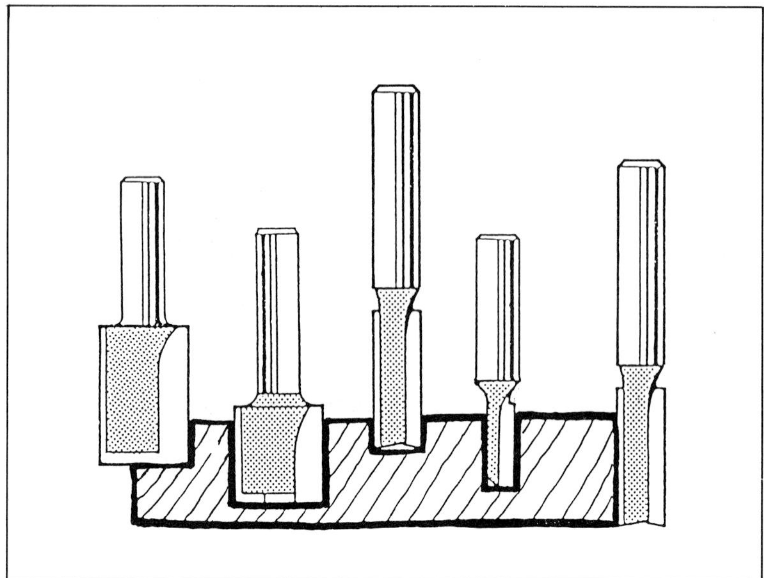

Fig 7.12 Rebates and grooves.

CUTTERS

Router cutters or bits are available in high-speed steel (HSS) or tungsten-carbide tipped (TCT). The latter last many times longer, but arguably are not as keen-edged as HSS, which also offer the advantage of home sharpening.

One company offering a re-sharpening service, as well as supplying probably the largest range of cutters available today, is Trend Tools & Machinery (see page 273). Trend offer a fast mail-order service for cutters of any description, including special cutters made up. Most, if not all, of the big names in the electric tool market offer routers, and some offer a range of cutters.

Cutter technology is so vast, there are so many shapes and sizes, that in these pages I can only attempt to cover the main types. These are best illustrated (Figs 7.12–7.18), and the point to

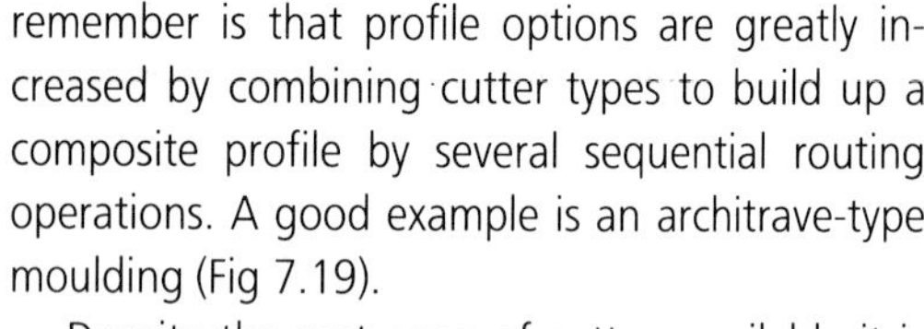

remember is that profile options are greatly increased by combining cutter types to build up a composite profile by several sequential routing operations. A good example is an architrave-type moulding (Fig 7.19).

Despite the vast array of cutters available it is quite possible to clock up a lot of creative mileage using just a handful, and in this respect the Trend

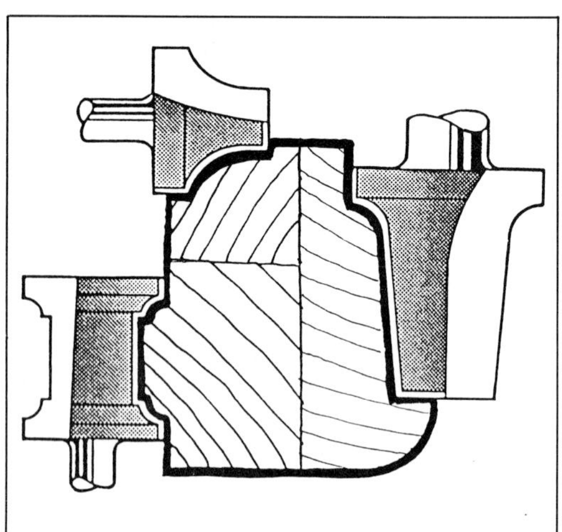

Fig 7.13 Ovolo and rounding-over.

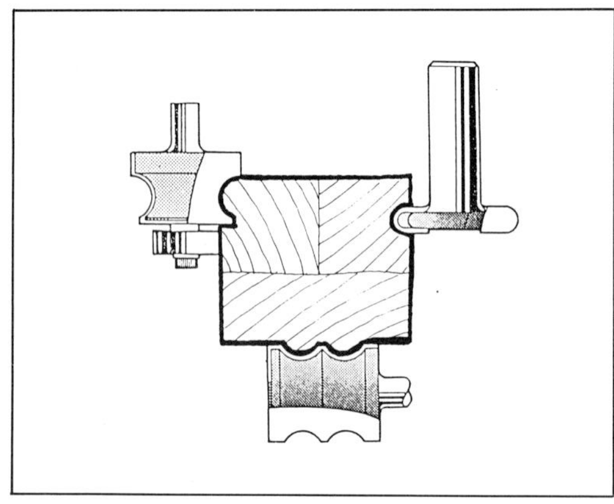

Fig 7.14 Beads and reeds.

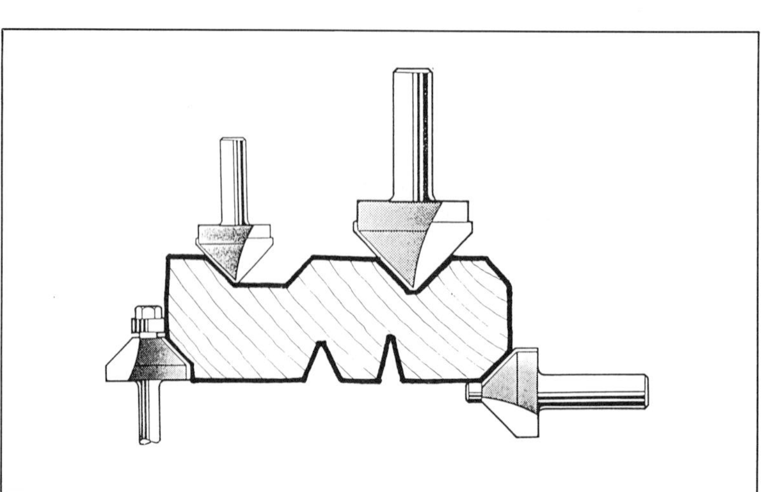

Fig 7.15 Chamfer and V-groove.

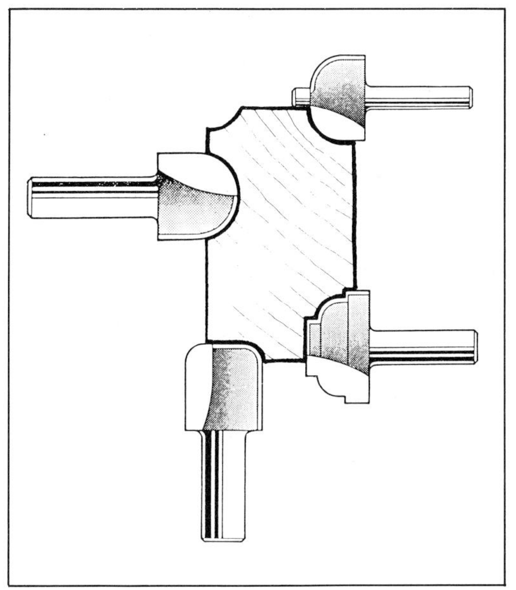

Fig 7.16 Radius.

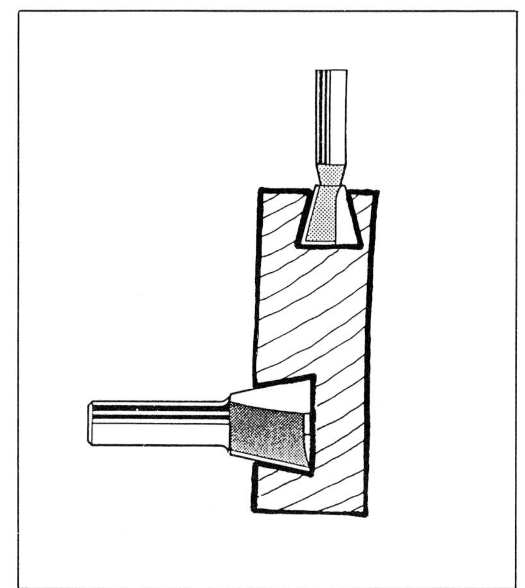

Fig 7.17 Dovetail.

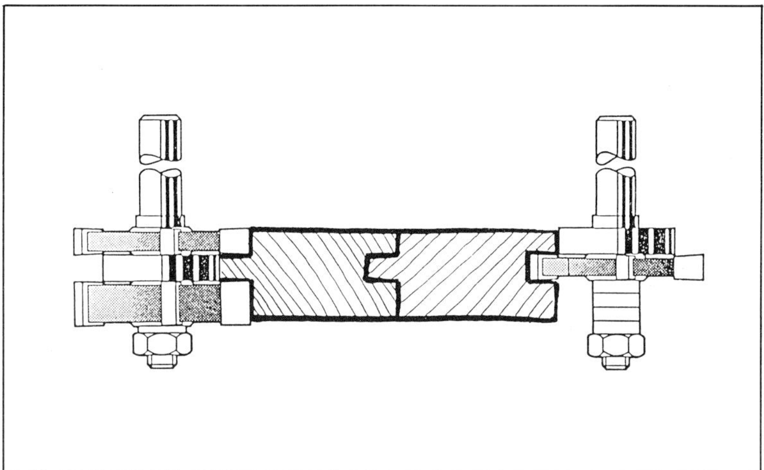

Fig 7.18 Slotting and grooving.

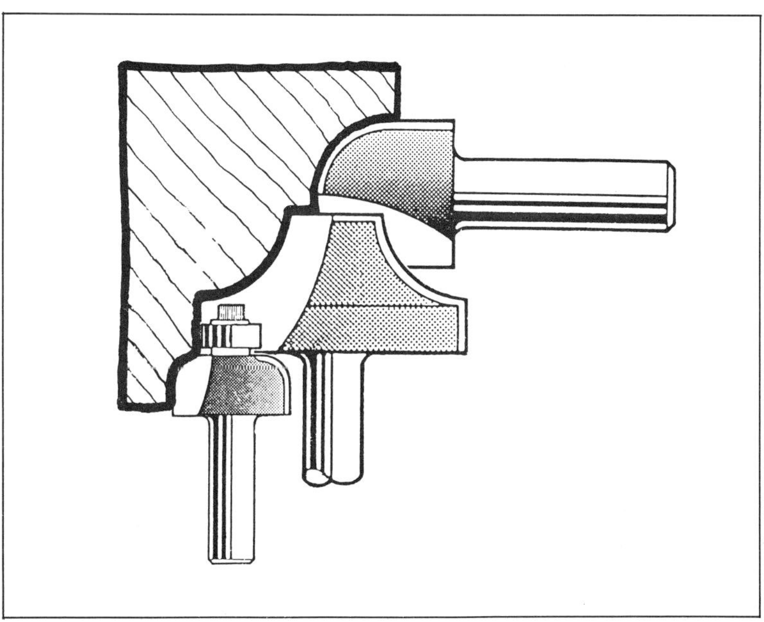

Fig 7.19 Compound profiles on a typical architrave moulding.

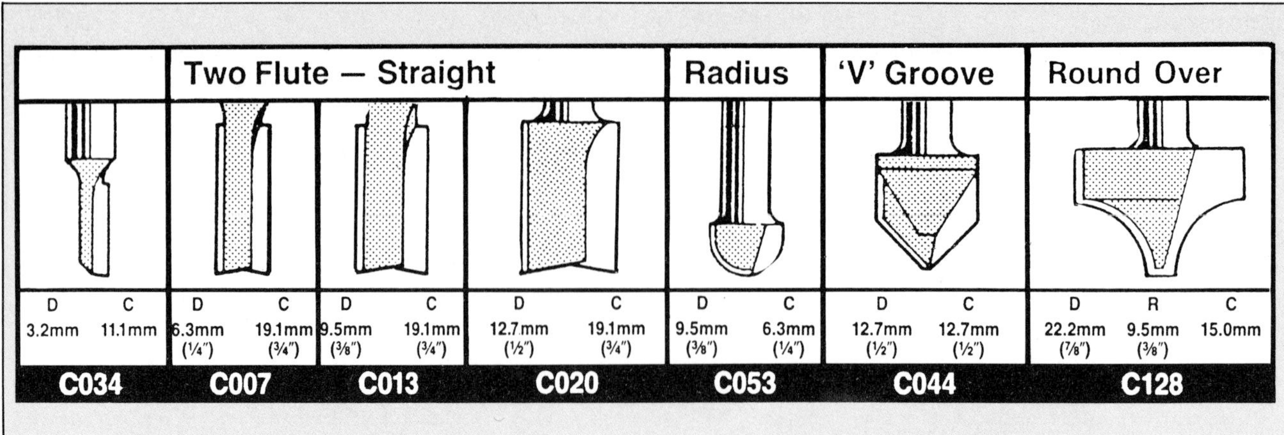

Fig 7.20 The Trend Craft Range of cutters.

Craft Range of seven popular cutters is extremely versatile (Fig 7.20). It also makes the point that some of the most creative design solutions can arise from quite limited resources – not that this cutter set is particularly limited! In my own work I probably use a straight cutter (of varying diameters) more than any other type – but then my design style tends to be characterized by long flowing lines!

There are also of course one or two special novel cutters, such as the massive (if expensive) finger joint cutter (Fig 7.21). It is designed primarily to edge-joint boards (Fig 7.22), which seems a waste as its decorative appeal is hardly appreciated, even though it makes an extremely strong joint.

Other novel cutters which catch my attention are 'T'-slotters and comb joint sets (Fig 7.23). They open up the field for creating routing beyond the uses for which they were originally intended.

Cutters are expensive, and a small collection can soon cost almost as much as the router itself. They are fragile bits of high technology ranging in

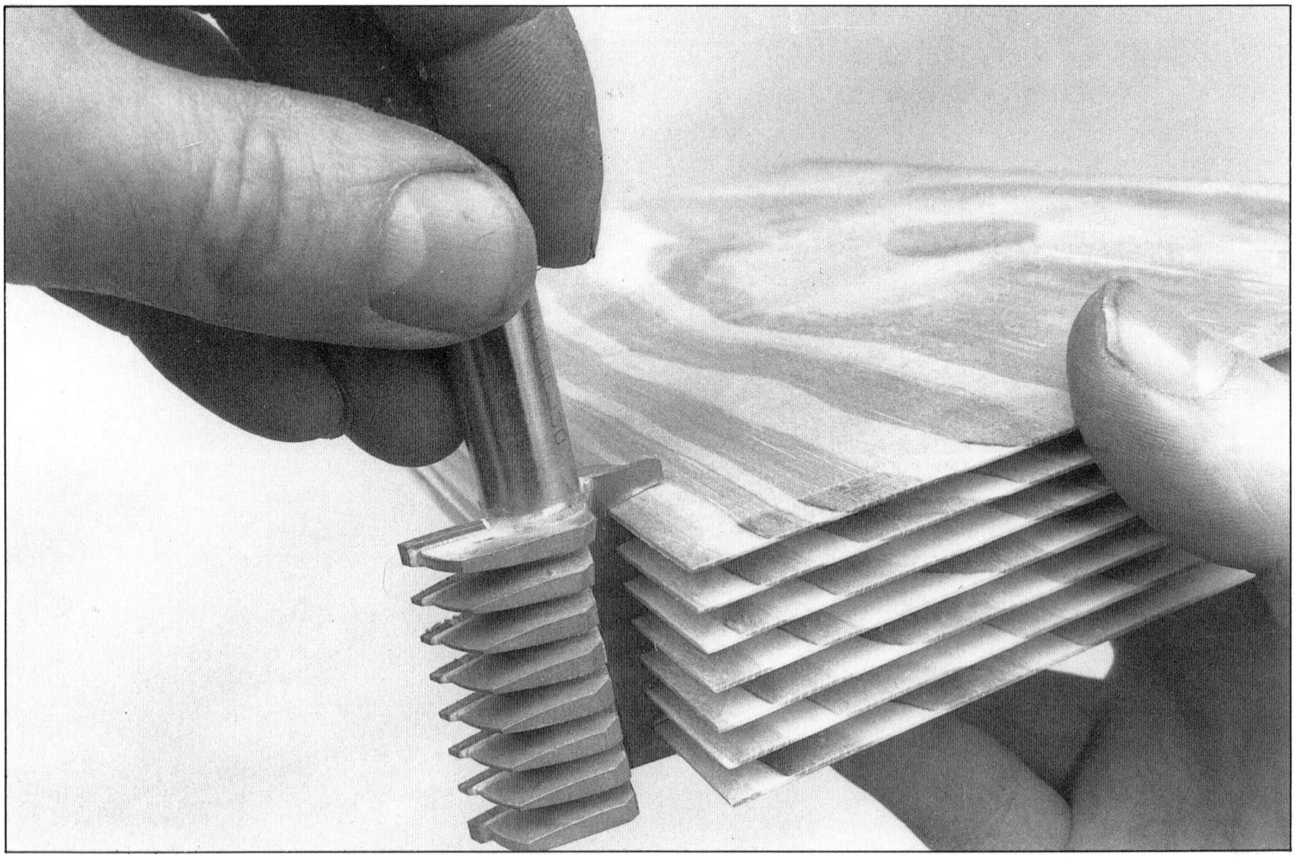

Fig 7.21 The massive finger joint cutter.

size from smaller than a match head to larger than a coin in diameter and should be handled with great care. If your workshop is subject to damp they will also rust. Trend cutters come encapsulated in a protective plastic gel and are well greased.

JIGS

I use the term 'jig' broadly as it includes the router itself and some of the standard attachments which come with it, such as the straight fence, roller attachment (for curved work – Fig 7.24) and guide bushes (Fig 7.25).

A jig is a guiding system to determine the path of the cutter. The fence enables the router to follow the edge of the work and therefore is commonly used for grooves and rebates (Fig 7.26). A batten G-clamped to the work also serves as a straight guiding jig against which the side of the router-base runs.

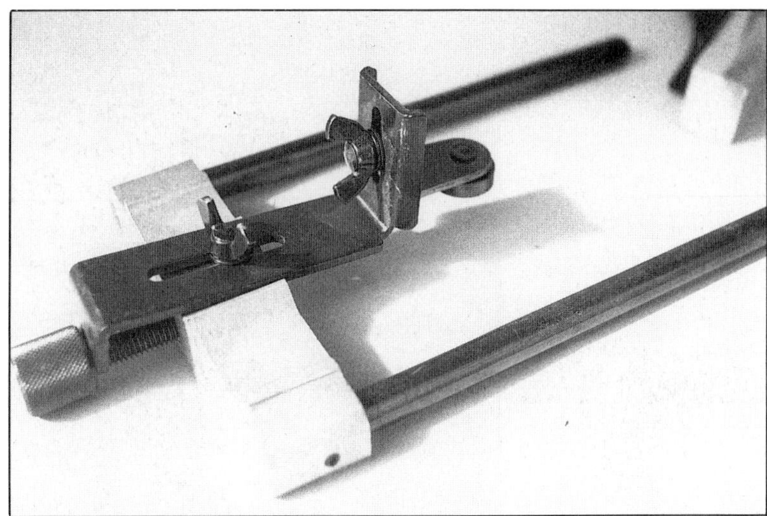

Fig 7.24 The roller and straight fence.

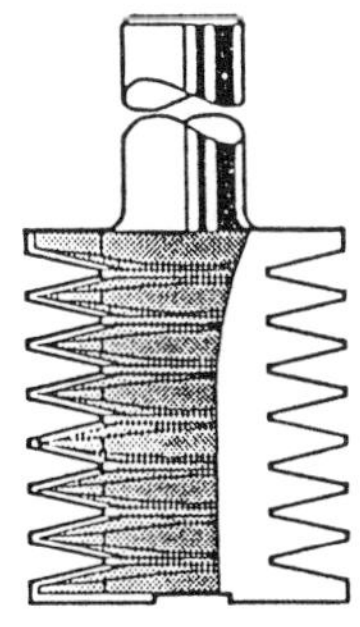

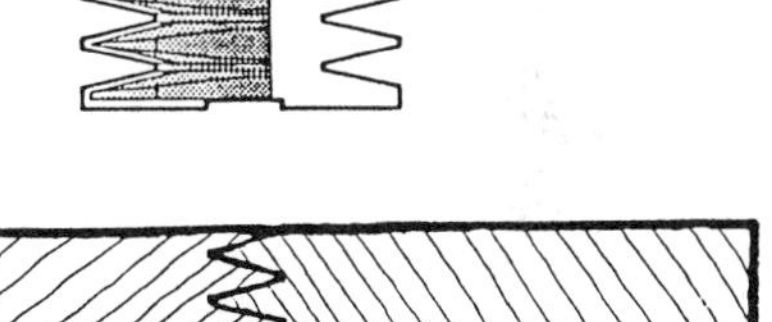

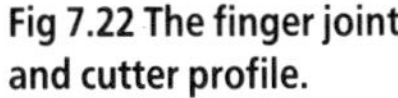

Fig 7.22 The finger joint and cutter profile.

Fig 7.23 The Trend TCT comb jointing set.

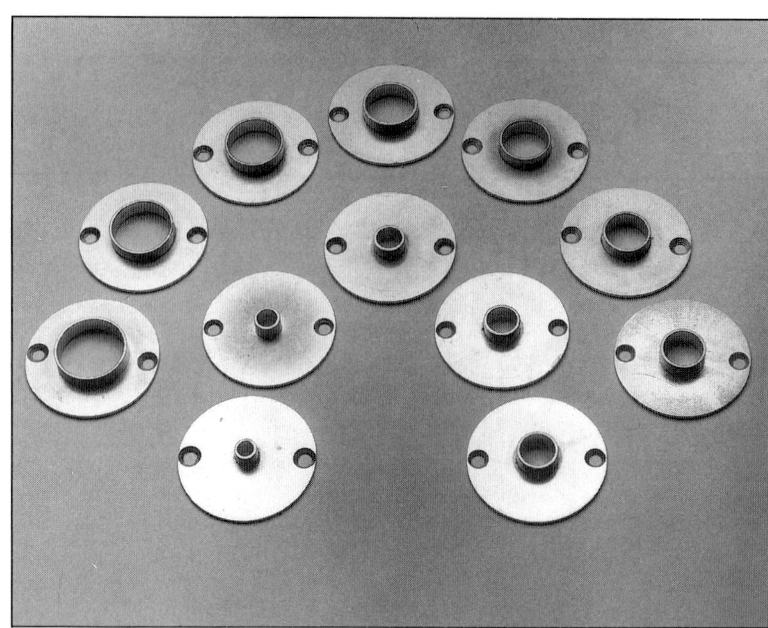

Fig 7.25 Trend guide bush set (the standard is 18mm).

Fig 7.26 Trend variable frame jig.

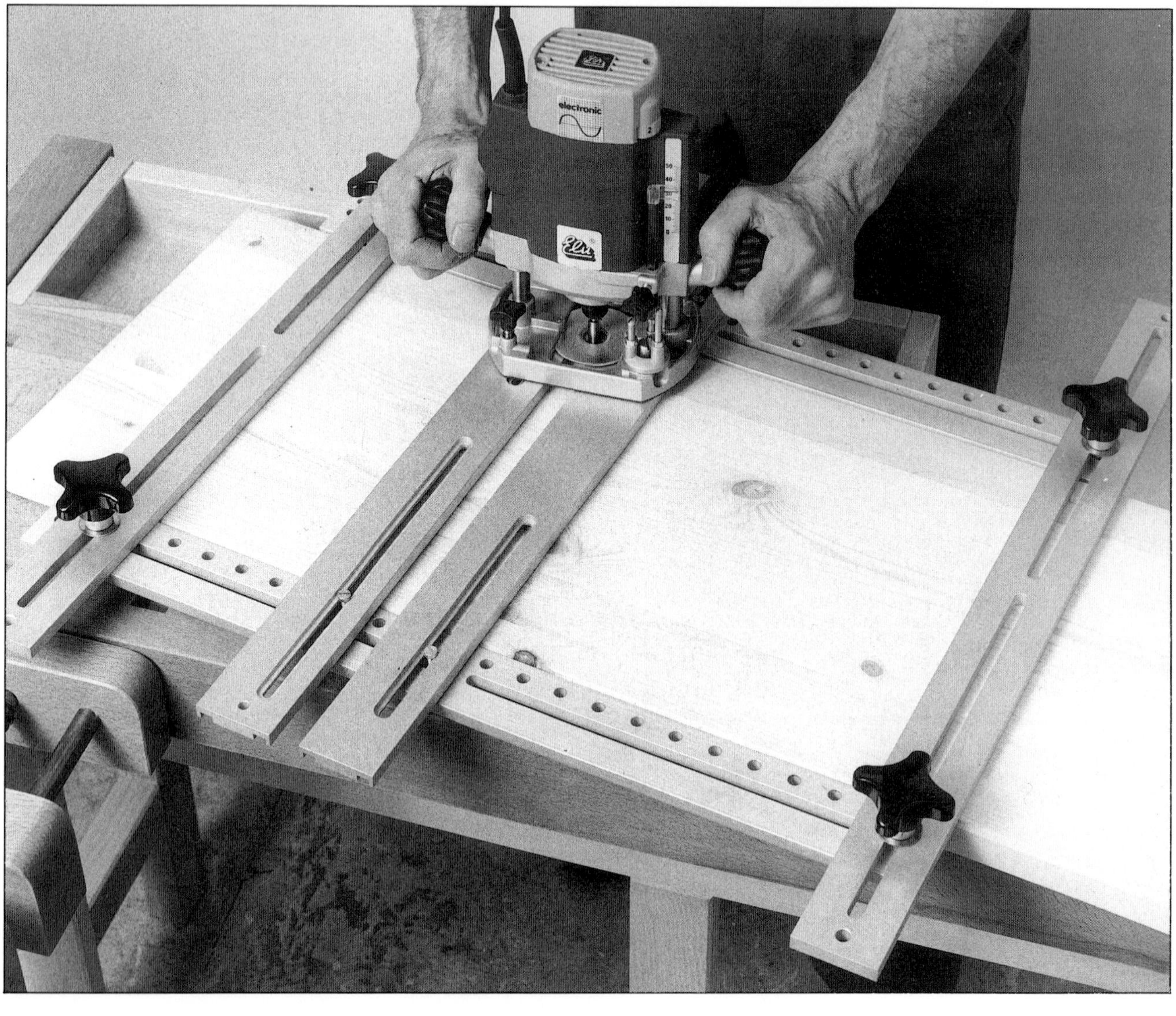

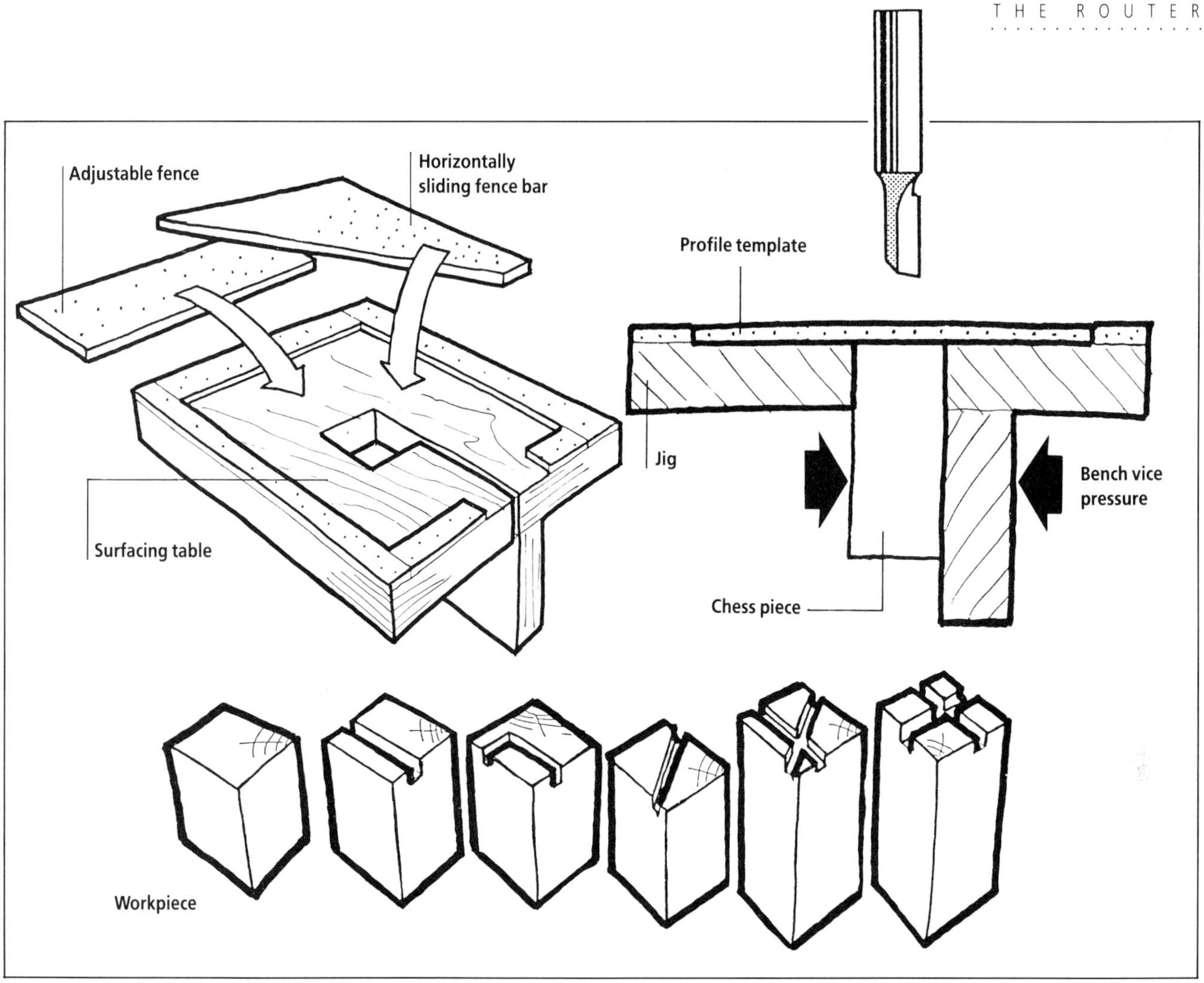

Adjustable fence

Horizontally sliding fence bar

Profile template

Jig

Bench vice pressure

Surfacing table

Chess piece

Workpiece

Fig 7.27 Chessmen jig.

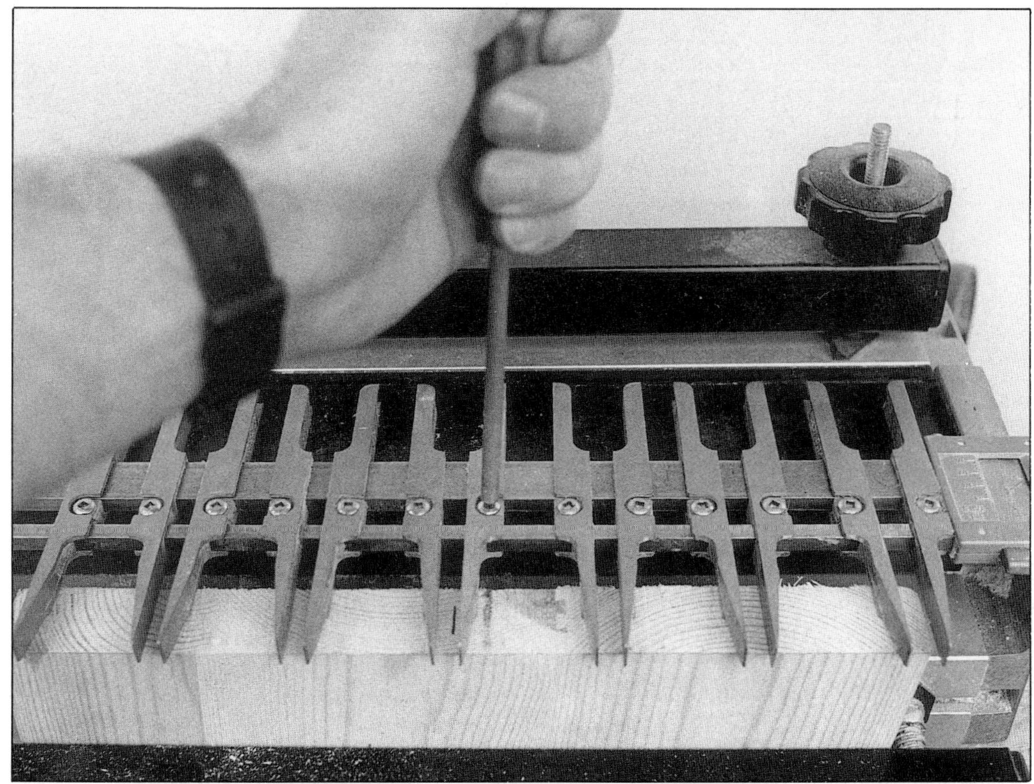

Fig 7.28 Close-up of the Leigh Dovetail jig.

Fig 7.29 The Woodrat dovetail and jointing device.

Guide bushes allow the router cutter to follow a determined path just off the edge of a profiled template attached to the work and are extensively used for shaped repetition work (Fig 7.25). Such templates and, indeed, special jigs are ideally made from MDF, usually 6mm thickness, hot-melt glued or pinned together.

Special jigs

In the history of furniture-making it is the jigs which are themselves almost more significant than the pieces. A clever jig makes the routing operation quick, easy and accurate. Jigs can be made inexpensively using 6mm MDF, hot-melt glued together or fabricated in any way that is appropriate (glue, nails etc.). My routing jigs are my real trade secrets and I am prepared to divulge just enough to whet the reader's appetite to make his/her own jigs.

A chess set I once designed (see *'The Incredible Router'* by Jeremy Broun, 1989) used a simple interchangeable jig for all eight chessmen (Fig 7.27). The chessmen were designed while I juggled mentally with the requirements of pieces which would graphically represent their respective moves. At the same time they had to be easy to manufacture in wood. (Traditional turned and carved Staunton chessmen are extremely labour intensive.)

If you can make jigs you will be in the fast lane of routing, and indeed any electric woodworking. The solution is just as likely to be found in your

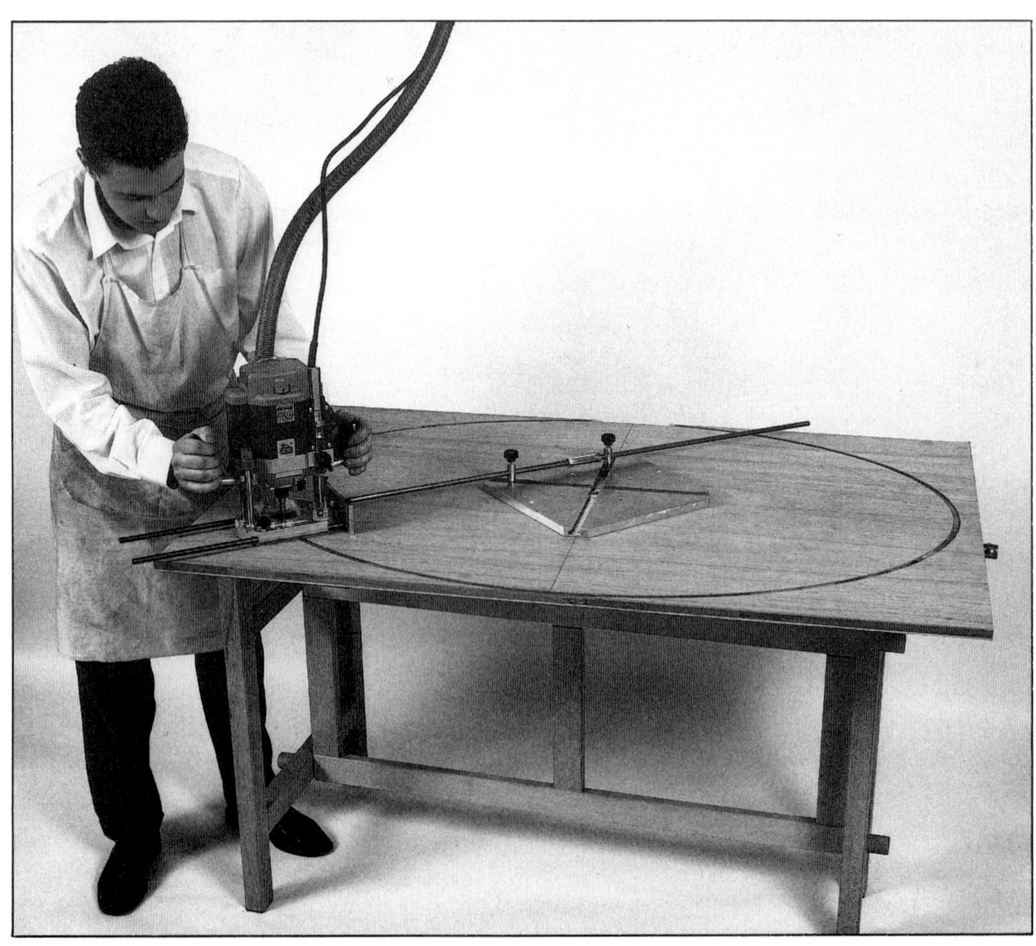

Fig 7.30 Ellipse cutting jig by Trend.

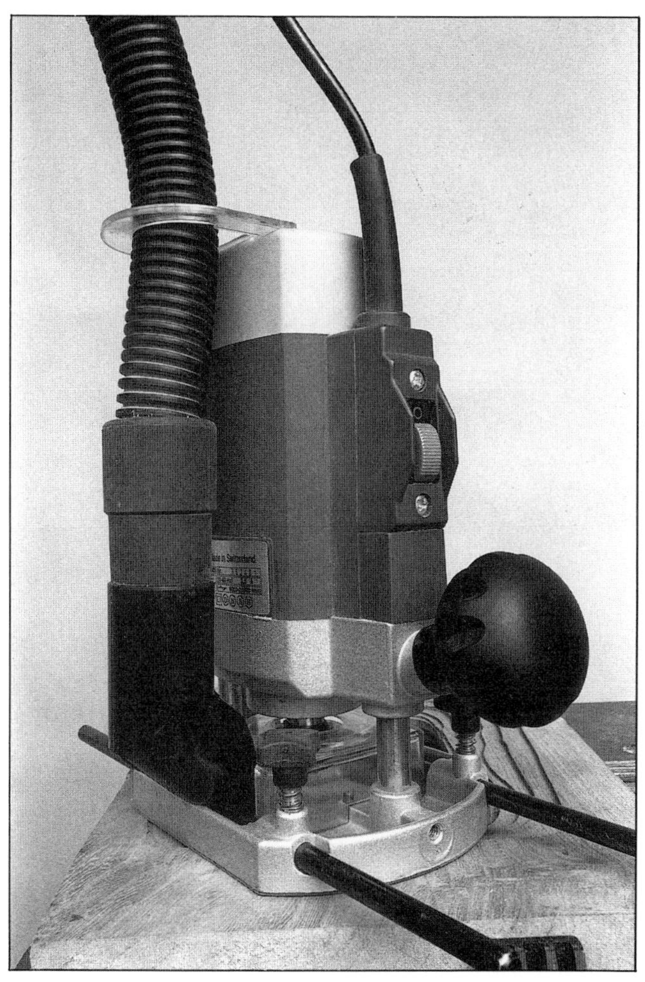

Fig 7.31 Dust extraction at source on the Elu MOF96E (left).

Fig 7.32 The router triggers the switch on the dust extractor (right).

head as in your pocket! However, having said that, I am impressed with one or two manufacturers' jigs, such as the Leigh Dovetail jig. This jig (Fig 7.28) accurately cuts a wide range of dovetails up to 24in wide and similarly the Woodrat dovetailing device (Fig 7.29) achieves attractive and precision-cut dovetails as well as other jointing configurations.

Various router jigs and templates are supplied by power-tool manufacturers such as Trend (Fig 7.30). (The reader is recommended to obtain the *Trend Product Guide,* see page 273, as this is an education in itself.)

SAFETY

The router can do a lot of damage to bare flesh, even when switched off, as its cutter is razor sharp. It should always be left with the cutter retracted from its plunging operation. When changing cutters the power should be turned off at the wall (it's even wiser to pull out the plug). The router can also do a lot of damage to your ears so it is imperative to use earmuffs. (It is probably the most anti-social of all electric tools.) Eye protection should also be worn as the chippings are blown out centrifugally and of all the tools the router is perhaps most likely to damage eyes. A dustmask should also be worn as both chippings and fine dust become airborne. I prefer to hang the power cable overhead rather than have it trailing across the floor or bench as there is always a danger of cutting through the cable, and a common problem with cables is trapping them as you pass the machine across the work, hence preventing free movement. **Keep the cable out of the way.**

DUST EXTRACTION

A dust hood attached to the router (Fig 7.31) and linked with flexible hose to a portable extractor (7.32) is an essential piece of equipment. Not only does it prevent chippings flying (see Fig 4.3) everywhere in the workshop, but it reduces the clogging up of slots etc. in the work being routed. It also keeps optimum visibility around the cutting action.

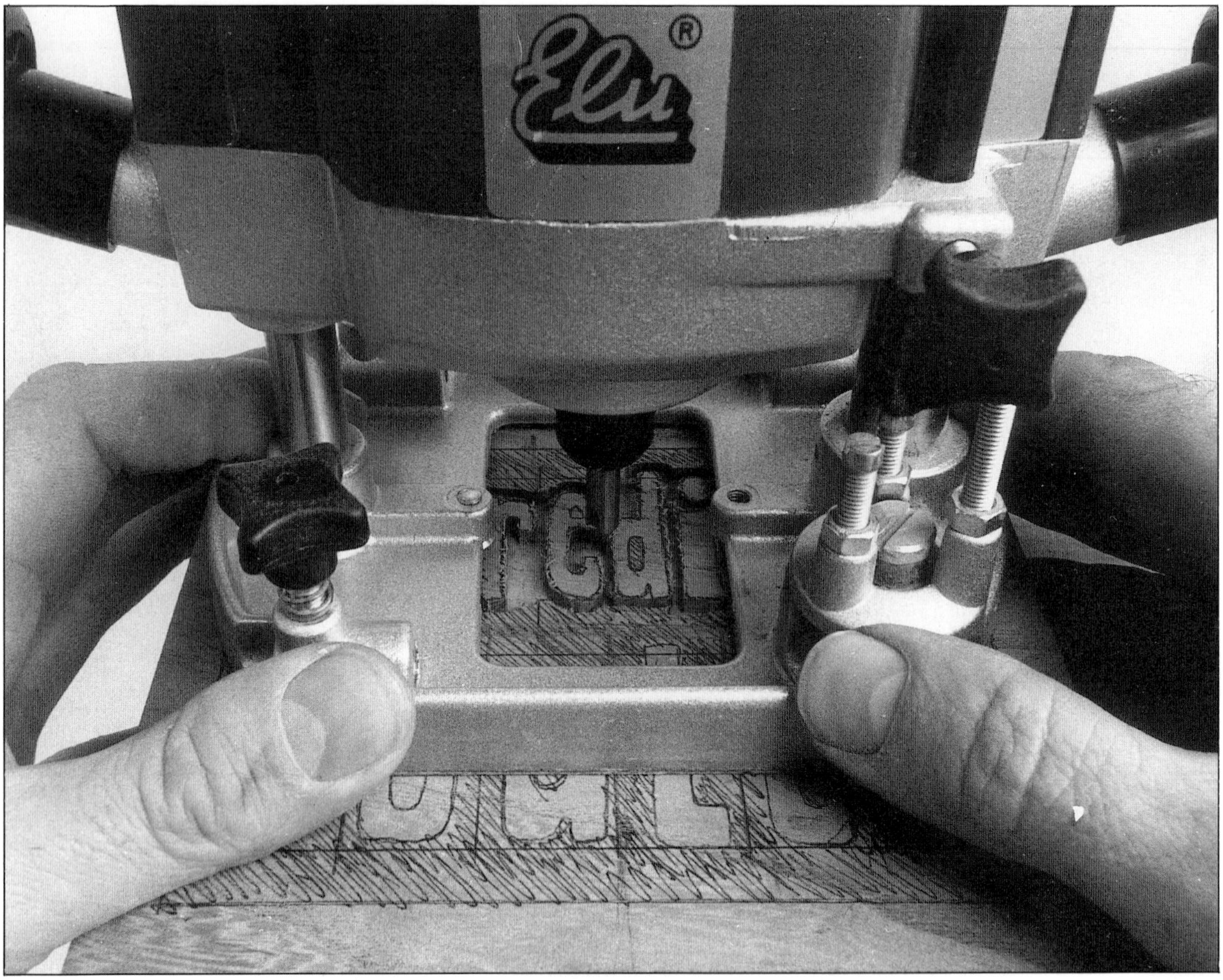

OPERATION

There are essentially three methods of routing:

- Hand-held routing (Fig 7.33)
- Inverted table routing – the router is fixed underneath a table (Fig 7.34)
- Overhead table routing – the router is fixed above the work table (Fig 7.35).

The choice of methods depends largely on the nature of the work. When hand routing the work has to be secured in a holding device, such as a vice, or with G-clamps. Table routing frees the hands to feed the work against the cutter and its jig. In general I am more comfortable holding the router so that the work is solid and secure and does not vibrate. The hands and arms 'sense' the performance of the router and its cutter engaging in the wood, and I would argue give better overall control. However, there are some operations which are better suited to table routing, e.g. where a

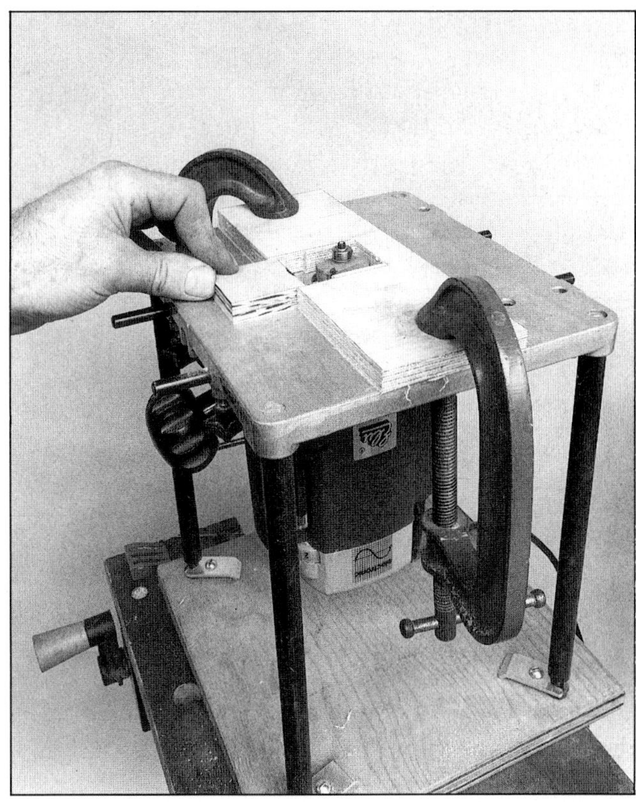

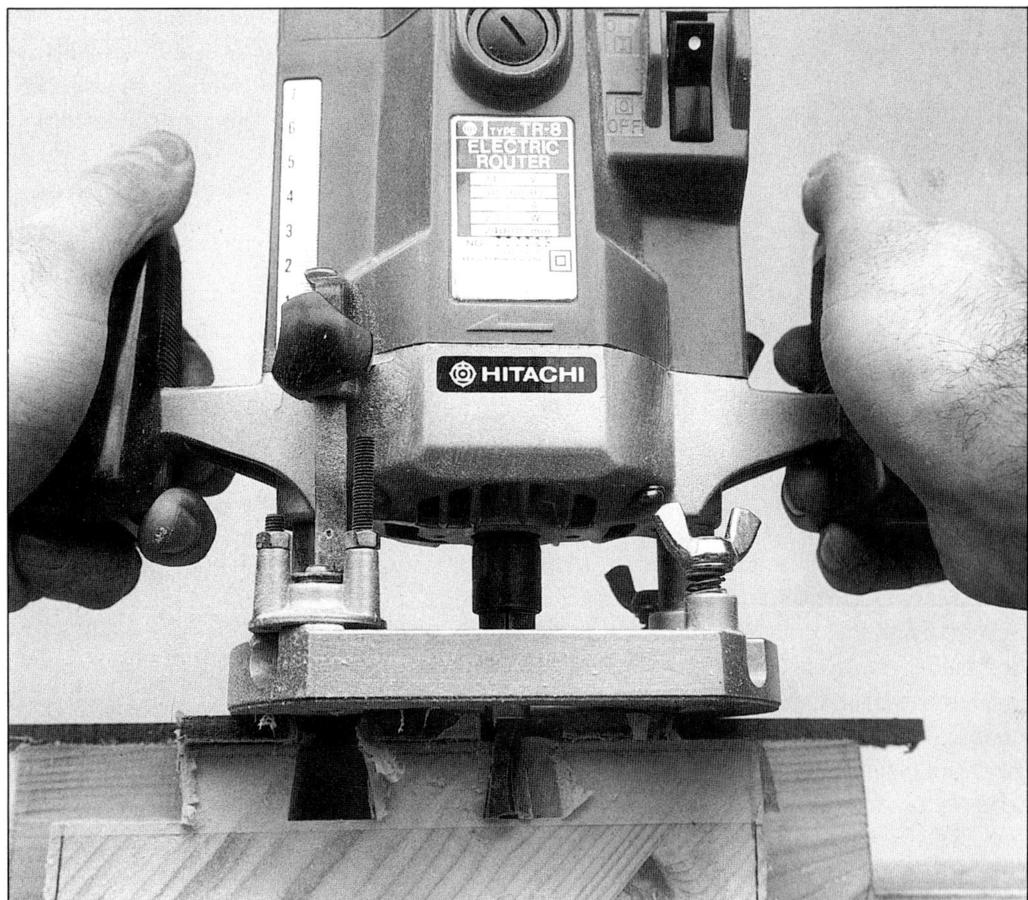

Fig 7.35 Overhead table routing (above left).

Fig 7.36 Using a router table for small and awkward work (above right).

Fig 7.37 A firm pair of hands is needed (right).

Fig 7.33 Hand-held routing (opposite above).

Fig 7.34 Inverted routing (using the JKB Universal Router Table) (opposite below).

large surface area is needed to support the work, or the workplace is too small and fiddly (Fig 7.36).

To master the router you need to hand hold it (Fig 7.37) and for this you need a firm pair of hands! It is wise when routing for the first time to pass the router over the work several times with the cutter retracted and the power switched off, just to get the feel of it.

When using a jig such as a straight fence the pressure has to be firmly in against the edge of the work. When plunging stopped grooves the cutter is lowered into the work at the beginning of the cut, locked with the lever, then released at the end of the cut.

Perhaps the most difficult part is knowing how quickly to rout across the work (make a pass). If you go too slow, the fast-rotating cutter will overheat and either dull or burn and break. If you go too fast, a small cutter will break and the router will probably go off course. Sometimes it is best to rout one way then the other to obtain a good finish, but rarely is the finish straight off the router adequate and it usually demands some sanding.

My choice would be to practise freehand routing first, without a fence (which serves as a crutch). This way you immediately get a feel of the character of the tool and you swiftly take command. The secret is to set the depth stop of the router to make a shallow cut. As a rule of thumb, if you cut to a depth half the diameter of the cutter in any one pass, you will have better control of the tool and the cutter is less likely to burn or break.

An excellent first exercise is to draw out in large letters in outline your name on a block of wood, and try to rout faithfully to the line. Set the depth to approximately half the diameter of the straight shank cutter.

APPLICATIONS

Joint cutting

Most traditional joints can be cut precisely with the router, though that is not to say it is *always* the best tool for any particular joint. For instance, it may be more efficient to make tenons on the radial arm saw (see Chapter 12), but there are some joints which are appropriate for the router. Dovetails, for example, can be made stylishly using various jigs (Fig 7.38).

The router lends itself to housing joints and mortices, although their radiused corners have to be allowed for when cutting the tenon. I use a routed loose-tongued mortice-and-tenon joint frequently as a very quick, strong and effective joint (Fig 7.39).

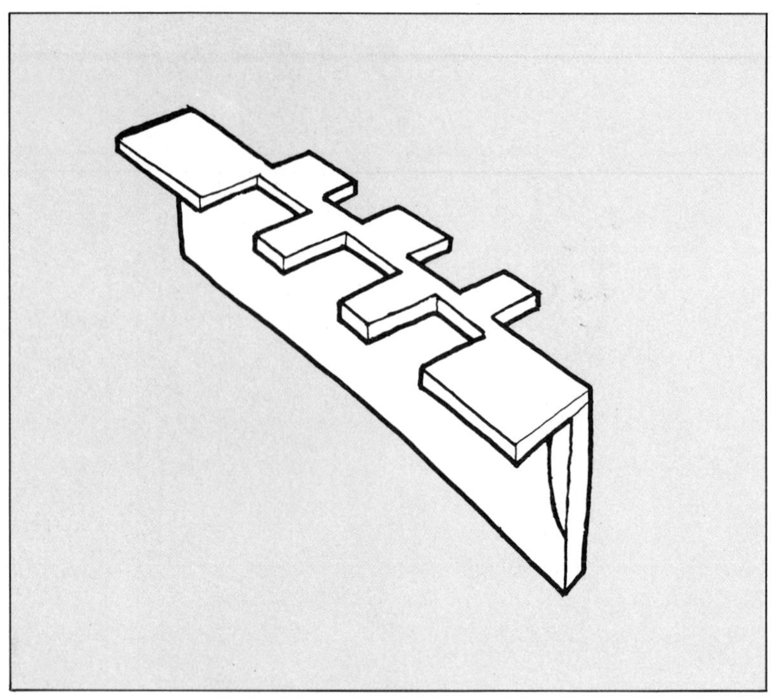

Fig 7.38 Jig for cutting dovetails on a 'millstone' table.

The router can be used for grooving inlays, cutting dowels and screw threads and can smooth wood flat, in particular trimming joints flush. It can also cut completely new joints such as my 'rout-kerf' joint, which is a combination of steam bending and saw-kerfing (Fig 7.40).

Router tables

It is an advantage to have a small router table which turns the router into a mini spindle moulder.

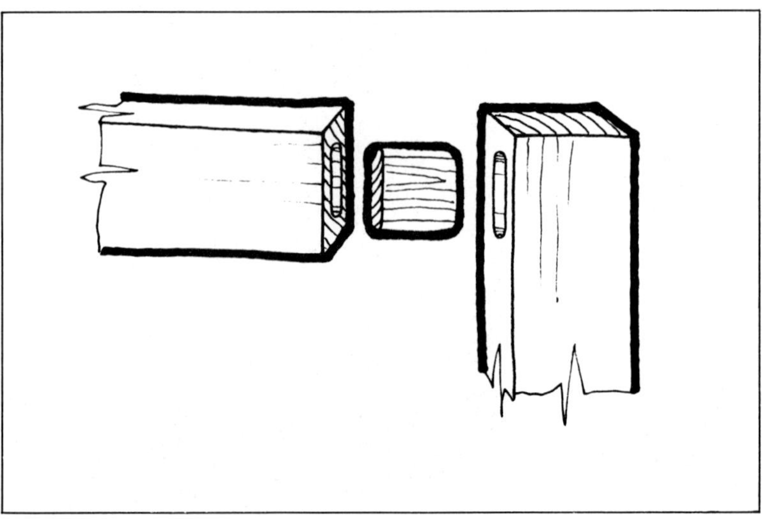

Fig 7.39 A loose-tongued mortice.

Fig 7.40 A new joint – the JKB rout-kerf joint.

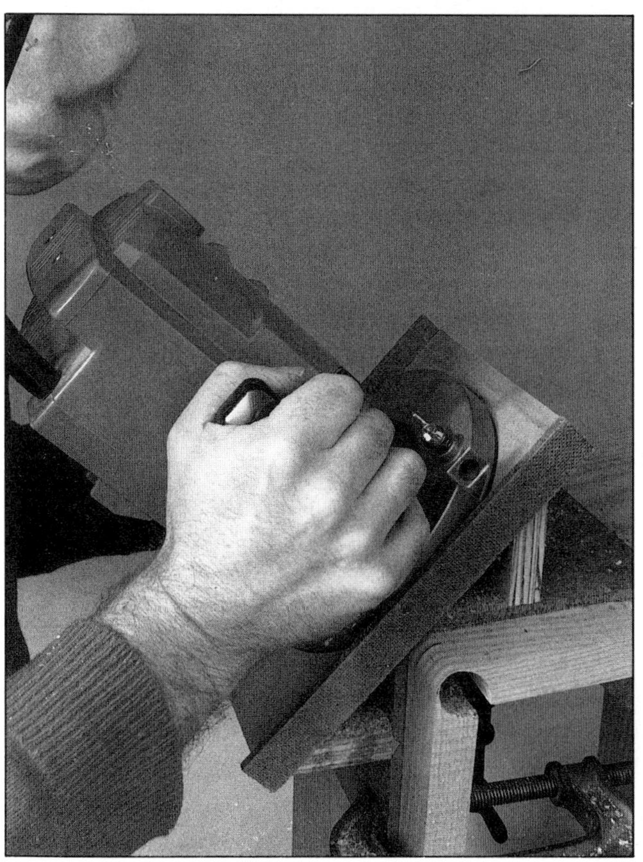

Numerous manufacturers supply these tables, either in pressed steel or cast aluminium, and of course the Triton and Pioneer workcentres include inverted routing facilities. The table set up with a straight fence or wheel guide for template work offers ease and speed of operation – such as re-bating edges of a panel or radiusing corners of components.

There are much larger router tables such as the Trend routing tables (Fig 7.41) and in some cases the work can be held down by vacuum clamping (Fig 7.42).

The JKB Universal Router Table

In *'The Incredible Router'* I introduced this plywood table which is inexpensive to build and versatile in its uses. It combines overhead, inverted and pendulum routing, and it is possible to mount more than one router at a time for ease of use.

The pendulum-routing facility is particularly novel as large, shallow 'adzed' dishes can be easily made. The table can be mounted on any bench and is particularly suited to that masterpiece of mass production – the Black & Decker Workmate, but it could also be mated with the JKB bench found in Chapter 18 of this book.

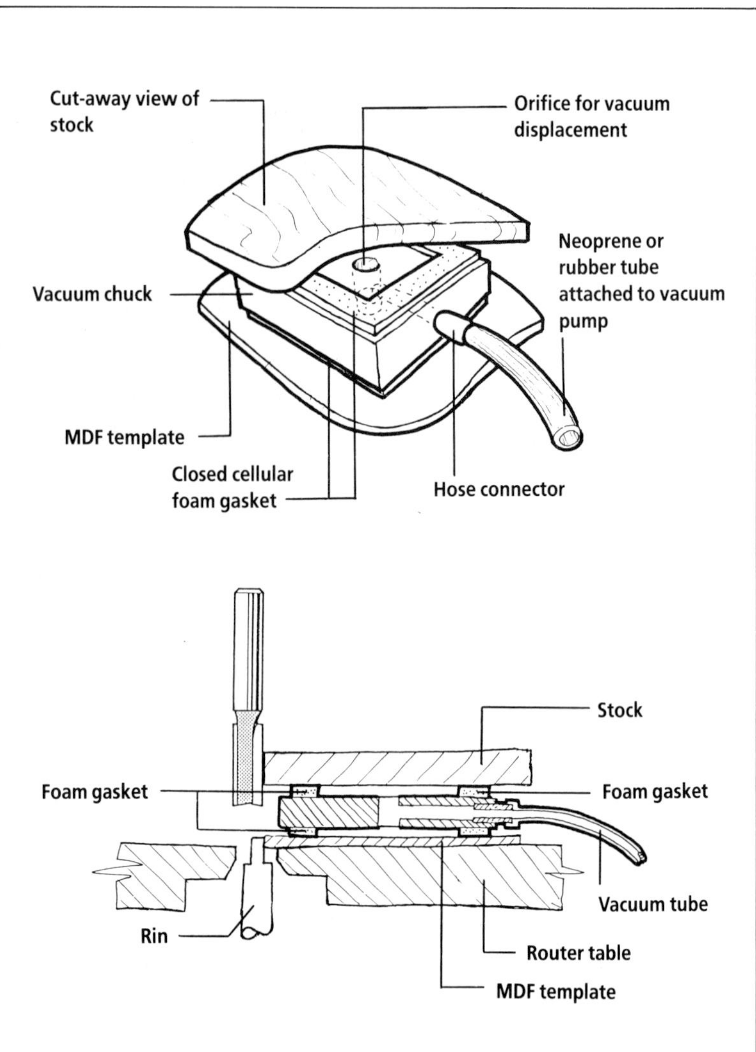

Fig 7.42 Vacuum clamping.

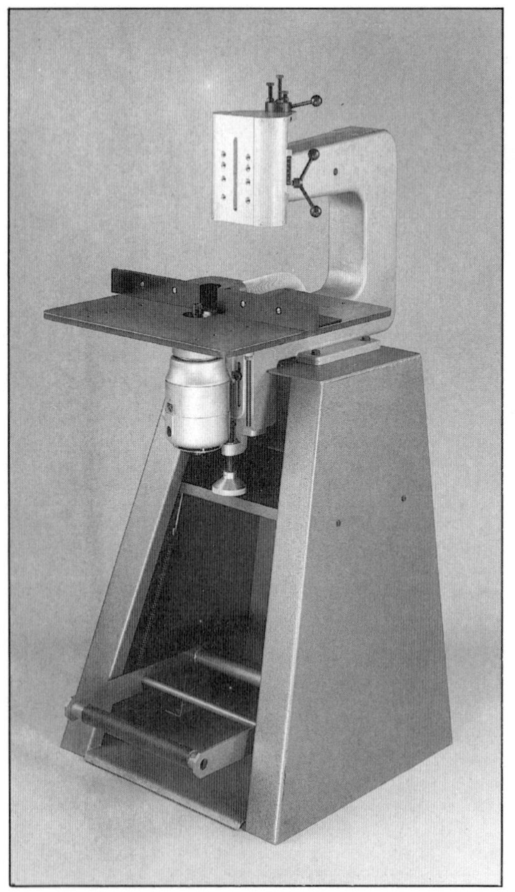

Fig 7.41 Trend inverted router.

CONCLUSION

Because the router is in a sense many tools in one, it can achieve virtually any woodworking task, but I have already mentioned that the *efficiency* of all tools has to be considered.

Although the router will cut wood straight through very cleanly and accurately, it would be slow and expensive in terms of cutters (and eventually routers). Obviously a tool such as a jigsaw, bandsaw or circular saw would be used nine times out of ten for this task. (The joy of electric woodworking is in using a variety of tools as a team to produce creative end results.) However, if I could only take *one* tool to my desert island – it would have to be the router!

8

THE BANDSAW

Not only is the bandsaw a top-priority electric tool for any workshop – because of its versatility – but there is something rather satisfying about its presence. In my experience it is one of the most 'friendly' machines, being easy to use and seldom idle.

Unlike the circular saw, which can be quite fearsome and noisy, the bandsaw quietly eats its way into the wood, making less fuss and less dust, but has a deceptive appetite. Even a tiny bandsaw with a narrow blade can happily cut through timber up to about 4in thick, and certainly most are at home cutting stock up to 2in thick all day. Its circular saw counterpart would have to be a much larger and more expensive machine.

Of course the circular saw is quicker for straight repetitive cuts, but the bandsaw will cut both straight and curved work, and waste less material as the saw-kerf is much narrower. And the bandsaw serves *all* woodworkers – cabinetmakers, turners, carvers *et al.* It can be used for 'roughing out', or as an extremely accurate tool with the correct blade and skilled use. I have gone so far as to cut accurate shoulder lines on larger finger joints, as well as cut the joints themselves, straight off the saw. Yes! (Fig 8.1)

PRINCIPLE OF THE BANDSAW

The bandsaw is a very basic concept. It is a linear cutting machine with a continuous-loop toothed blade passing over two or more wide-diameter rubber-lined wheels housed in a covered rigid frame (Fig 8.2) and exposing a minimal area of blade at the work table to which the work is fed. The blade passes through guides above and below the work feed area, the top ones being adjusted to the depth of the timber to be cut (Fig 8.3). The

Fig 8.2 The DeWalt BS/1310 bandsaw with cover removed.

Fig 8.1 Cutting large finger joints with precision on the bandsaw using a fine blade.

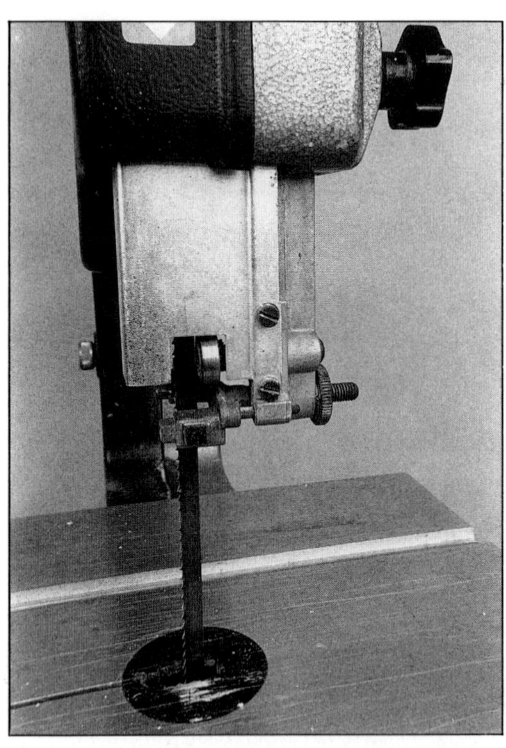

Fig 8.3 The upper guide assembly and plastic mouth.

blade also passes through a replaceable plastic mouth.

Apart from ensuring the blade is tensioned and tracking correctly there is really very little else to a basic bandsaw (Fig 8.4). It is of course powered by an electric motor, usually at least half a horsepower, and may have two speeds, but is quite happy working away at a fairly slow rate of knots.

This tool has the advantage of cutting both straight and curved work, and through tilting the table (Fig 8.5), it can achieve angled cuts.

Although not strictly a portable tool, the smaller bandsaws can be carried with relative ease and therefore can be used on site. I have used the well-proven DeWalt BS/1310 bandsaw (12in throat) since it first appeared in the 1970s and it has at times achieved the impossible – cutting heavy hardwood planks 4in thick down the grain (with support), and on one occasion cutting 150mm wide veneers 3mm thick out of a 6in thick board (to be later thicknessed down)!

Fig 8.4 The bandsaw.

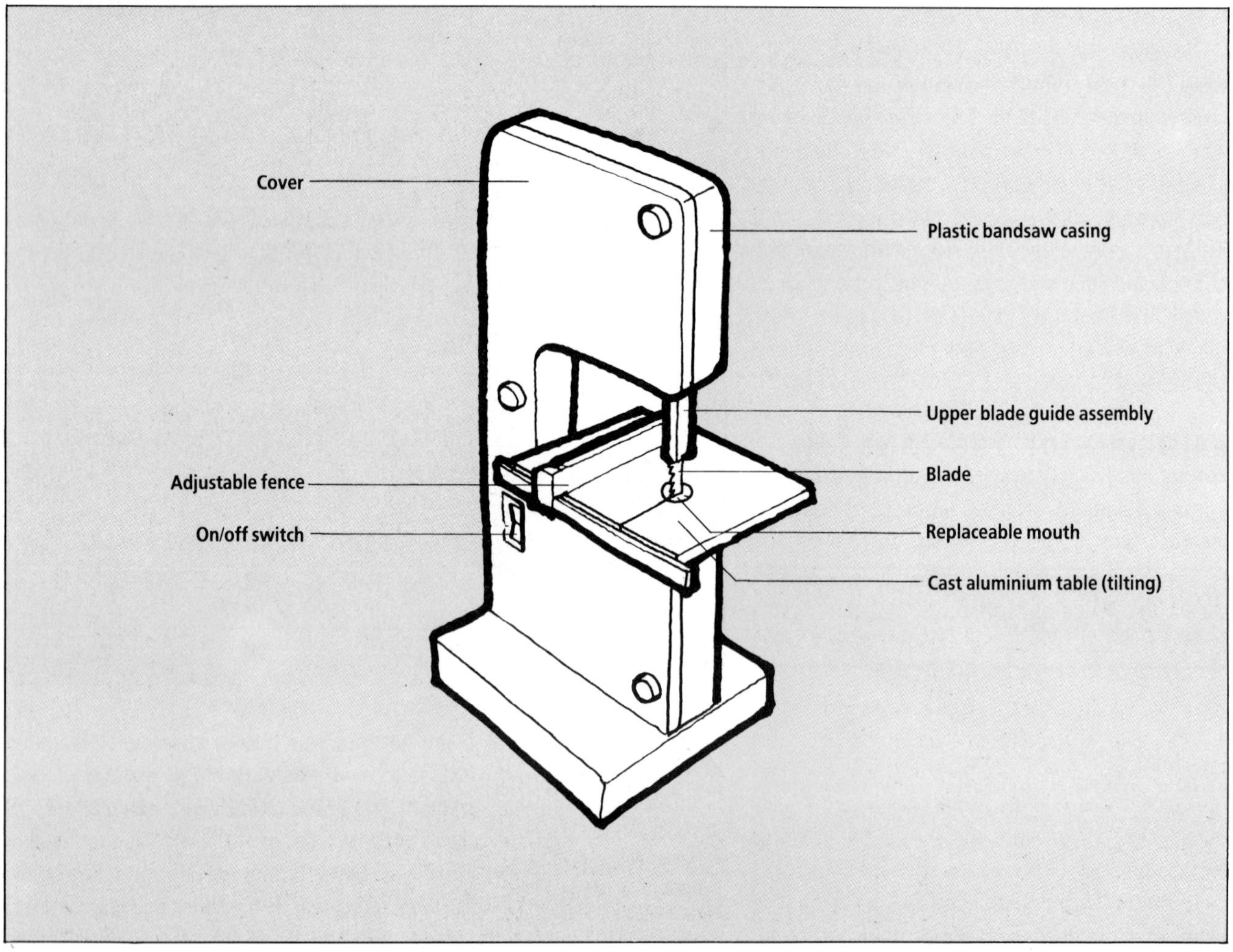

Cover
Plastic bandsaw casing
Upper blade guide assembly
Adjustable fence
Blade
On/off switch
Replaceable mouth
Cast aluminium table (tilting)

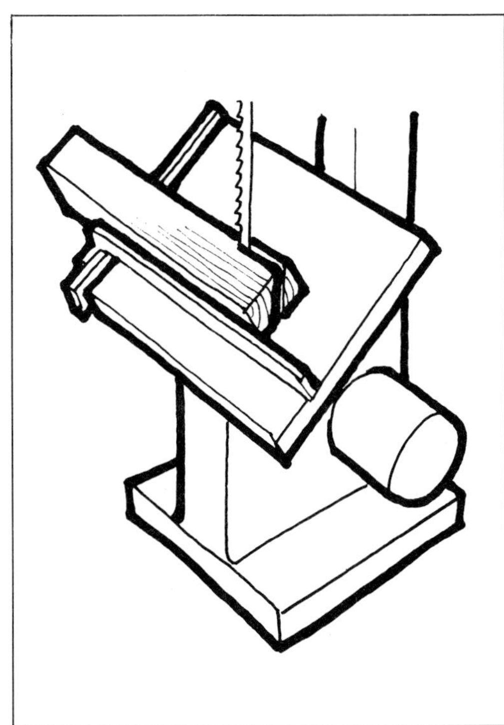

Fig 8.5 The table can be tilted to give angled cuts (0–45°).

THROAT CAPACITY

Some woodworkers consider that the most important feature of a bandsaw is its throat capacity (maximum width of cut) and that the wider it is the better. I am not one of them. There are of course times when a deep throat is required, but I believe the various manufacturers have got it absolutely right with the popular 300mm throat specification (Fig 8.6).

The vast majority of operations fall within this capacity, especially if you open your mind to the fact that a bandsaw is not limited to curved work, but is entirely at home cutting straight down the grain (reducing planks that are seldom over 12in wide – Fig 8.7). It is possible to overcome the throat problem by cutting a long piece of timber in half by making two opposed angled cuts (Fig 8.8).

WHEEL SIZE

Some of the smaller bandsaws achieve a wide throat capacity by driving the blade over three small wheels. It is the size of the wheels which in my opinion is more important than throat capacity. The larger the wheels the better. If you consider the continuous loop blade has to be joined by a solder joint, it is obvious the joint is the weakest part of the blade.

Constant blade-flexing over a small-diameter wheel in effect does the same as when you break chicken wire with your fingers – it is called 'fatiguing', and the blade is likely to break at the solder joint. In my opinion the wheels should be no less than about 12in diameter, giving a blade length of approximately 8ft. The flexing of the blade passing over the wheel is not seriously detrimental to the life of the blade, though in practice my blades need replacing either because they get blunt or because *very* occasionally a slight crack appears at the blade joint (which you can hear catching the guides).

THE BLADE

The secret of successful bandsawing is mostly in the attention given to the blade, the choice of it, and care of it. There are standard (serviceable)

Fig 8.6 Using the maximum throat capacity of the DeWalt bandsaw.

Fig 8.7 When ripping on the bandsaw a throat exceeding 12in is seldom needed.

blades and hardtipped (expendable) blades and I would use the latter every time. I have yet to see a college or training institution (where numerous people use the same machines) where the bandsaw does not produce more smoke than clean-cut timber in any working day because the blades used lose their edge almost as soon as they are re-sharpened! It is a false economy to use the cheaper but softer blades, and invariably when re-sharpened the set is incorrect (which can make the blade wander in the work).

The hardtipped blades, although throwaway, last many times longer and will accommodate 'insensitive woodworkers' who believe that if you push the wood hard enough through the bandsaw (irrespective of the density and thickness of the particular timber) it will cut cleanly!

The secret of economy is to buy these hard-tipped blades in 50m rolls and cut and solder them in a simple jig (Figs 8.9, 8.10, 8.11). Alternatively they can be purchased ready made up to length to suit your particular bandsaw. I have used a blade-soldering jig for years, making the cost of blades minimal. The moment they hint at getting dull, I simply throw them away.

The bandsaw demands a razor sharp and correctly set blade *at all times* – and one of the early signs of dulling is an inability to cut wood parallel to the fence . . . the blade will wander. The 'set' of the teeth, as with circular sawblades, creates the 'kerf', which in effect prevents the blade binding in the wood (Fig 8.12).

Some timbers – notoriously Parana pine – have a tendency to close in on the blade as the timber is

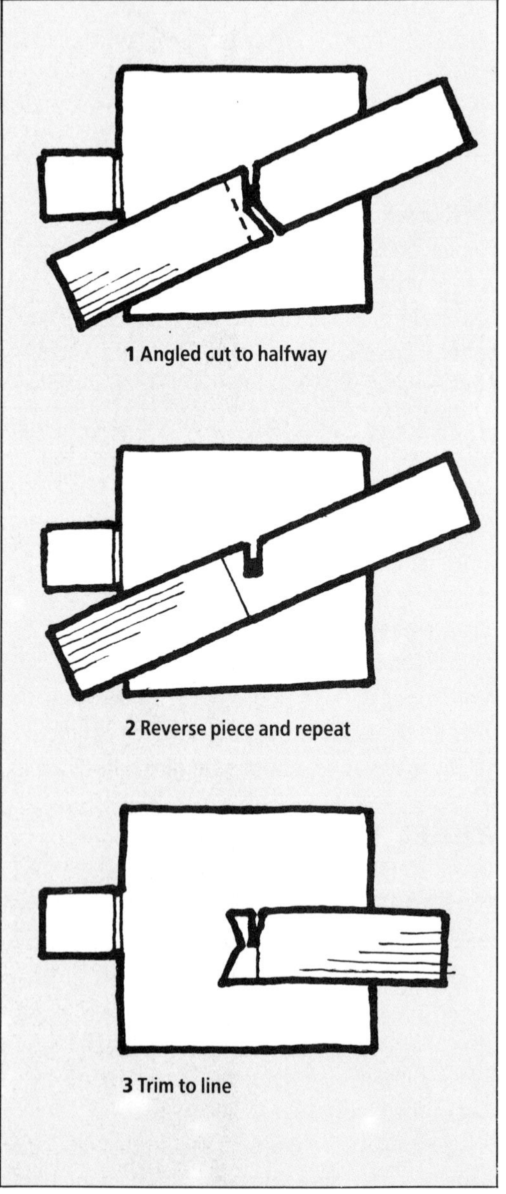

Fig 8.8 Cross-cutting a wide piece in three stages.

Fig 8.9 Using the Makita cordless grinder to scarf the ends of the bandsaw blade for joining.

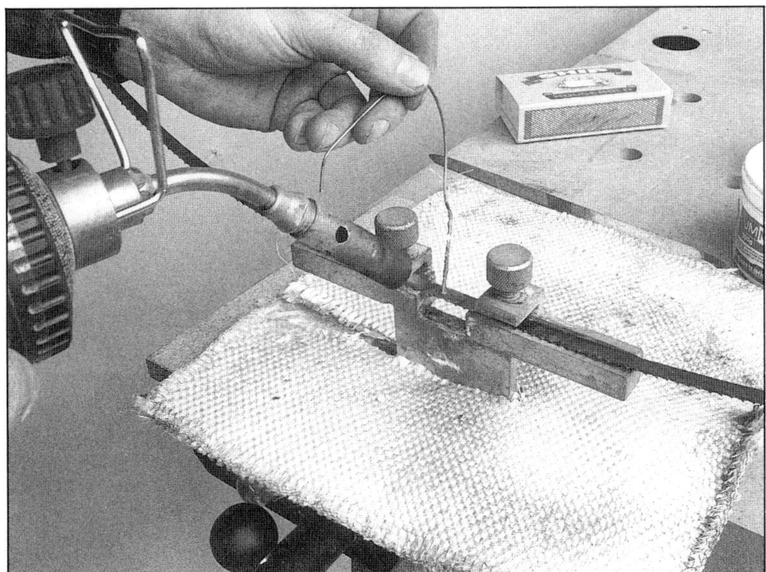

Fig 8.10 An easy-flow silver soldered joint is made.

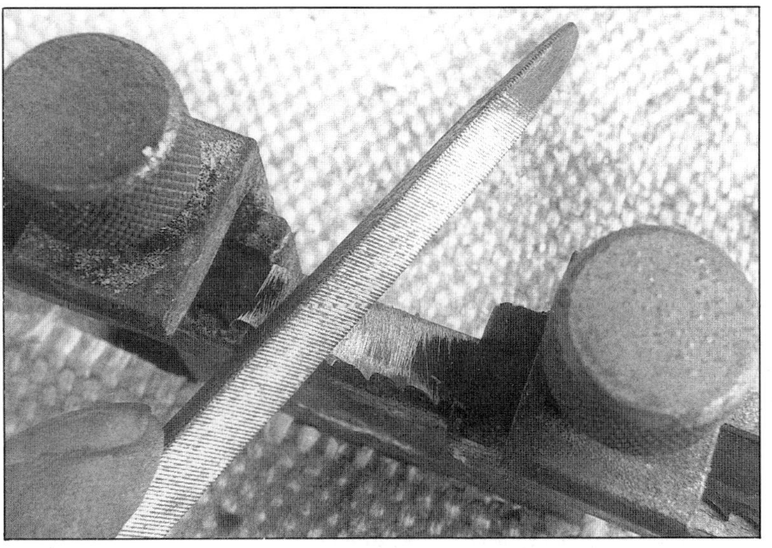

Fig 8.11 It is important to file the soldered joint perfectly flush otherwise it will catch in the bandsaw guides.

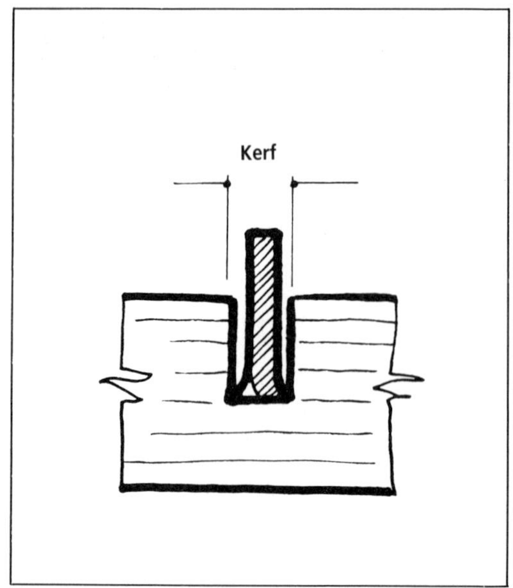

Fig 8.12 Saw-kerf.

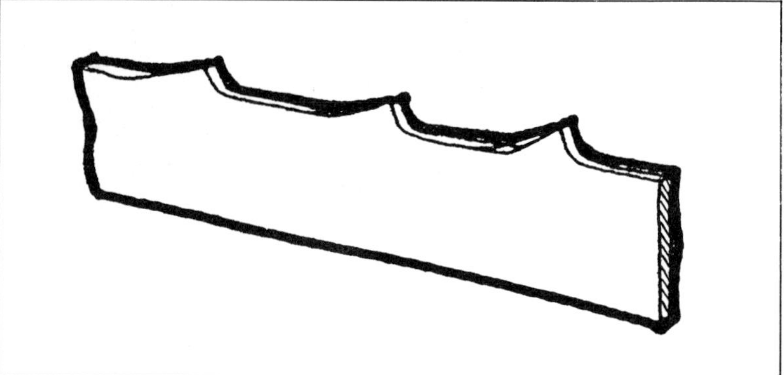

Fig 8.14 Skip-tooth profile.

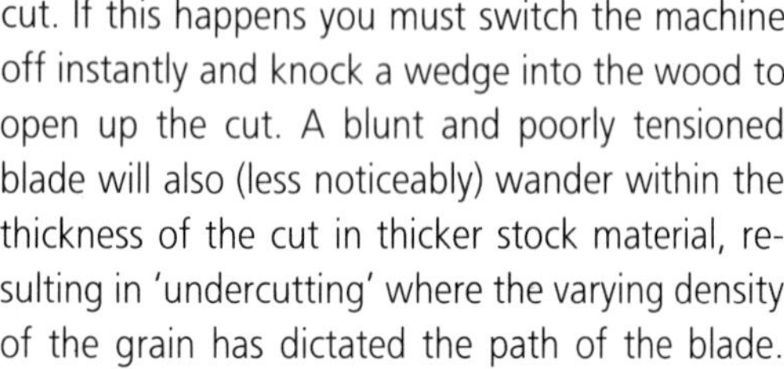

cut. If this happens you must switch the machine off instantly and knock a wedge into the wood to open up the cut. A blunt and poorly tensioned blade will also (less noticeably) wander within the thickness of the cut in thicker stock material, resulting in 'undercutting' where the varying density of the grain has dictated the path of the blade. This is one reason why I prefer to bandsaw to a line rather than use the fence on thicker wood – you can steer the wood to keep accurately to the line. (Of course I am referring to the smaller breed of bandsaws such as the DeWalt featured here.)

Blades are specified by their width, number of points per inch, and their shape (Fig 8.13). A typical '⅜in 6 skip' blade is ⅜in wide, with 5 teeth per inch (there is always one tooth less than the number of points), and the 'skip' is the profile of the tooth (Fig 8.14). There are standard tooth, skip-tooth and hook-tooth blades. The standard provides a smooth cut and is good for cutting

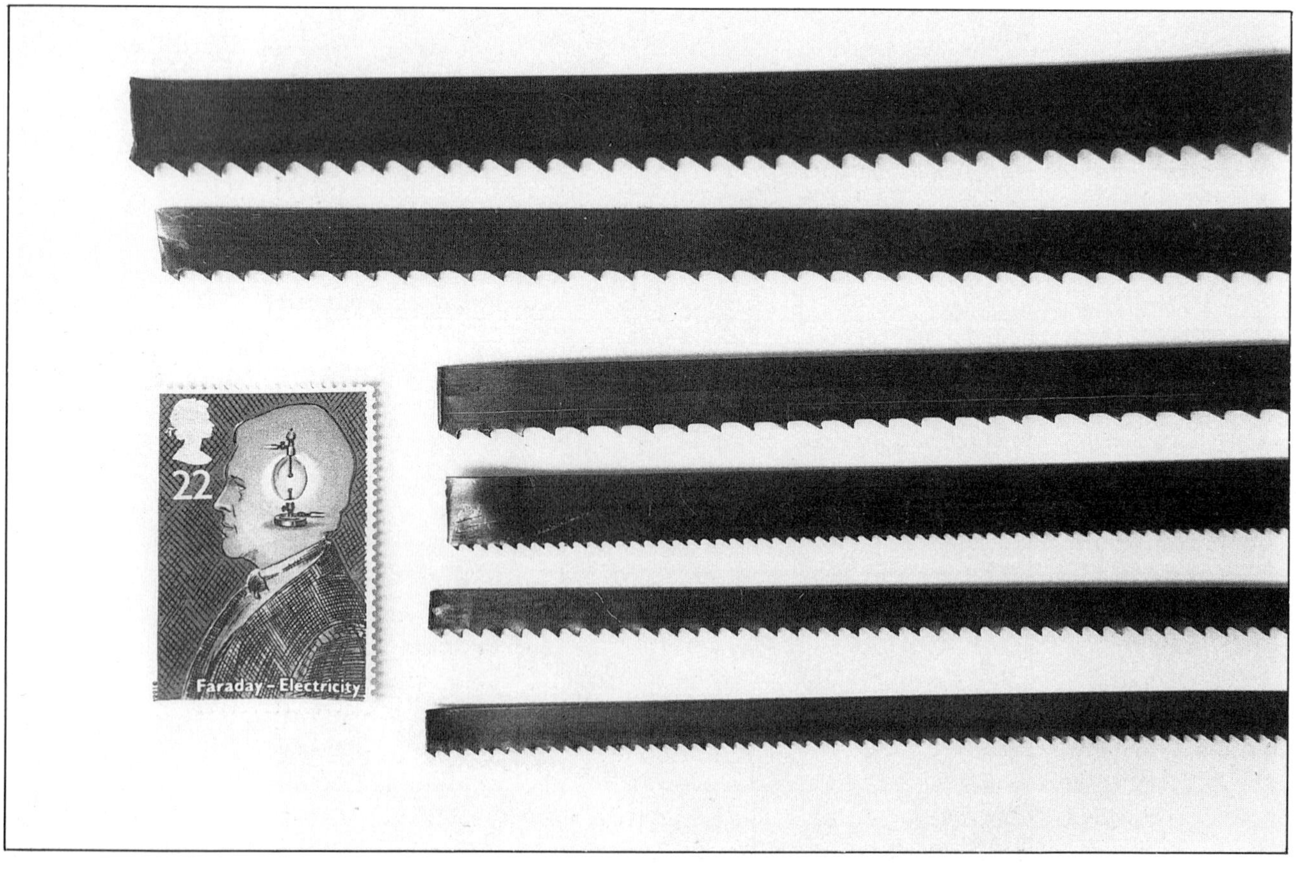

Fig 8.13 A selection of bandsaw blades (courtesy Simbles).

across grain. The skip-tooth cuts faster and is better for cutting with the grain and gentle curves. The hook-tooth is particularly efficient for cutting stock with the grain and when re-sawing.

Blades vary in width from 1/16in for the smaller bandsaws and in general a 3/8in is ideal for the small workshop. Wider blades are used for heavy-duty straight cutting. Obviously the narrower the blade, the tighter the turning curve.

SAFETY

The action of the bandsaw blade is relatively safe. The bandsaw is a linear cutting tool, and as I have said it is quiet and 'user-friendly'.

The machine should be mounted on a stand with a clear in-feed and out-feed area. The front of the casing should never be taken off while the machine is running, which is surely common sense.

Probably the worst that can happen when bandsawing is for the blade to break, and the sooner that happens to you the better because it sounds a lot worse than it is. The blade is immediately released from the wheels and the top end smacks the table – or more precisely the mouth – and the wheels continue spinning freely. You just switch the machine off and wait. Nothing gets mangled up, and if your fingers are in the way they are too close in any case as the point of contact is within about 25mm diameter of the blade path. So in practice it is a safe accident!

When I was a woodwork teacher not only did I insist on the 'one yard rule' (no pupil was allowed to stand nearer than that when another pupil was using a machine), but with the bandsaw I painted a 4in diameter ring around the blade mouth on the bandsaw table and no fingers were to be seen within that zone! Well, there were no accidents.

Earmuffs and a dustmask should be worn when operating the bandsaw. Eye protection is less important as chippings are unlikely to fly up because of the downward linear action of the blade, but really it makes sense to take full precautions and be safe rather than sorry.

OPERATION

One of the first things to learn is how to coil a blade for convenient storage. Folding long bandsaw blades into several coils is an amusing ritual to watch in specialist furniture colleges where the bandsaw is large and the blade taller than the user – the blade tends to whip out unexpectedly. The small bandsaw owner is spared this task as it should only be necessary to fold the blade into two coils, and this is relatively easy. Also when joining your own blades it is sometimes necessary to turn the blade inside out if the teeth are facing the wrong way.

Fig 8.15 Cleaning the works with a dust extractor.

Mounting the blade on to the bandsaw wheels entails making two adjustments – slackening off the top wheel (reducing its height), and tilting the top wheel to feed the blade on. The blade is hand-fed on to both wheels, ensuring any sawdust has been brushed off the rubber linings (Fig 8.15), and the blade is centralized across the width of the wheel (Fig 8.16). (Some smaller and medium-sized bandsaws operate with the blade teeth overhang-

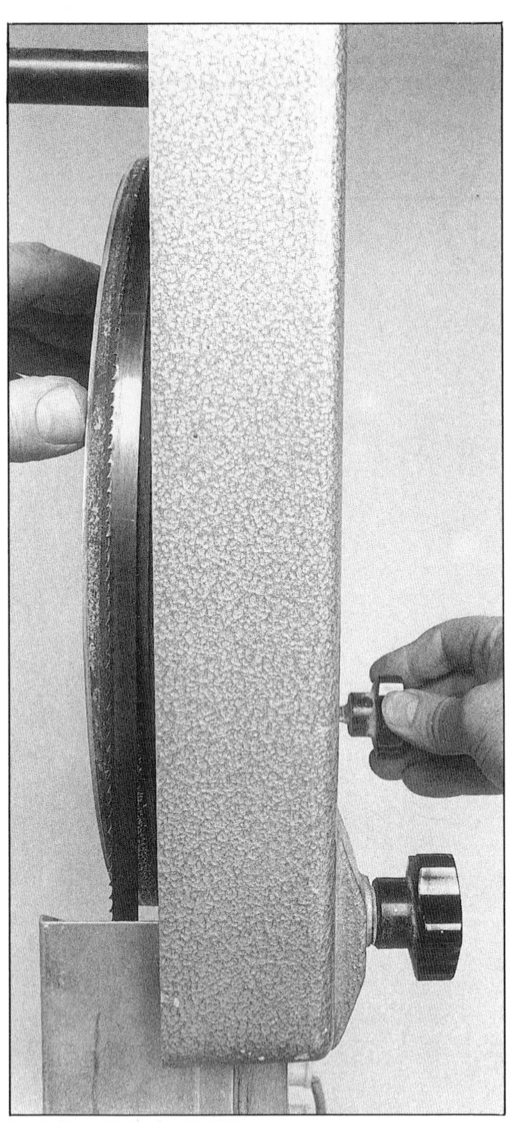

Fig 8.16 The blade has to be centralized across the rubber-lined wheel.

Fig 8.17 Adjusting the blade to the correct tightness.

ing the front edge of the upper rubber tyre.) The wheel is then rotated by hand and two adjusting screws tightened so that the blade is tensioned and running true. The blade should be about 1mm free of the ball-bearing guide of the upper guide assembly, should run freely between the side guides, and its tension should be set to give approximately ½in deflection over a 12in length of unsupported blade (Fig 8.17).

The bandsaw table should be checked for squareness with the inside edge of a try-square (I never rely on the calibrations of any machine) (Fig 8.18), and the final adjustment is made when the timber to be cut is placed on the table. The upper guide assembly should be set just above the thickness of the timber (about an inch) so that the blade is properly guided when it cuts through the timber (Fig 8.19).

When operating the bandsaw both hands should be spaced comfortably apart on the wood, away from the blade, for maximum control and safety (Fig 8.20).

Fence and freehand bandsawing

The fence can be attached to the table and adjusted to give parallel straight cuts (Fig 8.21). This saves the bother of marking lines on the wood for repeat work. I have to say I rarely use the fence other than for very thin work of a repeat nature. When using a fence there is a tendency for the blade to wander when it hits particularly dense patches in a thick piece of timber (even on much larger machines). I find it just as quick to pencil a line or use a marking gauge and bandsaw to the line. In this way you steer the timber so that the line is accurately followed, and the fact that you sometimes have to 'steer' it means the blade is in fact trying to wander.

Now this may be because I expect a lot from my small bandsaw, in so far as I feed quite thick pieces of wood into it, sometimes up to the very maxi-

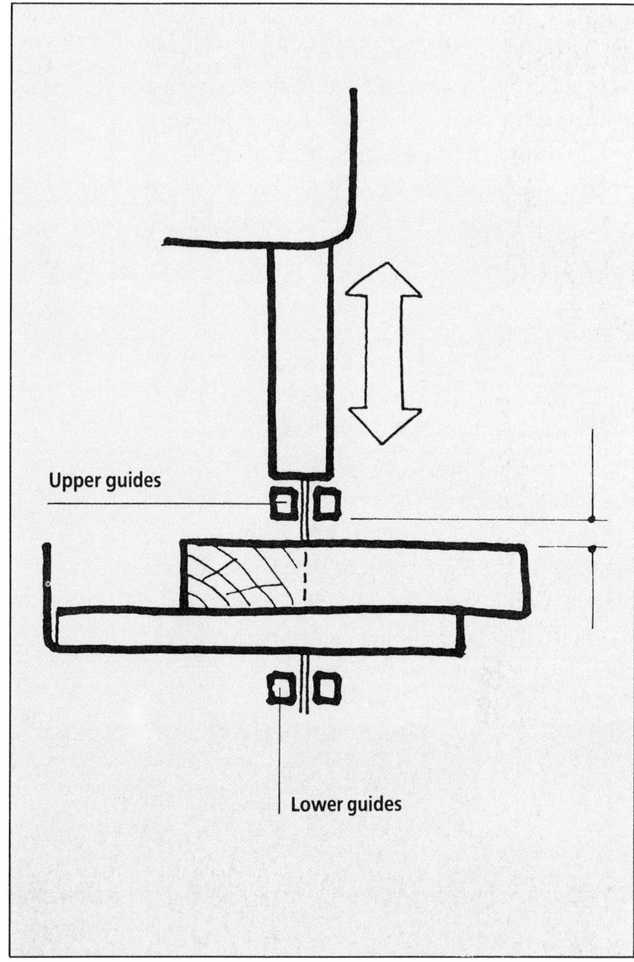

Fig 8.18 Check the blade is 'square' using the inside (accurate) edge of a small try-square (above left).

Fig 8.19 The guide should be set just above the work (above right).

Fig 8.20 Safe position of the hands.

mum cut, and often, say, 2in thick ash, but I *always* work to a line. And obviously for curved work you have to work to a line. (Indeed, working to a line is my preferred method for much electric woodworking, as I have mentioned elsewhere.) By working on the outside (or 'waste' side) of the line (Fig 8.22) you can later finish to the line by sanding (see Chapter 9, The Power Sander).

Deep cutting

Most cutting tools prefer to cut against the grain rather than with it. This may sound odd at first when you consider that an axe naturally cleaves the wood apart down the grain, but of course it follows the grain and not a prescribed line. A hand plane works most efficiently across the grain in breaking up the fibres and removing stock, though more smoothly with the grain, but meeting more resistance. The bandsaw (and other machine saws) behaves in the same way and meets less resistance

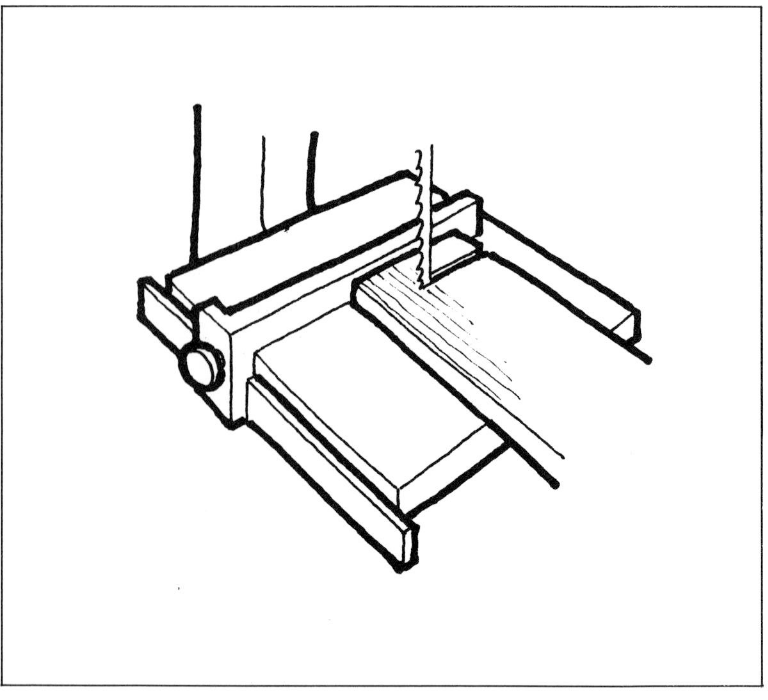

Fig 8.21 The fence is used for parallel cuts.

Fig 8.22 The author always prefers to work to a line.

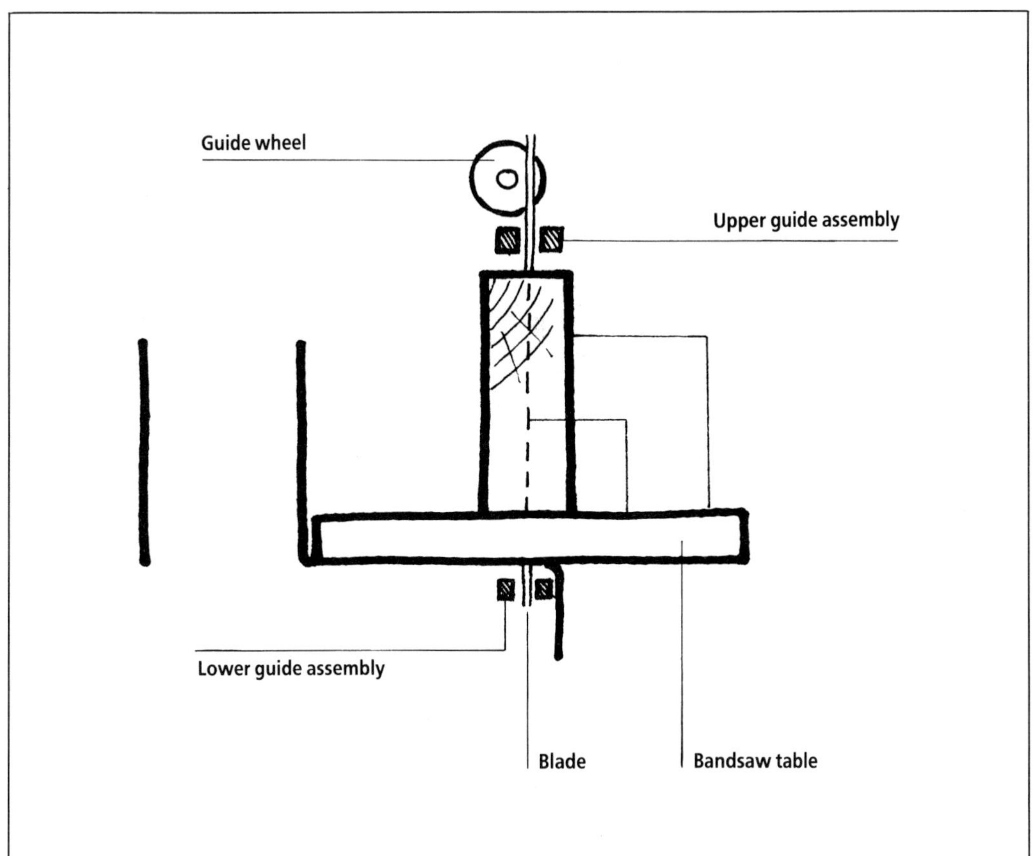

Fig 8.23 Deep cutting on the bandsaw – the work and table must be perfectly 'square'.

when cutting across the grain than cutting down the grain.

Perhaps the most difficult operation in band-sawing is deep cutting down the grain. The machine cutting speed should be slow, as should the feed-in speed. You must never be in a hurry or the blade will overheat and dull even more quickly. (When cutting curved work of course the resistance changes as the grain direction changes.) For deep cutting it is essential that the edge is perfectly 'square' (and should be machined on the planer-thicknesser) as any inaccuracy will be transferred to the angle of the cut (Fig 8.23). Here again, if a line is marked (marking gauge) it is sometimes best to check that the blade aligns before cutting.

My Pyramid Drinks Cabinet (see colour section) was made from a single 2in thick ash board. From this board I deep cut my own 'veneers' on a DeWalt bandsaw and thicknessed them on a planer-thick-nesser. Without giving away all my trade secrets (this particular piece has baffled a few fellow woodworkers), suffice to say that this piece could only have been made using predominantly four electric tools. I wonder what the other two tools were!

Fibre support

The problem with any saw blade is the rip-out of grain caused by the teeth as they cut. The gentle action of the bandsaw loaded with a medium-to-fine toothed blade minimizes this problem, but nevertheless it is still there. (Circular saws cause a bigger problem.) A remedy with the bandsaw,

Fig 8.24 A false platform to prevent fibres splitting.

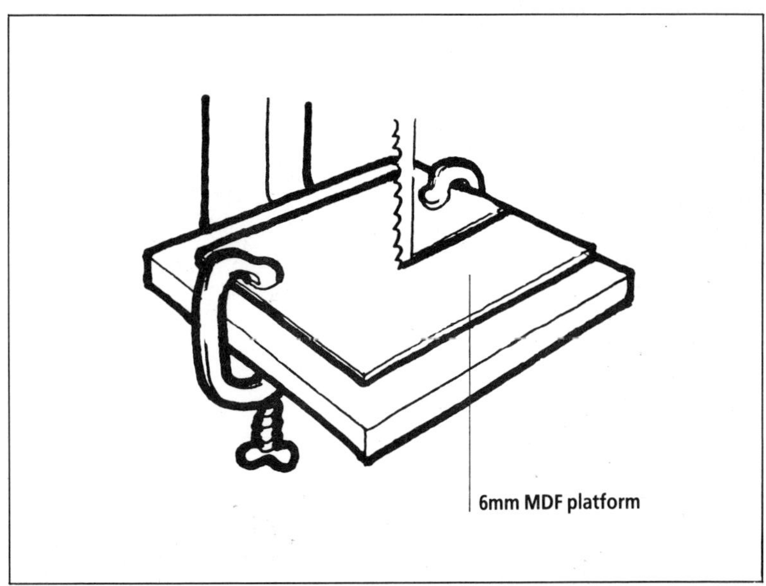

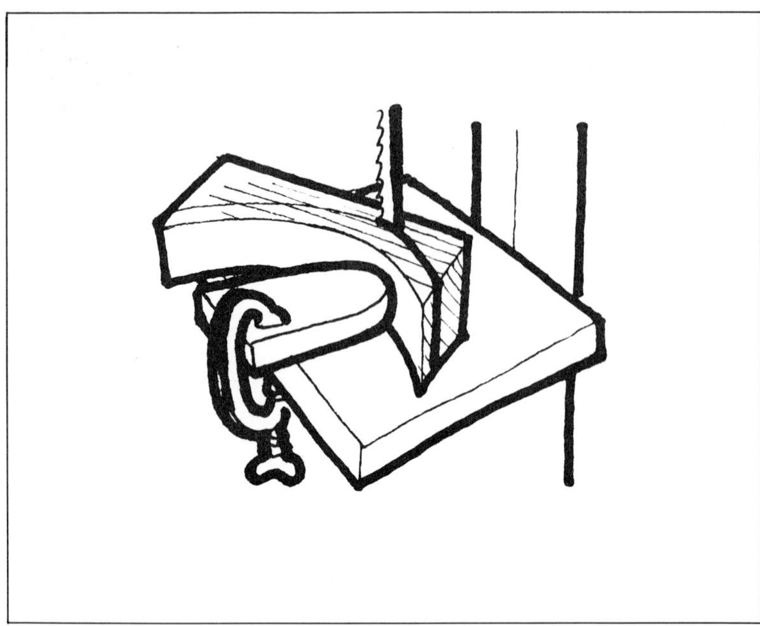

especially when producing fine work, is to back the blade with a piece of MDF or something similar. The replaceable mouth is not sufficient to support the fibres of the wood, and it also wears. The easiest solution is to feed a piece of 6mm MDF into the blade, G-clamp it down to the table and use it as a false platform (Fig 8.24). It will need feeding further in as it eventually wears, but can be jigged up for a specific cutting operation.

Fig 8.25 Batten and G-clamp jigging.

Fig 8.26 Making an 'internal' cut with the bandsaw.

JIGS

The use of jigs when bandsawing is as extensive as the user's imagination. There are depth-stop jigs which can cut shoulders on joints and can be used for saw-kerfing. There are angled and tapered jigs which can be easily made of wood and G-clamped down to the table. In fact a piece of wood and a G-clamp are the most useful jigging tools needed (Fig 8.25).

One thing you cannot do with a bandsaw is start an internal cut (as you can with a jigsaw with or without a drill). However, that is not to say that in some applications you cannot create an internal shape (Fig 8.26)! (See Chapter 26, TAO Board-game.) A good example is the chess-piece cutting jig I made and which can be seen in '*The Incredible Router*'. This MDF jig is accurately cut with a bandsaw. Where the square cut has been made there is an extended cut which allows the bandsaw blade to enter the wood. In this instance it served as a necessary spring to hold the chess piece, but if you stretch your imagination a little further, such a bandsawn shape can be totally enclosed by simply gluing and squeezing together the unwanted external cut. Of course this alters the dimension of the internal shape fractionally but it can have its uses. The important thing is to make the cut *down* the grain so that the glue join is strong. (The real

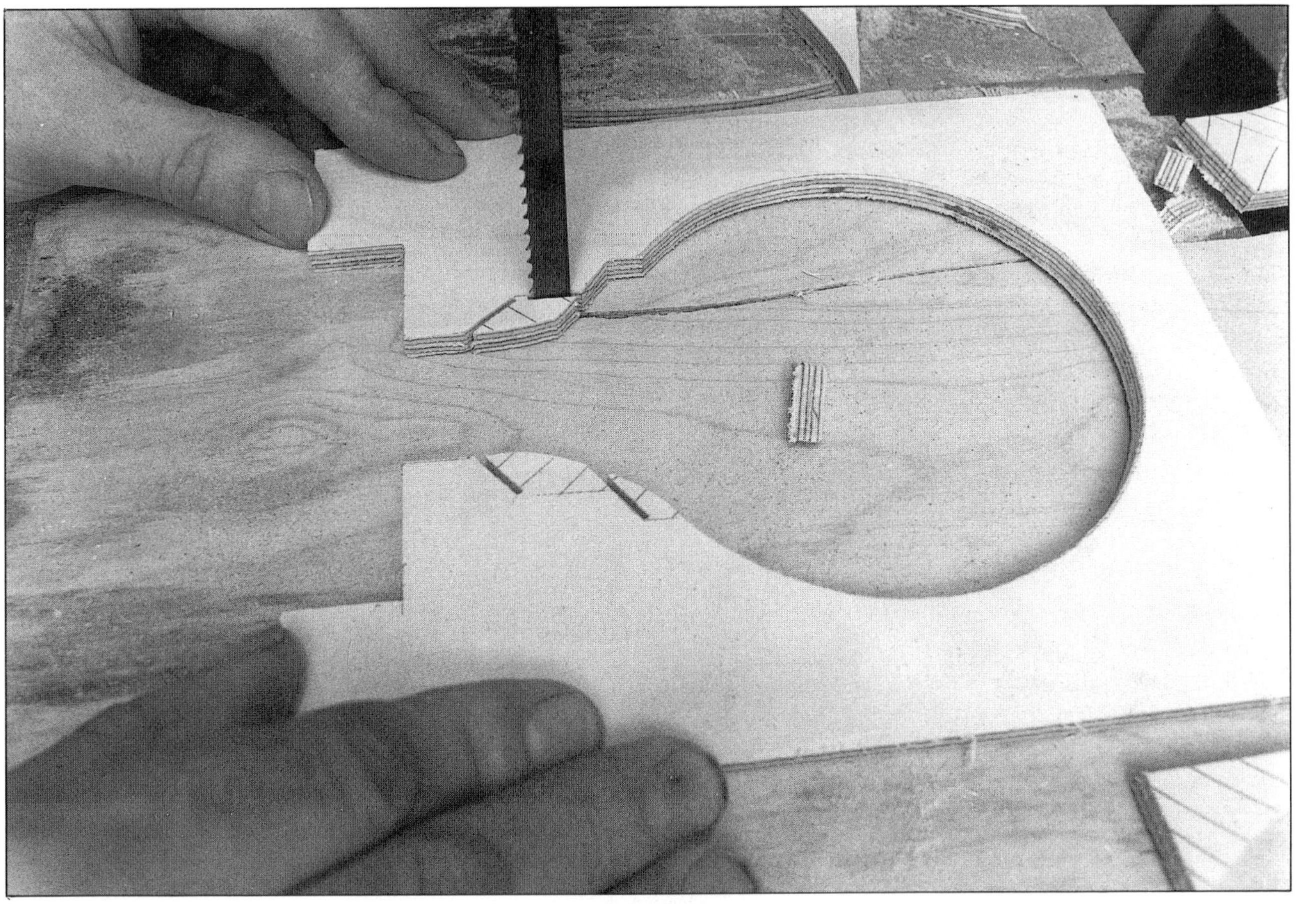

Fig 8.28 The bandsaw can be an extremely accurate shaping tool.

point is to use any tool to its fullest and turn a problem – or limitation – into a feature.)

APPLICATIONS

Most electric tools serve as valuable members of an efficient and creative team and rarely perform in isolation. In particular the bandsaw partnered with the planer-thicknesser can cover a lot of creative mileage – they are key players in my team.

Several years ago, when I used to make acoustic guitars, the bandsaw played a vital part in accurately cutting the formers and many of the guitar parts (Fig 8.27).

A design I first conceived in the late seventies is my 'Straight-from-the-tree' table (see colour section). I particularly wished to express the tool I used to make the table, which was predominantly a bandsaw. I deliberately left the blade marks on the edges of the curved members, contrasting texturally with the smooth top (planer-thicknessed). The stack-lamination configuration of the 'legs' of the table were also created with the bandsaw and came straight off the saw.

The table was made from timber from a tree blown down in Kew Gardens by the Great Storm of 1987. It was exhibited at the time of writing this book.

The bandsaw, therefore, is an extremely useful and creative electric tool (Fig 8.28). I would *almost* be tempted to rank it first!

Fig 8.27 The bandsaw finds another use.

9
THE POWER PLANER

Preparing timber accurately to size once it has been sawn is a prerequisite of any furniture-making activity. It is a slow, tedious and extremely skilful task to achieve consistent flatness and squareness when using a hand smoothing or jack plane, especially on a hard wood, but you cannot expect to make a piece of domestic woodwork well unless the timber is planed accurately to start with. Of course you can buy it already planed but it costs more and you are limited to certain species and standard sizes, and invariably it will warp out of 'square' before you get it home.

In this chapter I am going to deal with the 'mini' planer-cum-thicknesser (see colour section), which in my opinion is a *vital* tool for preparing timber to size and other dressing operations. Indeed it makes it a joy. I am also going to deal with the portable electric hand planer and its attachments (see colour section).

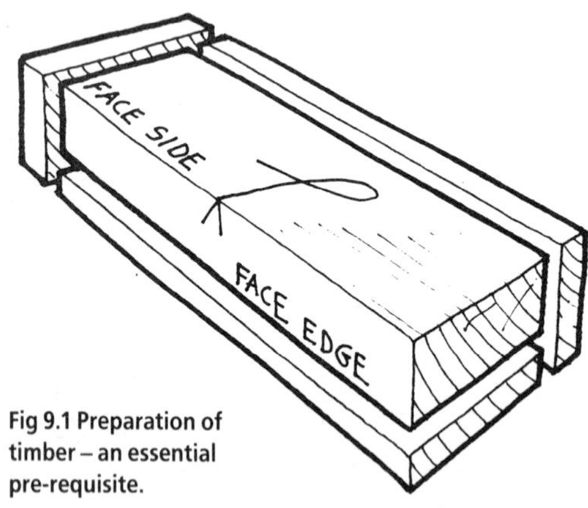

Fig 9.1 Preparation of timber – an essential pre-requisite.

Fig 9.2 If you can carry it under your arm – I'm happy to call it portable! (The Luna Woody.)

The planer (surfacer) gives flatness to the first (face) side, and flatness and 'squareness' to an adjacent (face) edge of the timber, and the thicknesser makes the other side and edge flat and parallel (Fig 9.1). Of course there are other creative applications for both these tools which I shall deal with later.

Although the planer–thicknesser is usually a heavy-duty and more expensive machine, with a width of cut upwards of 10–12in, the *mini* planer–thicknesser has recently become popular (6in cut), and far from being a 'toy', achieves exactly the same degree of accuracy as its larger brothers, but has the advantage of portability. If you can carry it

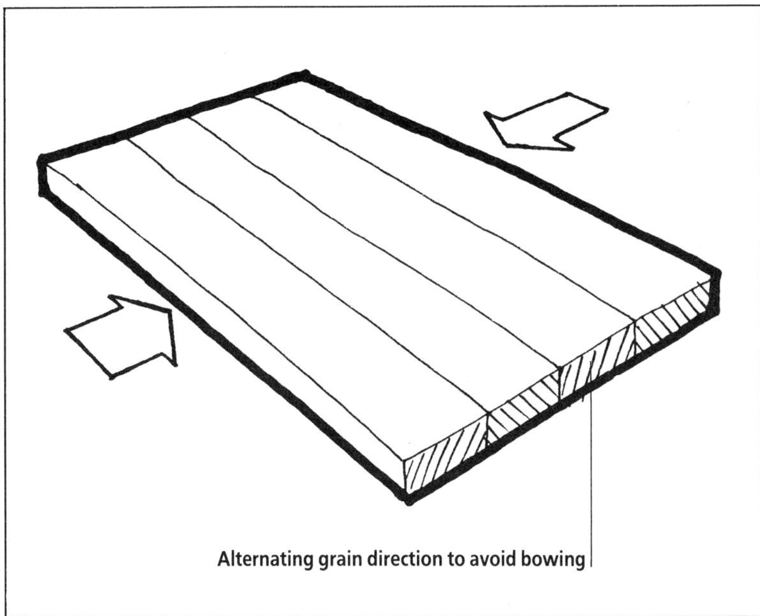

Fig 9.3 Edge-jointing narrow boards to make up panels.

under the arm I am happy to call it a portable tool (Fig 9.2), and one obvious application is on-site work.

Until the revolution in aluminium and plastics-forming it would have been absurd to imagine such portability. Even the 12in or 15in cast-iron machines weighed a ton and required a concrete floor for support, and of course needed a lot of operating space in front and behind. The portable planer–thicknesser can be positioned in the workshop to suit, then moved out of the way when not needed.

Now I rate the planer–thicknesser highly because I struggled for four years commercially with just a hand plane (and had the blisters to prove it!). I then purchased a Kity 6in × 4in planer–thicknesser in the late seventies which transformed my methods overnight!

It is said that necessity is the mother of invention. Whereas financial considerations determined my initial choice of this 6in planer–thicknesser, the apparent limitation of its width of cut introduced a useful feature to my work. Edge-joining narrow boards (Fig 9.3) for carcasses and table tops not only makes the timber more dimensionally stable (look at the way blockboard and laminboard is made up), but adds visual interest to a large surface.

The technique of laminating timbers (see Chapter 22, Laminated Bowl) is immensely useful in woodworking for building up strong and visually attractive sections of any dimension. In frame constructions sections greater than 6in × 4in are very rare, unless you are in the business of making railway sleepers!

When I later traded my little Kity for a larger machine, I found I missed it! In subsequent years I advertised unsuccessfully for a second-hand one (perhaps their owners would not part with them) and I was surprised and disappointed to learn that Kity had discontinued the model, although during the writing of this book a similar model has been reintroduced by Kity!

For the purpose of this book, however, I was able to obtain a similar mini planer–thicknesser called the Luna 'Woody', so perhaps at last the manufacturers have realized the huge potential of these 'Davids' amongst the 'Goliaths'.

The Woody is a 6in × 5in planer–thicknesser – referring to the width and thickness of a timber it can machine. In fact it is specified as the Woody 160 – and it cuts right up to 160mm wide (every millimetre counts!).

This particular machine, being extremely basic and 'matter-of-fact', is ideal for illustration purposes (irrespective of size). It does have one or two limitations but in general it is an excellent tool (Fig 9.4) and particularly appeals to me because it is so easy to move about.

PRINCIPLE OF THE PLANER–THICKNESSER

The concept is simple (Fig 9.5). A geared motor drives a rotating cutter block (normally two blades,

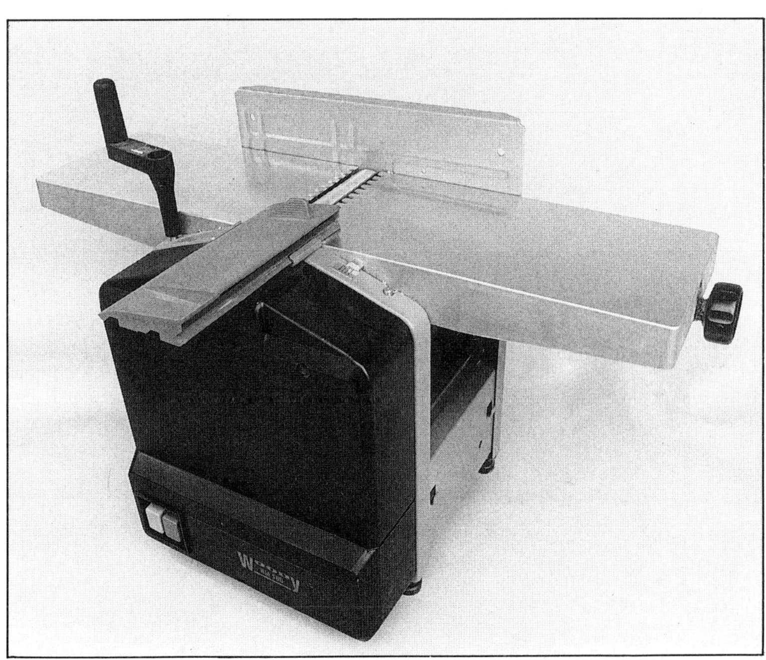

Fig 9.4 The Luna Woody 160 planer-thicknesser.

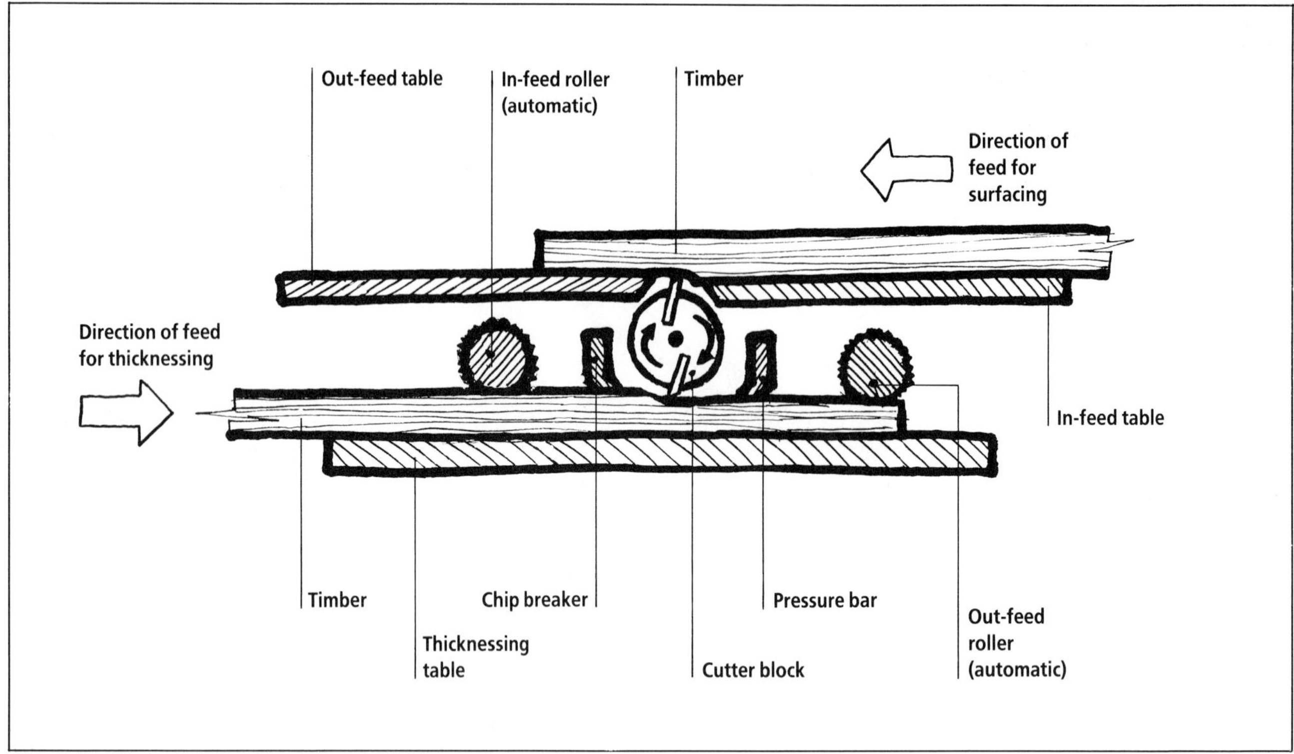

Fig 9.5 Section through a planer-thicknesser showing main parts.

but sometimes three) which is located in the middle of a feed table with the cutter fractionally protruding above the surface. (In front of the cutter is an adjustable 'in-feed' table and behind the cutter a fixed 'take-off' table.) The timber is hand-guided along the in-feed table, passed over the rotating cutters (approx. 6000rpm) and pushed along the take-off table. This is called surface-planing and the flatness is achieved by religiously keeping the timber in contact with the feed table which serves as a guiding jig. By using a 90° fence both side and edge of the timber can be accurately machined by pressing the wood firmly against feed table and fence. (The fence is also adjustable to give angled cuts – Fig 9.6).

For thicknessing, the timber is fed into the underside of the feed table (and under the cutters) and is guided along an adjustable thicknessing table

Fig 9.6 Adjustable fence on planer.

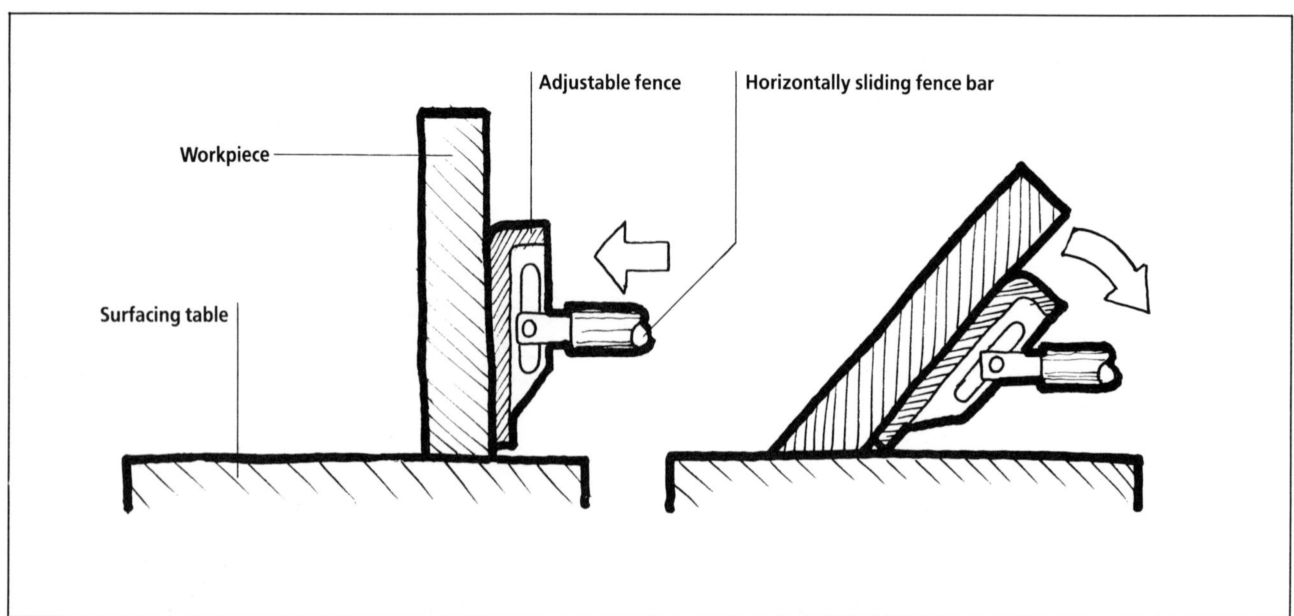

Fig 9.7 Adjusting for depth of cut when thicknessing.

which determines the required thickness of the timber. It engages with the automatic feed rollers which allow the timber to pass under the cutters at a steady rate (feed is around 6m per minute – quite slow).

The adjustments involve the correct initial setting-up and alignment of the cutters in the block, and the trueness of the 90° fence (don't rely on the manufacturer). The controls include wheels or knobs (Fig 9.7) for the rise and fall of the in-feed table for depth of surface-planing cut, and the adjustment in the thicknessing table for feeding in timber for that operation.

Some planer–thicknessers on the market have tilting table tops which swing out of the way for thicknessing operations. Dust extraction hoods are hooked on to the appropriate locations for surface-planing and thicknessing.

Now I prefer the non-tilting/swinging variety of planer–thicknesser tables because there is little fuss in the change-over operation between surfacing and thicknessing. In fact the only necessary adjustment is the switching of the dust-extraction hood to its alternative position. The advantage is that timber can be surfaced, squared, then thicknessed without moving and hence interfering with the fence which has been set up.

THE ACTION

One obvious difference between hand and electric planing is the way the tool cuts. With a hand plane the shaving is long, thin and continuous. An electric planer (thicknesser) chops the wood in a series of short concave cuts by its rotating cutter block.

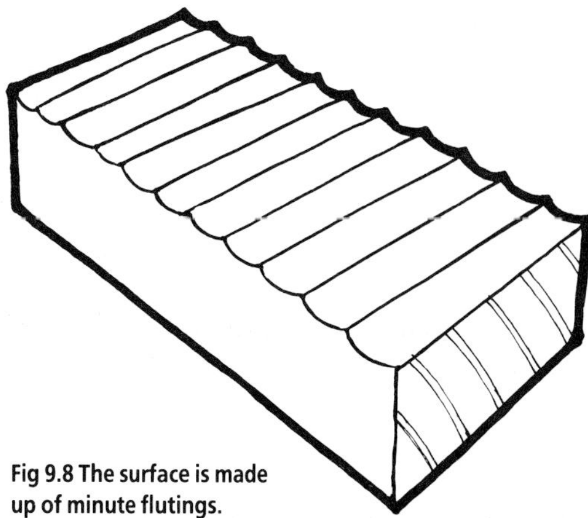

Fig 9.8 The surface is made up of minute flutings.

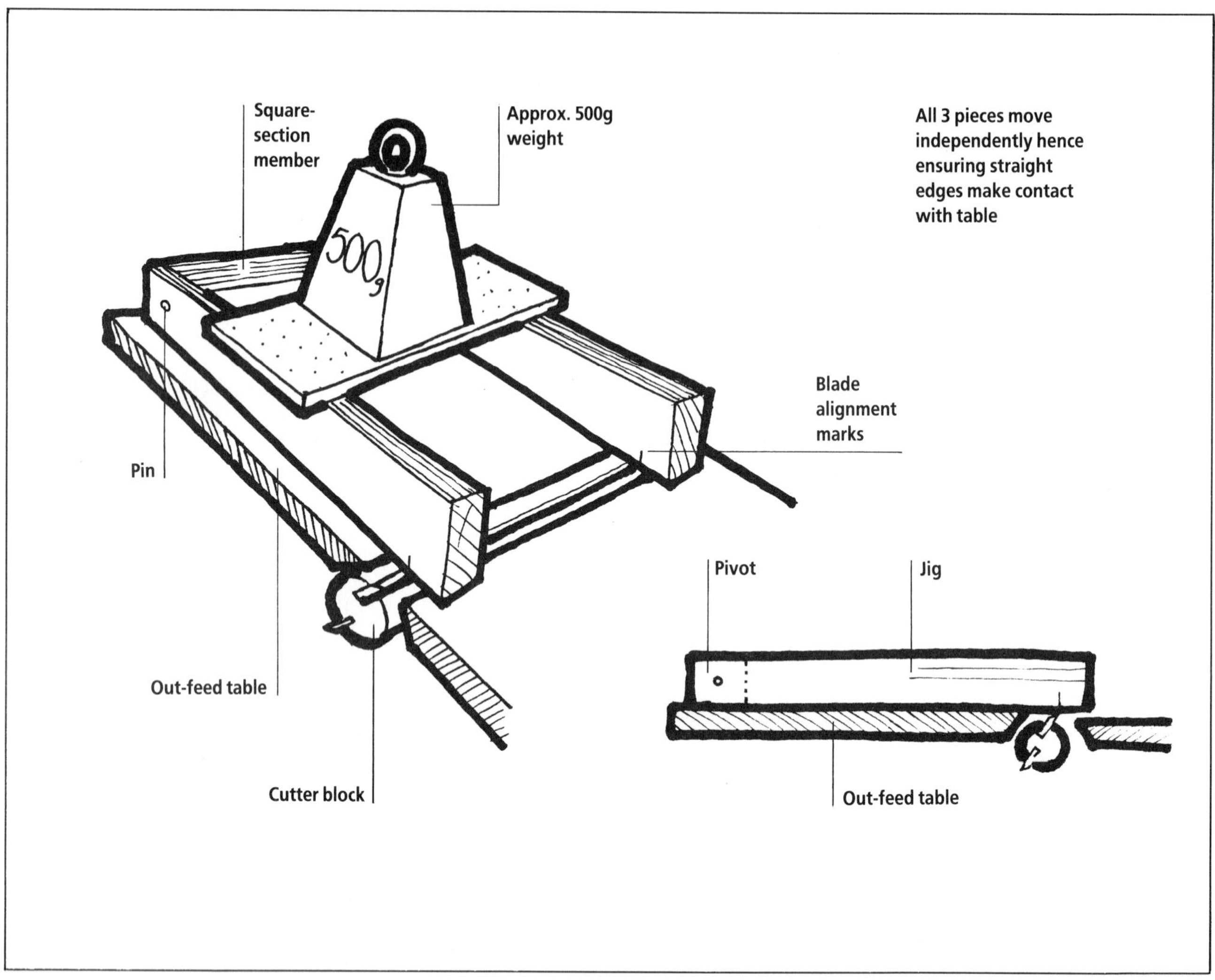

Fig 9.9 A blade-adjusting jig.

Each blow (about 12000 per minute!) creates a small chipping and if you look closely at the surface of the wood you will see a series of minute flutings (Fig 9.8).

Like a hand plane the electric planer can be adjusted to vary the depth of cut which in turn produces chippings ranging from a fine 'dust' to coarse particles. It is easy to monitor the performance of the cutter by the size of the chippings that are produced and also by the sound (pitch) of the machine, and in practice fine adjustment can be made as the timber goes through the thicknesser.

SETTING UP BLADES

It is important to know how to set up the blades (or knives) in the cutter block as they will need frequent re-sharpening. If they are out of true, or just one knife makes contact with the timber because the opposing one is set too low, it will not only throw the cutter block off balance but result in half the cutting speed – if it is a two-cutter block – and rapid dulling of the over-worked blade.

The blades are fixed in the cutter block by a compression-bolt assembly. For correct alignment of the blades a timber straightedge is placed along the take-off table so it just overlaps the cutter block. The blades should just 'kiss' the timber straightedge, or pull it fractionally forward as the cutter block is rotated slowly by hand (the electric plug has been taken out of the socket). In other words the tip of the blade is fractionally higher than the level of the take-off table – probably the thickness of a sheet of notepaper.

It is important that the blade is checked at both ends, and adjustments may have to be repeated to get it right as when tightening up the bolts the blade often slips slightly. It is crucial to get this right as the performance of the machine relies on it. The cutters are usually spring-loaded which makes them a little easier to adjust. The bolts should be firmly but not excessively tightened up. To reduce the time taken in this operation I have devised a simple blade-aligning jig (Fig 9.9).

The cutters are made of high-speed steel, or tungsten-carbide tipped, and in most planers are replaceable. I usually carry a spare pair of HSS blades for my 10in planer–thicknesser. Although TCT blades maintain their edge much longer, they are in fact more brittle and therefore less serviceable than HSS ones. Many woodworkers prefer HSS blades which they can easily service themselves, and argue that they have a keener edge than TCT blades. The TCT blades on the Woody are expendable, but relatively inexpensive, especially as they are reversible. (It costs almost as much to have HSS blades professionally sharpened.)

Although it is possible to hone blades with an oilstone, I find there is no real substitute for a cleanly and consistently machine-ground edge (normally 30–35°). I am sure it is possible to jig up a small router with a grinding wheel in its collett for re-sharpening blades in situ, but I have never got around to trying this!

Timbers vary enormously in their density and 'abrasiveness' and the consequent blunting of blades. (This also applies to hand planing. I often wondered why the school woodwork teacher always gave oak to the students – it kept them busier longer!) But timbers behave differently in the planer–thicknesser. Sometimes softwoods blunt the blades quicker, partly due to resins in the timber – the heat build-up caused by resin sticking to the blades reduces their working life. Remember, it all happens very quickly when the cutter is working 12000 times per minute. One timber to be especially wary of when machine planing is pitch pine as it can be resinous and may clog the rollers and slip.

SAFETY

If you regard the planer–thicknesser as an *extremely* dangerous machine, perhaps deceptively so, then you are approaching it in the right manner. Its noise does not carry the fearsome scream of a circular saw – indeed I would say it does not sound particularly dangerous at all – but the cutter block is lethal and will do untold damage to the fingers. **It is imperative that your fingers are kept well clear of the cutter block and that the bridge guard is used at all times.** The timber should always pass *under* the guard. This may not be the most natural way to feed the wood, but it is clearly the safest. Eye protection is necessary as chippings will fly everywhere if dust extraction is not being used. (The Woody was fitted with a modified bridge guard on all models in 1992.)

The stance is important and you should be positioned facing the machine at its centre with both legs astride so there is equal reach to feed the wood into the cutter and then out of the cutter, maintaining firm and constant pressure throughout the travel of the timber. Do not forget that when surface-planing you have to do what the automatic feed does when thicknessing.

The safety precautions for thicknessing are self-evident. Never place your hand inside the machine when it is switched on, particularly when lubricating the thicknessing table. If the timber jams, then instantly lower the table and switch off the machine. One common occurrence is the break-up of grain, either when a knot is hit, or 'short grain' in the middle or end of the timber is being knocked out. Usually it makes a sudden bang and often part of the debris will jam in the cutter block. This can be removed carefully with a chisel or screwdriver *after the machine has been switched off.*

Accidents can occur even when the cutters are stationary as they are razor sharp. In order to prevent the cutter block freely rotating while one of the cutters is being attended to, I simply jam the other cutter with a strip of softwood gently raised on the thicknessing bed.

MAINTENANCE

Apart from servicing and checking the blades as already mentioned, which is crucial to the performance of the machine, there are one or two points to look out for. When the drive casing is removed it can be seen that the drive mechanism is fairly lightly fabricated, relying on nylon and aluminium gears and pulleys with rubber belts and chains (Fig 9.10). There is not a lot of room for adjustment and the tensioning is fairly basic.

It pays to inspect the workings from time to time to blow away shavings or debris which might be trapped under the rubber belts and to lubricate the parts recommended by the manufacturer. The adjustable thicknessing table requires the four threaded height adjusters to be attended to as they tend to get clogged up. A wire brush and lubricant help, but lubricants can attract debris. A blower is a useful tool.

Fig 9.10 The drive belts and pulleys on the Luna Woody – a dusting down is occasionally required.

The in-feed roller can get clogged up after continual use of resinous woods (which should generally be avoided). The out-feed table should be removed, exposing the feed roller for cleaning with a wire brush.

The most common problem is the friction caused by wood passing over aluminium, especially when thicknessing. The thicknessing table on aluminium machines needs constant lubrication to ensure the wood does not stick, and manufacturers supply a special 'wax' for this. I sprinkle baby talcum powder over the table and rub it in and this works just as well! On some machines it is possible to buy a 'stick-on' stainless steel thicknessing sleeve, which in my experience also works quite well to eliminate the problem.

DUST EXTRACTION

Because the planer–thicknesser creates a lot of chippings and dust it is a priority machine for dust-extraction. Manufacturers usually supply an optional dust hood (see Fig 4.3) which clips on to the machine in its two modes – surfacing and thicknessing – to be linked by flexible tubing to a portable extractor. Ideally a fairly large-capacity extractor should be used and it may be necessary to purchase tube-reduction connectors to match the machines (see Chapter 15, The Electric Workshop).

PLANING

Surface-planing

Normally the first operation in using a planer–thicknesser is to surface-plane the first side of the timber. Naturally it may be slightly irregular – twisted and bowed, with a sawn surface. If this is

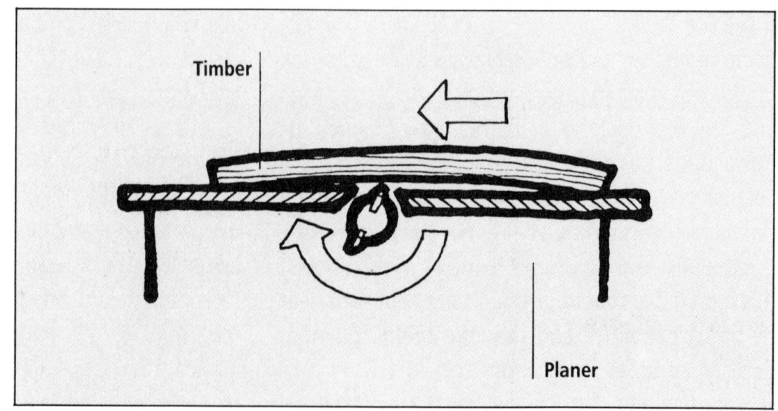

Fig 9.11 Feed the concave surface into the cutter block if wood is slightly bowed.

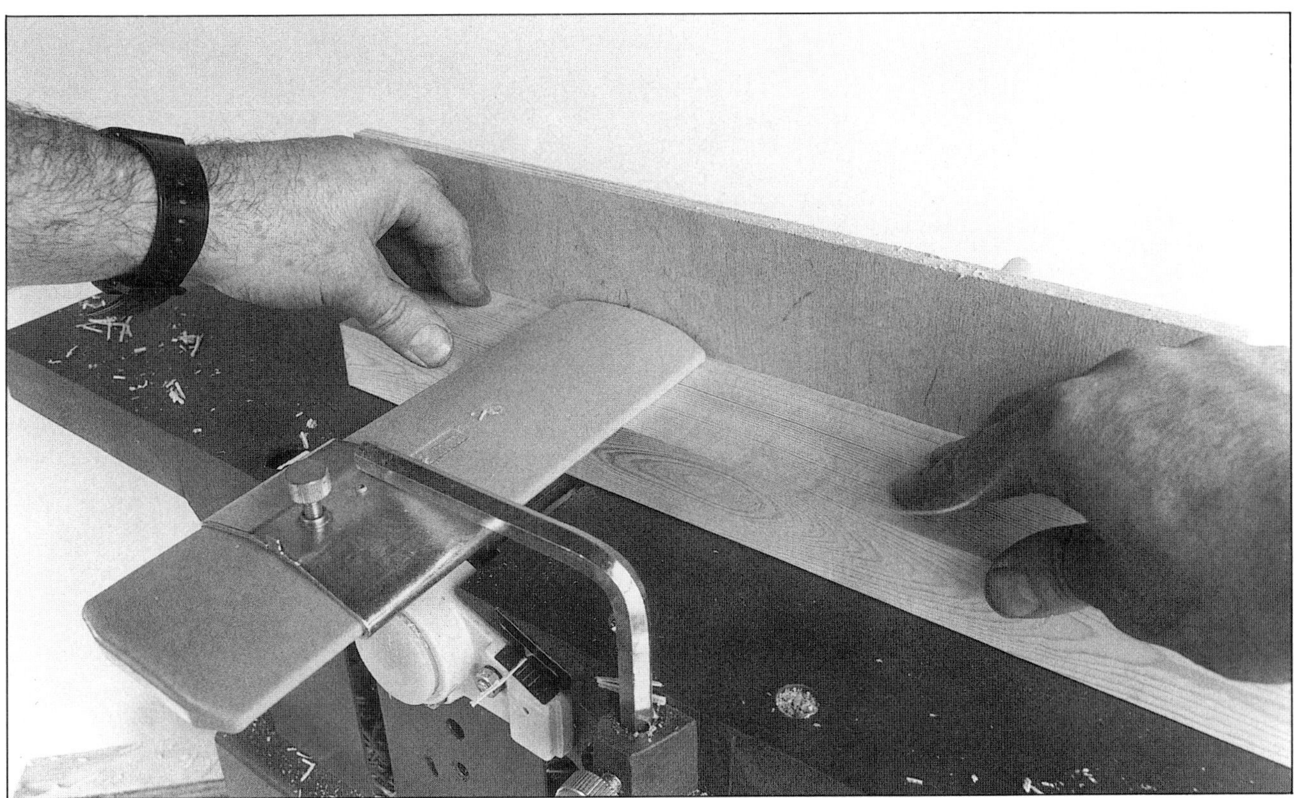

Fig 9.12 The position of the fingers plays an important part in the holding down and guidance of wood when surface-planing.

the case then the concave surface is offered to the cutters, otherwise the timber would rock on the table (Fig 9.11). Both hands are placed at either end of the timber (Fig 9.12), taking great care that fingers do not overlap the edge more than a *fraction* (it is largely a friction grip), and as the work is firmly pushed downwards along the table the hands should 'walk' across the bridge guard, which should be set just above the timber – without touching it – and therefore needs to be adjustable.

After the first two or three lightly set cuts (the in-feed table can be adjusted for depth of cut) you will probably notice that the planed surface is either smooth, or rough with evidence of the grain breaking up. This is because the grain direction of the timber seldom runs parallel to the surface of the timber (why should it!), and where the grain breaks you have in effect planed against the direction of the grain. You simply turn the board around and start again (Fig 9.13).

I usually mark a small arrow on the edge showing the feed direction as it is easy to stop halfway through the operation (because the telephone rings) and then pick up the piece again having forgotten which way it has to be fed into the machine – and you ruin your work in an instant. (How do I know!)

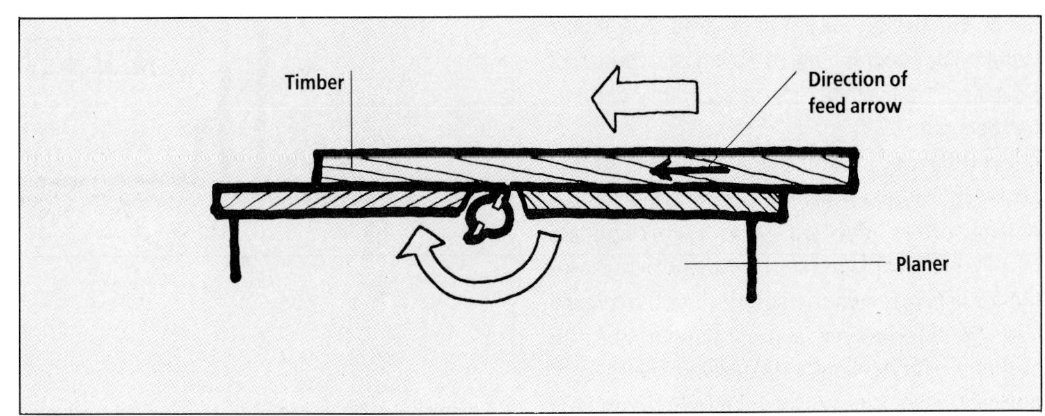

Fig 9.13 Mark the direction of feed with an arrow when the grain is not running perfectly parallel.

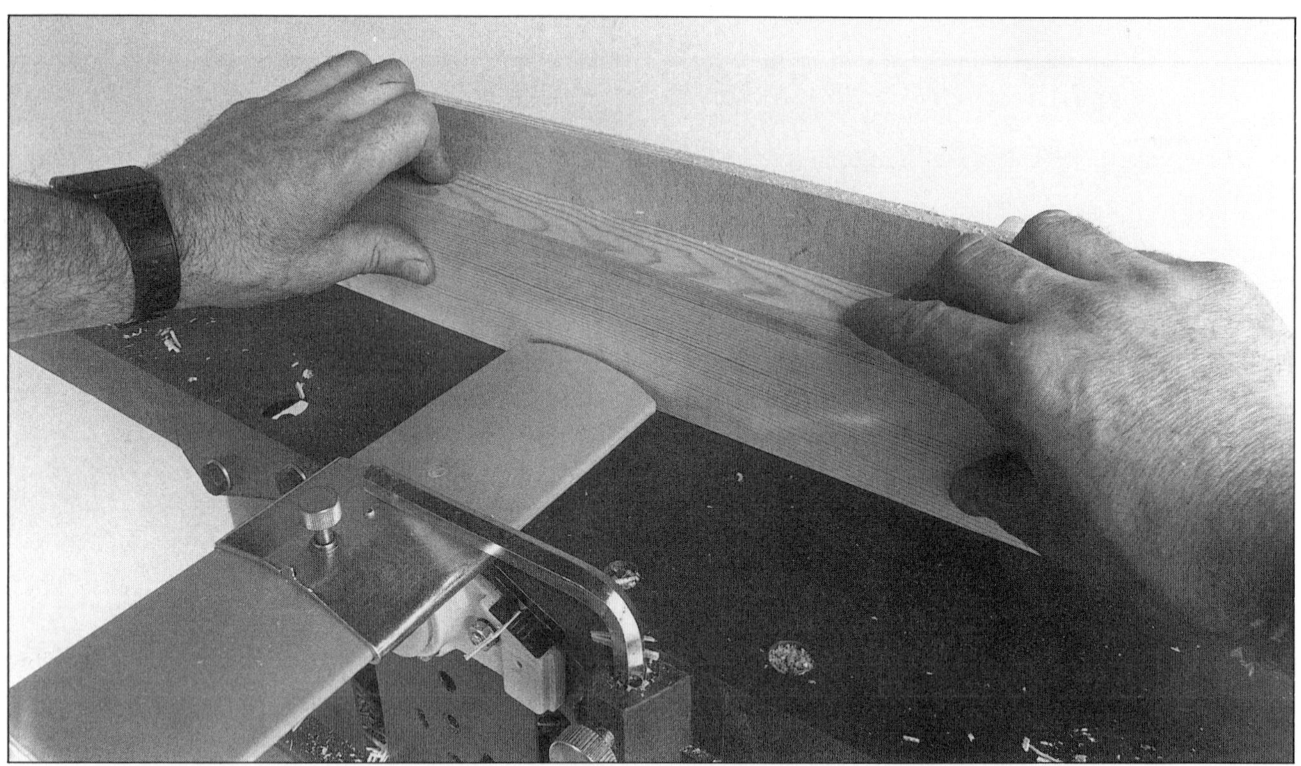

Fig 9.14 Similarly, pressure must be correctly applied to maintain accuracy – and safety – when planing.

Planing the edge square

On a new machine the square fence will need fine-tuning and facing with a piece of MDF sheet or something similar. A set-square can be used to check the angle of the fence to the surfacing table. Placing the face side of the stock material against the fence and ensuring pressure is even, the edge of the board is fed into the cutter to get it flat and 'square' (Fig 9.14).

Finger pressure against the fence is important, but take care not to place the fingers too near the surfacing table. The bridge guard should be adjusted right up to the material. It may require several passes to achieve a 'square' edge and I prefer to check the result with a try-square afterwards. This operation is one of the great joys of using the planer–thicknesser, as to get timber 'square' by hand is one of the most arduous of tasks and the machine does it accurately within a few seconds.

An effective use of the planer–thicknesser is in achieving flat and square edges on manufactured boards, such as chipboard. I prefer to cut chipboard initially with a fine-toothed jigsaw (which causes the least damage to the surface fibres) and then clean up the edges on the planer–thicknesser. This also applies to melamine-coated chipboard (Contiplas) as a circular saw, although giving a straight and square cut, tends to break up the lower surface, and when building kitchen units, for instance, an absolutely clean and square edge is crucial.

The excessive wear on the planer blades is a small price to pay as chipboard, with its glue resins, can even send off sparks. However, it teaches you to use the entire width of the blade by re-positioning the fence progressively across the table (Fig 9.15).

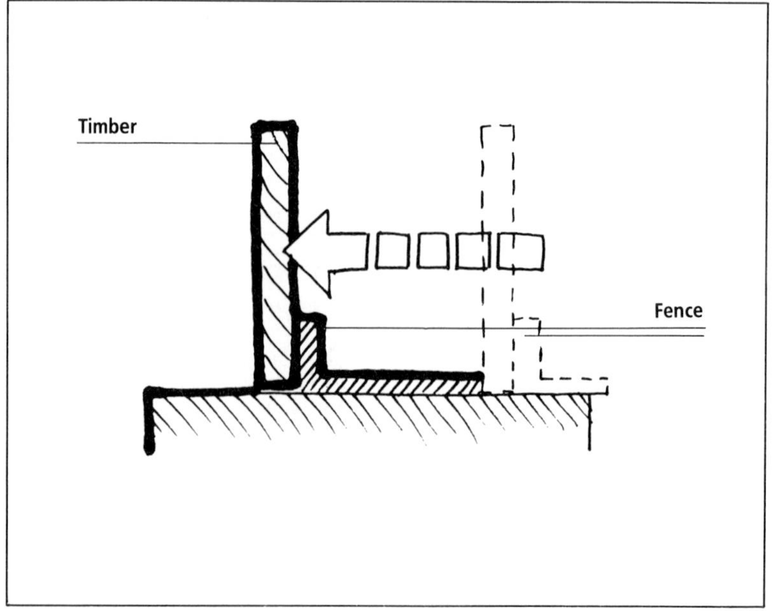

Fig 9.15 Manufactured boards can be 'square-edged' but the fence must be progressively moved across the cutter block to ensure even wear of the blades.

The Arbotech woodcarver – the skill of risk (see Chapter 3).

Dust extraction is essential in electric woodworking. One Elu automatically switches on another.

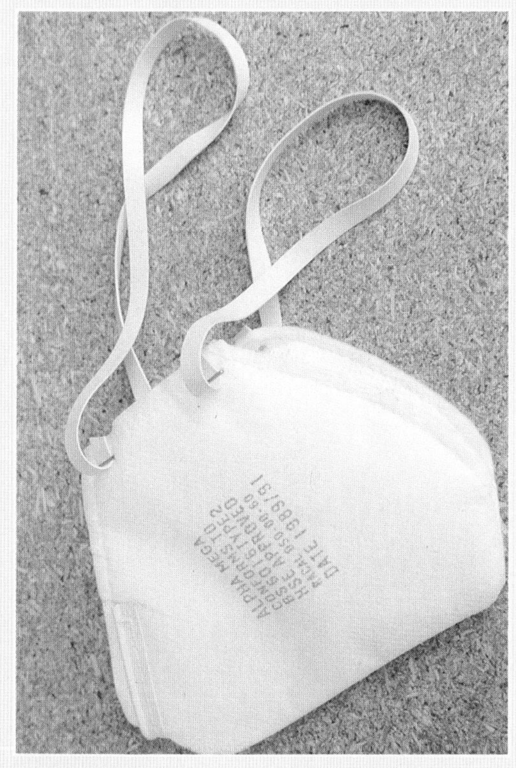

Check the shape of your nose before deciding on a dustmask! The author believes this Racal mask is the best in its class (or perhaps it fits his nose best!).

A classic power tool from Black & Decker.

A Hitachi cordless drill – forever useful in the workshop.

Reaching new heights – the Panasonic cordless drill.

Using a Hitachi orbital jigsaw to cut through 2in ash from Kew Gardens, a result of the Great Storm of 1987.

An AEG 12 volt cordless jigsaw – with no cable to trip over!

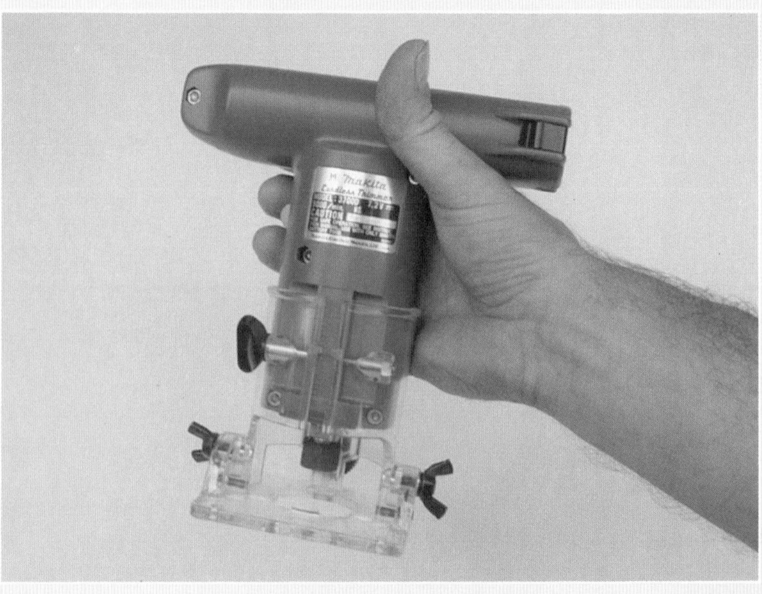

The Makita cordless trimmer.

A 'bench' of routers!

Manufacturer's router kit (Bosch).

Hitachi M12V router.

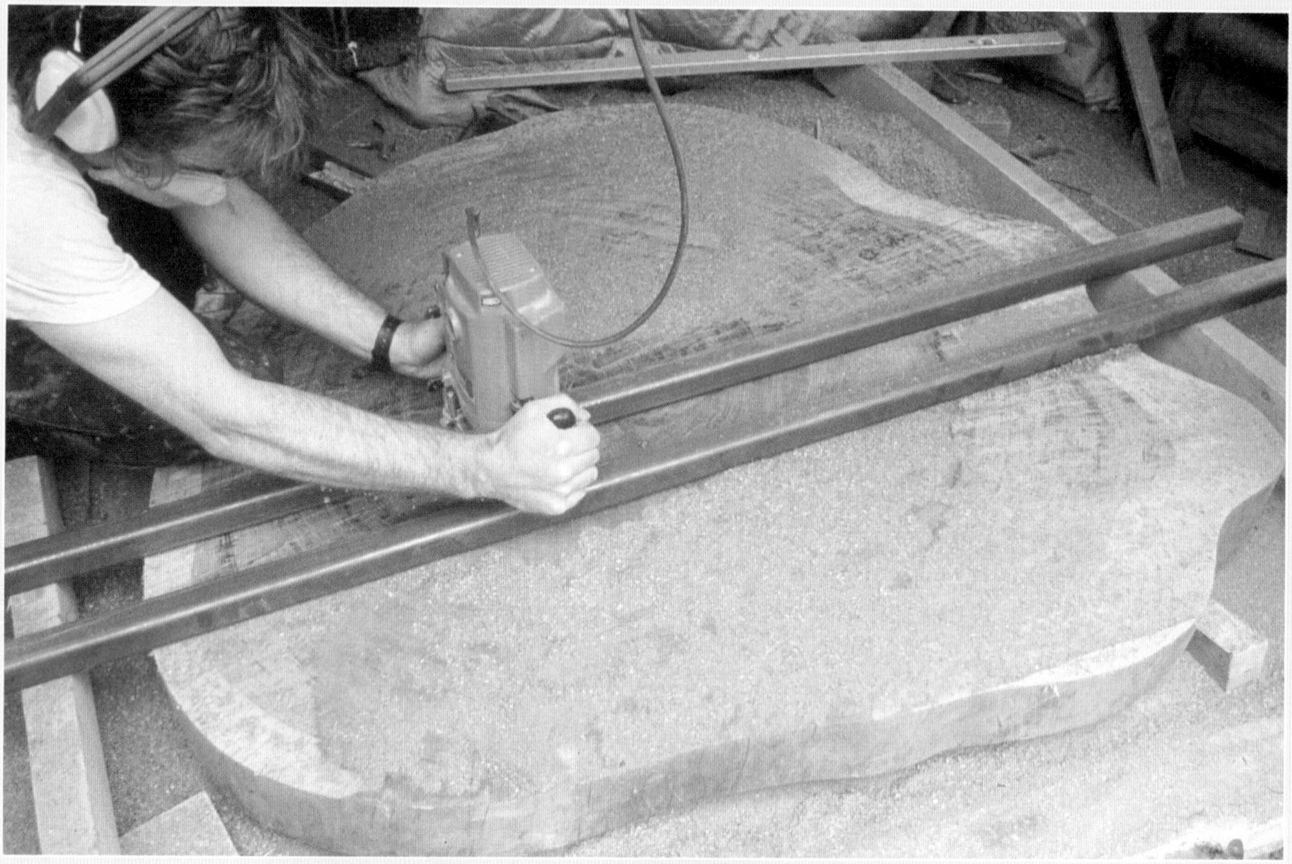

A simple router guiding jig for skimming the end-grain of a 65in wide butt of bubinga.

The author clocks up a lot of creative mileage from just one cutter – one of a range of thousands from Trend.

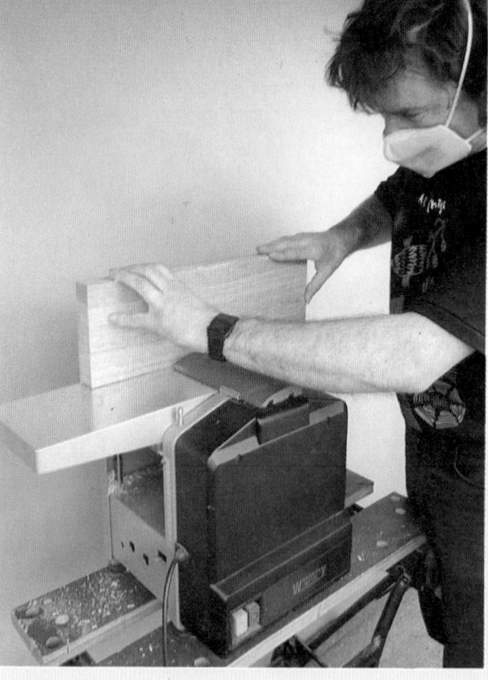

'Squaring' the edge of the Grid Table top on the Woody planer–thicknesser.

Marking guidelines for flat and consistent power planing.

Using an Elu biscuit jointer for the Grid Table top.

The router is used to create the 'rout-kerf' joint, a departure from tradition, yet based upon it.

The biscuit jointer in action on the top of the Grid Table.

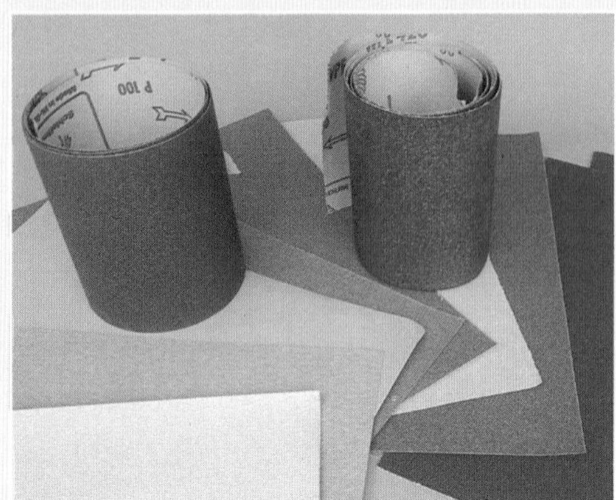

An assortment of abrasive sheets and rolls for sanding.

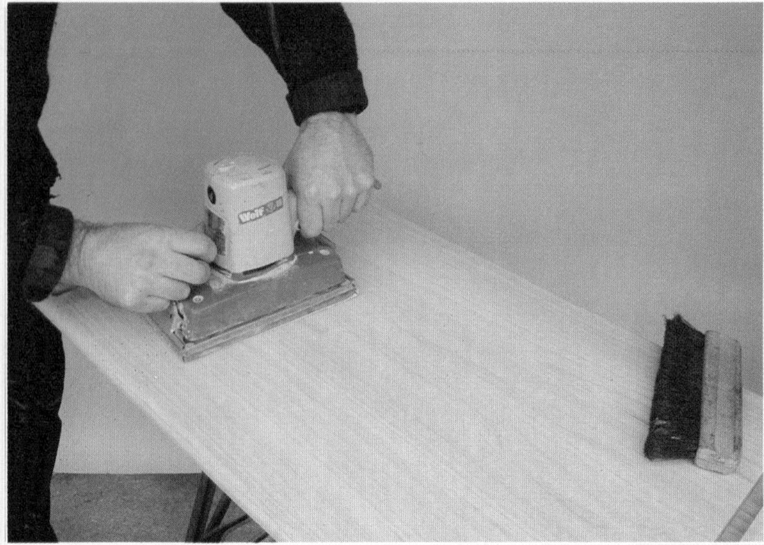

The author's 'old faithful' Wolf sander.

A superb, vital and inexpensive disc sanding attachment for the drill by Wolfcraft.

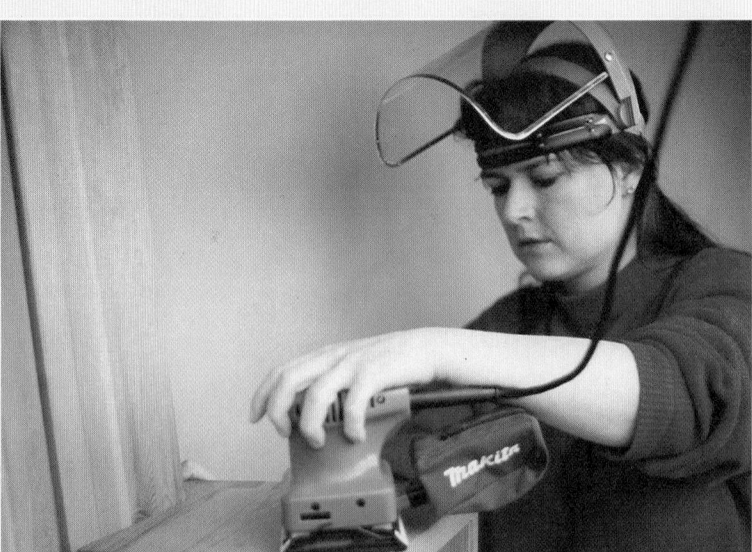

Using the Makita palm sander.

The Arundel J4 lathe with useful shop-made disc sanding attachment.

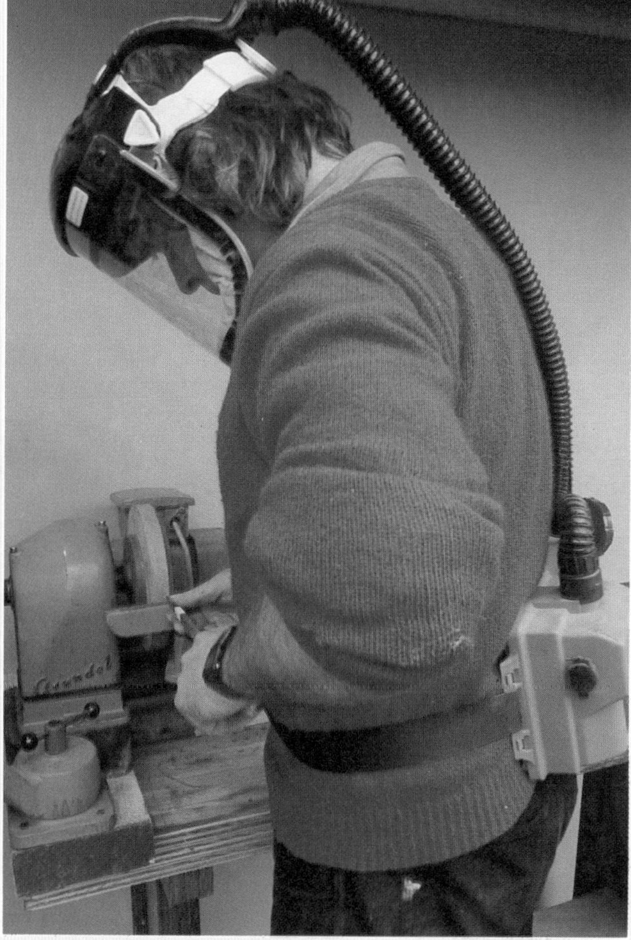

Effective headgear by Racal, used when operating the lathe.

'Aladdin's cave'!

The Wolfcraft Pioneer vice can also attach to the JKB bench.

The Kity Bestcombi compact universal machine.

A simple and efficient timber racking system.

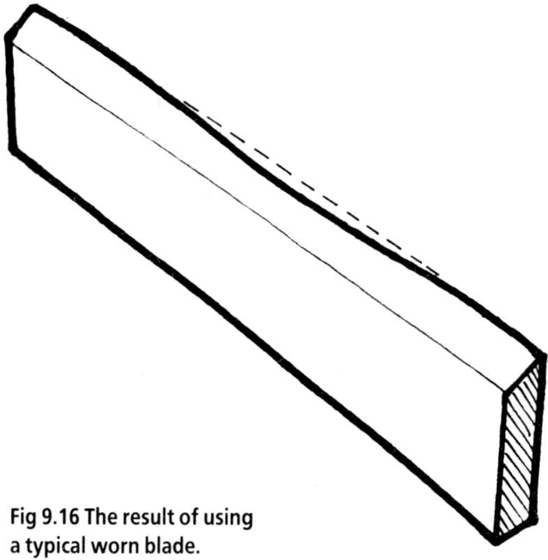
Fig 9.16 The result of using a typical worn blade.

There is a danger when planing or thicknessing any narrow-section timber of habitually using the middle portion of the blade. The result is that it will wear to a hollow (Fig 9.16), and this is never more evident than when machining chipboard. (Admittedly the machine is not specifically designed to edge chipboard, but it is the best method in my opinion of square-edging manufactured board, especially melamine-faced board!)

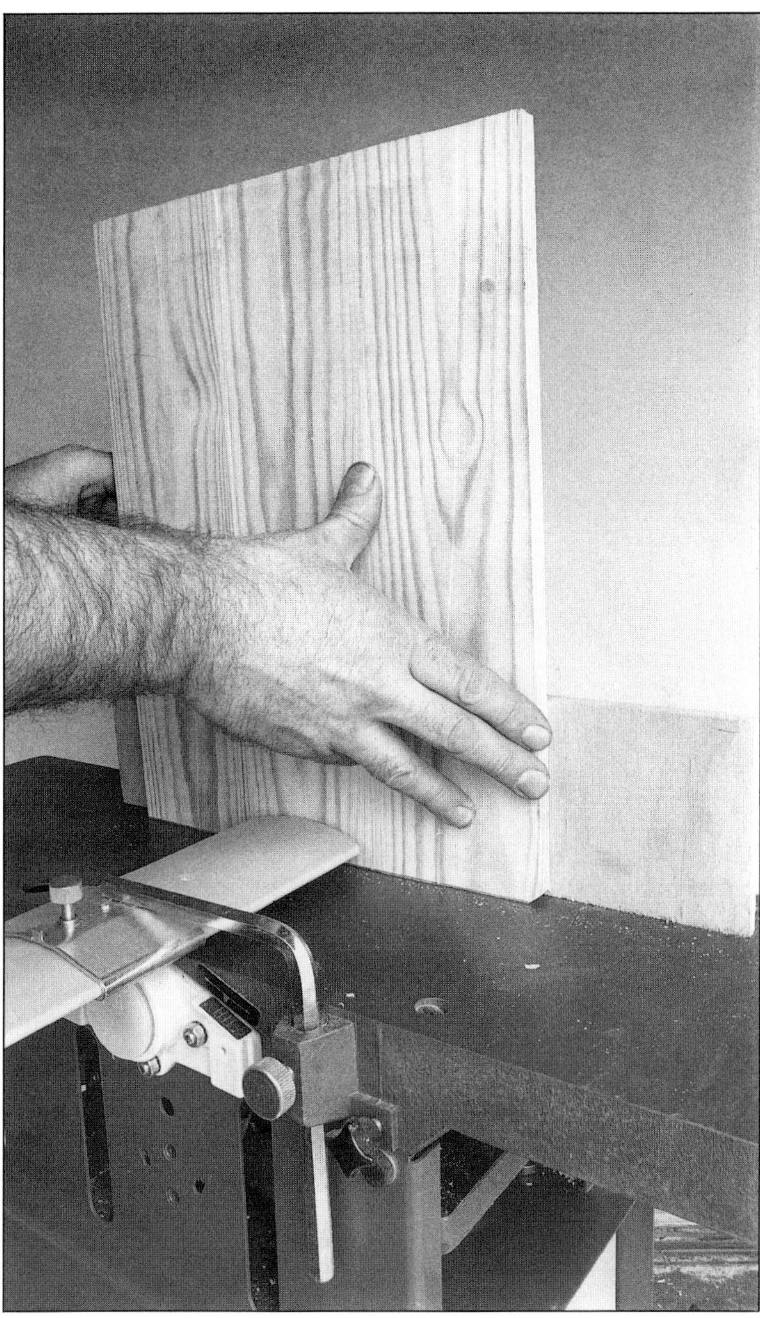
Fig 9.17 It is possible to 'square-off' end-grain on the surfacer – note the slight bevel to prevent the grain splitting.

Planing end-grain

Of course another thing you should not do is machine-plane end-grain, such as the end of a breadboard or small table top, as the fibres will violently split – well you can actually! By supporting the end fibres in much the same way as when hand planing, and by cutting a small bevel on the end, the planer will cleanly cut the end-grain provided the bevel remains (Fig 9.17). This can be taken off by machine-planing to width afterwards (Fig 9.18) and is a very useful method.

THICKNESSING

Thicknessing is usually done after the face side and face edge of the timber have been prepared on the surface-planer. These flat surfaces make contact with the thicknessing bed and the opposite surfaces are then fed into the cutters. If the timber is out of 'square' this will only be repeated when it is thicknessed (Fig 9.19). Normally the width is thicknessed first and then the edge.

The joy of thicknessing is in the automatic feed. Once the height adjustment has been set the timber is fed into the machine and you wait for it to come out at the other end (never bend down to look for it). The crucial thing is to adjust the thicknessing bed to the correct height. After the first two or three cuts the irregular edge becomes smooth (you can hear it).

Of course a small machine such as the Woody has a limited thicknessing depth (5in) which means you cannot thickness to its full width capacity of 6in, but that does not mean you cannot machine both edges. For any width of board you simply surface-plane the first edge against the 90° fence, mark a parallel line to the required thickness, and reverse the board and edge-plane it down to the line. For work of less demanding accuracy you can of course use the surface-planer to dress all four sides, but they won't be perfectly 'square' and parallel.

Thicknessing thin boards

A remarkable feature of the planer–thicknesser is its ability to reduce timber to a fractional thickness. The manufacturers claim 3mm, and I have pushed it a little further (I won't say how far!) in making my own 'veneers'. This is achieved by making a false platform out of 18mm MDF, or similar, which hooks on to the thicknessing bed (Fig 9.20). This effectively means that if you *keep on* raising the bed, the platform will keep engaging with the cutters, so it reduces down to zero. **This operation is clearly not for beginners!**

You need razor-sharp cutters, set perfectly parallel to the bed, and razor-sharp hearing as the sound of the machine resinating the thin wood tells you how much you dare take off in one pass. It involves micro-adjustment of the thicknessing wheel on each cut – and great patience, as only a dust will come off the timber. Too deep a cut and the blades will snatch the timber and shatter it in half a second, sending wood flying everywhere, and if you mistakenly feed the piece in the wrong way round (grain direction) your painstaking efforts will be wasted in half a second.

My 'Pyramid Drinks Cabinet' (see colour section) utilized the planer–thicknesser in this way. From a single solid board of 2in ash I bandsawed 6in wide pieces then deep cut them into 6mm thick sections.

Fig 9.18 Wide boards can be edged (to a line). This operation follows trimming end-grain.

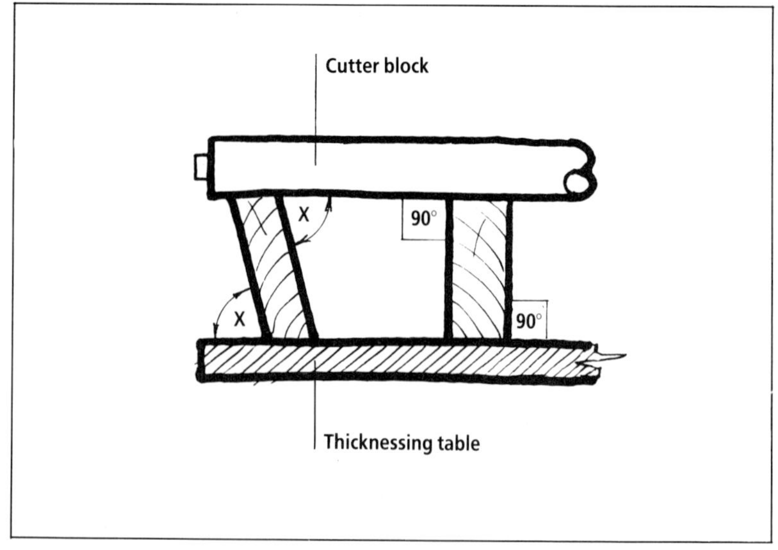

Fig 9.19 The thicknesser can only repeat the opposite surfaces.

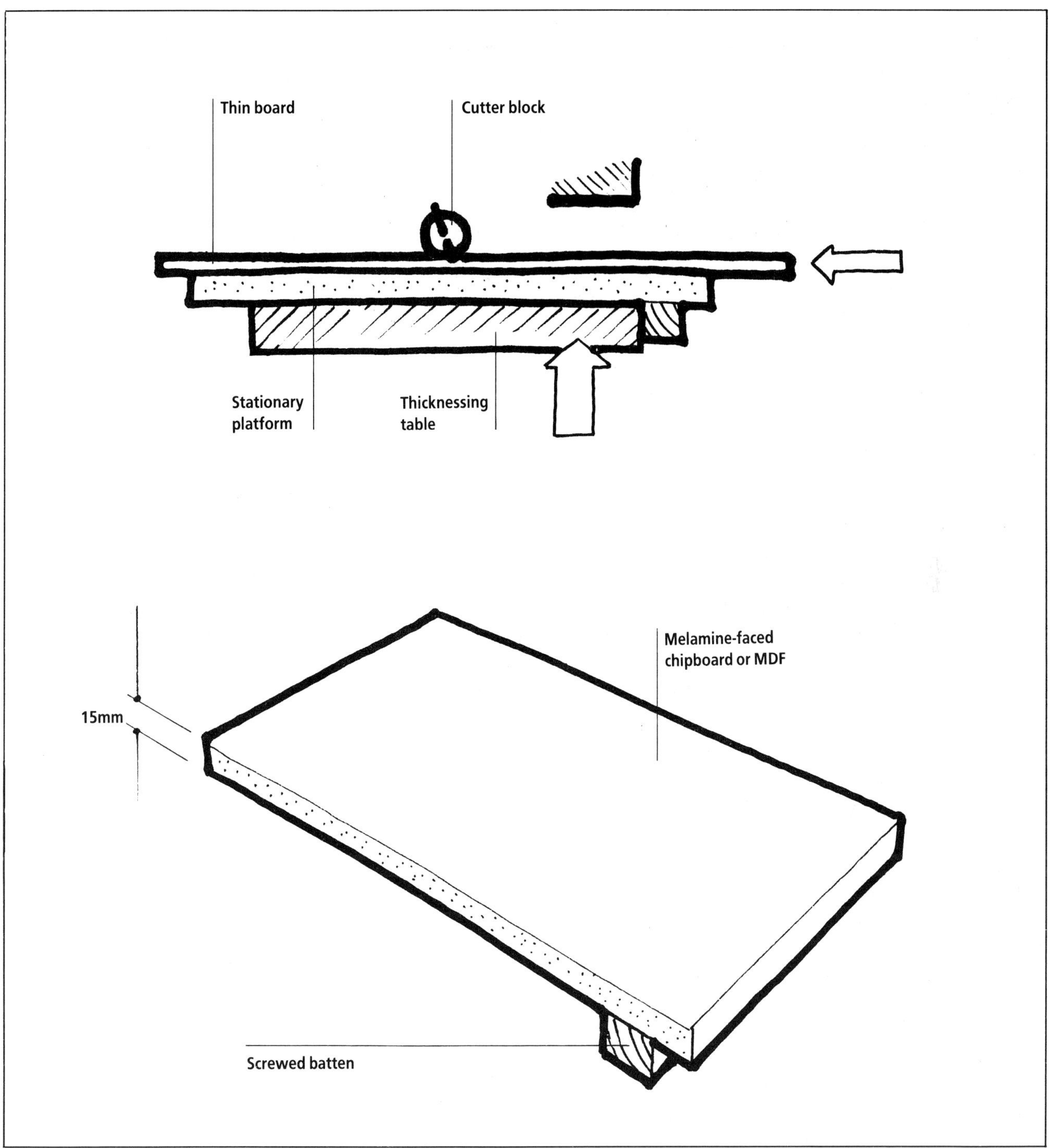

Fig 9.20 A thin board platform (stationary).

I then reduced these into 'veneers' which when edged-jointed were glued to both sides of a particle-board core. The result was perfectly matching grain on a manufactured-board panel from which the various components – doors, shelves etc. – were built and therefore gave continuing grain.

The design was a perfect example of the creative applications of electric woodworking techniques. It could not have been achieved by any other means and the other techniques I explored while making this cabinet are described in Chapters 6 and 7 on the jigsaw and the router. This is the real 'buzz' of electric woodworking.

JIGS

The use of jigs in conjunction with the planer–thicknesser, such as the veneer-cutting jig, open up various creative possibilities for the tool. A vari-

Fig 9.21 A moving platform for tapered and angled work.

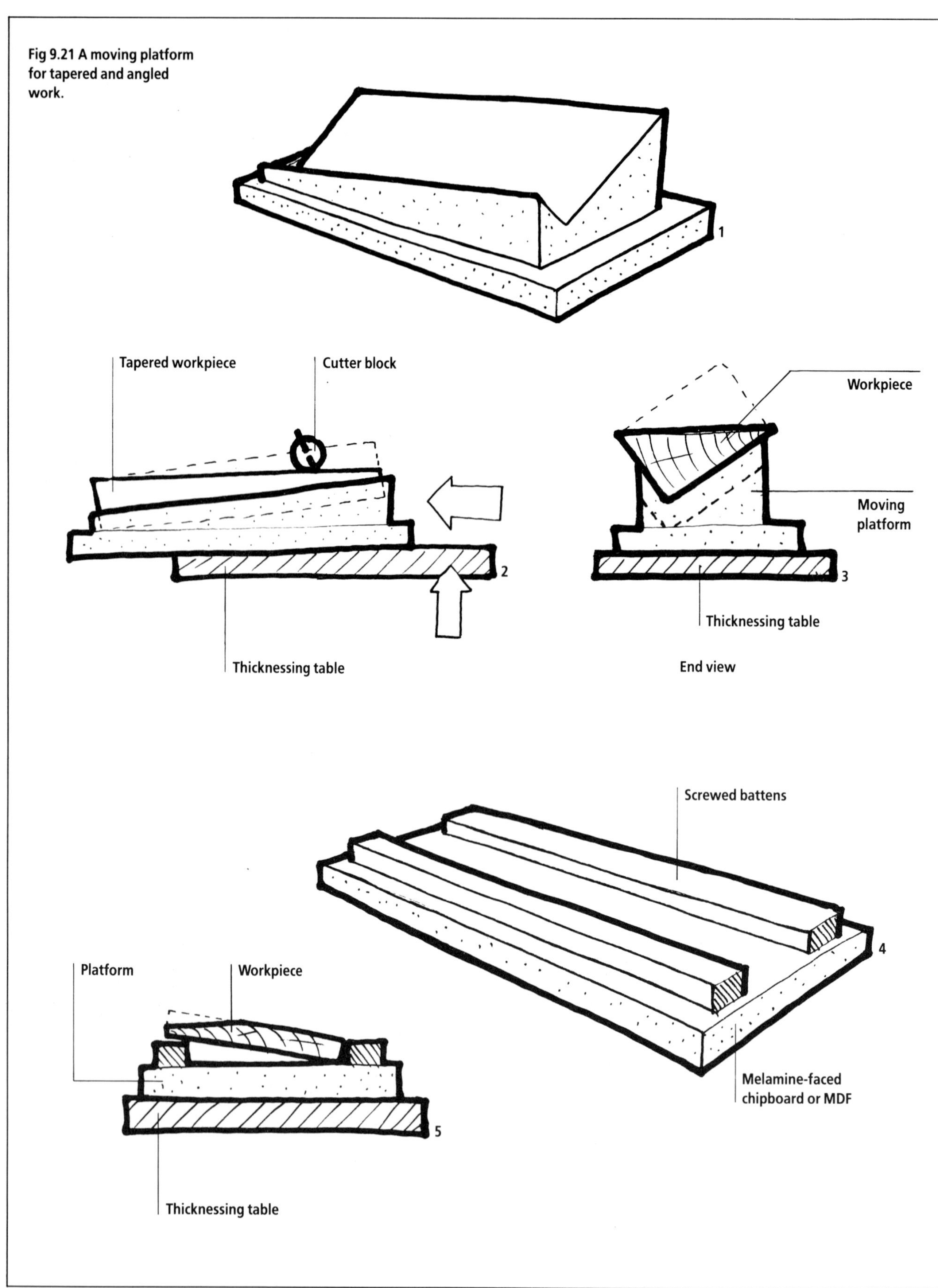

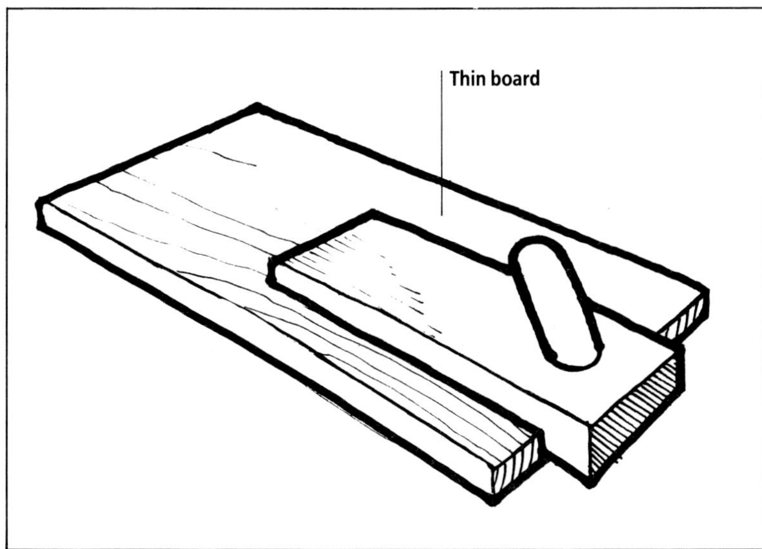

Fig 9.22 A hand grip for short and thin boards.

Fig 9.23 The power planer – ergonomically designed by Black & Decker.

ation of the false platform is an angled platform, which can be fixed or moving, allowing tapered or chamfered sections to be cut in the thicknessing mode (Fig 9.21).

If the taper is required lengthwise, then a travelling platform of this kind is needed. The jig and timber behave as one piece as they are fed through the thicknesser. But for the cross-section tapers and parallel cuts I prefer a fixed platform so that the only thing to be contended with is the timber as it comes out of the machine. I use melamine-faced board for my jigs because of their low-friction surface.

Various surface-planing jigs can be devised, such as an extended hand-grip jig which makes thin and short pieces safer to machine. This can be made inexpensively from MDF and softwood (Fig 9.22).

THE PORTABLE HAND PLANER

An extremely handy piece of kit, the portable hand planer is a relatively inexpensive tool for dressing timber (Fig 9.23). It cannot achieve the same degree of finish as the planer–thicknesser, although when attached to the thicknessing jig on some models it enjoys some success (Fig 9.24).

This tool is derived from a hand plane in shape and relies on a tiny revolving two-knife cutter block, similar to the planer–thicknesser.

Fig 9.24 The Bosch planer and thicknessing attachment.

The standard accessories usually include an adjustable fence, a dustbag, and a table for inverting the tool to act as a bench-top planer (Fig 9.25). Timber up to the width of the blades (approx. 82mm) can be accommodated in this mode, and strictly the same dimensions for freehand planing (although with care I 'skate' around a larger surface).

The blades, usually reversible, are available in HSS or TCT and are fixed in the cutter block by a series of Allen screws. Replacing them is easy as they have fixed locations and there are no other adjustments.

Safety

Dangerous is how I would describe this tool, especially to the *experienced* woodworker! Why? Because a woodworker brought up on hand planes will probably have got into the mental habit of wiping trapped shavings away from the blade mouth with his/her fingers. I do it all the time myself, and dread the day I unwittingly do it with an electric planer. The tool is also capable of wrecking your work by snatching into it if you set the feed too coarse.

The tool should be switched off after a cut and not placed on the bench until the cutters have come to a rest.

Operation

The portable hand planer should be set very finely for maximum control. The tool can be manoeuvred backwards and forwards briskly along the workpiece (Fig 9.26) in order to achieve consistency. It is not a tool to switch on and leave stationary in one place, as it will soon make a hole in the floor!

When planing wide boards or any board wider than its blade, a series of progressive overlapping cuts can be made to minimize grooves being left. For taking off the 'jacket' (rough planing), I often plane diagonally or across the grain as the fibres break up more easily this way, but care has to be taken not to split the edges. The important thing is to keep the tool on the move all the time, as you would with a belt sander.

The hand power planer can be used both freehand and bench-mounted for rebating and angled cutting. It is an ideal tool for site woodworking and for dressing small-sectioned timber in the workshop.

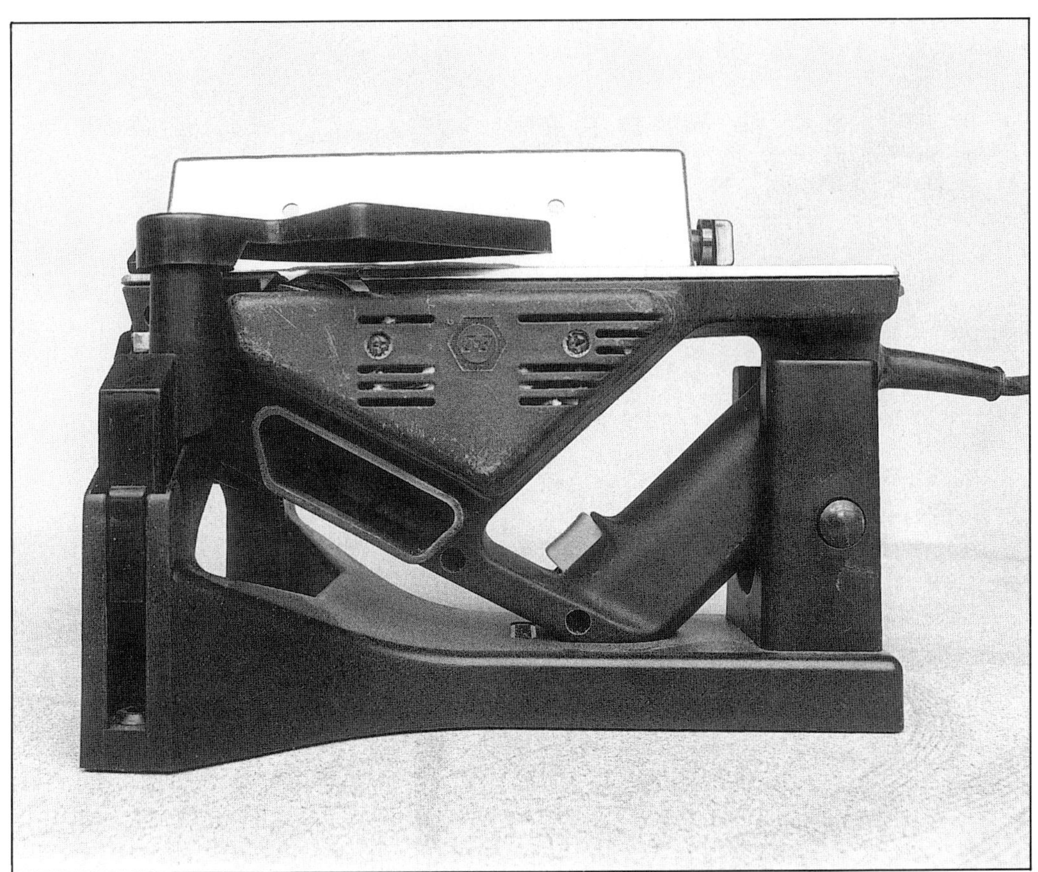

Fig 9.25 The Black & Decker planer inverted in its stand with fence attached.

Fig 9.26 The power planer is worked briskly and the sole adjusted for a fine cut. (The author cleans up the surface of the JKB bench – see Chapter 18.)

10
THE LATHE

Undoubtedly the most popular aspect of woodworking today is turnery. Just look at the advertisements in any woodworking magazine – the market for both lathes and weekend turnery courses is abundant. The fact that you can attend a 2-day course in this craft, purchase a lathe for a relatively modest price, and then go away and operate it in a relatively modest space says it all. In these pages I can only hope to whet the appetite of the reader as obviously this is the subject of entire books, written for novice and experienced turner alike.

The lathe is magnificently simple, and to use it is mesmerizing. It is a unified skill – the timber revolves, a tool is fed into it, and that's just about it – but such is the creative fervour surrounding wood turnery that it has led to world symposiums and world celebrities! If you want fame then the

Fig 10.1 The pole-lathe.

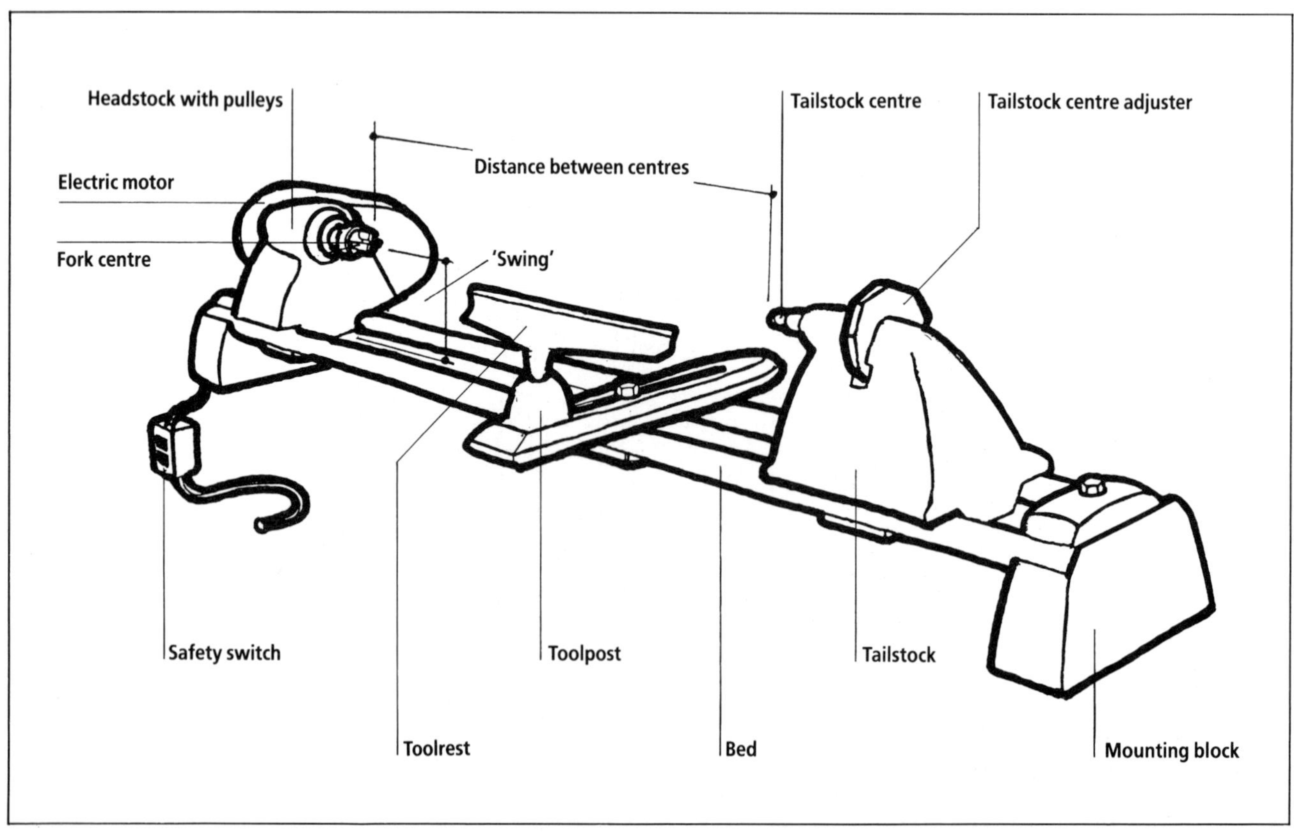

Fig 10.2 The parts of a lathe.

Fig 10.3 Easy gear change on the Record DML24 lathe.

Fig 10.4 The tapered drive centre.

Fig 10.5 Grease the live centre on the DML24 to minimize friction.

lathe will offer it more than any other tool! Of course, as with any other tool, there is no shortcut to the experience which gives complete mastery, but it is relatively easy to get started and achieve pleasing results.

On the lathe you can produce entire pieces ranging from bowls, boxes, condiment sets, egg-cups, goblets, lamps to 3-legged stools or just plain 'art form'. And it can be used to make components from cricket bails to the legs on Windsor chairs.

The modern electric lathe has evolved from the early pole-lathe (Fig 10.1) which was powered by a foot treadle pulling a piece of string attached to a springy pole. The string was double-looped around the work, usually a spindle, and it revolved first in one direction then the other. The chisel was fed into it in a rhythmic way, allowing for the alternating rotation. (The pole-lathe is currently enjoying a revival of interest.)

The electric lathe has developed in 3 ways from the pole-lathe (other than its power source and the use of steel in its construction):

1 The work to be turned can be varied in dimension, i.e. from a wide bowl to a drumstick.

2 The work rotates in one direction only and the tool can be fed into it constantly.

3 The speed at which the work rotates can be varied, thus allowing for different size work and cutting methods.

SPECIFICATION

The lathe is normally bench-mounted and powered by a ⅓ to 1HP motor (Fig 10.2). It comprises a motor housing (with switch) and headstock which delivers the power via a belt and pulley system of gears – usually three to four – to the threaded mandrel. On to the mandrel is screwed a faceplate or chuck, or a tapered drive centre (Fig 10.4). At the opposite end is the tailstock which slides and locks on to the lathe bed and contains a fixed or live centre (Fig 10.5). Also sliding along the lathe bed and fixed in position is the toolpost and toolrest, which is adjusted to be close to the work.

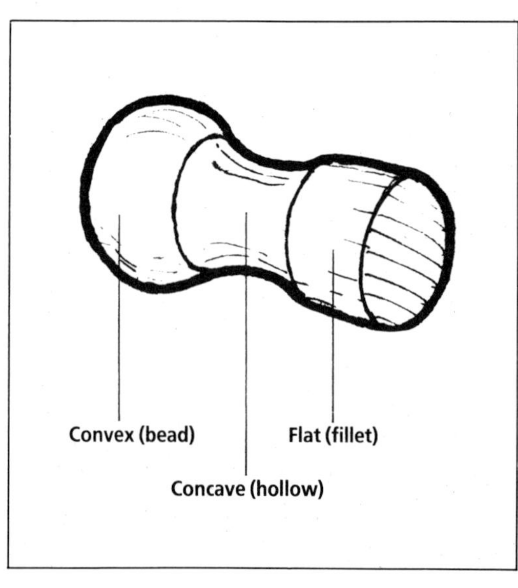

Fig 10.6 There are three basic profiles.

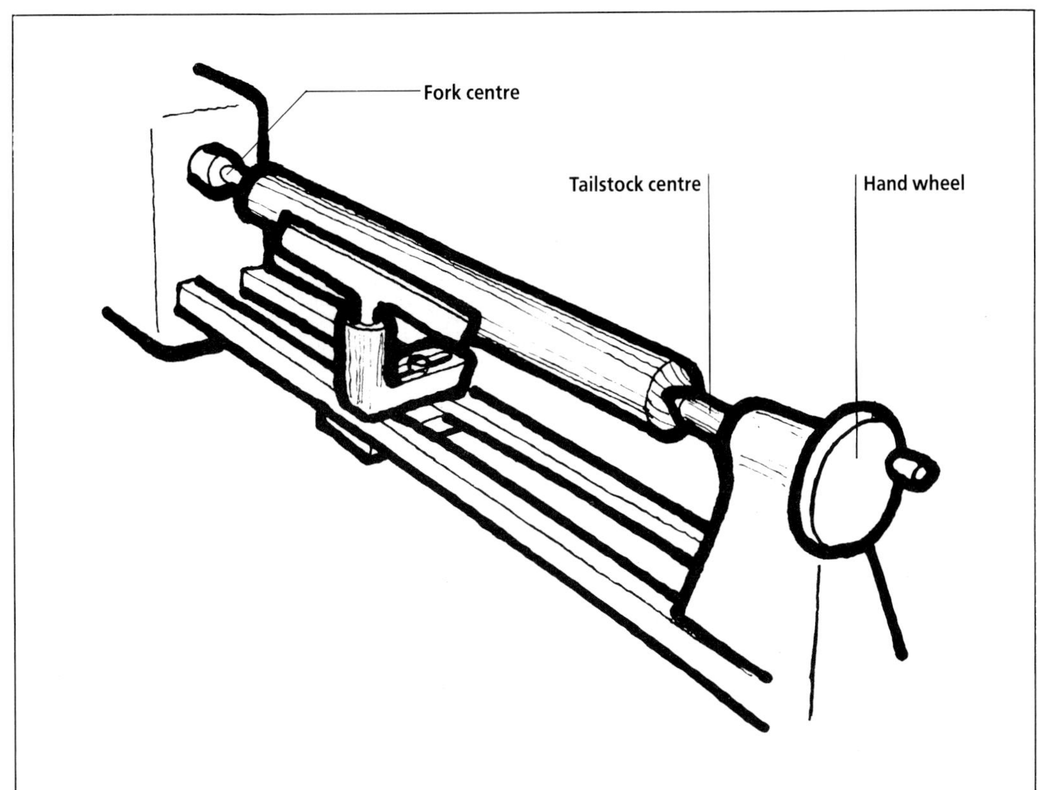

Fig 10.7 Turning between centres.

Fig 10.8 Use a soft mallet to drive the feed centre into the wood.

Lathes vary in bed length and drive-centre height (swing) and recent models feature a revolving headstock enabling wider-diameter work to be turned. This is a useful feature as it opens up the options for turning large salad bowls or small table tops on a relatively small lathe.

THE ACTION

The action of the lathe is to rotate the work at a selected speed, varying from 300 to 2500rpm (lower speed for larger diameter work), and to feed a lathe tool against the carefully positioned toolrest, into the work, through a series of controlled cuts.

There are basically three profiled cuts – flat, concave and convex (Fig 10.6). By using a variety of differently profiled tools – scrapers or gouges – any profile can be achieved, and many lathe workers, including myself, rely on a modest selection of tools to achieve a wide variety of turned work.

Before I elaborate on the tools, let us first consider the three main types of lathe work.

Turning between centres (spindle turning)

Turning between centres is used for long, small-diameter works. It involves the tailstock as well as the headstock for support of the work, and a conical tailstock centre is attached at one end and a forked drive centre at the other (Fig 10.7). The latter is carefully driven into the end-grain of the wood before mounting it on the lathe (Fig 10.8), and is then carefully inserted in a tapered hole in the drive centre. The work is then mounted and secured at the tailstock centre by a hand wheel at that end.

The toolpost accommodates toolrests of different lengths, and for spindle work a long rest is usually used. Its position can be varied, both in height and along the lathe bed. This method applies to any *long and thin work* where both ends are merely cut off (parted off). It is possible, for instance, to turn a billiard cue provided the lathe bed is long enough. (It has been known for some woodturners to cut a hole in a wall and extend their lathe into the next room!)

Turning from one centre

Turning from one centre involves small work held in a chuck. It utilizes the inner mandrel which has a left-hand external thread on to which a suitable chuck is screwed and the work mounted. A shorter toolrest is generally used and this method is usually used to make small boxes, eggcups and other small-diameter work where the *side and end* of the work is fashioned (Fig 10.9).

Faceplate turnery

Faceplate turnery is used in short wide-diameter work. The threaded mandrel is used for attaching a selection of varying diameter faceplates upon which the work is mounted (screwed). The thread has to be left-handed in order to prevent the work spinning off when the lathe starts. This method allows large diameter and generally short work to be turned, though longer work can be given extra support by attaching the tailstock centre to it. The most popular application is bowl turning, where both side and end are fashioned (Fig 10.10). Obviously a shorter toolrest is used for the side and a medium-to-long or even curved toolrest for the 'inside' of the bowl (Fig 10.11).

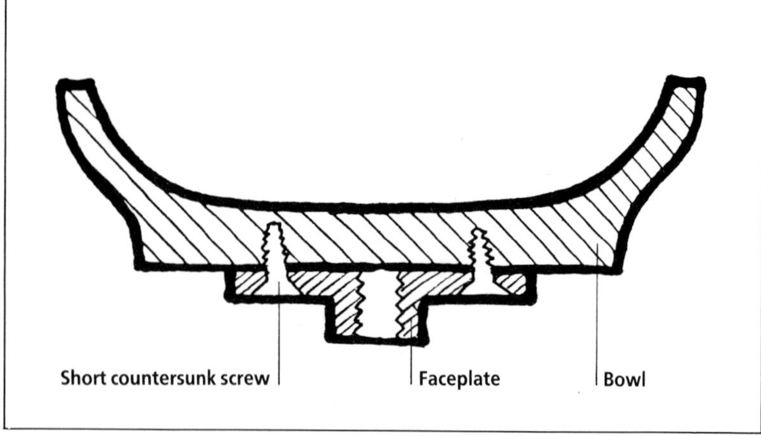

Fig 10.10 Faceplate turnery – section through faceplate and bowl.

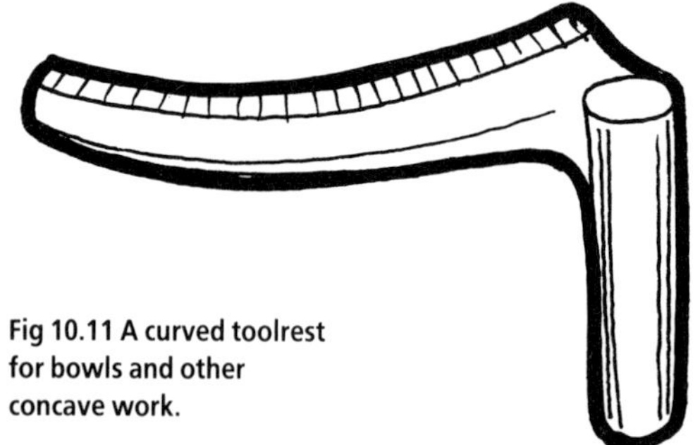

Fig 10.11 A curved toolrest for bowls and other concave work.

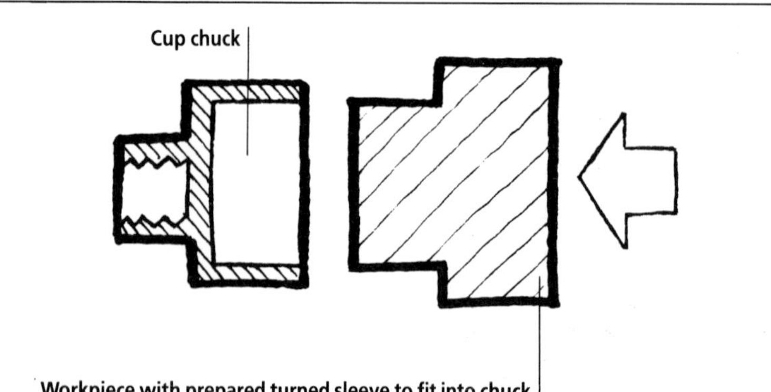

Fig 10.9 One-centre turning. A cup chuck which holds the work by friction.

TOOLS

The tools used in lathe work apply generally to both faceplate and centre methods, although woodworkers evolve preferences and grind their own customized tools. But there are essentially two types of tools – scrapers and gouges (Fig 10.12) – both made of high-speed steel or carbon steel, the former being superior.

Scrapers

Scrapers (Fig 10.13) are flat-sectioned tools which have a ground, shaped tip to suit different purposes (flats, concaves, convexes etc.). The tool is held horizontally in line with the centre of the work and the cutting action is relatively easy to master. The work normally demands subsequent abrasive paper finishing. Grinding the scraper is also relatively easy and it is essential it is kept keen to

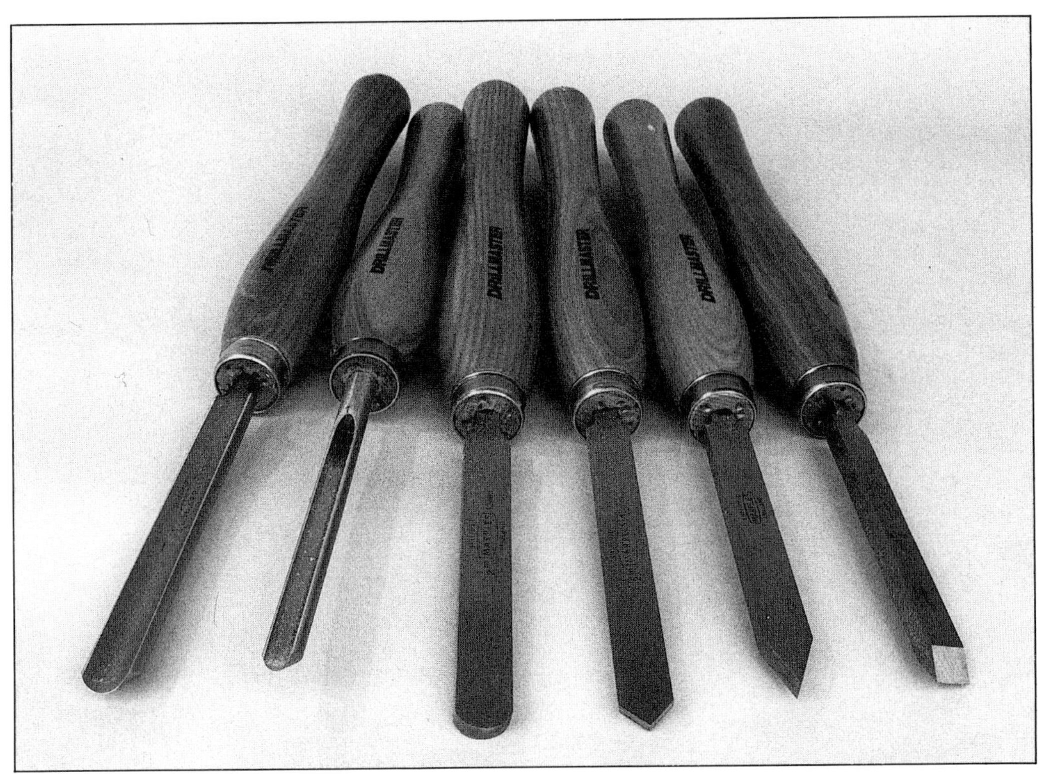

Fig 10.12 A selection of turning tools from Record.

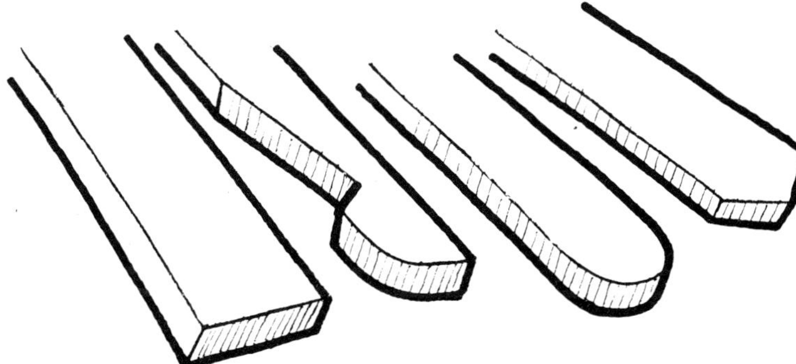

Fig 10.13 Scrapers.

minimize grain tearing, which is an inherent problem with scraping. (Converted files will suffice as scrapers, but check they are heat-treated.)

Gouges

Gouges (Fig 10.14) are hollow-sectioned tools with either a square or round edge to them. Their action is one of efficient slicing or peeling of the grain, and they are undoubtedly the choice of most professionals. They are more difficult to master, however, as they have a tendency to 'snatch' if fed into the work at the wrong angle. Gouges are held at a fairly steep angle to the work.

SHARPENING

Perhaps more so than in any other aspect of woodworking, lathe tools require constant sharpening (grinding). This is because the wood rotates fast and the tool is generally pressure-fed into it, causing heat which hastens the dulling of the tip. An electric grindstone should be at hand, ideally at the end of the lathe bench (Fig 10.15). It is wise to observe the correct angles for scrapers and gouges (Fig 10.16) but turners grind them to suit.

When grinding you feed the tool from right to left, and roll it in the case of the gouge. High-carbon-steel tools will 'blue' very easily, which softens their edge. Constant dipping of the tool in a jar of water helps prevent this. I tend to leave the burr from the grinder on the edge as it helps give the tool 'bite'. The tool should be touched up on the grinder every few minutes – it only takes a few seconds. Special tools will have to be ground in,

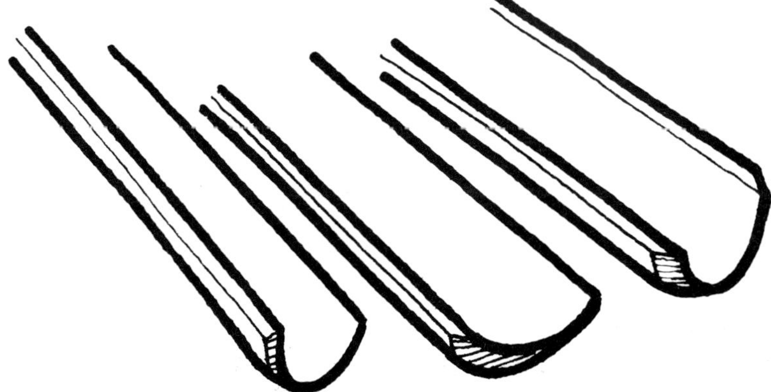

Fig 10.14 Gouges.

Fig 10.15 Grinding a scraper frequently throughout use.

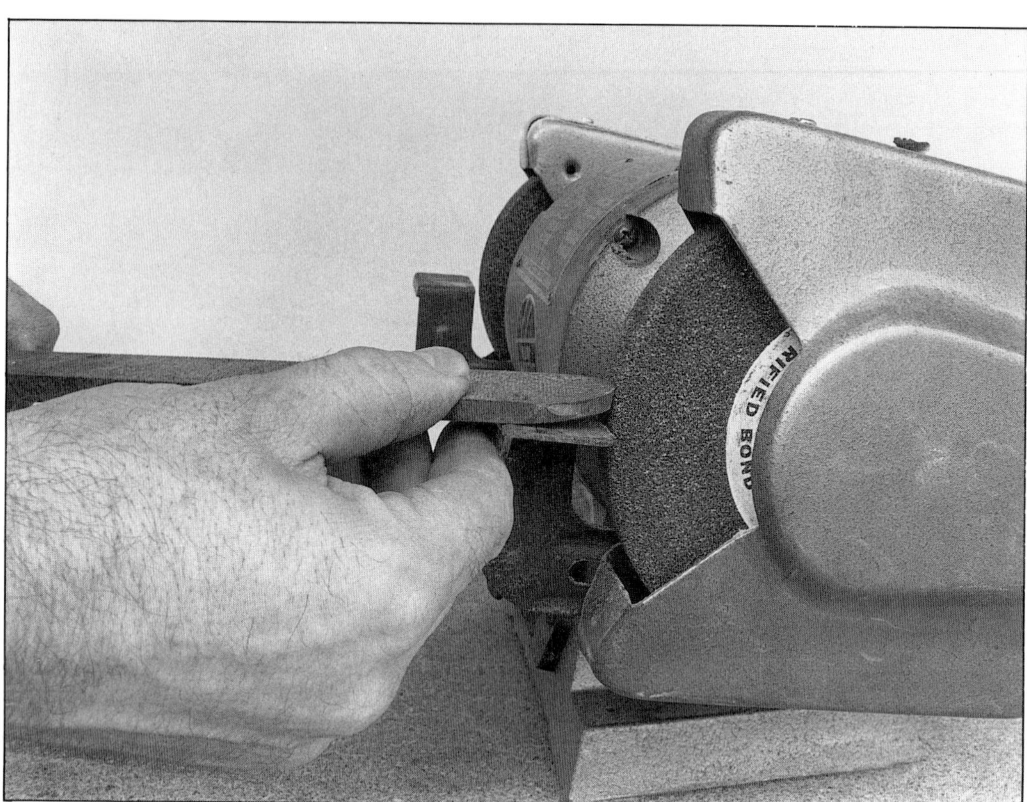

Fig 10.16 Grinding angles for scrapers and gouges.

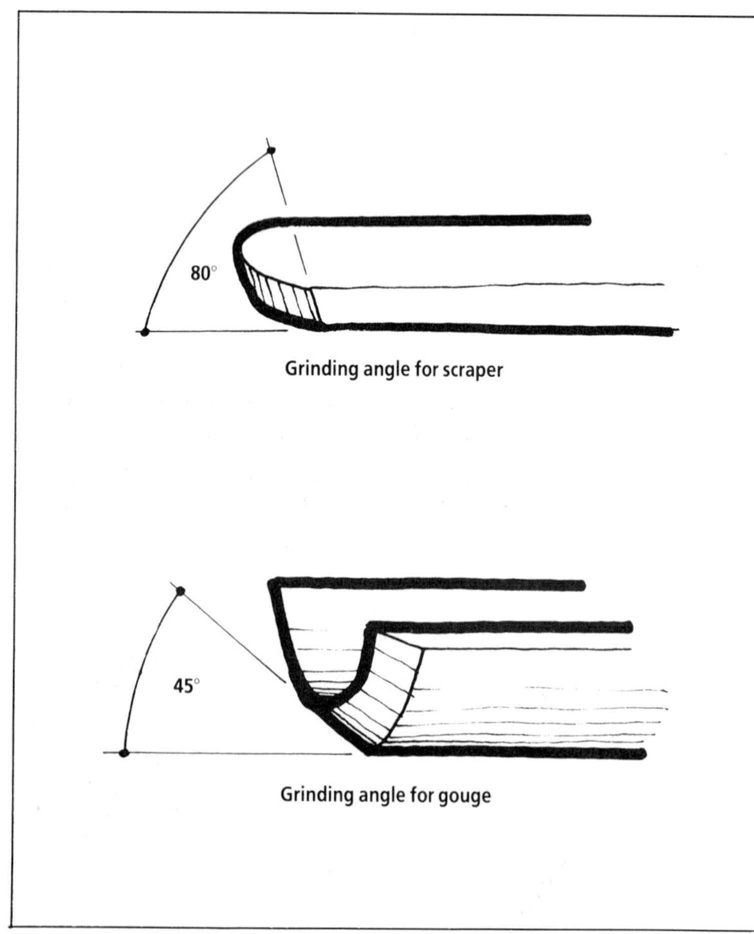

especially converted old files for scrapers, which are inexpensive and made from good-quality steel. They take time to grind, however, because of the 'bluing' problem. When grinding files it is necessary to heat-treat the cutting edge.

New tools will be ground by the manufacturer to a set angle. Often the side edges of the blade are raw and sharp and need softening with emery paper as they can be uncomfortable when held.

METHODS

'I'll do it my way' is a familiar cry amongst 'established' woodturners (Fig 10.17) and the freedom which turnery offers causes more heated debate over 'correct' methods than the more entrenched cabinetmaking traditions!

In 'respectable' woodturning circles the scraper tends to be less frequently mentioned than the gouge – indeed, it is probably frowned upon (although all metal-turning is done accurately and efficiently by a scraper – so the tool obviously 'cuts'!). In general, gouging is probably quicker and cleaner because it slices the wood, but it is more difficult to master as the rotating wood can snatch the gouge and not only ruin the work but also give a nasty shock.

Fig 10.17 'I'll do it my way!'

There are certain operations or particular features, however, where it is best to use a specially shaped scraper, so few woodturners can escape using one altogether. One argument against the scraper is that it tears the wood (similar to a flatbit in boring holes) and requires excessive sanding. This is not necessarily true in my experience. If the scraper is used *gently* and with a *razor-sharp* edge, minimal tearing will result (Fig 10.18) on the end-grain. Abrasive paper is necessary, but then it is also necessary in furniture-making generally (Fig 10.19).

My own experience is based on teaching young people how to master the lathe safely, confidently and creatively and I prefer the scraper. As a designer-maker in wood I have produced some fairly advanced turnery (at speed) using this method and I can only really share what I know. Others are more qualified to expound the virtues of gouging, but here is a brief mention.

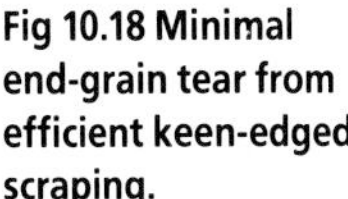

Fig 10.18 Minimal end-grain tear from efficient keen-edged scraping.

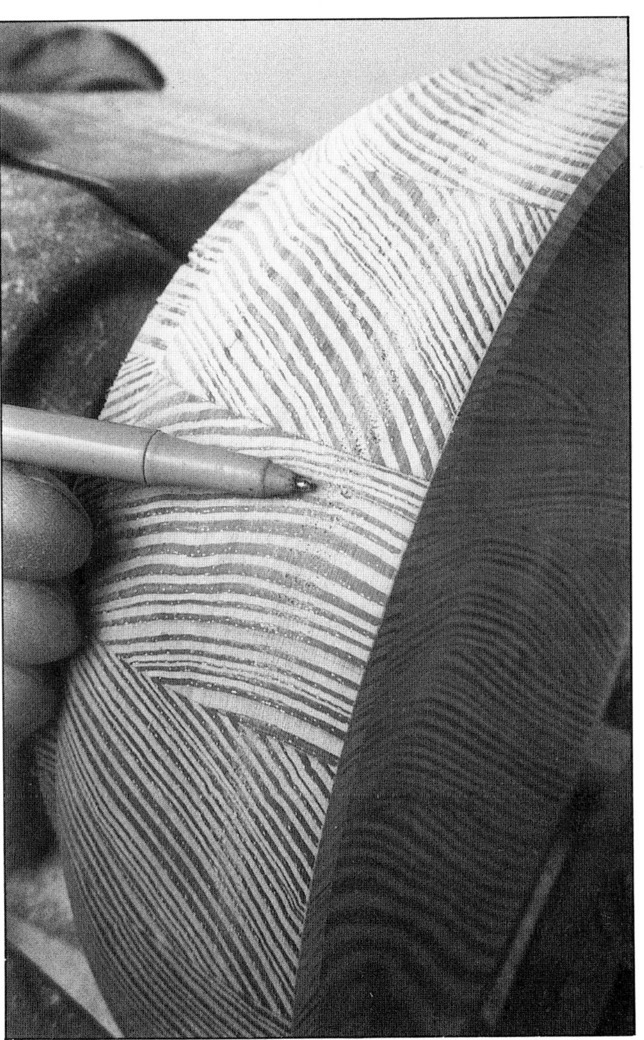

Fig 10.19 Using abrasive paper for the final finish.

Using a gouge

The gouge is held at an angle to the work so that it 'kisses' the top leaning edge (Fig 10.20). The cut is started by lifting the handle slightly to engage the tip of the tool. The gouge has to be inclined and rolled in the direction of the transverse movement (left or right), causing a slicing action.

It is important to hold the handle firmly midway down its length to prevent a levering action. Finger control of the tip is firm, the thumb offering downward support. Body stance is also important, leaning the torso in the direction of the cut.

Using a scraper

The essence of efficient scraping is to maintain a razor-sharp tool and to cut gently at the correct speed, otherwise the tool will tear the end-grain. The scraper is held horizontally and the upper edge of the tool held in line with the workcentre (Fig 10.21). It is easy to set the toolrest for height before work commences with the scraper resting on it.

When scraping for the first time it is better to wrap the knuckle around the tool and offer the side of the palm against the angled side of the toolrest (Fig 10.22). This allows excellent control of the tool as the give in the hand is all the movement that is needed. The hand remains tightly clasped around the scraper; the other hand grips the tool handle and prevents the levering action as the tool bites. (In fact with long scrapers I often hold the toolhandle against my hip as a steady – Fig 10.23.) The position of the fingers can be changed as confidence is established (Fig 10.24).

1

2

Toolrest

Gouge

Fig 10.20 The action of the gouge as it 'kisses' the wood.

Fig 10.21 Firm control of the scraper held horizontally.

Fig 10.22 Wrap the knuckles around the scraper for firm control (below left).

Fig 10.23 Dressed for action and holding a long scraper firm against the hip (below right).

Fig 10.24 Finger control with the scraper.

Fig 10.25 Cut a series of small stepped cuts – crucial to quick and efficient stock removal.

When removing stock quickly the shavings come off quite hot and the finish will not be particularly good when 'roughing'. I suppose my method is probably unconventional, but I have used it successfully for over 20 years; when doing shaped work I cut a series of stepped cuts (Fig 10.25) with a narrow scraper (often a mortice chisel, ground a little steeper), and then use a wider scraper (or firmer chisel) to form those steps into a 'flat' (Fig 10.26). The reason for using a narrow scraper is simply because the narrower the tool the less the resistance of the material (this principle applies to all woodworking). A wide chisel/scraper can be used, but only to cut 3mm wide steps.

It is possible to achieve a near-perfect tool finish with the scraper. Some sanding may be necessary, depending on how sharp the scraper has been (Fig 10.27).

SAFETY

Some experts may do it, but you should *never* make contact with your hand on revolving work, and never made adjustments while the work is spinning. The only exception is touching revolving work after it has been sanded and you use your hand to slow it down after the lathe has been switched off. The lathe should always be switched off when changing speed.

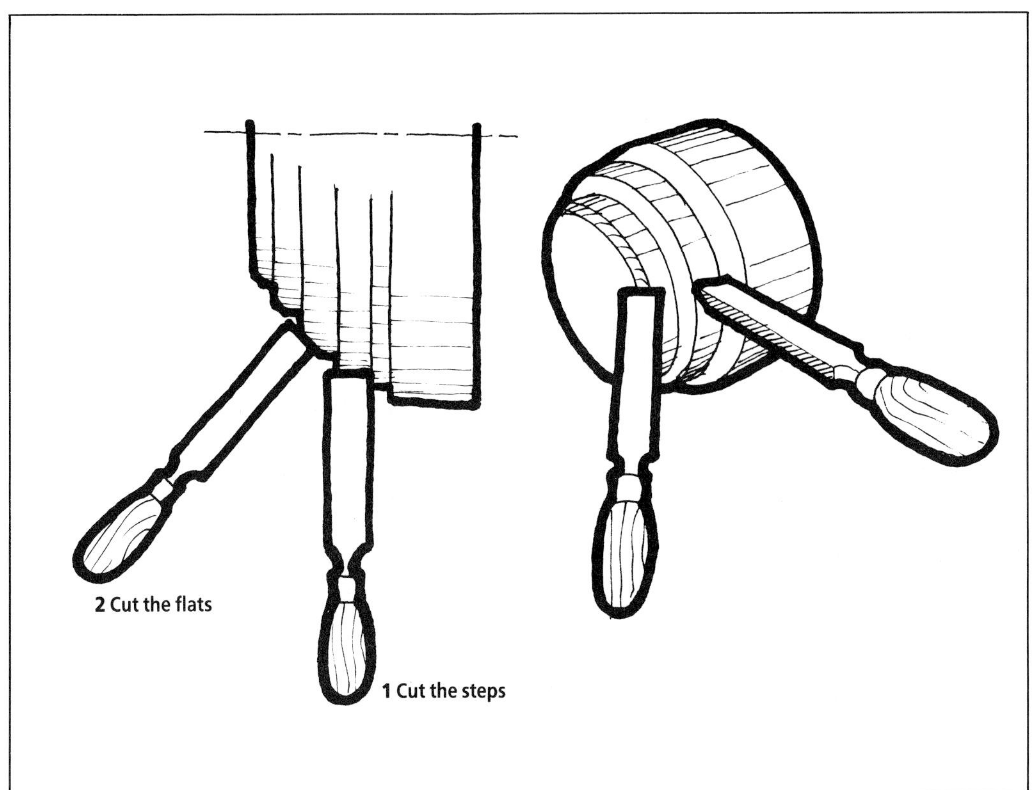

Fig 10.26 The steps are then cut into a flat with a wide chisel.

Fig 10.27 Excellent finish obtained from minimal sanding if the scraper is kept razor sharp.

Always wear eye and nose protection. Because of prolonged exposure or dust I prefer to wear a Racal Dustmaster 4 Mk2 (see Fig 10.23), which is a battery-powered system (see also Chapter 4, Health and Safety). Earmuffs are unnecessary – it is good to hear the performance of the tool. Never, never wear a tie, and if long hair is in fashion (again!) when this book is read, make sure it is tied up behind! The latter two points have caused some nasty accidents on the lathe.

The lathe itself should be firmly bolted down. Large work should be centralized first (see page 100) and turned at the slowest speed first. The floor area around the lathe is likely to get slippery if resinous shavings are trodden in. Abrasive strips glued on to the floor can help.

When sanding always feed the abrasive paper *under* the work and *away* from the direction of rotation (Fig 10.28). If you sand *into* the feed you can get your fingers knocked back if the abrasive paper snatches.

Good lighting is essential and an adjustable lamp can be positioned above the work.

Dust and chippings collection

Some form of dust and chippings extraction should be used (see Chapters 4 and 15, Health and Safety

Fig 10.28 When sanding feed away from direction of rotation.

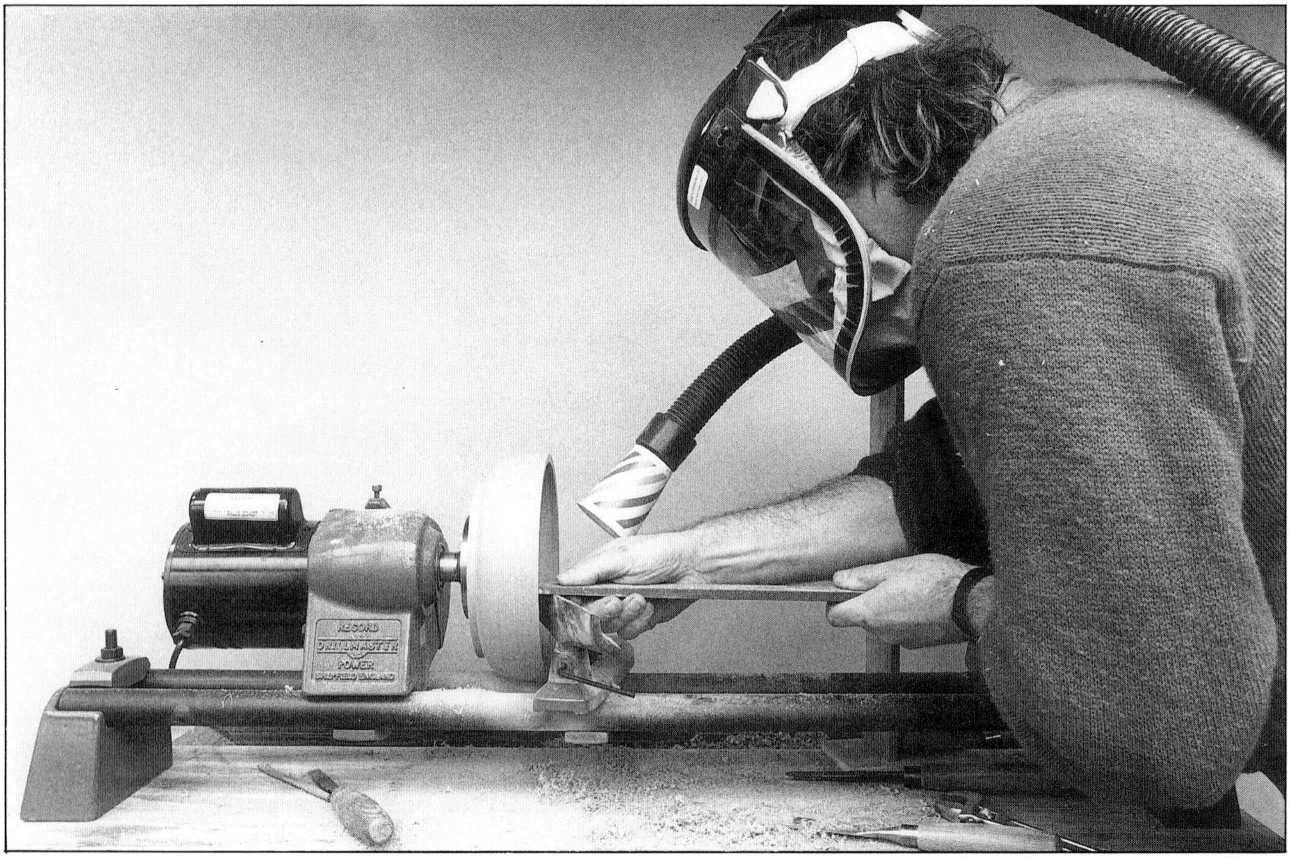

Fig 10.29 Improvised dust extraction – it all helps!

Fig 10.30 The revolving centre on the author's Arundel J4 Mk 2 lathe.

and Electric Workshop) and it is possible to custom-build some ducting and hoods, or improvise by linking up with a portable extractor (Fig 10.29). My simple method of presenting a dust 'funnel' to the work can be positioned precisely, depending on where the debris is flying in any particular cutting or sanding operation. However, its position should not inhibit the use or visibility of the tool as it cuts.

OPERATION

Before switching on the lathe the correct speed should be selected. Normally the gear change is crude on a lathe: the motor is tilted, the belt slackened and then manually lifted across the pulleys, taking care not to trap the fingers. A slow speed should be selected at first – the smallest pulley at the headstock – then the speed up-rated as work progresses.

Having selected the method of turnery (faceplate or centre) the work is positioned and tightened up appropriately. Rotate the work by hand first to check the clearance. The toolpost and toolrest are adjusted so that they are close to but not touching the work.

Obviously as the work is turned and reduced in diameter the toolpost will need re-setting closer. For long spindle work the long toolrest is used in stages, re-set each time to cover the full length. It should be checked for tightness.

When turning between centres the tailstock centre should be tightened periodically as the end of the wood will wear and eventually cause a chatter which quickly turns into a scream! It sounds worse than it is, and the work should not fly off immediately. This problem is overcome if a revolving centre is used (Fig 10.30).

CHOICE OF LATHE

Very difficult! There are now so many to choose from, but a few considerations are as follows:

- A robust and stable lathe bed.
- Some prefer the large, round centre-section as the toolpost can be swung out of the way for sanding.
- The centre-to-bed clearance (swing) should be good, allowing reasonable-size bowls to be turned (unless there is an end-turning facility especially for this).
- The various moving parts should slide and lock into position easily.

Fig 10.31 The Record DML24 lathe. An excellent lathe for the novice.

I have chosen the Record DML24 lathe for this chapter (Fig 10.31). It is a robust, economy lathe, suitable for the beginner and intermediate woodturner. Although it has a single mandrel end and a fairly narrow bed, it can take wood up to 24in between centres and up to 9in in diameter. (That does not mean a piece of wood 24in × 9in!)

A wide bowl-turning attachment (not available at the time of writing) necessitates the sliding of the motor housing up to the tailstock end. It is powered by a ⅓HP motor with speeds of 450, 950 and 2000rpm.

The model I was supplied with relied on three different sizes of Allen key to tighten the tailstock centre, the toolrest and the gear pulley lid. Apart from easily getting lost in the chippings I found this inconvenient and used Araldite to fix the Allen keys into their slots.

The other adjustments – to the toolrest, the sliding stock and belt adjustment nuts – were also different sizes, so the easiest remedy is to use an adjustable spanner or weld on a lever to the nuts (Fig 10.32). However, these small but irritating points are a small price to pay for an otherwise excellent lathe. The important thing is that it is robust.

My own lathe, a well-worn Arundel, has a larger capacity with double mandrel. The outer one I use as a disc-sander with table, an extremely useful attachment (Fig 10.33).

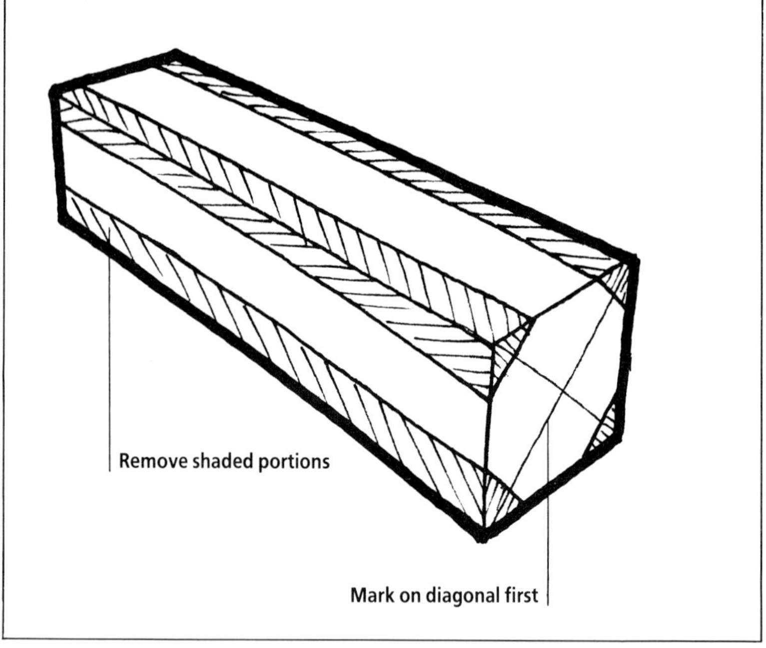

Fig 10.34 Preparation of stock for turning between centres.

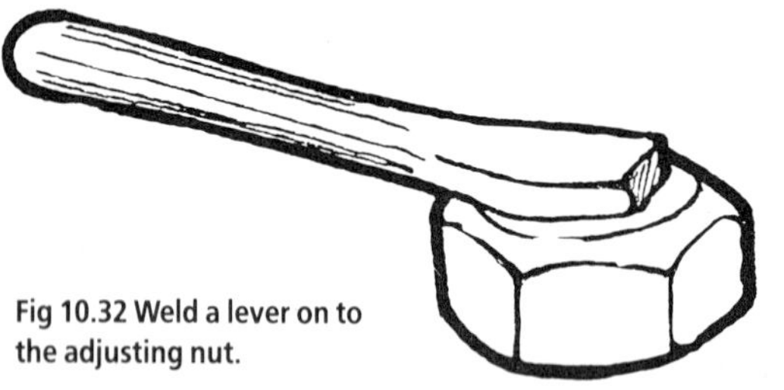

Fig 10.32 Weld a lever on to the adjusting nut.

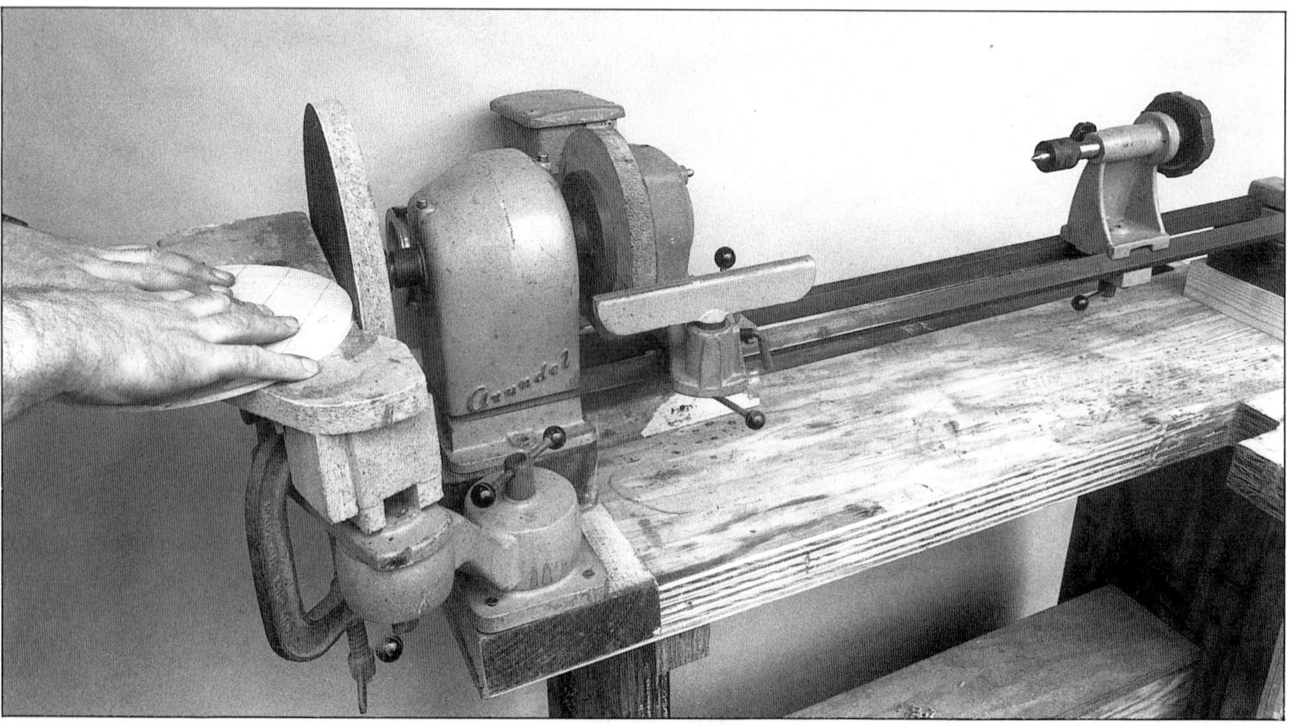

Fig 10.33 The author's Arundel J4 Mk 2 lathe with shop-made disc-sanding attachment.

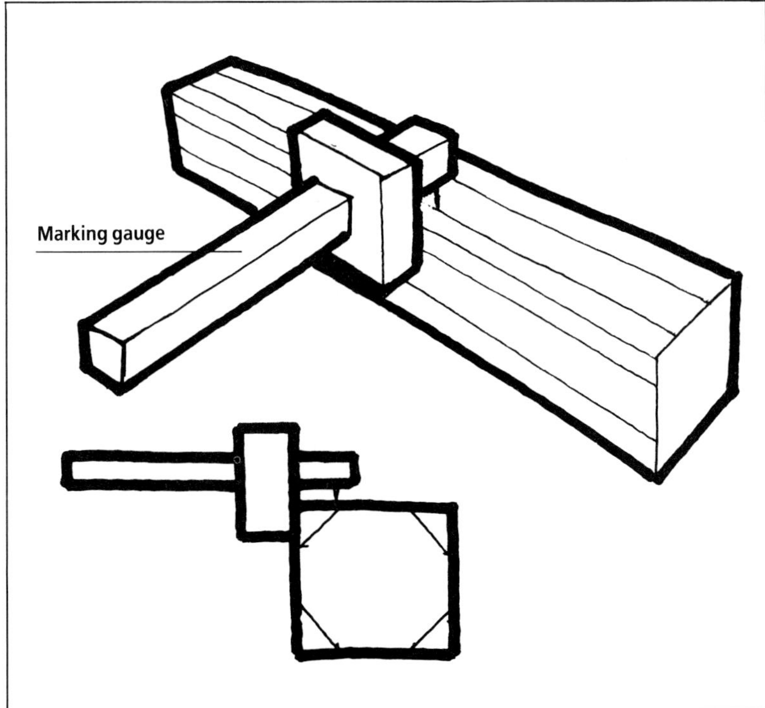

Fig 10.35 Use a marking gauge for marking out the octagonal section.

Fig 10.36 Tilt the bandsaw table to 45° and cut to the marking-gauge line.

PREPARATION FOR SPINDLE TURNERY

The 'Kneeling Stool' project, page 245, shows the application of this method. You will need to convert a square-sectioned piece of stock into an octagonal section by taking the corners off, but first diagonals should be drawn to find the centre on each end (Fig 10.34). (In some narrow-section spindle turnery it is possible to turn the square section, but the corners will virtually fly off when the tool is offered and this is generally reserved for advanced turners.)

The corners are then taken off, and my easy method is to use a marking gauge (Fig 10.35) and then cut to the line on the bandsaw (Fig 10.36).

Alternatively, a power plane can be used with the wood supported by its ends in the appropriate vice (such as the Zyliss clamp), or a planer–thicknesser can be used. I prefer the bandsaw, as it is quickest, with the table set to 45°.

A V-section saw-cut should then be made on one end to accommodate the fork centre (Fig 10.37) which should be driven in (against the bench top) with a soft mallet (see Fig 10.8). The work and fork centre are then mounted on the lathe and the tailstock centre fed into the other end and tightened.

The toolpost is set for height and clearance and the work rotated by hand to check this.

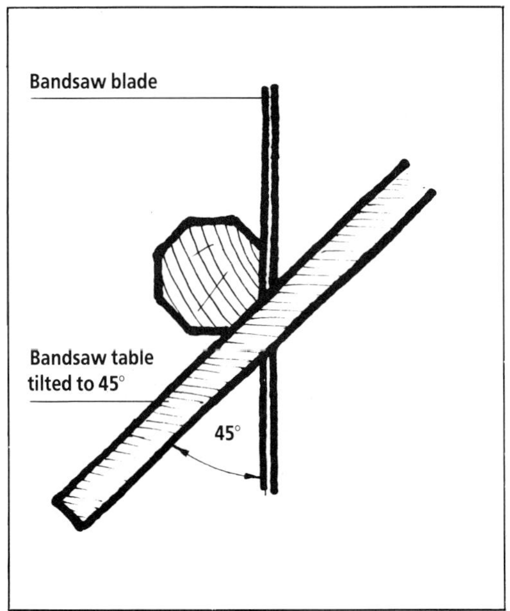

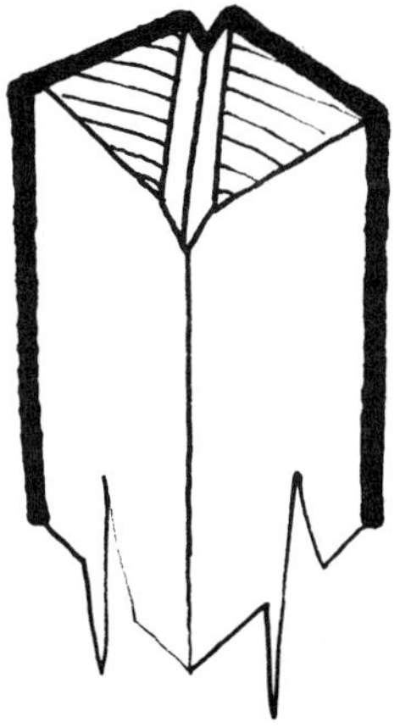

Fig 10.37 Cut a V-groove to locate the drive centre on the end of the work.

PREPARATION FOR FACEPLATE TURNERY

The 'Laminated Bowl' project, page 217, shows the application of this method. If circular bowl blanks are used a centre square is needed to find the faceplate centre (Fig 10.38).

If the blank is square section (cut from a plank), diagonals will need to be drawn to find the centre. Using a compass, two circles are drawn, one depicting the circumference to the bowl and the other slightly greater than the circumference of the faceplate, as a guide to aligning it. The blank is then bandsawn to shape and the faceplate screwed on. The shortest possible steel screws should be used, and plenty of them, taking care not to drill the pilot hole too deep as the thickness of the base of the bowl needs to be observed (Fig 10.39).

CHUCKS

This is fast becoming a subject in itself. Just as many of the great architects in the past have had a go at designing chairs, it seems that nowadays the leaders in the woodturning field all end up designing chucks. As John Haywood (Technical Editor of *Woodturning* magazine) says, 'There are now over 20 chucking systems available worldwide, so choosing the right one is like picking your way through a veritable minefield.'

Well, actually there are now 21, as there is the JKB Chucking System designed for the indecisive, impoverished, but imaginative woodturner – it's

Fig 10.38 Using the shop-made centre square.

Fig 10.39 Using the Panasonic drill-driver for faceplate pilot holes.

called a glue gun – not a chuck at all – and in fact does everything that all the other chucks do together at a fraction of the price! However, I shall deal with this later. I can only offer a basic survival guide to chucks here.

Firstly, the chuck generally accommodates smaller section work, and aims to give the maximum grip to the minimum amount of stock material. It allows open-end turning for objects such as eggcups, little boxes, etc. where the centrifugal force of the wood is fairly minimal and less leverage of the tool is in play (Fig 10.40).

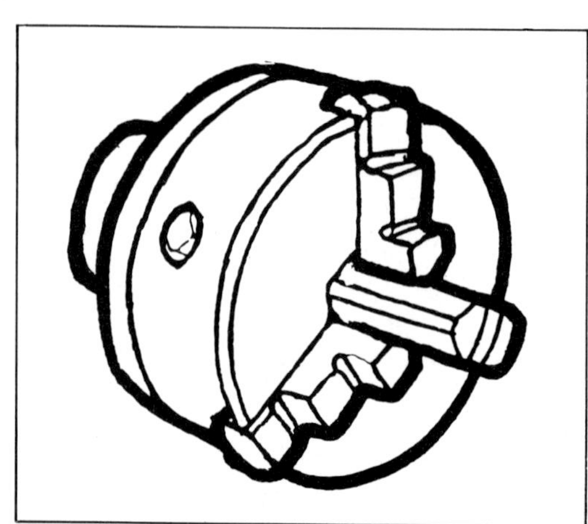

Fig 10.40 A chuck for the lathe.

The simplest chuck is a woodscrew chuck (Fig 10.41) with its left-hand thread. It requires minimal preparation (a flat base surface and pilot hole drilled into the wood) and has the advantage that the wood can be taken off easily; it is remarkably versatile.

Fig 10.41 A woodscrew chuck – a simple and effective method.

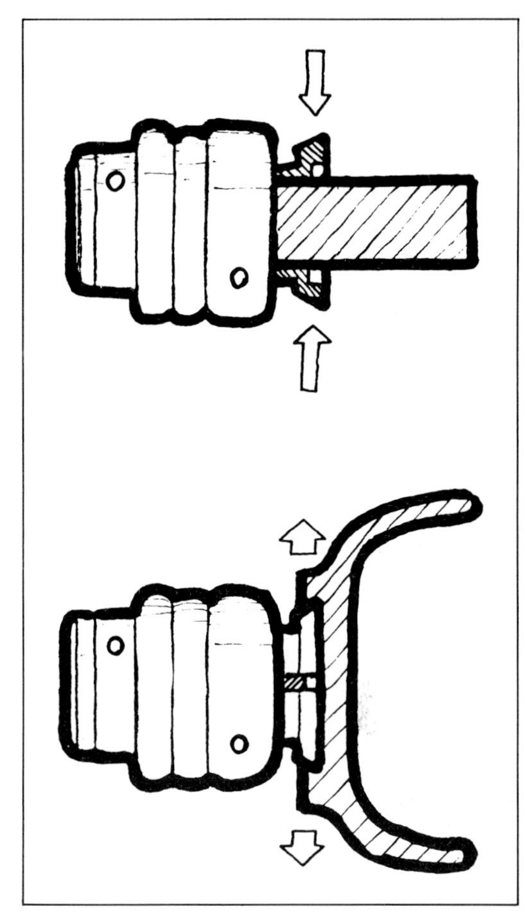

Fig 10.42 A collett chuck.

There are Jacobs-type chucks for narrow-diameter gripping, but they rely on circular-section stock.

There are 3- or 4-jaw chucks (which should appeal to those woodworkers with engineering backgrounds!). These are expensive, heavy, and in my opinion rather dangerous, with their protruding jaws, but many woodturners use them.

There is a self-centring 4-jaw chuck (available from Axminster, see page 272), which caters for round- and square-section work.

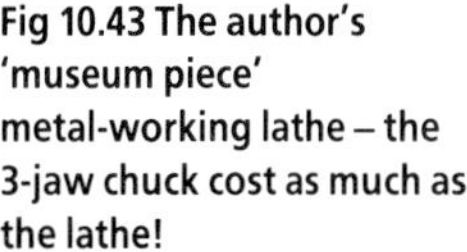

Fig 10.43 The author's 'museum piece' metal-working lathe – the 3-jaw chuck cost as much as the lathe!

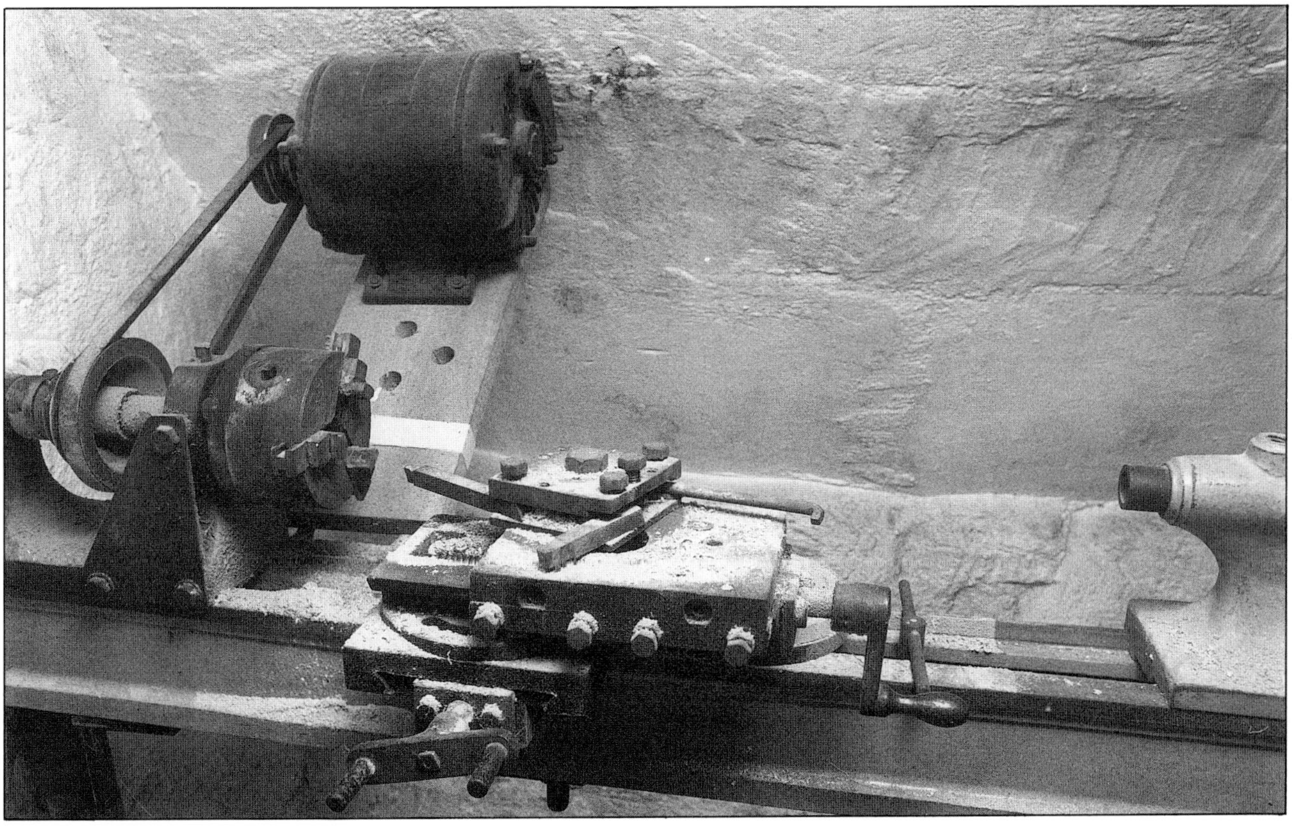

Fig 10.44 Concentric rings drawn on to the faceplate liner for easy location of work.

Fig 10.45 The JKB glue-chuck method – beats all others for simplicity and versatility!

There are collett and spigot chucks, which compress the timber (Fig 10.42), and one has to remember that the powerful mechanical action of some of these chucks will readily compress and damage the much softer timber.

When buying chucks you need to check thread patterns for your particular lathe. I acquired a wonderful 'Industrial Revolution' metalworking lathe, suitable for small wooden component turning. It has an automatic feed and cost £100, but it cost a further £100 to obtain a 3-jaw chuck (Fig 10.43)!

Glue gun/faceplate 'chucking'

This is a method I have used for as long as glue guns have been available (see also Chapter 13, The Mighty Glue Gun).

The work is hot-melt glued to a wood-lined faceplate. A circular wood blank is screwed to a faceplate and a series of concentric rings is pencilled or engraved on it with a parting tool while the lathe is running (Fig 10.44). The work is then simply glued in position (Fig 10.45), but you have to be quick! It is either parted off afterwards or carefully prized off with a chisel, depending on the amount of surface area glued. On no account should you hot-melt glue the wood to the metal faceplate – it just won't stick – and of course you can forget this method if you are turning wet wood.

Extra support on long work can be given from the tailstock centre when initially roughing the stock material to size. My only reservation about this method, apart from wet wood, is greasy wood, such as teak or some rosewoods. The thing to do is try it. Because the work is small it generally isn't the end of the world if it comes off, and I have seldom experienced a glue-chucked piece coming

Fig 10.46 The method is also quick and safe.

adrift. When parting off make sure the cut is not too close to the hot-melt glued base as rapid cutting can cause heat and the glue will . . . !

Lathe drilling

The lathe is unique in so far as in all other woodworking the work is stationary and the bit or cutter rotates. The opposite happens in lathe work, and can apply to the action of the drill also. The drill is fixed in a Jacobs-type chuck in the tailstock (Fig 10.47), and is simply wound into the rotating work. Various types of boring tool – twist drill or flatbit – can be used on the lathe.

TIMBERS

Most timbers will turn and part of the fun of using a lathe is to experiment. Generally the best (and safest) results are in medium- to close-grained timbers. Oak is a little brittle and coarse. Try to avoid toxic timbers such as afformosia and iroko. I prefer strong-grained timbers such as hobnolly pine. Yew is ideal for small and detailed work, but often has internal cracks to watch out for. Teak has traditionally been the ideal turnery timber for tableware, but is difficult to obtain nowadays. Elm turns well, especially wet, and takes a good finish such as linseed oil. Beech turns well, unless it is spalted, but is rather boring! Sycamore has a subtle lustre to it, and of course the burr woods are highly decorative. I have used burr oak for decorative bowls. It goes on . . .

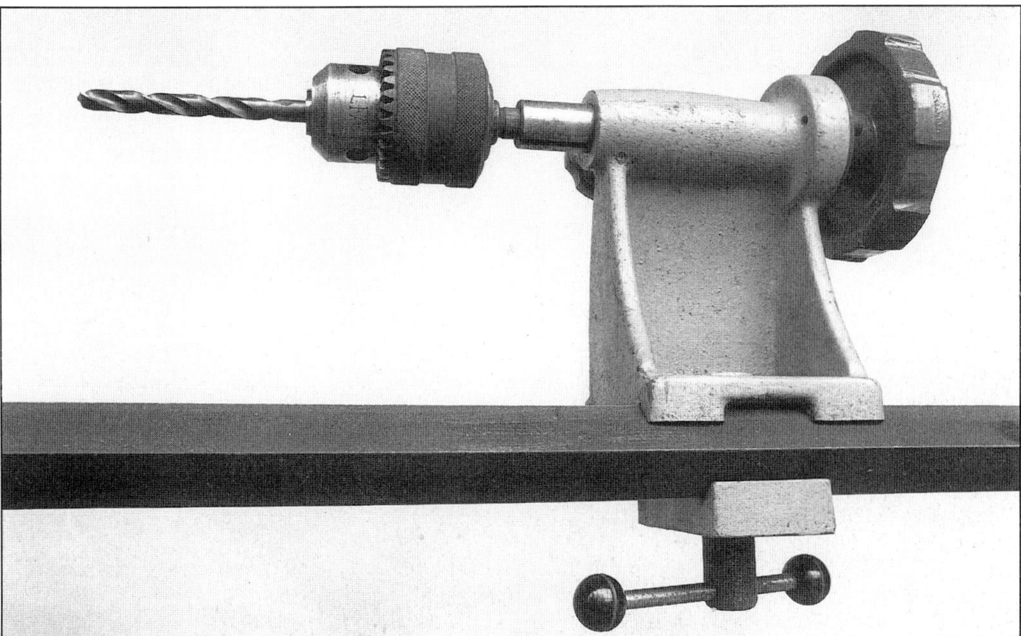

Fig 10.47 The drill is stationary as the work rotates.

11

THE BISCUIT JOINTER

The biscuit jointer (also referred to as a jointer-groover) has made a late debut to the power woodworking stage, although some professionals have used them for years. An experienced woodworking friend has told me that he wondered how he ever survived so long without one, but there are many woodworkers who still do not know what a biscuit jointer is – and what it can do. They happily plod away using other slower methods to achieve the same results.

I have to admit that until the writing of this book I had not had the opportunity to use a biscuit jointer either (the *only* tool, I may add!). However, one thing became immediately apparent – the biscuit jointer is remarkably quick and easy to use and opens up a whole new woodworking vocabulary.

Courtesy of Black & Decker, I tried out an Elu biscuit jointer for this part of the book (Fig 11.1).

Fig 11.1 Two views of the Elu biscuit jointer.

PRINCIPLE

A biscuit jointer is a hand-held rotary cutting tool, similar to a grinder, with a circular-saw-type blade. It is positioned accurately and independently over two pieces of timber to be joined, is plunged by a pivoting spring action into the wood to a pre-set depth (Fig 11.2), and cuts a shallow crescent-shaped groove into which an elliptical wood 'biscuit' is inserted with the addition of glue (Fig 11.3). This simple tool offers a quick, easy and accurate jointing system for solid timber and manufactured board in both framework and carcase construction. It is an alternative to many traditional enclosed joints, such as the mortice and tenon, housing and dowelled joints, and will join wood in virtually any configuration (Fig 11.4). It offers a completely new jointing system which makes it an exciting tool to use.

TYPES AND SPECIFICATION

There are several biscuit jointers on the market, made by Elu, Lamello, Freud, Bosch and Ryobi. Both Bosch models allow the motor component to be used as an angle-grinder, and the Elu and Bosch can readily be used as cut-off and trimming saws. There are also some biscuit-jointer attach-

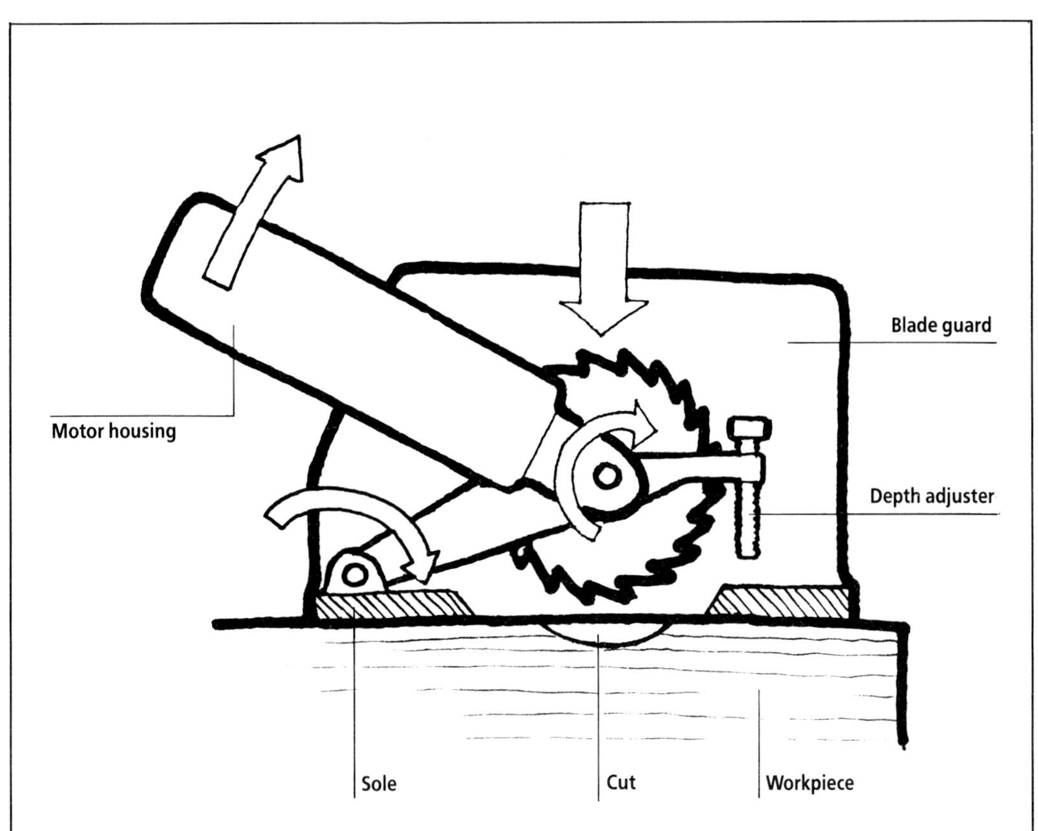

Fig 11.2 The principle of the biscuit jointer.

Fig 11.3 An elliptical wood biscuit is inserted into a crescent-shaped groove.

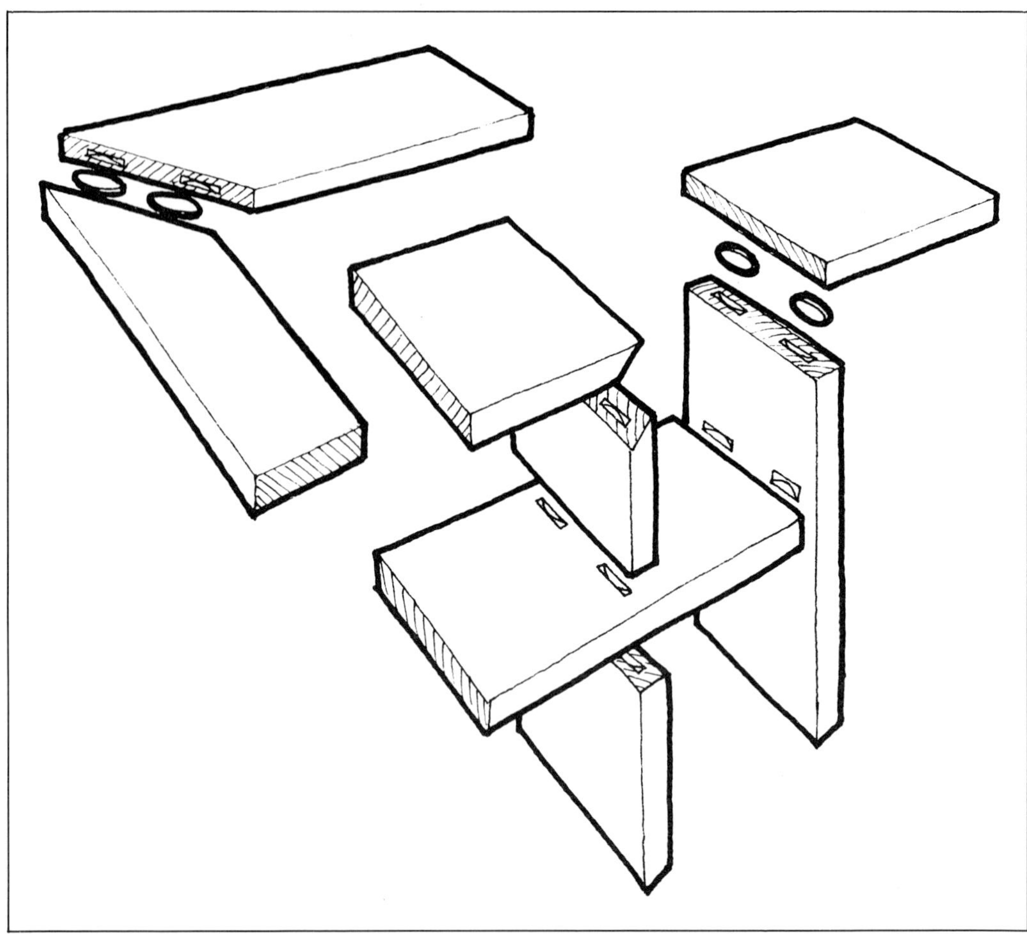

Fig 11.4 Wood jointing configurations.

Fig 11.5 The depth stop can be adjusted.

Fig 11.6 An adjustable fence is part of the biscuit jointer.

ments (e.g. Wolfcraft). They are normally power-rated at around 600 watts and have a TCT blade of 100–105mm diameter cutting a 4mm wide slot at approximately 10000rpm. The depth of cut is variable up to about 20–24mm, depending on the size of biscuit, and is adjusted by a depth knob (Fig 11.5). A side fence (Fig 11.6) and mitre fence (Fig 11.7) are part of the kit and fine adjustment to the positioning of the cutter can be made once the side fence is locked. Most biscuit jointers have dust extraction outlets – which should be used. As with planers, the chippings fly out fast and furiously!

BISCUITS

Biscuits are available in packs, and in 3 sizes for different board thicknesses – 0, 10 and 20 (Fig 11.8). They are made of beech, which is tough, close-grained and dimensionally stable. The grain runs diagonally and is compressed, giving the biscuit a deceptive strength. Plastic biscuits are also available, although these are used for test assemblies only. The biscuits swell when a water-based glue is applied, which calls for fairly swift assembly, but aids with the clamping.

STRENGTH OF JOINT AND USES

The joint has great strength, but obviously cannot match a mortice and tenon or dovetail as the mechanics of these are completely different – they have more fibre length, overlap and penetration. Because the joint – biscuit – tapers away from a maximum of 63mm × 12mm width to nothing, it is important to recognize its limitations and apply the joint in an appropriate way. A carcase, for example, which is in effect a box structure (Fig 11.9), achieves its strength as an integrated 3-dimensional whole, and no undue leverage occurs at any one joint as adjacent members act as a brace. The biscuit joint used in butt or mitre

Fig 11.7 A mitre fence can be attached to the biscuit jointer.

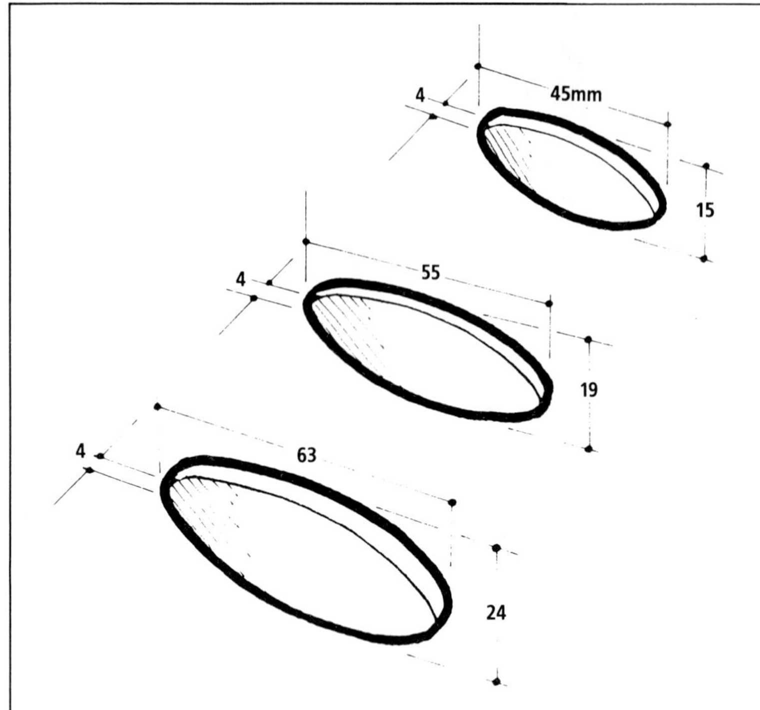

joints in this instance would be sufficiently strong. A biscuit joint in an unsupported L-configuration, however, would be weak, as the joint is virtually on the edge and would break out easily if stressed. In this case several biscuits would be used to maximize the bond.

A good application of the joint is in edge-jointing boards – as in the build-up of a table top – which traditionally would be dowelled, or even just edge-glued. Firstly the edge-to-edge grain of the timber gives the strongest bond, and secondly there is no leverage between pieces (Fig 11.10).

Where the biscuit joint really comes into its own, apart from edge-jointing solid boards, is in jointing manufactured board – chipboard, MDF and plywoods – where many of the traditional joints, which were designed for solid wood, are inappropriate. Even dowelling these materials can be awkward, as the drill can wander off course, but *biscuit jointing is an excellent locating system,* and this is an important consideration when assembling and gluing work. But of course the biscuit jointer can be equally at home with manufactured boards *and* solid timber.

It is important to note that biscuit joints offer

Fig 11.8 Biscuit sizes.

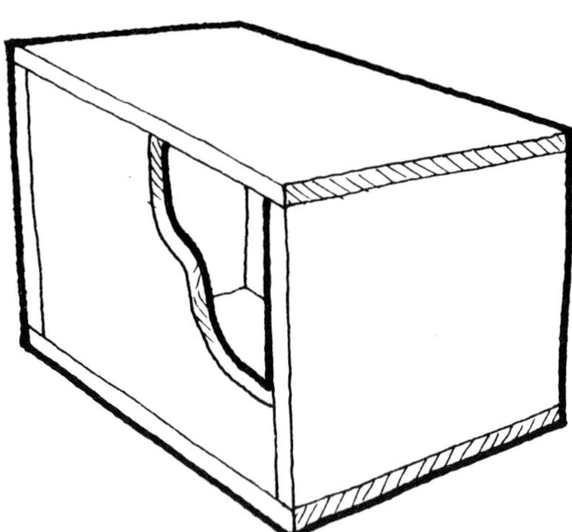

Fig 11.9 A carcase is an integrated 'box' structure.

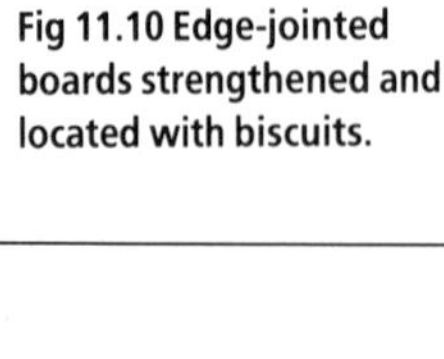

Fig 11.10 Edge-jointed boards strengthened and located with biscuits.

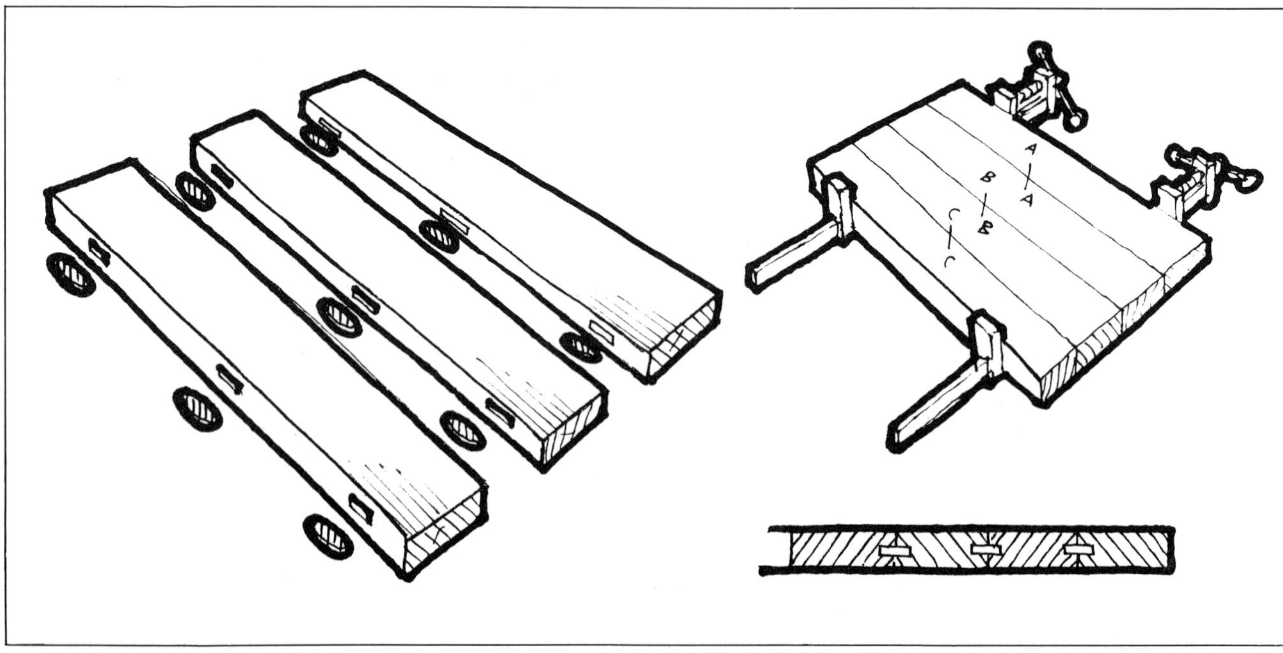

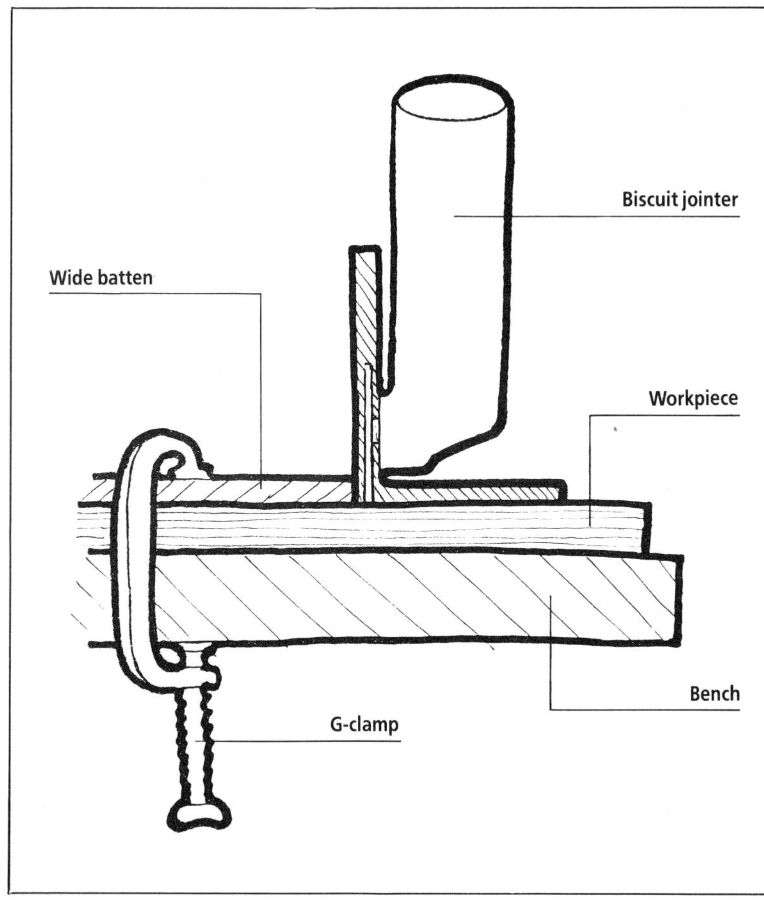

Fig 11.11 Using the biscuit jointer against a clamped batten.

an accurate self-locating system. For example when edge-jointing the boards for a table top which are likely to be slightly bowed, the inserted biscuits help keep everything flush and easier to cramp up (un-located boards slide around when glued and clamped).

SAFETY

The tool is fairly simple and solid in design, and its blade is automatically retracted by a spring-loaded mechanism. This means that little damage can occur even when the tool is switched on. It is also heavy enough not to wander about unduly and is therefore easy to control. The tool should be positioned first then the power switched on. The power should be switched off *before* the tool is lifted from the work and the tool should not be twisted in the work as a brake to slow the blade down.

OPERATION

The biscuit jointer can be used 'freehand', or against a clamped batten (Fig 11.11), and/or set against the side/bevel fence, depending on the joint configuration. Once the biscuit size has been decided and the blade-depth set, the positions of the pieces to be jointed and locations of the biscuits within the joint are easily marked out.

In the case of a carcase L-joint the fence is used for jointing both pieces and the centre point of the biscuits marked with a pencil (Fig 11.12). In a T-configuration carcase joint a try-square is first used to mark out the position of the edge of the adjacent piece. This is then placed on the first piece and the biscuit locations pencilled on to both pieces simultaneously.

The biscuit jointer can be used in one of two ways. Either 'freehand' on one piece, taking care to line up the side of the baseplate and its location marks against the square line (Fig 11.13), alternatively it can be set against a batten which has been clamped in line with the squared pencil line, then the other piece is jointed with the fence set against the edge (Fig 11.14). A hole in the side fence makes location of the marks easy (Fig 11.15). In fact it is all very easy (Fig 11.16).

For jointing framework structures in solid timber, any face of the timber section can be used for fence-jointing. The system very quickly becomes self-explanatory – the fence position corresponds

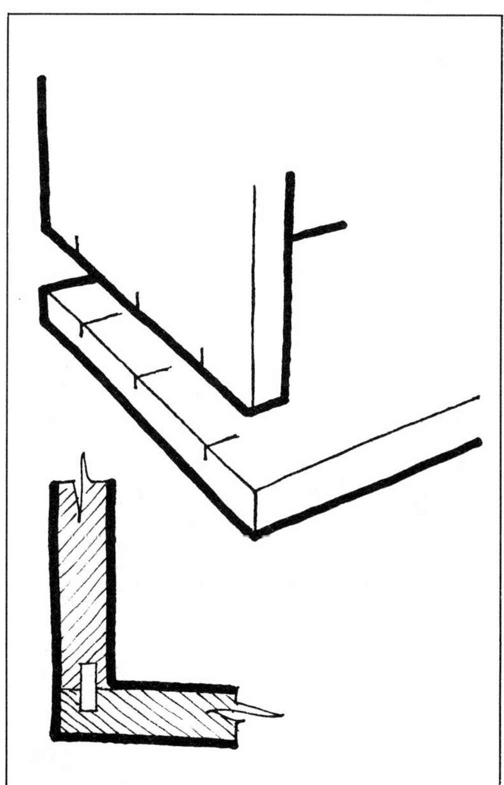

Fig 11.12 Both pieces are marked for an L-configuration joint.

Fig 11.13 The edge of the tool is simply lined up against a marked 'square' line on the wood, and the cutter plunged to the set depth.

Fig 11.14 The corresponding joint is cut with the fence set against the edge.

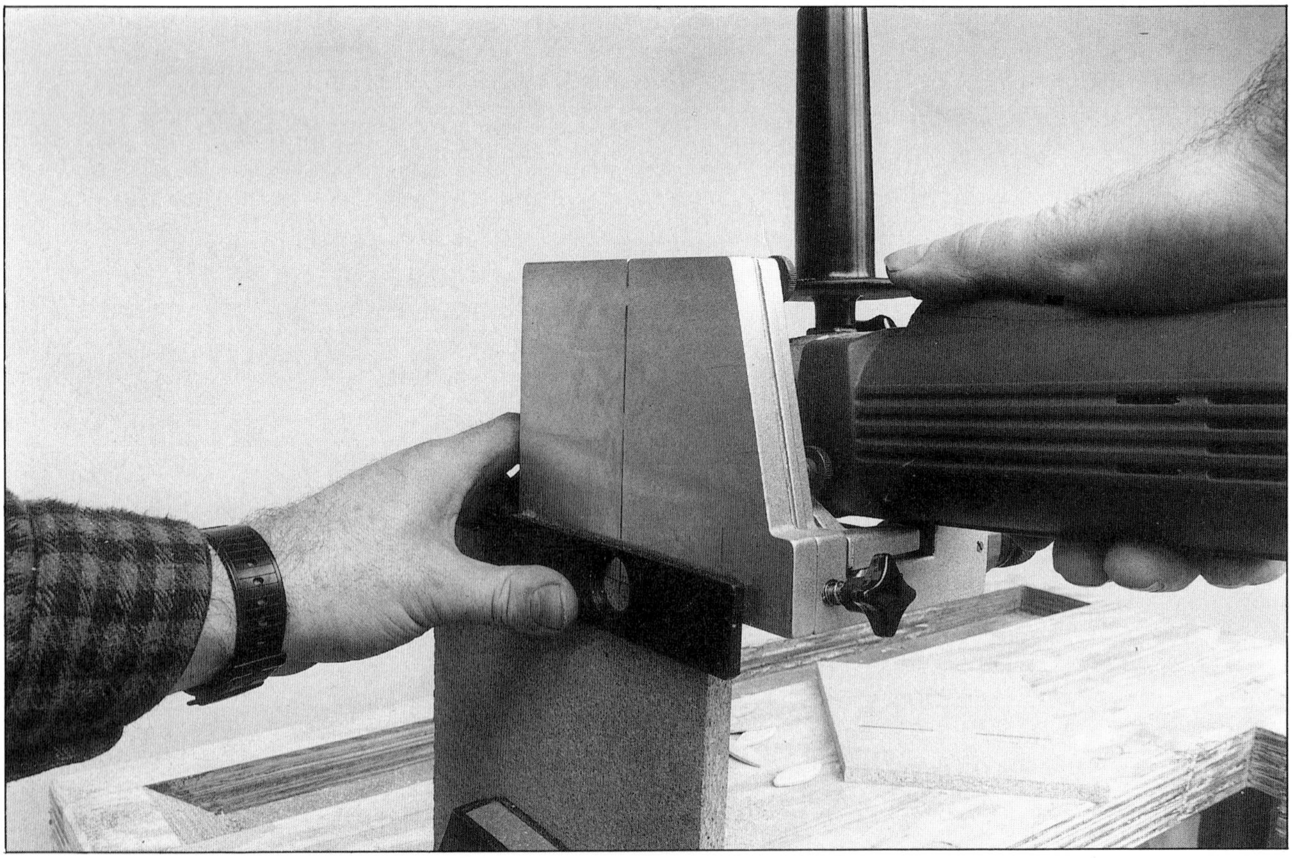

Fig 11.15 The centre line on the tool is lined up with the marked line on the work and can be seen through a hole in the fence.

Fig 11.16 The joint is delightfully simple.

Position of fence

Position of cutter

Position of biscuit joint for maximum strength

Fig 11.17(a) The position of the biscuit on a mitre joint is for maximum strength (above).

Fig 11.17(b) Section through mitre joint and position of fence and cutter (left).

Fig 11.18 Mitre joint cutting using a backing piece (below).

Fig 11.19 Several biscuits used for an L joint (right).

with the edge of the baseplate, and each is used as a guide respectively.

When applying biscuits to mitred joints, for maximum strength the fence is distanced to ensure the location of the joint is nearer the inside edge (Figs 11.17(a) and (b)). An alternative to the fence is the use of the mitre/bevel fence with the work set horizontally with a backing piece (Fig 11.18).

SPECIAL JIGS

Of course the biscuit jointer, like the router and many other tools, lends itself to special jigging systems, especially where repeat or batch work has to be achieved quickly. The batten is the simplest jig and if the tool is run along it, the resulting cut is a groove. Special jigs may be necessary for supporting the tool on the end of small section work.

The biscuit jointer offers a remarkably simple, easy and efficient method of jointing, and the serious woodworker will never run out of ideas for different applications. See page 227 for its use in the construction of the Grid Table.

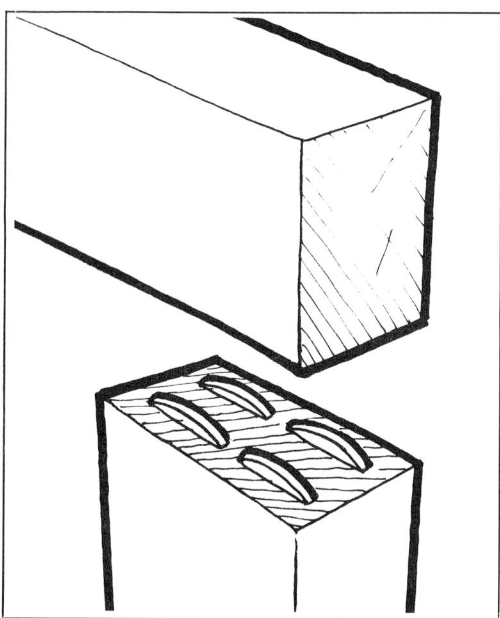

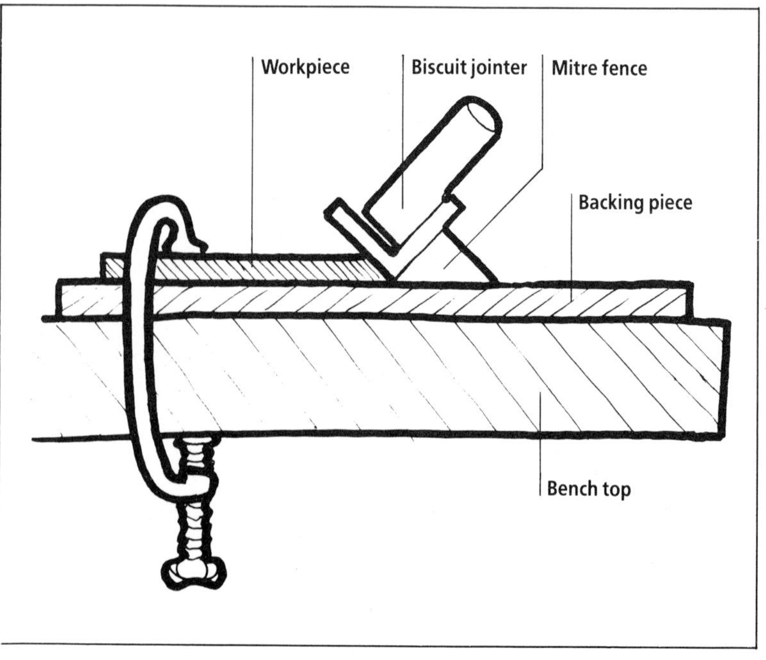

12
THE RADIAL ARM SAW

At its simplest the radial arm saw is an extremely efficient crosscut saw where the sliding machine head passes over the timber which is held stationary on a bed. However, it is a machine of *considerable* creative potential, as not only can the saw blade be angled universally – any direction vertically and horizontally – to crosscut, rip, bevel, mitre or make any compound angled cut, but it can be raised or lowered for cutting grooves and rebates. It can also be used as a vehicle for attachments such as the router (Fig 12.1) and drum sander (Fig 12.2), doubling up many of the above facilities. So in effect it is a useful and versatile shaping machine with many advantages over conventional saw benches. In fact it probably limits the perception of the tool to compare it with a conventional saw! The radial arm saw is *almost* a universal woodworking machine.

As a quick and efficient crosscut saw I rate it first because of its ease of use. Reducing timber to the required length is probably the first task in woodworking and it makes good sense to pass the saw *over* the timber rather than vice versa, especially with heavy timber. When using the circular saw for crosscutting you need an extension table to support cumbersome timber. With the radial arm saw you build a purpose-made bench which supports the stock material (Fig 12.3). Its main limitation (but not a serious one) is the reach of the arm, and consequently the length of cut – or should I say *width* of cut – the sliding carriage allows.

When I first set up a workshop the radial arm saw was my first machine. I bought an ex-demonstration DeWalt 10in model for £50 in 1972 and it still serves me well today. In fact the efficiency and versatility of the machine, and its ease of use, have played an important part in my design philosophy – the way I make things in wood being determined by the capability of the tools. Of course this particular machine does not possess the type of guard which current legislation requires on machines, but it has never been involved in an accident in almost twenty years of service.

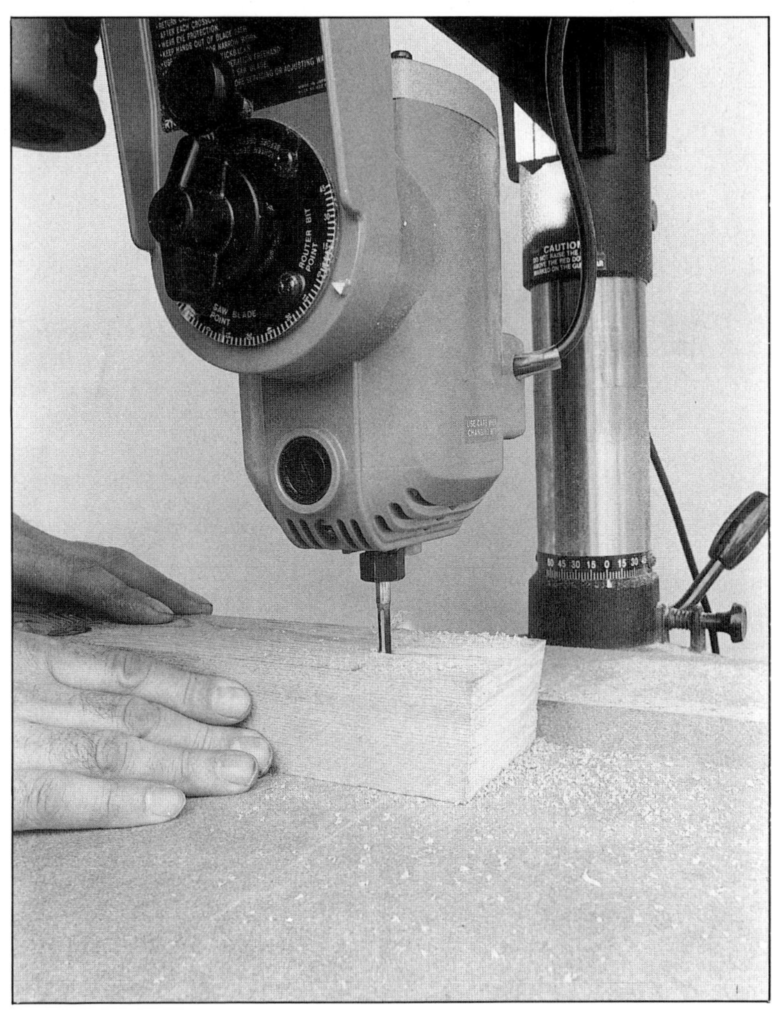

Fig 12.1 The Ryobi RA200 radial arm saw used as an overhead router.

In this chapter, and for the projects, I use my faithful old DeWalt and the compact and powerful Ryobi RA200 as fairly typical machines. The DeWalt runs at 2850rpm and the Ryobi at 5000rpm. Other models for both amateur and professional use are made by DeWalt and Sears, and there is also a heavier duty Ryobi.

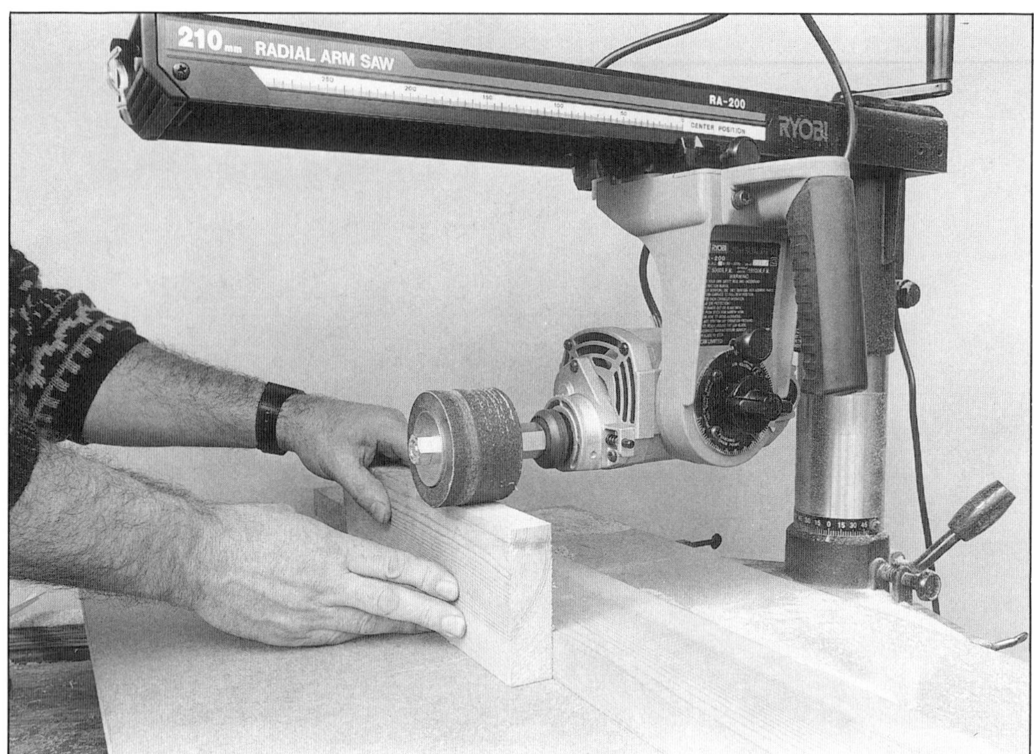

Fig 12.2 The radial arm saw as a drum sander.

210mm RADIAL ARM SAW
RA-200
CENTER POSITION
RYOBI

Fig 12.3 Purpose-built bench to give full support to the board.

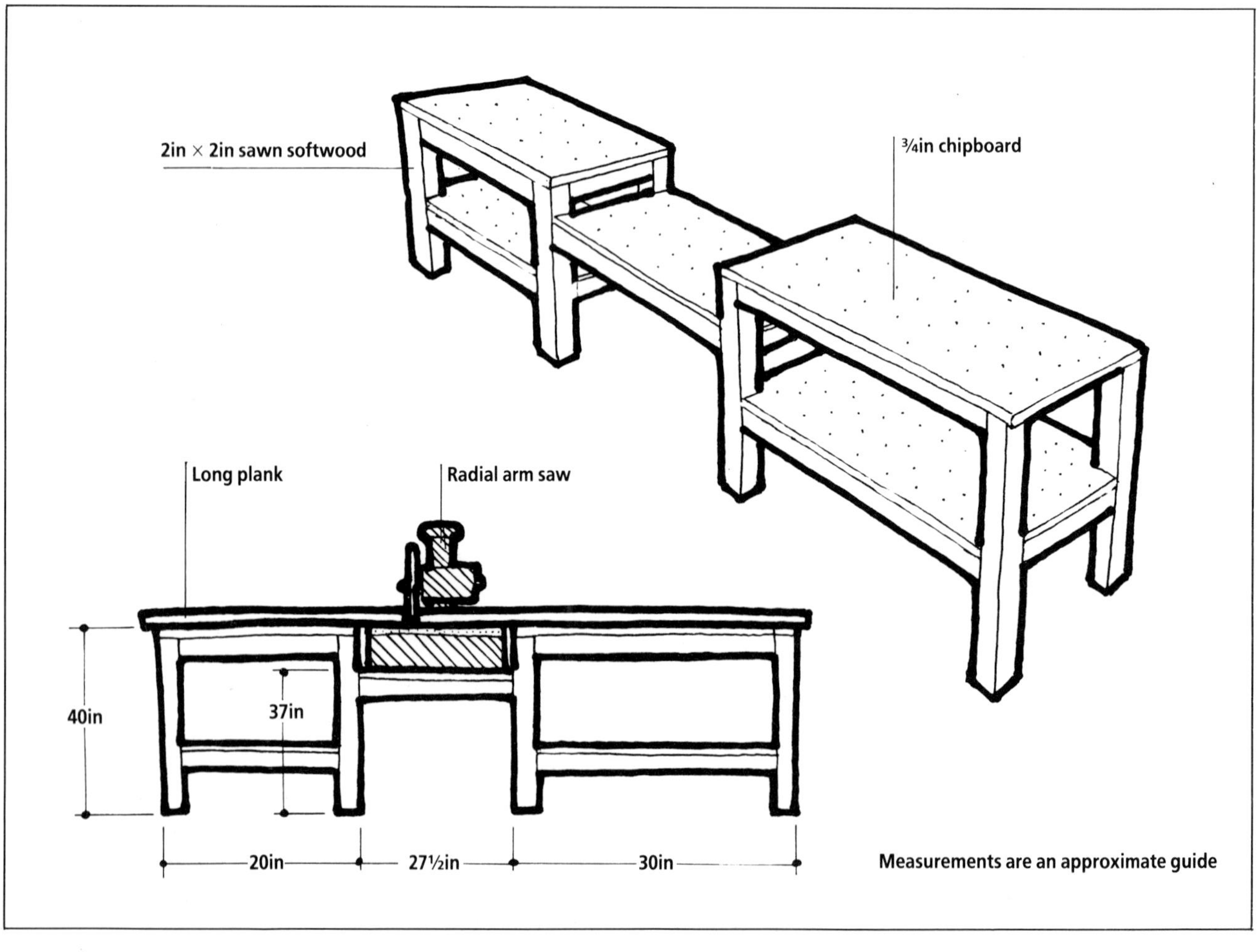
2in × 2in sawn softwood
¾in chipboard
Long plank
Radial arm saw
40in
37in
20in
27½in
30in
Measurements are an approximate guide

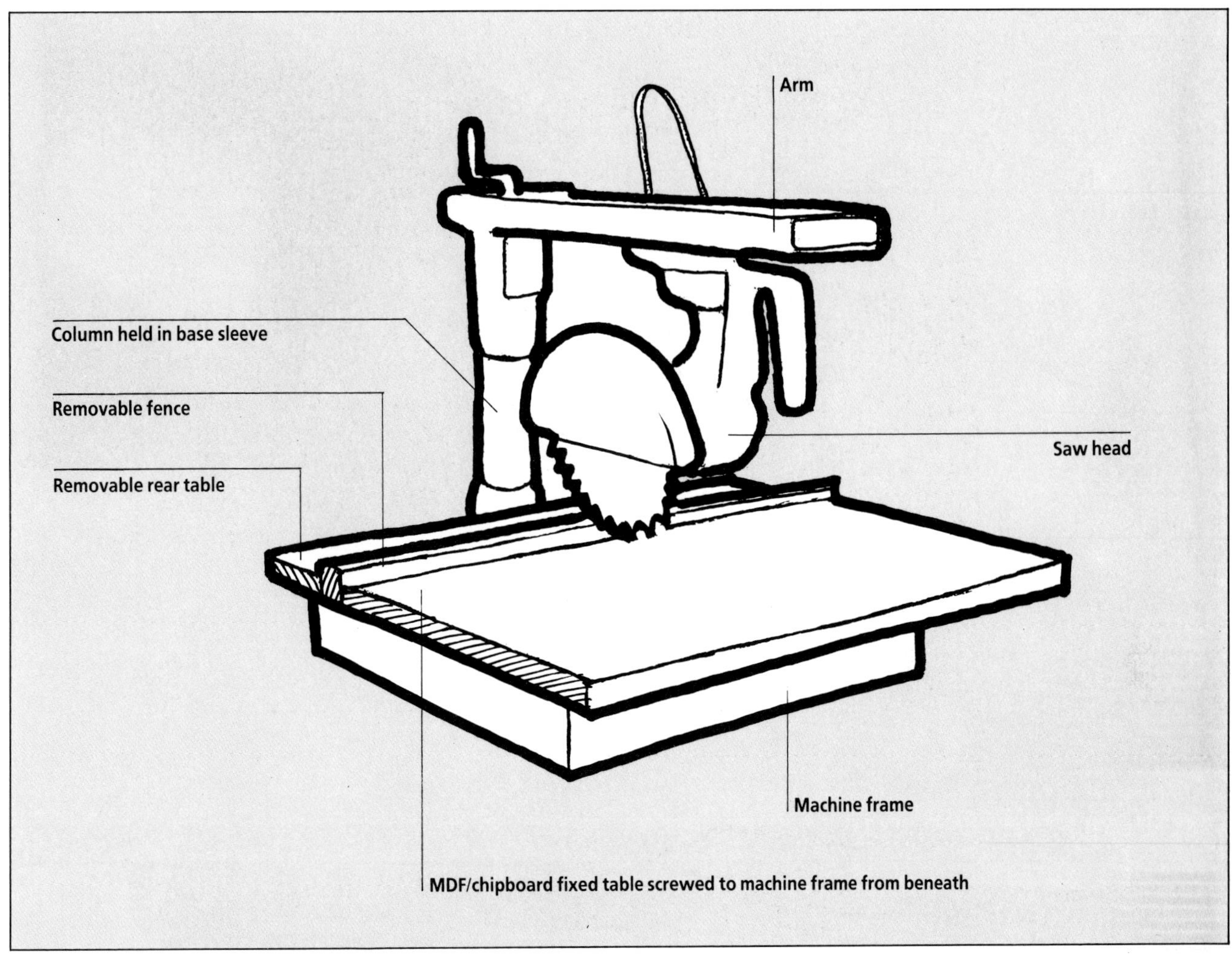

Fig 12.4 Assembly of the radial arm saw.

POWER AND SPECIFICATION

Radial arm saws range in power from about 1HP to 2.5HP with a blade diameter of 210mm to 250mm (although some of the heavy-duty industrial machines have blades up to 500mm diameter). The saw-spindle speed is between 2800 and 5000rpm. (The Ryobi RA200 has an accessory spindle speed of 18500rpm.) On popular machines the maximum depth of cut is 55–75mm, the crosscut capacity 280–310mm and the maximum ripping width 500–650mm.

The blade-spindle diameter is normally 30mm. The saw blade is covered with a guard which also holds a riving knife (for preventing timber closing up on ripping), and an anti-kickback assembly for ripping. The weight of the machine is around 24–32kg.

ASSEMBLY

Any new radial arm saw is likely to be packed flat in a box and requires assembly and careful setting up. Assembly is straight forward (Fig 12.4). A supplied manufactured-board top (usually 18mm chipboard) has to be screwed on to the base frame. The fence and inserts are floating and are clamped into position by two screws at the rear. The machine head column is then lowered into its seating and clamped. The Ryobi model has two extension feet which give extra stability to the base.

Setting up

As the action of the saw blade is in effect jigged (guided along the overhead arm, and the timber set firmly against the fence), it is important that the blade runs true. It is necessary to check the blade for vertical alignment (Fig 12.5) and the arm for 'squareness' in relation to the fence (Fig 12.6). Of course the locking levers on the base of the column (Fig 12.7) and the motor assembly (Fig 12.8) have set positions at zero, 45°, 90°, etc. for angle cutting operations, but they can be set at any desired angle and then locked.

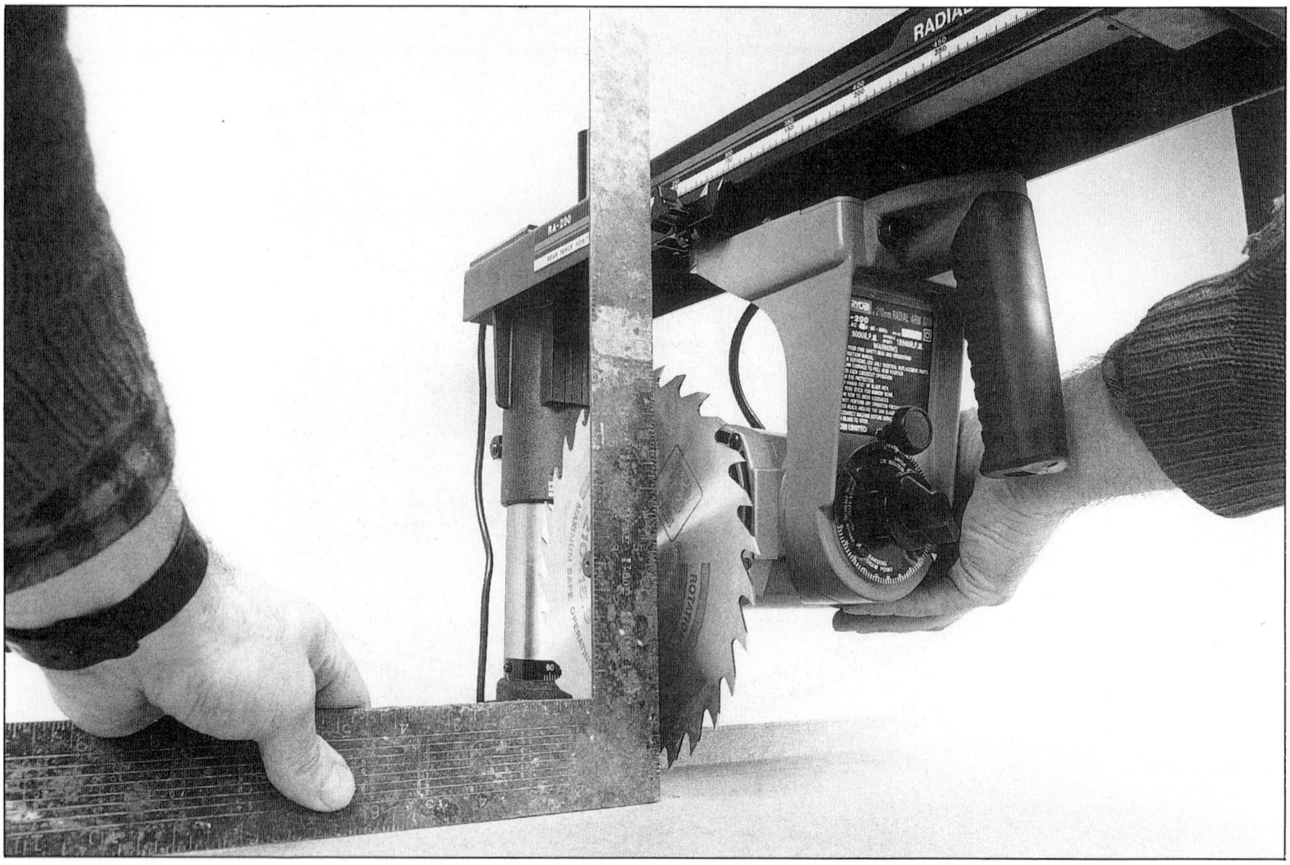
RA-200
RYOBI
ROTATION

RADIAL ARM SAW 210mm
RA-200
OUTRIP
INRIP
REAR FENCE POSITION
ROTATION

Fig 12.7 Column locking lever.

Fig 12.8 Locking the motor head at the required angle.

Fig 12.5 Checking the blade for vertical alignment (opposite above).

Fig 12.6 Checking the arm for 'squareness' to the fence (opposite below).

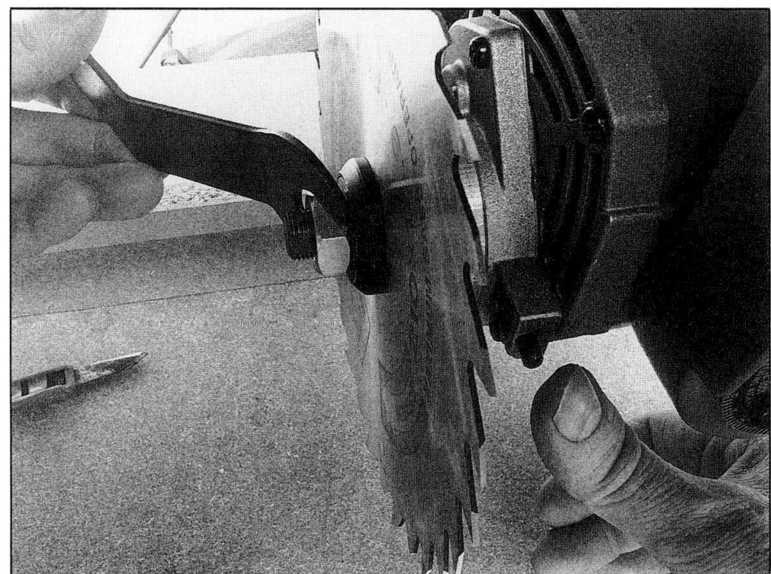

Fig 12.9 The spindle assembly locked with a spanner.

Setting up/changing the blade

The blade is normally mounted on a ⅝in spindle with a left-hand thread. The Ryobi machine has a 210mm (8¼in) blade which is set between two arbors. The spindle lock and spanner are used (Fig 12.9) to tighten the blade, checking the correct direction of teeth first.

Mounting the radial arm saw

The operating height of the tool is important and so too is the level support of boards to be cut. A purpose-built bench is advisable to optimize the capability of the tool and is best described by an illustration (see Fig 12.4).

When mounting the tool some clearance should be given at the back for the knuckles when operating the depth crank. It may also be advisable to attach a false top made from 6mm MDF to the table, which can be replaced when sawcuts begin to affect the fibre support under the blade. Of course the adjacent bench surface area should also be lined to maintain a flush surface for mounting planks.

DUST EXTRACTION

There is a dust-extraction take-off collar on the saw blade guard. It is strongly recommended that this be linked up to an extraction unit to minimize dust getting everywhere. Any circular saw will throw up a considerable amount of dust, especially as the saw-kerf is quite wide (3–4mm).

A useful place for a portable dust extractor is underneath the purpose-built bench for the saw (Fig 12.4).

Fig 12.11 Using the anti-kickback device when ripping.

SAFETY

Any setting up or adjustment to the saw should be done with the power off. The Ryobi radial arm saw has a locking key which has to be inserted before the motor will start up (Fig 12.10).

It is particularly important to check that locking levers are firmly tightened after the blade has been located in its swung position. Fingers should be kept well away from the blade, and its guard should be properly positioned with the anti-kickback device set when ripping (Fig 12.11).

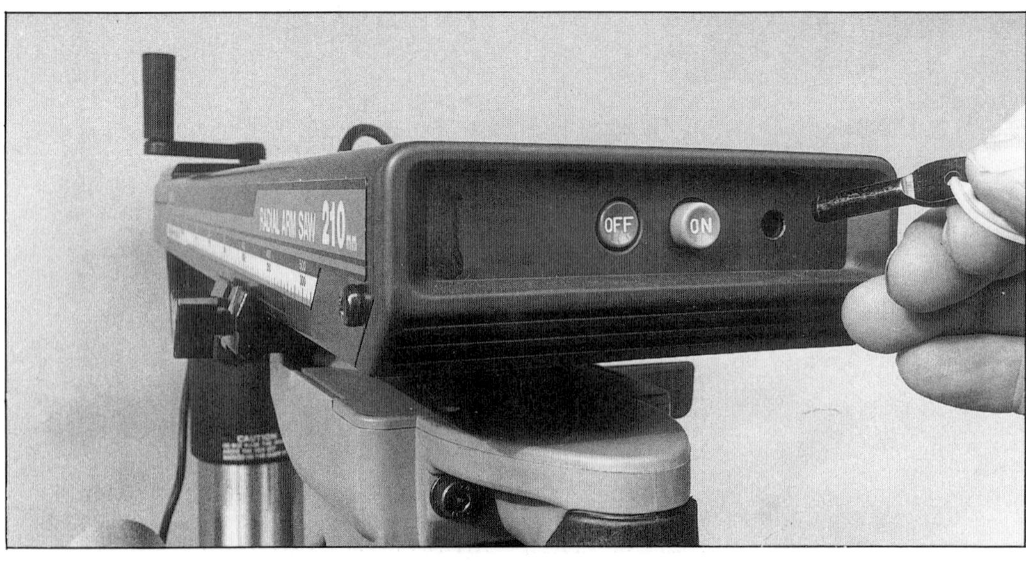

Fig 12.10 The locking key has to be inserted before use.

Fig 12.12 A simultaneous 'push-pull' action is required.

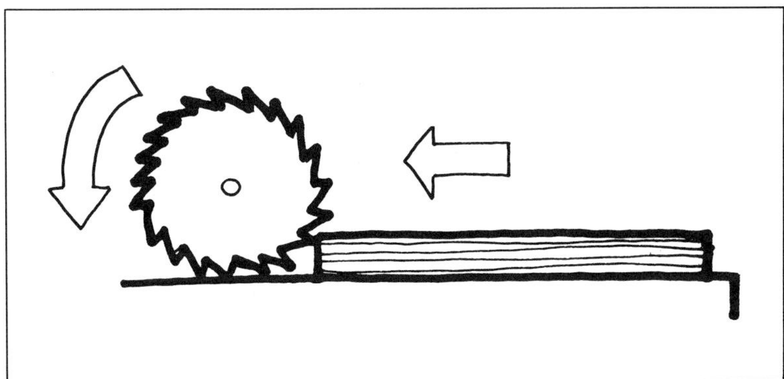

OPERATION

The saw blade will have a tendency to snatch the wood as it engages, so both machine head and wood have to be held firmly.

In the case of crosscutting, the wood is held firmly against the fence and the saw drawn across it. As the blade will want to pull back, the control of the hand is in effect pushing against it as it is drawn across (Fig 12.12). Too deep a cut will result in the blade wanting to snatch more and the motor suddenly stalling.

Fig 12.13 When ripping feed the wood *against* the rotation of the blade.

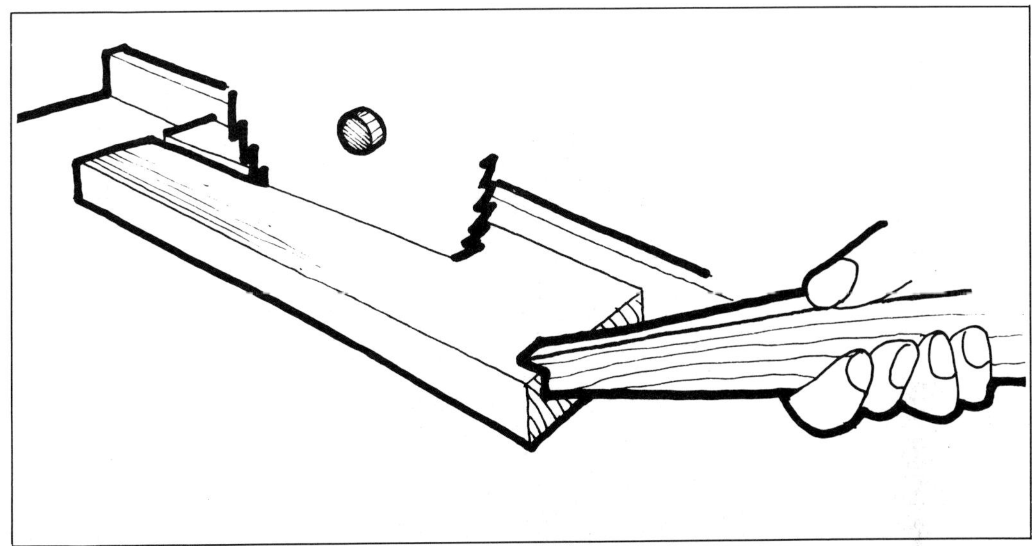

Fig 12.14 A push stick keeps fingers out of the way.

Extra wide boards

Although the Ryobi is specified to cut widths up to 380mm (Fig 12.15), it can in fact cut boards up to 510mm width by moving the table fence to the outside (up against the clamps – Fig 12.16). Obviously the saw head will be rotated so that the blade is on the outside. Here again, remember to feed the wood in *against* the rotation of the blade.

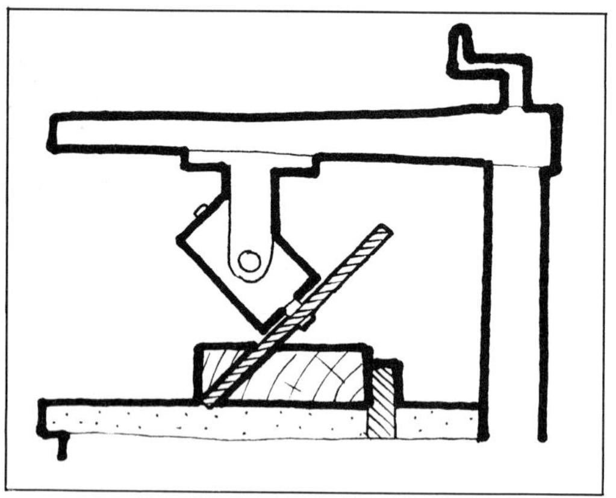

When supporting the wood an almost straight-arm position is desirable, with the fingers well away from the saw blade path. For ripping the head is swung around to 90°, locked, and the guard and anti-kickback device set in relation to the wood. The riving knife is then inserted. The width of cut is set (I prefer to use a ruler rather than rely on machine calibrations) and this is checked against a mark on the wood by 'kissing' the saw blade.

Both hands are used to feed the wood into the blade *against* its rotation. The wood is always fed against the cutting action of the blade – if you feed it in *with* the direction of rotation, it will be snatched and fly out at the other side (Fig 12.13). Push sticks may be necessary if timber sections are small (Fig 12.14).

Fig 12.15 A 380mm width of cut on the Ryobi.

Fig 12.17 Bevel cutting – used in the 'rip' mode.

Fig 12.18 Mitre cutting – the saw used in the 'crosscut' mode.

Fig 12.16 Widths up to 510mm can be achieved by moving the fence.

Bevel cutting

In the ripping mode the saw arm can be raised (for clearance) and the head tilted so that the blade is angled for bevel-cutting operations. The wood is fed in *against* the fence as in ripping (Fig 12.17).

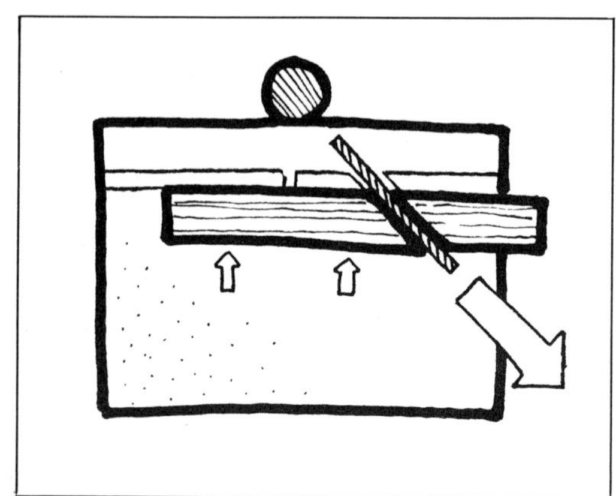

Mitre cutting

The saw blade is set at 90° and the arms swung to the 45° position. The saw is used in the crosscutting mode (Fig 12.18).

Compound angles

Any angle can be positioned from the arm (horizontally) and the saw blade (vertically), hence setting up the tool for cutting compound angles. The saw is operated in the crosscutting mode.

Fig 12.19 Raising the arm to its maximum.

Fig 12.20 Cutting a groove across the grain.

Grooving and rebating (dado cutters)

It is possible to cut any size groove or rebate across or along the grain by raising the arm (Fig 12.19), by turning the handle to the required depth of cut. The saw is used in the crosscutting mode, and by progressively moving the timber along the fence after each cut, a wider cut can be made (Fig 12.20). This is slow but controlled.

I use a method of cutting a series of narrow grooves, then breaking the waste off (short grain) and trimming the base line with the saw (Fig 12.21)

Alternatively dado cutters can be used. They are normally a series of smaller diameter 2-blade cutters carefully arranged on the spindle (Fig 12.22 – can you spot the mistake?), so that the full tooth configuration is set up (i.e. a cross, then diagonals). A wider cut is made on each pass, but of course for wide rebates or grooves the cutting will have to be done in progressive operations.

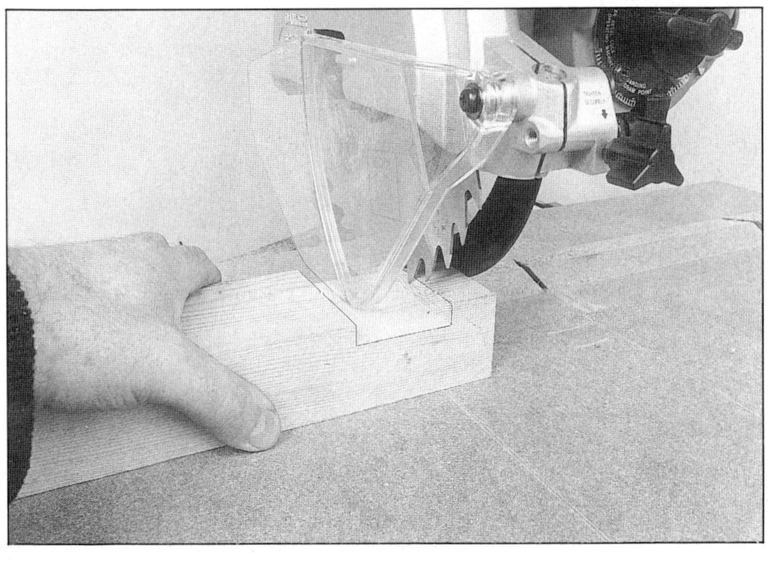

Joint cutting

This is where the radial arm saw comes into its own (Fig 12.23). By setting up 'stops' using battens clamped or pinned on to the table, repeat cuts can be achieved. Tenons can be quickly cut by setting the depth in two stages, using the same batten stop (Fig 12.24). Halving joints are cut in the same way.

Housing joints can be cut by marking the wood. I prefer to draw square lines across the wood and work to the line rather than rely on the accuracy of the tool. I say this because there is a small amount of give in the sliding action of the machine head in

Fig 12.21 The author's method of quick stock removal.

Fig 12.22 A set of dado cutters – but spot the mistake!

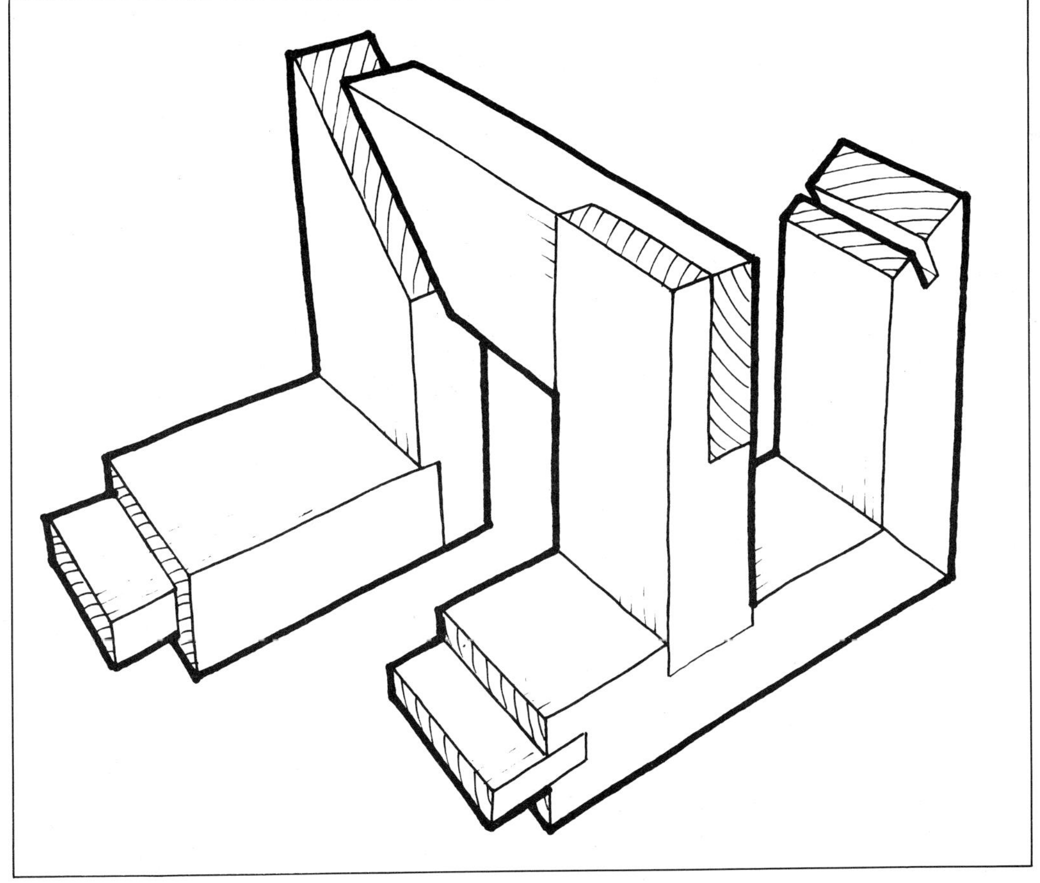

Fig 12.23 Joints which can be made on the radial arm saw.

Fig 12.24 Shoulder lines on tenons cut accurately against a clamped batten.

Fig 12.25 Saw-kerfing – achieves the bend but takes the strength out of the wood.

Fig 12.26 The JKB rout-kerf joint.

the arm which you can use to advantage by guiding the blade to a line on the wood. In all woodworking, the golden rule I observe is to work to a line, and leave the line on.

Saw-kerfing

Saw-kerfing is a novel method for achieving bends in wood (Fig 12.25). The only problem is the wood loses its strength as the fibres are cut through to all but a millimetre or two! (It is a useful method when the strength is *put back* into the timber, as in the rout-kerf joint (Fig 12.26) described in *'The Incredible Router'*.)

Saw-kerfing on the radial arm saw is in effect deep-groove cutting. The saw blade is set to depth and a couple of marks set on the fence to give equi-spacing of the saw-kerfs. The practised woodworker can saw-kerf quite rapidly (Fig 12.27).

Cutting a circle

A novel idea whereby the work is fixed, the machine head fixed, and the saw arm swung at the column a full 180°, resulting in a semicircle cut (Fig 12.28).

Routing

The Ryobi radial arm saw has a geared-up end-spindle (18000rpm) with a collett on the end which takes a ¼in shank diameter router cutter (Fig 12.29). This transforms the radial arm saw into an overhead router, hence opening up a whole new dimension to the tool. Now this is very useful (see Chapter 7, The Router), as the motor head can be pulled across the wood, as in the crosscutting mode, or fixed with the wood fed into it, as in the ripping mode.

The cutter can be 'buried' in the fence, similar to a spindle moulder (Fig 12.30), and with differ-

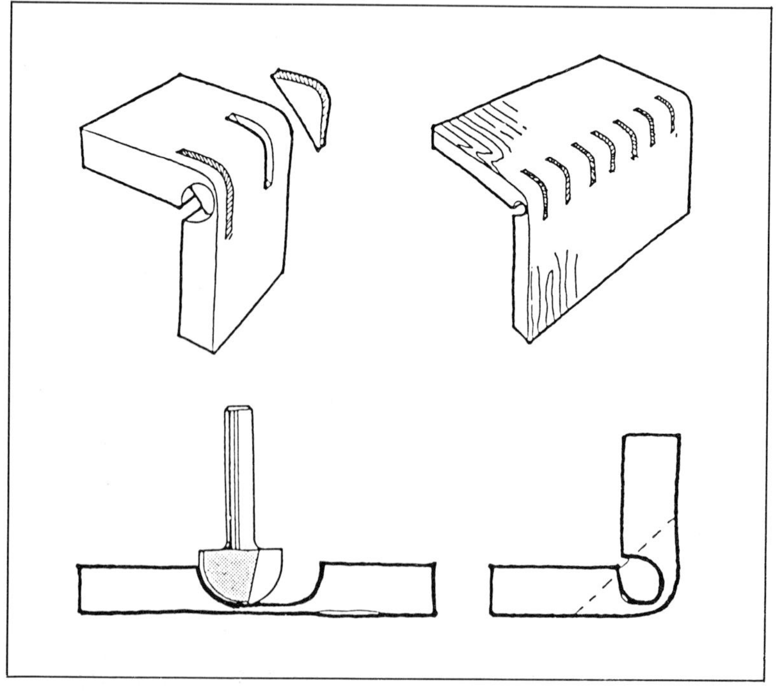

Fig 12.27 Saw-kerfing is in effect deep-grooving across the grain.

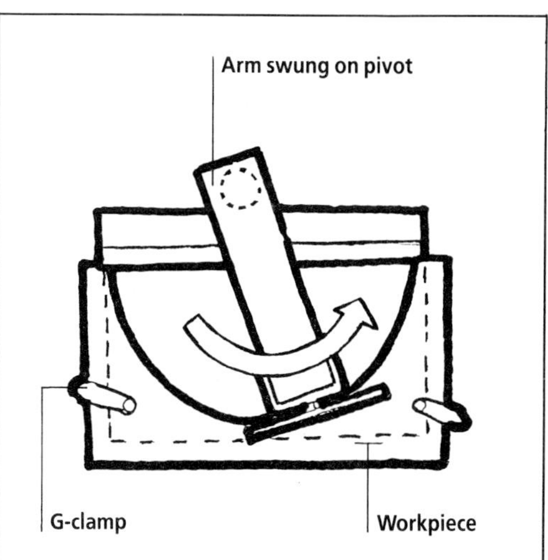

Fig 12.28 Cutting a circle on the radial arm saw.

ently profiled cutters various edge or groove features can be achieved.

A useful method for making a mitred box is to set up a wide-diameter straight cutter at a 45° angle in the machine head and lower it to all but a millimetre or so of the thickness of the material. Then mark the positions on the wood and draw the cutter across. If tape is stuck to the underside of the wood at the position of the cut it will give fibre support. The open joint is glued and the wood carefully lifted so the two mitres make a right-angle joint (Fig 12.31).

JIGS

Perhaps the most useful jig is the clamped batten which acts as a 'stop' for repeat cutting (see Joint

Fig 12.29 The 18000rpm spindle on the Ryobi for routing – opening up a whole new world.

cutting). The fence and table can be easily pencil marked for cutting locations, and jigs or battens hot-melt glued or pinned.

Not so much a 'jig', but certainly a jigging operation, is batch cutting whereby identical components to be sawn are taped together with masking tape and cut as one piece (see Chapter 23, Grid Table). (An early design of mine – the 'Metre Square' table in reclaimed church-pew pitch pine (© Jeremy Broun, 1976) – involved numerous cross-halving joints cut on my DeWalt radial arm saw.)

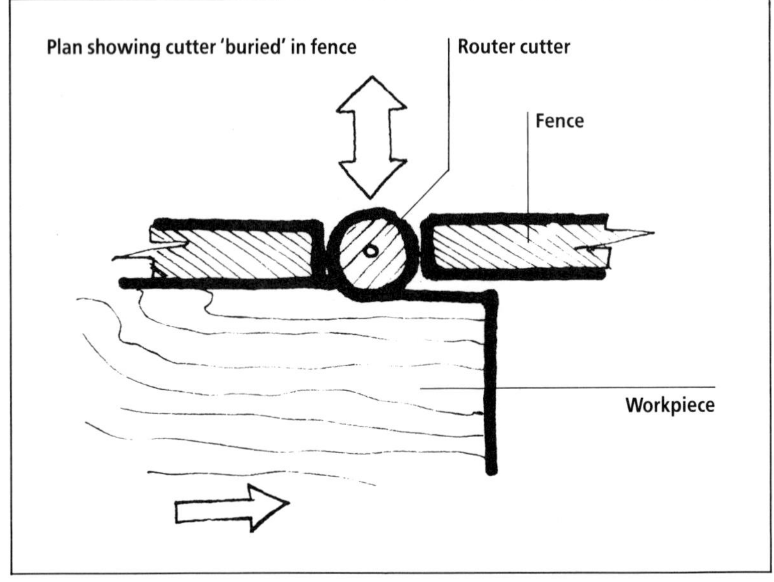

Fig 12.30 The cutter can be 'buried' in the fence.

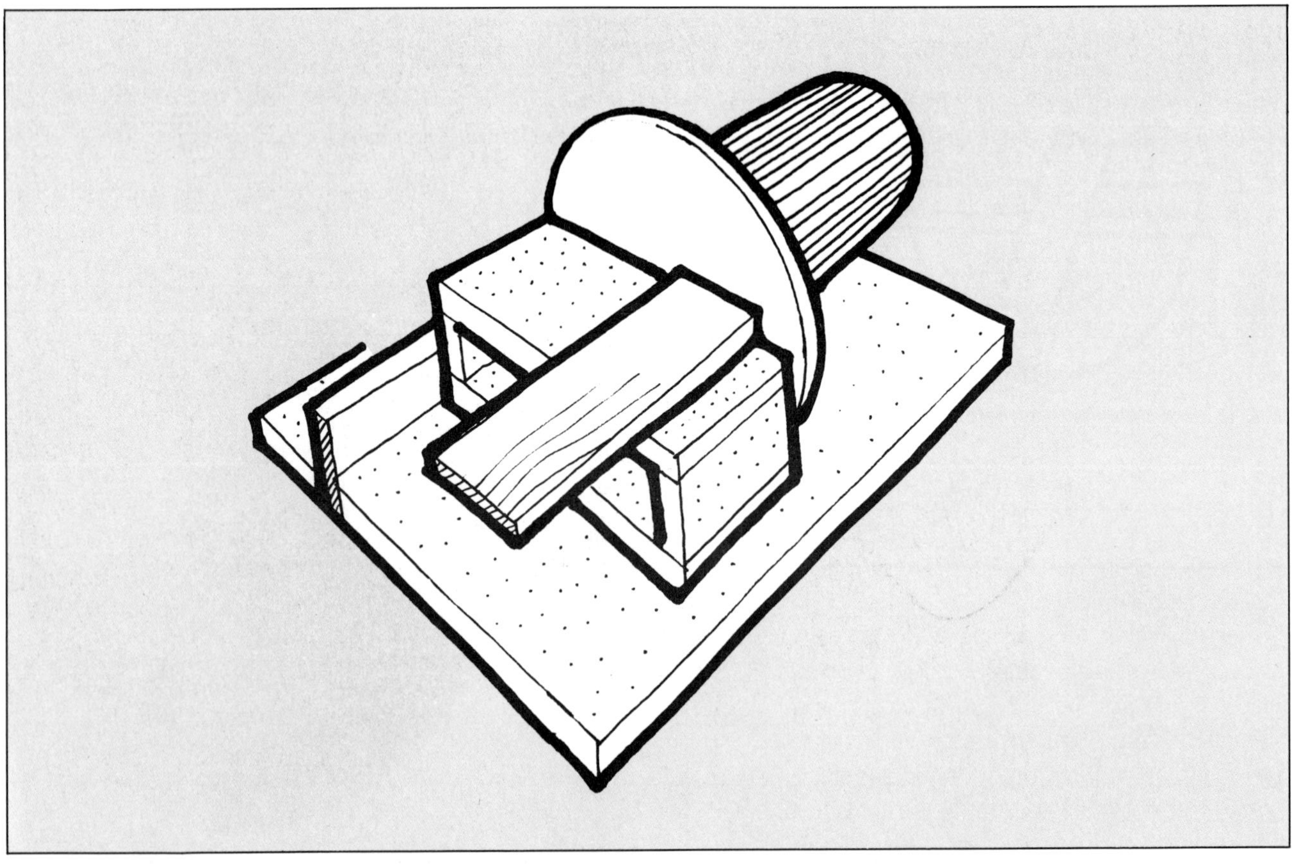

SANDING

The Ryobi radial arm saw accommodates a small diameter sanding drum on its saw blade spindle (see Fig 12.2) and the tool can be set up for free-hand or fixed sanding against the table and fence.

Disc sanding

It is possible to make up a large diameter disc (from MDF) and a purpose-built table and use the radial arm saw as an accurate disc sander (Fig 12.32).

Altogether the radial arm saw is an extremely useful and versatile tool, with a speed and easiness of use which gives it much appeal to the woodworker. It is an electric tool vital to my own needs. Once deemed not accurate enough for cabinet-makers, it has certainly earned its place in my workshop, being my very first machine and capable of achieving creative and precise results to the present day.

Fig 12.32 Shop-made disc sander and table.

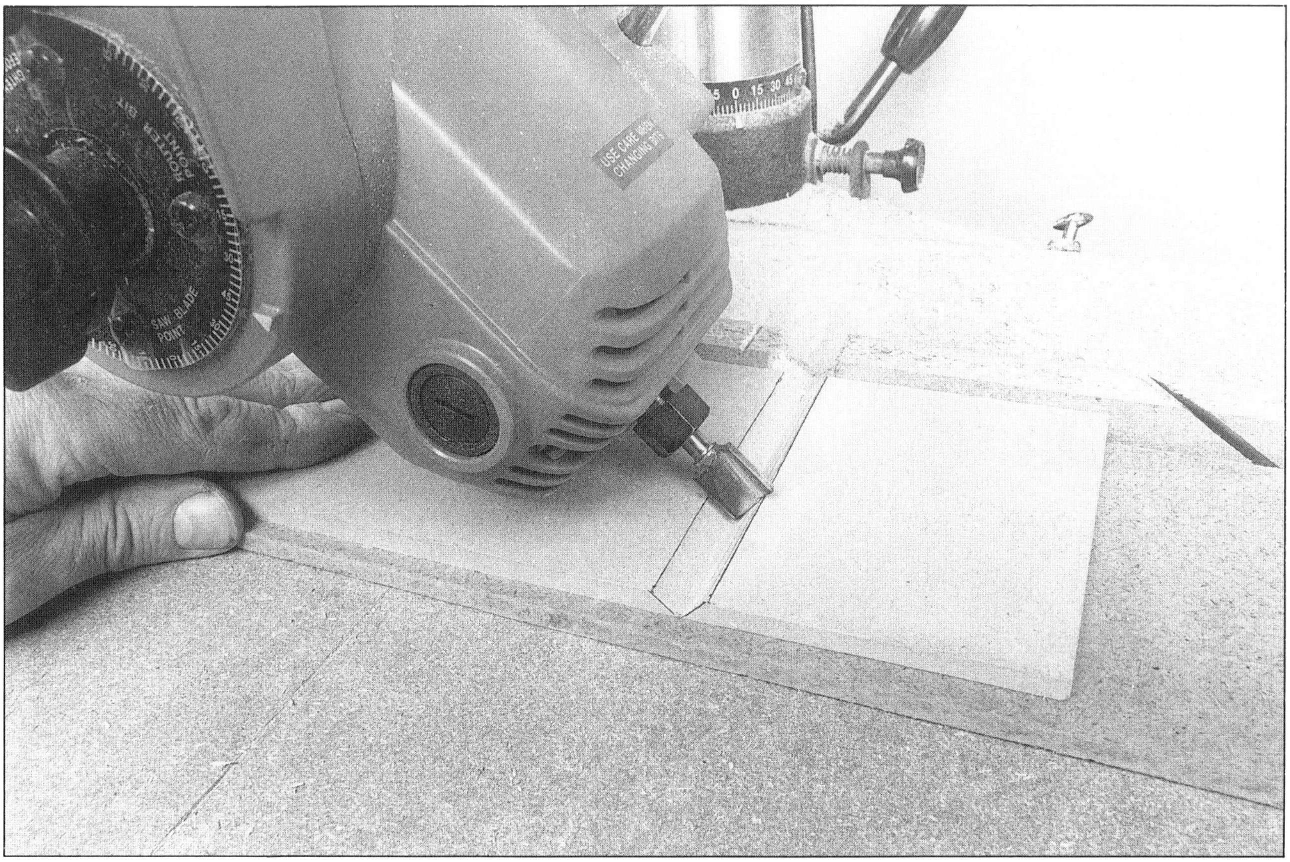

Fig 12.31 V-grooving on the radial arm saw to create mitre joints.

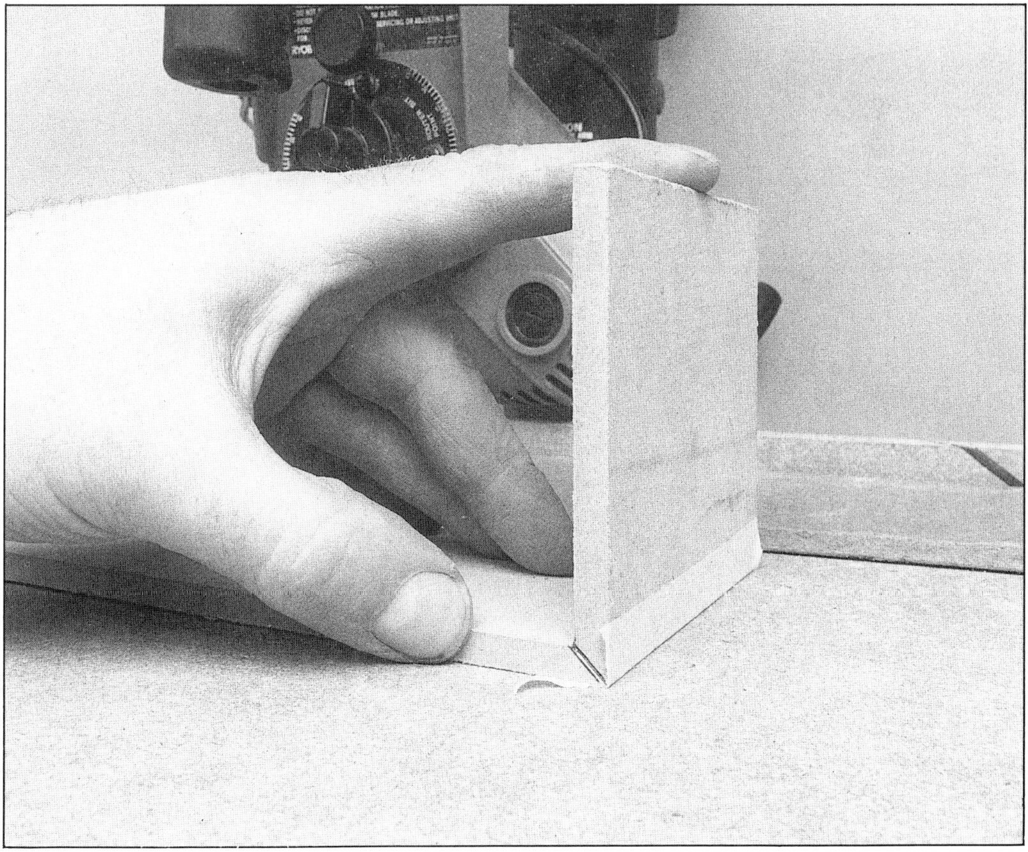

13
THE GLUE GUN

The hot-melt glue gun is perhaps the most underrated electric woodworking tool of all. Underrated because it is seldom perceived beyond its obvious function – to bond wood together! This it does with relatively limited success, but its very limitation becomes its greatest strength in my opinion, for at its most creative the glue gun is *an extra pair of hands*. Regarded as such, it has unlimited potential for the solo woodworker.

The glue gun made its début several years ago, and I suspect that the difficulty encountered when trying to obtain glue sticks from time to time indicates that its popularity is somewhat spasmodic, but more recently it has been enjoying a revival of interest.

It is a simple device. A steel-cased electric element within its body heats up a cylindrical thermoplastic stick (11mm diameter), and by pushing the stick through manually (Fig 13.1), or operating a trigger on the more expensive versions (Fig 13.2), a controlled flow of glue results. It is in effect an instant glue as it sets on rapid cooling, and 2 pieces of wood brought into contact in this way create a bond within a few seconds.

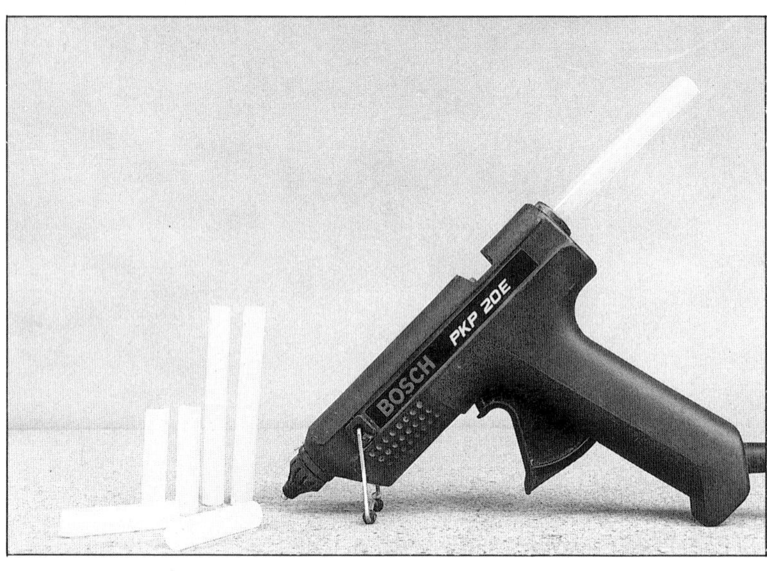

Fig 13.2 The Bosch trigger glue gun with an assortment of 11mm glue sticks.

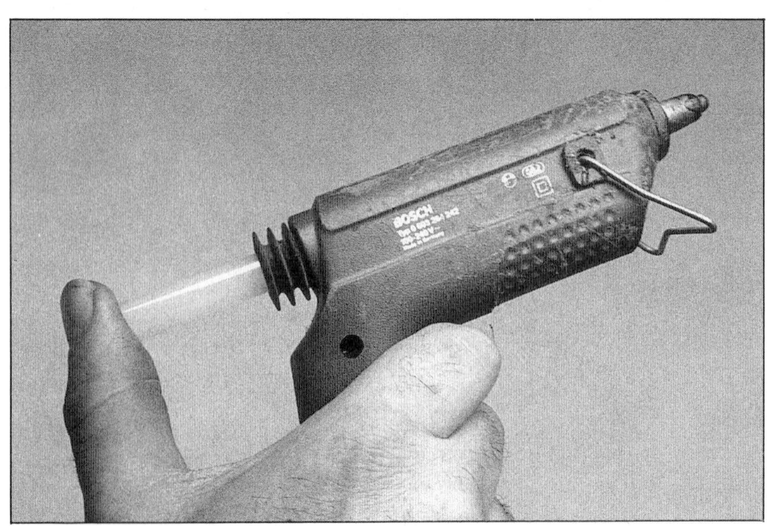

Fig 13.1 A triggerless Bosch hot-melt glue gun – the stick is pushed through manually.

Glue guns are either mains operated or cordless. The glue sticks are in different colours for different materials – clear sticks are generally designated for wood. The sticks are not exactly cheap, in fact whereas I wouldn't dream of robbing a bank, I might be tempted to raid a glue-stick factory! But, glue sticks apart, the value of the glue gun is in what it can do. It is a multi-purpose bonding device and probably more at home in the conventional sense in upholstery workshops and with other soft-materials applications. However, I would not be without one in a wood workshop as it is the unconventional applications which are of greatest value.

SAFETY

No doubt the glue gun is associated with a few horror stories, but then it is possible to drown in a cupful of water. I have only once resorted to the habit of wiping excess glue off the work with my finger (which one naturally does without thinking when using normal glues). The glue is not only extremely hot but it also sticks (!). It is also very unpleasant, giving a nasty burn which immediately takes off the skin.

When using the glue gun fingers and flesh should be kept well away from the tiny nozzle and the excess glue from the joint should not be touched for at least one minute after bonding. In the case of a burn the manufacturers of glue sticks recommend that the skin is immediately immersed in water (as with any burn). My proviso is to take care in an electric workshop where there is access to water as water and electricity are very good friends! The glue gun should not be left switched on for hours on end as there is the risk of it burning out.

Fig 13.4 The hot-melt glue method leaves a thick and unsightly glue line – not acceptable in cabinetmaking.

OPERATION

It takes five minutes or so for the glue gun to heat up after being switched on. Then it is ready for use with a glue stick inserted.

With triggerless glue guns you can only use the short glue sticks which you push through the gun with your thumb. The long sticks are just too awkward, although obviously they last longer. As the glue stick is spent and begins to disappear into the gun a new stick can be welded on to its end, making sure it is flush and in line (Fig 13.3).

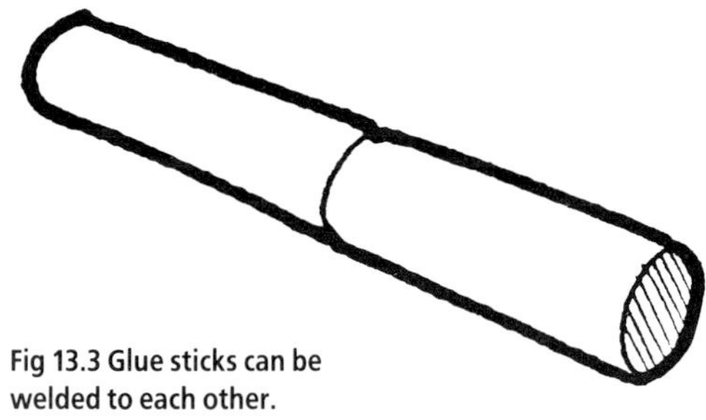

Fig 13.3 Glue sticks can be welded to each other.

Successful wood gluing relies largely on fibre penetration and there are no wood glues which can rival PVA, casein and urea formaldehyde glues (Resin W, Cascamite and Aerolite), and the more recent epoxy glues used primarily in boatbuilding (from SP Systems). The glue gun may heat the glue sufficiently to result in high viscosity as it comes out of the gun, but it is immediately cooled on contact with the cold and large surface of the wood. The glue therefore does not penetrate (or at least not very far). Considering this, it is surprisingly strong as a bonding agent, although subsequent shrinkage and moisture loss in the timber can reduce its bond over a period of years.

APPLICATIONS

In this respect using a glue gun for conventional wood bonding is a case of 'horses for courses'. I would not recommend it for cabinet work, not least because the glue line is highly visible because it is so thick (Fig 13.4). But it can be used as a general-purpose quick-bonding method, and it is surprisingly strong, although I would prefer to describe its characteristics as temporary rather than permanent. Occasionally it can be used as a 'first aid' measure (Fig 13.5) when re-gluing or repairing small damaged pieces in the wood, but here again the glue line can show, and it really

Fig 13.5 Everyone makes mistakes, but this one was easily remedied with a glue gun!

Fig 13.6 The glue has to be applied hot and quick.

Fig 13.7 Long contact surfaces are tricky because the glue will have dried before the end is reached.

Fig 13.8 Glue 'tacking' quickly covers the entire length.

needs swift but strong clamping pressure (to reduce the glue film).

One tip for dealing with this problem is to warm the pieces to be bonded with a hair dryer or hot air gun. After all, in traditional Scotch glue jointing, where the glue also cools rapidly, the pieces are ideally warmed (not heated) beforehand.

So, obviously when using a glue gun you have to be very quick after applying the glue, and this is not so much a problem with small section bonds (Fig 13.6). If you wish to bond the long edge of a piece of manufactured board, however, by the time you have laid all the glue down the first run will have cooled completely before the pieces make contact (Fig 13.7). In this case it may be better to use it as a glue 'tacker', applying blobs at intervals of a few inches (Fig 13.8). When glue has prematurely cooled you will be surprised at how easily it can be peeled off (which tends to underline my point about its suitability for quality cabinetmaking).

AN EXTRA PAIR OF HANDS

The glue gun really comes into its own as a temporary tacking agent. By controlled cooling (applying a 'blob' on one surface, then letting it cool before the other piece is joined) the fibre penetration is reduced and therefore the bond will be limited.

It is particularly useful in some routing operations when a conventional holding device such as a vice or G-clamp would get in the way of the router fence. Three or 4 glue blobs on the bench, left to cool for a few seconds before the work is pressed down on to them, make subsequent removal relatively easy (Fig 13.9). It takes a little practice but the grain should be left intact without tearing and the residue of glue cleanly chiselled off (or melted with an iron and brown paper).

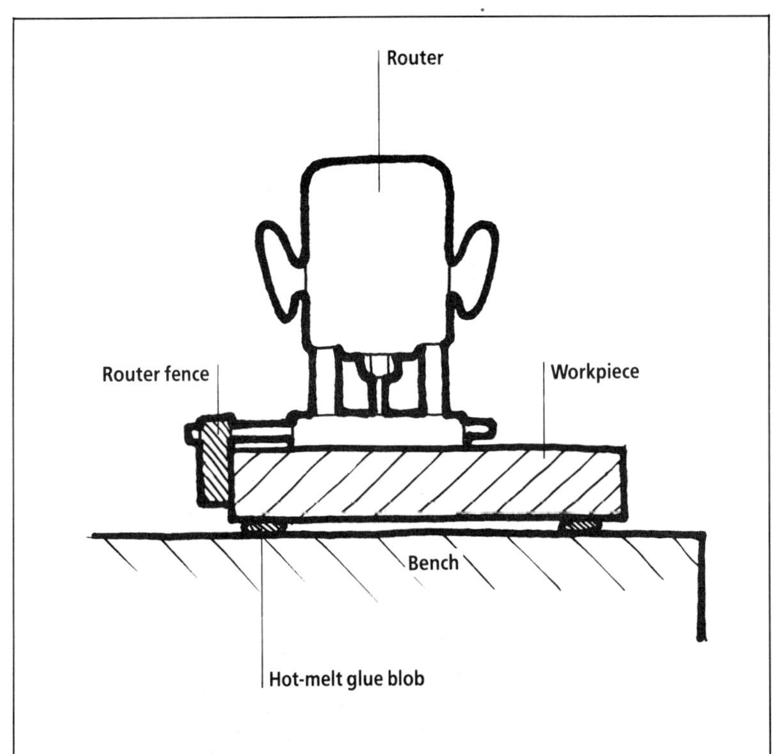

Fig 13.9 Section through workpiece mounting for routing operations.

As an example of its usefulness as an extra pair of hands, I could not have made a multi-angled sunroom at all without the glue gun as there was no one else around to assist me. This complex angled structure of fairly lengthy sections of 4in × 2in softwood is an excellent example of a 'marriage of methods'. Firstly, the framework was erected in 2 or 3 days. The construction relies on butt-joints and halving-joints reinforced with epoxy glue (from SP Systems, see page 273) and 6in nails.

Some of the members were partially tacked with the glue gun (the bulk of the sectional surface coated with a thixotropic epoxy glue). This gave an instant alignment of the pieces which were then immediately reinforced with the 6in nails (Fig 13.10). The glue-gun bond served purely as an extra pair of hands in *locating* the members, and played no part in the strength of the structure.

Half a dozen glue sticks at the most were used for the entire framework.

Long nail
Epoxy glue
Hot-melt glue blobs

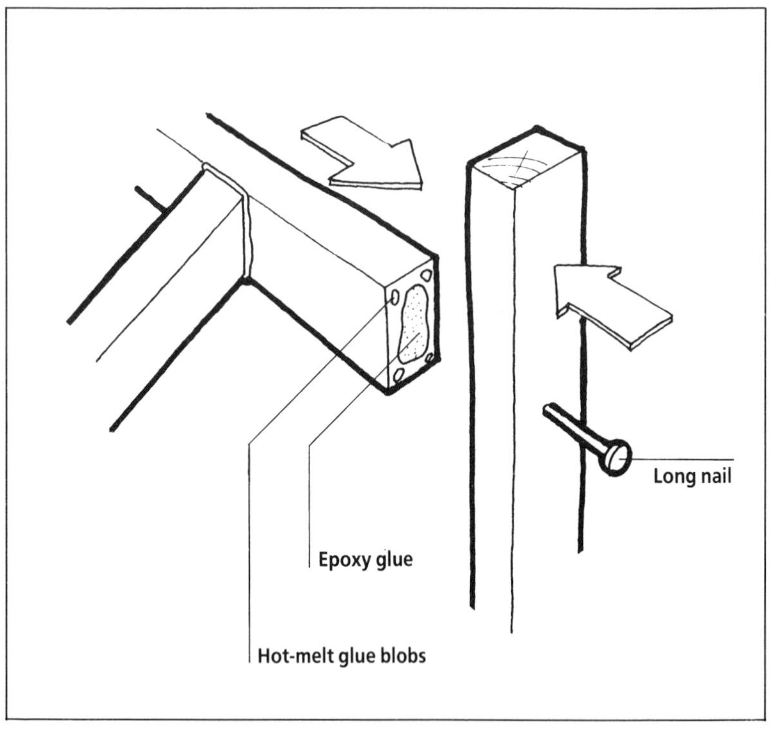

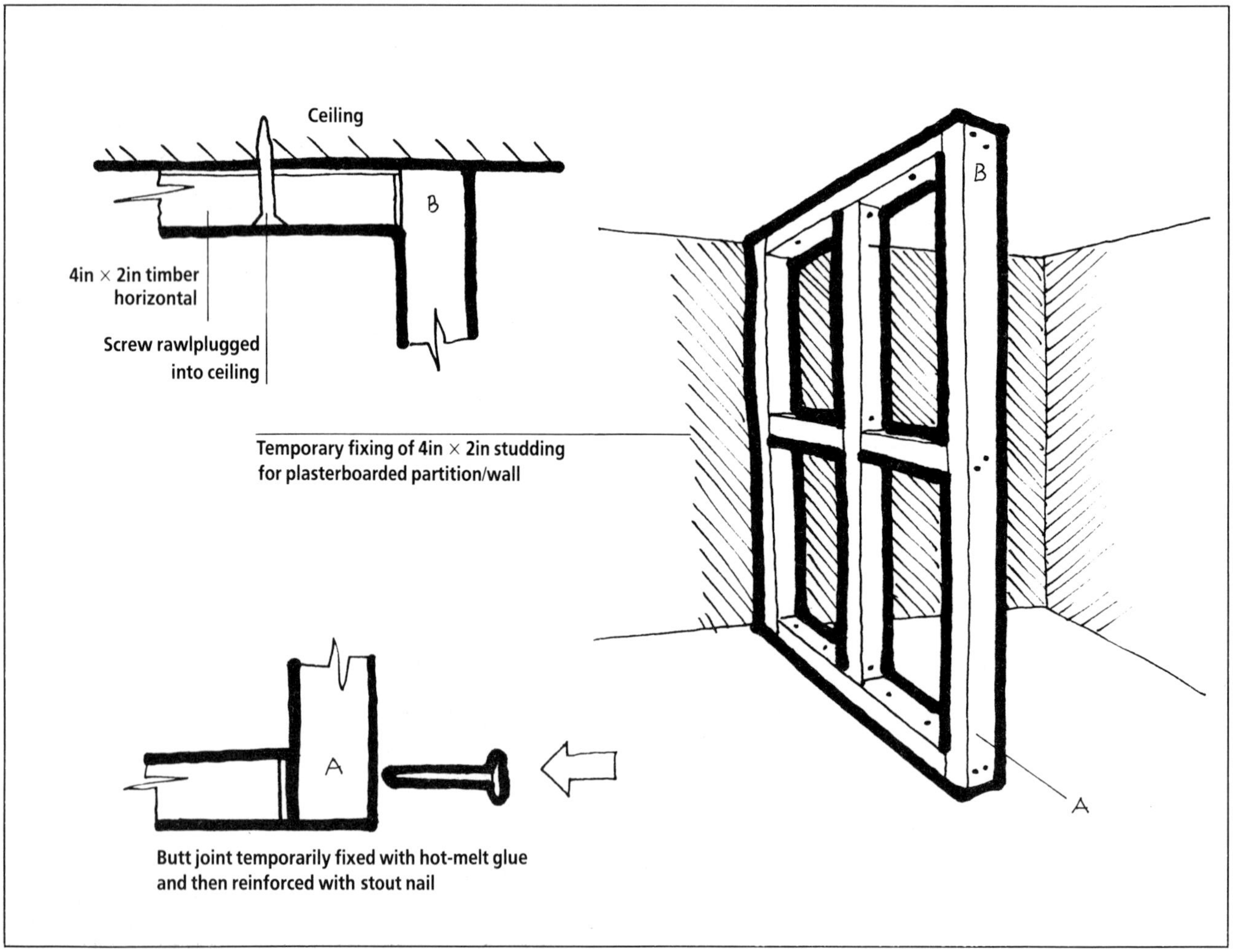

Ceiling
B
4in × 2in timber horizontal
Screw rawlplugged into ceiling
Temporary fixing of 4in × 2in studding for plasterboarded partition/wall
B
A
A
Butt joint temporarily fixed with hot-melt glue and then reinforced with stout nail

QUICK-BUILD STRUCTURES

The sunroom was of course an outdoor structure. I have made other internal studded structures using the glue gun as a quick-build aid followed by re-inforcement with long nails and screws as appropriate (Fig 13.11). A particularly useful application is a framework which attaches to the ceiling. Members can then be Rawlplugged and screwed to give a more permanent fixing after tacking with the glue gun.

Pine panelling can be attached to wall battens with the glue gun in situations where panel pins cannot be easily used. I would be hesitant to vouch for the long-term effectiveness of this method as the glue join restricts tongue-and-groove 'matchboard' from expanding and contracting. Apart from this the cost in glue sticks would be substantial.

Another useful application is in making beads around the back of a piece of mirror glass in its wood rebate (see Chapter 24, Picture Frame). It is not only neat and easy to flow the glue along the rebate where the back of the glass sits in the wood, but it is relatively easy to remove the glue bead if the glass should need replacing (Fig 13.12).

When designing chairs I find the glue gun invaluable for making quick mock-ups which help establish the angles and measurements of the seat and back from which the aesthetics evolve.

The glue gun can be used for 'split-turning' on the lathe where a temporary join is required (Fig 13.13) (see Chapter 10, The Lathe) and numerous other creative applications, which rely on one thing – the imagination of the woodworker!

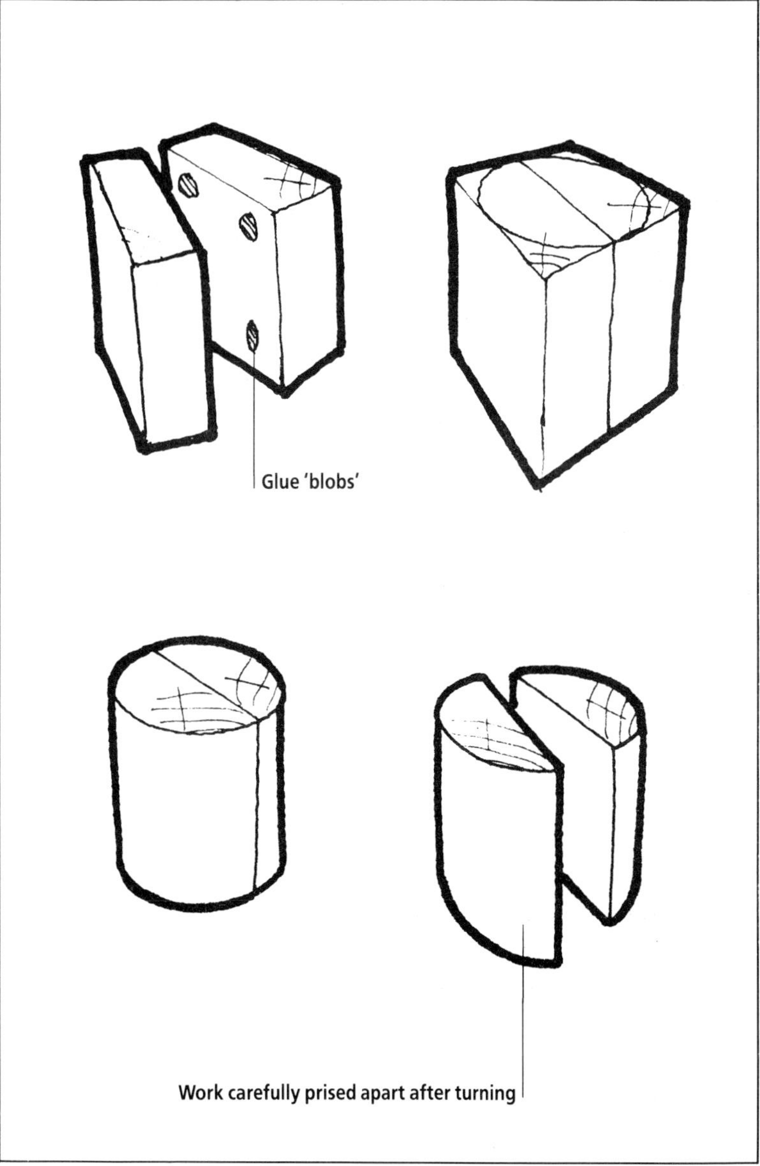

Fig 13.13 The glue gun can be used for 'split turning'.

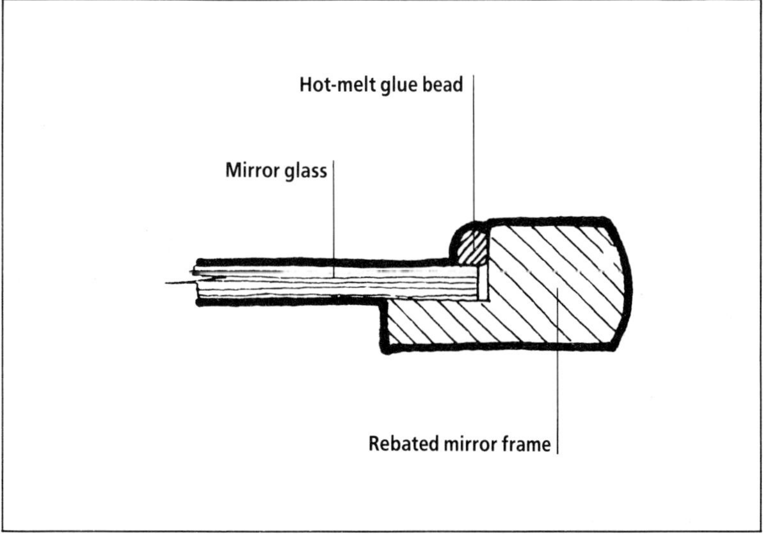

Fig 13.12 Beading a mirror glass into its rebate with hot-melt glue.

Fig 13.10 Joint detail of author's sunroom showing use of the glue gun (opposite above).

Fig 13.11 The glue gun can help erect a timber-studded partition (opposite below).

14
THE POWER SANDER

It takes almost as long to finish a piece of woodwork as it does to make it! It is the hidden operation. By 'finish' I mean the cleaning up of the piece as a final preparation for a polish or 'finish' to be subsequently applied.

It means the removal of superfluous marks caused by planing or sawing, pencil marks, hand grime, tiny blemishes etc. The most obvious signature to a piece of work that is unfinished is a scratch across the grain, and how easy it is to think that even the most minute scratch will be filled in or obliterated when the varnish is applied. No such luck – it often highlights the imperfection when it becomes shiny. So it is necessary to perfect the surface by a process of sanding – using an abrasive paper.

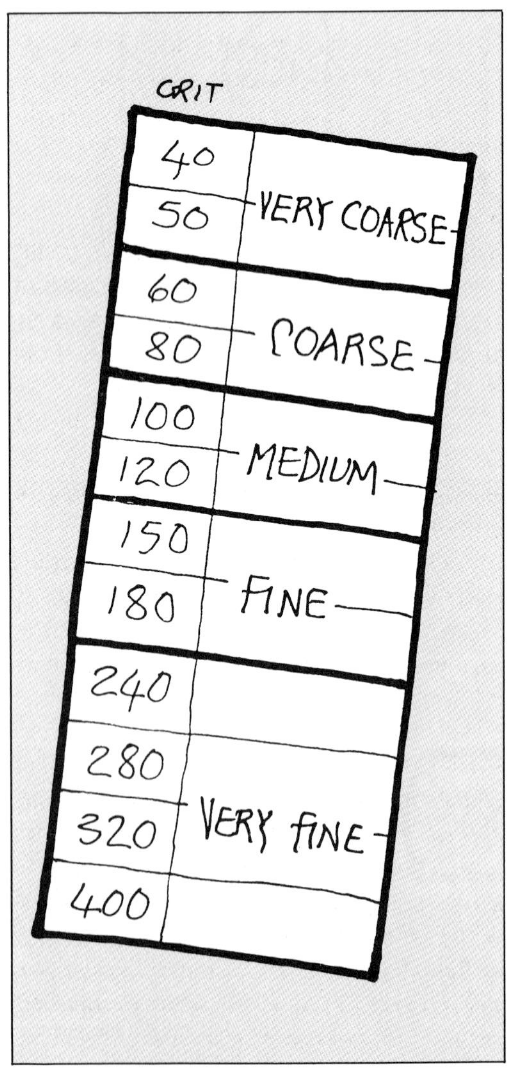

Fig 14.1 Abrasive grits.

Before the advent of electric woodworking all sanding operations were done laboriously by hand. The chair has been made, even sat upon and tested, but it is not completed until this ritual has been performed! We tend to be obsessed with finish. The early television sets in their real sapele veneer were highly glazed, not finished! The slightest scratch on a contemporary piece of furniture is seen to be the mark of the amateur, the yardstick by which all else is judged.

Electric woodworking has made the task much easier. It has not replaced hand finishing completely as the tool does usually leave its mark, which has to be finally taken out by fine hand sanding with the grain. Electric sanders are abrading tools and they use a variety of graded (grit) abrasive papers which attach to the sole of the machine. Apart from flexible-backed disc-sander attachments which tend to scour the wood (and which are therefore not really relevant here), the orbital, belt and table disc sanders are the most important types of power sander and they use flat abrasive sheets, abrasive belts and abrasive discs respectively.

I shall deal with these types of sander here because each has its own unique characteristics, although if pressed for choice the orbital sander would narrowly take first place in my electric workshop (as a first tool). Having said that I cannot imagine being without a disc sander and in a sense a belt sander does the job of the other two! However, before I deal with these power sanders let us first consider the abrasive paper they use.

ABRASIVE PAPER

Popularly but incorrectly called 'sandpaper' (it is not made of sand), abrasive paper is normally supplied as glass paper, garnet paper, aluminium oxide paper or silicon carbide paper in various grits, and to confuse the issue further the belt sander uses a cloth-backed abrasive paper for extra strength and therefore is not paper at all!

Grits range from 50 to 600 (Fig 14.1) and for power sanding generally I use a coarse to medium grit (60–100).

As to the choice of abrasive papers, glass paper loses its bite very quickly and is clearly a DIY choice, not that of the serious woodworker. Garnet paper (a stone) is tougher, but more expensive. Silicon carbide paper is often referred to as 'wet and dry', and although intended for metal abrading is excellent for woodfinishing used dry in its finer grades (400 grit). An excellent finishing paper of this type which I tend to use is Lubrasil paper (400 grit).

The most efficient and cost-effective for general sanding operations is aluminium oxide paper as it retains its 'bite' longest. It is available in full-size sheets (11in × 9in), and 100mm wide rolls from which you can cut the required sheet size for the sander (⅓ or ½), though this applies only to orbital sanders as belt sanders have their own purpose-made sanding belts. I always purchase either complete 100mm rolls or lengths from the roll as it is by far the cheapest method, and sanding is a material-consuming business! Varying diameter abrasive discs are available for manufacturers' models (e.g. Wolfcraft) and it is possible with care (I have been doing it for years) to make up a large disc out of 100mm sheets laid side by side on a shop-made disc sander (Fig 14.2).

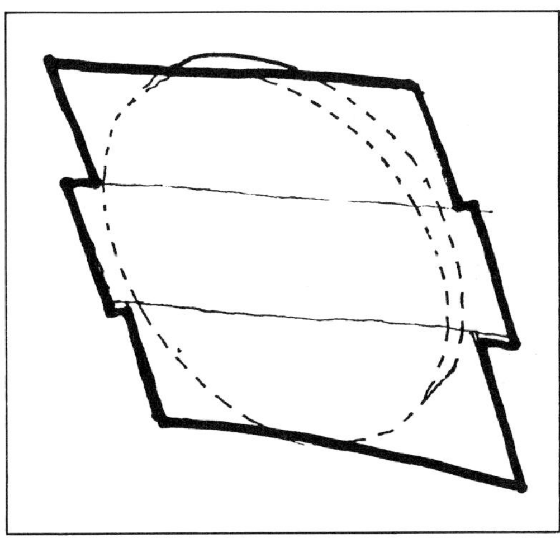

Fig 14.2 Large discs made up from 100mm abrasive roll using an impact adhesive.

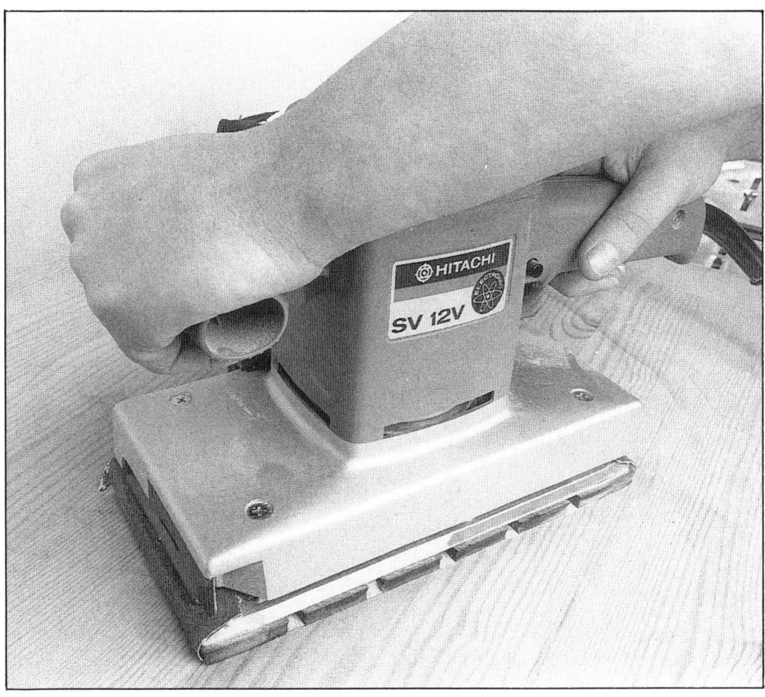

Fig 14.3 The orbital sander has a gentle, efficient action.

Of course all these abrasive papers can be used by hand (with a hand block), and indeed this is necessary to take out the tiny circular marks left by the orbital sander.

ORBITAL SANDER

The orbital sander is so-named because of the high-speed circular motion of its abrading action (Fig 14.3). An electric motor with its spindle eccentrically driving a baseplate causes the plate to 'vibrate' in a continuous tight elliptical motion. An abrasive sheet is stretched and clamped across the felt- or rubber-lined sole of the baseplate and when the tool is operated a series of minute circular abrading actions results.

The weight of the machine is sufficient pressure for the abrading action and it should not be unduly pressed down (Fig 14.4). The tool is kept on the move in any direction. It does not have to faithfully follow the grain of the wood.

Specification

Orbital sanders are generally ⅓ or ½ sheet size. They are very easy to use – indeed, I even find they have a therapeutic quality! By gently stroking the wood the high-speed buzz and vibration of the machine can be quite mesmerizing!

The rate of sanding is specified in orbits per minute (20000–25000), generally the higher the better. Variable-speed sanders are useful for a

Fig 14.4 Very little downward pressure should be used – the weight of the machine is virtually all that is needed.

Fig 14.5 The Makita palm sander achieves 14000 orbits per minute.

Fig 14.6 The palm sander is easy to use.

Fig 14.7 The palm sander is ideal for confined spaces.

variety of materials but in general a single high speed is quite appropriate for woodworking. Because of the rectangular shape of the sanding plate the orbital sander can be worked into tight corners, unlike the belt sander. It can also cope with slightly curved work.

I have a high regard for the orbital sander as it is no mean performer when loaded with a medium-to-coarse grit paper (60 grit) for what I call rough but fast sanding – it can remove a fair amount of wood. You then change papers and work through the grits to achieve a finer finish (100 grit) and then complete the task by hand with a Lubrasil paper (400 grit).

An important question is how do you know when the paper needs changing? Apart from the obvious signs of clogging (caused by resinous woods) it will just dull gradually. My philosophy is to change paper fairly frequently – you will notice the difference as the new paper has much more 'bite'. Rather than throw away half-spent papers I store them for hand-sanding operations, especially those which a power sander cannot easily achieve.

One point worth mentioning is that of all electric woodworking tools the power sander is probably used for the longest duration, perhaps several minutes continuously. It therefore pays to buy a good-quality 'industrial' model which can take the pace. When choosing any power sander make sure it has an integral dustbag.

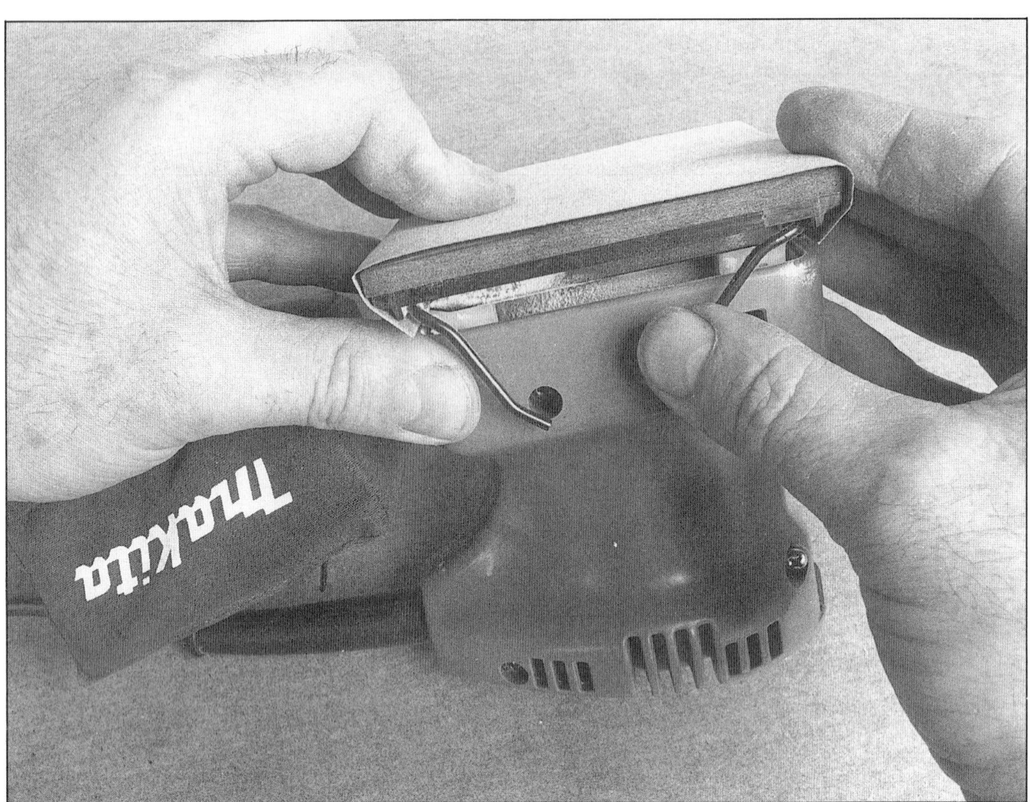

Fig 14.8 Attaching an abrasive sheet to the palm sander.

PALM SANDER

The smaller brother to the orbital but working on the same principle, the palm sander orbits at a higher rate (Figs 14.5 and 14.6). It is very comfortable and easy to use and particularly useful for confined spaces (Fig 14.7), and for final finishing with Lubrasil paper. When changing abrasive sheets the new paper is pressed firmly around the rubber-lined sole, and held down by the clips (Fig 14.8) and the dust-escape holes punched in with the manufacturer's template (Fig 14.9).

Fig 14.9 The manufacturer's template punches holes through the abrasive sheet to match the dust-extraction ducts in the baseplate.

BELT SANDER

The belt sander is a fast and furious tool (Figs 14.10 and 14.11). It has a much greater appetite than an orbital sander and is a little more difficult to use. Instead of abrading in a circular motion its sanding belt gives a continuous linear abrading action (Fig 14.12), which is effective *across* the grain for fast results and *with* the grain for clean results, working up the grades of belts. Because of the 2 belt-suspending rollers the tool cannot sand right up to a corner, but the roller profile does offer flexibility for shaped work.

It can be inverted in a stand as a mini linisher (Fig 14.13) or indeed clamped upright on the bench with a table attached at 90° for edge-grain sanding.

The edge of the front roller can also be used (carefully) for freehand contour sanding (Figs 14.14 and 14.15).

The belt sander is available in either 75mm or 100mm models, referring to the belt width. The tool usually includes a detachable sanding frame (Fig 14.16) which is used for sanding large flat panels (Fig 14.17) and provides more accuracy and makes the tool easier to use. The belts are spring-loaded (Fig 14.18) and adjusted by a screw on some models (the Skil model automatically self-aligns).

Fig 14.10 The Skil 4in belt sander.

Fig 14.11 The Skil belt sander with dustbag, sanding frame and spare 100mm belts.

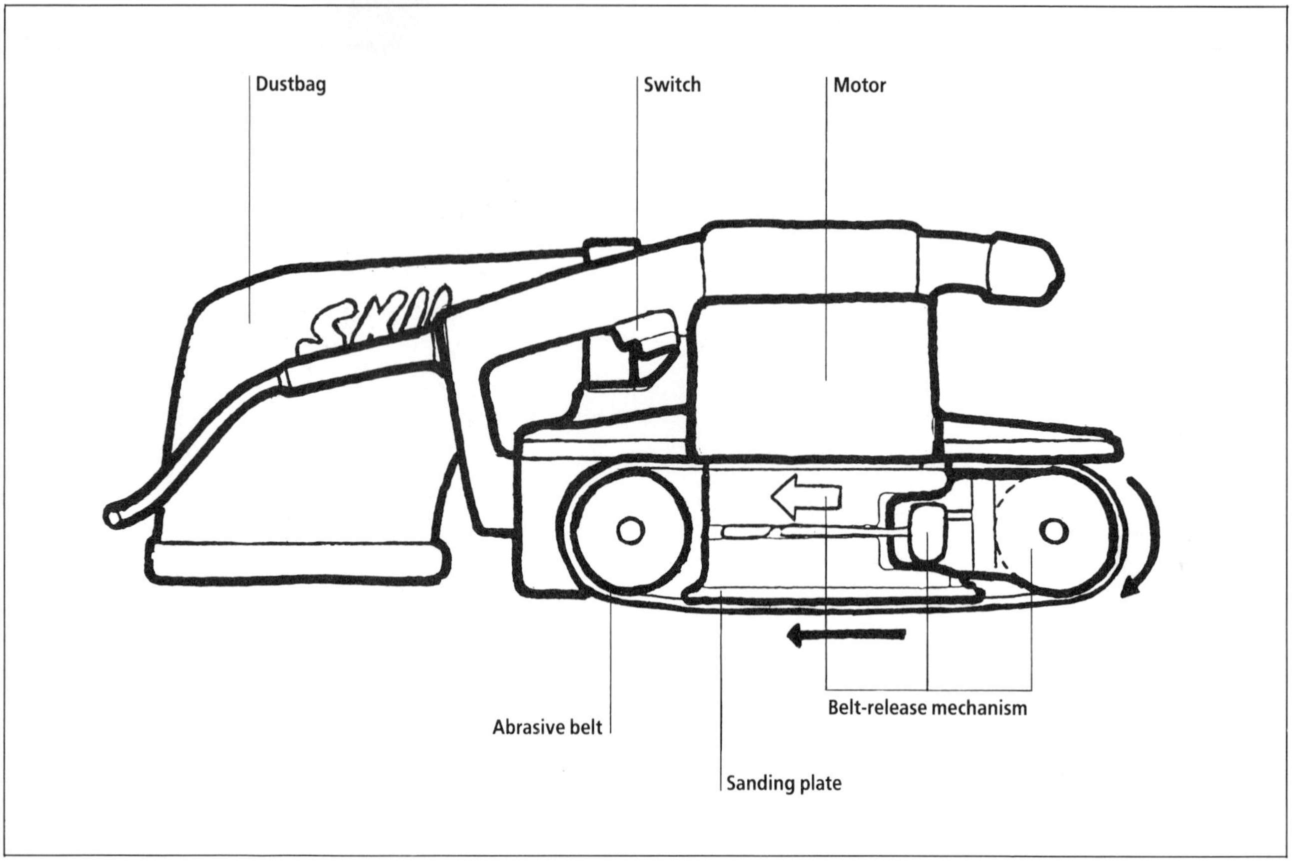
Dustbag
Switch
Motor
SKIL
Abrasive belt
Belt-release mechanism
Sanding plate

Fig 14.12 Section through a belt sander.

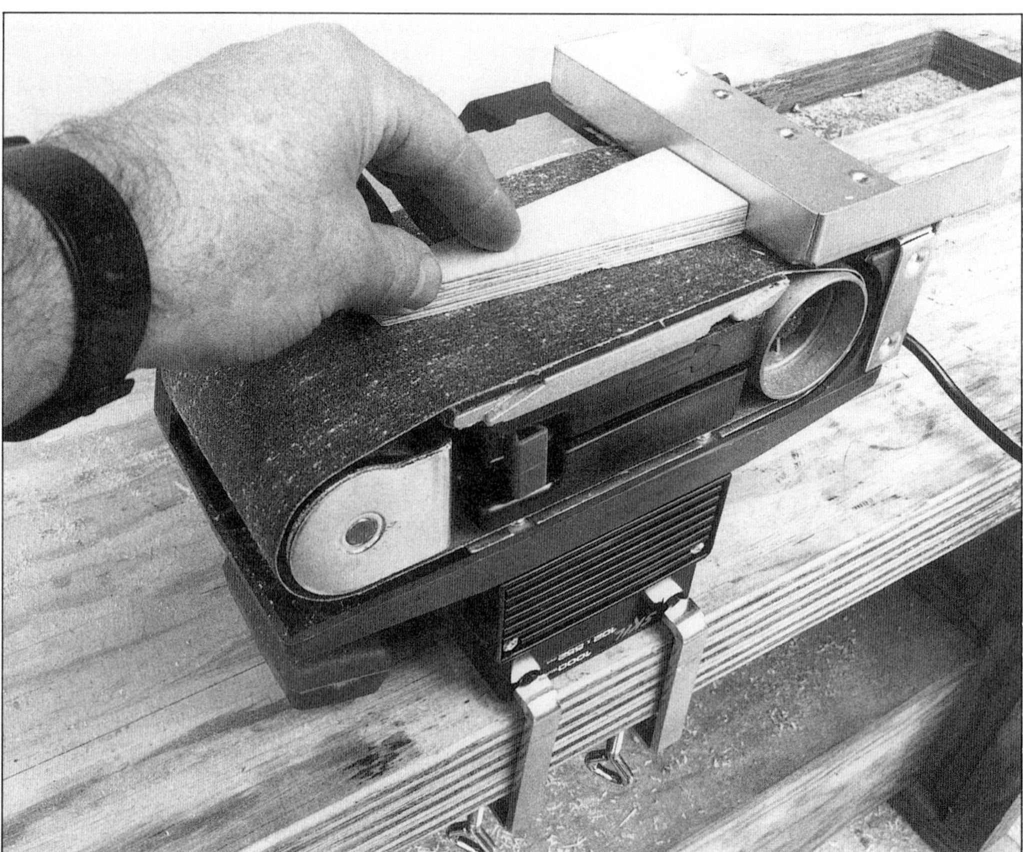

Fig 14.13 The belt sander is inverted to act as a linisher.

Fig 14.14 The belt sander can be used for contoured abrading.

Fig 14.15 Contoured abrading again.

Fig 14.16 The sanding frame is adjustable for height and includes dust brushes. It helps maintain flatness on large work.

Fig 14.17 The belt sander used with sanding frame on a carcase (see Chapter 29, Chest of Drawers).

Fig 14.18 Changing the belt is easy – a lever releases the roller tension and the belt slides out.

Fig 14.19 Awkward work can be supported when sanding flat.

The belt sander is an extremely useful and creative tool for flat and shaped work and in particular for cleaning up small and sometimes awkwardly shaped components (Fig 14.19) (See Chapter 28, Electric Lamp). It is an invaluable tool for any electric workshop, but in the hands of the unwary can produce disastrous results instantly. It is a good idea to practise on scrap wood first.

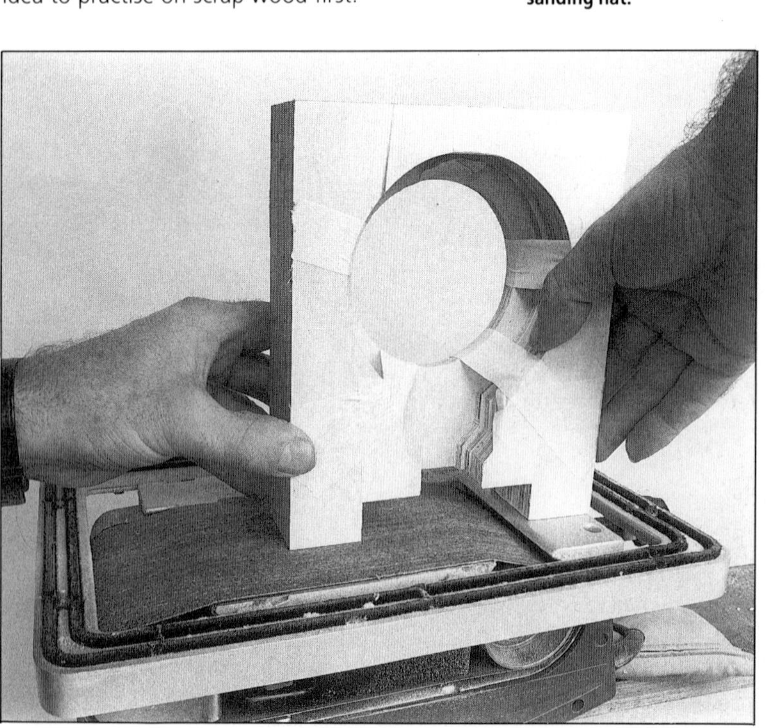

THE TABLE DISC SANDER

The table disc sander accurately sands flat work, or rather, applies accurate flats to the work. It is bench-mounted with a disc diameter of sensibly no less than 8in and the adjustable table and fence (Fig 14.20) act as a jig for angled sanding (see Fig 5.26). When I say that it will apply a 'flat' to the workpiece I mean that by rotating the wood or keeping the wood moving a curve can be achieved, i.e. for trimming large discs and indeed making wheels (Fig 14.22), or any shaped work. If you consider that you can shape the end of a large dowel into a pencil end, or indeed a round-nosed end (with skill), the disc sander is truly versatile.

Various manufacturers supply independent disc-sanding machines for electric drills. It is possible to shop-build your own, perhaps as an attachment to the lathe (Fig 14.23). The larger the disc diameter the better.

Where I rate table disc sanding highly is for edge-sanding, especially end-grain to a line (Fig 14.24).

Although the manufacturers' models include a fence I prefer to work to a marked line which leaves the sanding table free. This is because it is important to keep the work moving across the disc surface (Fig 14.25) to avoid heat build-up and clogging of the abrasive disc. Gentle pressure should be applied, and generally a coarser grit disc will clog less. The Wolfcraft attachment (see Chapter 5, The Drill) includes Velcro-backed abrasive

Fig 14.20 'Squaring' the end of a dowel on the Wolfcraft table disc sanding attachment.

Fig 14.21 Sanding accurate angles using the adjustable fence.

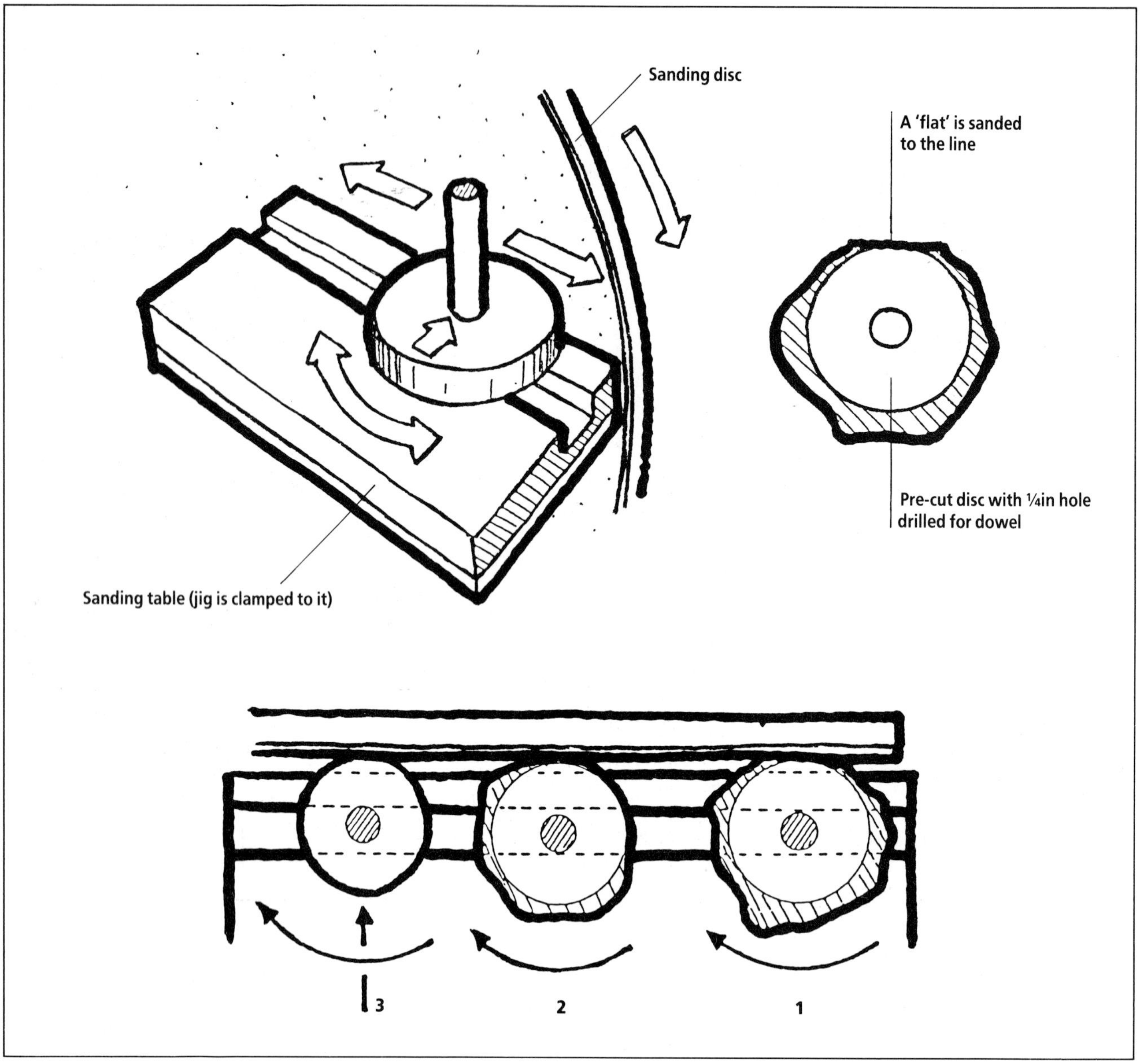
Sanding disc
A 'flat' is sanded to the line
Pre-cut disc with ¼in hole drilled for dowel
Sanding table (jig is clamped to it)
3
2
1

Fig 14.22 The JKB wheel-cutting jig (1971, courtesy *Woodworker*).

EVO-STI
IMPACT
ADHESIVE

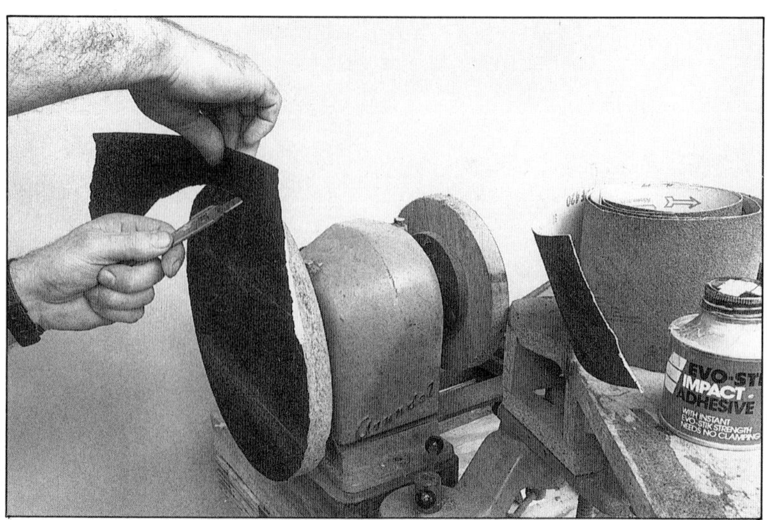

Fig 14.23 The author makes up his own abrasive discs from 100mm abrasive rolls on his shop-made table sander.

Fig 14.24 End-grain trimmed to a line on the table disc sander.

discs. Abrasive disc and belt cleaners are available which prolong the life of the belt or disc and increase efficiency.

DUST EXTRACTION

As much wood-shaping nowadays is done by abrading, it is essential that adequate dust extraction is provided. Most portable power sanders include integral dustbags, which are quite efficient. Dust gets everywhere so it makes sense to remove as much as possible at source.

Shop-made extractor hoods (Fig 14.26) which link up to a portable extractor unit can be inexpensively built using MDF and a glue gun and attached to table disc sanders and bench-mounted linishers.

It really is essential to extract dust, which is not only a workshop nuisance, but a fire hazard and health risk. When the sun shines through your workshop window even the smallest of airborne dust particles are made visible, which gives an indication of the problem. These particles remain airborne for several hours.

Fig 14.25 Keep the workpiece moving across the disc to minimize clogging.

6mm MDF

Hole to suit extractor hose

Fig 14.26 A shop-made extractor hood for a table disc sander.

15
THE ELECTRIC WORKSHOP

One of the obvious benefits of power tools is the opportunity they afford woodworkers to capitalize on the space – often limited – they have available to pursue their craft. As tools and machines have become smaller, the planning and setting up of a workshop have become attractive aspects of a craft where adaptability and flexibility are paramount.

There was a time when it would have been a major commitment to consider setting up a powered woodworking workshop. Machines used to weigh a ton, and took up acres of space on a suitable concrete floor. These machines would also need much operating space around them, and this would greatly affect the siting of workshops, which would also be more expensive to run – not least because of the heating bills.

Modern lightweight and compact power tools and machines have given a whole new dimension to both professional and amateur woodwork. Not only do they perform the same tasks as much larger and heavier machines have done in the past (some do much more), they also have the enormous advantage of being able to be moved into position, operated, then moved out of the way afterwards, maximizing on limited space.

In my early career as a woodwork teacher I usually inherited a complete mess of a workshop from the previous teacher and my priority was to totally reorganize it. It takes little imagination to realize that a stimulating, well-planned, orderly and attractive workshop fires the imagination for creative activity!

My very first workshop was a tiny converted cattle shed which was just large enough to accommodate a second-hand radial arm saw and a museum-piece bandsaw. I then spent the next 5 years in a very narrow underground workshop

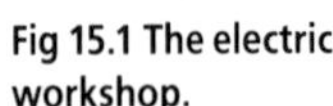

Fig 15.1 The electric workshop.

Fig 15.2 'Aladdin's cave'.

without natural light (I called it the smallest workshop in England)! But each workshop was a creative environment evolving around my particular needs – and one thing I certainly ought to know about is how to organize a small space (Fig 15.2)!

First you have to identify the problems or requirements:

- You have a potential work space or building of a certain size.
- Within the confines of its size and shape you wish to site various tools, machines, workbenches, storage facilities and sundries, with adequate room to move about and operate.
- The workshop needs to be insulated for noise and warmth.
- It needs to be wired up safely and efficiently with plenty of easily accessible power sockets.
- It should be well lit and it should include dust extraction for reasons of health and cleanliness (see Chapter 4).
- It should be warm enough to prevent tools rusting (it is surprising how little heat you require once you start woodworking).

Depending on the kind of work you are likely to be engaging in, your requirement for tools and equipment might include some or all of the following.

General requirements

- A solid workbench (free-standing or fixed – see Chapter 18, JKB Bench).
- An ancillary workbench such as a Workmate (Fig 15.3).
- A power tool workcentre such as a Triton (Fig 15.4(a)), or a combined bench and workcentre such as a Wolfcraft Pioneer (Fig 15.4(b)).
- A set of hand tools (see Chapter 19, Toolbox).
- A toolbox and/or racking system (see Chapters 19 and 25, Toolbox and Tool Rack).
- Various clamping/holding devices (Fig 15.5).
- Storage for ironmongery, glues, polishes etc. (Fig 15.6).
- Timber board storage.
- Manufactured board storage (Fig 15.7).
- Veneer storage (Fig 15.8).
- Offcuts storage (Fig 15.9).
- Special jigs.

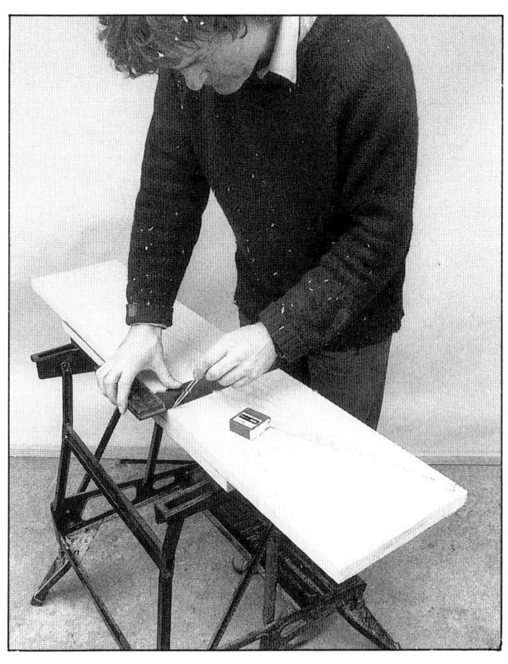

Fig 15.3 The Black & Decker Workmate – a superb device.

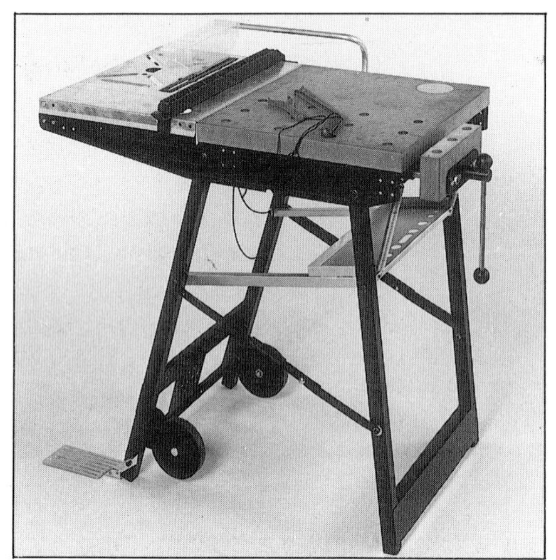

Fig 15.4 (a) The Triton power tool workcentre.

Fig 15.4 (b) The Wolfcraft Pioneer workcentre.

Fig 15.5 Clamping and holding devices.

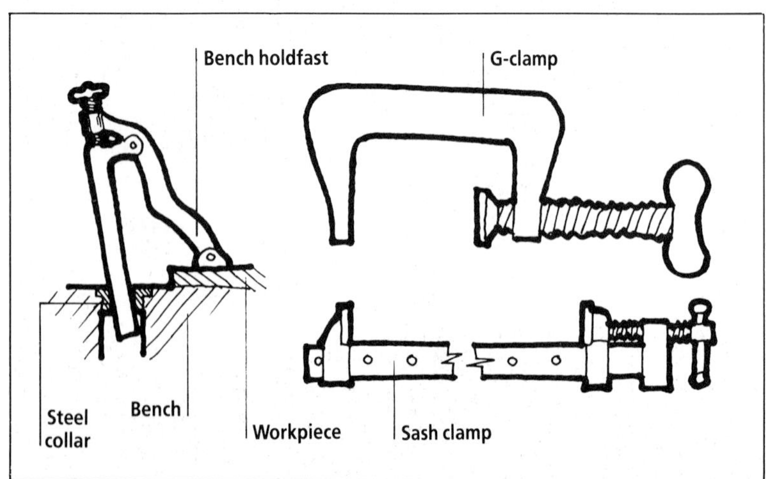

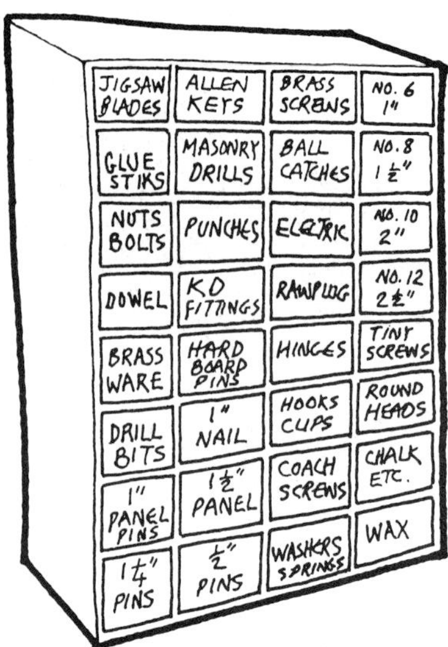

Fig 15.6 Storage and woodworking oddments.

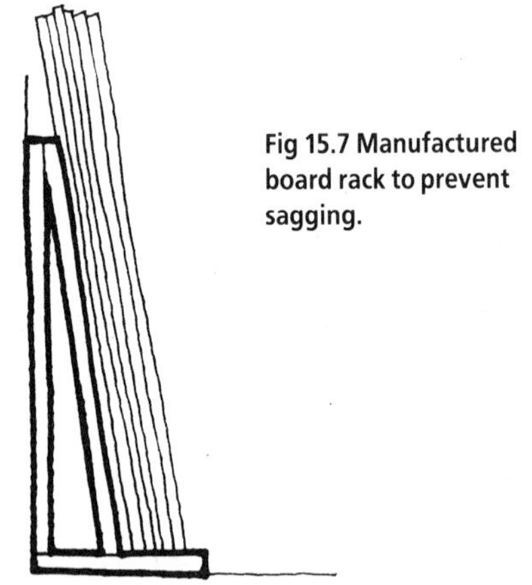

Fig 15.7 Manufactured board rack to prevent sagging.

Fig 15.8 A simple veneer hanging system.

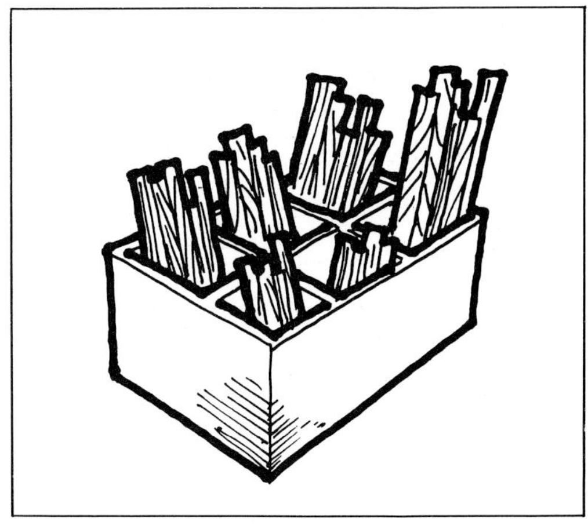

Fig 15.9 Offcuts storage.

Essential electric tools/machines

- Hand drills (one fixed in drillstand)
- Jigsaw
- Orbital sander
- Router
- Bandsaw
- Planer–thicknesser
- Portable dust extractor
- Grinder (or attachment)

Other desirable electric tools/machines

- Radial arm saw
- Lathe (with disc sander)
- Glue gun

Optional electric tools/machines

- Additional router(s)
- Belt sander
- Linisher
- Circular saw
- Biscuit jointer
- Palm sander
- Orbital disc sander
- Portable planer
- Chopsaw/pullover saw/mitre saw

THE IDEAL WORKSHOP

Of course your needs will change as you progress, but it is worth planning ahead a little. Every workshop will be different and will largely be dictated by what space is available and what you wish to fill it with and choose to do.

I know a prominent local woodturner who operates a Goliath 'ex-Industrial Revolution' lathe from a lean-to building more akin to a narrow corridor. In fact he leans against one wall while turning! (One of the joys of woodturnery is that it takes up surprisingly little space.) There are other stories of holes being knocked through walls to allow a long piece of turnery to extend through and be supported in the next room! Equally, in my previous shop/workshop I once had the planer–thicknesser sited diagonally to dress a long, laminated staircase member as it was fed through the window into the street outside! I do not recommend these practices, and obviously safety is paramount, but improvisation is often the order of the day.

Safety (see Chapter 4)

Apart from a safe working area, and one where you are not likely to trip over yourself or make accidental contact with tools and machines, it is essential that the floor is strong and sound, and there are no fire risks (a smoke detector and fire extinguisher should be installed). Electrics and dust extraction must also be dealt with properly.

Electrics and lighting

A correctly wired workshop is essential and it would be advisable to buy a book on home electrics. The 240 volt supply should be properly earthed and overload protected ('trip' switches at the master unit and even in the workshop). 13 amp sockets should be carefully planned and installed in a loop and appropriately fused. I prefer all power sockets to be well above bench-top height, giving easy access and minimizing trailing power-tool cables.

It is always useful to have extension cables, either in a reel or as flexi-cable. When operating

Fig 15.10 Energy-efficient lightbulbs using one fifth the electricity for the equivalent lumens.

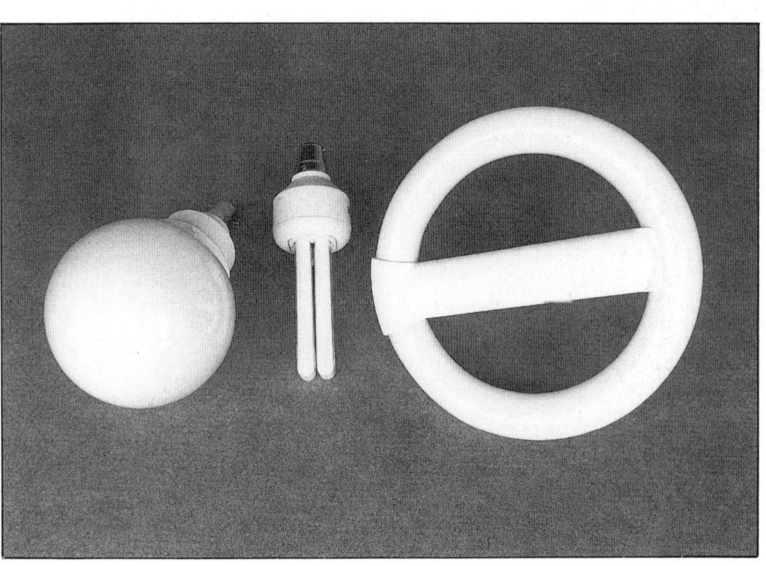

reel cable it should always be fully unwound, otherwise it acts as a resistor and potentially will melt.

Your lighting requirements should be wired on a separate fused loop and ideally the workshop should have plenty of natural light, although modern artificial lighting is not a strain on the eyes. The new energy-saving fluorescent lamp technology (see Chapter 28, Electric Lamp) offers excellent lighting and it is my preferred choice. For example, a 32 watt bulb gives the equivalent of 150 watts, consumes one fifth the electricity, and lasts five times longer than a tungsten bulb (Fig 15.10). Despite the high initial cost it makes economic sense in the long run (Fig 15.11). In fact these lamps are not new, and I have been using them myself since the late seventies.

Fig 15.13 The author's improvised – but effective – lathe dust-extraction system.

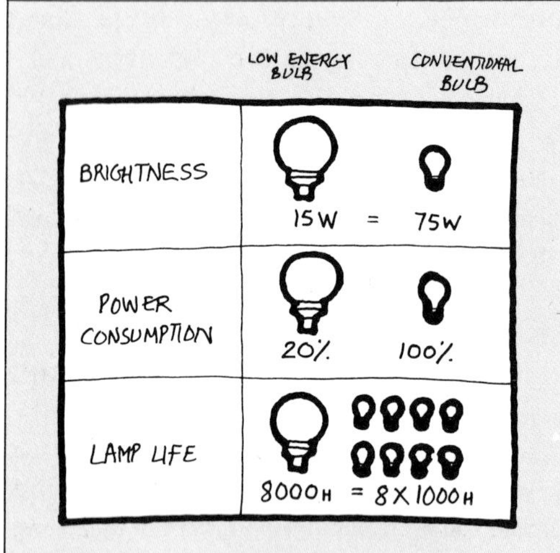

Fig15.11 The facts about low-energy bulbs.

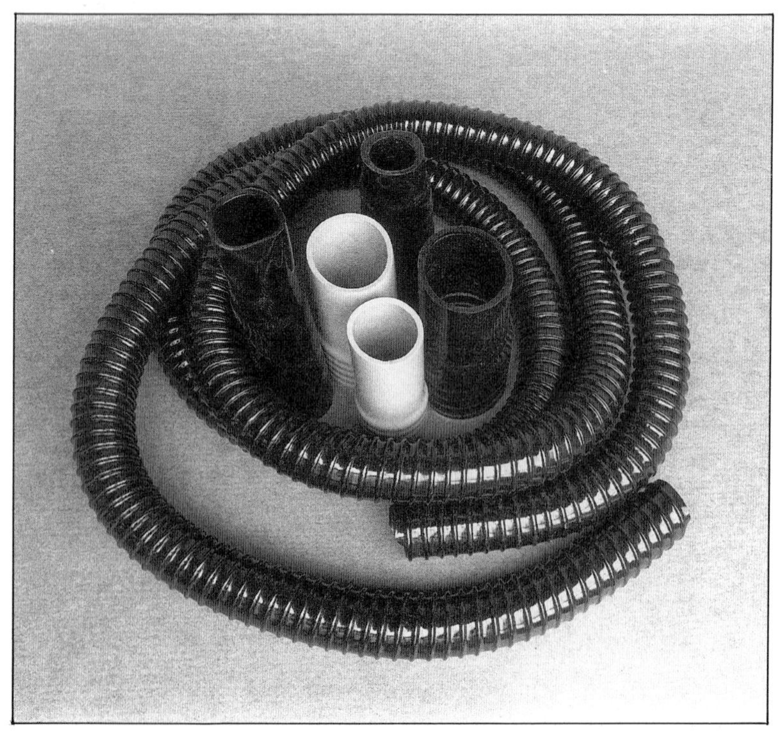

Fig 15.12 Cable and connectors for dust extraction from Trend.

It is best to experiment with lighting as its effects are quite important. It may be that specific tools or machines, such as the lathe, need focused lighting, or the lamp illuminating your main bench carefully positioned to avoid shadows. Good work depends on good light.

Dust extraction

Dust is a menace. It gets everywhere. It not only poses a health hazard for the woodworker (see Chapter 4), but it can be a fire risk (instantaneous combustion) and will get into the armatures of electric tools. Furthermore, tool bits, etc. can easily get lost amidst dust and chippings – especially expensive router bits.

It is possible to achieve a high standard of cleanliness in a workshop, or at least strive towards it. Probably the best solution is a portable dust extractor which can be taken to each tool or machine (see Fig 7.32). Some models, such as the Elu, are automatically switched on by the switch on the power tool when the latter is plugged into the extractor.

Various nozzle profiles (Fig 15.12) can be purchased, or home built, to suit different machines (Fig 15.13). It was good thinking on the part of some manufacturers to bevel the end of the hose nozzle as it makes the cleaning down of machines and awkward components much easier (Fig 15.14).

Fig 15.14 An intelligent bevel on the end of an AEG dust-extraction hose for cleaning awkward parts.

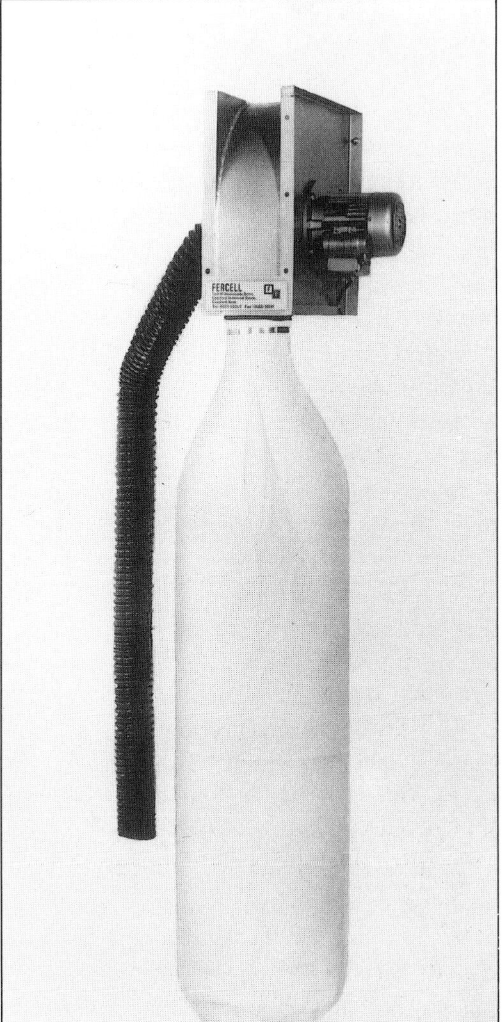

Fig 15.15 Wall-mounted dust extractor.

It is obviously a priority to connect a dust extractor to a sander or sander attachment. (Most electric tools tend to throw up dust and chippings centrifugally.) Other priority tools are the planer–thicknessers, the lathe and circular saws.

The portable dust extractor can be stored under a bench or sited conveniently within range of the tools or machines. A more permanent arrangement would be the use of an octopus piping system whereby priority machines are independently linked, and if such tools are permanently sited it makes sense to use this method.

Available also are large-volume extractors, both portable and wall-mounted (Fig 15.15). They have 100mm diameter wire-reinforced flexible hoses and can be attached to individual machines.

A small tip for extracting dust which accumulates in ironmongery chests of drawers is to place a piece of expanded aluminium mesh over the tray, turn it upside down and shake the contents around with the extractor hose up against the mesh. The dust disappears down the tube and not your ironmongery – hopefully (Fig 15.16)!

Sociability

Power-tool woodworking can be very unsociable from a noise point of view. Certain tools such as circular saws, routers and planers create noise pollution, and can be heard beyond the 4 walls of

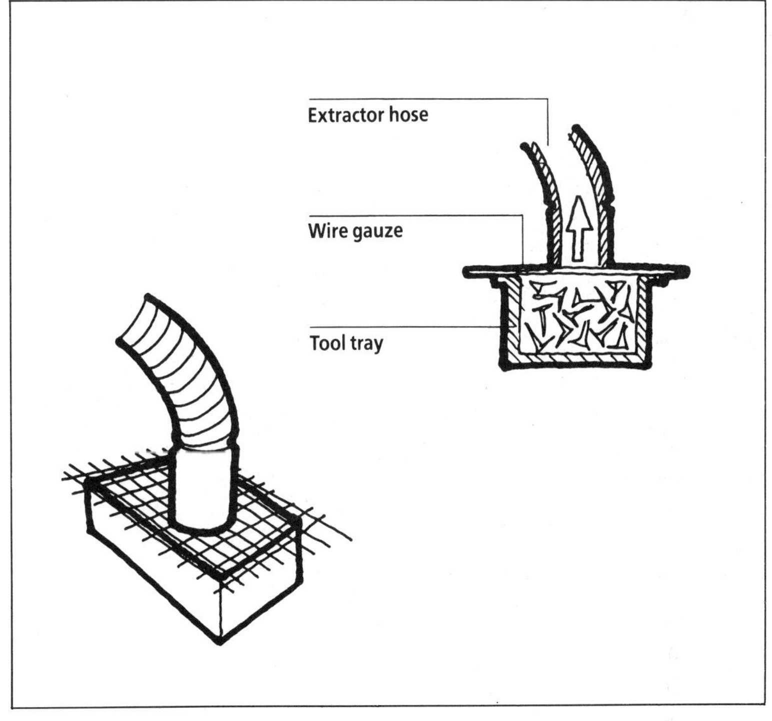

Fig 15.16 Cleaning dust out of a tray of screws.

your workshop. The responsible woodworker will remedy the problem as far as possible, but a certain level of noise is inevitable. Some machines, such as circular saws, resonate through the machine itself and insulation material can be attached to reduce the problem.

Insulation materials include softboard (Cellutex), polystyrene, rigid polyurethane foam and car sound insulation felts and rubbers. (Bear in mind that polystyrene is a fire hazard and the fumes are toxic.) Softboard is probably the least expensive and is available in 8ft × 4ft sheets which can be cut with a Stanley knife. It is ideal for lining walls and roofs for sound and heat insulation. It can be nailed to battens and joins taped and whitewashed afterwards.

Fibreglass wool (Rockwool) or roof insulation fibreglass is another combined insulation material. It is 4in thick and is most effective when applied to walls, but it can be used above and below. Double glazed window panels help insulate against sound, although the optimum cavity is wider than for heat insulation and is approximately 4in, making this measure more drastic, but these ideas are food-for-thought for anyone in a position to purpose-build a timber workshop, such as the one I built some years ago for a musical-instrument maker. He tells me it is so well insulated that a small electric convection heater keeps him 'as snug as a bug in a rug' during the winter months, and relatively cool in the summer, which can only be good news for the musical instruments as well.

Universal and combination machines

Many woodworkers consider a universal or combination machine to be a serious alternative to several independent machines. There are a number of manufacturers who supply a whole host of machines, such as Kity, Startrite, AEG, Luna etc. The obvious advantage is that the universal machine is a space saver and may in some cases be a cheaper option, although shopping around for independent machines makes this is an arguable point. Universals tend to be necessarily heavier and therefore require a robust floor, and of course for maximum effectiveness are likely to be sited somewhere near the middle of the floor, putting some stress on floor joists.

As Jacks-of-all-trades they need careful consideration and my opinion is that certain priority machines can be combined and others are best purchased as independents. Universals use either one motor or several, the latter facilitating quick access to separate functions. In general, change-over functions can be slow and at times the jigging up of a specific operation will hinder the other uses of the machine.

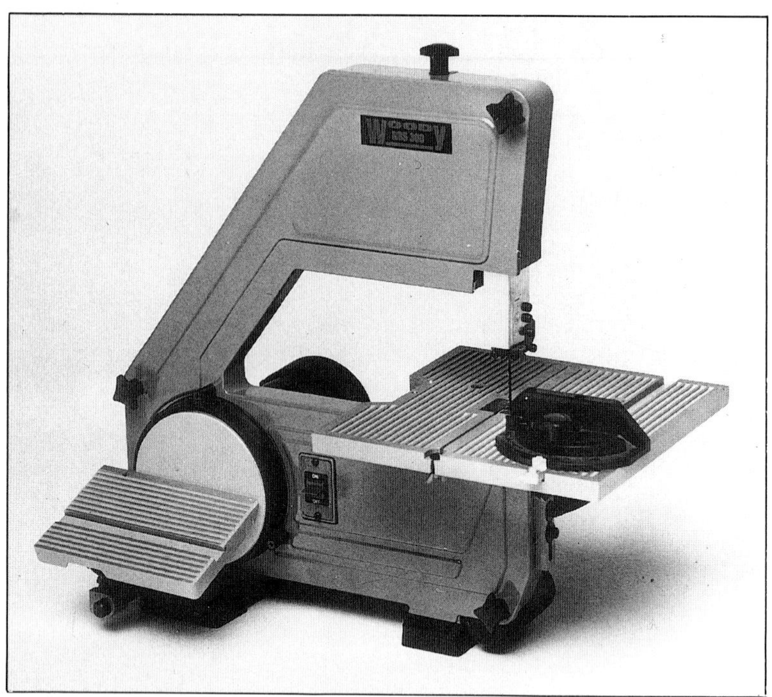

Fig 15.17 The Luna bandsaw/sander.

Universal machines generally offer

- circular saw,
- planer–thicknesser,
- spindle moulder
- slot-morticer

and sometimes a bandsaw and lathe.

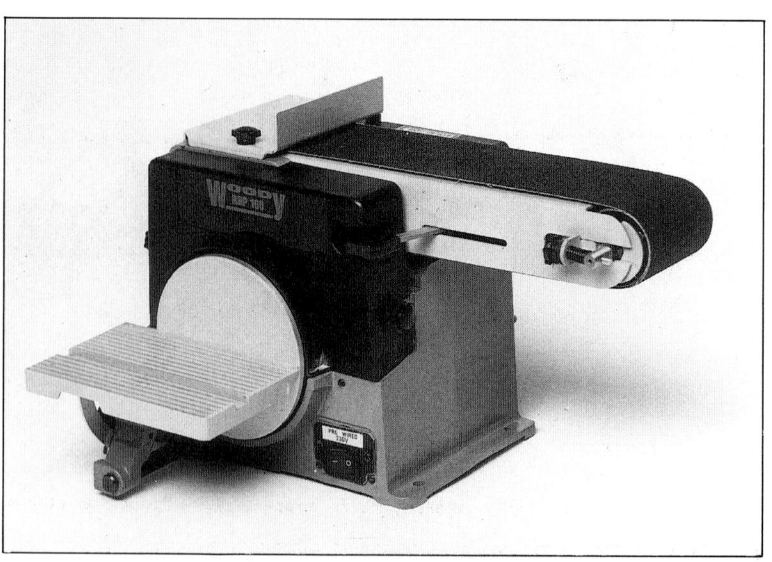

Fig 15.18 The Luna belt and disc sander.

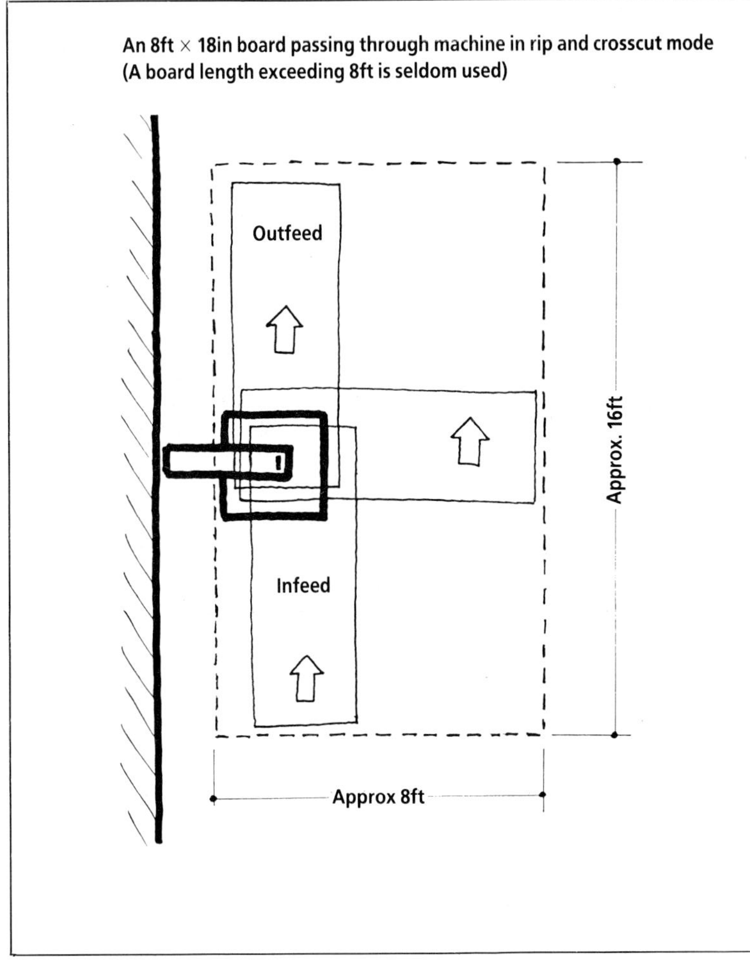

Fig 15.19 The operating space requirements of a bandsaw.

Combination machines generally offer

- bandsaw and disc sander (Fig 15.17) *or*
- planer–thicknesser and circular saw *or*
- planer–thicknesser, saw and slot-morticing attachment
- belt and disc sander (Fig 15.18)

OPERATING REQUIREMENTS

The design and planning of the electric workshop relies largely on the operating requirements of tools and machines. In some cases it is best to have a free-standing machine which can be moved about to accommodate some operations. I seldom bolt my machines down, and indeed have a purpose-built bench (see page 194) where machines can be set at different heights depending on which is being used.

Let's consider some essential tools/machines.

Bandsaw

The work is fed in and out of the table area and needs free operating space sideways for curved manoeuvres. A small bandsaw such as a DeWalt 12in model requires a working area of approximately 12ft × 6ft (Fig 15.19).

Radial arm saw

The machine itself takes up little room but needs an operating space (long narrow bench) of little more than twice the length of a plank maximum, say 13ft × 2ft (Fig 15.20).

Planer–thicknesser

Has similar requirements to radial arm and circular saws, and needs approximately 6ft clearance from either end of the machine for in-feed and out-feed. Extension rollers, adjustable in height, are useful for supporting long work (Fig 15.21).

Lathe

Requires a small operating space a little larger than the machine itself. A solid bench is required, ideally

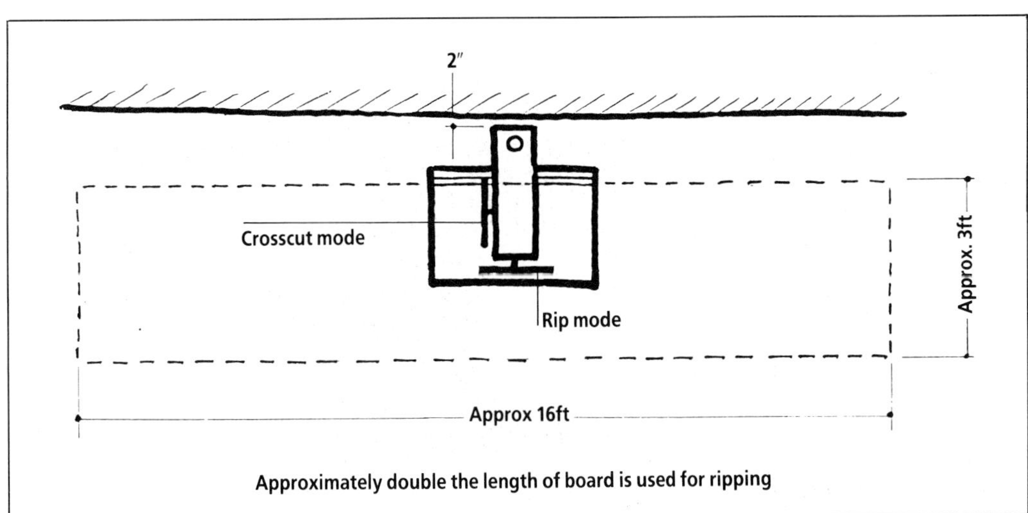

Fig 15.20 The operating space requirements of a radial arm saw.

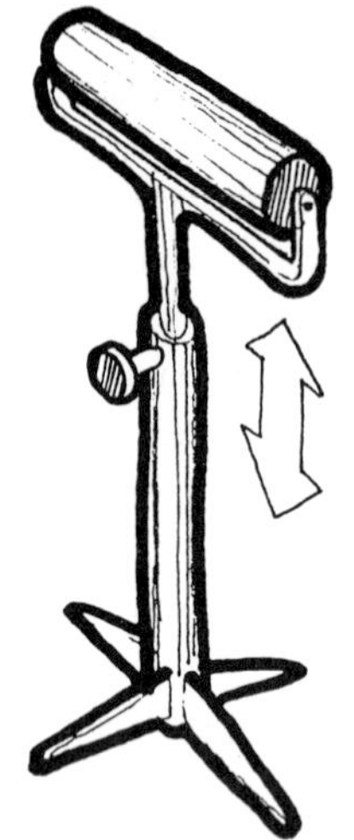

Fig15.21 Extension roller for the planer–thicknesser.

firmly anchored to the floor and wall. Lathe tool storage should be integral, and in my opinion so too should dust and chippings collection.

The workcentre

There are various workcentres on the market. First and foremost the **Black & Decker Workmate** is in my opinion an ideal general-purpose 'workcentre'. As a bench it offers remarkable stability for its light weight. It can be folded away and carried easily. Its integral vice-tabletop will grip virtually anything and with modification (insets) will accommodate various power tools. It is not designed to take heavy poundings with mallets or hammers, but is essentially a stable gripping device.

The **Triton** is an excellent and highly popular workcentre. Australian designed and made of brightly painted steel (does it ever rust?), it is an ingenious system whereby power tools (a router, circular saw and jigsaw) are either fixed or slide along the bench top. The tops rotate and interchange at two levels and the system offers a circular-saw bench and inverted router, plus an overhead saw akin to a radial arm saw in its action. The table has an extension and I look forward to the manufacturers deciding to include an optional top with a vice. Care should be taken over choice of power tools for this device as the larger circular sawblade diameters do not necessarily give the maximum depth of cut, as it depends on the design of the tool.

It is strange how handy a vice can be in a workshop, and the **Wolfcraft Pioneer** workcentre seems to meet the bill. Although at first it seems rather flimsily built – but nevertheless built to a good price – it contains sawbench, inverted router, inverted jigsaw actions on one half and a very chunky MDF bench top and vice on the other. The plastic dogs also allow for odd-shaped work to be clamped. This particular workcentre is nice and compact. The bench top includes a thoughtful feature – a solid metal insert for hammering against. Perhaps for flattening the ends of nails before they are used? (Fig 15.22)

The electric bench

Not to be confused with the electric chair, this bench is my own speciality and one which *evolved*

Fig 15.22 (a) The Wolfcraft Pioneer.

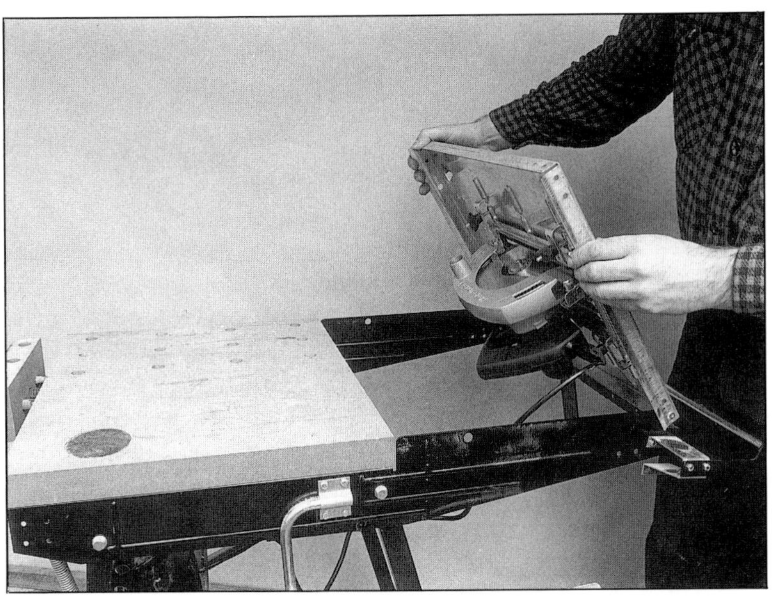

in my workshop, rather than being 'designed'. It is particularly useful where space is at a premium. It is fixed to the wall and floor and essentially allows a large plank or board to be crosscut, ripped and bandsawn. It is an integral bench supporting a small bandsaw, a radial arm saw at one end, and a milling machine (which could alternatively be a pillar drill) on the other end with a bench grinder. Such a bench could be modified to take other tools. It does not claim to accommodate everything but it does capitalize on limited space by sharing it (Fig 15.23).

The important thing is that the table height of the bandsaw and radial arm saw is lowered or raised, by packing, depending on which tool is being used. Also, the bandsaw can be swivelled on its base and moved backwards or forwards, hence

Fig 15.22 (b) Another feature of the Wolfcraft Pioneer.

Fig 15.22 (c) Lightweight and easy to store.

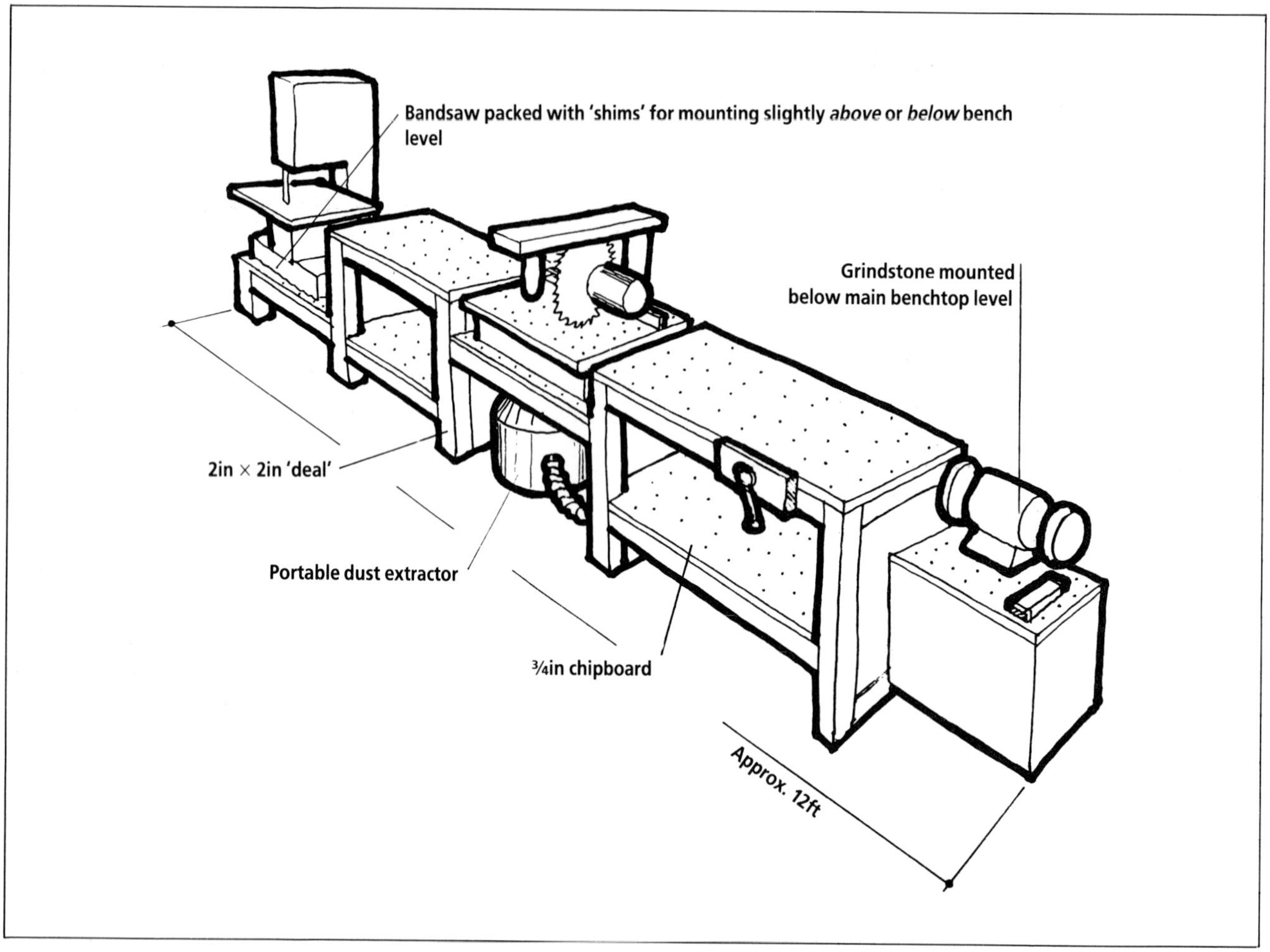

Bandsaw packed with 'shims' for mounting slightly *above* or *below* bench level

Grindstone mounted below main benchtop level

2in × 2in 'deal'

Portable dust extractor

¾in chipboard

Approx. 12ft

Fig 15.23 The electric bench.

allowing long pieces of timber being cut (ripped) on the radial arm saw to pass freely in front of or behind the blade. It works!

If you are spoiled for space, you cannot have enough bench space, but then like extra lanes on motorways – the capacity quickly gets filled.

Tool racks and storage

Wall space should be properly organized so that tools and other equipment can be easily accessed. A simple system of tool racking is offered as a project (Fig 15.24) (see Chapter 23, Tool Rack) and you may wish to purpose-build specific racks. Open racks are easy to use but may attract dust. Wall-hung cabinets are useful and there are numerous sliding box cabinets for ironmongery etc. on the market which can be fixed to the wall. Many woodworkers use old jamjars for storing an array of small items. An easy system of holding G-clamps is via a chunky dowel drilled into the wall. Various flat manufactured boards can be screwed to the wall and fixings attached.

The humble nail is an excellent hanging supporting device for some tools, bandsaw and circular saw blades, and even sash clamps can be hung from a stout nail – but the fixing has to be strong – into brick or stonework ideally. I am a great fan of the 6in nail. (I haven't dared use them in my designs, though others apparently do!) I hang all my sash clamps from stout nails with the

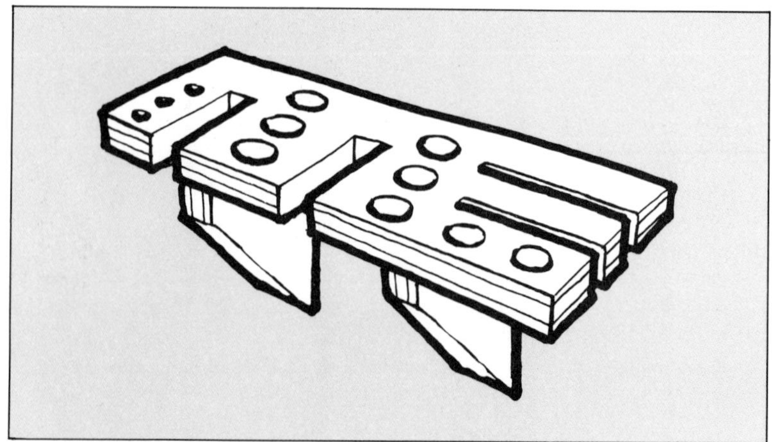

Fig 15.24 A simple tool rack.

heads removed and rounded slightly – they are driven in at a slight angle. If you are fixing into a wall you can drill and rawlplug a nail! You don't have to stick to convention. What works, works.

TIMBER AND MATERIALS STORAGE

Solid timber board

Depending on the amount of work you do, it is important to have some kind of organized racking system for timber and other materials. Timber board up to about 12in wide can be horizontally racked in adjustable steel shelving systems, or steel tube drilled into 3in × 2in softwood bolted to the wall. It is important to have access to individual planks and allow breathing space between planks (Fig 15.25).

Manufactured board

Manufactured boards (8ft × 4ft sheets) take up room and should be stacked carefully, so they do not sag, near to the entrance of the workshop and in a position where they can be easily cut up.

Veneers

Veneers invariably get damaged when handled. They are expensive and need careful handling and storing. A simple system I devised many years ago for schools is a vertical wall-clamping system where the veneers hang and are cut with scissors when specific lengths are needed (see Fig 15.8). Such a valuable material can get torn very easily.

Offcuts

Offcuts are always a cumulative problem. There comes a time when some have to be burned, but in the main it is a good idea to put aside offcuts for future use. The simplest storage system is probably a teachest or similar box, or a series of labelled boxes for different species. The offcuts can be stored vertically and any length can be contained and subsequently selected.

The electric workshop is a highly personal environment. I can only share my own particular experience, that based on playing 'Red Adair' to school woodwork over a period of years in my early career. Organization is vital, but I would guess that not all woodworkers are tidy by nature. Despite the high degree of organization in my own workshop it quickly becomes a disaster area when I use it. I therefore have a periodic 'blitz' when there is no room to stand or no available space on the bench.

A simple early-forming habit for anybody taking up this wonderful craft is – put the tool away *immediately* after you have used it and clean the bench and floor at the end of the day! That way the electric workshop is a joy to use at the beginning of each new day.

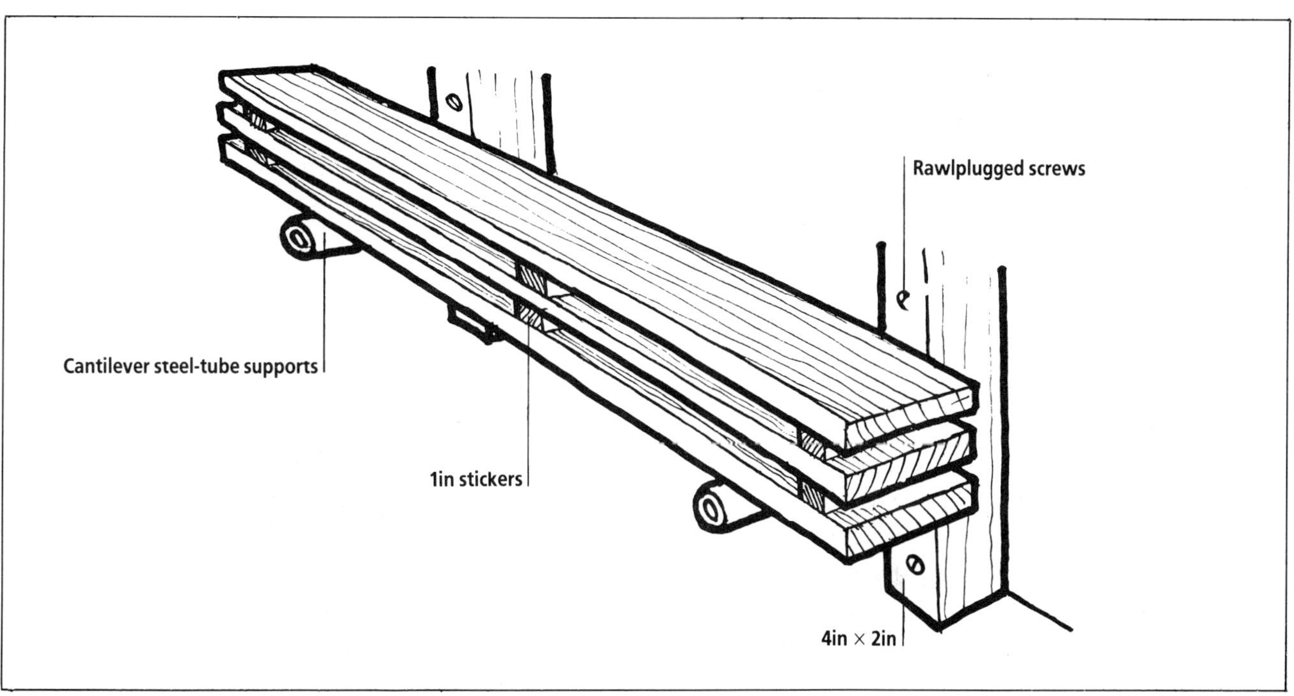

Fig 15.25 The boards should be 'sticked' for air circulation.

16

THE CORDLESS REVOLUTION

Cordless has come of age! In recent years it has become the most exciting and rapidly developing aspect of power-tool woodworking, and today there are few woodworkers who do not possess a cordless power tool of some description or other.

Cordless or battery-powered tools are clearly the tools of convenience (Fig 16.1), and even though they can never compete in power capacity with mains-operated tools, they are becoming increasingly popular for trade and leisure use. They are fast becoming state of the art (Fig 16.2), and apart from being convenient, battery-powered tools are also very safe because of their low voltage.

Cordless tools are not only the obvious choice for on-site or remote woodworking, but also find their place in the home and professional workshop. The latter may seem strange as mains electricity is on tap, but it is interesting to note that the automotive industry, for example, uses cordless power

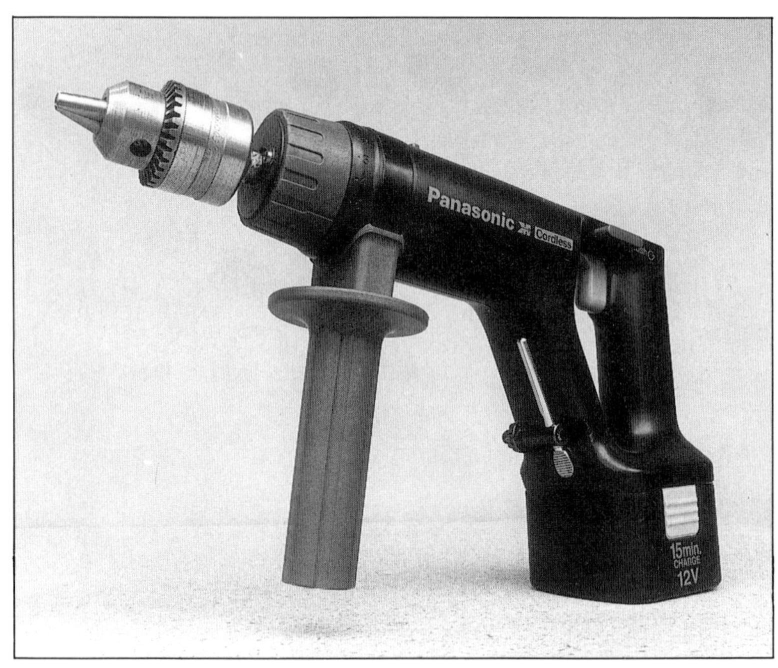

Fig 16.2 Panasonic 'Force 12' cordless drill and driver – a meaty performer.

Fig 16.1 Reaching those awkward parts with a cordless drill (Hitachi) (left).

Fig 16.3 A Hitachi cordless drill used away from the mains (right).

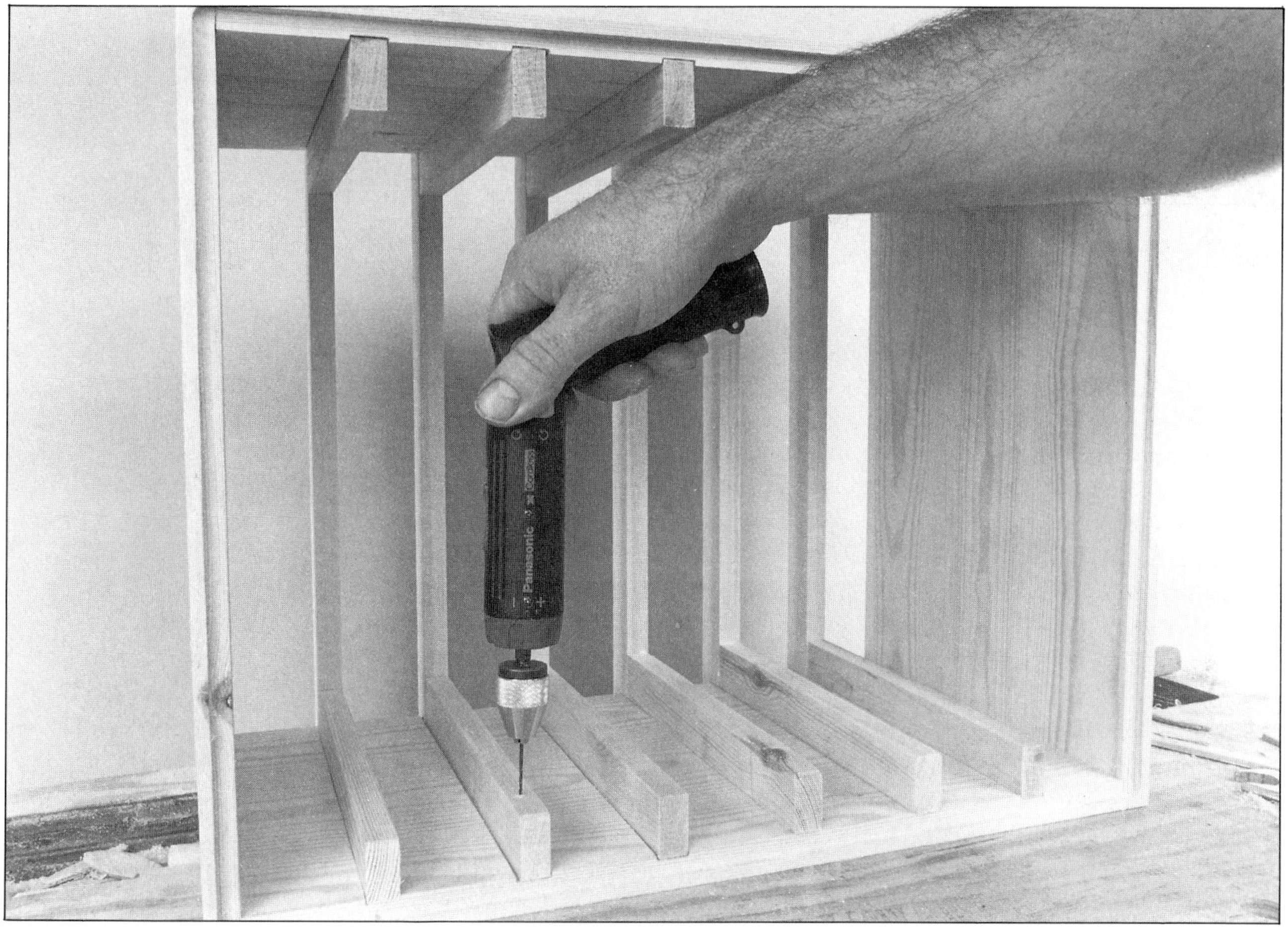

Fig 16.4 Using a Panasonic 2.4 volt drill-driver in a confined space.

Fig 16.5 The author uses the versatile and neat Hitachi D10DF drill-driver for sinking screws.

Fig 16.6 AEG 12 volt orbital jigsaw – a very useful tool.

Fig 16.7 Using a compatible battery, the AEG circular saw.

tools, especially for interior fitting where a compact, clean and easily manoeuvrable tool is required whose power cable will not get in the way. And these tools work 18 hours a day, 5 days a week.

For the woodworker an extra drill which is cordless can be used away from mains electricity, in the garden shed, or outdoors generally (Fig 16.3), or can be equally useful for specific functions in the workshop such as drilling pilot holes (Fig 16.4) or indeed as a screwdriver (Fig 16.5).

The range of cordless tools is fairly extensive and includes screwdrivers, jigsaws (Fig 16.6), circular saws (Fig 16.7), orbital sanders, tackers (Fig 16.8), trimmers, glue guns and grinders (see Fig 13.2), to mention a few. Indeed I can envisage 'caravan woodworking' whereby a cordless drill is set up in a lathe attachment offering a little weekend woodturning away from it all!

There is one cordless tool I would personally like to own and that is a cordless glue gun (see Chapter 13, The Mighty Glue Gun), as the power

Fig 16.8 Metabo 9.6 volt tacker for staples and pins.

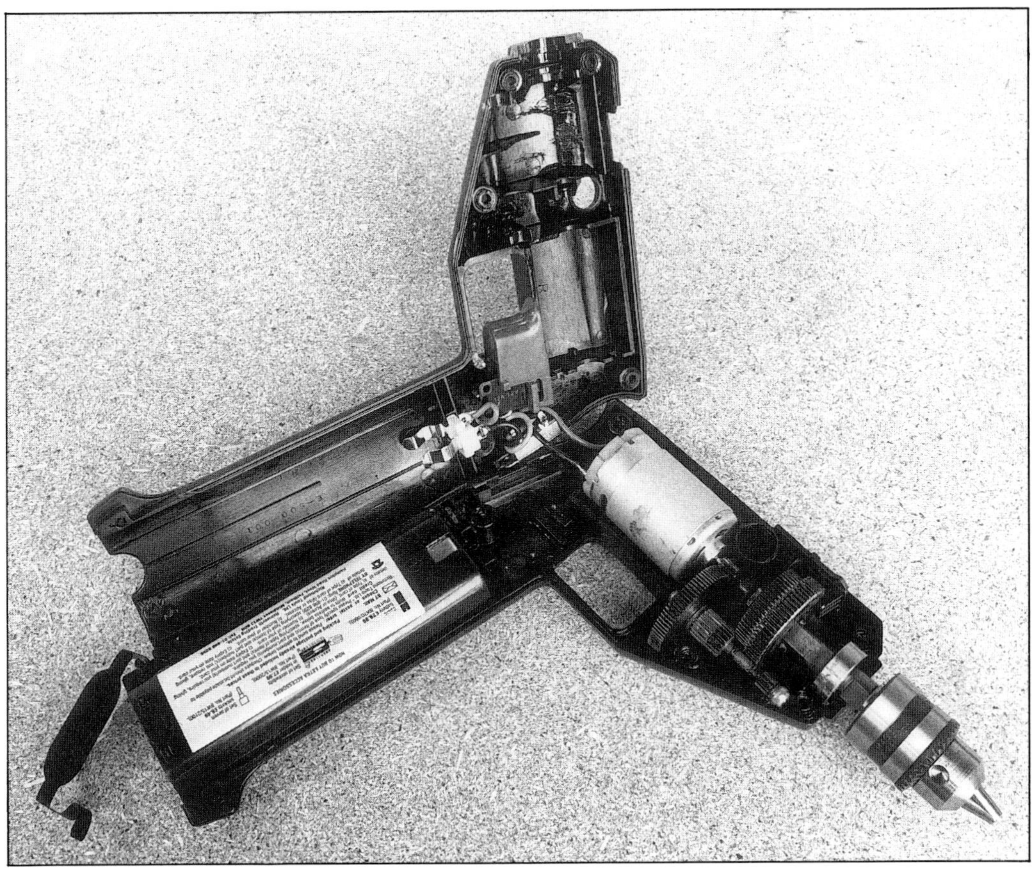

Fig 16.9 Inside the Richmond cordless drill.

cable on the mains version is not only too short, but the relative weight and thickness of it tends to knock the glue gun over!

Not exactly a power tool, but certainly cordless, is the Racal Dustmaster (see Fig 4.9). It runs for 10 hours on one charge and the battery is then charged overnight.

Of course the most versatile and popular cordless tool is undoubtedly the drill (Fig 16.9); indeed, the early cordless tools were drills. Their batteries were quite large, some of them being integral to the handle casing, which meant that the drill was rather heavy and unbalanced and had to be thrown away when the battery was worn out. These early

Fig 16.10 The clip-on battery being charged (Hitachi).

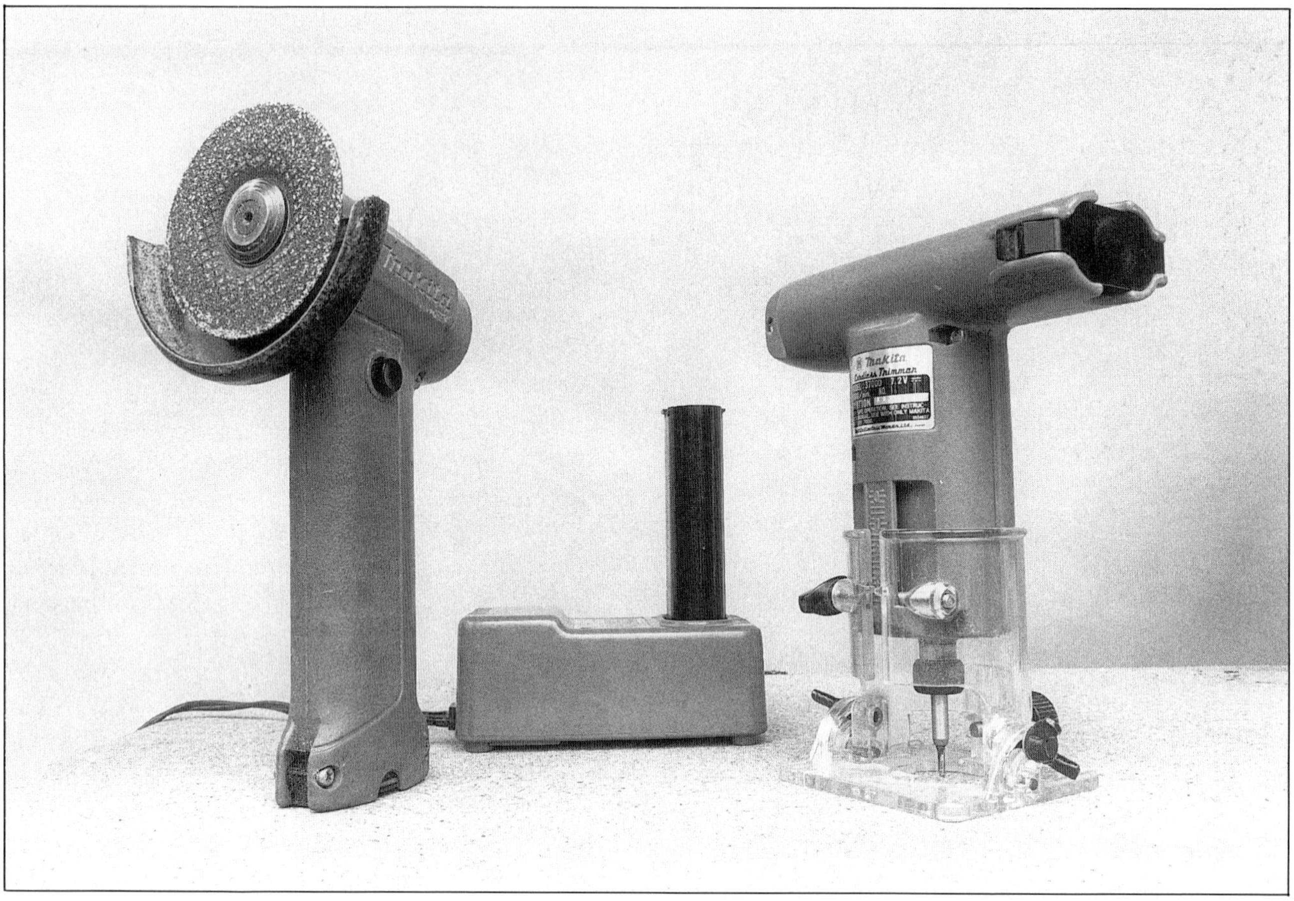

cordless tools took 12–16 hours to charge, generally referred to as 'trickle' or 'overnight' charging. Clip-on batteries with separate chargers (Fig 16.10) were developed and the range of tools expanded to include just about every conventional tool.

Most manufacturers today offer a system of cordless tools where the same battery is shared, so spare batteries are always on hand (Fig 16.11). The charge time of batteries has been significantly reduced and in recent years the industry standard of 1 hour has fallen significantly. A useful gadget is a timeswitch (Fig 16.12) which can be set to automatically cut off the power to the charger. (For convenience I use this on the longer charge devices such as the Racal Dustmaster batteries.)

BATTERIES AND CHARGING

The type of battery commonly used is nickel-cadmium, although lead-acid batteries are used to a lesser degree. The batteries are similar to any rechargeable battery used in torches, music centres and toys. They are 1.2 volt cells attached in series (Fig 16.13) and encapsulated in the manufacturer's particular pack.

Manufacturers offer a range of voltage systems based on multiples of the 1.2 volt cell, e.g.:

AEG 2.4, 7.2, 9.6, 12 volts
Black & Decker 7.2, 9.6, 12, 13.2 and 24 volts
Hitachi 2.4, 7.2, 9.6, 12 volts
Makita 7.2, 9.6, 10.8 volts
Metabo 4.8, 7.2, 9.6, 12 volts

Fig 16.11 The Makita cordless grinder and trimmer share the same battery type.

Fig 16.12 A useful timeswitch.

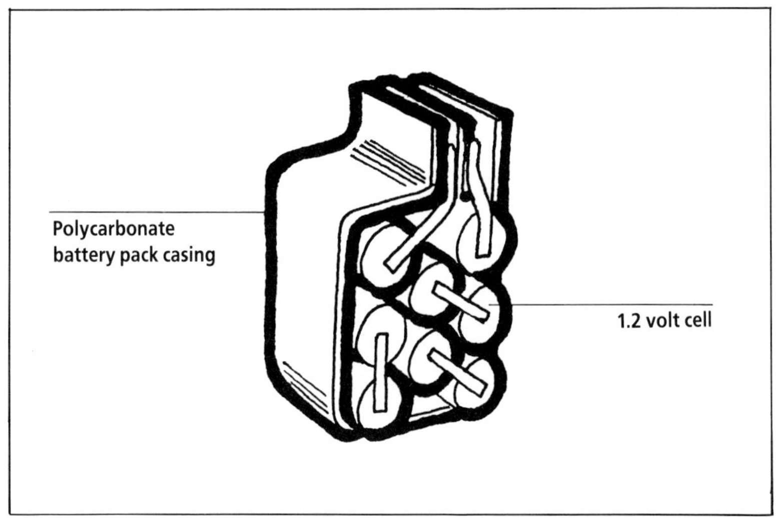

Fig 16.13 A series of 1.2 volt cells make up the pack.

The main advantage of higher voltage cordless tools is that they work longer, i.e. a cordless drill might perform for 30 minutes instead of 15 minutes on one battery charge.

Now the heart of cordless technology is in the battery, and it is here that development is fast-moving. Indeed, fast-charging or 'coffee-break' charger cordless tools were the state-of-the art at the time of writing this book (Fig 16.14). Of course, having reduced the charge time of a battery from 1 hour to 5 or 15 minutes is academic when you are on-site without access to mains power for the charger, and you would always carry a spare battery!

Whether it takes an hour or just 5 minutes to charge, the life and performance of the battery are greatly affected by how the battery is both discharged and charged. This is called 'cycling' Manufacturers claim several hundred re-charges (250–1000) before the battery is spent. Significantly longer life can result from proper cycling and 'smart-charge' technology. Metabo, for instance, claim up to 3000 charges (under laboratory conditions) on a 10 minute 'pulse' charge. In effect the battery plates undergo an electrolysis reaction and the 'pulse' method of charging has been found to be more effective and kinder to the battery. (Throughout the charging process the battery heats and gases need to be vented.)

It is important to remember that heat is the enemy of the battery and will cause it to degrade. 'Pulse' charging is intermittent charging where the split-second off-charge allows cooling, but there is more to it than that. What also has to be remembered is that the battery has a memory, as this is what can determine its performance. When a

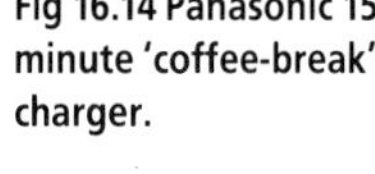

Fig 16.14 Panasonic 15 minute 'coffee-break' charger.

Fig 16.15 Lazy cells.

cordless tool is used spasmodically it is easy to just put it on charge when it is *thought* to be low, rather than when it is known to be fully discharged. If, for instance, 10 per cent of the charge is remaining in the battery and it is then placed in the charger, it will charge up the remaining capacity which is 90 per cent. On the subsequent charge the memory will cause it to charge up 90 per cent of 90 per cent, so it is important to fully discharge the battery before recharging. Should the performance of the battery wane noticeably, it should be cycled by fully discharging then fully charging as the memory may be playing up!

THE SMART CHARGER

Originally pioneered by PAG (well known for broadcast television and military power requirements), and first adopted in the power-tool market by Metabo, the 'smart' or fast charger is not simply a trickle charger switched to boost mode. The charger contains complex microcomputer circuits which sense the state of discharge in the battery, monitor the heat build-up in each cell as it is charged, regulate that charge from an initial precharge to main charge, and balance (cell) charge to a maintenance charge. This 'intelligent' devicing is measured and controlled in milliseconds. The net effect is a battery which is charged correctly and evenly throughout all its cells (there can be lazy cells – see Fig 16.15), avoiding overheating eliminating battery memory problems and maintaining maximum charge. This results in long service life which, as Metabo claims, can be up to 3 times the normal battery pack life.

FRIEND TO THE ENVIRONMENT?

In short, it is *you* who has to be environmentally friendly as the nickel-cadmium battery certainly is not. Despite the considerable life expectancy of the battery, perhaps several years, there will come a day when it has to be disposed of. In no event

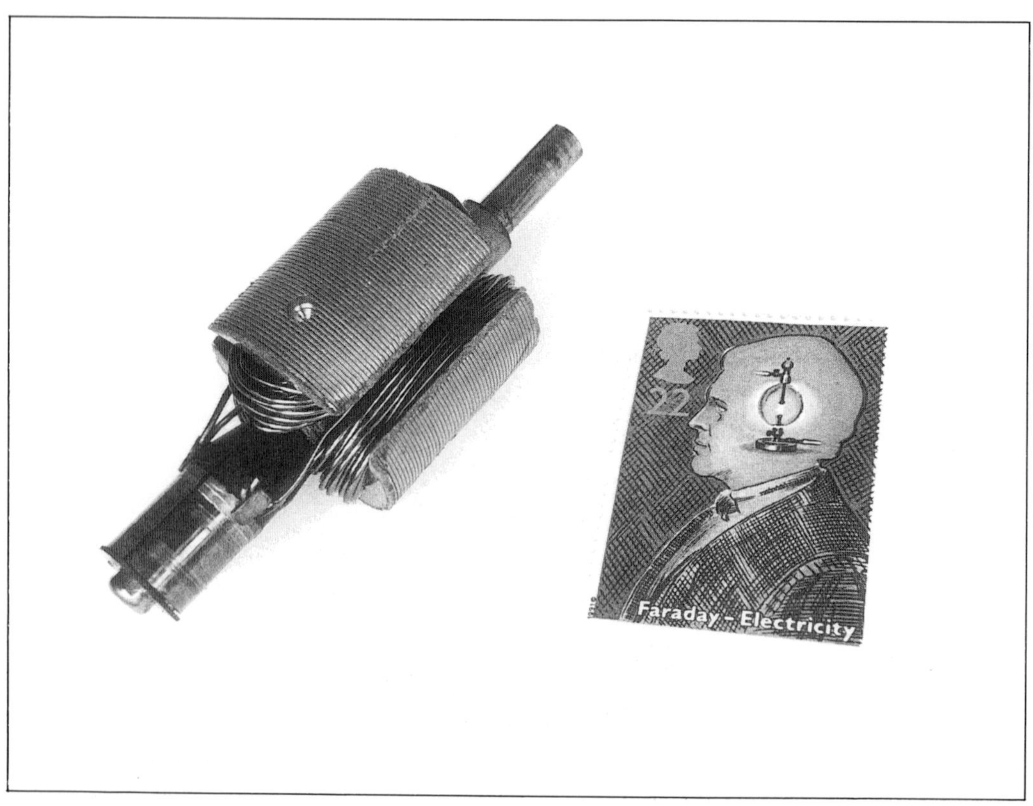

Fig 16.16 Hitachi cordless motor pictured against the man who pioneered it all.

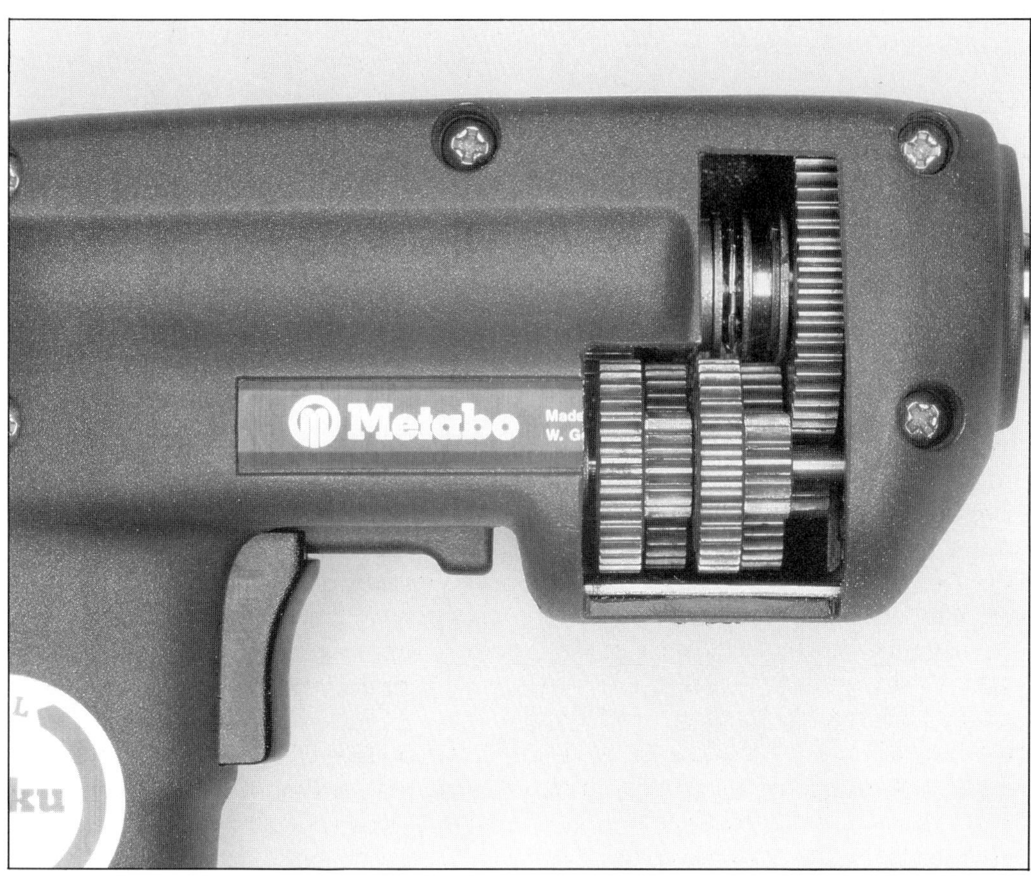

Fig 16.17 Spur gears in a Metabo drill.

should a spent battery be simply put in the dustbin (or incinerated) as it will inevitably be destined for a shallow land-fill or worse. Cadmium is a highly toxic heavy metal similar to mercury and exposure to it will cause damage to the central nervous system. Spent nickel-cadmium batteries should be returned to your local council for 'safe disposal', or returned to the tool merchant. An initiative taken by Metabo is to offer 10 per cent off new batteries for old ones, a practice which should become standard. The technical term 'cycling' may be applied to the way the battery is charged and discharged, but might also apply in the *environmental* sense.

THE CORDLESS MOTOR

The cordless power tool uses direct current (DC) motors, and these are generally more compact as they have high power magnets (rare earth), heat-resistant motor brushes and built-in cooling fans giving more torque at the chuck (Fig 16.16).

THE GEARBOX

Most power tools use spur gears (Fig 16.17), and some use planetary gears (Fig 16.18), such as the Panasonic range which is generally more compact.

The cordless power tool is a revolution in itself and a wonderful development of electrical power. At the time of writing this book, many new developments will be on-going. It is likely that the most dramatic changes to come will be in the nature of the battery, its capacity and stamina, but who can be sure of the future?

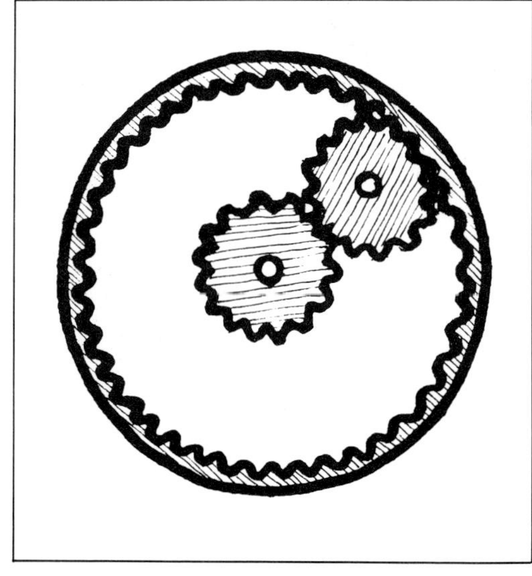

Fig 16.18 Planetary gears in a Panasonic cordless drill.

17

AN A-Z OF ELECTRIC WOODWORK

ABRASIVE DISC

Aluminium oxide or silicon carbide sanding disc. 5in diameter in various grades or grits for attaching to rubber backing disc and 6mm arbor assembly for drills.

ABRASIVE FLAP WHEEL

For use with portable power drills for shaping and finishing wood. 6mm shank diameter, 80 grit paper (Fig 17.1).

ALLIGATOR SAW

A power saw by Black & Decker. Similar in principle to a chain saw, it has a single reciprocating tooth system held in a conventional handsaw blade – it is therefore self-guiding and can achieve accurate cuts. 1100 watts. TCT and HSS blades. 260mm square cutting capacity (Fig 17.2).

ANGLE GRINDER

Although predominantly used for cutting and shaping masonry and metal, a useful tool for the woodworker for grinding and sanding. Replaceable glass-fibre reinforced resinoid discs in various diameters: 100mm, 115mm (mini), 180mm and 230mm. Power ratings 450–2000 watts. 6000–10000rpm.

ARBOTECH WOODCARVER

A simple and ingenious rotary 'chainsaw' cutter which attaches to a hand-held grinder. It is a versatile shaping tool for applications such as sculpture, and for plumbers and electricians to chase in pipes and wires, etc. (Invented by Kevin Inkster, an Australian who first used it to sculpt his own chair seats.) The blade is modified from a chainsaw tooth configuration to cut on its edge and side (see Fig 2.17).

BANDSAW

A bench- or floor-mounted machine with a continuous loop blade (min. 8ft length

Fig 17.1 Abrasive flap wheel.

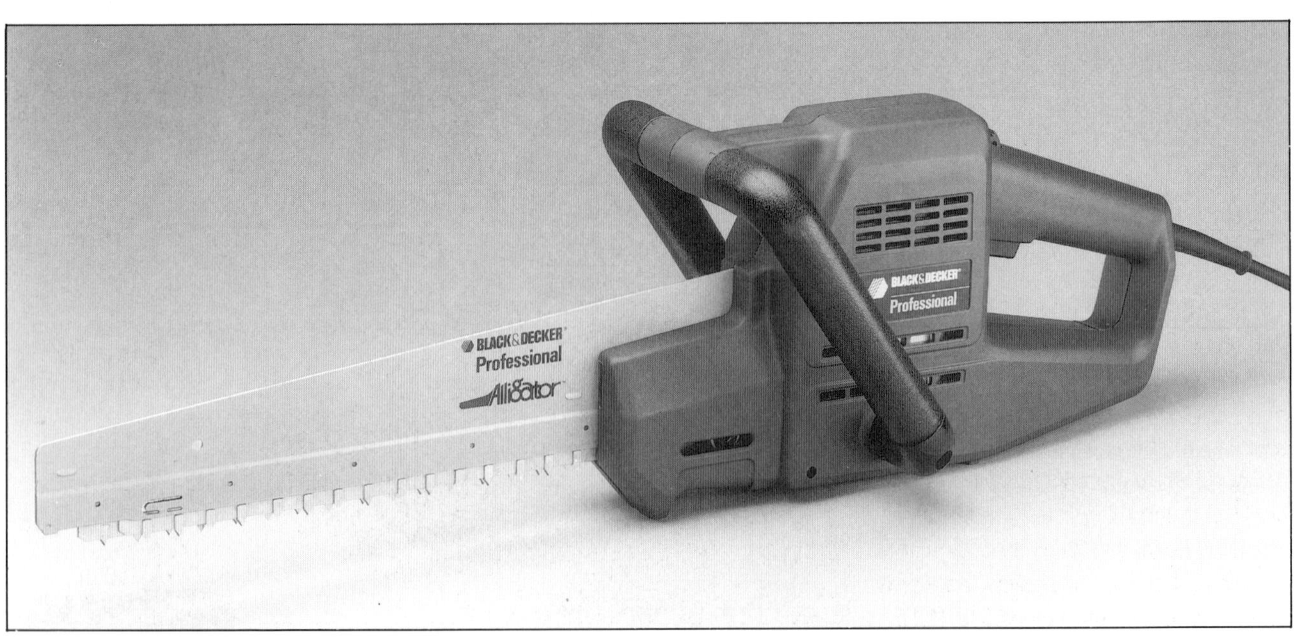

Fig 17.2 Black & Decker Alligator Saw.

Fig 17.3 Bench grinder.

recommended) for cutting curved, straight and angled work. A priority machine (see Chapter 8).

BELT SANDER (portable)

For fast surface removal rather than finishing, the belt sander normally uses a 3–4in wide belt suspended between two rotating drums.

BELT SANDER (bench mounted)

Using a longer belt than its portable counterpart (i.e. 100mm × 910mm), the bench-mounted model is designed to finish smaller dimension work. Some models have a combined disc-sander function.

BENCH GRINDER

An essential tool for servicing chisel and planer blades, carving and turning gouges and scrapers. Coarse and fine aluminium oxide wheels, 5–8in diameter. Power ¼ to ½HP (Fig 17.3).

BISCUIT JOINTER

An ingenious and simple grooving tool. A blade is plunge cut into two pieces of wood to be jointed, making a crescent-shaped indentation into which a compressed wood biscuit is glued (Fig 11.1).

Fig 17.4 Makita buzz saw.

BLOWER

A handy, portable, mains-operated tool for cleaning dust from machines.

BUZZ SAW (Makita)

A 9.6 volt cordless mini circular saw with 85mm narrow kerf blade for ripping, crosscutting and grooving (Fig 17.4).

CARBORUNDUM WHEEL

A grinding wheel of various diameters for using in the chuck of a portable drill (Fig 17.5).

Fig 17.5 Carborundum wheel.

CHAIN MORTICER

A narrow bar with toothed chain, similar to a chainsaw, held in a vertical column. Average max. cutting width – 30mm; depth – 160mm; clamping width – 50–185mm.

CHAINSAW

A modern lumberjack's tool for felling trees and cutting branches. Electric

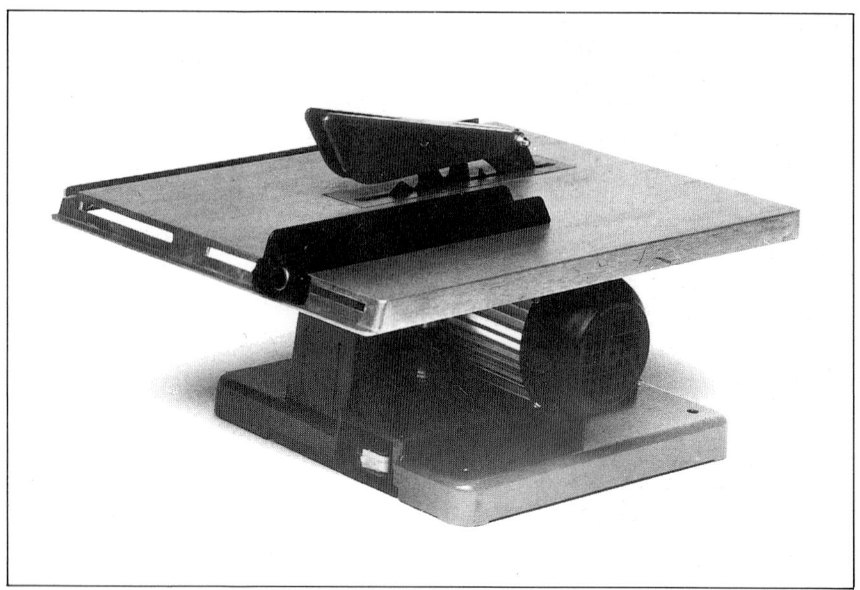

Fig 17.6 The Luna Woody TS 210 circular saw.

models are smaller than the petrol-driven type, with blades approximately 16in long.

CHARGER

A mains-operated battery-charging device for cordless tools. The industry standard is 1hr (1991), and "fast" chargers reduce this to as low as 5 minutes. 'Pulse' or 'smart' chargers are fast chargers which sense and monitor the state of the battery extending performance and battery life considerably. (See also Universal Charger)

CHIP COLLECTOR

An essential piece of equipment in any electric workshop. Either free-standing or wall-mounted–1–2HP. Large capacity bags with filtration bag. Hose diameter usually 120mm.

CHUCK (geared)

Attached to drills for gripping bits. The chuck key is tightened on all three locations for maximum grip. There are different sized chuck keys for different drills. Capacities – ¼–½in, the latter preferred.

CIRCULAR SAW (table)

Either pressed steel or cast aluminium in various sizes by various manufacturers, although some still have cast-iron tables, especially universals. Bench mounted or floor standing. Circular saw usually attached (Fig 17.6).

CIRCULAR SAW (portable)

Blade diameters: approx 150–265mm. 900–1900 watts. Accessories include straight fence (Fig 17.7).

COMPASS DRILLING STAND

A versatile drilling and milling stand with sliding table.

Fig 17.7 Black & Decker portable circular saw.

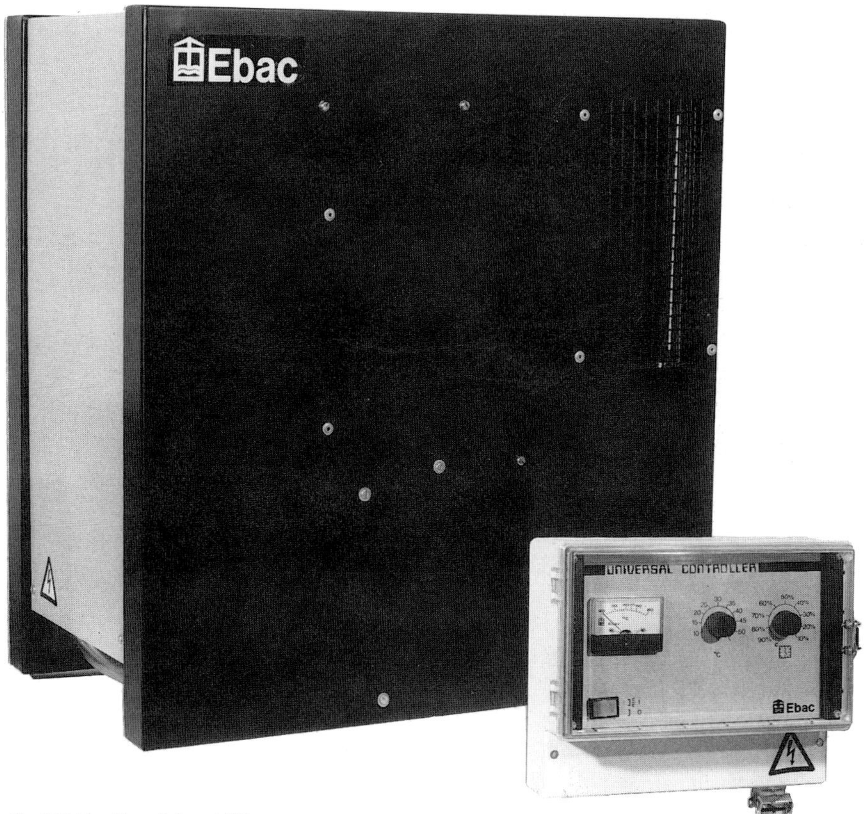

Fig 17.8 The Ebac dehumidifier.

COMPRESSOR
An electric motor driven pump. It compresses air in a cylinder for storage and controlled release to power various tools such as hammer guns, drills and spray guns.

COPY CARVING JIG (router)
A simple router jig for three dimensional carving/shaping.

CUSHION DRUM SANDER
A rotary attachment for drills and radial arm saws. Abrasive belt is backed with a high-density foam.

DADO CUTTER
A series of blades packed together on the same spindle to make up a wide grooving cutter for use in a radial arm saw (see page 125). They can also be used with a circular saw if the table has a removable cut-out.

DEHUMIDIFIER
An electric kiln drying device for timber. It extracts moisture slowly and inexpensively via a system of tubes placed in a sealed and insulated container in which the timber is stacked (Fig 17.8).

DISC SANDER
An essential tool or tool attachment for the electric workshop. A minimum diameter of 8in is recommended (small discs clog up). Ideal for precision sanding of end-grain, and shaping where 'squareness' or flatness is essential.

DOVETAIL JIG
A simple pressed-steel or cast-aluminium jig for using with the router and supplied by various manufacturers. These simple jigs give fixed spacing dovetails with rounded shoulder lines (Fig 17.9). See under **LEIGH** and **WOODRAT** for more accurate and flexible jigs.

DOVETAIL JIG (router)
Made by various manufacturers, a simple template for cutting dovetails.

DOWEL BIT
For use in a portable or pillar drill and with a dowel jig. Similar to a twist drill but with a centre point and two spurs for accurate locating and clean cutting. Size coincides with available dowels. (Also called a brad-point bit.)

DOWELLING JIG
A precision-built guiding system for drilling holes for 6mm, 8mm and 10mm standard dowel. A drillbit depth stop is usually included in the kit. (Fig 17.10 (a) and (b))

DRILL
The original power tool, from which most other power tools evolved. Basically an electric motor with a handle, switch and chuck. There are countless drills on the market by numerous manufacturers (see Chapter 5).

Fig 17.9 The Wolfcraft dovetailing jig.

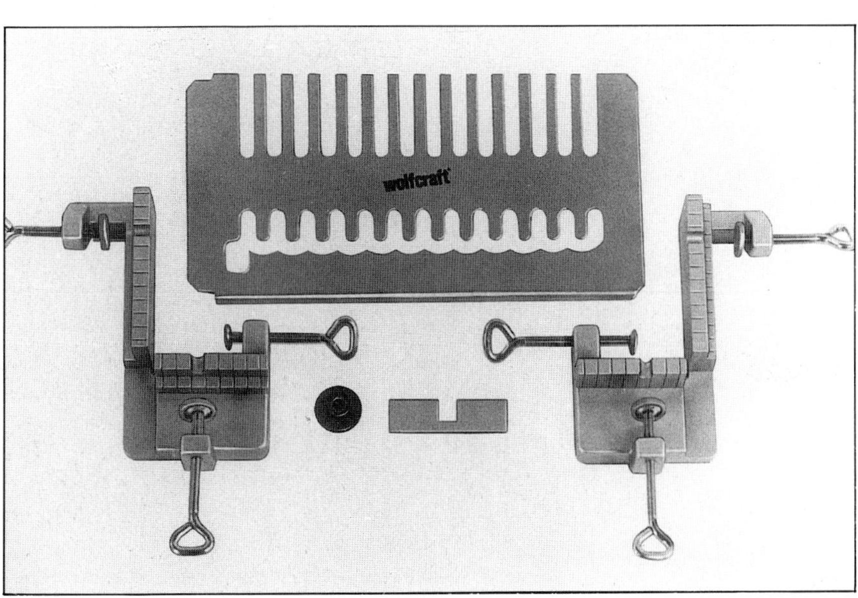

Fig 17.10 (a) and (b) The Wolfcraft dowelling jig.

DRILL-DRIVER

A mains-operated or cordless drill with various features – 2-speed, variable, keyless chuck, torque control etc. – with one differentiating feature: reverse action for taking screws out as well as putting them in.

DRILL AND MILL ATTACHMENT

A versatile drill guide and router head attachment for straight and angled cuts (Fig 17.11).

DRILLSTAND

Extremely useful and inexpensive guiding jig for a portable drill and router with 43mm collar. Most stands have adjustable depth stops and some include head swivelling facility (Fig 17.12 and Fig 5.23).

DUPLI-CARVER (copy carving jig)

An American router jig for accurate 3-dimensional carving in a fraction of the time it would take to do by hand. Ideal for gun butts, ornamental carving, swags, plaques etc.

DUSTMASK

Vital health protection wear for the electric workshop where high-speed wood cutting and abrading creates potentially dangerous dust and chippings. Main suppliers: Racal and 3M. The fit around the nose is most important. (See Chapter 4.)

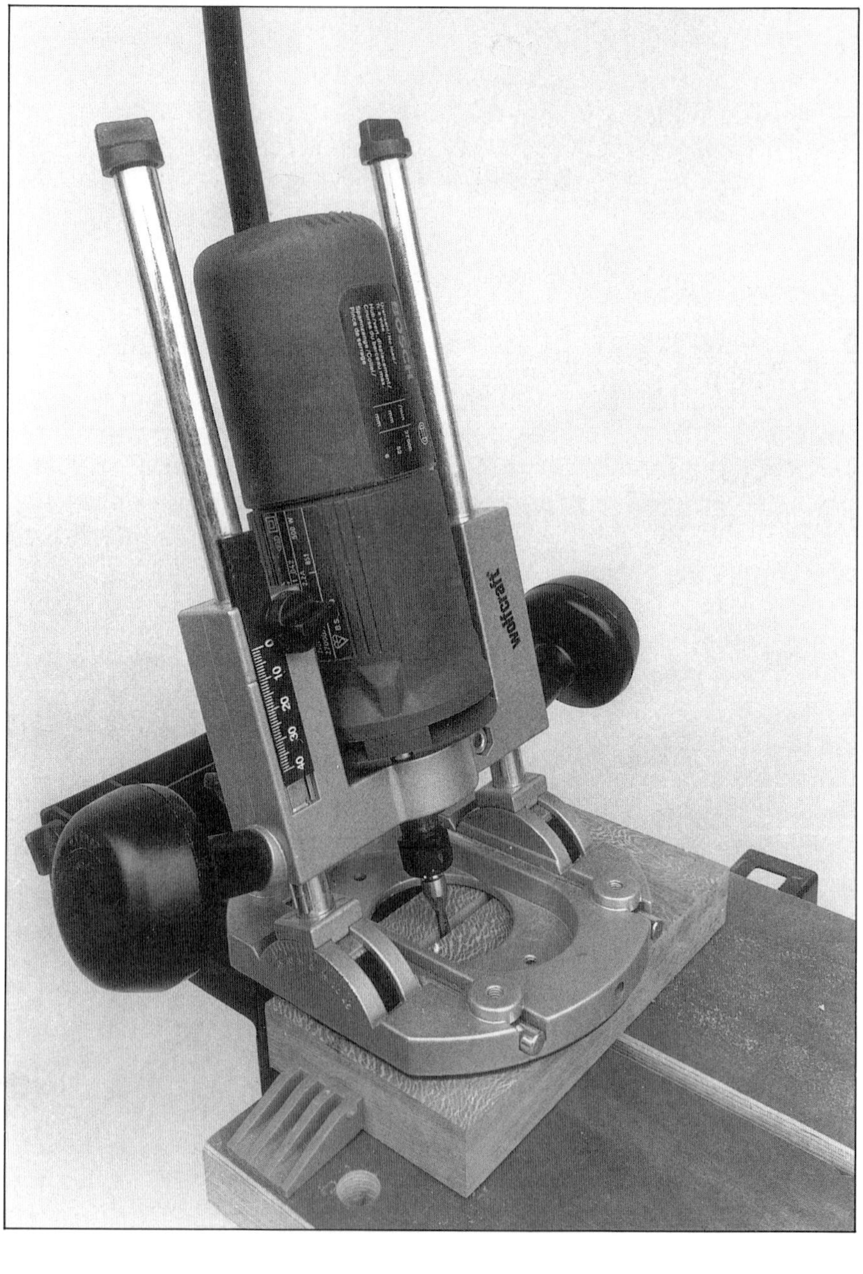

Fig 17.11 Wolfcraft Master Router and Drill Guide.

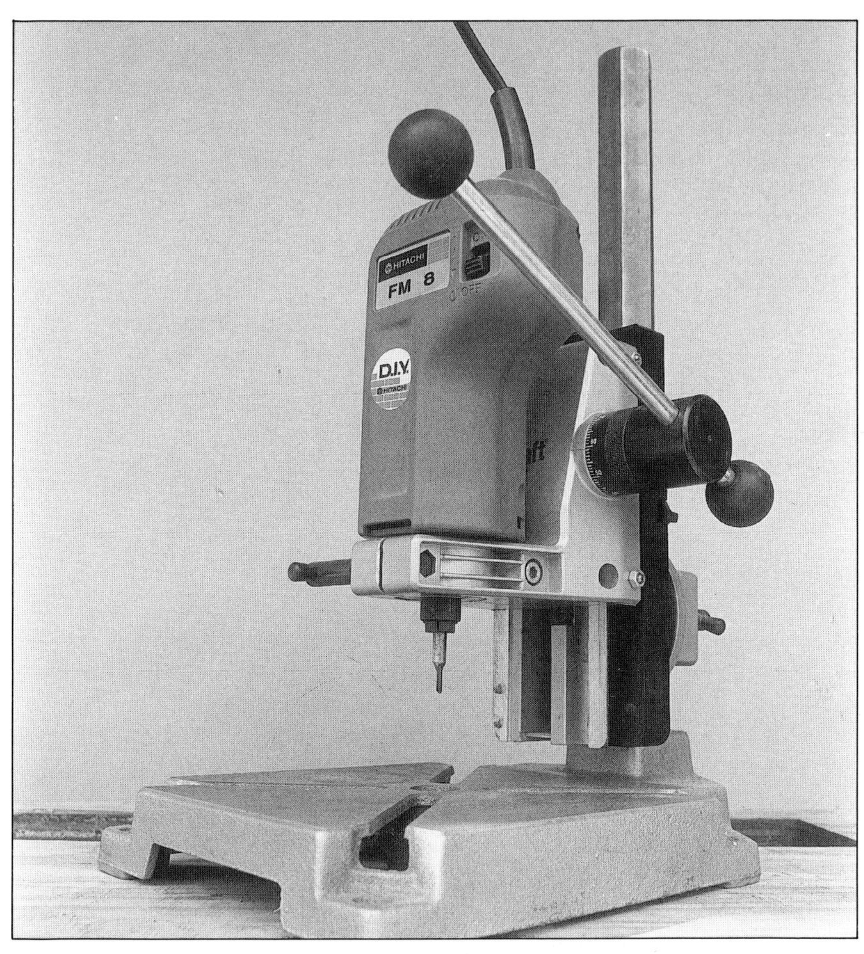

Fig 17.12 Hitachi drillstand.

DUSTMASTER (Racal)
A sophisticated head harness with separate cordless filter pack. The harness incorporates a sealed, high-impact polycarbonate visor (Fig 17.13). The Dustmaster 4 Mk2 provides clean, filtered air to the face, and eye protection.

DUST BAG
Usually a cotton bag with zip. Attaches to numerous electric tools drawing the dust or chippings away from the source. The fabric design acts as a filter as air passes through it.

DUST EXTRACTOR (heavy duty)
Wall- or floor-mounted, fixed or portable dust-extraction units are supplied by various manufacturers to collect dust and chippings. Power capacity generally 750–1000 watts.

DUST EXTRACTOR (bin type)
Similar in power rating but usually with a smaller collection capacity than the bag collector systems, and narrower diameter

Fig 17.13 The Racal Dustmaster 4 Mk2.

Fig 17.14 AEG dust extractor.

Fig 17.15 Black & Decker flexible drive.

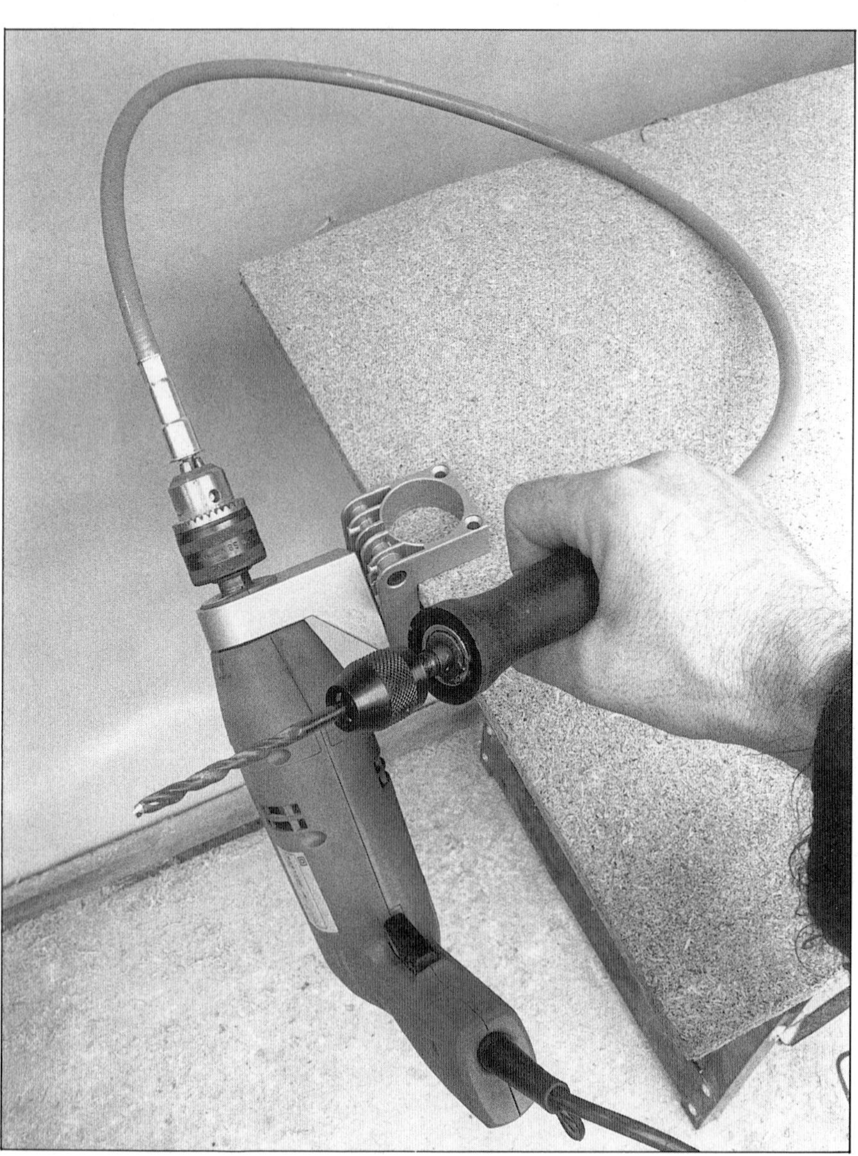
Fig 17.16 The Woody RKS 330 fretsaw from Luna.

hoses (50mm). Particularly suited to power tools (Fig 17.14).

ENGRAVING PEN

An actuating electric tool for wood, metal and other materials.

EXTENSION CABLE

PVC cable in varying lengths in open or closed reels with 13amp fused sockets. Also flexible coil cable useful for extending power tools in the workshop.

FLATBIT

A wonderful invention! Flat, forged-steel boring tool cutting holes from 6–38mm. Relatively inexpensive. Can be easily reground and tailored to suit specific tasks (see Fig 5.10).

FLEXIBLE DRIVE

For use with a portable drill, and with a small hand-tightened chuck on the end for reaching awkward spaces (Fig 17.15).

FRETSAW

A reciprocating saw with fine blade for intricate curved work up to 50mm thick (Fig 17.16).

GLUE GUN

Hot-melt glue gun for quick bonding of wood and other materials. 11mm gluesticks supplied in various lengths in packs. An invaluable extra pair of hands for temporary fixing. (See Fig 13.2.)

Fig 17.17 Makita cordless grinder.

GRINDER (cordless)
An extremely handy tool for cutting, abrading and tool-sharpening (Fig 17.17).

HAMMER DRILL
A portable drill, usually 2-speed, with hammer action for drilling into stonework or concrete. Switchable to normal drilling action, this is probably the most useful type of drill for general work.

HEAT GUN (hot air)
Versatile DIY tool for stripping varnish and paint, but also used for speeding up glue bonding or assisting the flow of glue with a hot-melt glue gun (Fig 17.18).

HOLE SAW
For use with a portable or pillar drill. Has hardened steel cutters of varying diameters which screw on to a universal mandrel with HSS pilot drill.

Fig 17.18 A Black & Decker heat gun.

HOLLOW CHISEL MORTICER
Basically a precision bench drill with clamping table. A drillbit (similar to the old brace and bit) turns within a square-edged chisel, combining drilling with compression cutting. Mortice bits: ¼in, ⅜in and ½in (Fig 17.19).

JIGSAW
A versatile reciprocating saw for wood,

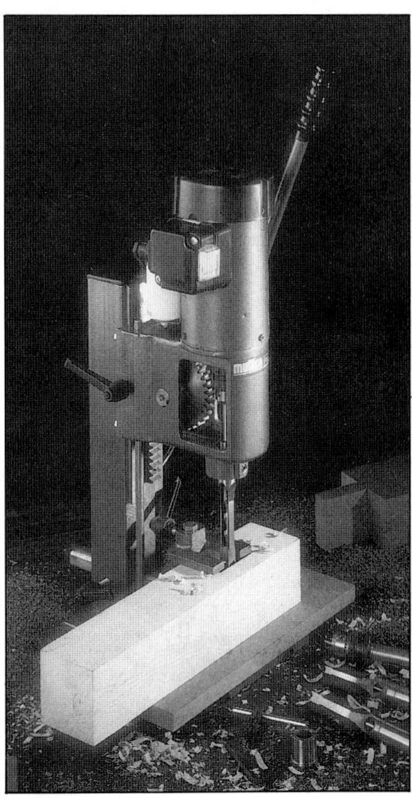

Fig 17.19 The Multico PM-12 portable hollow chisel morticer.

metal and plastics. Various types of disposable blade. Used for curved, straight and angled cutting. The most efficient jigsaws have an orbital cutting action (Fig 17.20).

JIGSAW TABLE
Saw table for converting portable jigsaws. Includes parallel fence.

KEYLESS CHUCK
Hand-tightened friction-grip chuck for most drills. Overcomes the frustrating problem of woodworkers losing chuck keys! (See Fig 5.4.)

LATHE
A bench- or floor-mounted rotary wood-

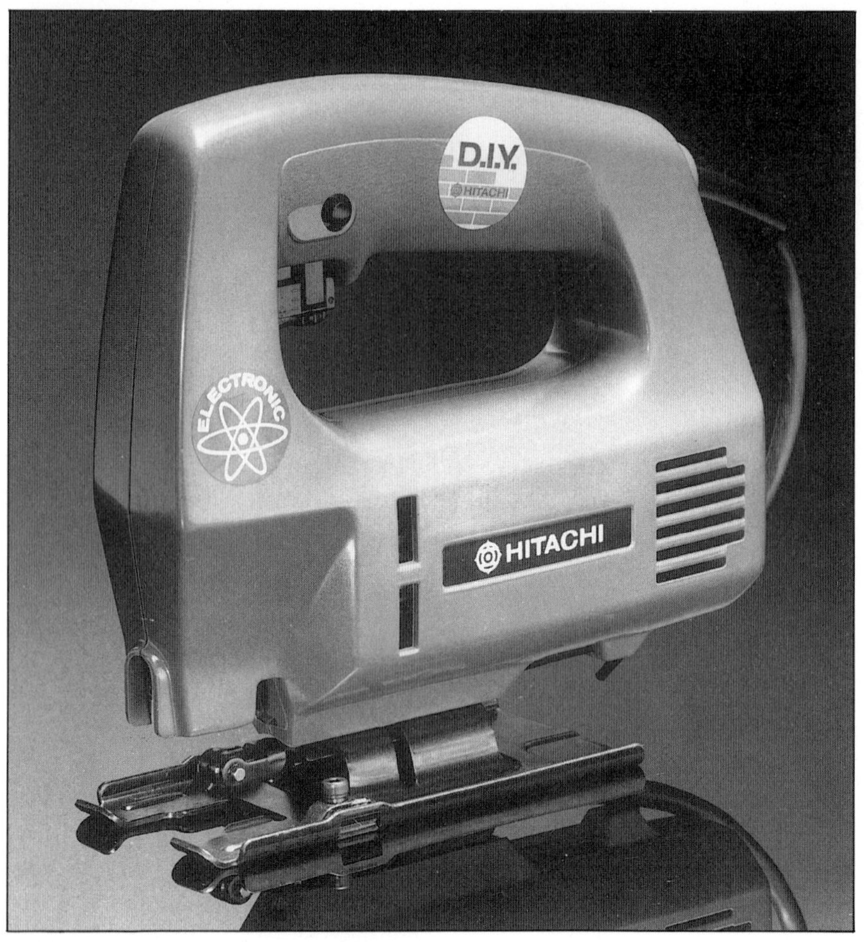

Fig 17.20 A jigsaw from Hitachi.

fashioning device. The wood is held in a faceplate, chuck or between centres, revolves at speed (350–2000rpm), and a chisel, scraper or gouge is fed into it, against a toolrest. Complete objects can be made ranging from bowls, chair legs and pepperpots to cricket bails (Fig 17.21).

LEIGH JIG

A simple, sturdy aluminium jig for accurate and highly attractive tailor-made dovetails up to 24in wide – and using any router. A range of dovetail variations can be cut quickly. (Originally developed and marketed in Canada by its British inventor.) (Fig 17.22)

LINISHER

A long bench-mounted belt sander for finishing flat or curved pieces of wood accurately (Fig 17.23).

MILLING MACHINE

Essentially a metalworking machine but with potential for woodworking. An overhead drill and router with sliding table carriage (Fig 17.24).

MITRE SAW

Made by various manufacturers, a pivoting crosscut saw, with adjustable arm for varied or set angles, for precision cutting. Blade diameters approx.: 255mm. 1400 watts average.

MOISTURE METER

An electronic field resister device for measuring the relative water or moisture content of timber. Two electrodes are plunged into the wood and a reading shows on a dial. Accurate readings are taken from the centre of the wood, so a cut may be required.

MORTICER

See Slot Morticer.

MULTI-PURPOSE WOOD JOINTER

A biscuit jointing attachment for use with angle grinders. Includes 100mm cutter.

ORBITAL SANDER

A popular and easy-to-use finishing sander. Either ⅓ or ½ sheet size. Power ratings: 18–550 watts. 5500–12000 orbits per min.(opm). The higher the better. (See page 146.)

OVERHEAD ROUTER

A purpose-built table which guides the router over the work, giving clear visibility, but relying on perfectly parallel thickness work.

PALM SANDER

A miniature orbital sander for small areas and getting into cramped spaces. 12000–14000 rpm.

Fig 17.21 The Luna Woody SV 300 woodturning lathe.

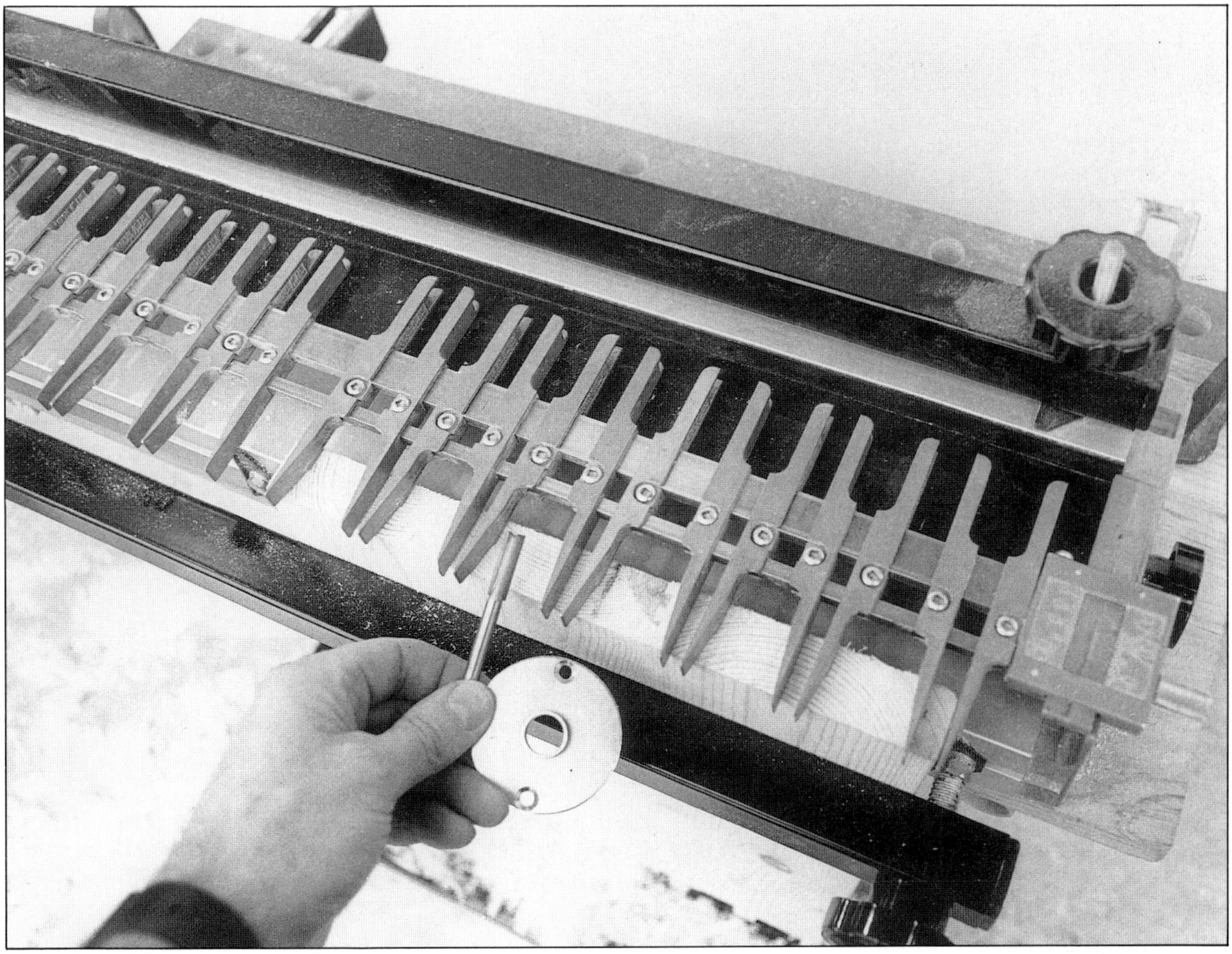

Fig 17.22 The Leigh dovetail jig.

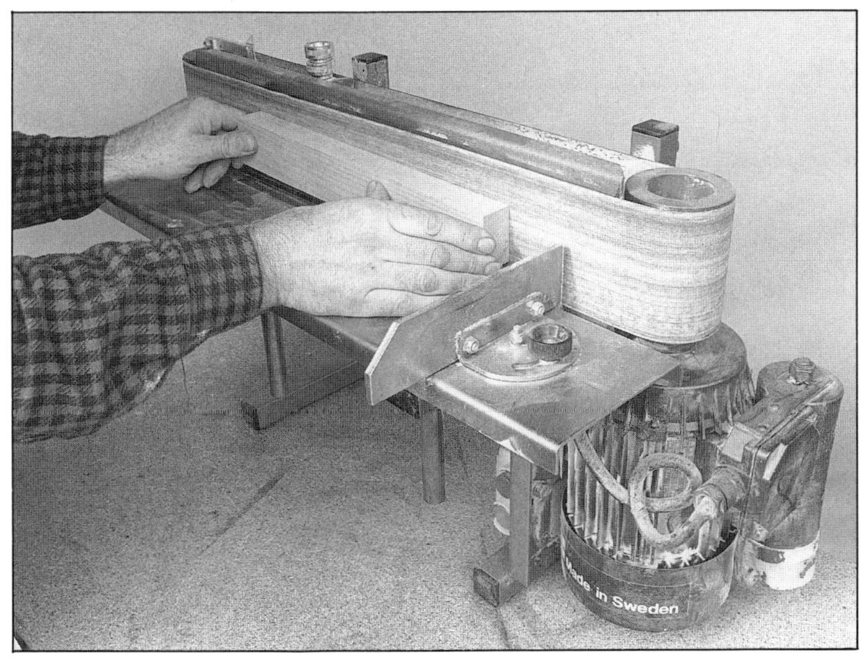

Fig 17.23 The linisher in action (below).

Fig 17.24 The author's Alpine milling machine.

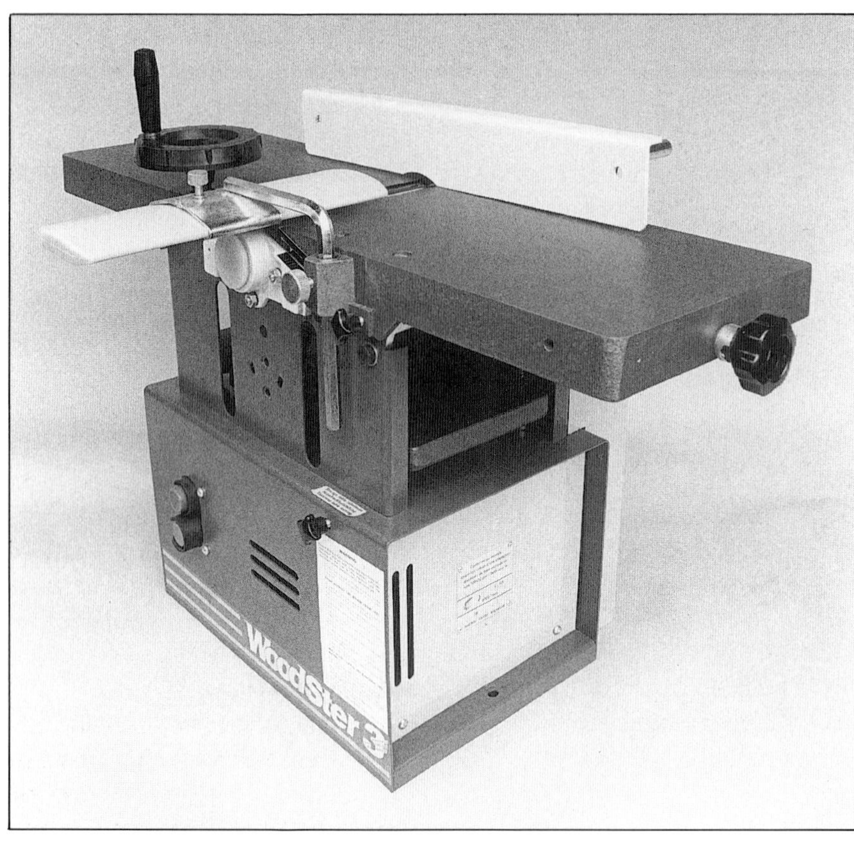

Fig 17.25 The Kity Woodster 3 planer–thicknesser.

PANEL SAW

A jigged circular saw for cutting manufactured board up to 8ft × 4ft to accurate dimensions (see page 125).

PENDULUM ROUTER JIG

A swinging router jig made of metal or wood for shaping concaved recesses and 'adze'-type finish (see Fig 7.7).

PERCUSSION DRILL

See Hammer Drill.

PLANER (portable)

A hand-held power planer with 2-blade cutter block, similar to the bench-mounted machines. Up to 122mm width of cut. For surfacing and rebating (see Chapter 9).

PLANER–THICKNESSER (mini)

Approx. 6in × 4in capacity. Power: 750–950 watts. Cutter speed: 6000–7500rpm. Thicknessing rate of feed approx. 8 metres/min. 17–31kg (Fig 17.25).

PLUNGING ROUTER

The popular modern router. It has a retractable spring-loaded base so that the cutter is guided or plunged into the work

Fig 17.26 (b) The business end of the Powerfile.

Fig 17.26 (a) The Black & Decker Powerfile with integral dustbag.

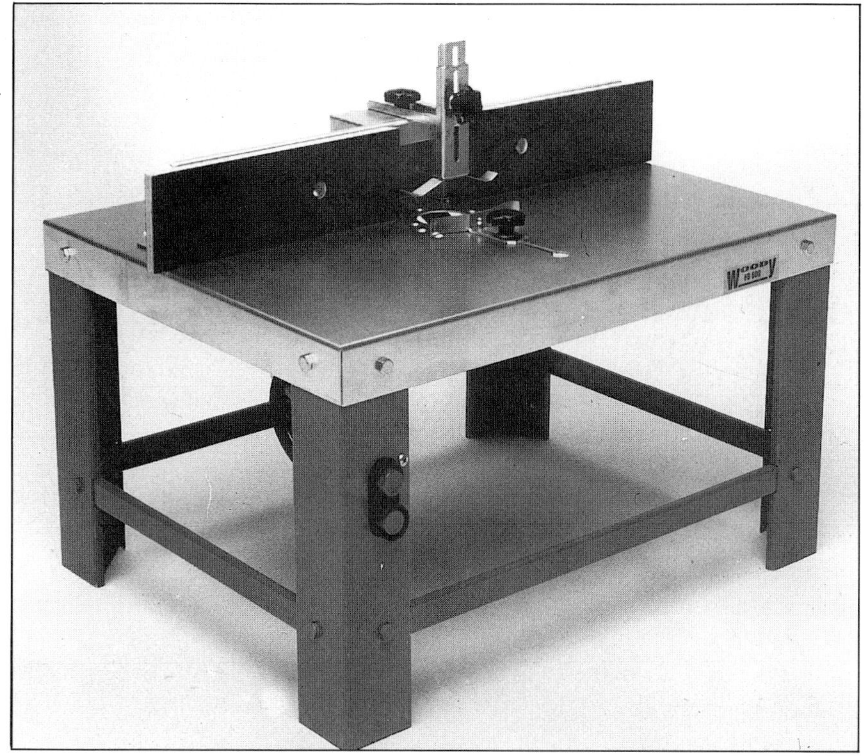

Fig 17.27 The Luna Woody FB 600 router table.

then released clear of the work at the end of the cut. The cutter can be depth-adjusted and locked as part of its plunge action. (See Chapter 7.)

POLISHING BONNET

Attached to rubber disc for use in portable drill. Normally 4in diameter. Lambswool for buffing waxed finishes etc.

PORTABLE GENERATOR

Petrol-driven 110–240 volt (110 is safer for outdoor work). Wattage: 550–2400. Single phase A/C current.

POWERFILE

A portable, narrow, belt-sanding tool by Black & Decker for filing, carving, and shaping. It has an integral dust bag (Figs 17.26 (a) and (b)).

RADIAL ARM SAW

Essentially a crosscutting saw where the work is table-mounted and the saw-head drawn across it. Blade can be positioned to cut in any angle or direction, raised or lowered, and optional functions include routing, drum sanding and drilling. (See Chapter 12).

ROTARY ORBITAL SANDER

A combination of disc and orbital sander – the abrasive disc moves eccentrically while rotating. Suitable for small contours (concave and convex). (See page 147.)

ROTARY RASP

For shaping/abrading wood in various profiles and diameters. 6.35mm shank.

ROUTER

See Plunging Router.

ROUTER TABLE

Supplied by various tool manufacturers for inverted routing (Fig 17.27).

SANDER

See Orbital, Belt, Palm, Disc and Linisher.

SCREWDRIVER

See Drill-driver.

SCROLLER JIGSAW

An omni-directional jigsaw whose blade is rotated to the required direction of cut. Slightly more difficult to master than an ordinary jigsaw as pressure has to be maintained behind the direction of the cut.

SLIDE COMPOUND SAW

A precision universal-angle circular saw working on a sliding arm. Various pre-set angle cuts, 920 watt motor. Can cut timber up to 65mm thick and 305mm wide (Fig 17.28).

Fig 17.28 Hitachi slide compound saw.

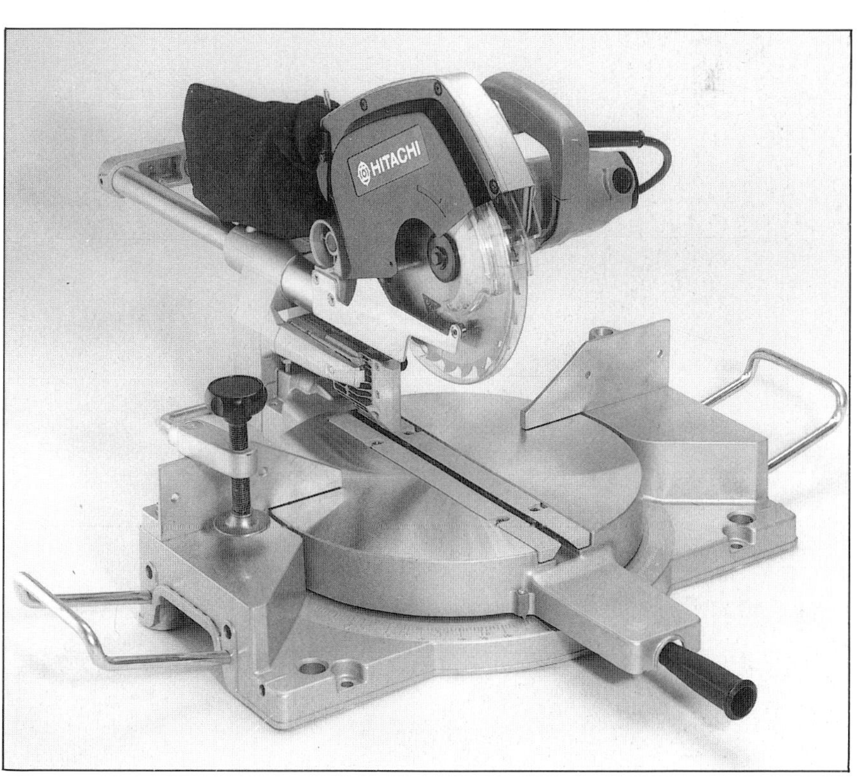

Fig 17.29 Ross SS 26 wide panel sander for the small workshop. Capacity up to 26in wide, 6in thick.

SLOT MORTICER

A horizontally mounted milling attachment with a bit similar to a router cutter usually attached to a planer–thicknesser or universal woodworking machine. Cutters range from 6mm to 16mm. The work is clamped to a table which slides by means of a lever.

SPINDLE MOULDER

A giant inverter router with larger cutter block (average 32mm spindle). Generally used in industrial workshops, though superseded by current large-capacity portable routers. Used for edge treatment of long boards and other repeat work – curved components etc.

SPRAY GUN

Actuating integral motor links up with an electric compressor for applying cellulose and acid catalyst lacquers. Requires properly ventilated work area (industrial applications mainly).

STAPLEGUN

See Tacker.

SURFACING PLANER

A large, flat-bedded 2- or 3-cutter block planer for getting boards flat and 'square'. Thicknessing is done on a separate thicknesser.

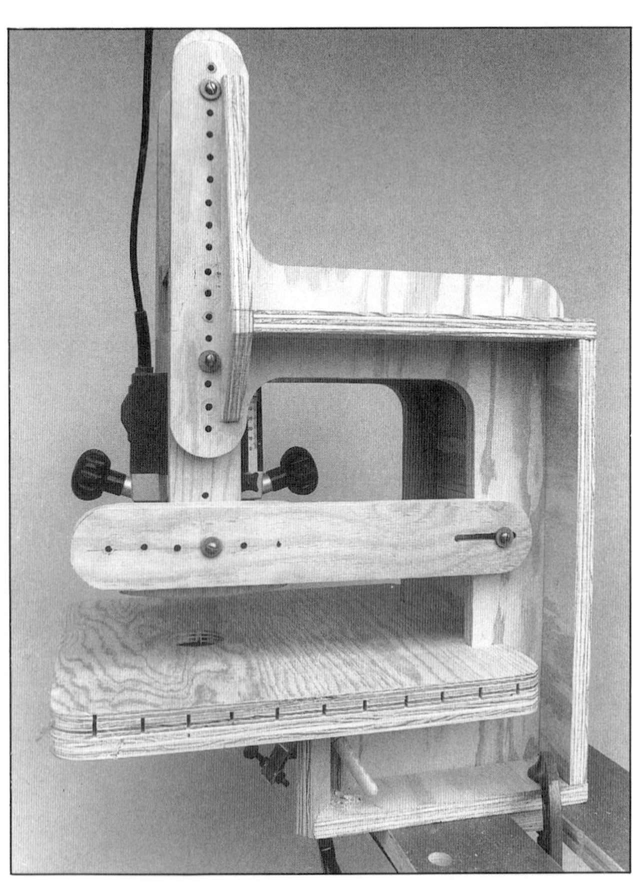

Fig 17.30 (a) The JKB universal routing table in overhead routing mode.

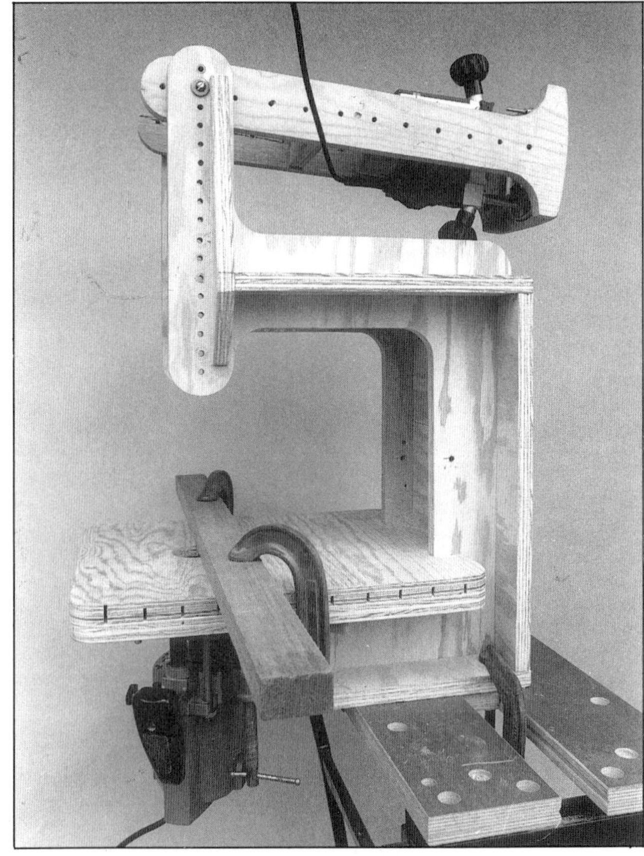

Fig 17.30 (b) The table with the pendulum arm and router swung back out of the way.

Fig 17.31 The Woodrat wood-jointing system.

TABLE SAW
A circular saw, usually with rise and fall and tilt facility. Blade diameters: 140–300mm. An ideal small workshop size is 250mm. Normally the depth of cut is about one third of the saw-blade diameter. A rip and mitre fence is included and some larger saws have extended sliding carriages for cutting large panels. Models vary from relatively inexpensive pressed-steel versions to heavy cast-iron or aluminium.

TACKER
An adjustable impact tool for driving in staples and nails up to approx. 19mm. Ideal for upholstery, and thin wood panel and sheet fixing. (See Fig 16.8.)

THICKNESSER (attachment)
An aluminium attachment for linking to a power planer enabling surfacing and thicknessing of limited dimension, e.g. up to approx 75mm. It is also available for use with some surface planers, i.e. stationary machines such as those from Myford and Coronet. (See Fig 9.24.)

THREE-DIMENSIONAL CARVING JIG (see copy carving jig, dupli-carver)

TRITON WORKCENTRE See Fig 15.4 (a).
A multi-purpose power tool bench which operates in various modes for utilizing electric tools such as jigsaw, router, circular saw. An extension table is available.

TWIST DRILL
For use in a portable or pillar drill. HSS with two helical flutes, 1.6mm–12.8mm diameter. Metal drills better for wood. Tips ground at 45–59°.

UNIVERSAL DRILL CLAMP
A robust cast-aluminium device for clamping a power drill in any position on or beside the workbench. Adjusted with an Allen key.

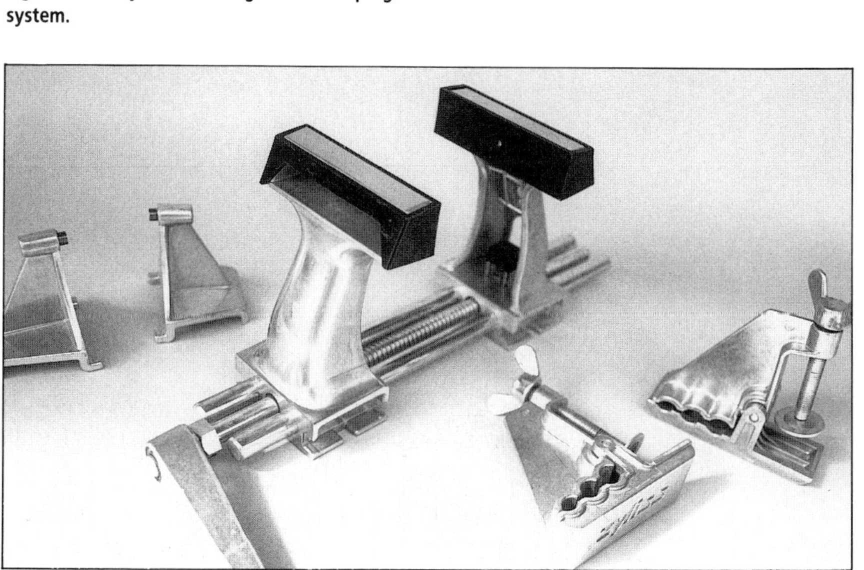

Fig 17.32 The Zyliss Profi-King bench-clamping system.

UNIVERSAL MACHINE
A multi-function woodworking machine with space-saving advantages. A variety of sizes and types available combining saw, spindle moulder, slot morticer, planer–thicknesser and bandsaw. (See Chapter 15.)

WIDE PANEL SANDER
For small workshops, a thicknessing sander with continuous belt up to 26in wide × 6in thick with automatic feed (Fig 17.29).

UNIVERSAL CHARGER
For charging most brands of detachable nickel cadmium battery packs. The Black & Decker Rapide Universal will fully charge batteries from 2.4-13.2 volts in 13 minutes or less. Such chargers cost many times more the manufacturers' slower designated chargers. (See also Charger.)

UNIVERSAL ROUTING TABLE
A 3-mode routing table (inverted, overhead pendulum) by Jeremy Broun (Figs 17.30 (a) and (b)).

WOLFCRAFT PIONEER
A versatile space-saving worktable for planing, shaping and sawing for a wide range of applications. Regular and awkwardly-shaped work can be held in the vice and dogs (see Fig 15.22).

WOODRAT
A wood-jointing device capable of cutting attractive precision dovetails in stock as thin as ⅛in and as thick as 2in. Batch jointing, tenon and housing cutting etc. (Fig 17.31).

WORKMATE (Black & Decker)
A truly intelligent clamping, holding and supporting device which is lightweight, compact and stable. The benchtop accommodates irregular-shaped work and can hold dowel while sawing.

ZYLISS CLAMP
An ingenious bench-clamping system made from aircraft aluminium (Fig 17.32).

ZYLISS LATHE ATTACHMENT
Similar in construction to the Zyliss vice, this attachment accommodates any drill with 43mm universal collar. Integral revolving 'live' centre.

RONSEAL
SATINCOAT

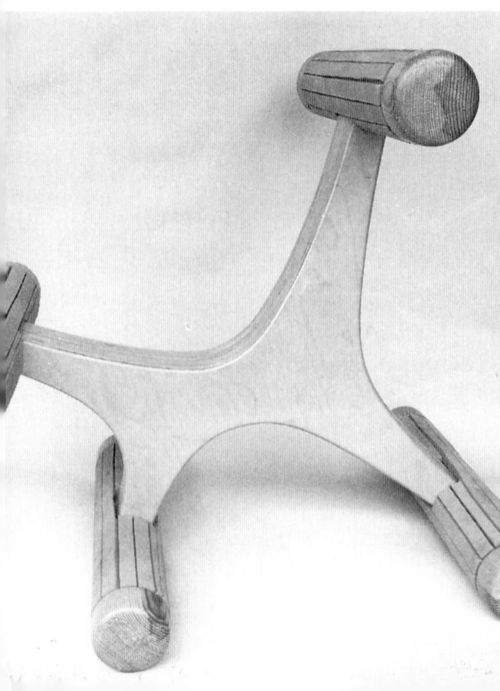

PROJECTS

18

JKB BENCH

Woodworking benches in general tend to be standardized and expensive, and there is a tendency to look backwards in terms of the design rather than meet current needs. Of course I am not talking about those ingenious, lightweight folding appliances such as the Workmate, but there must surely be life beyond the solid beech, traditional bench!

One of my first benches, and one I still use, was made from pitch pine railway sleepers and plywood, and it is perfectly adequate for what I call 'heavyweight woodworking'. Bear in mind that the Workmate and similar devices are not really designed to take a pounding from a mallet or hammer, and when using such tools the work should never be placed in the vice but supported on the bench top.

Here is a bench (Fig 18.1) which I designed in the workshop as I went along – with a few requirements in the back of my mind – setting myself the challenge of using only a single sheet of 8ft × 4ft plywood in its construction to keep down the cost.

The result is:

- It is made from a single sheet of 18mm manufactured board. (I used douglas fir shutter ply, but birch or even 18mm MDF could be used.)

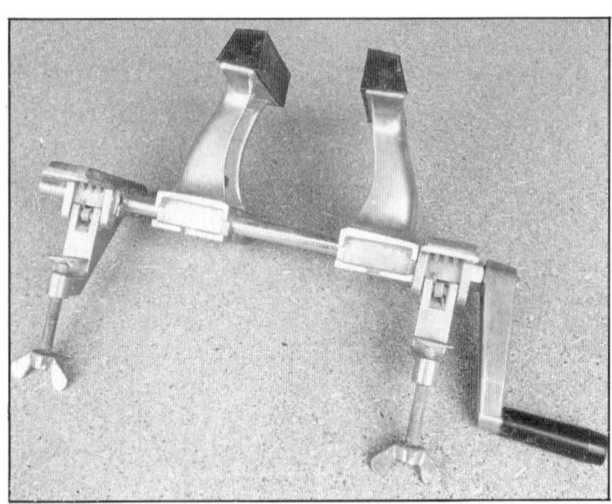

Fig 18.1 The JKB workbench made from a single sheet of plywood.

Fig 18.2(b) The versatile Zyliss vice.

Fig 18.2(a) An inexpensive, if slightly limited, aluminium vice.

- It is relatively easy to build (see power tool options).
- It is strong, solid and compact.
- It is 'knockdown', allowing for easy freighting or storage.
- It will take a variety of vices (Figs 18.2(a) and (b)).
- It has a novel method of clamping 'dogs'.
- Its 'hook' is useful for stabilizing large panels.
- It has under-bench top storage for the Toolbox (see Chapter 19).
- Its top is easy to clamp to, being 54mm thick,

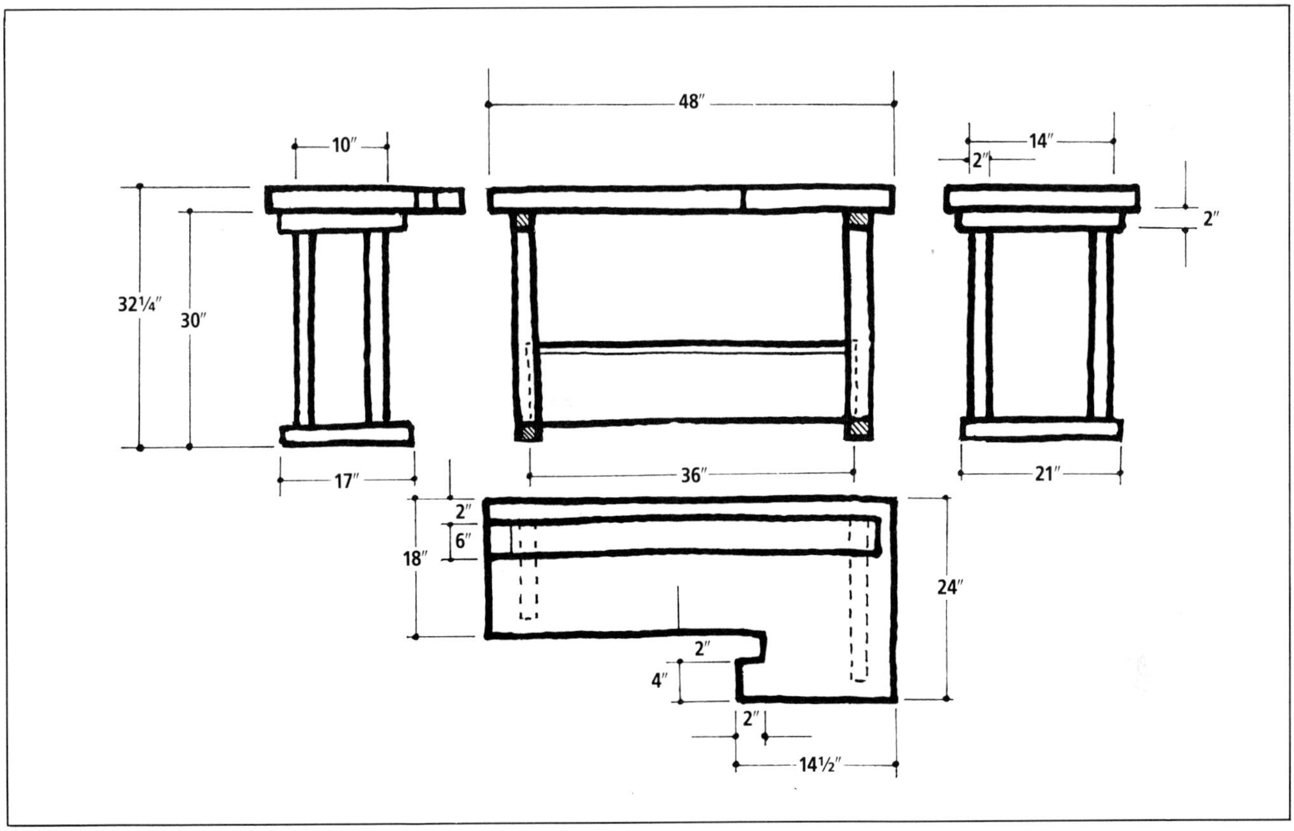

Fig 18.3 The JKB bench.

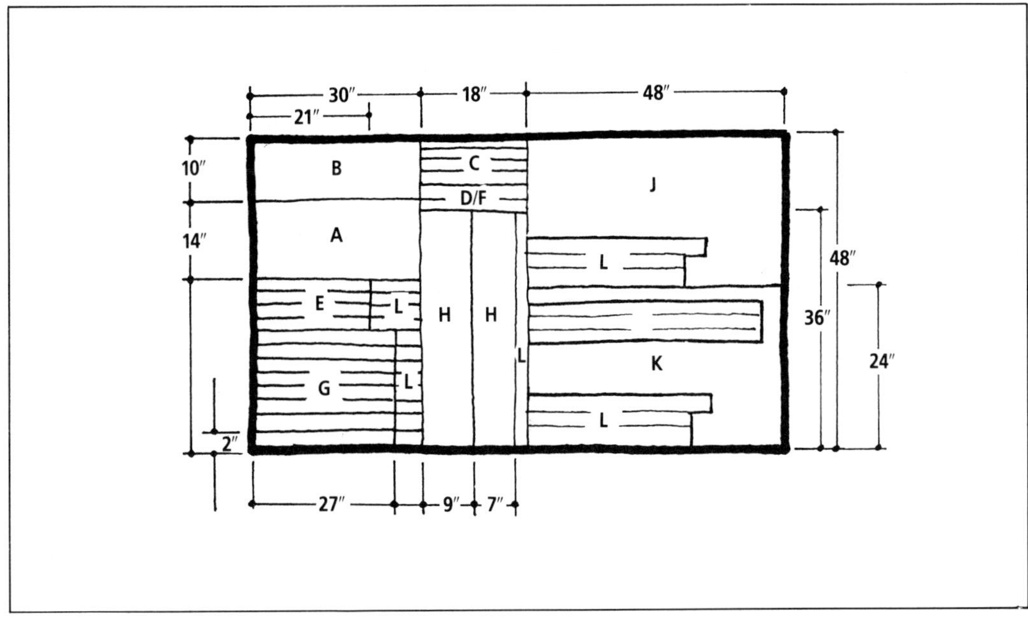

Fig 18.4(a) All the components fit into an 8ft × 4ft sheet of ply.

easily conforming to manufacturers' clamping systems (e.g. Wolfcraft, Zyliss).

PROCEDURE

1 Select a good sheet of plywood. It is likely to be slightly warped (which can be remedied by laminating), but avoid heavily plugged sheets (they do vary enormously). Shuttering plywood is sold as 'one good face', meaning the other face is likely to be heavily plugged (knots removed).

2 Mark out the components and code them (Figs 18.3 and 18.4 (a) and (b)).

3 Cut the components. I used a jigsaw with a medium-toothed blade.

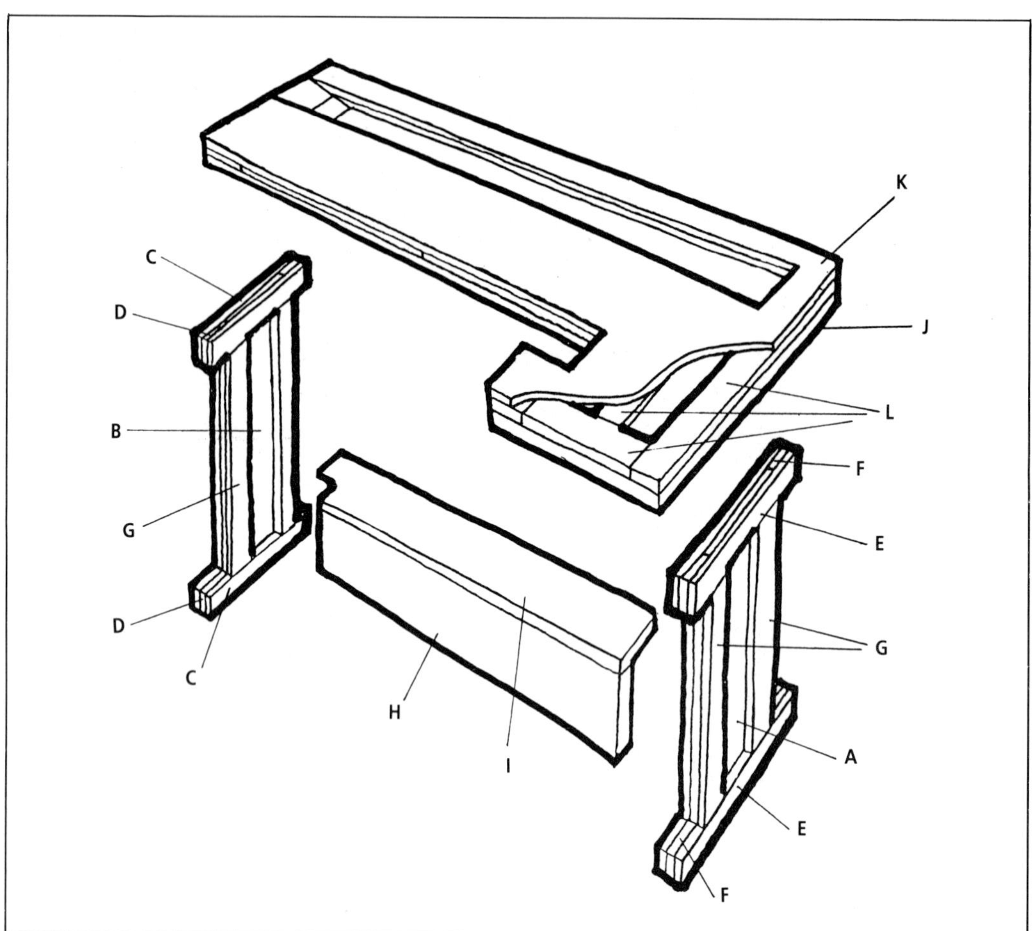

Fig 18.4(b) Exploded view showing main components.

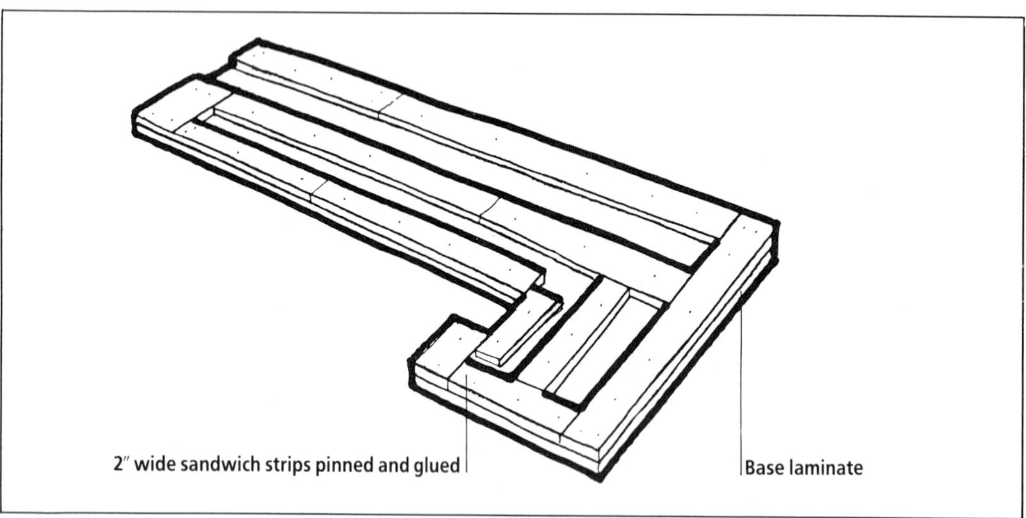

Fig 18.5 The economic construction of the bench top.

4 Trim the components. I used a planer-thicknesser to dress those edges which will show. Internal edges do not matter. The thicknesser is set to the standard width of the 'ribbed' members (Fig 18.5).

5 Glue and clamp the laminates to form the bench top, and the two uprights. If you do not have enough G-clamps you can pin the laminates together using sunken nails – they will hardly show when a plastic wood filler is used.

6 Clean up the laminated edges with a power sander (Fig 18.6).

7 Locate and drill holes for coach screw fixings for bench top and uprights (Fig 18.7).

Fig 18.6 Cleaning up the plywood edges with an orbital sander.

Fig 18.7 Drilling holes for the coach screw fixings.

Fig 18.8 The coach screws are tightened up.

8 Construct centre piece and locate and drill fixings into uprights using clamps to position the pieces.
9 Bolt bench together (Fig 18.8).
10 Cut tapered section for tool trough – this is for easy cleaning and chippings removal (Fig 18.9).
11 Fix vice of choice to bench top (Fig 18.10).
12 Clean up bench top with a power sander or planer (setting it very finely).
13 Mark out and drill holes for 'dogs' (Fig 18.11) using a 20mm flatbit. It will accommodate plastic dogs from other workbenches.
14 Construct dogs and wedges, turning the dowel on the lathe (Figs 18.12 and 18.13). Clean up the wedges on the disc sander (Fig 18.14) and glue the dowels in.
15 Varnish or paint the bench if desired.

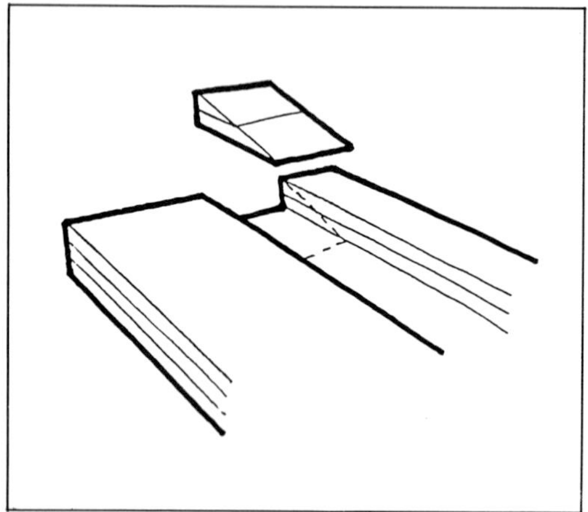

Fig 18.9 The end of the tool trough is tapered for easy cleaning with a brush.

Fig 18.10 Facing the vice with a suitable hardwood.

Fig 18.11 Drilling holes for the dogs.

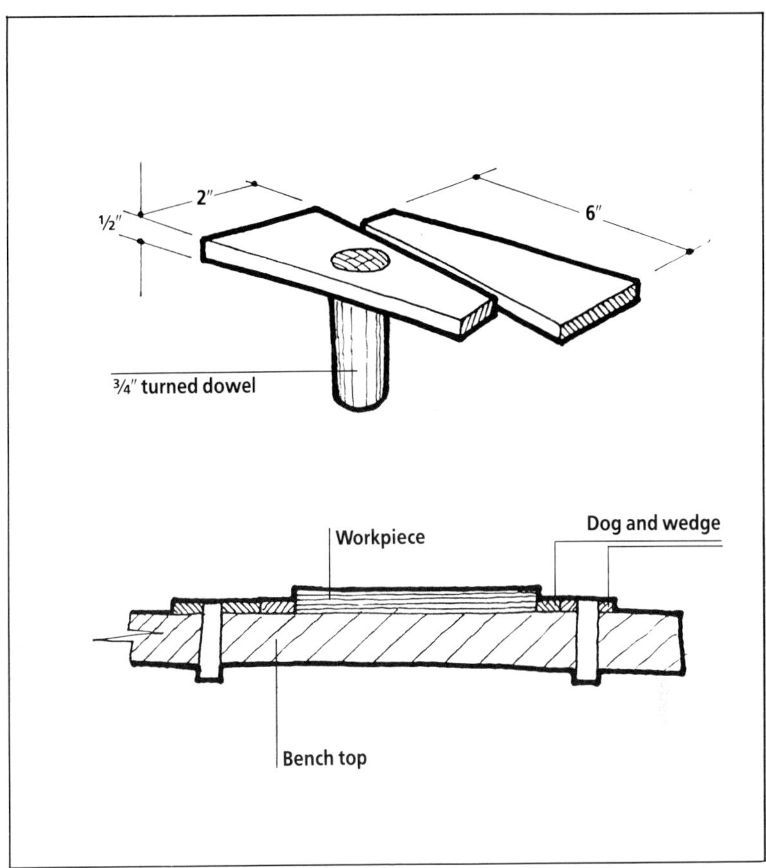

Fig 18.12 A length of hardwood turned on the lathe for the dogs.

Fig 18.13 Dogs/wedges (above right).

Fig 18.14 Sand all edges of the dogs/wedges on the disc sander.

TOOLBOX

This toolbox is not my design (Fig 19.1) – indeed, some readers may recognize it as the standard issue toolbox from days past at colleges such as Shoreditch. I made one during my first week at Shoreditch College in 1963. It was to accommodate a full range of hand tools and I have not come across a better design (and I still use the tools).

I am deliberately including a toolbox for *hand tools* in this book because it should be emphasized that hand tools are essential in any woodworking. *Sole* reliance on electric tools would not only be Philistine, it would also be impractical.

Whereas many cutting operations are better done with electric tools, there is still a need for tools such as handsaws (which occasionally are quicker and don't need setting up), and in particular marking out and measuring tools. It seems to me good sense to start off with a basic set of hand tools, which needn't cost a lot of money. In my case I have a collection of tools from my student

Fig 19.1 Toolbox.

Fig 19.2 Some basic hand tools.

Fig 19.3 Designate the more handy tools to the lid.

days, together with odd second-hand planes and inexpensive chisels etc. which I have picked up since. In fact I occasionally browse through my local Saturday afternoon market on the lookout for old (and interesting) tools.

Before discussing the toolbox design, let's consider what a *basic toolkit* might include (Fig 19.2):

- steel rule (24in rule/straightedge)
- try-square
- marking gauge
- hammer
- mallet
- handsaw (up to 26in)
- tenon saw
- dovetail saw
- sliding bevel
- drill (electric drill–driver)
- G-clamp(s)
- jack plane
- spokeshave
- coping saw
- set of twist drills/flatbits
- centre punch, nail punches
- shallow tray for holding: screws, pins, glue, pencils, etc.

The challenge with a toolbox is how to combine compactness with ease of handling and access. Ideally, tools should be secured in allocated positions, and there is no single, simple, fixing method. Whereas 'Terry clips' may adequately support chisels and many other tools, a handsaw or try-square will need a different kind of fixing.

Of paramount importance is the *ease of access* of tightly packed tools, and it is here that the flap-down design is hard to beat. It pays to spend some time thinking about what tools should go where, and to play around with a glue gun temporarily 'tabbing' tools or their fixings to see what works out best. The most commonly used tools should be positioned where they can be easily accessed, and I have chosen to designate certain tools to the flap-down lid (Fig 19.3). This leaves the box cavity (below the shelves) as a 'free' area, offering flexibility as to what tools are stored. For instance, if you are going to work in someone's house and they do not have a bench, a portable vice such as the Zyliss clamp, which clamps on to an ordinary table, can be stored in the tool-box. Similarly, various compact electric tools such as drills, small routers and jig-saws can be packed into this free space, although the final decision is a personal one. It may be that the toolbox contains a combination of small electric tools *and* some essential hand tools.

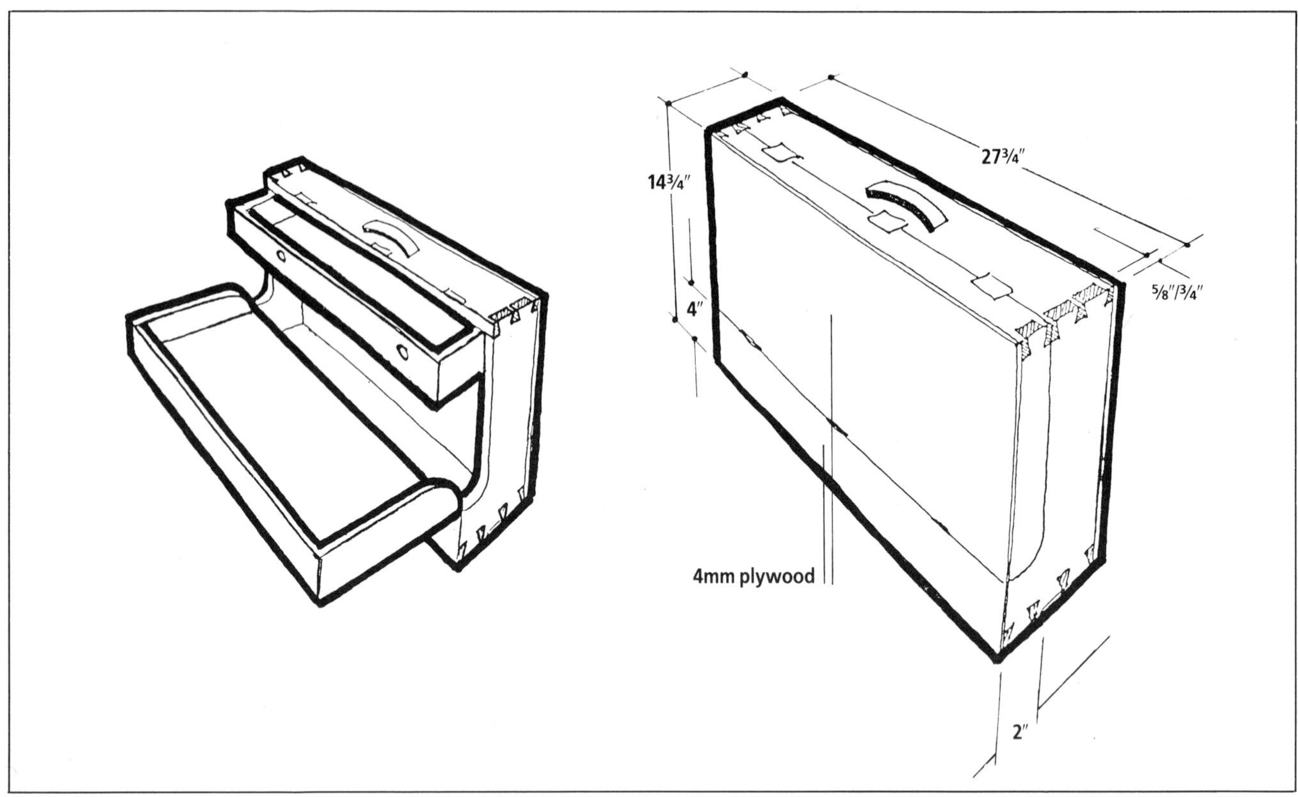

Fig 19.4 A well-proven and time-tested toolbox design.

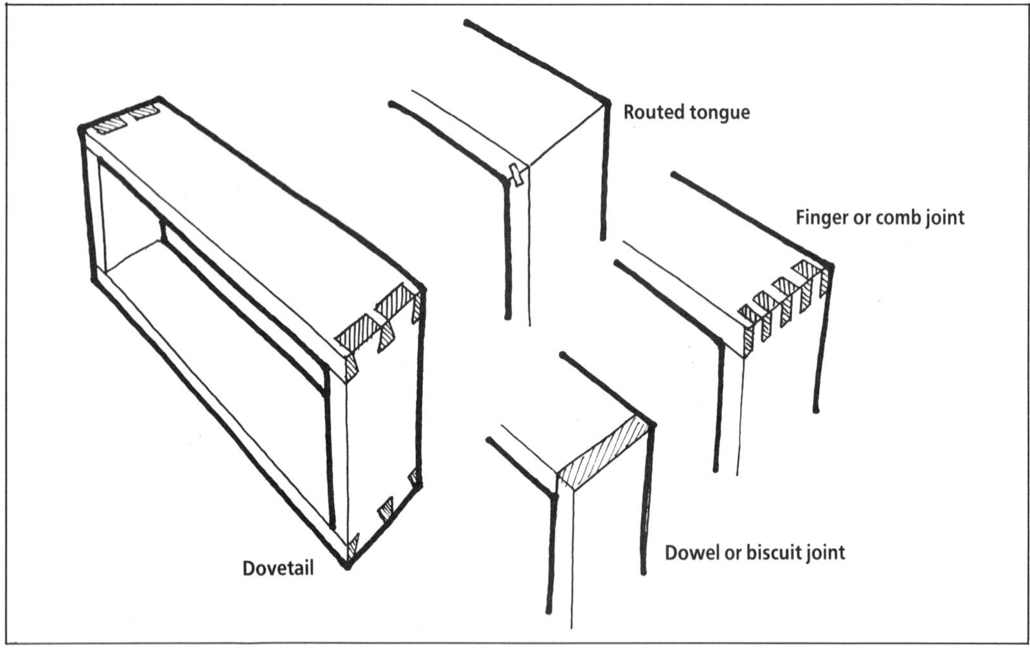

Fig 19.5 Some joint options for the carcase.

The design of this toolbox is a standard 4-sided narrow carcase construction in solid pine (top, sides and base), with plywood panels glued and pinned (front and rear), and the lid 'split' and hinged afterwards (Fig 19.4).

The choice of carcase joints is wide open, ranging from dovetails (using the Leigh or Woodrat jigs), to butt, mitred and reinforced joints (using the radial arm saw, biscuit jointer etc.) (Fig 19.5).

The toolbox contains 2 loose drawers which can be made of MDF, and the ironmongery includes handle, hinges, lock and clasps, and a piece of chain to support the opened lid. The base has 'skis' and the lid is lined with a thin rubber strip

(Fig 19.6) to seal it. I have also fitted a mortice lock on my toolbox.

With a full complement of tools this design offers a compact and practical solution for workshop or site use and it complements the bench (page 194) by adding a little more weight to it by locating it under the bench top (Fig 19.7).

PROCEDURE

1 Prepare toolbox carcase members to size. You may wish to use a wide-board material or you can edge-joint narrow boards. Make sure the face side and edge marks are put on each piece.

2 Cut corner joints. I chose to use through/ common dovetails. These can be cut on a Leigh or Woodrat jig (see pages 59 and 60).

3 Clean up inside surfaces with an orbital sander and glue and clamp carcase, checking for squareness (Fig 19.8).

4 Trim edges of carcase (it's easier with a hand plane). Prepare the front and back panels from 6mm plywood (birch is stouter). Make these slightly oversize.

5 Power sand (orbital) the inside faces of the plywood and glue and pin to carcase, checking again for squareness.

6 Trim edges of plywood flush with the carcase and soften them with abrasive paper. Using a marking gauge, scribe lines for the parting of the lid (4mm gap for saw kerf). Shade waste area. Mark curve for the radiused lid.

7 Carefully cut the lid off using a jigsaw (to start the cut you may wish to use a handsaw at one

Fig 19.6 Rubber strip is used to seal the lid.

Fig 19.7 The JKB toolbox adds weight to the JKB bench!

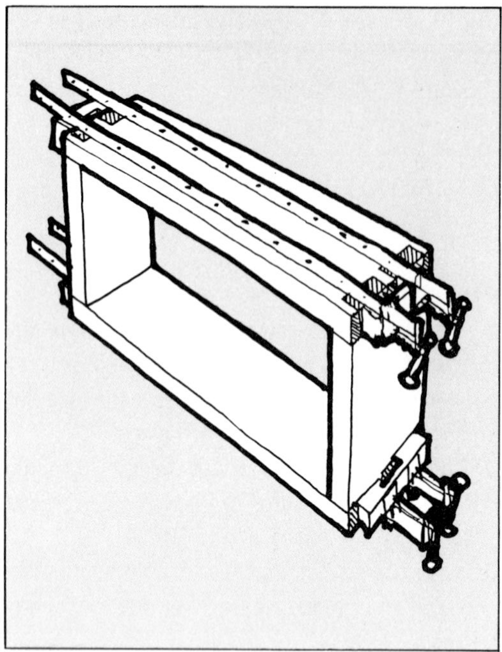

Fig 19.8 Clamp the carcase joints together.

corner). Alternatively, a portable circular saw can be used with the fence set to make the straight cuts, but this is a tricky operation and the cut must fall within the tramlines marked out (the carcase will probably need to be held in the vice). The lid will gently come away from the carcase as the cuts join up.

8 Trim the sawn edges carefully with a hand plane or power planer set extremely finely. An abrasive stick may be necessary as well, especially on the curve.

9 Mark out and cut the hinges – a small router with a fence can be used for this. Attach the hinges.

10 Mark out and attach the catches, and cut a mortice for a lock if one is required (the router can be used for this). Attach a suitable handle.

11 Attach 'skis' to the base.

12 Prepare tray material and construct two narrow trays. Attach tray runners to the carcase.

13 Attach rubber strip lining to the opening edge of the toolbox.

14 Fit out the inside to match your requirements (Fig 19.9).

15 The drawers can be partitioned to suit (Fig 19.10). The area of space immediately above the drawer is designated for hand saws and try-square (Fig 19.11).

16 Remove catches and handle, clamp box closed and power sand with an orbital sander. Soften all edges with abrasive paper.

17 Apply several coats of polyurethane varnish, either matt or gloss (Fig 19.12).

18 I used dry transfer to identify my toolbox, but a more permanent effect could be achieved with a router with a V–groove cutter.

19 Apply more varnish and replace the handles and catches (Fig 19.13).

Fig 19.9 Using a Skil screwdriver to fix Terry clips for the tools.

Fig 19.10 The space above the trays is for hand saws and try-square. The space below is 'free'.

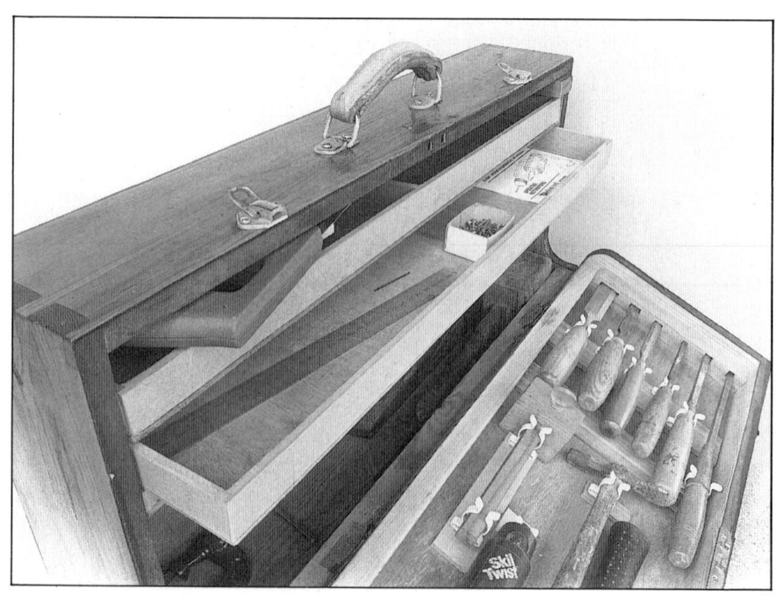

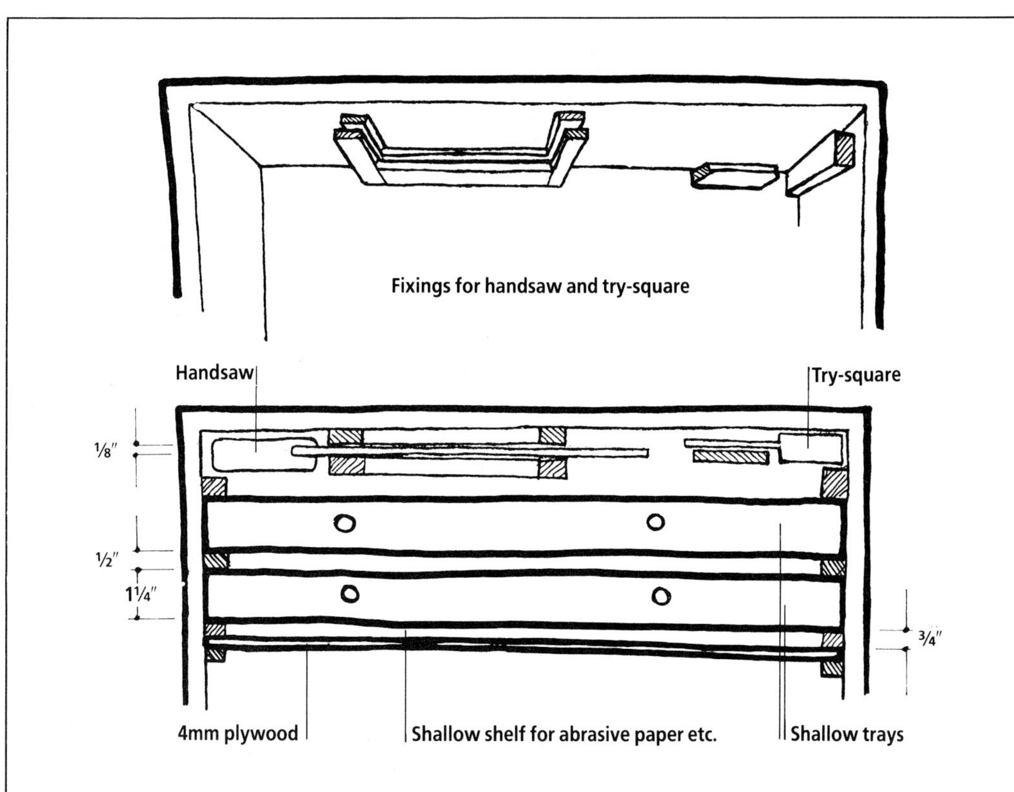

Fig 19.11 The fixings for hand saws and try-square.

Fig 19.12 Applying a robust finish to the toolbox.

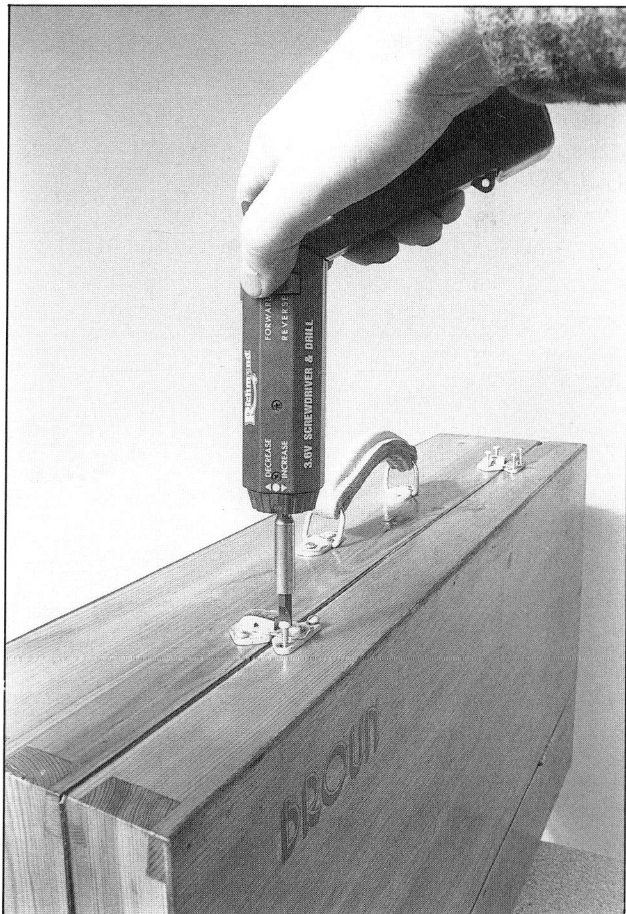

Fig 19.13 The Richmond drill-driver quickly fixes the catches and handle.

20

NEST OF TABLES

An appropriate description of a well-designed piece of furniture was once given by the Germany company Braun, 'It is rather like the traditional English butler – always there when you need him and you don't notice him when you don't need him!' And so it is with the nest of tables. A very useful piece of furniture but one which should take a back seat when not required.

This simple design is both visually understated and highly practicable, offering not only three tables in one, but a system which is easy to use (Fig 20.1). Many traditional designs tend to be top heavy, leggy and awkward, which means that both hands are needed to lift the tables into position, and that means putting down the tea tray somewhere else while you are doing this! The nest of tables shown here is designed for ease of use and one-handed operation. While the tray is in one hand you simply *slide* the table (or tables) into position with the other.

I have chosen to build this design (Fig 20.2) from solid ash, edge-jointed in narrow strips. It

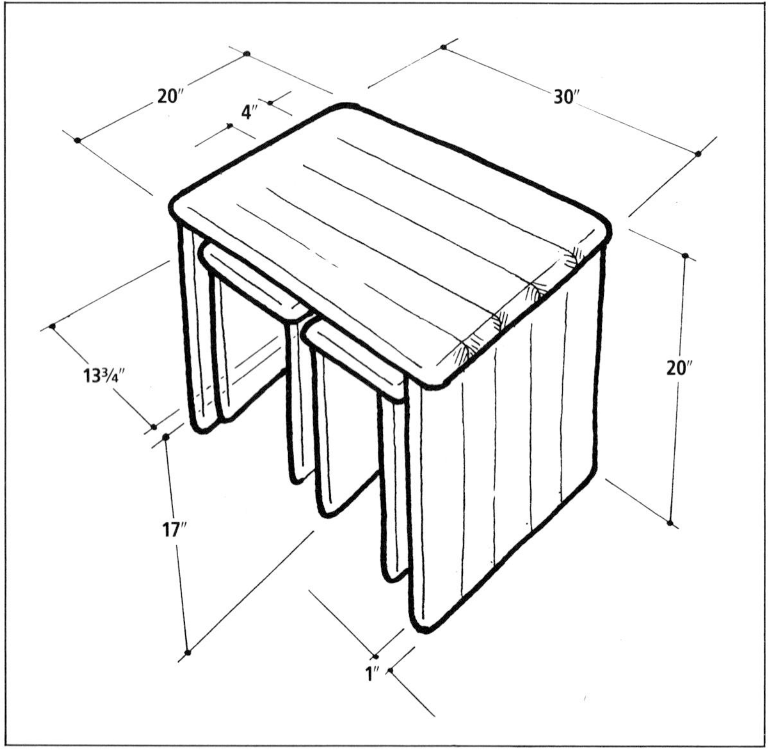

Fig 20.2 The nest of tables showing dimensions.

Fig 20.1 Nest of three tables in ash.

could be made from alternative timbers such as oak or cherry, but essentially it is designed to be made from the solid – not manufactured – board because the edges are fashioned. It is important to note that the grain direction of components is similar, thus allowing the timber to move all as one.

A clear matt polyurethane varnish finish is applied by hand, giving a relatively hard heat-, water- and chemical-resistant finish.

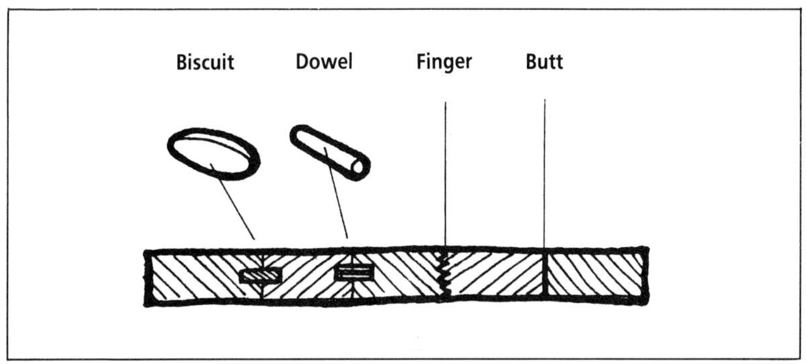

Fig 20.3 Joint options for the edge-jointed panels.

Fig 20.4 Gluing and clamping edge-jointed boards together, using Cascamite.

PROCEDURE

1 Prepare the laminates to size for edge-jointing into extended boards for the three respective tables. (Top and sides of each table are cut later.) Number or code each piece for identification and assembly. The planer–thicknesser is used for this (see Chapter 9).

2 Decide how you are going to edge joint the pieces. A butt joint is sufficient with modern glues, but you may with to consider using biscuits or dowels (Fig 20.3). Cut the edge-joints. For this project I used butt joints, but it should be pointed out that biscuit joints will help maintain all surfaces flush, making cleaning up easier.

3 Using sash clamps glue the laminates together,

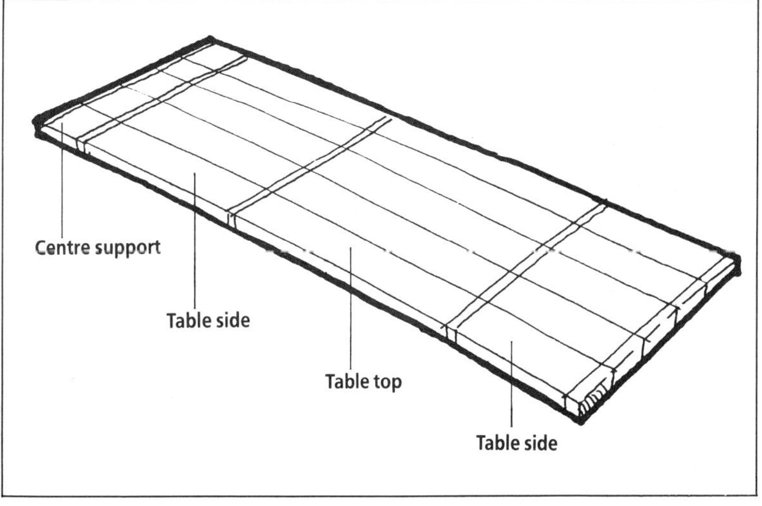

Fig 20.5 The table components are prepared as one extended board and separated later.

Fig 20.6 The Black & Decker power hand planer used across the grain.

ensuring they are flat, and wipe excess glue off with a damp cloth. If using Cascamite leave to cure for at least 8 hours (Fig 20.4). Resin W should be left for at least 2 hours at 60°F and Cascorez for 1 hour. Remember that the large table top needs to include the width of the central support (Fig 20.5), which will be cut off afterwards.

4 Carefully trim the laminates flush – they should already be fairly flush – using a portable power planer. Use it across the grain or diagonally, taking off very light cuts (Fig 20.6). Keep the planer moving all the time. If this is done carefully orbital sanding only will be needed to remove superfluous marks, although I prefer to use a belt sander first.

5 Use an orbital sander with 80–100 grit paper and sand all components flat.

6 Using a large roofing square, square off the ends of the laminated components to size (Fig 20.7), cutting lines for separating the extended boards into 'top' and 'sides'. A 3mm dividing line is left for separating the pieces with a jigsaw (Fig 20.8).

7 Use the planer–thicknesser to clean up the end-grain, but ensure a bevel is left to prevent grain splitting. The bevel is planed off when dimensioning the sides (see page 80).

8 Using the planer–thicknesser reduce the components to the required width. A line can be pencilled on.

9 Code each component and add face marks.

10 Rout joints for each table using a straight cutter and a straight fence (Fig 20.9).

Fig 20.7 Using a roofing square for accurate marking.

11 Using a router set up with a rounding-over cutter, profile the edge of the table components.

12 Calculate the positions and rout out the concave grooves on the inside of the main table sides which serve as a sliding support for the two smaller tables (Fig 20.10).

13 Power sand the radiused edges and internal

Fig 20.8 Electric woodwork at its best – an attractive edge-jointed panel built up and cut with a variety of power tools.

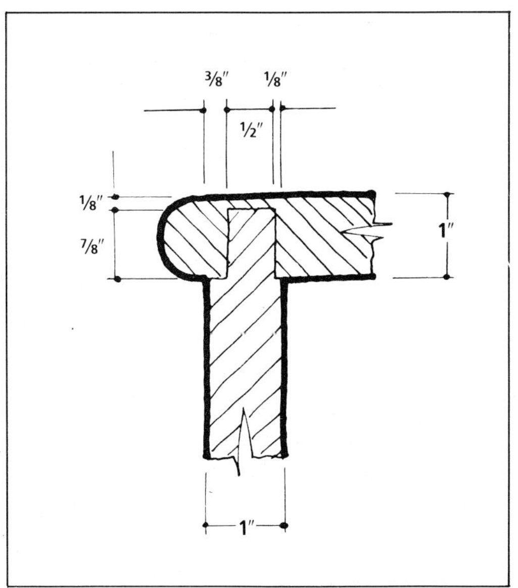

Fig 20.9 The table top/side joint.

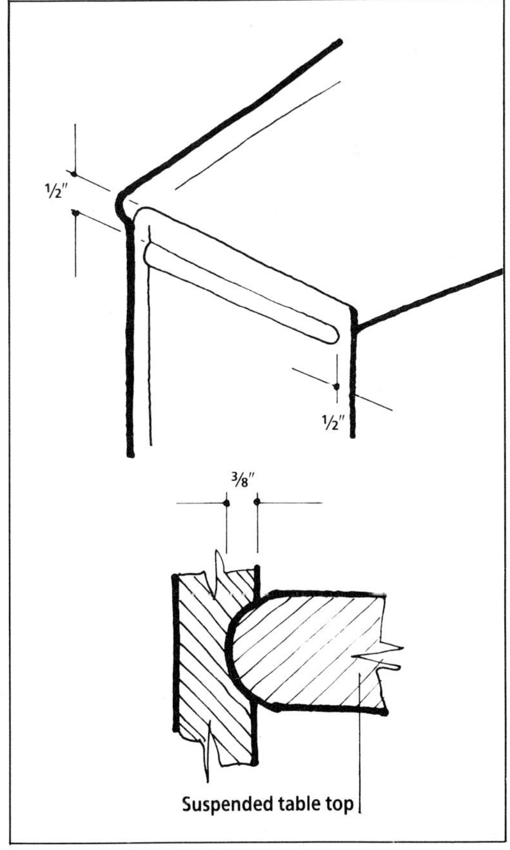

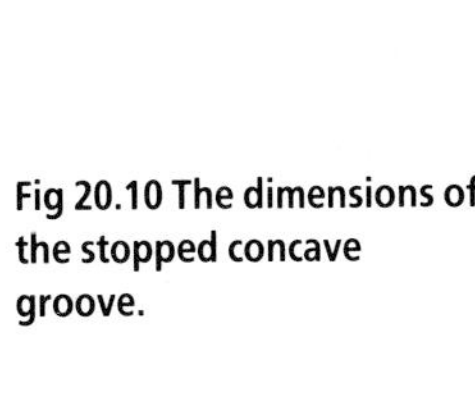

Fig 20.10 The dimensions of the stopped concave groove.

Fig 20.11 Use Cascamite and a fine wood spatula to coat the joints in the nest of tables.

Fig 20.12 Checking for 'squareness' with a roofing square when gluing and clamping.

Fig 20.13 The author *always* wipes off excess glue with a damp cloth – even if it raises the grain, it can be power sanded afterwards.

surfaces of the 3 tables. Use a curved sanding stick and hand sand the concave grooves, taking care not to round over the edges.

14 Glue and clamp the main table (the smaller ones are done later). I used Cascamite, which has a longer pot life (Fig 20.11). Check the components are square with a roofing square (Fig 20.12) and wipe off excess glue with a damp rag (Fig 20.13).

15 Now here is the tricky bit – mount the two small table tops into their respective grooved channels, checking for parallel and 'squareness', and calculate the profile of the central support (Fig

Fig 20.14 Using a piece of paper to calculate the profile of the central support.

20.14). This is tailor-made at this stage to get the crucial perfect fit, and I used a piece of paper as the most accurate measuring device.

16 The central support has already been cut from the large extended board (Fig 20.5), and is now jointed and featured using the router. Groove the underneath of the main table top to accommodate the central support (Figs 20.15 and 20.16).

17 Dry assemble the central support (Fig 20.17) and slide in the table tops to check everything works freely. There should be a minimal amount of

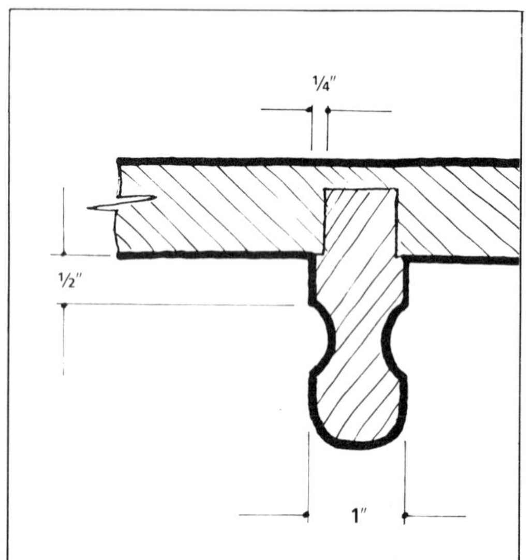

Fig 20.15 Section showing the centre support fixing into the main table top (above left).

Fig 20.17 The central support in the nest of tables.

Fig 20.16 Using a Hitachi router with clamped batten to joint in the centre support.

Fig 20.18 Checking the operation of the three tables.

'play', to allow for varnish and timber movement.

Any necessary trimming should be done to the table-top edges – which is probably why I left the jointing up of the smaller tables till later.

18 Glue and clamp the central support, wiping off excess glue. I recall leaving the smaller table tops *in situ* while gluing this support, hence ensuring correct alignment.

19 Check the small table tops are accurate, as the sliding operation of the suspended tables is crucial. Then, joint the sides of these tables in the same way as the main table. Power sand, glue and clamp as before.

20 Finally, check the operation of the three tables (Fig 20.18). Clean up all surfaces with an orbital sander using medium-to-fine abrasive paper and work through to Lubrasil paper.

21 Apply a clear matt polyurethane varnish (Fig 20.19) – perhaps 2 coats – finely sanding between coats. I prefer not to wax my furniture as I find it subsequently attracts grime, especially to light-coloured and open-grained timbers such as ash.

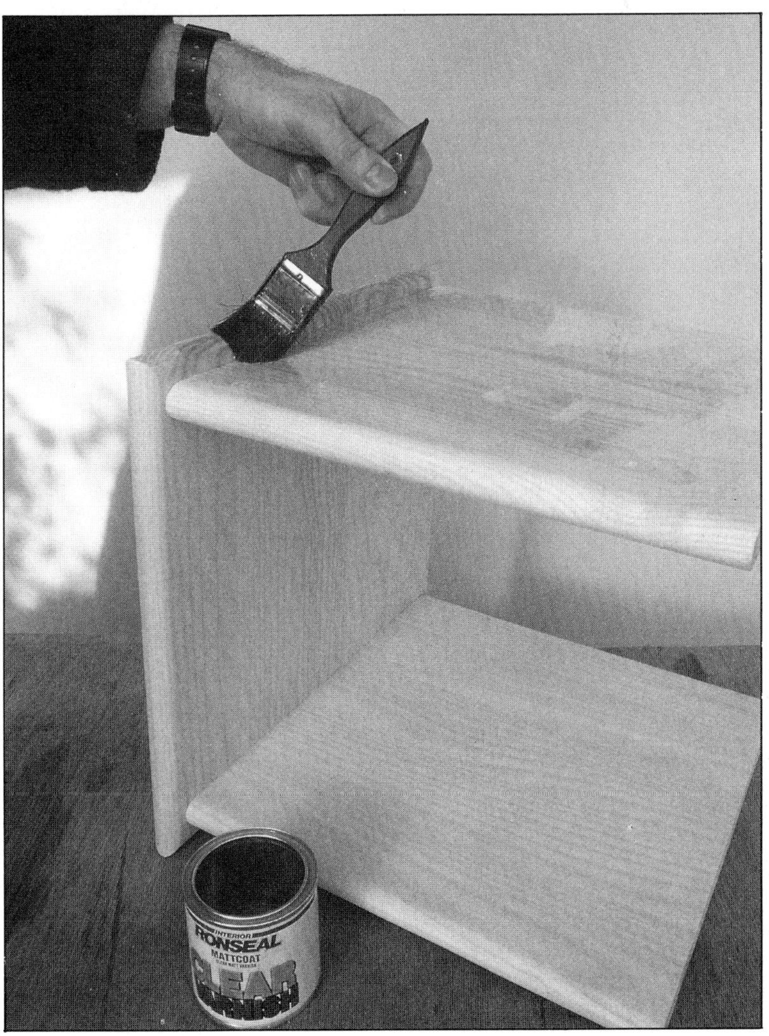

Fig 20.19 Applying a coat of polyurethane matt varnish to the nest of tables.

21 BEDSTATION

This multi-purpose design is primarily a space-saver – in fact it creates space. By allowing extra floor space it can turn a boxroom into a study bedroom, and it's fun as well!

The bedstation (Fig 21.1) is based on existing ideas, but is made from sturdier-than-usual materials. It is constructed from 8ft × 4ft sheets of 18mm Douglas fir shuttering plywood, or birch plywood or MDF (the latter would need to be painted) (Fig 21.2).

Fig 21.1 The bedstation made from 18mm plywood.

It is an integral 'knockdown' design comprising:

- bed
- ladder
- wardrobe
- desk
- drawer unit

The fittings are readily available wood screws, angle-and-plate brackets (Fig 21.3), hinges and a

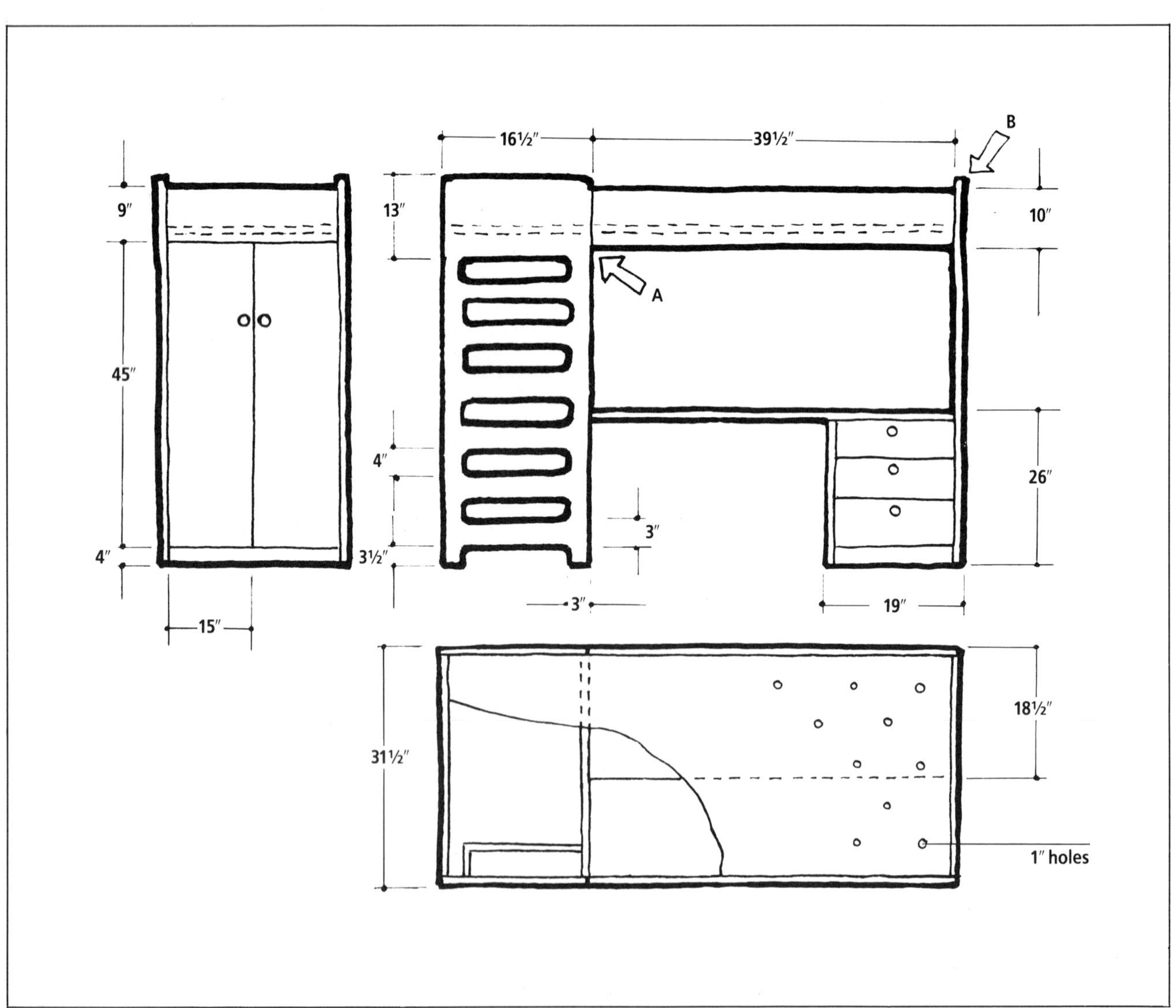

Fig 21.2 The bedstation.

hanging rail. This particular example has been customized with a router-engraved name sign and is finished in matt polyurethane, but it could easily be colour varnished to suit individual taste.

PROCEDURE

1 Select some good-quality 8ft × 4ft sheets of 18mm Douglas fir plywood (the quality varies) and mark out the components.

2 Using a jigsaw, cut out the components. A fine-toothed blade will minimize grain tear.

3 Trim the edges of the components with a power planer set very finely, or a belt sander. Mount the pieces in a Workmate or something similar while working the edges. A power sander will be necessary to clean up the radiused profiles.

4 Using a drill to start the cut, jigsaw out the ladder profile to the line.

5 Set up a router with a small-radius cutter with bearing guide, and radius the edges of the components.

6 Set up the router with a 6mm straight cutter and router 'engrave' a name on the top of the ladder panel if required (Fig 21.4).

7 With the router, mark out and cut recesses for angle and straight brackets.

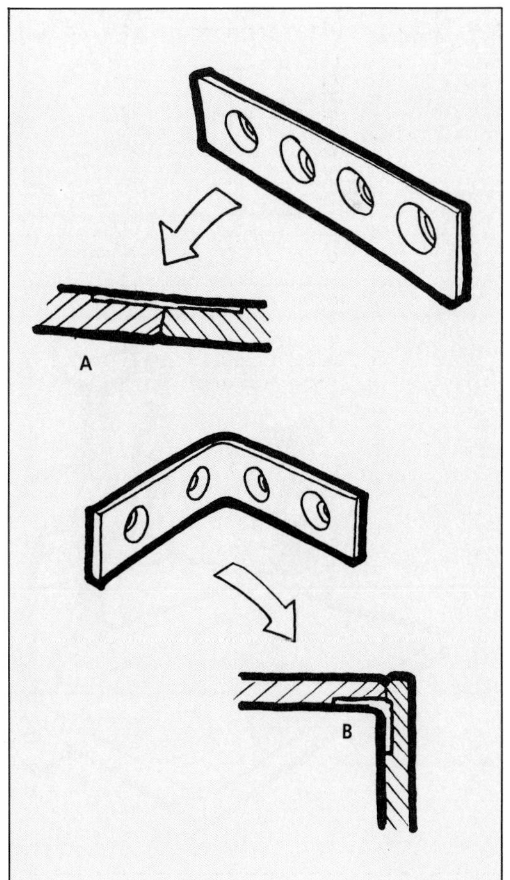

Fig 21.3 Angle brackets and plates used for the KD construction.

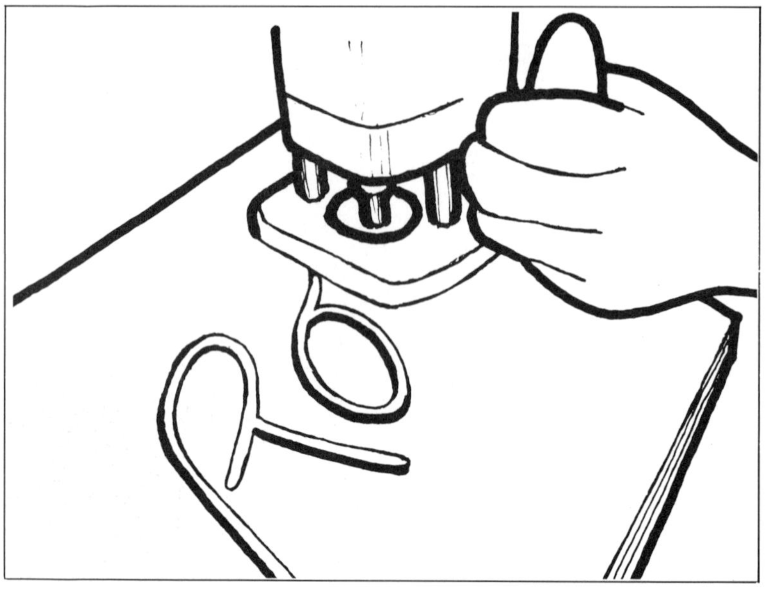

8 Mark out and sink the wardrobe hinges in, using the router with a straight fence.

9 Construct the chest of drawers. There are various joint options, ranging from dowels to biscuit joints (Figs 21.5 and 21.6).

10 Attach the various supporting strips (Fig 21.7).

11 Assemble the bedstation and drill and screw brackets in place. Construct the bed platform and drill air holes for the mattress.

12 The bedstation can be stained or varnished while assembled, or it can first be taken apart. Apply 2 or 3 coats of polyurethane varnish, sanding in between coats with an orbital sander.

13 Cut the wardrobe hanging rail to length with a hacksaw and attach.

14 Attach magnetic catches to the doors and door frame.

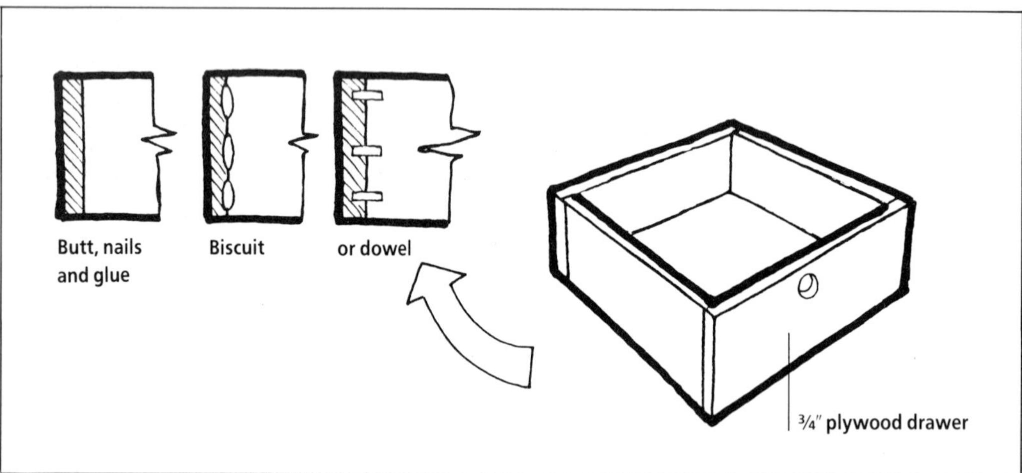

Fig 21.4 Engraving a name with the router (above).

Fig 21.5 Joint options for the chest of drawers.

Fig 21.6 Glue and clamp drawer runners to chest carcase side (below left).

Fig 21.7 Add the supporting strips (below right).

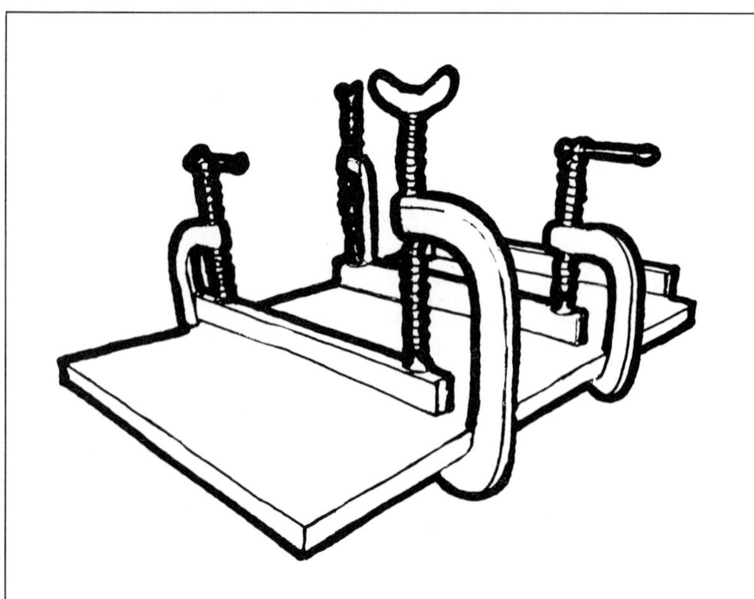

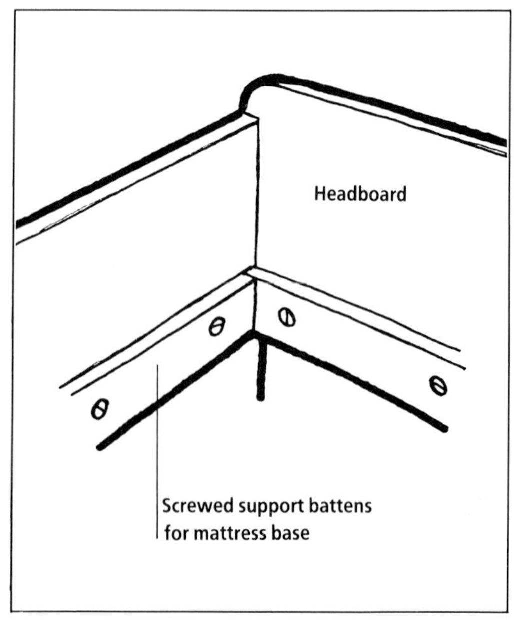

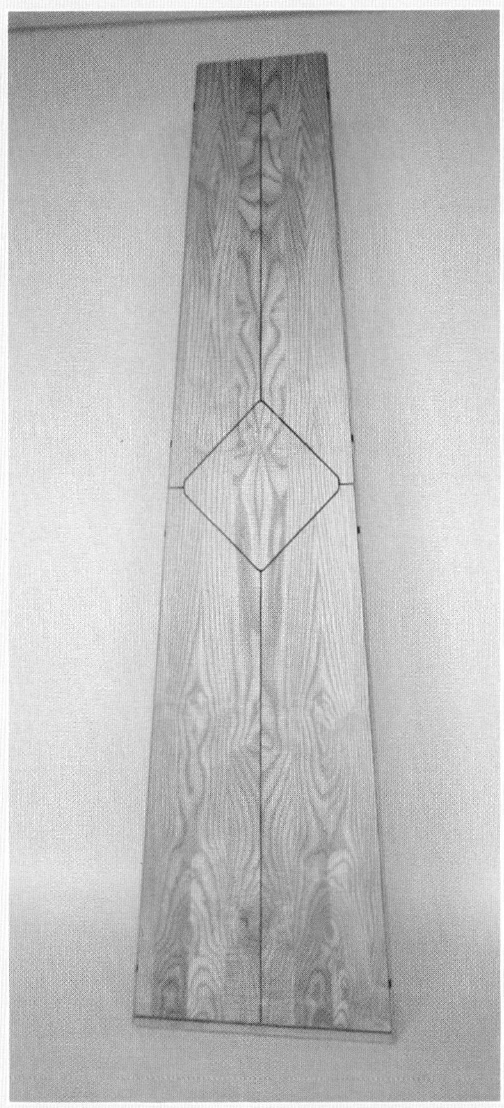

'Pyramid Drinks cabinet' (© Jeremy Broun 1980) – made from a single 2in board of ash and cut into 'veneers' using various electric tools such as the bandsaw and planer–thicknessers.

The novel centre flap in the cabinet with no handles – this design is a classic example of electric woodworking.

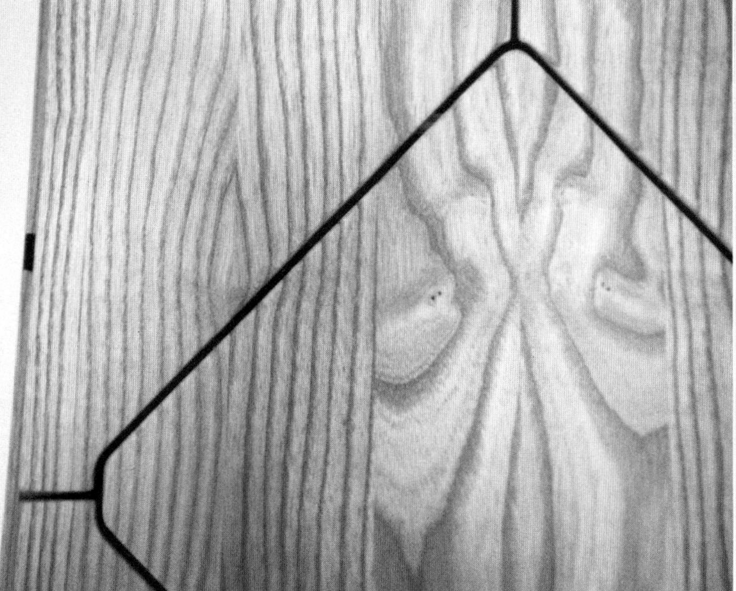

The continuing matching grain on the doors and centre flap of the cabinet, only made possible by unconventional construction techniques using a jigsaw, planer–thicknesser and router.

The author's 'Zigzag' table in bubinga 48in span × 13in (© Jeremy Broun 1978)

The unique centre-joint of the 'Zigzag' table – precision woodworking. The joint is highlighted by a 1.6mm 'Danish shoulder'.

'Straight from the tree' low table, made from Kew Gardens storm timbers (© Jeremy Broun 1987)

The JKB workbench, well worn and well tested, inexpensively made from a single sheet of 18mm plywood!

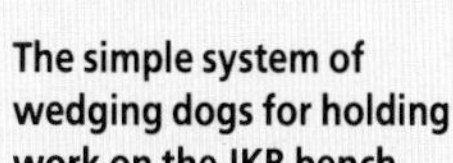

The simple system of wedging dogs for holding work on the JKB bench.

'Shoreditch' design toolbox – deceptively versatile.

The nest of tables is designed to meet functional requirements.

The simple sliding system which makes the tables easy to use.

Bedstation in Douglas fir plywood.

Laminated pitch pine bowl made from an old church pew.

Close-up of the laminated bowl. Epoxy glue is used for the laminations.

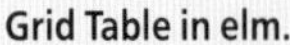

Grid Table in elm.

Picture frame in elm.

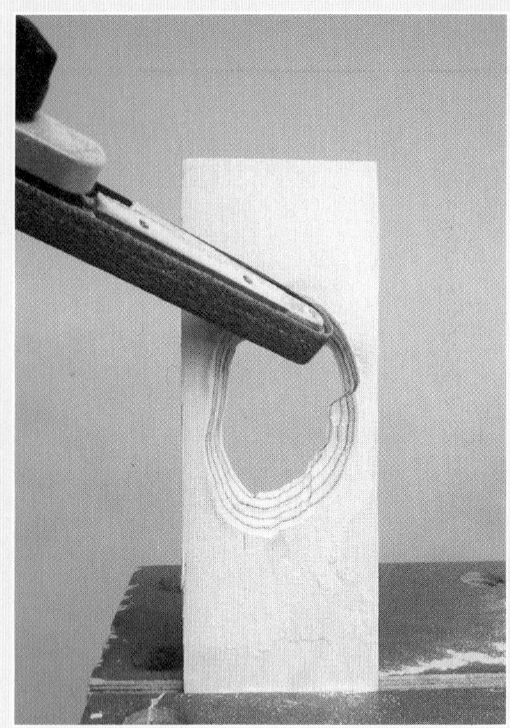

Sculpted effects in plywood made with the Black & Decker Powerfile.

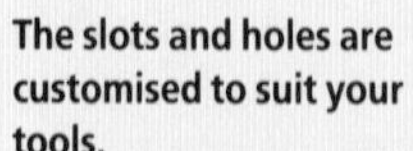

The slots and holes are customised to suit your tools.

The JKB toolrack – a simple and versatile system.

The TAO boardgame designed by Paul Cresswell (© Paul Cresswell 1989)

Applying stain varnish to the TAO game.

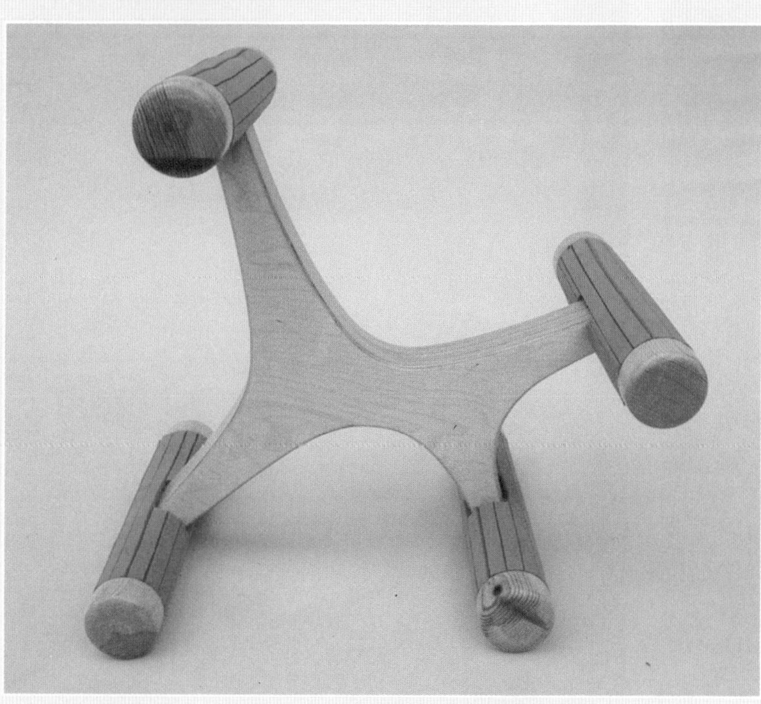

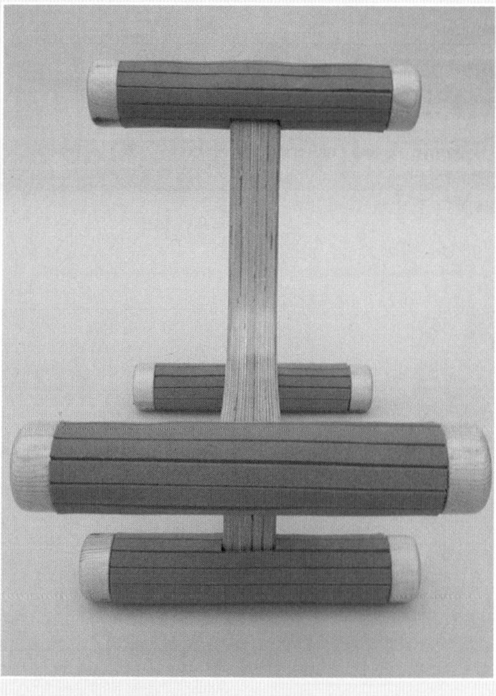

Kneeling stool in birch ply, pine and foam rubber.

Is it a bird, is it a plane?

Electric lamp in birch plywood using an energy efficient 15 watt bulb.

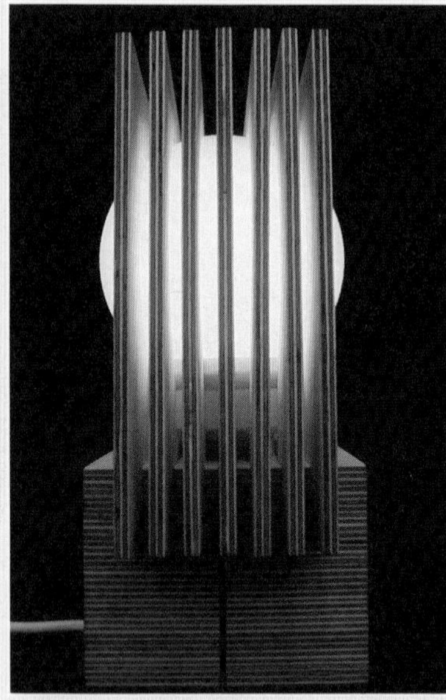

The electric lamp creates an ambience when switched on.

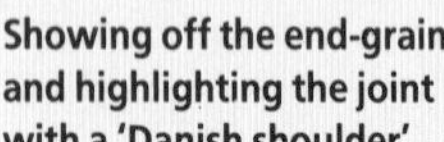

Showing off the end-grain and highlighting the joint with a 'Danish shoulder'.

Chest of drawers – carefully selected pine.

22
LAMINATED BOWL

A bowl must be one of the most satisfying objects to make, and to be further enjoyed when used. It is one of the most primitive receptacles, and a wooden bowl especially has a certain magic. (Perhaps it is partly because it reminds us of the tree from which it came. So much wooden furniture is rectilinear and has undergone complex processes and been embellished, which makes it easy to forget its origins.) Using the lathe is mesmerizing enough, so there is nothing better than making a turned bowl (Fig 22.1).

It strikes me that there is much wastage of material in bowl turning, as all but a thin-wall diameter of the material is kept. The rest lands up as a pile of shavings on the workshop floor, and this could be as much as 90 per cent of the material! This is partly why I chose to laminate my bowls as you can use narrow-section timber and build them up economically (refer to template) out of a wide variety of timbers. You can also laminate up to any desired dimension within the capability of your lathe.

A laminated structure also adds visual interest in a strongly figured timber, and minimizes subsequent timber movement as the laminates create an equilibrium of stresses. (Lamination is a technique I use in woodworking generally.)

During and after turning most bowls warp a little (in wet-wood turning this is more drastic), and if subjected to repeated wetting and drying e.g. during washing up, the bowl will move, so it is important to use the appropriate glue – a water-soluble glue would be disastrous for gluing the laminates! I recommend a boat-building epoxy glue (available from SP Systems, see page 273), which is strong enough to ensure the bowl is safe

Fig 22.1 The laminated bowl in reclaimed pitch pine.

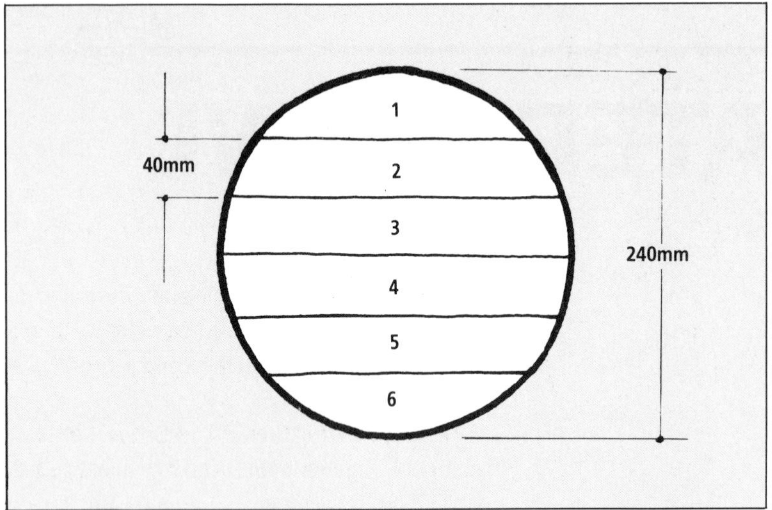

Fig 22.2 The bowl blank template from which pieces are individually numbered and measured for preparation.

when turning (laminates don't disintegrate), and will hold together under any atmospheric conditions. (Or use Cascamite.)

(I might add that so-called laminated or 'segment' turnery was eventually banned from many educational establishments because glue joins were found to be suspect and bowl blanks made up of different species of timber resulted in different shrinkage rates and bond properties.)

This design uses just one timber. (Make sure the timber is not on the list of toxic timbers.) I chose to use some pitch pine which came to hand from some old church pews I acquired years ago. It is one of the hardest softwoods and fairly resinous, with a distinctive attractive figure which is highlighted when laminated and finished. The finish is a matt polyurethane varnish applied by hand while the bowl is still on the lathe but stationary.

PROCEDURE

1 First, construct a plywood or similar template and mark out the laminates (Fig 22.2) coding each one. Choose what size diameter bowl you wish to turn. This one is 9in diameter, the maximum which would fit on to the Record ML24 lathe.

2 Using the planer–thicknesser prepare a length of timber calculated on the template codings.

3 Glue and clamp the sections together ensuring they are aligned to a series of marks (Fig 22.3).

4 Bandsaw the bowl blank after tracing the outline from the template (Fig 22.4).

5 Fix a lathe faceplate on to the base side of the bowl blank using 6 short screws (Fig 22.5 and see Fig 10.39).

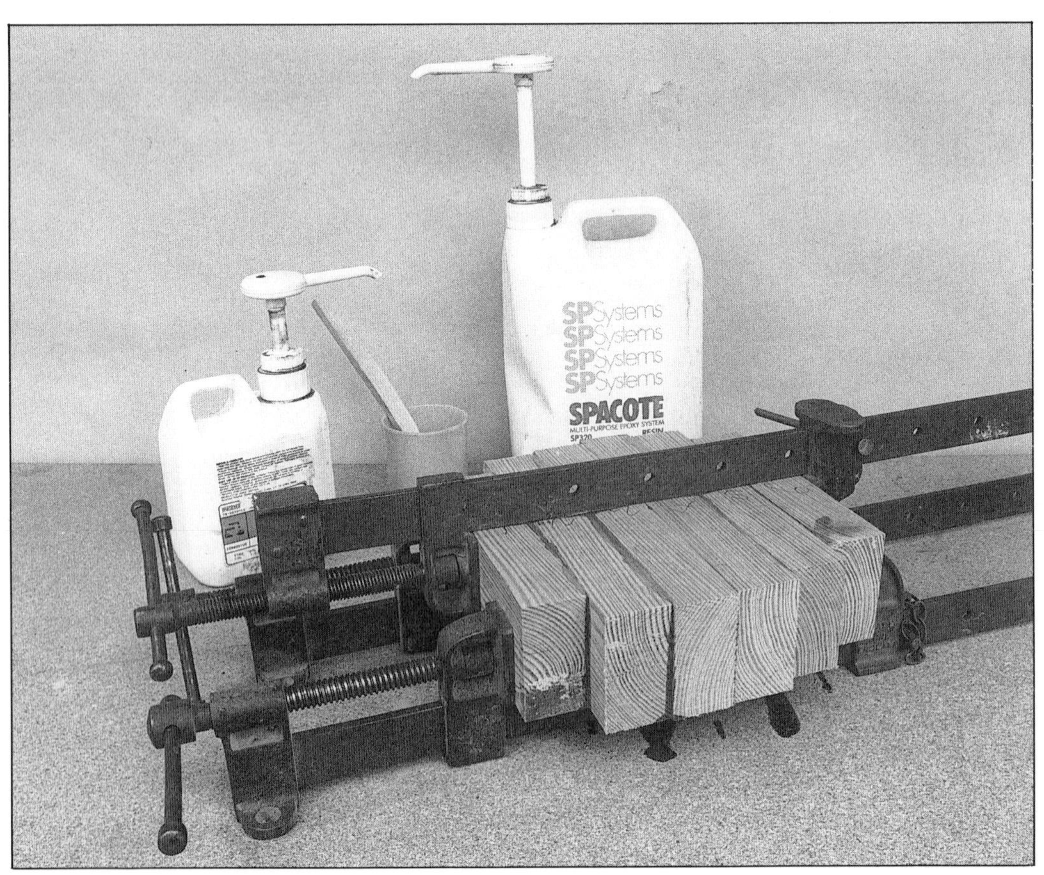

Fig 22.3 The bowl laminates are numbered and glued together – using SP Systems epoxy glue – and clamped.

Fig 22.4 Bandsaw the laminated bowl blank accurately to the line – note the economy of material.

6 Mount the bowl blank on the lathe. Set to the slowest speed and adjust the toolrest and toolpost to position for profiling the bowl edge.

7 Use a flat narrow scraper or chisel to trim the outer wall perfectly circular. Apply one edge of the tool and make progressive cuts across the bowl thickness, about 3mm each. This is quick and efficient stock removal. Reduce the bowl to the required diameter (Fig 22.6).

8 Profile the outer edge of the bowl by cutting a series of steps (Fig 22.7) and then taking the corners off (see Fig 10.26). Here again the edge of the tool is used for quick removal (the narrower the cut the less the resistance of the material) –

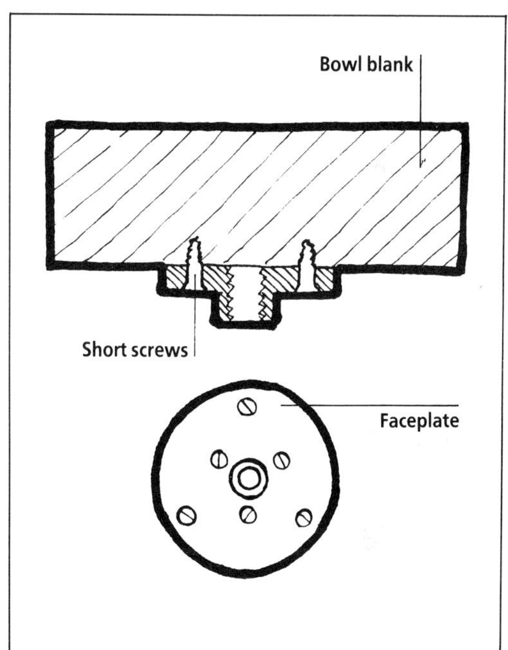

Fig 22.5 Section through bowl showing fixing to faceplate.

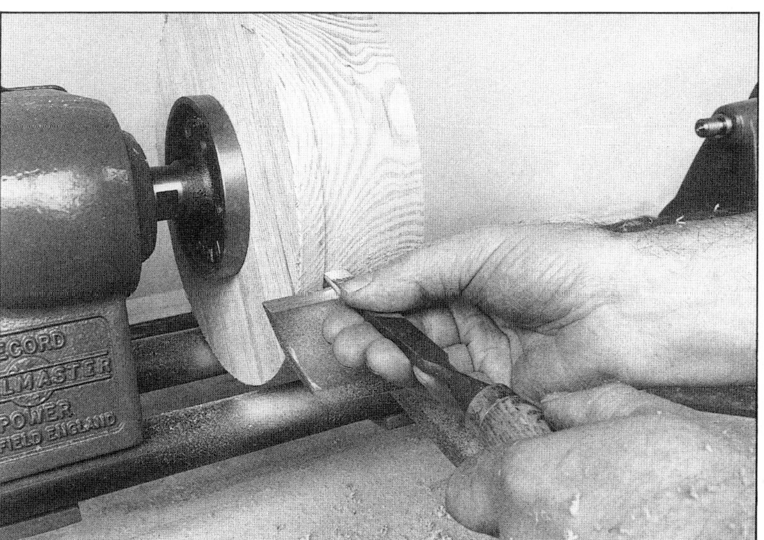

Fig 22.6 Using a scraper/chisel to get the wood circular.

Fig 22.7 The JKB method of efficient stock removal – by edge-cutting a series of steps (above left).

Fig 22.8 The final contour achieved with a curved scraper (above right).

Fig 22.9 Narrow cuts, started from the centre, minimize tool 'snatching' when using a long-handled chisel.

you may wish to use a flat or curved scraper (Fig 22.8). Fashion a small lip for the base – final finishing of the edge can be done later. You may wish to step up the speed for these shaping operations, but do not use the fastest speed.

9 Move the toolrest to the face of the bowl and use a narrow chisel to turn the inside. (I use a mortice chisel ground slightly steeper.) Work from the centre outwards as there is less resistance and the overlapping cuts give maximum control (Fig 22.9). (The tool will need to be held firmly to stop it snatching.) Work in to full depth progressively in a series of steps (Fig 22.10). Masking tape can be wrapped around the scraper/chisel to the required depth which can be checked with a ruler (Fig 22.11).

10 Use a curved scraper to profile the inside edge of the bowl (Fig 22.12), and use a wide flat firmer chisel to ensure the inside base is flat (Fig 22.13). If the lathe has 4 speeds, engage the third for final skimming to improve the surface. A dust will be taken off and small tears caused by the scraping action can be virtually eliminated, so only minimal sanding will be required (Fig 22.14). The tool should be constantly reground as a keen edge is vital –

Fig 22.10 Use the JKB method again.

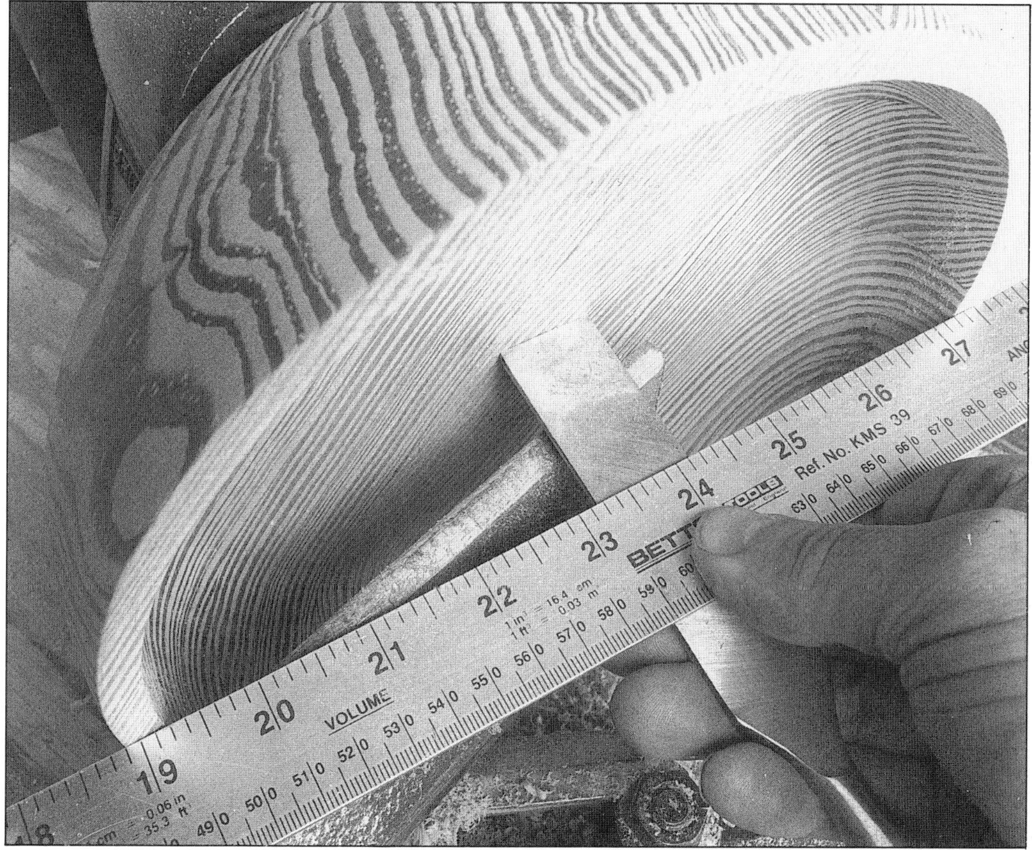

Fig 22.11 A simple depth-checking method.

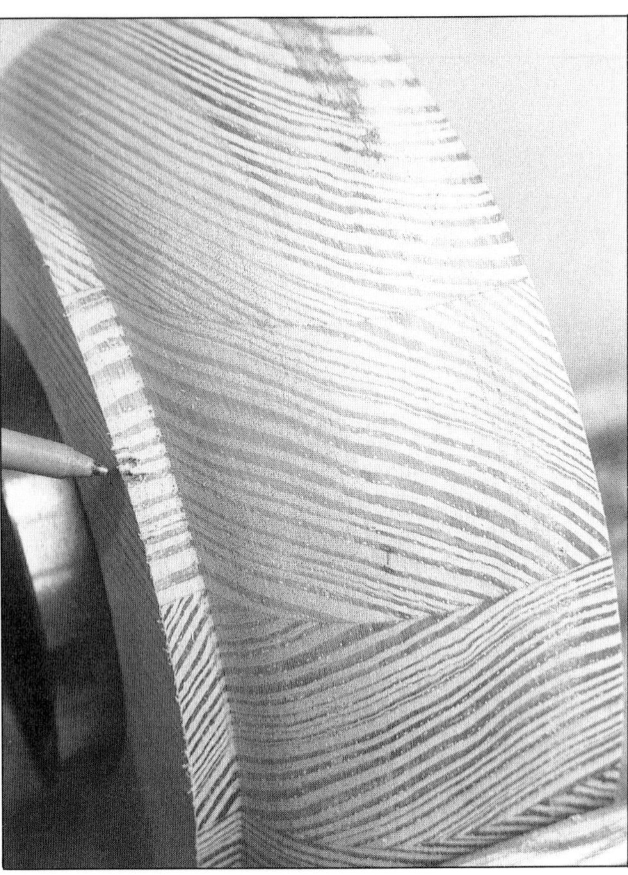

Fig 22.12 A wide curved scraper is used to carefully trim the inner profile.

Fig 22.13 A flat wide chisel is used for the bowl floor.

Fig 22.14 Minimal grain tear (end-grain) from the scraper – to be removed by subsequent sanding.

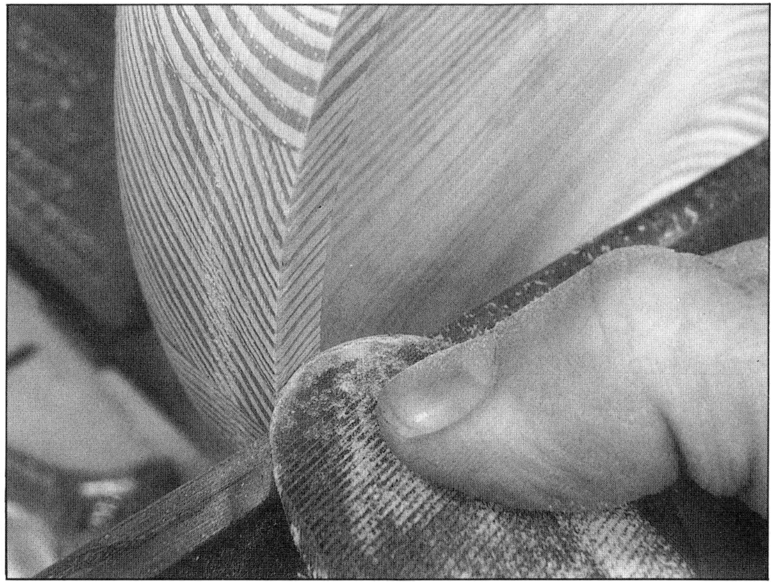

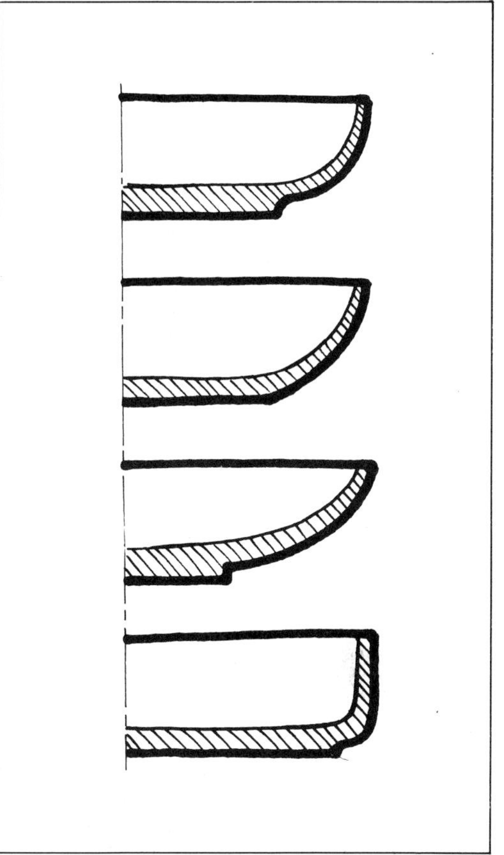

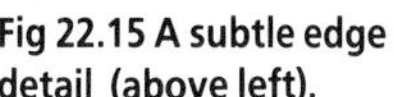

Fig 22.15 A subtle edge detail (above left).

Fig 22.16 Section through bowl wall – design options.

you will feel it bite. (Don't take the burr off the tool as it is part of the cutting action.)

11 Reshape the outer edge so that inner and outer profiles blend. Fashion the upper lip of the bowl – a plain flat is boring! Add a little subtlety (highlighted when light reflects on the finished bowl) by fashioning a slightly inturned concave (Figs 22.15 and 22.16).

12 Remove the toolpost and sand the entire bowl working through the grades. Ensure that you always sand away from the rotation (Fig 22.17). (The abrasive paper will get hot, especially with pitch pine.)

13 I prefer to hitch up a dust-extraction hood to minimize dust getting everywhere. Finish off with a fine Lubrasil paper – try to keep edges crisp but not razor sharp.

14 Dust down the bowl and apply finish. You may wish to burnish the bowl with a handful of shavings (Fig 22.18), or apply a couple of coats of matt polyurethane which gives a serviceable finish (Fig 22.19).

15 Remove the bowl from the faceplate and plug the screw holes with a tapered section of the same timber. Lightly sand with a block or against a disc-sanding attachment (Fig 22.20) and apply lacquer to base to complete the sealing of the bowl.

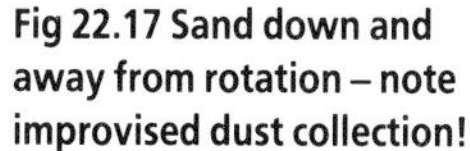

Fig 22.17 Sand down and away from rotation – note improvised dust collection!

Fig 22.18 Using shavings to burnish the wood at speed.

Fig 22.19 Apply a matt polyurethane varnish by hand on the lathe.

Fig 22.20 The base of the bowl is accurately trued on a disc attachment to the author's Arundel lathe.

23

GRID TABLE

This table is a simple, understated design for the modern home (Fig 23.1). The one shown is made of elm although any interesting timber such as oak or ash could be used. The centre 'grid' is loose fitting and can be taken out, allowing a plant pot, for example, to be placed in the middle.

The design can be modified so that the grid is set lower in the top and a piece of glass laid over it flush with the surface – for those traditionalists who think an open grid top is completely impractical! And if you also think you would have to employ a full-time home help to clean dust out of the grid – think again, as the humble electric vacuum cleaner will take care of that. (Personally, I think it would be a shame to 'inhibit' the design with a sheet of glass.)

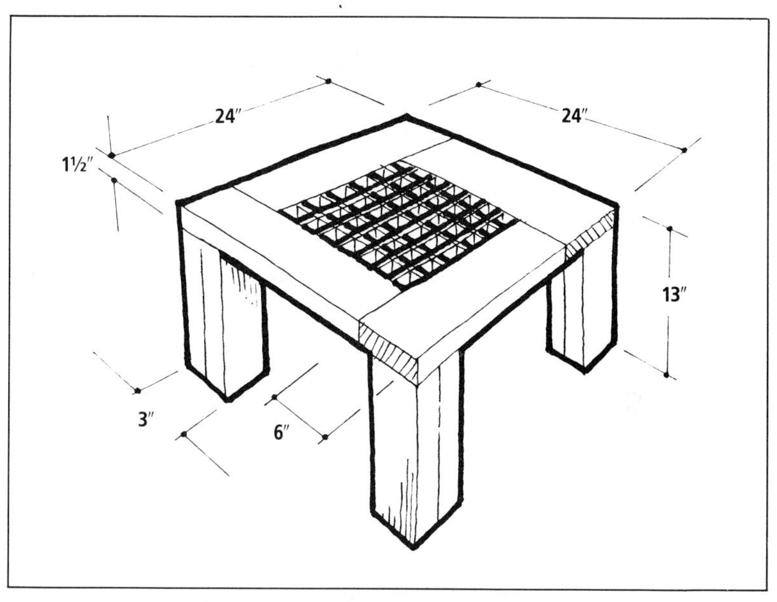

Fig 23.2 The grid table with dimensions.

Fig 23.1 The grid table in elm.

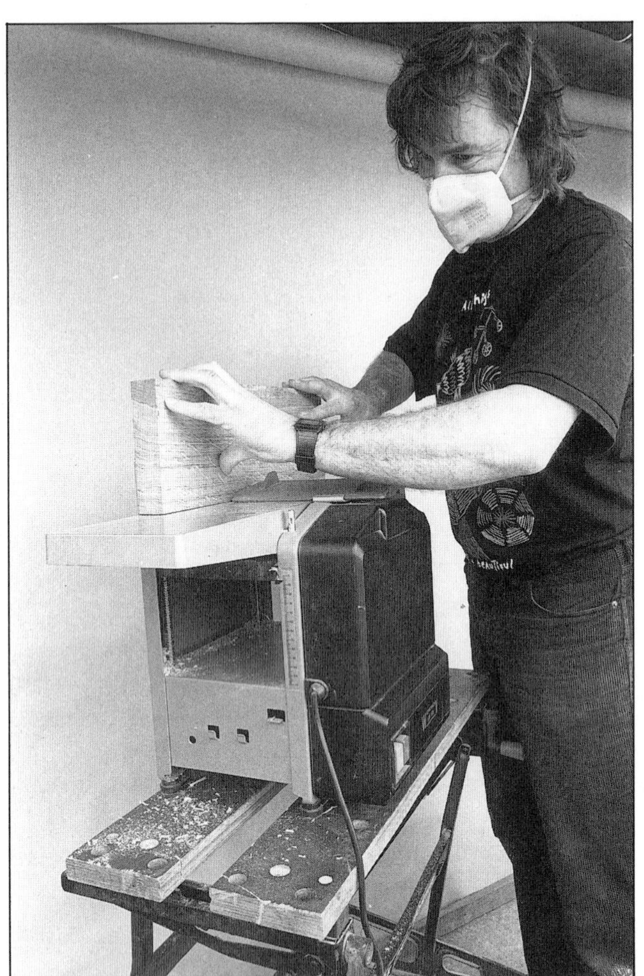

Fig 23.3 Using the Woody planer-thicknesser to square the edges.

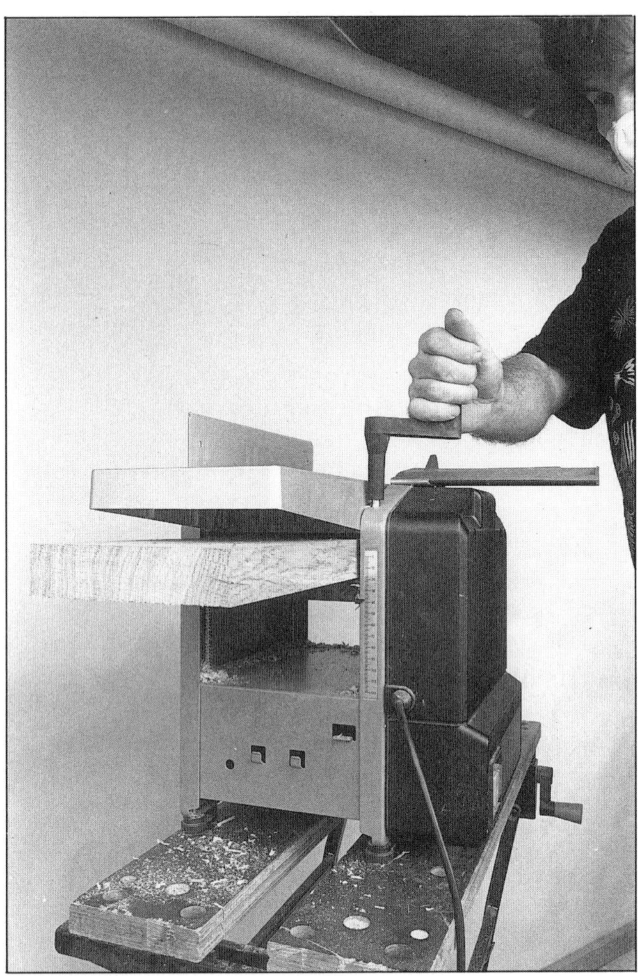

Fig 23.4 Thicknessing the table top.

Fig 23.5 Code the table top joints and cut the chosen joint.

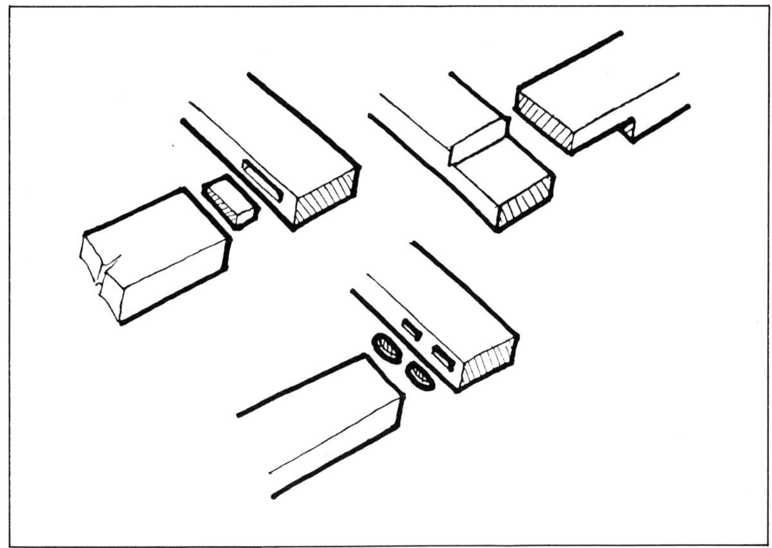

The finish for the elm version is linseed oil. The dimensions can be enlarged slightly (Fig 23.2) and wider boards for the top built up by edge-jointing. Alternative timbers other than ash and oak are pine and cherry.

The table offers several construction options involving the use of various electric tools. However, when I first designed it the process centred largely around my radial arm saw and mini planer–thicknesser.

PROCEDURE

1 Select a board of seasoned elm and cut the components using a jigsaw and bandsaw. Code them.

2 Prepare the pieces to size using a planer–thicknesser or, if built up, a power planer and thicknessing attachment (Figs 23.3 and 23.4).

3 Alternatively, the pieces can be edge-jointed using narrower stock to build up the full width, and then glued and clamped.

4 Clean up top members and joint together (Fig 23.5) using either biscuit joints, dowels or loose tongues (Fig 23.6). Glue and clamp.

5 Clean up top after gluing, checking outer edge is flush. A power sander (belt and orbital) could be used.

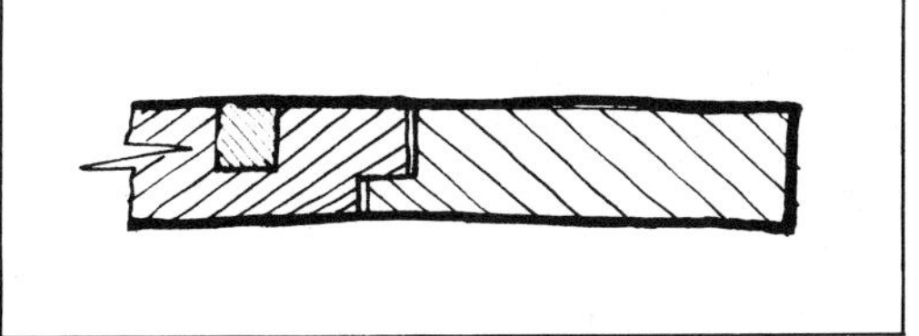

Fig 23.6 Joint options for the top.

Fig 23.8 'Danish shoulder' highlighting the laminated 2-piece leg build-up.

Fig 23.9 Mortice and tenon joint for the leg and table top.

Fig 23.7 Section through the table top showing routed rebate for grid.

6 Set up a router with a 12mm diameter straight cutter with a roller fence and rout the grid-housing rebate in the top (Fig 23.7).

7 Prepare material for the 4 legs. I joined two pieces together to make up the square section, routing a 'Danish shoulder' along the glue line (Fig 23.8).

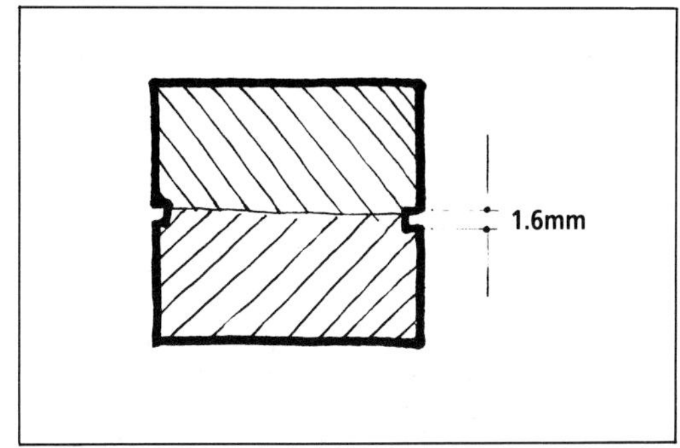

8 Cut the joints where the legs meet the table top. Joint options include biscuit joints, dowels or a shallow mortice and tenon. I used the latter, cutting the tenons on the radial arm saw (see Chapter 12) and the mortices with a router. Round off the edges of the tenons to match the radiused mortice corners (Fig 23.9).

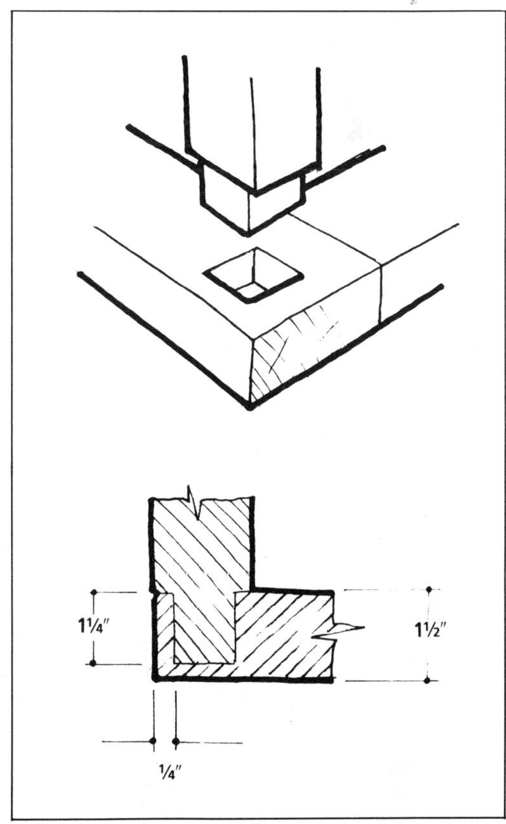

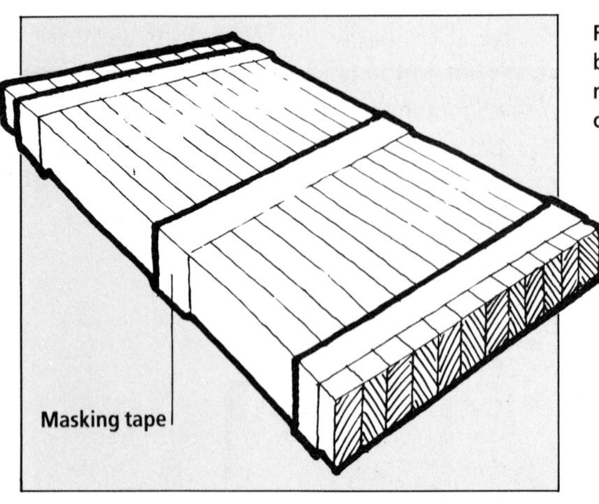

Fig 23.10 The grid members bundled together with masking tape ready for cutting the halving joints.

9 Prepare to size the strips for the grid and bundle together using masking tape (Fig 23.10).

10 Accurately mark out the distances for the cross halving joint (Fig 23.11). Make sure waste is shaded.

11 Set the radial arm saw to half the depth and carefully cut the grid bundle to the lines already marked out (Fig 23.12). An extra piece serves as a checking piece for tightness (Fig 23.13).

12 Untape the grid bundle and dry-assemble the grid halving joints (Fig 23.14) using a chiselled 'leading edge' on the inside of joints (Fig 23.15).

Fig 23.11 The halving joints are marked out as a batch.

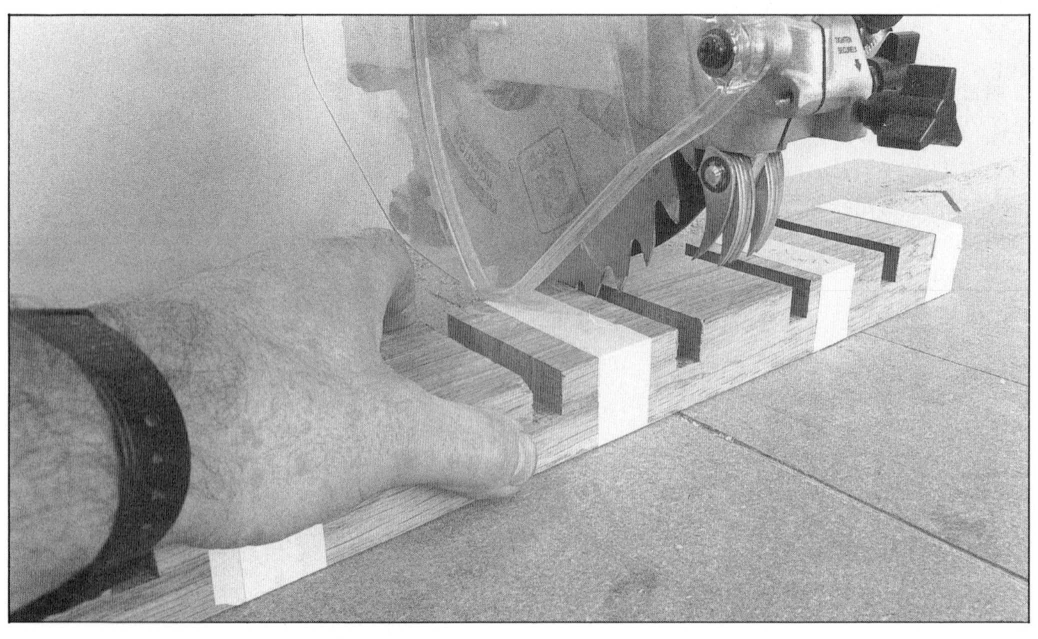

Fig 23.12 The Ryobi radial arm saw accurately cuts the halving joints taped together in a bundle.

Fig 23.13 I use a spare member to check each joint for tightness.

Fig 23.14 The grid is easily constructed.

13 Clean up with a power sander and soften all edges by hand. Glue grid together – if the joints are tight it should not require clamping. I used minimal glue on the horizontal surfaces of the joint leaving the joint walls 'dry tight'.

14 Check the loose grid fits easily into its housing.

15 Clean up entire table and apply linseed oil.

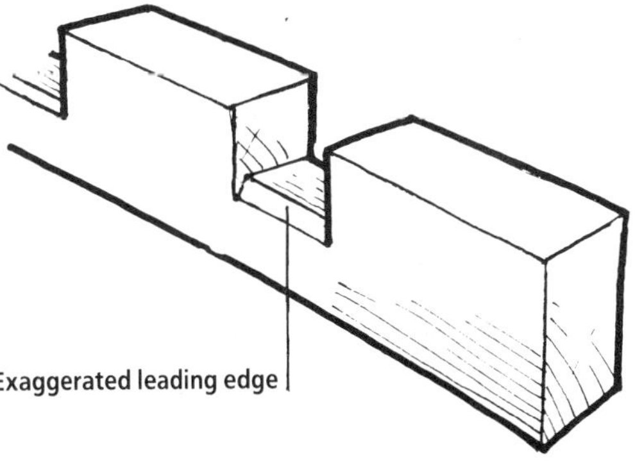

Fig 23.15 'Leading edge' cut with a chisel to ease tight joints.

24

PICTURE FRAME

This simple picture frame (Fig 24.1) can be made in any attractive timber and can vary in size and shape.

It is made from solid timber – this particular one is in elm, and linseed oiled – and is predominantly an exercise in free-hand routing. The picture glass is rebated into the rear, and with its picture and backing board is fixed with a hot-melt glue gun. A small locating hole is routed into the back for hanging on a screw rawlplugged into the wall. The design lends itself to a mirror as well.

This particular example was originally inspired by a picture of some burial mounds which needed framing, and the wany edge of the piece of timber also strongly dictated the overall design.

Fig 24.1 The picture frame in elm.

PROCEDURE

1 Having chosen a picture to be framed and established the required size, select a nicely figured piece of wood. This is quite important and it is worth remembering the each piece of timber is totally unique in grain configuration.

Cut the piece of timber to size using a jigsaw or bandsaw.

2 Draw a freehand profile for the opening of the picture frame (Fig 24.2), drill a hole through, and cut with a jigsaw. Start the cut by inserting the blade in the hole.

3 Use a glue gun to fix the piece of timber to the bench top, tacking it with 4 'blobs'. These will later be removed, but they serve as a securing device for freehand routing. The rear side will be uppermost.

4 Trace the profile of the picture glass equidistantly to the frame wall already cut. This is to be rebated (Fig 24.3).

5 Set a router up with a small-diameter straight cutter – say ¼in – and carefully rout a shallow rebate along the drawn line. This is for the picture and glass and backing material to house into (Fig 24.3). Enough depth should be allowed for a small hot-melt glue fillet which will secure the assembly (Fig 24.4).

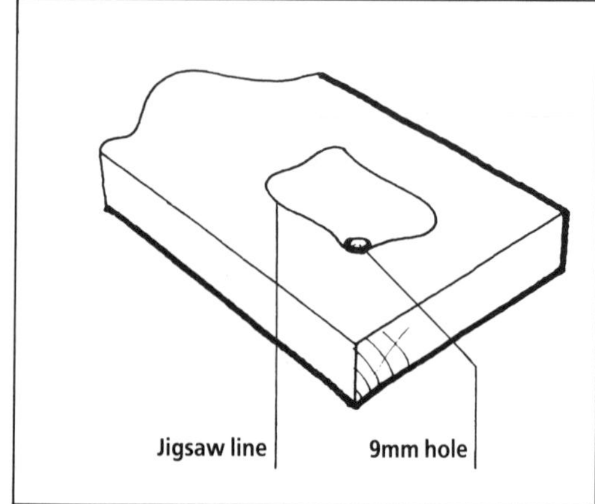

Fig 24.2 The frame is marked out and a hole drilled to start the jigsaw cut.

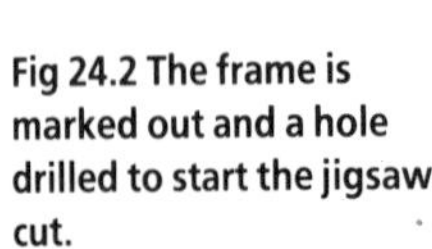

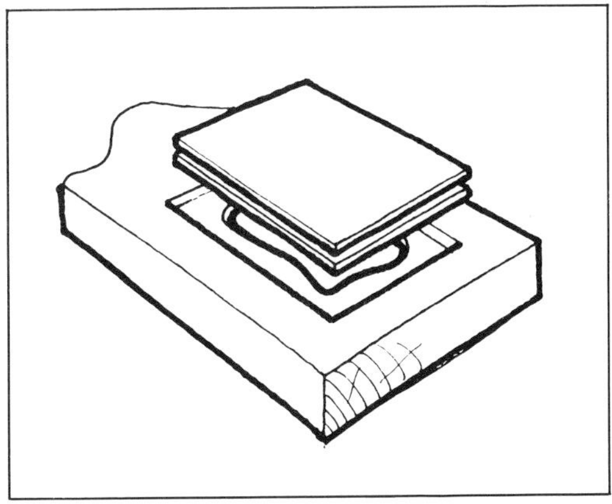

Fig 24.3 Exploded view showing the picture glass and its rebate at the back.

6 Carefully prise the frame off the bench and reverse the fixing using the glue gun again. Apply 4 small blobs so that the face is uppermost.

7 Rout a series of concentric freehand 'stepped' rebates to give an interesting contoured visual effect on the front of the frame (Fig 24.5).

8 Carefully prise the frame from the benchtop and clean it up with an orbital or palm sander, softening the edges slightly. A disc sander can be used on the straight edge (Fig 24.6).

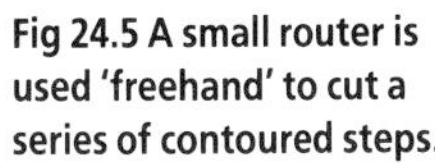

Fig 24.5 A small router is used 'freehand' to cut a series of contoured steps.

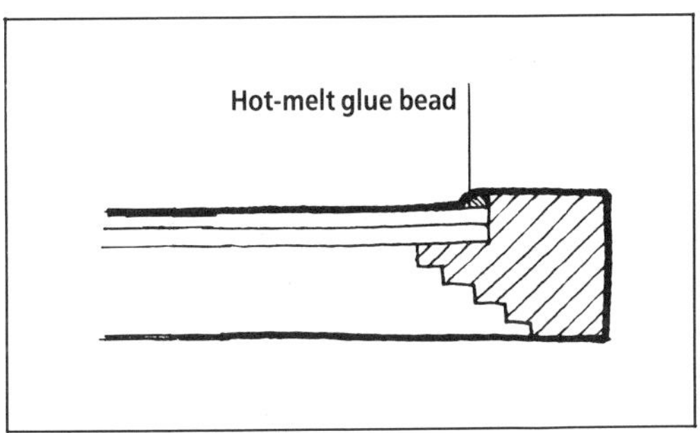

Fig 24.4 Section showing the method of fixing the picture assembly.

9 Rout or drill a small hole in the back of the frame for fixing on a wall.

10 Apply lacquer or linseed oil to the frame. If using elm, linseed oil is particularly attractive – perhaps 3 coats over a period of 24 hours. Take care not to oil the rebate itself, however, as this has to be hot-melt glued.

11 Set the picture glass, picture and backing material into the rebate and glue-gun a fillet along the entire rebate (see Fig 24.4).

Fig 24.6 A disc sander can be used to clean up the straight edge of the picture frame.

UNIVERSAL TOOLRACK

This toolrack is an extremely simple and useful idea which can be quickly made and designed for the workshop to accommodate your own particular set of tools (Fig 25.1). (See Chapter 15.) You may require several racks in different locations for different purposes, as I have (Figs 25.2 and 25.3).

The main consideration is ease of access and flexibility of use. In my early days as a woodwork teacher I devised all sorts of toolrack systems, but never found a completely idiot-proof one (and I have seen some pretty inefficient ones in my time!).

The traditional (and painstaking) solution was to paint a profile of each tool on a board behind its designated area, which of course showed up those tools which were missing. However, this method always seemed to me to be wasteful in space and was visually unattractive. This toolrack is designed for the solo user, although its use could be shared, but the important thing is that it does not matter particularly where tools are replaced on the rack in general, hence its name – universal (Fig 25.4). This is quite an important consideration for the busy woodworker, who isn't going to make a career out of finding the designated area for each tool every time – and the tools can be added to.

Plywood or MDF can be used, but preferably not a solid wood because of the problem of short and weak grain. A variety of electric tools can be used, such as the jigsaw, bandsaw, router, radial arm saw and drill (flatbits). The angle brackets can be hot-melt glued and the rack is fixed on to the wall with screws and rawplugs.

Fig 25.1 The toolrack made from 22mm birch plywood.

Fig 25.2 Fig 25.3
The author's toolracks.

Fig 25.4 The slots and holes are customized to suit your tools.

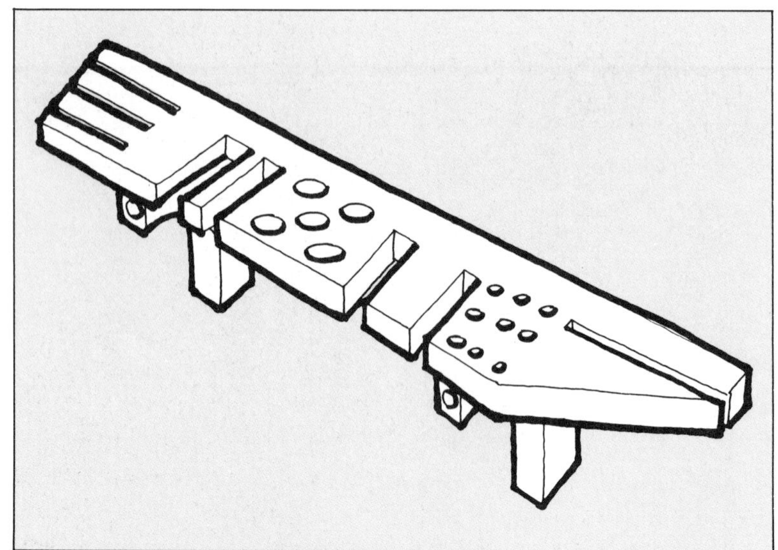

Fig 25.5 The toolrack.

Fig 25.6 Marking out the positions for the tools – actually I didn't use a ruler!

Fig 25.7 (a) Cutting out the features in a series of cuts with a jigsaw.

PROCEDURE

1 Decide on the dimensions of the toolrack – let's say 30in × 4in. Cut the material from a board using a jigsaw.

2 Clean up the edges with a power planer or on the planer–thicknesser.

3 Decide what tools you wish to rack and calculate the width of openings and diameter of holes to be drilled. Mark out the positions (Fig 25.5) and shade waste (Fig 25.6).

4 Cut out the openings with whatever tool you choose. I chose a jigsaw and drill exclusively (Figs 25.7 (a), (b) and (c)). A bandsaw will not have a deep enough throat to cut all the rack features unless you design the appropriate cut-outs at each end and reverse the marking out so that the blade feeds in from the right side.

5 When using the jigsaw insert a metal cutting blade to minimize grain tear (Fig 25.8).

6 Select the appropriate diameter flatbit and drill the required number of holes (Fig 25.9). You may have holes of varying diameters (Fig 25.10).

7 Construct the support brackets from a thicker material (Fig 25.11) so that the fixing screws can easily pass through its thickness. Counterbore holes (Fig 25.12) to sink the screw heads in deep (Fig 25.13), and drill out for the screw shanks using the appropriate size flatbits (I used No. 12 screws).

8 Clean up the profiled angle brackets with a drum sanding attachment to the drill (Fig 25.14).

9 Hot-melt glue the support brackets to the toolrack (Fig 25.15).

Fix the toolrack to the wall by drilling with a masonry bit, rawlplugging and screwing.

Fig 25.7 (b)

Fig 25.7 (c)

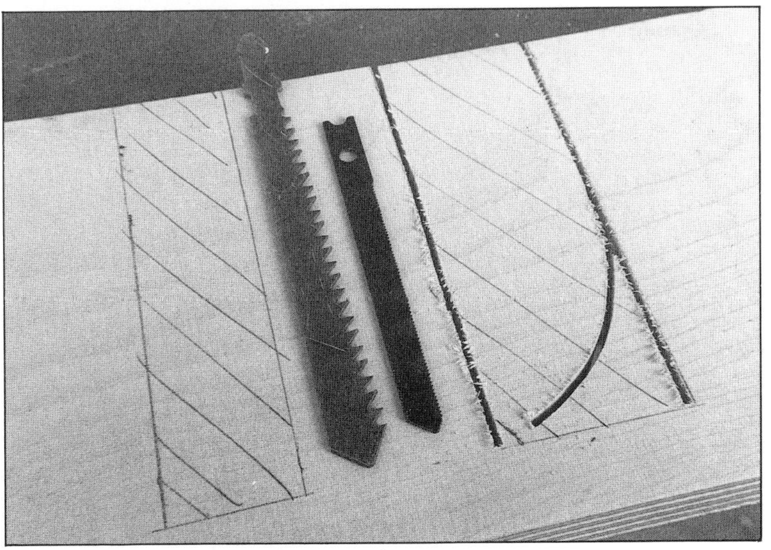

Fig 25.8 On the left – a wood cutting blade, on the right – a metal cutting blade. Now which do you think I used!

Fig 25.9 Hold work very firm while drilling with a flatbit and ensure bracket makes contact with scrap wood to prevent fibres tearing underneath.

Fig 25.10 A small diameter twist drill is also used.

Fig 25.11 The brackets are carefully cut to the line on a bandsaw.

Fig 25.12 Hold the bracket firm while counter-boring with a flatbit.

Fig 25.14 The brackets are cleaned up on the drum sander attachment.

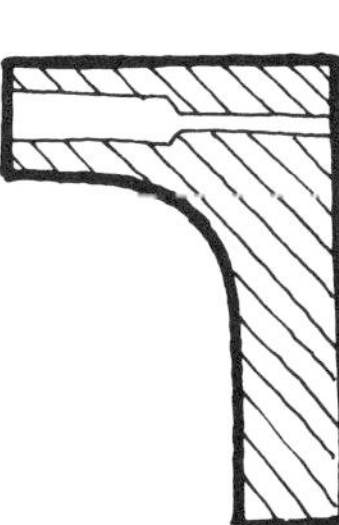

Fig 25.13 Section through a bracket.

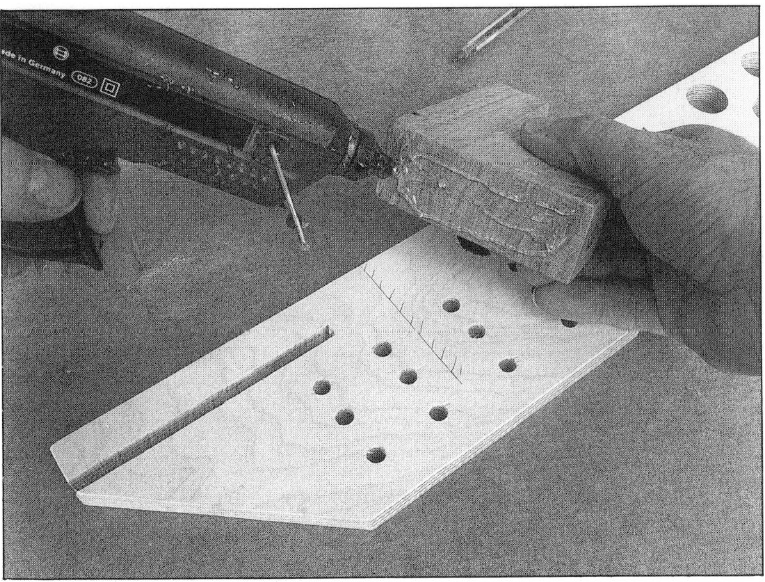

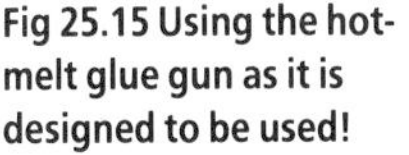

Fig 25.15 Using the hot-melt glue gun as it is designed to be used!

26
TAO BOARDGAME

TAO is a completely new boardgame designed by a friend of mine, Paul Cresswell who claims 'It is the game the world has waited 3000 years to play!' (Fig 26.1).

Anyone who has visited a maze like the one at Hampton Court will know how fascinating such places can be. If you combine the idea of a maze with some of the basic principles found in the best games of skill and strategy, such as chess and Nine Men's Morris, you will come near to understanding what this remarkable, new and original boardgame TAO is all about.

The name TAO is Chinese and means 'the perfect way' or 'the effortless path', and in this game 'the way to win is to win the way'. First and foremost TAO is a race game (first home wins), but equally important it is a game of skill and tactics. However, tactics alone cannot win, nor can serendipity. To succeed the player must balance intuition with judgement right up until the end.

TAO is a puzzle, a living maze whose avenues are in a constant state of flux. This is because the TAO board is made up of 32 individual square tiles, each designed to be lifted and rotated so that the turn of a single tile can dramatically alter the balance and complexion of the game by changing the course of the paths. It is along these paths that the playing pieces (3 per player) travel in whatever direction the player decides. TAO is very easy to learn and great fun to play. It is elegant in its simplicity yet mischievously deceptive.

Fig 26.1 Jeremy Broun and Cherry Coad try the game of TAO.

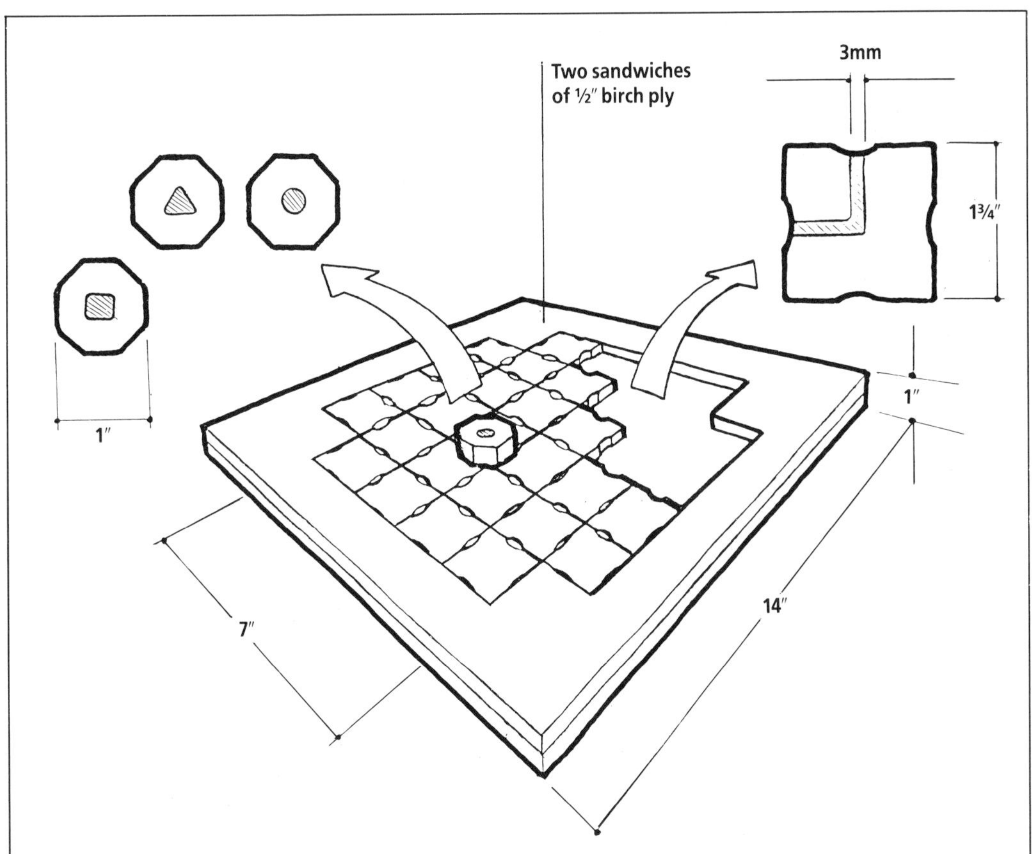

Fig 26.2 The TAO board and pieces.

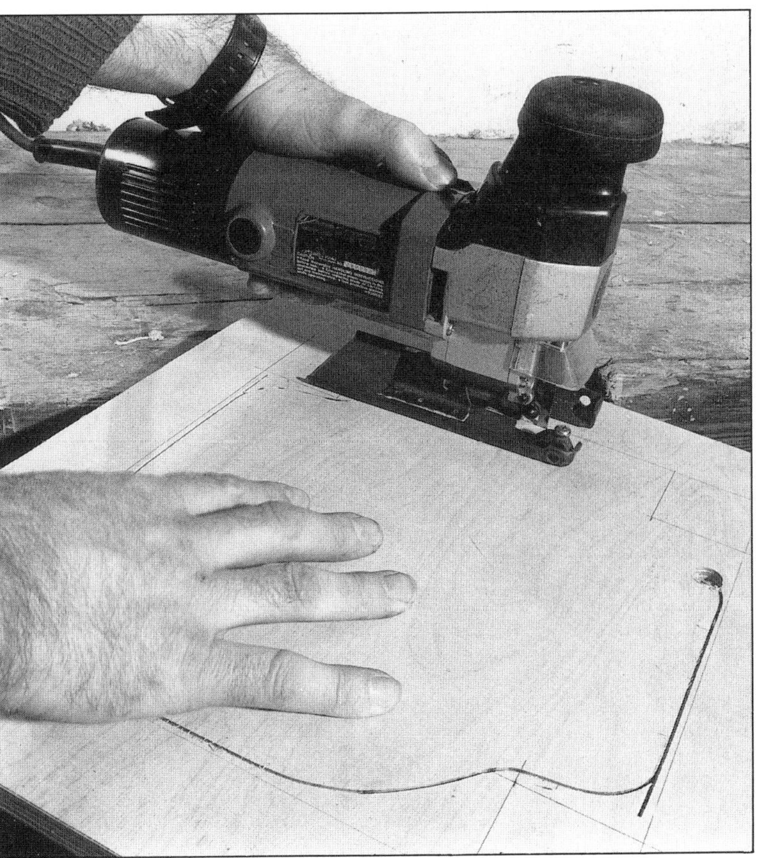

Fig 26.3 Cutting the top laminate of the board with a jigsaw.

If the world has waited 3000 years to play this game, then it has taken that long to find the tools to make it with! Now, with the permission of the game's inventor, I have devised a way to make it in wood using electric tools. In order to play the game, a copy of the rules can be obtained from Virgo Games (see page 273).

The game comprises a board with 32 square tiles and 6 pieces – 3 per player – and marked with the ancient symbols:
square – (earth)
triangle – (fire)
circle – (water).

PROCEDURE

1 There are several ways to make the game, and various materials to choose from, though it makes sense to use a manufactured board for the board because it is less likely to warp. I have chosen to use two laminates of 6mm birch plywood for the board and a short length of sycamore for the pieces (Fig 26.2).

2 The top laminate of the board is accurately marked out and cut using a drill to start the jigsaw cut (Fig 26.3).

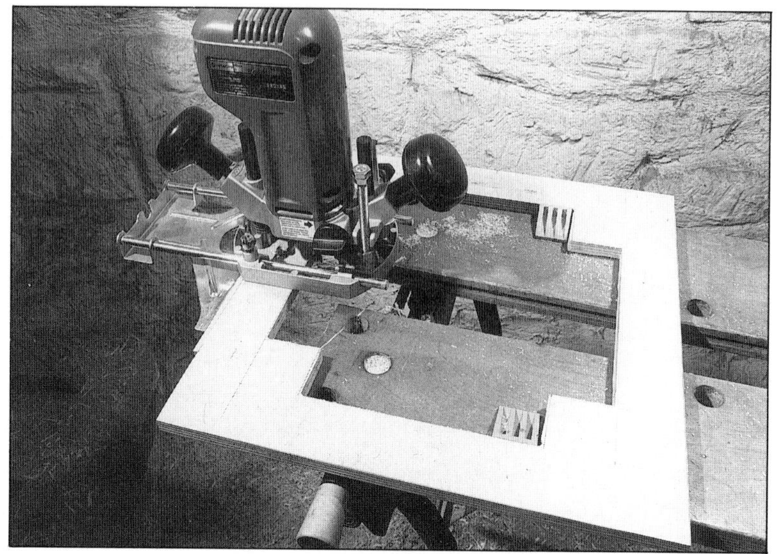
Fig 26.4 Trimming the top 'frame' with the router.

Fig 26.5 Taking the corners off the pieces blank.

Fig 26.6 Carefully plane the octagonal section, checking the angle of the fence.

3 The top 'frame' is then trimmed using a router set up with a fence (Fig 26.4) and ¼in straight cutter. A Black & Decker Workmate with its plastic dogs was used to effect. The slightly radiused edges left from the cutter are chiselled square afterwards.

4 After cleaning the edge up with a file or abrasive stick, the 2 laminates are glued together to form a 'tray'. The length of sycamore is machine-planed and thicknessed perfectly square, and then bandsawn with the table tilted to 45° to marking gauge lines depicting the octagonal section (Fig 26.5).

5 The adjustable fence on the planer-thicknesser is set to surface-plane the bevel on 2 adjacent sides (Fig 26.6).

6 The opposite sides are then thicknessed, and both bevelled sides can be progressively thicknessed to the line – this is the most accurate way of achieving an octagonal section. In other words, the final cut to each surface is always done from the thicknesser because the automatic feed (finely adjusted cut) gives the best finish.

Fig 26.7 The jig has 3 insets for inserting the square, triangle and circle.

7 I have devised 2 simple router jigs for this game: one for the octagonal section pieces and the other for the square tiles. The first jig has three insets for routing the square, triangle and circle (Fig 26.7). The measurements (Fig 26.8) relate to a standard 18mm guide bush fixed to the router base with a 3mm diameter straight cutter inserted.

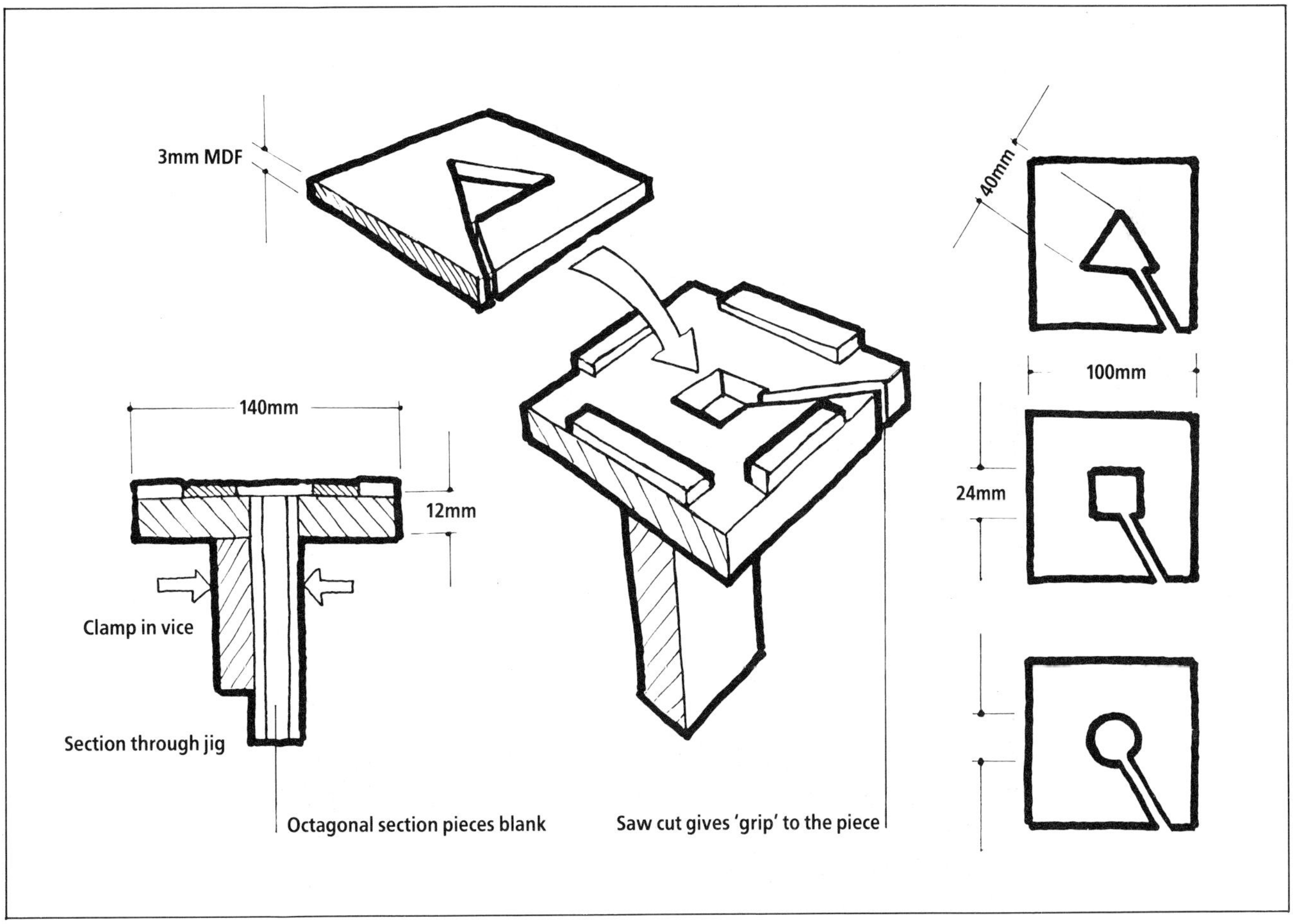

Fig 26.8 The pieces jig and 3 insets.

3mm MDF
140mm
12mm
Clamp in vice
Section through jig
Octagonal section pieces blank
Saw cut gives 'grip' to the piece
40mm
100mm
24mm

Fig 26.9 The pieces blank is inserted in the jig ready for routing.

Fig 26.10 Cutting off the pieces using the bandsaw and fence.

Fig 26.11 **The router jig for grooving the pieces.**

8 The octagonal-section blank is pushed through the matching opening in the jig base and clamped in a vice. The appropriate symbol inset is then used to rout a shallow cut 2 mm deep. Both ends are first disc-sanded square then routed (Fig 26.9).

9 The ends are then cut off to 8mm using the bandsaw (Fig 26.10), or slightly over to allow for final sanding with a disc sander.

10 The 32 square tiles are cut from a piece of 6mm thick birch plywood. A radial arm saw can be set up, but a fine blade should be used to minimize splitting fibres. Alternatively the bandsaw can be used to first make an MDF or acrylic template and then trace around it; then, cut just outside the line and disc sand to the line. The square should fit neatly in the jig, but more importantly, should fit loosely in the board (tray).

11 An inset is made for the router jig (Fig 26.11) for cutting the right-angle groove (Fig 26.12), and the same cutter and guide bush are used.

12 To ensure the square tile is firm when routing, it helps to stick some double-sided tape under the right-angle inset. The L-section is carefully routed on all 32 pieces (Fig 26.13). (It pays to have one or two extra tiles.)

13 The final operation on the square tiles is to rout a slight recess on each face. This gives a finger-nail grip for lifting the tiles when playing the game. I decided the quickest way to rout 128 recesses was

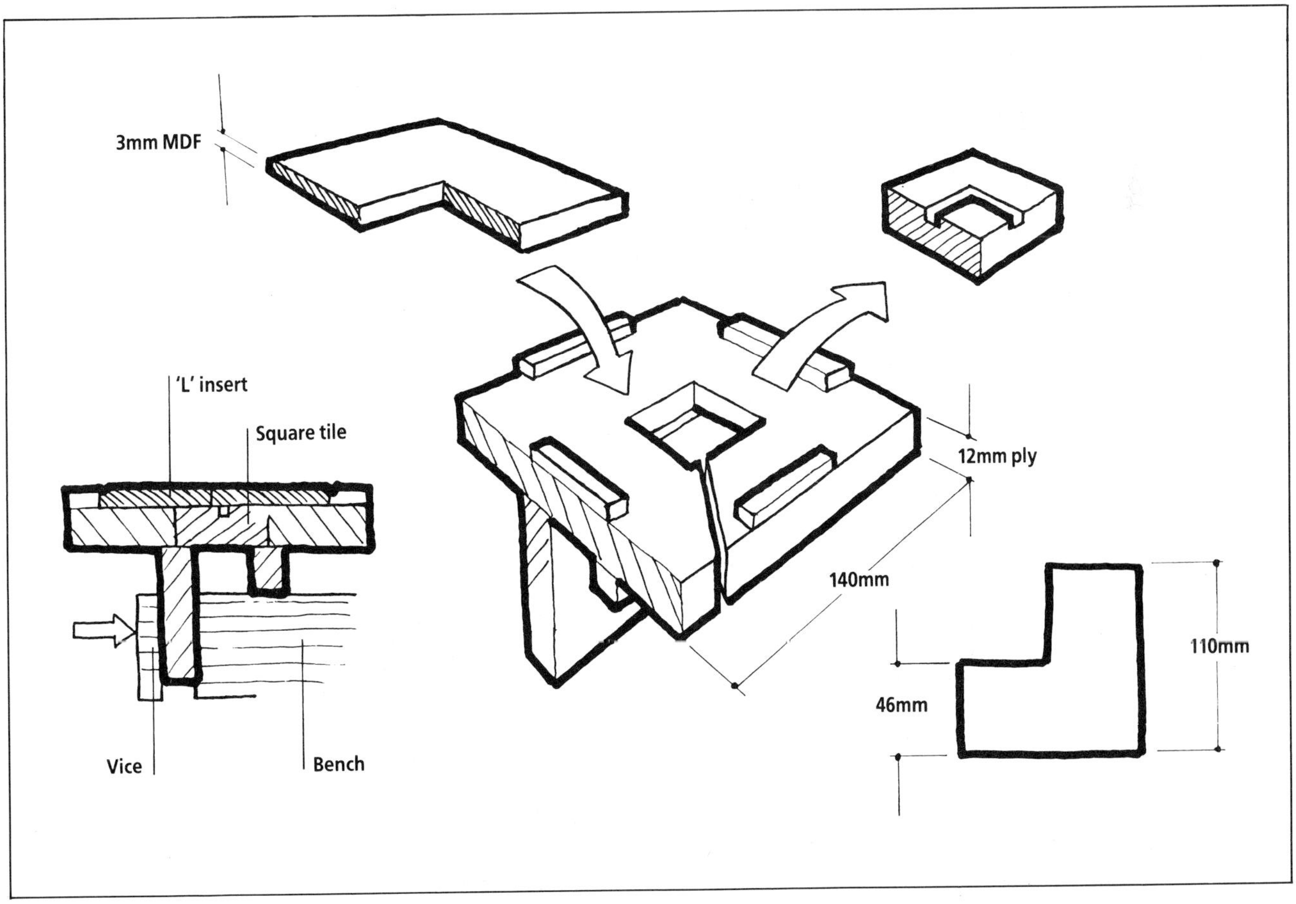

3mm MDF
'L' insert
Square tile
Vice
Bench
12mm ply
140mm
46mm
110mm

Fig 26.12 The L-groove jig insert for the tiles.

to set up a router table with a simple jig (see Fig 7.36).

14 The board and pieces are carefully sanded and all edges softened with a fine flour or Lubrasil paper.

15 Apply a matt polyurethane varnish to the board, the 6 pieces and the 32 tiles. Apply 2 coats, leaving 6 hours between them. Rub down lightly with Lubrasil paper.

16 Apply black lacquer to the perimeter of the board (Fig 26.14).

17 Using a fine artist's brush apply black lacquer next (turps-based, not cellulose-based) to the L-grooves in the tiles and in the 3 pieces of one player (Fig 26.15). Use a turps-soaked rag to wipe excess off the top. (The reason the tiles are lacquered in clear varnish first is to prevent the black lacquer subsequently running into the grain.)

18 Apply white lacquer in the three pieces of the opposing player. I used Humbrol modellers' paint applied with a fine brush. Apply a second coat if necessary.

Fig 26.13 Routing the L-groove in the tiles with a Hitachi FM8 router (above left).

Fig 26.14 Paint the board perimeter black, wiping off any excess on the edges (above right).

Fig 26.15 Painting the 3 black pieces and 32 tiles with a fine brush. Excess is wiped off with a turps-soaked rag.

27

KNEELING STOOL

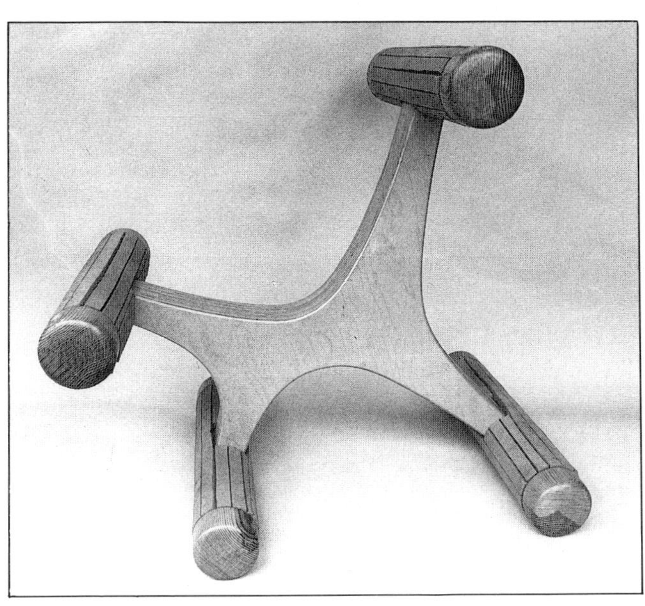

Fig 27.1 The kneeling stool designed by the author in 1985.

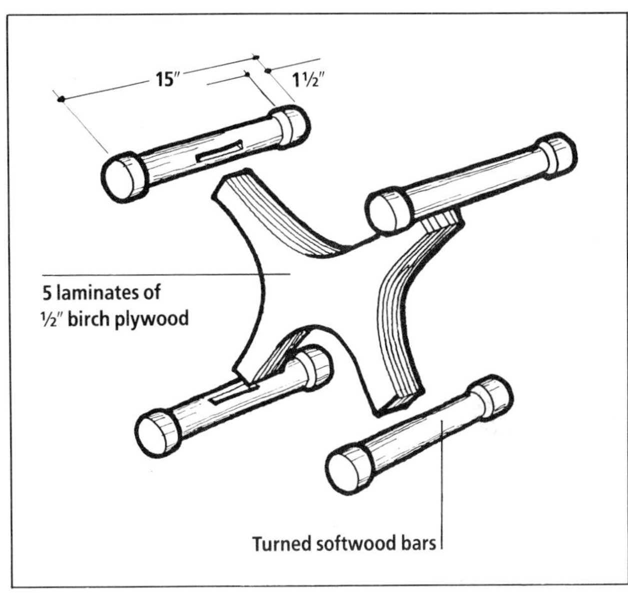

Fig 27.2 Exploded view of the main stool components.

In recent years much attention has been given to our posture when we sit. It is believed that conventional seating bends the spine in an unnatural way, compressing internal organs and restricting the flow of blood. The Scandinavian kneeling or 'Balans' stool came on to the market several years ago and variations of the design have since appeared. The basic principle is that the spine is arched rather than curved, which relieves strain on the inter-vertabraeic discs. Such stools are used in some offices and within the Health Service.

This kneeling stool (Fig 27.1), which I designed as a prototype in 1985, is an attempt to resolve the problem of accommodating people of varying sizes. Like a pair of shoes, a single chair cannot be expected to fit everyone! (See Thinking Hand Video: The Chair, page 273.) This design works on an inverted principle. The body-contact points are also the feet of the stool when turned upside down. Their lengths vary, thus allowing for 2 sizes of person. An added bonus is that if the stool is turned on its side and a sheet of plate glass placed on top – it serves as a coffee table!

The kneeling stool is made from five ½in birch plywood laminates stacked to make up a stout structure (Fig 27.2). The cross members are made from pine turned on the lathe and covered with camping roll-mattress foam rubber. A deep tenon links the frame with the turned arms.

A variety of electric tools can be used to make this design, and the turned bars can be cut on a lathe or lathe attachment (Fig 27.3). The kneeling stool is finished in matt polyurethane varnish applied by hand.

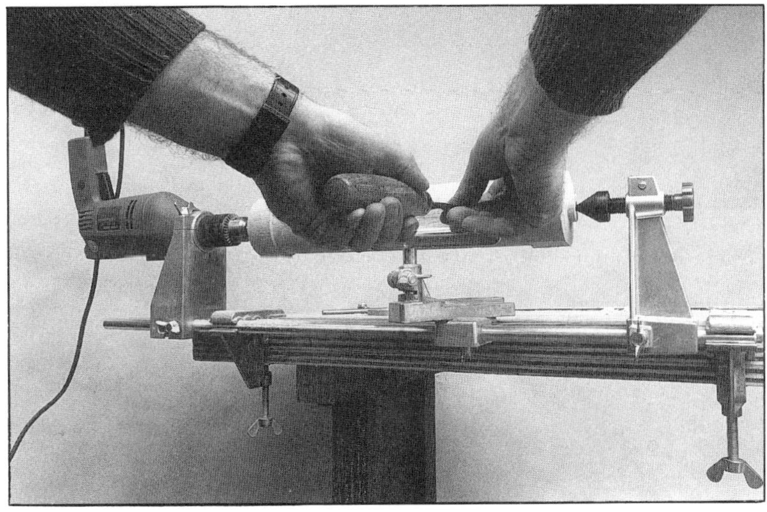

Fig 27.3 Lathe-turning the bars.

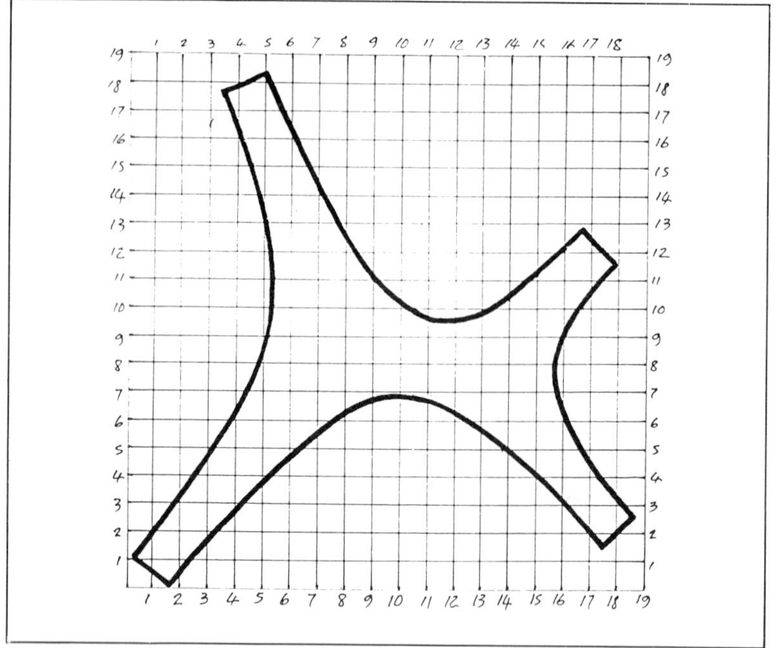

Fig 27.4 Drawing the profile from the enlargement grid.

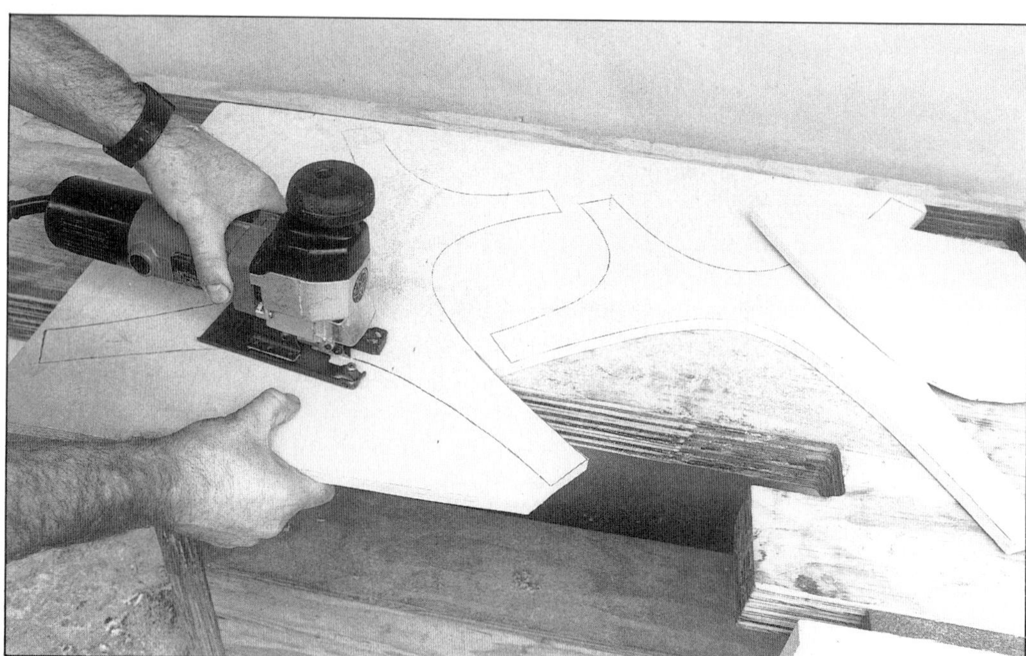

Fig 27.5 Cut the laminates with a jigsaw loaded with a metal cutting blade to minimize grain tear.

PROCEDURE

1 Construct an enlargement grid (Fig 27.4) on a piece of 6mm MDF or similar and draw the stool profile which will serve as a template. Cut the template with jigsaw and bandsaw.

2 Select a well-figured board of ½in birch plywood and trace the template on to it, making economic use of the material. I used a board measuring 48in × 20in and cut 3 complete laminates (Fig 27.5), using the offcuts to fabricate the other two (Figs 27.6 and 27.7). When cutting the laminates allow a little extra for trimming. The easiest way is to cut one slightly over-size and use that as the template for subsequent ones.

3 Glue the laminates together using Cascamite or a PVA glue. Use G-clamps to ensure even pressure and check that the laminates do not slide out of line (Fig 27.8).

4 Retrace the MDF template on to the laminated structure and trim to the finished profile. This can be done on the bandsaw, then with a belt sander (see Fig 14.15). Alternatively, a slightly smaller

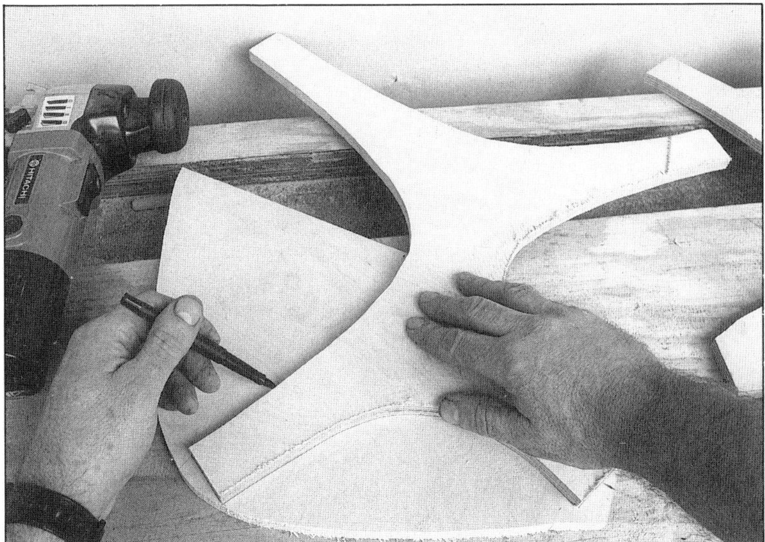

Fig 27.6 Offcuts are used to build up laminates 2 and 4.

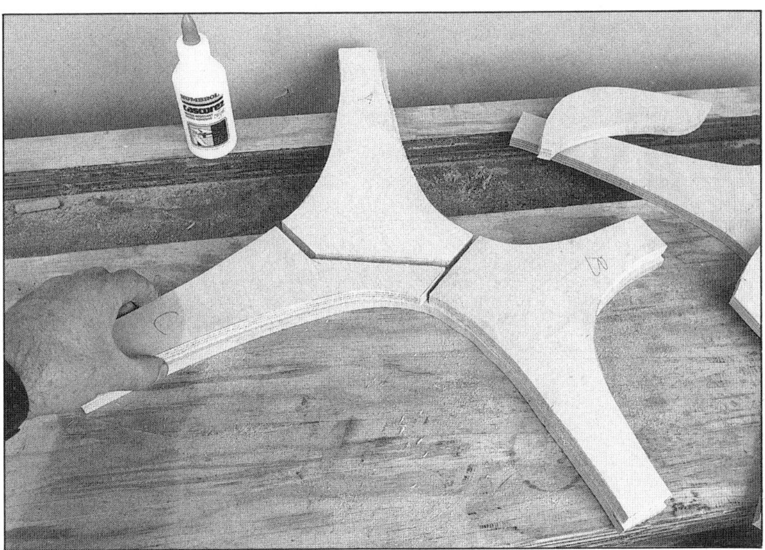

Fig 27.7 Laminates are carefully fabricated.

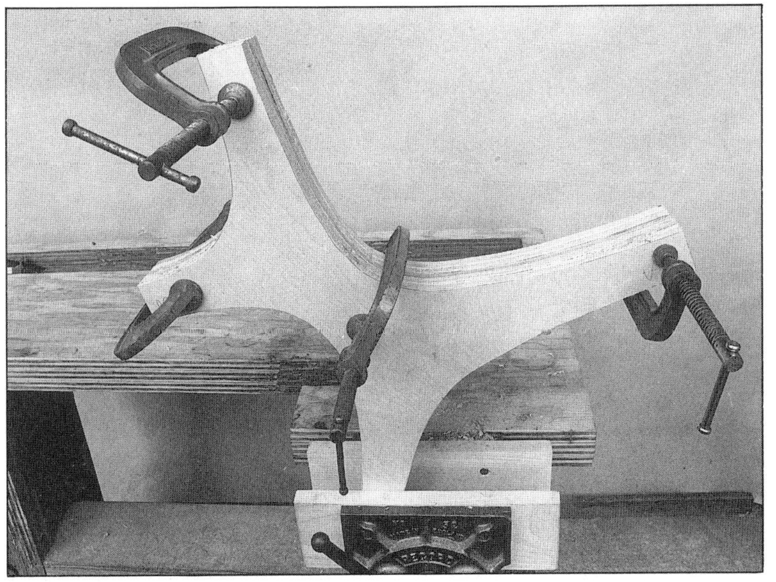

Fig 27.8 Glue and clamp the 5 laminates.

Fig 27.9 Using the Hitachi M12 V router to trim the laminates.

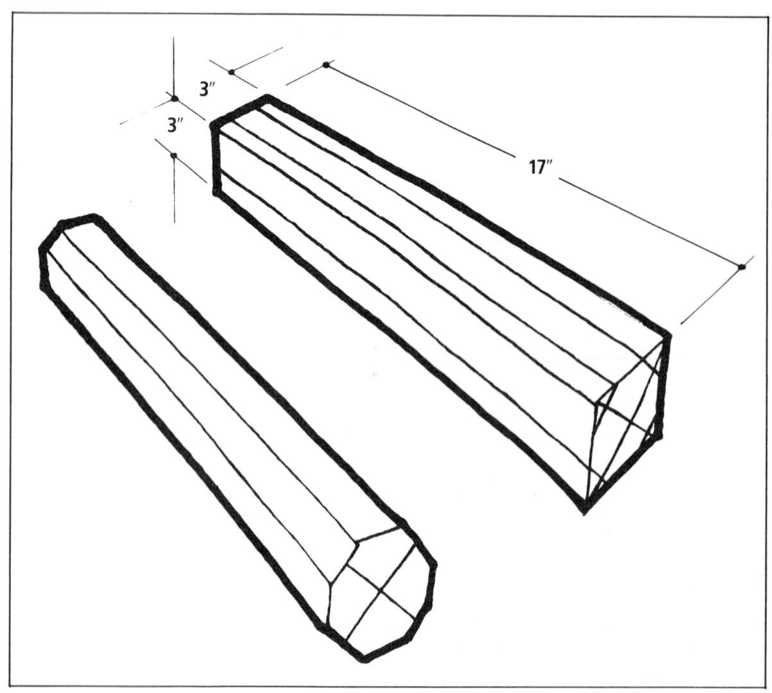

Fig 27.10 The softwood bars are prepared to an octagonal section and diagonals marked on for centres.

template can be made and a router and guide bush used with a long straight cutter – it will need to be plunged in stepped depths (Fig 27.9). The work is hot-melt glued to the bench.

5 Prepare 4 softwood pieces for the bars (16in × 3in). Square-section pine is available and the corners can be removed to make an octagonal section (Fig 27.10). Diagonals will be marked on the ends for centre locations – locate the drive centre in one end.

6 Mount the bar components consecutively on the lathe and reduce to diameter with a scraper or gouge (see Fig 10.24). Mark and incise the ends to 15in length for parting off later (Fig 27.11). Cut the long recess on each leg (Fig 27.12).

7 Partially part off the bars to all but sufficient to support the work while sanding (Fig 27.13). Radius the edges (Fig 27.14).

8 Use abrasive paper, working through the grades, and clean up the exposed ends of each

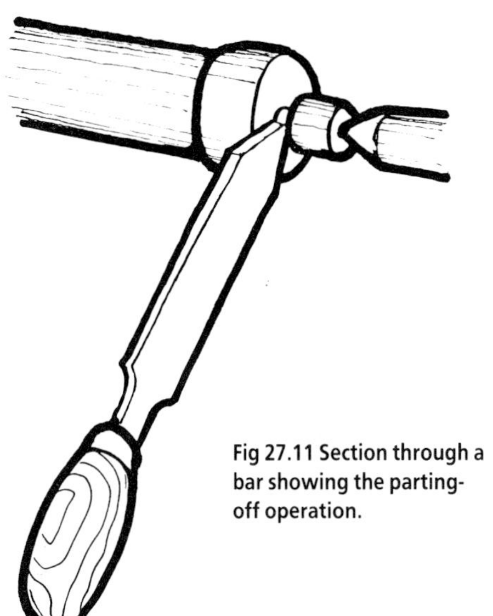

Fig 27.11 Section through a bar showing the parting-off operation.

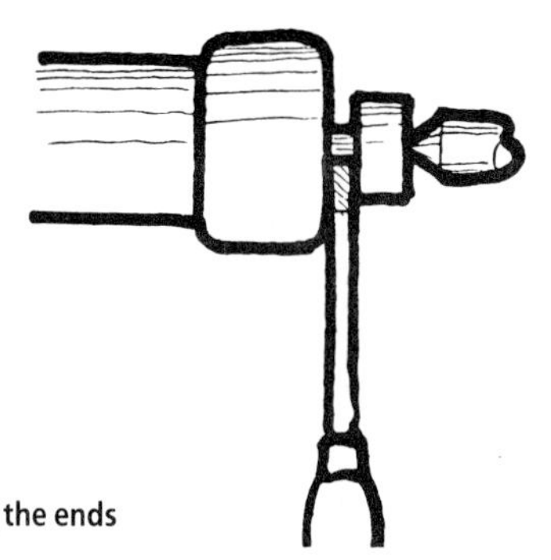

Fig 27.13 Cutting the ends off – almost.

Fig 27.12 A wide chisel/scraper is used to cut the long recess, checking with calipers (above and top).

Fig 27.14 The edges are softened.

Fig 27.15 Abrasive paper is used to clean up the exposed parts of the bars.

Fig 27.16 Router jig for cutting the mortice in the bars.

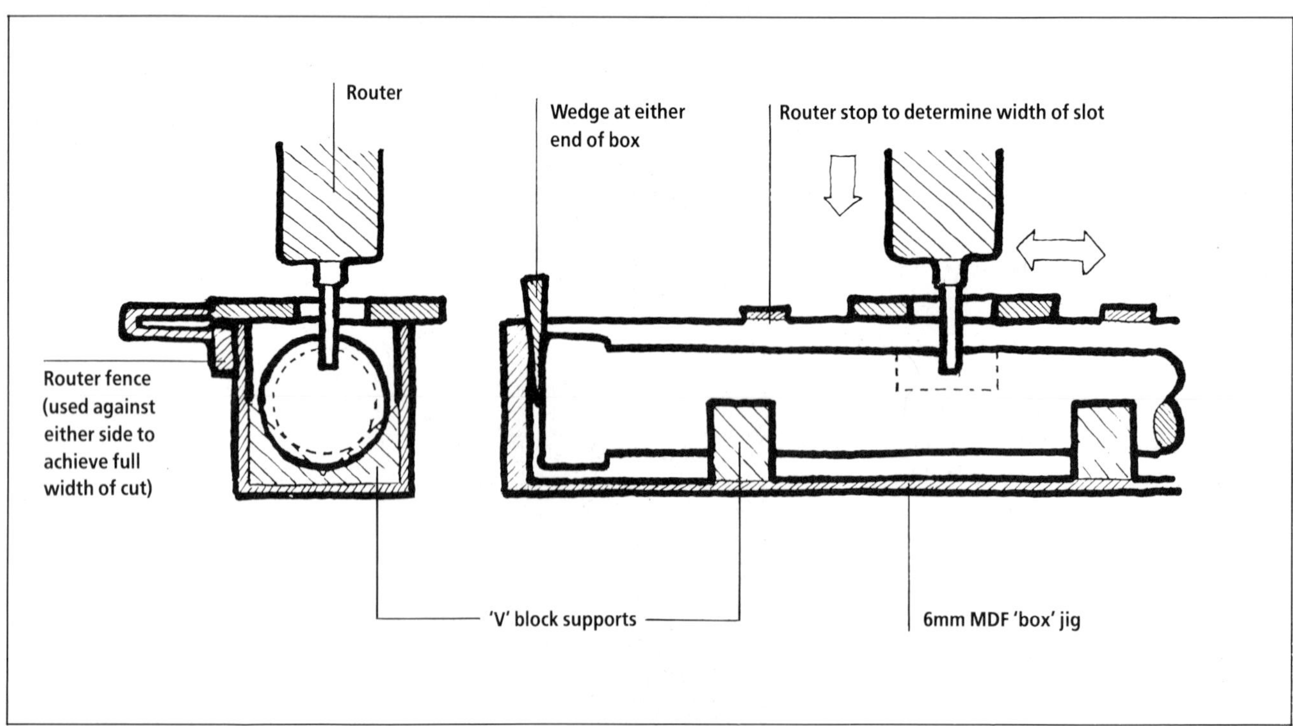

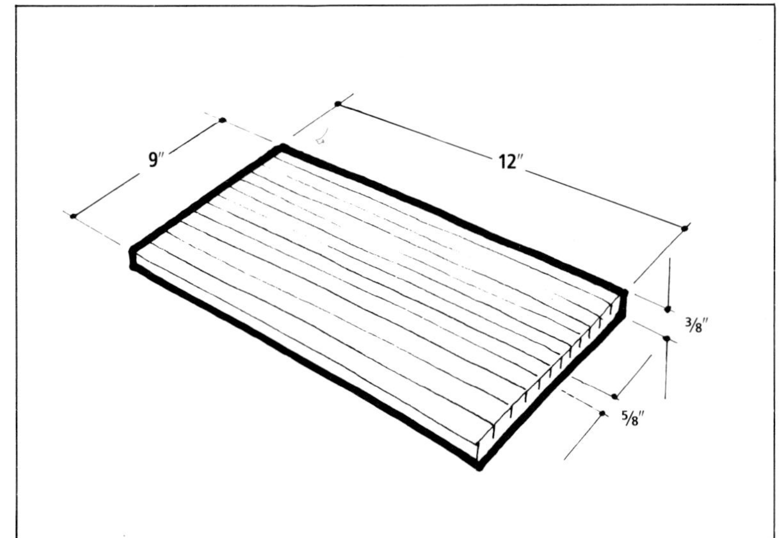

Fig 27.18 Camping foam is cut to size and incised with a Stanley knife against a straight edge to give a ribbed effect.

Fig 27.17 Section through the laminated centre piece showing radius cut with a router.

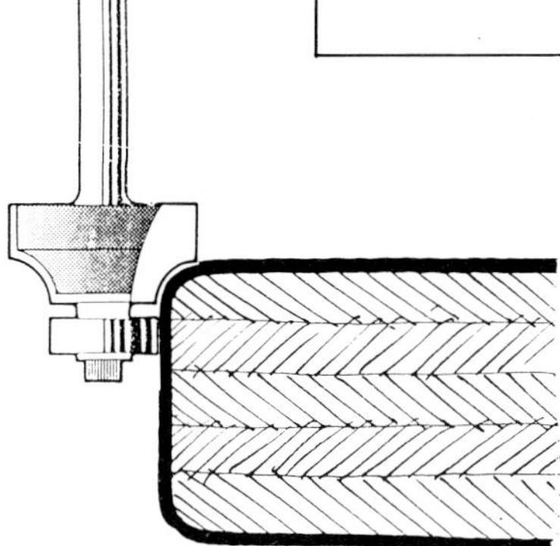

Fig 27.19 The camping foam 'upholstery' is hot-melt glued to the kneeling stool bars.

component. (The recessed portion is left from the tool as foam rubber is glued to it.) (Fig 27.15)

9 Finally, part off each bar component and hand finish the end with abrasive paper.

10 Mark out the centre of each bar component and set up in a router jig to cut in a mortice. Using a medium to heavy duty router, cut the mortice in each bar (Fig 27.16).

11 Radius the corners of the plywood laminate 'tenons' to fit into their respective mortices.

12 Radius the edges of the plywood centre structure with a router set up with a wheel fence (Fig 27.17) and clean up with an orbital sander prior to assembly.

13 Glue the leg components to the centre structure checking alignment with a large try-square. Use Cascamite or an epoxy glue for the joints.

14 Apply 2 or 3 coats of matt polyurethane varnish to the stool.

15 Cut to size some ½in thick camping foam and use a Stanley knife to incise a ribbed effect (Fig 27.18). Glue the foam strips around the legs using a hot-melt gun (Fig 27.19). Allow for slight cutouts around the joints.

28
ELECTRIC LAMP

Lighting is an extremely important aspect of the domestic environment and clearly gives ambience to a room, whether it be kitchen, study, bedroom or living room.

This design for a lamp (Figs 28.1 and 28.2) not only attempts to give a little ambience to a room, but also expresses that wonderful material – plywood. I have always liked the edge of plywood, especially plywoods like Douglas fir or birch. In the past it has been hastily disguised with lippings, but its structure has an inherent beauty of its own. My desire to express the 'material within' also extends to the way I wish to use the light source – the bulb – which is equally attractive.

The design utilizes the new energy-efficient fluorescent bulb technology. Actually, it's not that new – I used these bulbs when they first became available from Philips in the early 80s and was impressed with their cool running characteristics. They can be hand-held, and this opens up possibilities for integrating them into close-fitting wooden structures without the risk of burning.

This lamp design uses a 15 watt bulb (Fig 28.3) which gives out the equivalent of 75 watts. Its 'goldfish bowl' shape and opaque luminance made me ask why a shade is necessary at all. So I decided to integrate the bulb into a wood structure, which results in a fairly open and unusual design (Fig 28.4).

The lamp was designed as I went along in the workshop, and in hindsight can be simplified further (Fig 28.5), as it turned out to be quite difficult to make – it has to be made accurately. The sandwiched plywood base is 'split', giving access to the bulb and bulb holder. The bulb holder is a readily available plastic type with a bayonet fitting. (Ideally, the holder should be 'screw-in' as it makes the bulb more stable, but these can be more difficult to get hold of).

Different materials and different dimensions could be used. Instead of plywood for the 'shade', an opaque white acrylic sheet could be used. This would create a 'fibre optic' effect on the edge, but it would be a more difficult material to fashion, although the same woodworking tools could be used. Alternatively, veneers could be sandwiched together to make up an ultra-thin plywood to serve as each rib. (Really, you can do anything in wood!)

Fig 28.1 The electric lamp in birch plywood.

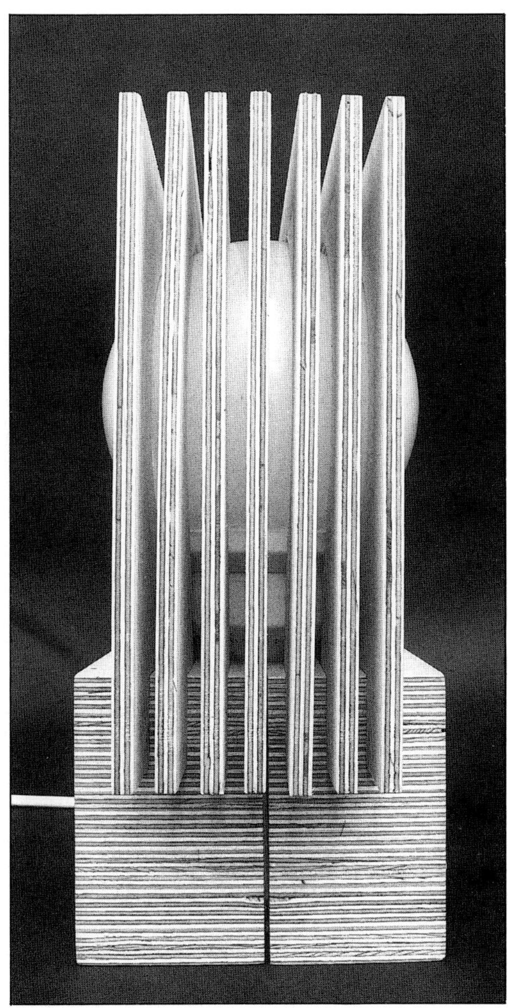

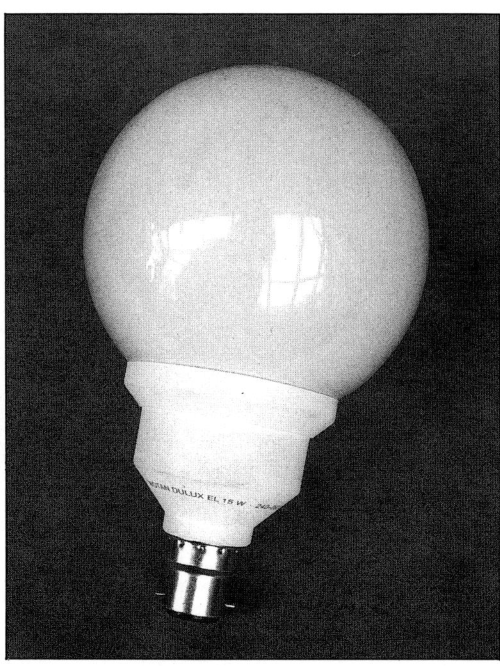

Fig 28.2 (far left) The electric lamp – side view.

Fig 28.3 The low-energy 15 watt bulb which gives out 75 watts.

Various electric tools can be employed in this project. I used a jigsaw extensively, with a metal cutting blade to minimize fibre tear. I also used a bandsaw and a belt sander in its bench-mounted position for accurately 'squaring' and trimming the edges. Alternatively, a disc sander could be used. The lamp-holder orifice is drilled out with a large flatbit, but could be mounted on the lathe and turned from both ends. The 'split' base-fixing offers

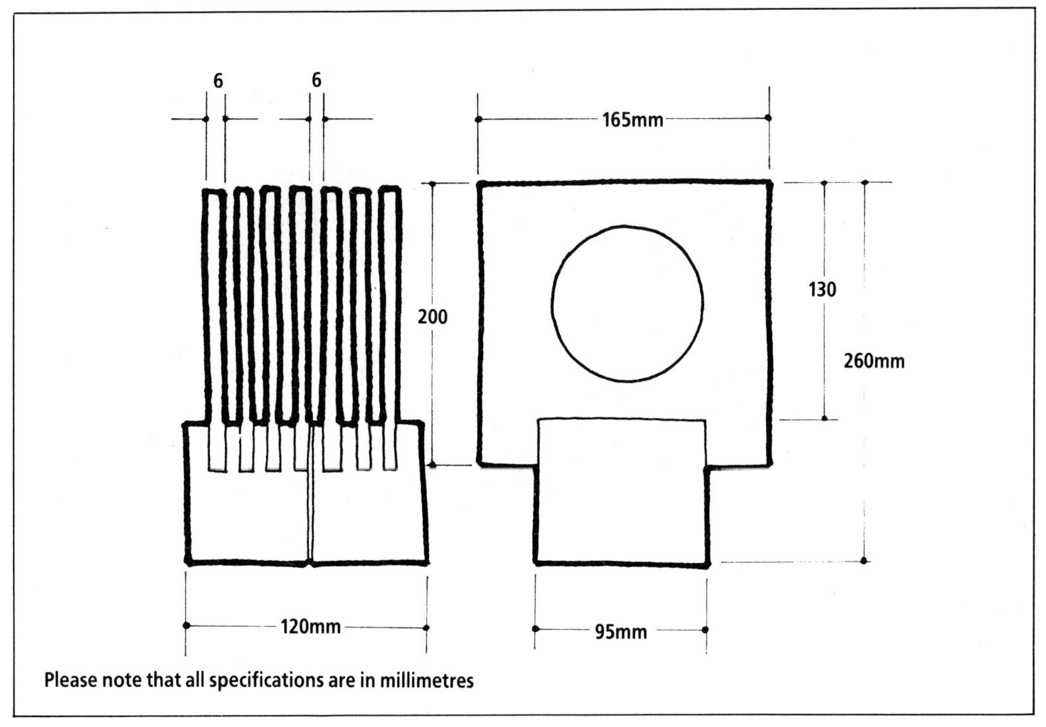

Fig 28.4 The electric lamp design.

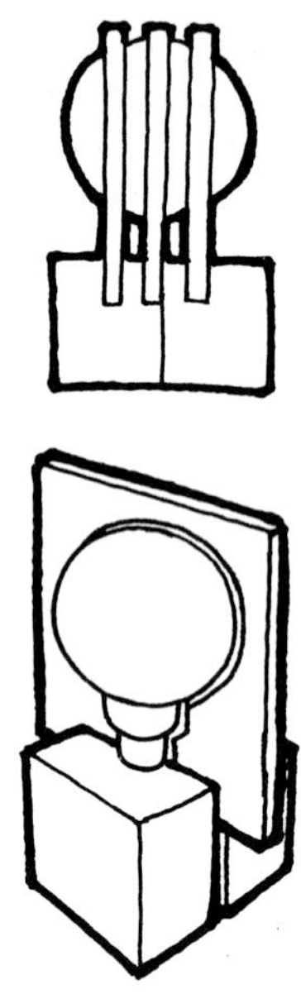

Fig 28.5 Some simplified design options.

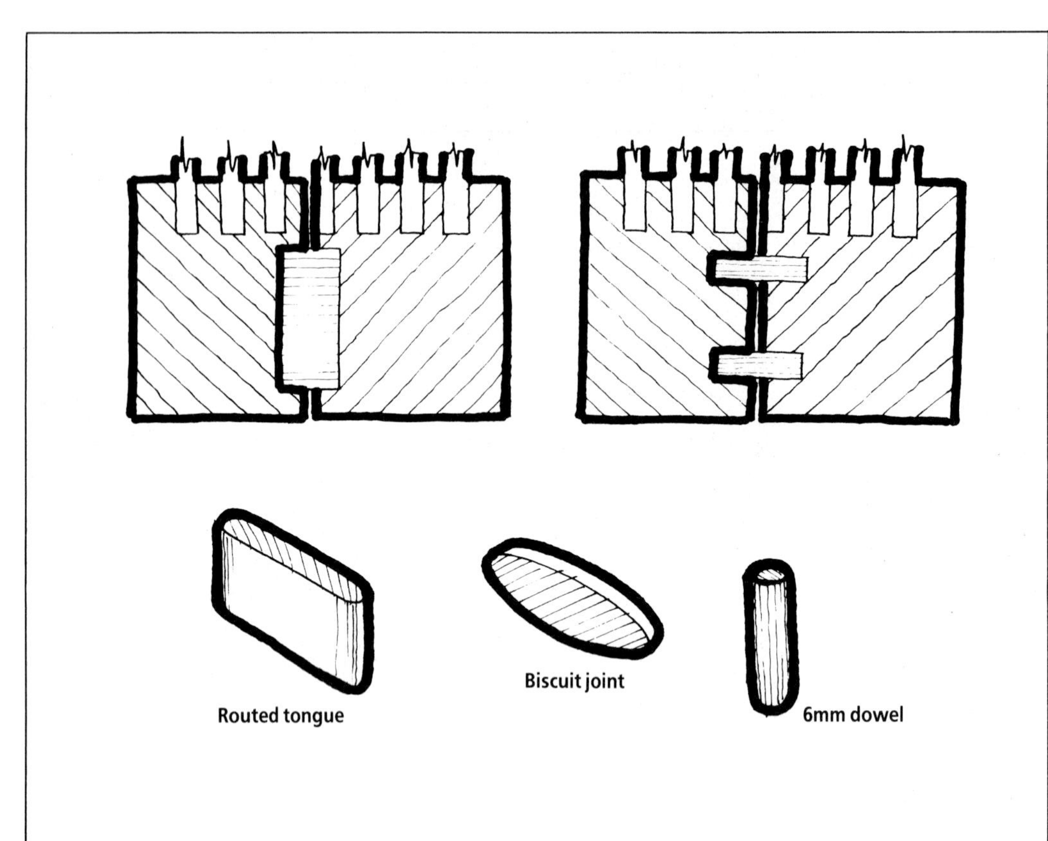

Fig 28.6 Options for joining the base.

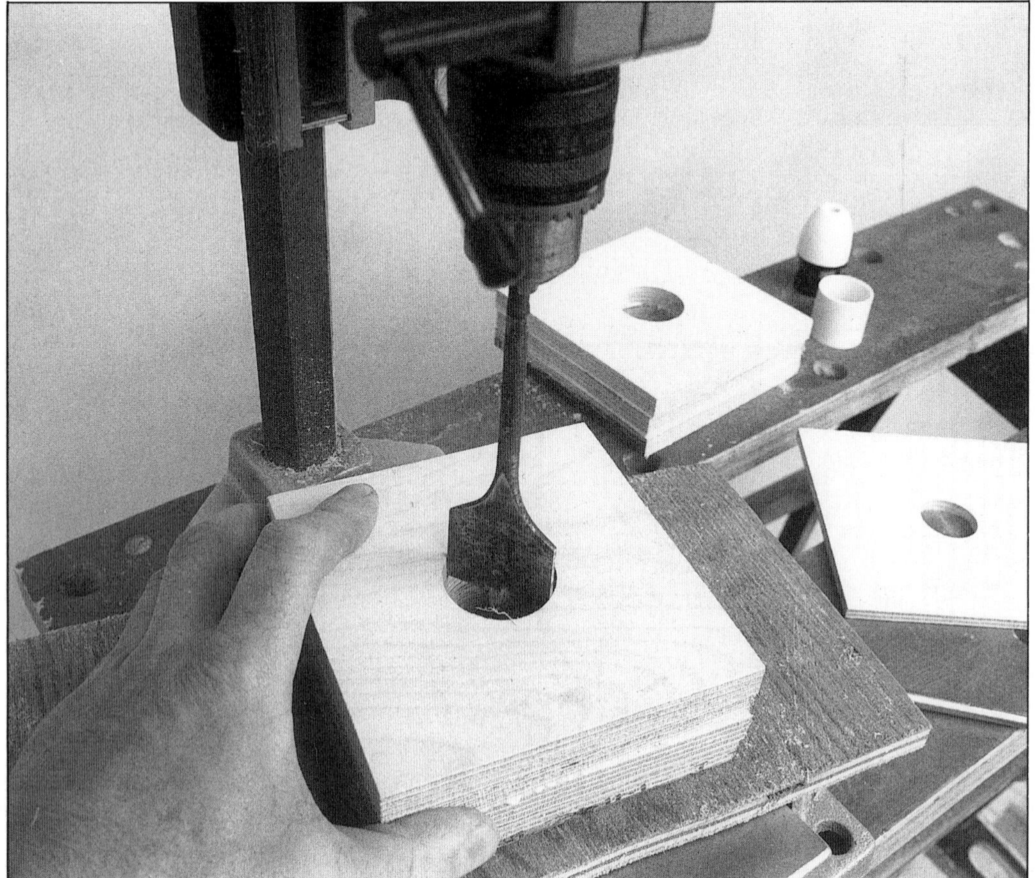

Fig 28.7 Hold work very firmly when drilling with a flatbit.

Fig 28.8 Creative use of the jigsaw – cutting the lamp holder hole accurately in a series of cuts.

various options, from dry dowel joints to routed loose tongues (Fig 28.6).

PROCEDURE

1 Select a board of ½in birch plywood, checking that 'plugs' are avoided. Prepare oversize the pieces for sandwiching the base (Fig 28.4). The middle laminate is made of 6mm birch plywood and has a smaller hole drilled in it for supporting the lamp holder.

2 I glued together two sets of laminates separately. When dry, I drilled them with a 38mm flatbit (Fig 28.7). I then cut out the hole in the 6mm blank with a jigsaw as I did not have a flatbit of the correct diameter (Fig 28.8). The hole is traced around the screw thread of a standard plastic lamp holder.

3 The three parts of the base are then glued together, taking care to align the holes concentrically (Fig 28.9). You may wish to construct the base in a different way, i.e. by turning the complete

Fig 28.9 Masking tape is used to 'clamp' the base laminates while gluing.

Fig 28.10 Careful trimming of the base block on the bandsaw to a line. Check blade is running 'square' to the table.

Fig 28.11 Using the Skil belt sander to smooth the base block.

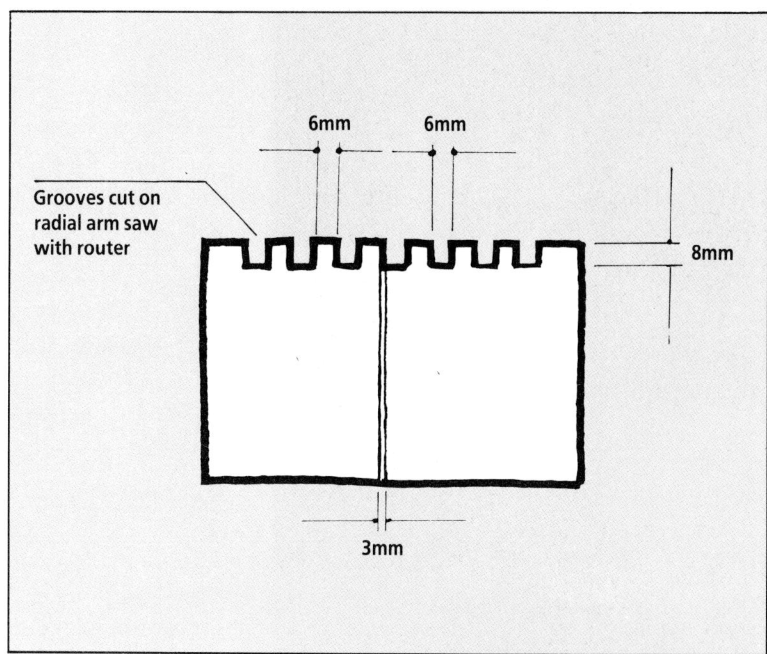

Fig 28.12 The marked positions for the 'shade' ribs.

blank on the lathe from both ends to achieve the same inner profile.

4 Mark out the base block accurately to finished size and trim using the bandsaw (Fig 28.10) and a sander (Fig 28.11). Check for 'squareness' with a try-square.

5 Mark out the positions of the 'shade' ribs (to be made from 6mm birch plywood). The base will be 'split' on the edge of the centre rib (Fig 28.12).

6 Prepare accurately the shade ribs to size (Fig 28.4) and trim on the sander (disc or belt).

Fig 28.13 The radial arm saw is used to cut the rib grooves (my old DeWalt does not have modern guards).

Fig 28.14 Very careful 'splitting' of the base to the line.

Fig 28.15 Routing in the loose tongues with a Hitachi FM8.

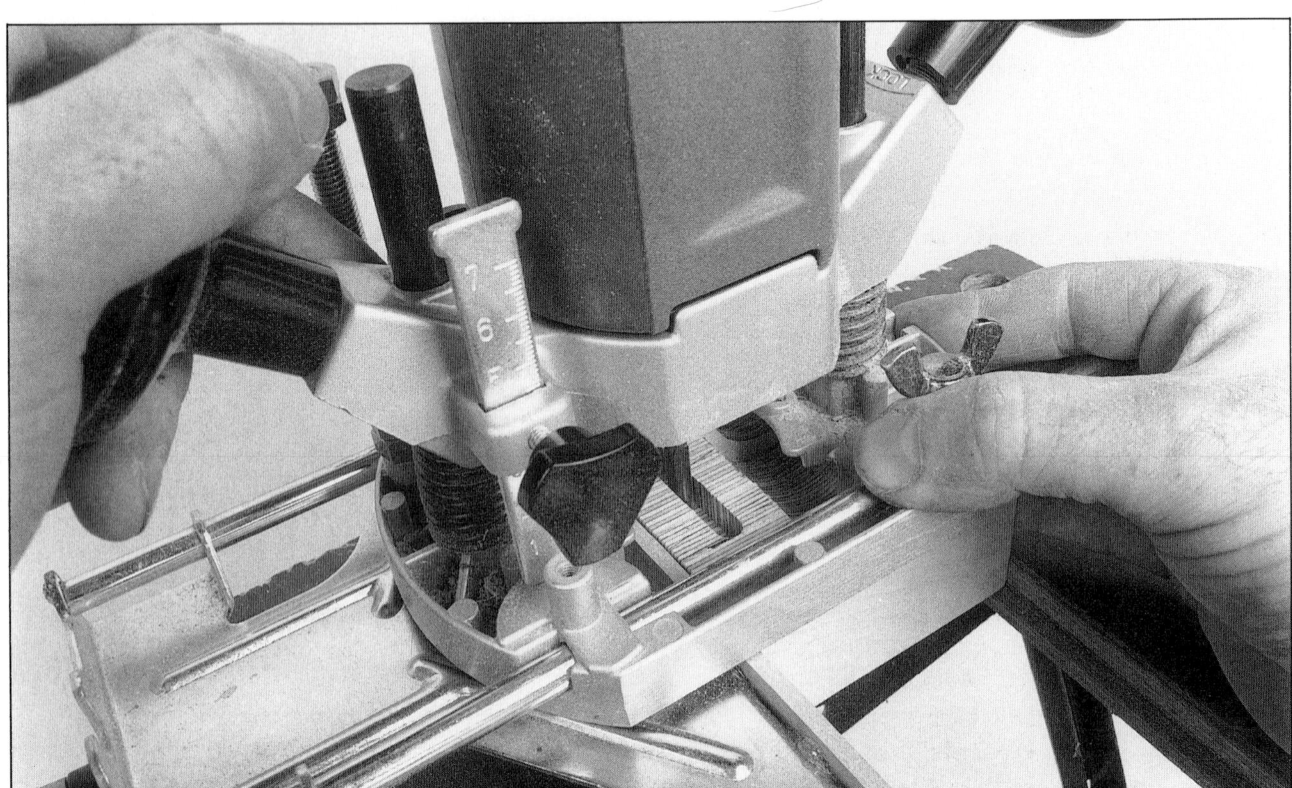

Fig 28.16 Drill the flex hole from the outside.

Fig 28.17 The rib profiles.

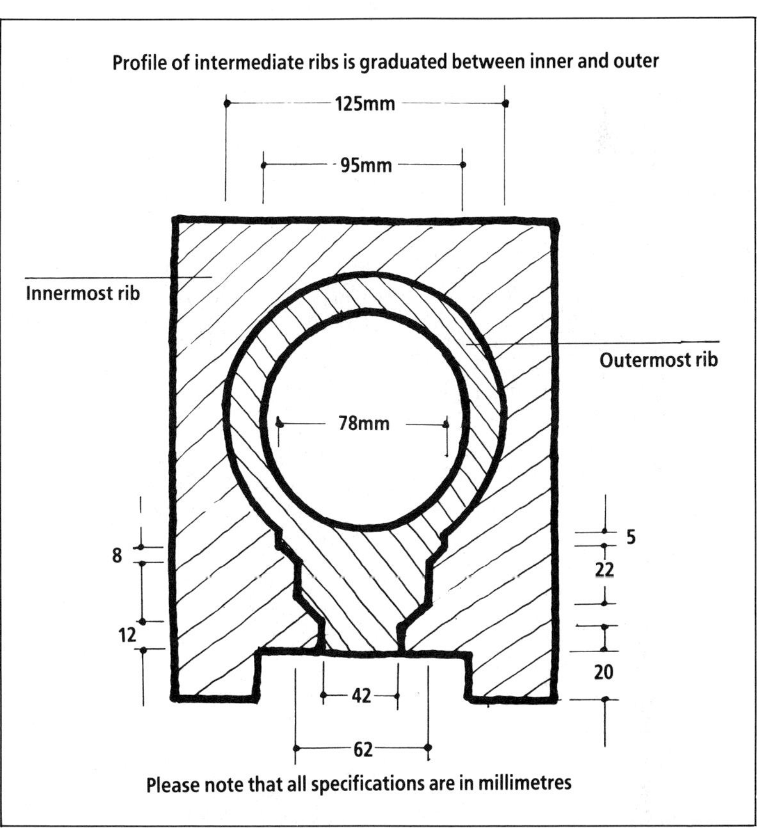

7 Cut the rib recesses into the top of the base. I used a radial arm saw (Fig 28.13) and worked accurately to the line, checking with a piece of 6mm plywood for fit. Alternatively a router set up with a straight fence can be used.

8 Mark out the 'split' line on the base and very carefully bandsaw it apart (Fig 28.14). Minimal cleaning up on the sander will be done to the inner faces.

9 Decide on the method of fixing the 2 parts together (Fig 28.6). I routed a loose tongue in (glued into one side only) (Fig 28.15). The tongue was fractionally oversize, creating a slight shadow line on the join. (If you can't disguise it, feature it!)

10 Fix the bulb holder into its housing (screw collar). A small amount of fine trimming is needed with a chisel.

11 Mark out and drill a 6mm hole in one half of the base for the flex (Fig 28.16).

12 Now comes the tricky part – accurately marking out the ribs to follow the profile of the spherical lamp bulb. The diagram is a guide (Fig 28.17). You may wish to mock up one of the ribs in MDF or a spare piece of plywood. In effect a gap of

Fig 28.18 Bandsawing the rib inner profiles.

Fig 28.19 The 2 outer ribs are drilled then cut accurately with a jigsaw.

Fig 28.20 Use a drum sander attachment on the drill to clean up the rib profiles.

approximately 3mm exists between the plywood edge and the surface of the bulb. You need to attach the bulb and bulb holder to check your calculations.

13 Cut the profiled ribs, having marked out with a compass and try-square. I used a bandsaw for the open-ended ribs (Fig 28.18) and a drill and jigsaw for the 2 end ribs which are circles (Fig 28.19).

14 If you use a backing piece on the bandsaw (false platform) the fibres will not tear and a reasonable finish straight off the saw is possible. Final cleaning up of the internal profile can be done with a drill set up with a drum sander attachment (Fig 28.20).

15 Power sand the outer edges of the ribs. Either trim individually using a table disc sander or bundle together with masking tape and trim as a block (see Fig 14.19). I used the belt sander mounted inversely.

16 Carefully check each rib fits correctly. You will need to code each member, marking it where the glue joint will be so that the mark does not show.

17 Dry assemble the entire lamp with the bulb inserted to check for clearance. You may find the bulb holder you use is slightly different to mine. That is why it is important to check measurements before you cut (Fig 28.21).

18 Glue the ribs into the base members using a PVA glue, and wipe excess off with a fine wood spatula. If you wish to varnish the lamp you may be best advised to varnish the ribs *before* they are glued, although it is possible to varnish them afterwards. All edges should be slightly softened with Lubrasil paper.

19 Attach 2–3 metres of light flex to the bulb holder, threading it through the 6mm hole in the base, and fix a plug on the end – switch on!

Fig 28.21 The components of the lamp ready for assembly.

29

CHEST OF DRAWERS

Fig 29.1 **A mini chest of drawers for holding A4 documents.**

The great thing about tradition is that it can be a springboard for ideas – not something stagnant, to be preserved in a 'heritage' museum. Techniques used today are bound to be a continuum of tradition, and 'contemporary' or 'modern' work should not be divorced from what has gone before.

So although it was my original intention to present a 'traditional' miniature chest of drawers (Fig 29.1) as a project for this book, knowing that it would have popular appeal, somehow I seem to have made a few changes on the way! The finished result may seem modern, but it was in fact inspired by tradition!

Firstly, this chest of drawers was designed to hold A4 paper, to suit my own needs, but obviously it can hold all sorts of things. However, the drawers are fairly shallow, and therefore suitable for filing papers, or as a collections' cabinet.

The design is a solid wood carcase, and when I was deliberating over the visual appearance of an overlapping moulded top, with drawers set within the framework of the carcase – the 'traditional' method – I decided to simplify things and have everything flush, with the drawers sweeping across more freely and exposing that wonderful feature of wood – end-grain! The reason for this is simple: we live in an age when solid wood is increasingly rare and thus treasured. The proof that a piece is solid and not veneered is in the end-grain, so why not show it!

The carcase is made up of edge-jointed boards from standard 4in × ¾in deal. It utilizes the jigsaw, bandsaw, planer–thicknesser, or hand planer and thicknessing attachment (Fig 29.2).

After gluing, the pieces are dressed with a belt sander and orbital sander. The back of the carcase is made of 4mm plywood and the drawers are made of solid deal with similar thin plywood bottoms.

The construction of the carcase offers various options – dowelled joints, Leigh or Woodrat cut dovetails, or biscuit joints (Fig 29.3). I chose the latter, and it took longer to apply the glue to the joints than it did to mark out and cut them – such is the wonder of the biscuit jointer! (See Chapter 11.)

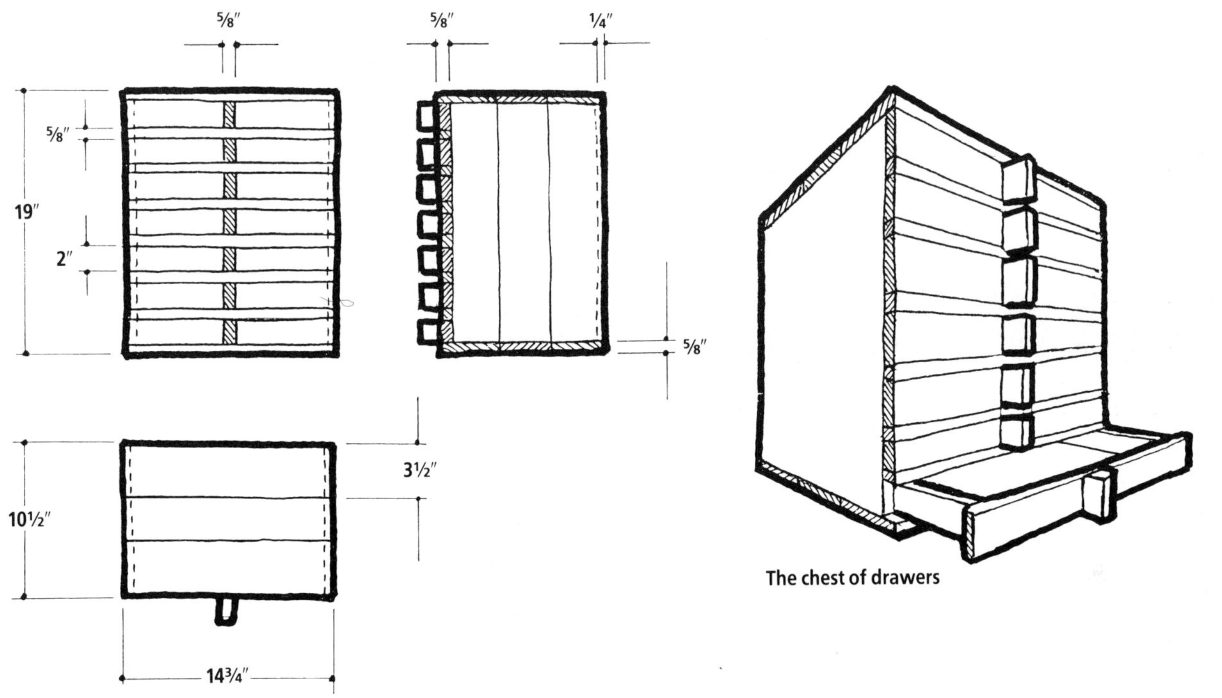

Fig 29.2 Pictorial view and elevation of the chest of drawers.

The drawer spacers and guides can be biscuit jointed, or recessed with a router and glued and screwed. The drawers offer similar construction options (Fig 29.4), including the above, and the use of the radial arm saw for grooved joints.

Another departure from tradition, and one I constantly practise, is the *progressive* build-up of a partitioned carcase rather than building and gluing all in one go. It would be a nightmare to assemble, glue and check for squareness numerous components, especially as the pot-life of glue is limited. It makes sense to me to design the object in such a way that partitions can be jointed in *after* the main carcase has been glued, and this is only possible using tools such as a small router or a biscuit jointer which is equally compact. All in all, this is truly an *electric* project!

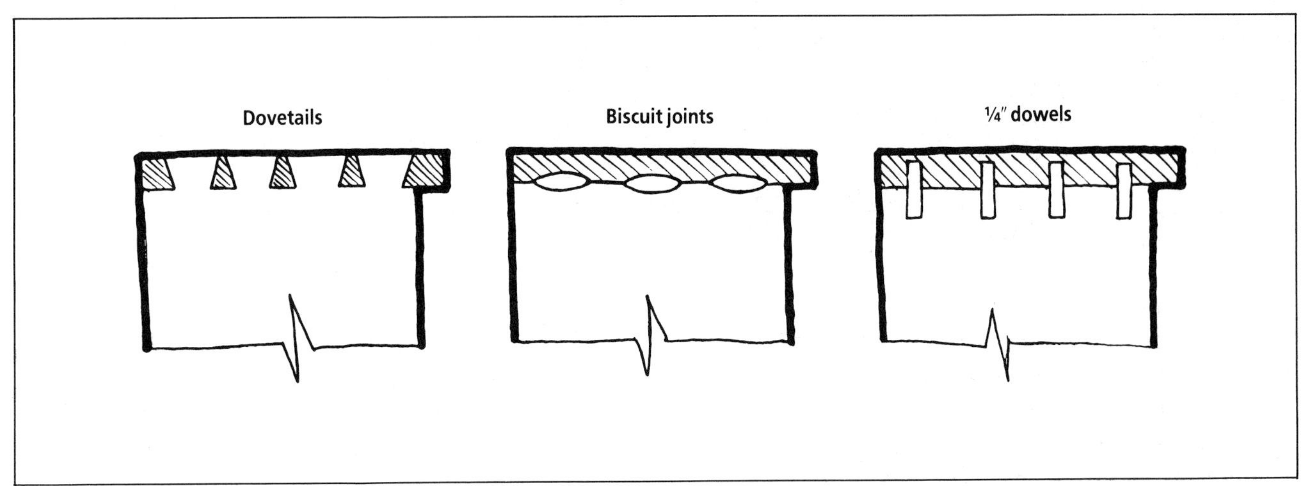

Fig 29.3 Carcase joint options.

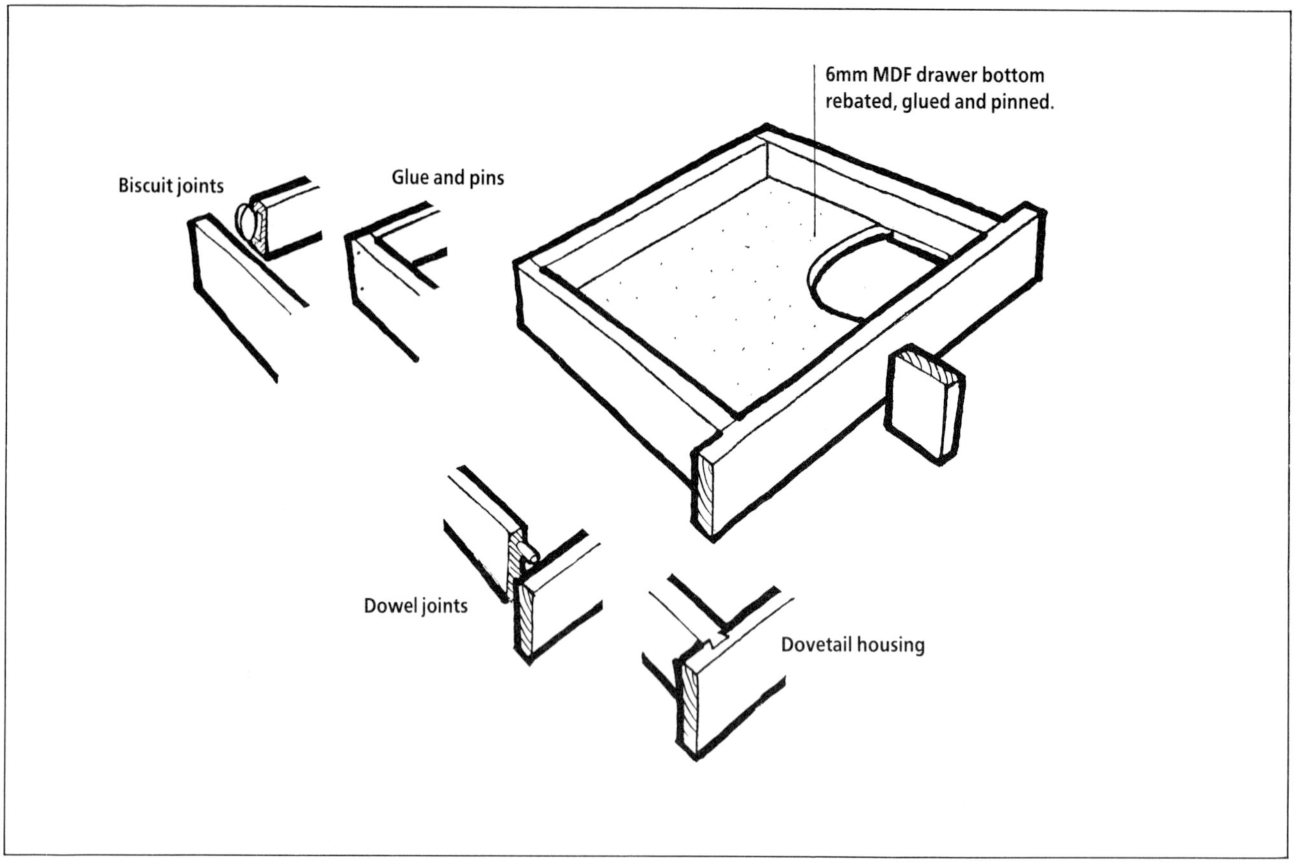
6mm MDF drawer bottom
rebated, glued and pinned.
Biscuit joints
Glue and pins
Dowel joints
Dovetail housing

Fig 29.4 Drawer joint options.

EVO-STIK
WOOD
ADHESIVE

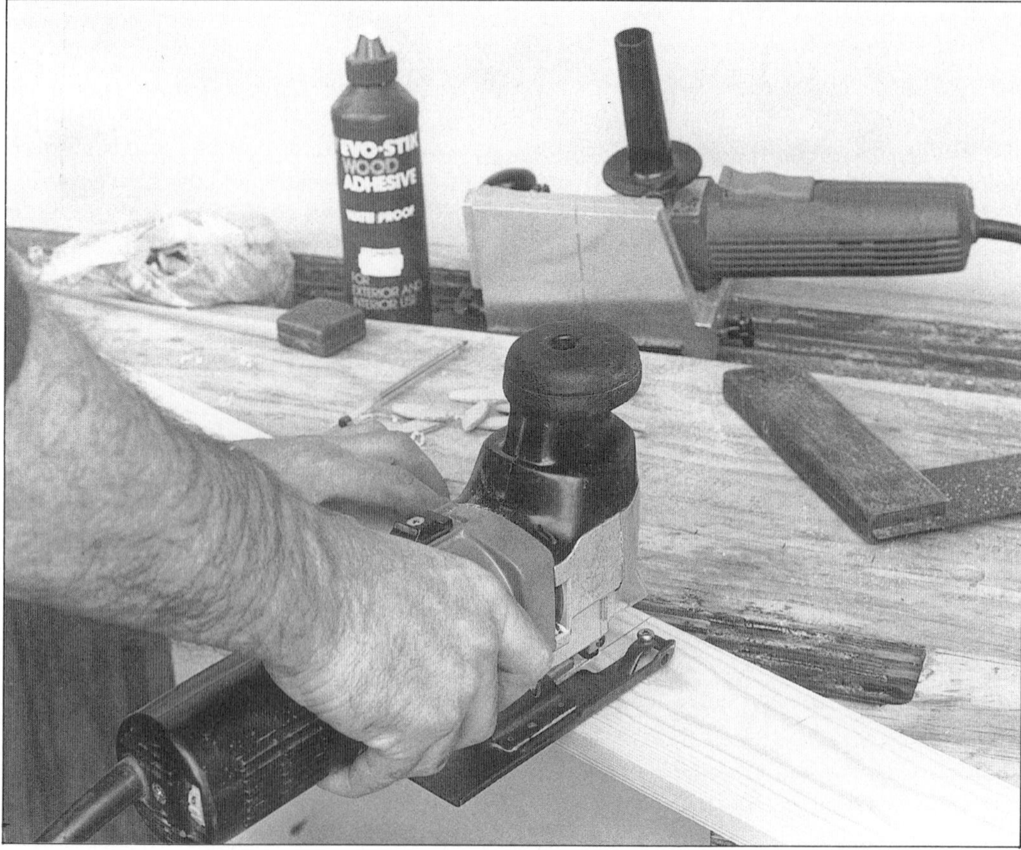

Fig 29.5 Using the Hitachi jigsaw to cut the pieces.

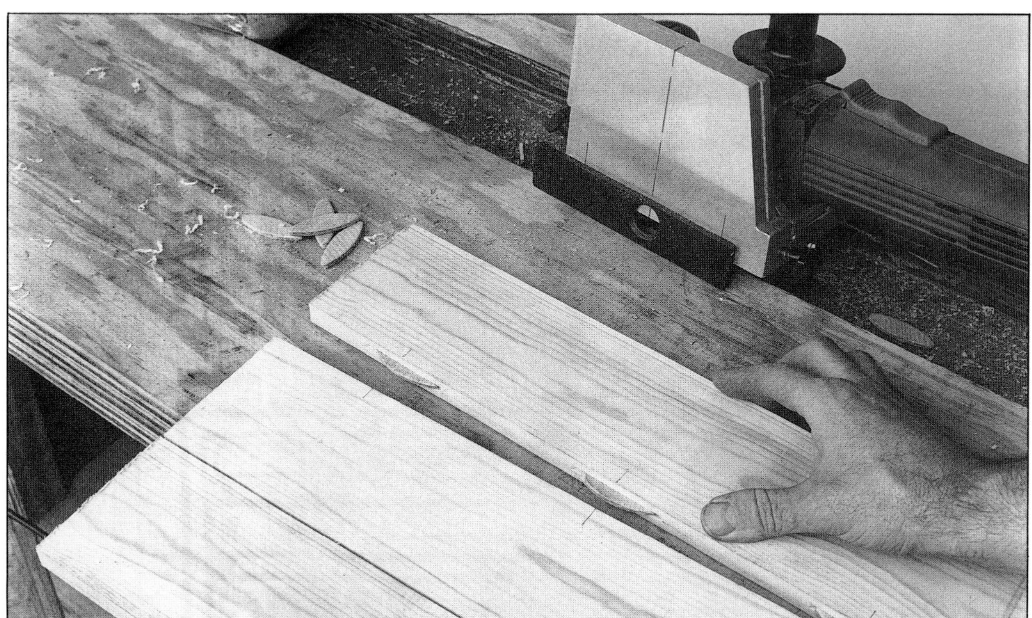

Fig 29.6 Edge-jointing the carcase members with the Elu biscuit jointer.

Fig 29.8 Trim the edges on the bandsaw to a marked line – always leave the line on.

Fig 29.7 The edge-jointed pieces are glued and clamped together.

PROCEDURE

1 Prepare the carcase components to length (Fig 29.5) and machine plane to dimension. Code all components. For cutting pieces to length initially I use a jigsaw with a fine metalworking blade to avoid fibre tear across the grain.

2 Edge-join the carcase members using the biscuit jointer (Fig 29.6). (It is also acceptable to butt the edges together without a biscuit or dowel joint.) Glue carcase members together and clamp. I used Cascorez glue which takes 30 minutes to set, but I prefer to leave it longer in the clamps (Fig 29.7).

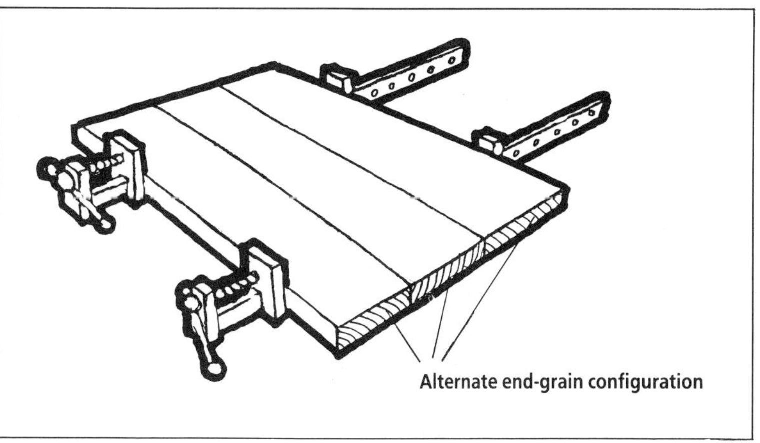

Fig 29.9 Clean up the edges on a Black & Decker power planer.

Fig 29.10 (a) Using the Elu biscuit jointer for the carcase members . . .

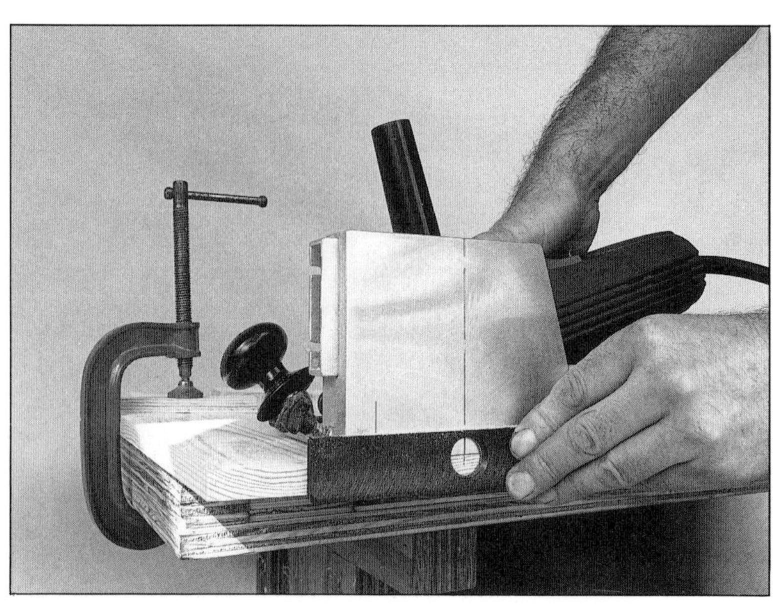

3 Clean up the surfaces of the carcase members. The joy of biscuit jointing is that it leaves everything flush, hence minimal cleaning up is necessary. I used a belt sander to smooth the surfaces, followed by an orbital sander (see Fig 14.10).

4 Cut pieces to length and width on the bandsaw (Fig 29.8) finishing on the power planer (Fig 29.9). The end-grain can be carefully planed, ensuring a bevel is left at the end (see Chapter 9).

5 Mark out and cut joints with a biscuit jointer and code each piece (Figs 29.10 (a), (b) and (c)).

6 Clean up insides of carcase members, and glue and clamp using PVA or Cascamite glue. Wipe away excess glue with a slightly damp cloth. Check the carcase for squareness with a roofing square or large try-square.

Fig 29.10 (b)

Fig 29.10 (c)

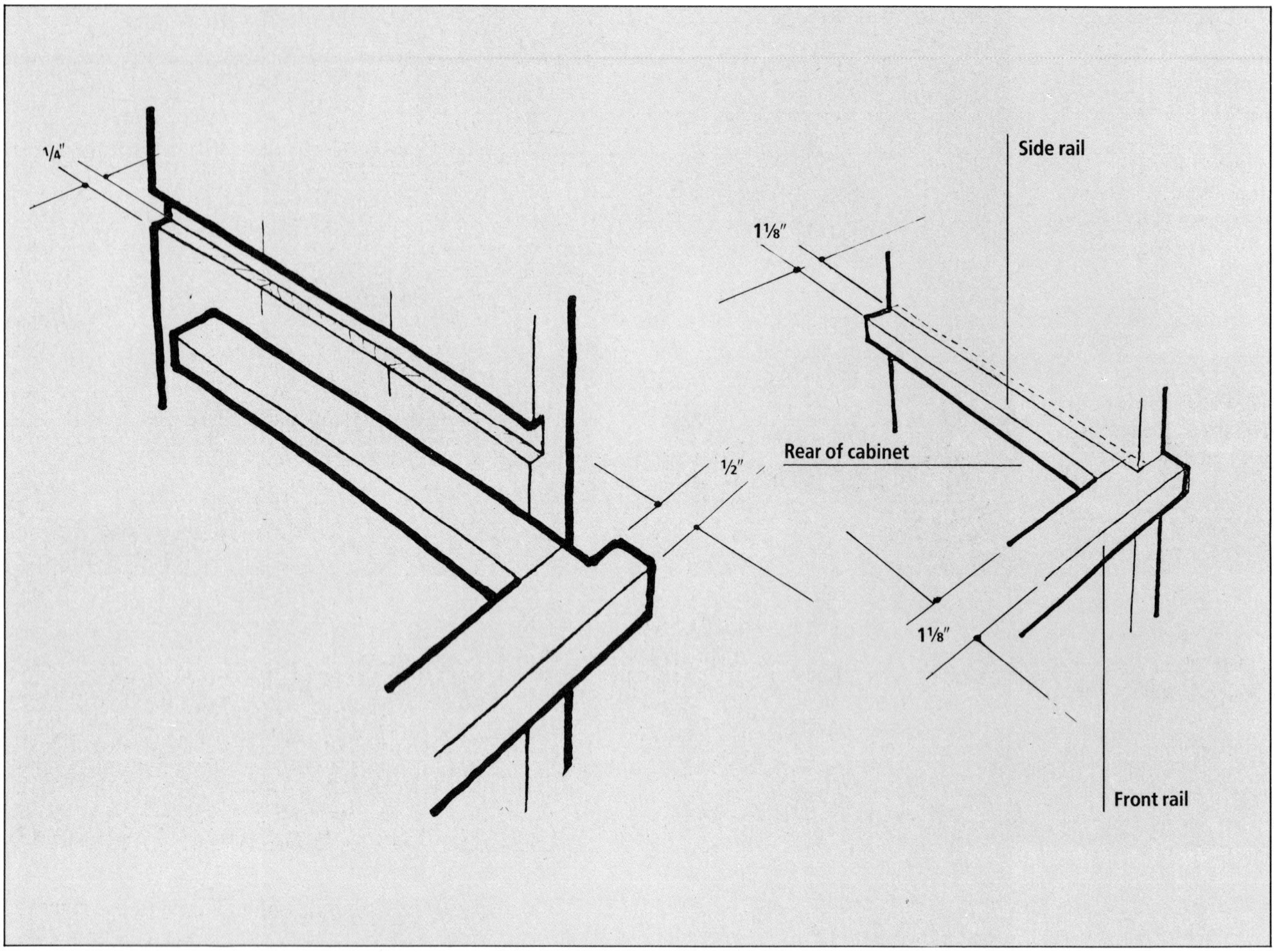

¼″
1⅛″
Side rail
½″
Rear of cabinet
1⅛″
Front rail

7 Clean up the outside of the carcase carefully with a belt sander, clamping it to the bench top. Mark out positions for drawer guides and front rails (Fig 29.11). Clean up carcase edges.

8 Prepare to size the required number of drawer guides and front rails and code them.

9 Set up a small router with a 12mm diameter straight cutter. Prepare thin space battens, and using a batten and G-clamps rout each drawer guide groove (Figs 29.12 and 29.13). I calculated and marked the equidistant positions with a piece of paper.

10 Attach a straight fence to the router and, using the same cutter, rebate the back for the back panel (4mm plywood) (Fig 29.14).

11 Accurately mark out and bandsaw the front drawer rails, code and dry assemble. Fit respective drawer guides in place, trimming to length carefully to be flush with the back rebate.

12 Clean up inside of carcase, removing pencil marks and burrs etc. with a small sander (see Fig 14.7).

Fig 29.11 View of carcase showing dimensions for drawer guides (opposite above).

Fig 29.12 The wall of the carcase is used to guide the first cut, with a thin spacer (opposite below).

Fig 29.13 Battens are carefully positioned to guide the small router.

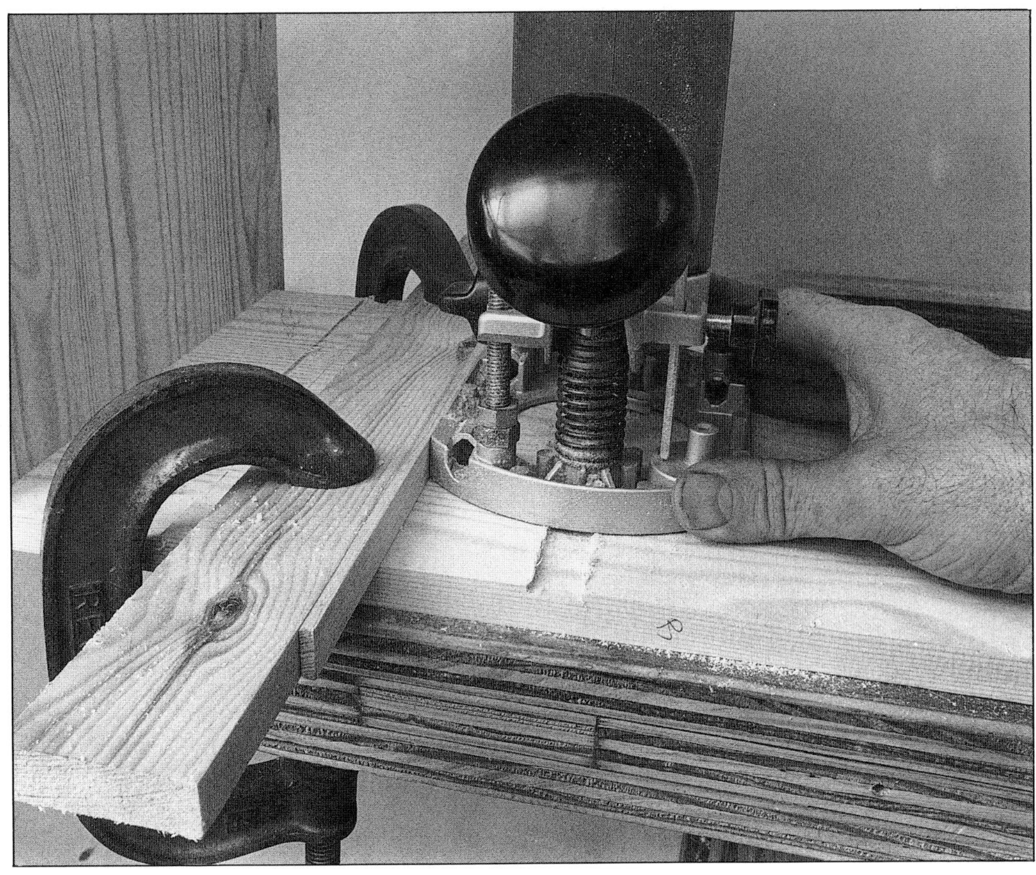

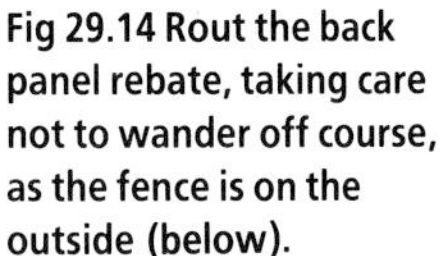

Fig 29.14 Rout the back panel rebate, taking care not to wander off course, as the fence is on the outside (below).

Fig 29.15 Fitting the rear panel to the carcase. (below right).

13 Glue drawer guides and front rails into place, checking they are square and flush. Additionally, or as a jointing alternative, the drawer guides can be attached with small screws (see Fig 16.4).

14 Prepare to size, power sand and fit the plywood back panel, radiusing the edges to match the routed rebate corners. Glue and pin, sink and fill! (Fig 29.15).

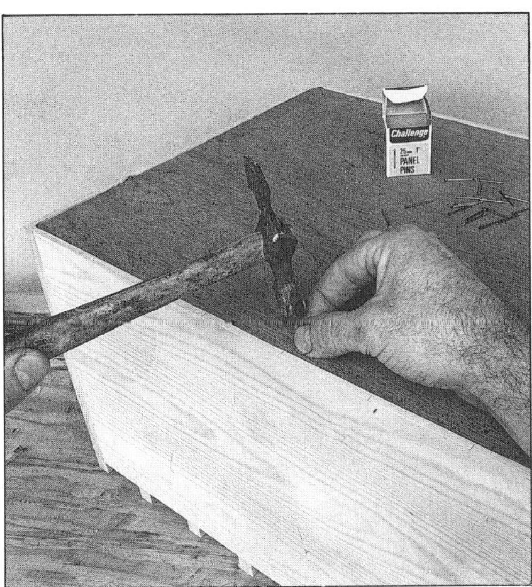

Fig 29.16 A disc sander (Wolfcraft attachment) accurately trims the ends of the drawer fronts.

15 Now, here is the tricky part – and the divulgence of a huge trade secret. Getting drawers to fit perfectly is one of the highpoints of this craft. Why not tailor each drawer in turn and make it *around* the dimensions already dictated by the cabinet built so far? Traditionally, drawers are made from their jointed (dovetailed) shoulder lines. I chose to make these drawers from their external dimensions, which obviously match the internal dimensions of the drawer guides and rails.

16 Carefully prepare and code each drawer front to fit exactly, in length and width. I used a disc sander attachment to square off the ends perfectly flush (Fig 29.16).

17 Prepare material for the drawer sides and back pieces (Fig 29.17) and joint together (Fig 29.4).

18 Clean up the insides of the drawer components and glue and clamp.

19 Clean up the drawers with a power sander.

20 Rebate the drawer bottoms with the router in the same way as the carcase back panel was rebated. The drawer will need to be hot-melt glue-tabbed to the bench, or set in the bench dogs.

21 Glue and pin the drawer bottoms into their rebates, checking first that their squareness matches the carcase (insert drawers).

22 Insert completed drawers into the carcase (they are of course coded) and mark out positions for handles. You can design your own handles – turning knobs on the lathe, for instance. I decided to maintain the visual harmony of the piece and kept the handles straight (Fig 29.18).

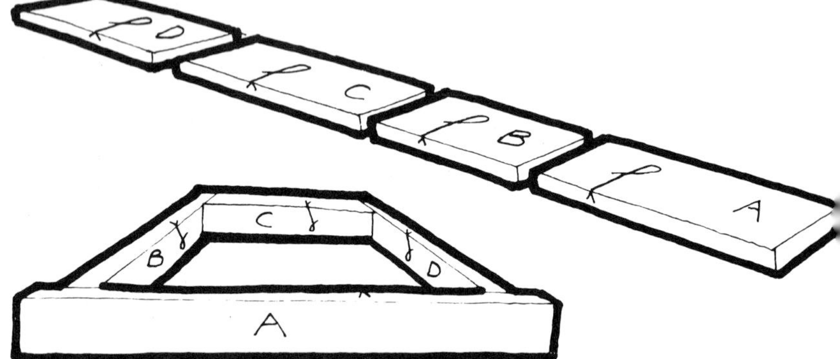

Fig 29.17 The drawer sides and back are made from a single piece, coded and face marked (below).

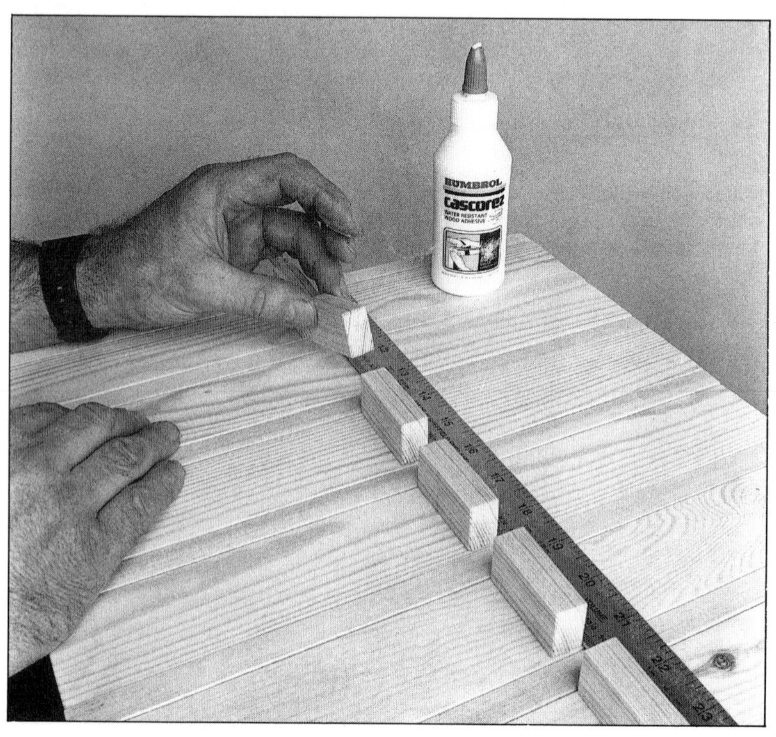

Fig 29.18 Ensuring the handles are glued perfectly in line.

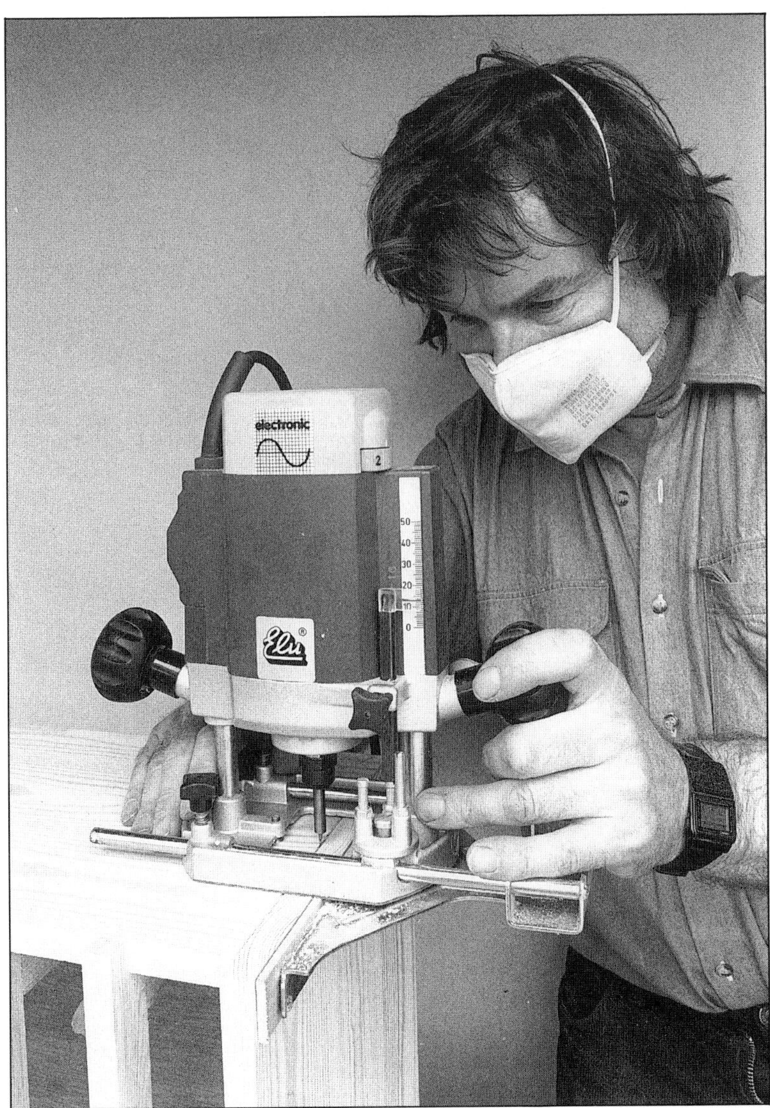

Fig 29.19 The author uses his incredible router to make a 'Danish shoulder' which gives the chest of drawers a finishing touch.

23 A small signature to this piece is to rout in a 'Danish shoulder' with a 1.6mm straight cutter along the glue line of the carcase joints (Fig 29.19). Without it I feel the result looks a little crude (Fig 29.20).
24 To match this shadow line 'inlay', I also slightly bevelled the edges of the drawer fronts creating a similar shadow line (Fig 29.21).
25 Finally, clean up the entire chest of drawers with a palm or orbital sander and soften all edges slightly with Lubrasil paper (see Chapter 14), and apply a varnish. I used 2 coats of a matt polyurethane varnish.
26 It may be desirable to use a little wax to ease the run of the drawers.

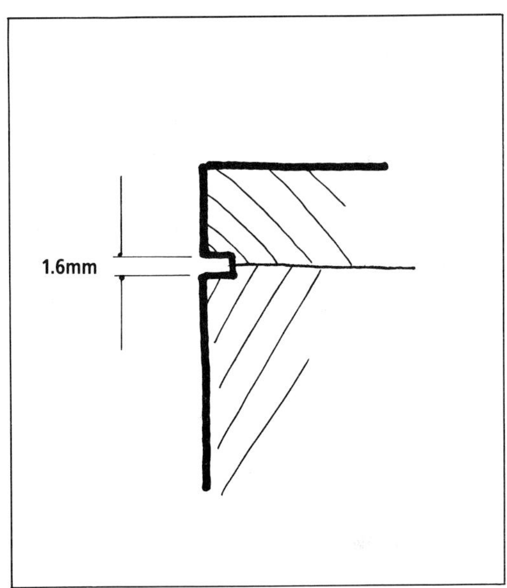

Fig 29.20 Section showing the cutting of a 'Danish shoulder'.

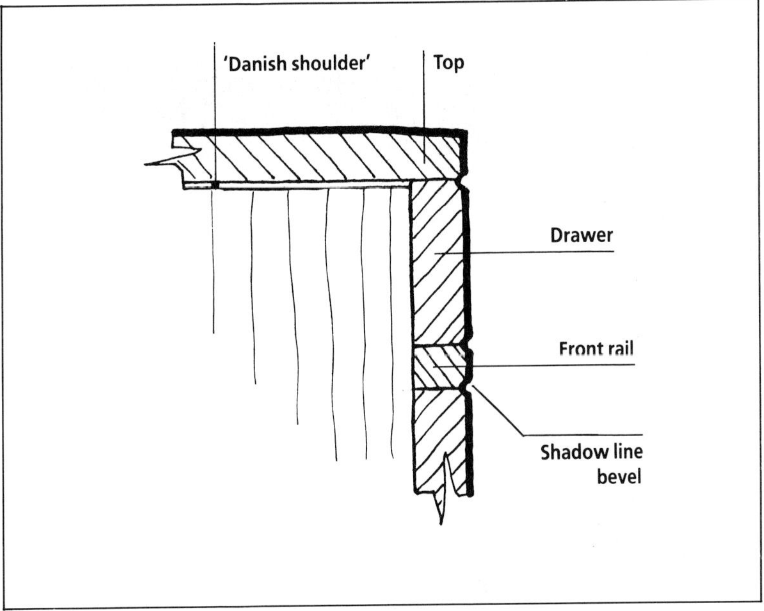

Fig 29.21 Section through cabinet showing shadow line bevel.

SUPPLIERS

AEG (UK) LTD
Power tools
217 Bath Road, Slough SL1 4AW

AXMINSTER TOOL CENTRE
Power tools and equipment
Chard Street, Axminster, Devon EX13 5DZ

BLACK & DECKER LTD
Power tools and accessories
Westpoint, The Grove, Slough, Berks SL1 1QQ

BOSCH, ROBERT LTD
Power tools
PO Box 98, Broadwater Park, North Orbital Road, Denham, Uxbridge UB9 5HJ

CHALKLINE ENERGY
Low energy bulbs
32 Littleport Spur, Slough, Berks SL1 3JD

EBAC LTD
Timber de-humidifiers
St. Helen Trading Estate, Bishop Auckland, Co. Durham DL14 9AL

ELU
see Black & Decker

FERCELL
Dust extraction
Unit 60, Swaislands Drive, Crayford Industrial Estate, Crayford, Kent DA1 4HU

GOMEX TOOLS LTD
Circular sawblades
Finedon, Wellingborough, Northants NN9 5JF

HEALTH AND SAFETY EXECUTIVE
Information about COSHH regulations etc.
HMSO, Freepost, Norwich NR3 1BR

HITACHI POWER TOOLS (UK) LTD
Precedent Drive, Rooksley, Milton Keynes MK13 8PJ

HUMBROL LTD
Cascorez and Cascamite glue
Marfleet, Hull HU9 5NE

KITY UK LTD
Independent machines, combinations and universals
Rawdon Machine Sales Ltd, 6 Acorn Park, Charlestown, Shipley, Yorks

LUNA TOOLS AND MACHINERY LTD (RYOBI)
Presley Way, Crownhill, Milton Keynes MK8 0HB

MACHINE MART
Drum sanding kit, accessories
211 Lower Parliament Street, Nottingham NH1 1GN

MAKITA ELECTRIC UK LTD
Power tools
8 Finway, Dallow Road, Luton, Beds LU1 1TR

METABO (DRAPER TOOLS)
Hursley Road, Chandlers Ford, Eastleigh, Hampshire SO5 5YF

MICOM LTD
Copy-carving machines
7 Industrial Estate, The Street, Heybridge, Maldon, Essex CM9 7XP

M & M DISTRIBUTORS LTD
Arbotech, Triton, Routermaster etc.
PO Box 128, Bexhill-on-Sea, East Sussex TN40 2QT

MULTICO LTD
Bandsaws, saw benches, morticers, accessories etc.
Brighton Road, Salfords, Redhill, Surrey RH1 5ER

PANASONIC INDUSTRIAL UK
Power tool division
Willoughby Road, Bracknell, Berks RG12 4FP

PORTER CABLE
Tools, jigs, cutters etc.
P B Conseng Ltd, 2 Dovedale Close, High Lane, Stockport, SK6 8DU

RACAL SAFETY LTD
Dust masks, ear protection, visors etc.
No. 1 Building, Beresford Avenue, Wembley, Middx HA0 1QJ

RECORD POWER LTD
Tools by Coronet, Elektra Beckum, Drillmaster, Ridgway, Arundel etc.
Parkway Works, Sheffield S9 3BL

RICHMOND TOOLS LTD
Cordless drills and drivers
Hanworth Trading Estate, Hampton Road West, Feltham, Middx TW13 6DH

ROD NAYLOR
Dupli-carver 3 dimensional copying machines
208 Devizes Road, Hilperton, Trowbridge, Wilts

RYOBI, *see* Luna

J R SIMBLE & SONS
Tools, attachments, bandsaw blades, jigs, sundries, etc.
The Broadway, Queens Road, Watford, Herts WD1 2LD

SHEPPACH, *see* Multico

SKIL
Power tools, sanders etc.
Fairacres Industrial Estate, Deadworth Road, Windsor, Berks

SMS WOODWORKING MACHINERY
Danesforde, Pamber Road, Silchester, near Reading RG7 2NU

SP SYSTEMS LTD
Epoxy glues and reinforcing materials
Cowes, Isle of Wight PO31 7EU

THINKING HAND VIDEO (JEREMY BROUN)
Woodworking videos: 'Five Ways to Fashion Wood', 'The Chair', 'British Craftsmanship in Wood' etc.
PO Box 658, Bath BA1 6ED
Tel. 0225 332738

TREND CUTTING TOOLS LTD
Router bits, accessories
Unit N, Penfold Works, Imperial Way, Watford WD2 4YF

VIRGO GAMES
TAO boardgame
3 George Street, Bath, Avon

WESTMINSTER TRADING CO. LTD
Zyliss vice and lathe attachment
72 Albert Street, London NW1 7NR

WOLFCRAFT UK
Drillstands, attachments, accessories, Pioneer worktable etc.
39 Walnut Tree Lane, Sudbury, Suffolk CO10 6BD

WOODRAT
Dovetail and jointmaking jig
The Old School, Godney, Wells BA5 1RY

WOODFIT LTD
Furniture fittings
Kem Mill, Whittle le Woods, Chorley, Lancs PR6 7EA

INDEX

D

E

L

M

N

P

Other titles available from GMC Publications Ltd

BOOKS

Woodworking Plans and Projects *GMC Publications*
40 More Woodworking Plans and Projects *GMC Publications*
Woodworking Crafts Annual *GMC Publications*
Turning Miniatures in Wood *John Sainsbury*
Woodcarving: A Complete Course *Ron Butterfield*
Pleasure and Profit from Woodturning *Reg Sherwin*
Making Unusual Miniatures *Graham Spalding*
Furniture Projects for the Home *Ernest Parrott*
Seat Weaving *Ricky Holdstock*
Green Woodwork *Mike Abbott*
The Incredible Router *Jeremy Broun*
Woodturning: A Foundation Course *Keith Rowley*
Upholstery: A Complete Course *David James*
Making Shaker Furniture *Barry Jackson*
Making Dolls' House Furniture *Patricia King*
Making Tudor Dolls' Houses *Derek Rowbottom*
Making Georgian Dolls' Houses *Derek Rowbottom*
Making Period Dolls' House Furniture *Derek & Sheila Rowbottom*
Heraldic Miniature Knights *Peter Greenhill*
Furniture Projects *Rod Wales*
Restoring Rocking Horses *Clive Green & Anthony Dew*
Making Fine Furniture: Projects *Tom Darby*
Making & Modifying Woodworking Tools *Jim Kingshott*
Multi-centre Woodturning *Ray Hopper*
Turned Trickery in Wood *David Springett*
Complete Woodfinishing *Ian Hosker*
Making Small Wooden Boxes *John Bennett*
Members' Guide to Marketing *Jack Pigden*
Woodworkers' Career and Educational Source Book *GMC Publications*

GMC Publications regularly produces new books on a wide range of woodworking and craft subjects, and an increasing number of specialist magazines, all available on subscription:

MAGAZINES

Furniture Woodturning Woodcarving Business matters

All these books and magazines are available through bookshops and newsagents, or may be ordered by post from the publishers at 166 High Street, Lewes, East Sussex BN7 1XU, telephone (0273) 477374. Credit card orders are accepted. Please write or phone for the latest information.